LENIN

A BIOGRAPHY

ROBERT SERVICE

LENIN

A BIOGRAPHY

The Belknap Press of
Harvard University Press
Cambridge, Massachusetts

Printed in the United States of America

First United Kingdom publication in 2000 by Macmillan Publishers Ltd.

Library of Congress Cataloging-in-Publication Data

Service, Robert.
    Lenin—a biography / Robert Service.
       p. cm.
    Includes bibliographical references and index.
    ISBN 0-674-00330-6 (cloth)
    ISBN 0-674-00828-6 (paper)
       1. Lenin, Vladimir Il'ich, 1870–1924.   2. Heads of state—Soviet Union—Biography.
    3. Revolutionaries—Russia—Biography.   4. Russia—Politics and government—1894–1917.
    5. Soviet Union—Politics and government—1917–1936.   I. Title.

DK254.L4 S4323 2000
947.084'1'092—dc00
[B 21; aa05 01–14]

                                               00–021394

To my family

CONTENTS

Preface

This book was read in draft by Adele Biagi, David Godwin, Heather Godwin, Martyn Rady, Arfon Rees and Tanya Stobbs, and John Klier read the first chapter. Their suggestions made for very welcome improvements. Several helpful tips were also offered by Philip Cavendish, Myszka Davies, Norman Davies, Bill Fishman, Julian Graffy, Riitta Heino, John Klier, Richard Ramage, Arfon Rees, Kay Schiller and Faith Wigzell. I should also like to thank John Screen and Lesley Pitman in the School of Slavonic and East European Studies Library in London and Jackie Willcox in the St Antony's Russian Centre Library in Oxford for their assistance in getting important material on to the stacks. David King generously introduced me to the wonders of his personal collection of Soviet photographs and posters, and I am immensely grateful for his permission to use some here. A particular debt is also owed to the staff of the Russian Centre for the Conservation and Study of Documents of Contemporary History, especially Kirill Anderson, Larisa Rogovaya, Yelena Kirillova, Irina Seleznëva and Larisa Malashenko; and to Vladimir Kozlov at the State Archive of the Russian Federation. Russian fellow historians who have given me useful ideas for research include Gennadi Bordyugov, Vladimir Buldakov, Oleg Khlevniuk, Vladimir Kozlov and Andrei Sakharov.

Lenin is a subject of great political and emotional resonance in Russia and I am grateful for the encouragement given by Russian friends to undertake this biography. I am aware that as a foreigner I may be walking into sensitive areas, perhaps even with hobnailed boots. Then again this is perhaps what the biography of Lenin requires.

For several years on my way to work in central London I used to cycle past buildings where Lenin lived, edited or researched. One route took me through Highbury (where *Iskra* editors had their Russian mail sent) and on to the St Pancras district (where Lenin lived in 1900), across Gray's Inn Road (with its pubs where Lenin drank with party comrades in 1905) and along Tavistock Place (where he lived for some months in 1908). It strengthened a feeling that my subject was not quite as exotic as it sometimes appeared. But of course it is in Russia that fuller perspective on his life and times must be obtained. The Kremlin, Red Square and the Smolny Institute are buildings that have to be visited in order to acquire a sense of time and place. I have tried in the following chapters also to give a sense of personality. In this connection it was a pleasure to meet and spend an afternoon with Viktoria Nikolaevna Ulyanova, one of the few people alive who knew the Ulyanov family members mentioned in the book. Her generosity of spirit – a trait not shared by Lenin, her husband's uncle – demonstrates that not everything that happened in Russia earlier this century was absolutely inevitable.

Lastly, I want to thank my family – my wife Adele and our boisterous descendants Emma, Owain, Hugo and Francesca – for discussing the contents of the book. Each of them has read lengthy sections and helped with the editing. They have displayed the same attitude as those millions of Soviet citizens who, while acknowledging Lenin's huge historical significance, took an interest in his private – and occasionally comic – foibles. I have tried to write a book that brings together the public and private aspects. Until the opening of the Moscow archives in the 1990s a biography of this kind was unfeasible. And I hope the chapters provide material for my family as well as for readers more generally to go on resolving the enduring questions of Lenin's career and impact.

Robert Service
Oxford, May 1999

Note on Transliteration and Calendars

The system of transliteration employed in this book is a simplification of the system developed by the US Library of Congress. The first difference is the dropping of both the diacritical mark and the so-called soft *i*. Secondly, the *yoh* sound is rendered here as *ë*. By and large I have kept to the Russian versions of Russian proper names, but some sound too exotic in English. *Aleksandr Ulyanov*, for example, therefore appears as *Alexander Ulyanov*. The Julian calendar was maintained in Russia until January 1918, when Lenin's government introduced the Gregorian version. Unless otherwise indicated, the dates mentioned in this book correspond to the particular calendar in official use at the time.

List of Illustrations

Section One

1. The Ulyanov family home on Moscow Street in Simbirsk.
2. The Ulyanov family, 1879.
3. Alexander Ilich Ulyanov.
4. Anna Ilinichna Ulyanov.
5. Dmitri Ilich Ulyanov.
6. Maria Ilinichna Ulyanov.
7. Vladimir Ulyanov.
8. The leaders of the Petersburg Union of Struggle for the Liberation of the Working Class.
9. Georgi Plekhanov.
10. Yuli Martov, 1896.
11. Vladimir Ulyanov, 1895.
12. Nadezhda Krupskaya, 1895.

Section Two

13. Clerkenwell Green.
14. 21 (now 36) Tavistock Place.
15. Cartoon cat Lenin attacked by Menshevik mice.
16. Cartoon cat Lenin counterattacking Menshevik mice.
17. Georgi Gapon.
18. Alexander Bogdanov and Lenin play chess, 1908.
19. Lenin's letter of re-application for a British Museum reader's ticket. (*Copyright © The British Museum*)
20. Inessa Armand.
21. Lenin, 1914.
22. Country house in Poronin rented by Lenin and Krupskaya, 1914.
23. Herr Titus Kammerer outside his shop on Spiegelgasse, Geneva.

Glossary of Names of Lenin and his Family

Lenin

Ilich – Respectful nickname for Lenin, used mainly inside the party
Lenin – The most famous of the 160 pseudonyms he used
V.I. – Lenin. Short version of Vladimir Ilich
Vladimir Ilich – Lenin's Christian name and patronymic
Vladimir Ilich Ulyanov – Lenin's name at his christening
Volodya – The diminutive of Lenin's first name

His Close Family

Alexander Ilich (Ulyanov) – First name and patronymic of Lenin's elder brother

Anna Ilinichna (Ulyanova) – First name and patronymic of Lenin's elder sister

Anyuta – Diminutive first name of Lenin's older sister Anna Ilinichna Ulyanova

Dmitri Ilich (Ulyanov) – First name and patronymic of Lenin's younger brother

Ilya Nikolaevich – First name and patronymic of Lenin's father

Manyasha – Diminutive of Christian name of Maria Ilinichna (Ulyanova)

Maria Alexandrovna (Ulyanova) – First name and patronymic of Lenin's mother

Maria Ilinichna (Ulyanova) – First name and patronymic of one of Lenin's younger sisters

Mitya – Diminutive first name of Lenin's younger brother Dmitri Ilich Ulyanov

Nadezhda Konstantinovna (Krupskaya) – First name and patronymic of Krupskaya, Lenin's wife

Nadya – Krupskaya's diminutive first name

Olga Ilinichna (Ulyanova) – First name and patronymic of one of Lenin's
younger sisters

Olya – Diminutive of Christian name of Olga Ilinichna Ulyanova

Sasha – Diminutive of Christian name of Lenin's elder brother Alexander
Ilich Ulyanov

Maps

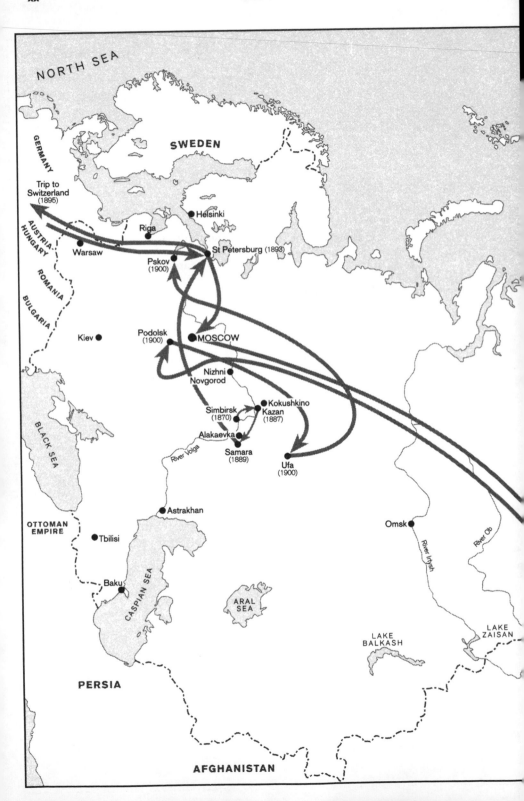

NORTH SEA

SWEDEN

GERMANY

Trip to
Switzerland
(1895)

AUSTRIA-
HUNGARY

ROMANIA

BULGARIA

Helsinki

Riga

Warsaw

St Petersburg (1893)

Pskov
(1900)

Kiev

Podolsk
(1900)

MOSCOW

Nizhni
Novgorod

Simbirsk
(1870)

Kokushkino

Kazan
(1887)

Alakaevka

BLACK SEA

River Volga

Samara
(1889)

Ufa
(1900)

Astrakhan

OTTOMAN
EMPIRE

Tbilisi

Omsk

River Irtysh

River Ob

Baku

CASPIAN SEA

ARAL
SEA

LAKE
BALKASH

LAKE
ZAISAN

PERSIA

AFGHANISTAN

**LENIN'S EARLY YEARS
Volga, St Petersburg, Siberia
1870 to 1900**

Route of Lenin's travels

ARCTIC OCEAN

PACIFIC OCEAN

River Lena

River Angara

Krasnoyarsk
(1897)

Shushenskoe
(1897)

Sakhalin

Irkutsk
LAKE
BAIKAL

Chita

Khabarovsk

Vladivostok

CHINESE EMPIRE

JAPAN

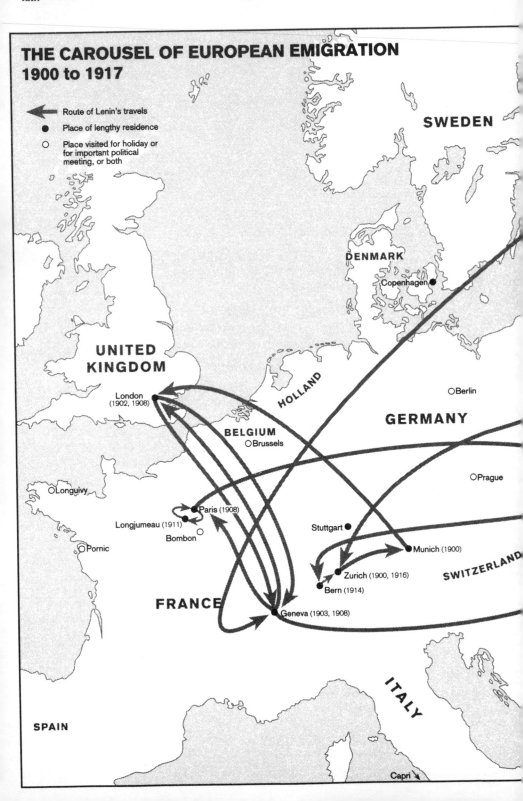

THE CAROUSEL OF EUROPEAN EMIGRATION 1900 to 1917

Route of Lenin's travels

● Place of lengthy residence

○ Place visited for holiday or for important political meeting, or both

SWEDEN

DENMARK

Copenhagen ●

UNITED KINGDOM

London (1902, 1908)

HOLLAND

BELGIUM
○ Brussels

GERMANY

○ Berlin

○ Prague

○ Longuivy

Paris (1908) ●

Longjumeau (1911) ●
Bombon ○

Stuttgart ●

Munich (1900) ●

○ Pornic

Zurich (1900, 1916) ●
Bern (1914) ●

SWITZERLAND

FRANCE

Geneva (1903, 1908) ●

ITALY

SPAIN

Capri ↘

Tampere

Terijoki
Kuokkala (1906)
St Petersburg (1905)

Stockholm

Pskov (1900)

Moscow

RUSSIAN
EMPIRE

Kraków (1912, 1913)
Biały
Dunajec (1913)
Poronin (1914)
Zakopane

AUSTRIA-
HUNGARY

ITALY

ROMANIA

BLACK SEA

Capri

BULGARIA

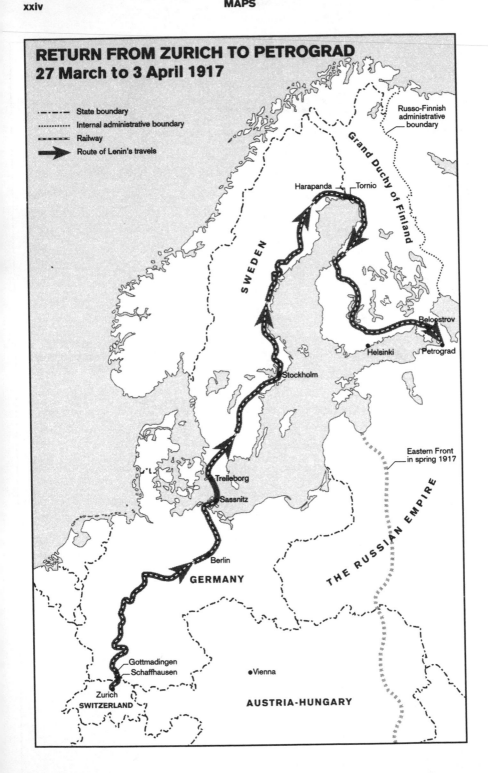

RETURN FROM ZURICH TO PETROGRAD
27 March to 3 April 1917

- ·—·—·— State boundary
- ············· Internal administrative boundary
- - - - - - Railway
- ➔ Route of Lenin's travels

Russo-Finnish administrative boundary

Grand Duchy of Finland

Harapanda — Tornio

Beloostrov

Helsinki   Petrograd

SWEDEN

Stockholm

Trelleborg

Sassnitz

Eastern Front in spring 1917

THE RUSSIAN EMPIRE

Berlin

GERMANY

Gottmadingen
Schaffhausen
Vienna

Zurich
SWITZERLAND

AUSTRIA-HUNGARY

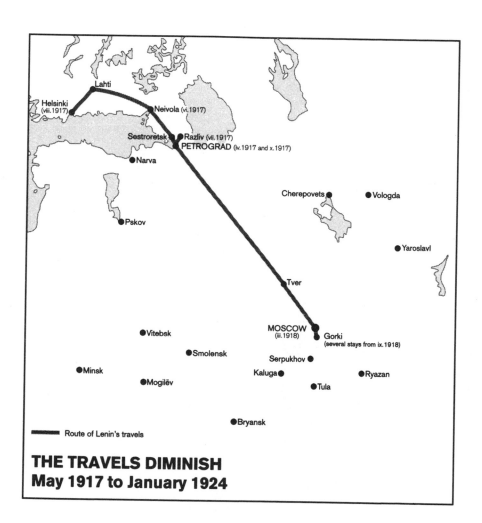

Lahti

Helsinki
(viii.1917)

Neivola (vi.1917)

Sestroretsk

Razliv (vii.1917)
PETROGRAD (iv.1917 and x.1917)

Narva

Cherepovets

Vologda

Pskov

Yaroslavl

Tver

Vitebsk

MOSCOW
(iii.1918)

Gorki
(several stays from ix.1918)

Smolensk

Serpukhov

Minsk

Kaluga

Ryazan

Mogilëv

Tula

Bryansk

Route of Lenin's travels

THE TRAVELS DIMINISH
May 1917 to January 1924

INTRODUCTION

Lenin was an exceptional figure. He founded a communist faction, the Bolsheviks, which he turned into a party that made the October Revolution of 1917. The world's first socialist state was proclaimed. This state – which was the territorial core of what eventually became the USSR – survived against the odds. Lenin and the communist leadership withdrew Russia from the First World War and won the Civil War. By setting up the Communist International, they imprinted themselves upon politics across the continent. The USSR was a beacon to the world's far-left socialists and a dangerous rock to conservatives, liberals and other socialists. Lenin's interpretation of the doctrines of Marx and Engels became holy writ for communists, and at his death was designated as Marxism–Leninism. After the Second World War the communist model – the one-party state, ideological monopoly, legal nihilism, militant atheism, state terror and the elimination of all rival institutions of authority – was transferred to eastern Europe, China, south-eastern Asia and eventually parts of the Caribbean and Africa. Communism was dismantled in eastern Europe in 1989 and in the USSR at the end of 1991. But no one had made a greater impact upon the development and establishment of the communist order than Lenin.

This could never have happened if Lenin had not spent his early life in an extraordinary society at a unique period of its development. Growing up in the Russian Empire in the late nineteenth century, he and others of his generation were caught in a vortex of historical change. The potential of the world's largest country was beginning to be exploited. The old cultural and social constraints were being undermined. International contacts were being improved and the cultural and scientific achievements made the Russian Empire a marvel to the world.

Yet the transformation was at a preliminary stage and most educated Russians were dismayed by the slowness of their country's progress. Many thought Russia was too vast, variegated and tradition-bound to change. They had a point. It was five thousand miles from the Polish lands in the west of the empire to Vladivostok on the Pacific coast. From the White Sea down to the Persian and Ottoman frontiers it was two thousand. The roads were poor and rivers froze in the long winter months. The rail network was rudimentary: the Trans-Siberian Railway was started in 1891 and not completed until 1903. On every border there were problems. To the west was the threat from Germany and Austria–Hungary. To the south there were tensions with the Ottomans – and war broke out in 1876. In the east, Russia feared that other powers would despoil China. Japanese power too was on the rise. Russian armed forces had long lost their reputation for invincibility. In the Crimean War of 1854–6 a limited expeditionary force of the British and French came close to victory over the Russian defence. The Russians were more successful against the Turks but there was no room for complacency. The international power of the Romanovs no longer had the weight it had won in global relations after Napoleon's retreat from Moscow in 1812.

Society in Russia was ill prepared for change. Russia had 'missed' the Renaissance and, to a large extent, the Enlightenment. The reforming tsar Peter the Great had reinforced feudalism at the beginning of the eighteenth century by forcibly tying peasants to their landed masters. Educational standards were woeful. Legal norms went unheeded. Poverty was awesome. The Romanov police-state banned political parties, trade unions and public protest, and administrative arbitrariness was pervasive.

Emperor Alexander II tried to nudge the country towards modernity in 1861 by freeing the peasants from compulsory personal bondage to the landed nobility, and he followed this with a series of alterations in judicial, military and educational institutions. But there remained a massive gap between rich and poor. The legendarily rich Yusupov family had estates all over the country – land equivalent in size to a small European country – and retainers, Old Master paintings, fine clothes and meals shipped by train from Germany. At the other end of the range there were the households of the Russian poor. Most peasants lived in their native village and rarely strayed beyond it. Each wore bast shoes and a smock, let their beards grow long and feared God in a traditional way unassociated with Biblical study. Peasants were highly credulous and had little idea of the broader concerns of public life. Exploited as a human resource by successive tsars, they were subject to discriminatory legislation including even flogging. Resentment against the authorities and the propertied elites was acute. Across the country there were other groups that objected to the social structure. The so-called 'Old Believers' had fled from the reformation of the Church ritual in the seventh century. There were also various sorts of sectarians. Sparsely inhabited areas of Siberia existed where the police barely penetrated – and Siberia was used as a dumping ground for convicts as Australia was used by the British.

Disgruntlement was growing not only in the Russian heartland but also in the 'borderlands'. Poland had been partitioned among Russia, Prussia and Austria in the eighteenth century and the Poles who were under Romanov dominion revolted in 1830 and 1863. The Finns were surly and looked down on the Russians. The Caucasus mountains were in rebellion through the later years of the nineteenth century. Even the Ukrainians, who had seldom given much trouble to the tsars, were becoming restless. It was not a quiescent empire.

Yet the potential of the country was enormous. Raw materials existed in unrivalled abundance. The Russian Empire had coal, iron, diamonds, gold and oil. It had vast spaces where grain could be cultivated. It had opportunities to import foreign capital to intensify its industrial drive. It had a ruling elite that was refreshed by contact with foreign countries, and increasingly official opinion favoured a rapid attempt to catch up with the achievements of the advanced industrial countries to the west. Russia and its borderlands had an ever more buoyant high culture. Russian novelists Tolstoi, Dostoevski and Turgenev were taking Europe by storm. Russian scientists, led by Mendeleev, gained acclaim. Russian composers Rimski-Korsakov and Chaikovski had a continental reputation and, although Russian painters were not yet known abroad, they were superb exponents of their craft. Throughout the Russian Empire there was educational progress. And there was an expanding professional middle class that strove to build social institutions and practices independent from the state administration. Local agencies of self-government were being formed and schooling was being spread to the sons and daughters of the poor, especially in the towns. Architecture, dress and popular behaviour were undergoing change. Even the tsarist bureaucracy was becoming less dominated by the traditional nobility than had once been characteristic.

It was a turbulent transformation. Political passions rose high as rival ideologies were attacked and defended. The less tolerant critics of the status quo were turning to violence against an Imperial state that for centuries had practised repression upon society. The agrarian socialists (*narodniki*) in particular were conducting propaganda from the 1860s, and some of them were engaged in assassination attempts. Liberal political groups also existed. But from the 1880s it was Marxism that became the most prominent ideology of assault upon the Romanov monarchy. It was a race against time. Would the tsarist system sustain its energy and authority for a sufficient period to modernise society and the economy? Would the revolutionaries accommodate themselves to the changing realities and avoid the excesses of violent politics? And would the tsarist system make concessions to bring this about?

Lenin was one of those many intellectuals demanding Revolution. The political and economic structure was offensive to him; the social hierarchy disgusted him. The opportunities for consensual development in Russia held no appeal for him. He hated the Romanovs and Old Russia. He wanted a New Russia, a European Russia, a Westernised Russia. His specific admiration for Germany was enormous. But Lenin's approval of 'the West' was selective. He admired Marx, the German Marxist movement and contemporary German industry and technology. But he wanted the West too to change. There had to be a European socialist revolution that would sweep away the whole capitalist order. He was determined at the same time to liquidate those phenomena in Russia and elsewhere that appeared to him to be backward and oppressive. Lenin belonged to a particular type within his generation in his country. He believed in Enlightenment, Progress, Science and Revolution. In each instance he offered his own interpretation. Nothing shook his confidence that he had the right ideas.

It was not only his own actions that gave him his practical importance. Environment was immensely significant. The fact that fellow Bolsheviks shared his political vision meant that a party existed for all-out Revolution even when he was geographically isolated or physically incapacitated. Without that party's zeal and practicality, Lenin would have been a political nullity. He was also helped by the widespread antagonism among Russia's intellectuals, workers and other social groups to tsarism and to many aspects of capitalism. And the peculiar nature of Russia – its political tensions, its administrative fragility, its internal national and social divisions, its violent popular culture – played into his hands. The final crisis of the Romanov monarchy was induced by the First World War. The fighting on the eastern front brought disaster as transport, administration and economy started to implode. There can therefore be no doubt that luck was on the side of the Bolsheviks in 1917–18. If the Germans had won the First World War in 1918, the military plans of the Kaiser were to turn upon Russia. Lenin's government would have been strangled in its cradle. Without all these factors counting in his favour, Lenin would have been a bit-player on the side of the stage of twentieth-century world history.

He has, of course, been written about frequently. But not until recently was it possible to get access to crucial materials about his life and career. Important documentary collections were published under Mikhail Gorbachëv. Then in 1991, as the USSR collapsed, Boris Yeltsin gave direct admittance to the central party archives themselves. During those years I was writing a trilogy on Lenin's politics, trying to explain the connection between his practical activity and his doctrines within the framework of a revolutionary party that founded the world's first socialist state.

The analysis I have offered – both then and now – differs in basic ways from other works on Lenin. The most obvious contrast is with successive official Soviet accounts and with various Trotskyist accounts, which have represented him as an unblemished thinker, politician and humanitarian.[1] But there are also books which, despite not eulogising him, give him the benefit of too many doubts. Thus I do not share Neil Harding's conviction that Lenin thought out his ideas thoroughly and exclusively from Marxist principles and that his actions derived entirely from 'orthodox' doctrine.[2] It is equally difficult to agree with the notion of Rolf Theen that Lenin secretly derived all his fundamental notions from non-Marxist Russian revolutionaries.[3] The following chapters dissent, too, from Marcel Liebman's claim that Lenin strove to minimise authoritarianism in his party and the Soviet state (as well as from the claim in Alexander Rabinowitch's generally useful works that the Bolshevik party was highly democratic in organisation in 1917).[4] Nor, to my mind, does the evidence support the suggestion by Moshe Lewin and Stephen Cohen that, shortly before he died, Lenin tried to reform communism in the direction of eliminating its association with dictatorship, class war and terror.[5]

Lenin's ideological commitment remains a bone of contention. E. H. Carr saw him as a politician who, as the years passed, was more interested in building up the state institutions than in pushing through with his revolution.[6] As regards foreign policy, Adam Ulam asserted that export of revolution was no longer a primary goal for Lenin within a few months of the communist seizure of power, and Orlando Figes has pushed this to the extreme by suggesting that Lenin ordered the invasion of Poland in 1920 for purely defensive reasons.[7] The following chapters affirm that Leninist ideology is crucial to an understanding of the origins and outcome of the October Revolution.

Much has been written, too, about Lenin's personality. But Richard Pipes is surely wrong to portray Lenin in power as merely a psychopath to whom ideas barely mattered and whose fundamental motivation was to dominate and to kill.[8] Likewise this book takes issue with Alexander Solzhenitsyn and Dmitri Volkogonov, who argue that Lenin and Leninism were wholly alien to Russian traditions;[9] it also contests the anti-semitic case of Valentin Soloukhin that Lenin's ideology was largely a product of the Jewish element in his ancestry.[10] A somewhat less demonic portrait of Lenin emerges from the work of Ralph Carter Elwood, Dietrich Geyer, Leopold Haimson, John Keep and Leonard Schapiro.[11] But in the past couple of decades it has been suggested, notably by Sheila Fitzpatrick and Ronald Suny, that the way to explain Lenin is anyway not to concentrate attention upon him but to look at broader phenomena in the state and society of both Imperial Russia and the Soviet Union.[12] My own earlier work highlighted the political and organisational pressures which pushed Lenin into doing what he did or which, in some instances, stopped him from doing what he wanted.[13] Even Alfred Meyer and Martin Malia, whose writings convincingly indicate the importance of ideology, underestimate the obstacles in the path of Lenin's complete freedom of self-expression.[14] So there is certainly a need to look at Lenin in the context of his times. But in the final judgement – as I hope to show – his personal impact upon events in his time and later was crucial.

The aim is not just to give an analysis different from the other serious ones that are available. I also wish to provide something that has hitherto been impossible to achieve: a biography. The Lenin of history was screened from us by the Soviet state. Those documents and memoirs which did not support the contemporary official image were kept hidden. The first revelations under Gorbachëv were memoirs by Lenin's relatives and by Bolshevik party members. Some of the Politburo records from the revolutionary period were also published. The result was a large increase in our knowledge about Lenin, but always there was the problem that historians were not allowed into the archives to read things for themselves. This changed in 1991. (I was fortunate to be in Moscow on the day when the central party archives were 'unsealed' after the abortive *coup d'état* against Gorbachëv and to use the new historical freedom.) Steadily the files became declassified. The Politburo, Central Committee, Conference and Congress minutes became accessible in their original form. Even material on Lenin's campaign to unseat Stalin in 1923 could be scrutinised. Lenin as a politician became a more comprehensible figure as a consequence.

This was already an enticement to take another look at Lenin. What has made the project irresistible is the access more recently granted to the archival correspondence and memoirs of his family. Long-held suspicions were proved correct. Even the version of Lenin's wife's memoirs that appeared under Gorbachëv turns out to have been subject to politically motivated cuts. Then the reports by his sisters, brother, doctors, bodyguards and nurses were cleared for inspection. At last a biography in a full sense became feasible.

This book starts from the premise that Lenin the revolutionary and Lenin the man are inexplicable without reference to each other. His mixed ethnic background was not without significance. But the idea that this was enough in itself to make him 'anti-Russian' or 'cruel' is implausible. The point about his family is that its members were marginal elements seeking incorporation into the official Imperial order – and ultimately they failed to achieve this. Like other such families, the parents pushed their offspring hard to achieve educational success. The children were subjected to heavy pressure and not all of them survived unscathed. Lenin was one of the successful ones, but his compulsion to work intensively and meet deadlines stayed with him until his last illness. The contents of his education also left their mark. What has not previously been understood is that Lenin's schooling involved deep but narrow study. The effect was that his mind was left exposed to other influences, including revolutionary ideas in particular. Lenin's education enabled him to read foreign languages and to respect science, but also left him open to the attractions of any ideology that seemed to make sense of the society in which he lived.

He was an able suppressor of outward emotion. He acted calmly even after the trauma he suffered when his elder brother Alexander was hanged; and later he was to find steady satisfaction in his work alongside his wife. But things were not always on an even keel. We can see in some detail how other women tempted him and that one of them, Inessa Armand, held his heart for a while. But by and large, he was a manipulator of women. In securing their help, he played them off one against the other – and this meant putting his wife Nadezhda Krupskaya at the mercy of his less than kindly sisters. These women provided him with a regular support in day-to-day organisation. Krupskaya did not always fall for his charm. But mostly she did. In particular she returned to his side when he became mortally ill in 1922. Lenin was a bit of a hypochondriac and, if he had not been able to count on the active sympathy of his family, he would probably have erupted. There was always the possibility of an explosion: Lenin was a human time-bomb. His intellectual influences thrust him towards Revolution and his inner rage made this impulse frenetic. Lenin had greater passion for destruction than love for the proletariat.

His personality is closely linked to the kind of politician he became. His angry outbursts were legendary throughout the party before 1917; shortly before he died they became so acute that serious questions arose about his mental equilibrium, even his sanity. But usually he took a grip on himself and channelled his anger into a controlled form of aggression. He was a political warrior. This has never been a secret, but the intensity of his militant style can now be seen more clearly. Even in the moments of retreat, as when he introduced the New Economic Policy in 1921, he was wild in his declarations and proposals. It is true that he moderated his ideas after consultation with colleagues and acquaintances. But he stayed loyal to certain key understandings. His occasional restraint came from a man who wanted to fight hard but saw the advantage of temporary and partial withdrawal. He modified policies, sometimes in drastic ways when his power was under threat. But from its formulation at the beginning of the 1890s to his death in 1924 there was little change in his basic thinking. He could live for years in a locality – be it London, Zurich or Moscow – and fail to draw the conclusions about his surroundings that came easily to others without his hardened prejudices. He lived and died a Leninist. In his basic assumptions about politics Lenin was no chameleon.

The influences on him were not just Marxist. For some time we have known that he was influenced by the Russian agrarian-socialist terrorists of the late nineteenth century. Indeed there is no need to choose between Marxism and populism as if they were polarities: the two tendencies of thought massively overlapped each other. But there were other influences that are less familiar. Lenin's childhood reading, from *Uncle Tom's Cabin* onwards, had a lasting effect. So too did Russian literature – and some of his favourite authors such as Gleb Uspenski, who wrote stories about the Russian peasantry, strengthened his scepticism about the pleasanter side of contemporary peasant attitudes. In later life he picked up further ideas from writers such as Machiavelli and Darwin. He also assimilated ideas from chance acquaintances even if they happened to be hostile to Marxism. Thus the figure of Father Gapon, Orthodox priest and critic of the Romanov order, had a significant impact. Marxism was the primary ingredient of Lenin's thought, but it gained a lot of its solidity from combination with other ingredients.

While Lenin stuck to his basic assumptions, he felt free to alter strategy even when it caused acute annoyance to his colleagues. On some questions he ignored them entirely. He relished the disputes over the October Revolution, the Brest-Litovsk Treaty and the New Economic Policy. But he was also a party boss who let his associates argue with each other to deflect criticism from himself. He was almost a one-man court of appeal. Lenin alone was respected by all sections of the Bolshevik party and his patriarchal style strengthened his dominance at least when he was in reasonable health. He also handled the party with finesse, managing to sound radical even when he was recommending moderation. Lenin could be evasive; he could also play down secondary dispute in pursuit of the supreme goal of the moment. More than most politicians, furthermore, he could speak in several registers at once. While using Marxist terminology, he could also develop popular slogans. The Party Congresses were always victories for him. He had a gift for ruthless and yet inspiring leadership. Steadily he learned how to widen the range of his political techniques. He never lost his teacherly style or his odd enunciation of words. But his force of personality and ideological commitment reinforced the message and he learned to trust his instincts.

Nevertheless he was not infinitely adaptive. Lenin's austere personality had its counterpart in his narrow approach to politics. It took a huge effort for him to become a reasonable public speaker. He was a man of the printed word, a fanatical reader and writer. In fact the most effective exponents of twentieth-century political techniques in 1917 were the anti-Bolshevik premier Alexander Kerenski and Lenin's fellow Bolshevik Lev Trotski.

And the common idea that Lenin was always a widely known figure is nonsense. Few knew what he looked like when he came back to Russia in 1917. His writings were familiar only to well-informed Marxists. In 1917 neither *Pravda* nor the other newspapers carried his visual image. Even in the Civil War he had difficulty in getting recognised by the general public. It was only after the inception of the New Economic Policy in 1921 that he became generally famous. This is of importance for a consideration of his political impact. Lenin was often absent for decisive moments in the history of his party and government. In Siberian exile and in European emigration he was frequently removed from the centre of action; in 1917 he could not return until April, and then in July he fled to Finland until the beginning of October. Furthermore, he was recurrently incapacitated by serious illness. We can now see that his health had been failing him since his early manhood. Ulcers, migraine, insomnia, St Anthony's fire and both minor and major heart attacks laid him low. He had to leave much administration to others and, to his chagrin, his leading colleagues showed that they could run the state quite adequately without him.

Nonetheless Lenin did make history. In the *April Theses* of 1917 he drafted a strategy for the party to seize power. In October he insisted that power should be seized. In March 1918 he fended off a German invasion of Russia by getting a separate treaty signed at Brest-Litovsk. In 1921 he introduced the New Economic Policy and saved the Soviet state from being overwhelmed by popular rebellion. If Lenin had not campaigned for these strategical shifts, the USSR would never have been established and consolidated.

Not everything done by Lenin was carefully conceived. In particular, he had little foresight about what he was doing when he set up the centralised one-party state. One of the great malignancies of the twentieth century was created more by off-the-cuff measures than by grandiose planning. Yet the creation was far from being a complete accident. Lenin, even at his most improvisational, thought and acted in accordance with his long-held basic assumptions. He liked what he had done in his career. He was proud of his doctrines, his party and his revolution. And his influence was not confined to the events of his lifetime. His institutional legacy was immense. Lenin set up the Sovnarkom and dispersed the Constituent Assembly. Lenin created the Cheka. Lenin convoked the Communist International. More basically he had an impact upon assumptions. Lenin eliminated concern for ethics. Lenin justified dictatorship and terror. Lenin applauded the political vanguard and the need for firm leadership. Lenin convinced his party that his Marxism was pure and that it embodied the only correct policies. In strategy, institutions and assumptions Lenin had a lasting impact upon far-left socialism for his country and the world.

PART ONE

THE REBEL EMERGES

'I'd like to arise from my grave in about a hundred years
and have a look at how people will be living then.'

Lenin's grandfather, Dr Alexander Blank

1

THE ULYANOVS AND THE BLANKS

On 10 April 1870 the river Volga – the dominant natural feature of the provincial town of Simbirsk in Russia's south east and the largest river in Europe – was showing the first signs of spring. The temperature had risen to 5° centigrade. The huge field of ice across the channel between the banks of the river was heaving and beginning to crack. Spring was arriving, and the long-awaited change of season caused excitement in every house in Simbirsk except for one on Streletskaya Street, where a baby boy was being born. His parents Ilya and Maria Ulyanov already had two children and the whole family attended his baptism some days later in the St Nicholas Cathedral, where the priest sprinkled water over his head and christened him Vladimir Ilich Ulyanov. The godparents were Arseni Belokrysenko, an accountant in the Imperial civil administration and Ilya's chess partner, and Natalya Aunovskaya, who was the widowed mother of one of Ilya's colleagues.[1] After the christening Ilya Ulyanov departed for St Petersburg to attend a pedagogical conference and left Maria Alexandrovna to recover from her labour with the assistance of the family's new nanny Varvara Sarbatova. Life in the house on Streletskaya Street returned to normality.[2]

Vladimir Ilich Ulyanov entered the history books as Lenin, the main pseudonym he used in the Russian revolutionary movement. It was also as Lenin that he bequeathed his name for a set of doctrines, Marxism–Leninism. Yet when his native city had its name changed in his honour in 1924 it was not called Leninsk but Ulyanovsk. And Ulyanovsk it remains to this day.

In the nineteenth century there was a widely held idea that places like Simbirsk were somnolent places and that bustle and enterprise was confined to St Petersburg. Foreign travellers had this impression. Many Russian observers – including tsars, ministers and intellectuals – thought this too. The static nature of Russia's provincial way of life was part of the conventional wisdom. The assumption was made that the further a city was from the capital, the sleepier the urban scene was likely to be.

In fact the cities in the Russian provinces were anything but quiet. Simbirsk, a Volga port a thousand miles from the capital, bustled with the struggle of its inhabitants to make enough money to survive. At its highest point, the town stood 450 feet above the water level. But most of the town was long and low-lying and stretched eleven miles along the waterfront. The quays were the main places where goods entered or left the city. Fishing was an important source of urban employment; sturgeon was the prime catch. Simbirsk lay along the route from central Russia to the Caspian Sea. Barge-haulers, who were the *burlaki* immortalised in the 'Song of the Volga Boatmen', pulled the heavy, flat vessels up and down the river. There was hardly any large-scale manufacturing. A few clothing factories and the old Simbirsk Distillery were the extent of the province's industrial development. Although trade with the Ottoman Empire and Persia was on the increase, Simbirsk was not an economic centre at the level of St Petersburg and Moscow. There was no metal-working factory, and no significant foreign industrial presence existed. The buildings were mainly of wood and there was little sign of the architectural panache of the Imperial capitals.

Peasant agriculture was the other mainstay of economic activity. The peasantry sold their produce to middlemen with their businesses in Simbirsk and the other towns. The main crop was rye. Potatoes, wheat, oats and barley were also grown. In 1861 there had been a great jolt to the traditional way of treating the province's peasants, when the Emperor Alexander II had issued an Emancipation Edict freeing them from the personal control exercised by noble landowners. But the land settlement was particularly disadvantageous to the peasantry of Simbirsk. The soil in the Volga region was as fertile as any in Russia, and the noble landlords contrived to keep all but a small proportion of it in their hands. And so the peasants could seldom live by agriculture alone. Many of them eked out their existence by means of various handicrafts. Simbirsk province was covered by forests, and woodworking was a common craft and trade. Carts, wheels, sleighs, shovels and even house-hold utensils were wooden goods produced locally. The markets were colourful and the biggest of them was the Sbornaya Market in Simbirsk, where it was possible to buy anything made in the province.

By far the largest proportion of Simbirsk province's inhabitants – 88 per cent – were members of the Russian Orthodox Church (and the proportion rose to 97 per cent for the town of Simbirsk itself). Two per cent were classified as 'sectarians' of various Russian sorts. This was the official designation for those Russian Christians who declined to accept the authority of the Orthodox Church; they included the so-called Old Believers, who had rejected the reforms in liturgy and ritual imposed by Tsar Alexei in the middle of the seventeenth century. In the province, too, there were Christians whose faith derived from foreign sources. Among these were Lutherans and Catholics. There were also about four hundred Jewish inhabitants. But the second largest group after the Orthodox Christians were the Moslems, who constituted 9 per cent of the population. They lived mainly in the villages of Simbirsk province and were diverse in their ethnic composition; most of them were Mordvinians, Chuvashes or Tatars. They had been there for centuries and were generally despised by the Russians as being their colonial inferiors. The great St Nicholas Cathedral at the heart of Simbirsk was an architectural reminder that the tsars of old Muscovy would brook no threat to Russian dominion in the Volga region.

Yet the central authorities in St Petersburg had experienced grave problems in maintaining their grip on the entire Volga region, and the problems were not caused exclusively by non-Russians. The Orthodox Christian peasants of Simbirsk province had played a part in the great revolts led against the holders of the throne by Stenka Razin in 1670–1 and Yemelyan Pugachëv in 1773–5. Care was consequently taken to equip an army garrison in Simbirsk, and the civil bureaucracy administered the province in the authoritarian style that was characteristic of tsarism. The governor of the province was personally appointed by the emperor and was empowered to do practically anything he saw fit to impose order.

After the Emancipation Edict, Emperor Alexander II introduced a reform of local administration whereby provincial councils – zemstva – were elected to take charge of schools, roads, hospitals and sanitary facilities. This was a limited measure, but it marked an important break with the past. However, Simbirsk province was known for the traditionalism of its social elite; it was one of the so-called 'nests of the nobility'. Yet even in Simbirsk there was enthusiasm among the landed nobles to take up the new opportunities for self-government. The zemstvo was a hive of busy initiatives. The town had had its own newspaper in the form of Simbirsk Provincial News since 1838, and in 1876 the provincial zemstvo started up its own publication. The schooling network, too, was given attention. Funds for this were allocated from St Petersburg. By the end of the nineteenth century there were 944 schools of various sorts across the province. The pinnacle of this educational establishment was the Simbirsk Classical Gimnazia (or Grammar School), which took pupils up to the age of seventeen. Although Simbirsk lacked a university, the Imperial Kazan University was only 120 miles to the north.

Inhabitants of Simbirsk had cultural achievements to their name. One of Russia's greatest historians Nikolai Karamzin, who died in 1826, had hailed from the province. So, too, had the writer Ivan Goncharov, whose novel *Oblomov* – published in serial form in the 1850s – has become a European literary classic. Admittedly Simbirsk was not a centre of cultural and intellectual effervescence. The Karamzin Public Library did not have a very large stock and the bookshops were few; no literary circle existed there. But those individuals aspiring to a role in public life were not incapacitated by having been brought up there. It may even have been an advantage for them. Many of the most original Russian writers, thinkers and politicians came from a provincial milieu. Such intellectuals benefited from spending their early years outside the claustrophobic cultural atmosphere of St Petersburg. They developed their ideas on their own or within a small, supportive group, and did not have the originality and confidence crushed out of them. Often they were the ones who attacked the conventional wisdom of the day and were the country's innovators – and there was to be no more innovative revolutionary thinker and politician than the man who had started life in Simbirsk as Vladimir Ulyanov.

The Ulyanov family had moved to Simbirsk in autumn 1869, a few months before the birth of Vladimir. The father, whose full name was Ilya Nikolaevich Ulyanov, had been appointed as Inspector of Popular Schools for the province. He brought his pregnant wife Maria Alexandrovna Ulyanova and their two children, Alexander and Anna, to the home they would rent from the Pribylovski family on Streletskaya Street.[3] Ilya's post had been created as part of the government's scheme for a rapid expansion of schooling in the mid-1860s. He immediately became a prominent figure in the affairs of the town and province of Simbirsk.

Ilya and Maria Ulyanov had a heterogeneous background. The Soviet authorities were to try to keep secret the fact that Maria was of partly Jewish ancestry. Her paternal grandfather Moshko Blank was a Jewish trader in wine and spirits in Starokonstantinov in Volynia province in the western borderlands of the Russian Empire. Starokonstantinov was a small town and most of its inhabitants were Jews. Moshko was frequently in conflict with his neighbours, including his son Abel. He took Abel to court for verbal and physical abuse.[4] But the result stunned him. The judge did not believe Moshko and fined him rather than his son. In 1803, Moshko himself was prosecuted when his Jewish neighbours brought an action against him for stealing hay. Two years later he was charged with selling illegally distilled vodka. In both cases he was found innocent. But in 1808 his luck ran out when he spent several months in prison on a charge of arson. Eventually he was again cleared of guilt, and he moved with his family to the provincial capital Zhitomir. Yet he did not forget his humiliation in Starokonstantinov. In 1824, he appealed for a judicial review of the arson case and secured the fining of the families who had prosecuted him. Moshko was no man to trifle with. It was a feature that one of his descendants was to share.[5]

Moshko Blank was not a practising Jew. His parents had not brought him up to observe the Jewish faith, and he had not sent his own children to the local Jewish school. By tradition they ought to have gone to the Starokonstantinov *heder* to learn Hebrew and study the Torah. Instead Moshko entered them for the new district state school where they would be taught in Russian. When Moshko's wife died, he broke the remaining connections with the faith of his ancestors. He approached the local priest and was baptised as an Orthodox Christian.[6]

Perhaps Moshko Blank underwent a spiritual experience, but he may have had a more material motive. Conversion to Christianity would eliminate obstacles to his social and economic advancement. Few Jews had lived in the Russian Empire until the three partitions of 1772–95, when Austria, Prussia and Russia divided up Poland among themselves. The result was that the tsars acquired a large number of Jewish subjects. Catherine the Great feared unpopularity if she were to allow them to move outside the western borderlands since religious and economic hostility to Jews was common to Russians of every rank. She therefore issued a decree confining them to a Pale of Settlement in the western borderlands. Only the very small proportion of wealthy Jews was permitted to live outside the Pale and Jews could not attain the rank of nobleman. The solution for an ambitious, unbelieving Jew was to seek conversion to Orthodox Christianity. Any such former Jew was automatically registered as a Russian and was relieved of the burden of discriminatory legislation. Moshko Blank no doubt felt unusually hampered by his Jewish status since, by his own account, he had no religious or educational affiliation to Judaism.

Yet few apostates behaved quite as aggressively to their former co-religionists as Moshko Blank, who wrote to the Ministry of the Interior suggesting additional constraints upon Jews. He proposed to ban the Jews from selling non-Kosher food (which they could not eat themselves) and from employing Christians on the Jewish sabbath (when Jews could perform no work). He particularly urged that the Hasidim, the fervent and mystical Jewish sect, should be prohibited from holding meetings. Moshko's militancy was extraordinary. He called upon the Ministry of the Interior to prevent Jews in general from praying for the coming of the Messiah and to oblige them to pray for the health of the Emperor and his family.[7] In short, Moshko Blank was an anti-semite. This point deserves emphasis. Several contemporary writers in Russia have argued that Lenin's Jewish background predetermined his ideas and behaviour. The writers in question tend towards anti-semitic opinions.[8] But, in trying to pursue a Russian nationalist agenda by an emphasis upon the Jewish connections of Lenin, they avoid the plain fact that Moshko Blank was an enemy of Judaism and that no specific aspect of their Jewish background remained important for his children.[9]

Moshko's sons, Abel and Srul, equalled him in their desire to dissolve their Jewish ties. Indeed they underwent conversion to Christianity before their father Moshko, who had sent them to study at the Medical-Surgical Academy in St Petersburg. Evidently Moshko did not hold a grudge against Abel for the violent clash that led them to appearing against each other in court in Zhitomir. Abel and Srul were choosing a career, in medicine, that was attractive to many who wished to rise from the base of Imperial society. The 'free professions' offered a route to public prominence by dint of technical competence. Abel and Srul studied hard to become doctors in St Petersburg. In 1820, after making known their wish to become Christians, they were given baptism in the Samson Cathedral in St Petersburg's Vyborg district. As was the convention, they were accompanied by Russian nobles who had agreed to be their godparents. Abel and Srul took Christian names: Abel became Dmitri while Srul became Alexander. One of the godparents was Senator Dmitri Baranov, who had conducted a survey of Volynia province on behalf of the Imperial government in 1820 and who actively helped young Jews who converted to Christianity.[10]

The Blank brothers qualified as doctors. On graduating in 1824, Alexander (Srul) Blank took up practice initially in Smolensk province. Thereupon he appears to have made his own way in his career. If he kept contact with his father, there is little sign of this in the official records. Alexander was his own man. This was true of him even in his attitude to his studies. While learning the recommended textbooks at the St Petersburg Medical-Surgical Academy, he also read about unorthodox techniques of medicine.[11]

Alexander Blank married a Christian, Anna Grosschopf, in 1829.

Anna was a Lutheran from St Petersburg. She was of German and Swedish ancestry: her father Johann Grosschopf was a notary whose family came from Lübeck while her mother, Anna Estedt, was of Swedish background. In any case, both the parents of Anna Grosschopf were long-term residents of St Petersburg.[12] This was where she met and married Alexander Blank. Since her fiancé had become a Russian Orthodox Christian, she was supposed by Imperial law to adopt Alexander's faith as a prerequisite of the marriage. She went through the formalities; but the fact that she was to bring up her daughters as Lutherans shows that she had not really abandoned her Lutheran faith. She also stayed loyal to a number of customs not yet shared by most Russians. Germans at Christmas placed a decorated fir tree in the house. This was a custom that Anna passed down to her children and her grandchildren, who regarded it as characteristically 'German'.[13] Alexander Blank and Anna Grosschopf were assimilating themselves to a Russian national identity, but they did not take the process to its furthest possible point. Anna in particular retained traces of her ancestral past; and Alexander, while relegating his Jewish past to oblivion, did not insist that his wife should forswear her own heritage.

By continuing to adhere to Lutheranism, Anna was breaking the law. But in practice the state authorities only rarely forced Orthodox Christians to stay strictly within the bounds of Orthodoxy, and Alexander and Anna could proceed to concentrate on establishing themselves in Russian society. Alexander had a decent but unspectacular career as a doctor. He moved from post to post in St Petersburg and the provinces. His was not an untroubled career. In Perm he clashed with his professional superiors and lost his job. His appeal against his treatment failed, but he eventually secured appointment as the medical inspector of hospitals in Zlatoust and restored his reputation. With this last posting he automatically became a 'state councillor' and a hereditary noble.[14]

But Anna's health was frail and she died, before she was forty, in 1838; she left behind six children. There was one son, Dmitri, and five daughters: Anna, Lyubov, Yekaterina, Maria (Lenin's mother) and Sofia. Alexander Blank could not cope on his own. He turned for help to his wife's side of the family, and one of his wife's sisters, Yekaterina, agreed to take her place in bringing up the children. Yekaterina von Essen – née Grosschopf – was a widow. Alexander Blank had several reasons to be pleased about her. Not only did she take responsibility for her nieces but also she had a substantial legacy and was willing to help with the purchase of the estate of Kokushkino, twenty miles to the north-east of the old Volga city of Kazan (where she had lived with her now-deceased husband Konstantin).[15] The last reason is somewhat less seemly. Apparently Alexander Blank and Yekaterina von Essen were living together as man and wife soon after Anna Blank's death. Alexander applied for permission to marry her without divulging to the authorities that Yekaterina was his deceased wife's sister. Such a marriage was illegal, as he must have known, and the application failed. But Alexander and Yekaterina were undeterred from their liaison; they stayed under the same roof until Yekaterina's death in 1863.[16]

The Blank family resided in Kokushkino in 1848 and Alexander Blank, having retired from his medical work in Penza in the previous year, became a landowner with personal control over the lives of forty peasant males and their families. Kokushkino had a substantial manor house with two storeys and a mezzanine floor. There would be plenty of room for all the Blanks. The boy Dmitri went to the Kazan Classical Gimnazia, but the five girls were educated at home. Aunt Yekaterina supervised formal academic studies as well as the musical training, especially at the piano; her efforts were supplemented by the hire of teachers who came out from Kazan to the Kokushkino estate. The girls were brought up with a knowledge of Russian, German, French and English. Aunt Yekaterina was a very demanding taskmistress, but her nieces were to appreciate the educational benefit they received from her.

As for Alexander Blank, he had a passionate interest in hygiene, diet and dress and wrote a booklet on the advantages of 'balneology'.[17] This was a medical fashion involving wrapping up patients in wet blankets; the idea was that enclosure by water helped to prevent ill health. Blank applied the method to his young family. He disliked to hand out medicine except in exceptional circumstances, and insisted on a plain diet: the girls were not allowed tea or coffee except when they were served these beverages on visits to their neighbours. The Blank children had to wear clothes with open necks and short sleeves even in winter.[18] They had reason to think, in adulthood, that they had had an idiosyncratic upbringing.[19] It is true that their father also had a sense of humour; but his jokes were usually made at someone else's expense. On 1 April, for example, he played tricks around the house. On one occasion he fooled everyone by placing powdery snow on the dinner plates.[20] But usually he and Aunt Yekaterina had erred on the side of strictness. Although the girls loved their father and aunt, they were more than a little in awe of them.

Young Dmitri was intensely unhappy. In 1850, shortly after the move to Kokushkino, while he was still a student, he committed suicide.[21] Exactly what upset him is still not known. It may be that his mother's death unhinged him or that something disturbed him in his relations with his father. Perhaps he felt himself to be under excessive pressure of expectations either from his family or from his tutors. Or possibly he was simply a victim of psychological illness.

Yet life for the Blank children was generally a lot more pleasant than for the peasants on the Kokushkino estate. When the Emancipation Edict freed them from their personal ties to the newly arrived Dr Blank, they refused to accept the maximum amount of land available to them since this would have entailed their agreement to pay him compensation. Instead they opted for the scheme whereby they received a minimal amount but did not have to pay anything for it. On the neighbouring estates the peasants had taken the maximum amount on offer, and Dr Blank, a tall, thin individual with dark eyes, asked his peasants to reconsider. He warned them that they would sink into penury if they stuck to their decision. But they did not trust him. Presumably they believed the unfounded rumours circulating among the discontented peasantry that all the land was about to be transferred free of charge to those who themselves cultivated it. They lived to regret their decision. But it was too late: the Blanks would not allow them to go back on the original settlement. The troubled condition of Russian agriculture in the nineteenth century was a topic that was understood at close quarters by Blank family members – and they did not take a kindly approach.

Maria Alexandrovna Blank had been born in St Petersburg in 1835. Her husband Ilya Nikolaevich Ulyanov had come into the world four years earlier. Ilya had belonged to a commercial family in Astrakhan, where the river Volga debouches into the Caspian Sea. He was the youngest of four children; his brother was called Vasili, his sisters were Maria and Fedosya. Their father Nikolai Ulyanov was a tailor.[22] Official Soviet historians claimed that the Ulyanovs lived in straitened circumstances; but there is nothing to substantiate this. Nikolai Ulyanov lived in a stone house with a wooden superstructure and his business flourished.

Although the family's ethnic and religious background is not completely clear, Nikolai probably descended from peasants who came to Astrakhan from the upper Volga province of Nizhni Novgorod in the eighteenth century. Originally their name, it seems, was not Ulyanov but Ulyanin; such a shift in orthography was common in those years. The possibility that they came from near Nizhni Novgorod, one of Russia's greatest cities, has given rise to the suggestion that they were Russians. Quite possibly they were. But the province of Nizhni Novgorod, like several provinces of the Volga region, was inhabited by a mixture of ethnic groups, and it cannot be excluded that the Ulyanovs belonged to one of the indigenous ethnic groups conquered by the Russian tsars in the sixteenth century. Thus the Ulyanovs could have been Chuvashes or Mordvinians. Even more obscure is their religious affiliation. If they were Russians, they may have been Orthodox Christians; but it is equally conceivable that they belonged to one or other of the local Christian sects. If Chuvash or Mordvinian, they could have been pagans or Moslems or even converted Christians. All that is beyond challenge is that Nikolai Ulyanov – Lenin's grandfather – brought up his family as Russian Orthodox Christians and had them educated in Russian schools.[23]

There also remains uncertainty about the identity of his Astrakhan grandmother. Even her first name is problematical. According to some sources, she was Alexandra, whereas others have her as Anna. It cannot wholly be discounted that she was a Russian by birth. But certainly Lenin's sister Maria was convinced that their Astrakhan forebears had a Tatar ingredient in their genealogy; and Maria may have had her grandmother in mind when she referred to this. Most writers have her as a Kalmyk but it is conceivable that she was a Kirgiz. The Kalmyks were a mainly Buddhist people living in the southernmost regions of the Russian Empire. Their ancestors were the nomadic tribes which had overrun the Russians in the thirteenth century with the Mongol Horde. Most of the Kalmyks and Kirgiz who lived in Astrakhan were poor; some were even slaves. Only a few rose to become urban traders. They were disliked and despised by the Russian authorities as 'Asiatics'.

Nevertheless the possibility that she was a Russian is not wholly discountable since the records are so scanty and imprecise. Mysteries continue to exist. But later generations of the family believed that a non-Russian element ('Tatar', as Anna Ilinichna Ulyanova put it) entered their ancestry in Astrakhan and it is difficult to believe that they invented this.[24] Alexandra was younger than Nikolai Ulyanov, who had delayed marrying until middle age. Indeed he reportedly bought his wife out from a prominent Astrakhan merchant family. This has encouraged the speculation that she had been converted to Orthodox Christianity. But in truth a cloud of unknowing covers the matter. Another piece of guesswork is even more peculiar. This is that Nikolai Ulyanov already shared a surname with his bride Alexandra. The suspicion has been aired that Nikolai and Alexandra were related by blood, even quite closely related. Nothing has been proven and, in the absence of documents, probably never will be. The only fair conclusion is that Lenin could not claim a wholly Russian ancestry on his father's side; indeed it is possible, but by no means certain, that he lacked Russian 'blood' on both sides of his family.

Yet Nikolai and Alexandra, whatever their origins, brought up their family in Russian culture, raised them in the Orthodox Christian faith and sent the boys to Russian schools.[25] The Ulyanov family was taking its opportunities to establish itself in the lower middle class of Astrakhan society. Its ambition survived the death of Nikolai at the age of seventy-five in 1838. The eldest son Vasili, who never married, took his family responsibilities seriously and paid for his brother Ilya – thirteen years his junior – to enter the Astrakhan Gimnazia and to proceed to the Imperial Kazan University, where he completed a mathematics degree in 1854. On graduation Ilya took a succession of teaching jobs. His first post took him to Penza, where he worked in the Gentry Institute. It was there that he met Maria Alexandrovna Blank, who was staying with her sister Anna, the wife of the Gentry Institute's director I. D. Veretennikov.[26]

The marriage of Ilya Nikolaevich Ulyanov and Maria Alexandrovna Blank took place in Penza in August 1863. They shared many interests and a general attitude to life. In particular, they had a common passion for education. This brought them together despite the many contrasts in their backgrounds. Ilya adhered to Orthodox Christianity whereas Maria was a tepid Lutheran. Ilya had an Asian background, Maria a north European. Ilya was a man of the Volga. He lived his whole life near that great river: in Astrakhan, Kazan, Penza, Nizhni Novgorod and finally Simbirsk. Maria had lived her early years in St Petersburg and the western area of the Russian Empire. Whereas the Ulyanovs had only recently become comfortable in material terms, the Blanks had always been so. Ilya was a university graduate; Maria had been educated only at home. None of these differences mattered to them. What counted was their educational commitment. Maria was as zealous about this as Ilya; she too trained as a teacher even though she did not proceed to teach in a school. Education was the focal point of their lives. The Blanks had been brought up this way. Not only Maria but also two of her sisters married teachers who rose up the hierarchy of educational adminis-tration. Ilya and Maria were united by their zeal, which they successfully transmitted to the next generation.

Ilya had intellectual pursuits outside schooling. He was fascinated by meteorology, and he published learned articles based on his scientific observations. His training at the Imperial Kazan University had sharpened his intellectual appetite. Wind, rain, sun and humidity were recorded by him. Ilya Ulyanov was devoted, as his children would also be, to the rational investigation of their environment. For Ilya the object of attention was the weather; for his offspring it would be the politics of the Russian Empire.

Although Ilya was academically gifted, Maria outshone him in at least one respect. When speaking German, he had trouble with his *rs* as if he were speaking French. (In fact he had the same problem with the Russian language.) The results could be comic to the ears of his school pupils. On one occasion, for instance, he asked some of them what the German word was for 'very'. A pupil answered 'sekhr', with the heavy aspirate of the Russian language, instead of *sehr*. But when Ilya tried to put him right, his own attempt was no better: 'sehl'. Ilya pretended not to notice the class laughing at his mispronunciation.[27] Yet simultaneously he let everyone know that he was always looking for high standards. His standards were applied not only to pupils but also to teachers. He never failed to reprimand any of his protégés who did not come up to scratch. But the successful ones held him in admiring respect and were proud to be called the Ulyanovites (*ulyanovtsy*). Ilya's accomplishments provided him and his family with prominence and status in Simbirsk. He had done well for the province.

His success was made possible by his wife's efficiency in running the Ulyanov household. Ilya even left it to her to buy his suits.[28] Although he was a tailor's son, Ilya could not be bothered to try on clothes. His preoccupation was with his work, and everything was subordinate to it. At home Maria enjoyed his total confidence and Ilya received her unstinting support. They lived a rather isolated existence. Ilya liked the occasional game of chess and whist. But he could find only the elderly civil servant and accountant Arseni Belokrysenko – his son Vladimir's godfather – as his chess partner;[29] and he played whist only with the town's teachers.[30] Maria Alexandrovna was even more withdrawn from local society. A few friends came to the family house on Streletskaya Street, but she seldom paid them any visits in return. Ilya and Maria travelled around the Volga region in the summer. Yet their trips were always to members of one side or the other of their family. In Ilya's case this took them to Astrakhan, in Maria's to her relatives in Stavropol and Kokushkino. Thus the Ulyanovs rarely ventured outside the milieu provided by professional activity or by family. To that extent they remained, despite Ilya's manifest achievements, on the margins of the provincial elite.

They do not seem to have minded much about their seclusion. Their wish was not to climb up the social hierarchy of old Russia so much as to help to construct a new Russia. They focussed their hopes on Ilya's career and upon the education of their sons and daughters. Eight Ulyanov children were born in quick succession. First came Anna in 1864. Then there arrived Alexander two years later. These were followed by Vladimir in 1870, Olga in 1871, Dmitri in 1874 and Maria in 1878. These were not the only ones born to the couple. There had also been an earlier Olga in 1868 and a Nikolai in 1873, both of whom died as babies. This was not unusual for those days, when health-care was rudimentary by twentieth-century standards. In any case the deaths did not discourage the Ulyanovs from continuing to increase the size of their family.

Ilya was not a talkative person and often shut himself away in his study when he was at home. He showed enthusiasm when he was chatting about education and lived for his work. He did not yearn for praise from others, and was rather stingy in praising others when they did well at work. Indeed both Ilya and Maria were emotionally undemonstrative. It took something wholly extraordinary to make them show their feelings – when the younger Olga died as a baby, Ilya sobbed his heart out.[31] But Ilya and Maria were otherwise stolid, quiet individuals. As young adults they already looked middle-aged. Ilya was self-conscious about his premature baldness, and tried to disguise it by brushing forward what was left of his hair. Yet his burning ambition as a kind of cultural missionary was unmistakable; and he and his wife Maria – whose inner calm was extraordinary – were a couple who impressed everyone with their commitment to cultural enlightenment.[32]

Ilya's job as Inspector of Popular Schools was not one he could discharge from his study on Simbirsk's Streletskaya Street. By the last year of his life there were 444 primary schools and more than twenty thousand pupils in Simbirsk province.[33] He had to travel around an area of nearly sixteen thousand square miles, and was frequently away for weeks at a time. Ilya had been appointed as Inspector only eight years after the Emancipation Edict of 1861; his job in the early years lay not so much in the inspection of pedagogical standards as in the supervised construction of suitable buildings in appropriate locations. This required much initiative. In town and village he had to ensure that things were being done to a proper level of efficiency and safety. From spring through to early autumn Ilya would take a tarantas to visit the provincial schools. The tarantas was not the most comfortable horse-drawn vehicle of its day since it had no springs. But it was sturdy and the roads in Simbirsk province were primitive. In any case things were better for Ilya in the winter when he could travel by sleigh. Whatever the season, however, the energy he expended in his early and middle career was extraordinary.

The Ulyanovs spent their summers in the Blank house at Kokush-kino. Before Vladimir was born, they had also taken a trip with their children Anna and Alexander to visit Ilya Ulyanov's surviving relatives in Astrakhan. Ilya's mother Alexandra and elder brother were still alive. Anna Ulyanova never forgot the affectionate fuss made of herself and her brother Alexander. It was so different from what she was used to at home. Her mother Maria, however, disapproved. As often happens in families, she applied a regime of emotional austerity to her children even though she thought her own parents had been too severe towards her and her sisters. Maria Alexandrovna also thought her children were being 'excessively spoiled' by her Astrakhan in-laws.[34] The Astrakhan trip was not repeated, and when the Ulyanovs visited relatives from then onwards, it was always to Maria Alexandrovna's side of the family.[35] Dr Blank was delighted to see his new grandson Vladimir, who was brought to Kokushkino with the rest of the family in the early summer of 1870. Old Dr Blank was not at home when the party arrived, and had to ascend the stairs to find Maria Alexandrovna. She met him proudly on the landing with the baby in her arms. Her father proceeded to make a medical examination of Vladimir and to ask questions about his progress.[36]

But Vladimir was to have no memory of his grandfather because, on 17 June, Dr Blank suddenly died. The estate at Kokushkino passed into the joint possession of the old man's daughters, who kept it as a place for their families to relax together in the summer months. Their joys did not include the obligations of manual work. July was the time when the harvest was taken in and when the peasants of Kokushkino worked their hardest. They sweated in the fields where food and drink was brought out to them at midday; in the evening, folk songs were sung with gusto. This environment was familiar to the visiting Ulyanovs, but they took no part in it. They were on holiday. They were escaping the cares of their urban existence; but they refused to romanticise their rural sur-roundings. Peasant life was not very appealing to them – and the distrust shown by the recently emancipated serfs to Dr Blank cannot have helped matters.

Meanwhile Ilya Ulyanov had risen still higher in society. In July 1874 he was promoted from Inspector to Director of Popular Schools for Simbirsk province. Automatically he thus emulated Dr Blank and became a 'state councillor' and hereditary nobleman entitled to be addressed as 'his Excellency'. Ilya's absences continued to be frequent and lengthy, but Maria was more than capable of handling the situation. Like other middle-class families of the period, the Ulyanovs employed a cook to relieve the burden upon Maria, and nanny Sarbatova looked after the children from 1870. Workers, too, were hired when snow needed to be cleared or wood sawn. The Ulyanovs were similar to any other middle-class family.

Ilya and Maria were also loyal subjects of Alexander II and were committed to the reforms initiated with the Emancipation Edict of 1861. During the Russo-Turkish War of 1877–8, Ilya patriotically collected voluntary contributions for the care of wounded troops.[37] In turn he was proud to accept the various awards, including the Order of Stanislav (First Class) in January 1887, which were conferred in respect of his professional achievements. Ilya and Maria avoided contact with anyone who caused trouble to the authorities. But they made an exception in respect of Dr Alexander Kadyan, whose subversive political opinions had led him to being sent into administrative exile in Simbirsk. This meant that he was obliged to stay within the limits of the town and remain under police surveillance. Ilya and Maria became acquainted with him and asked him to act as their family physician. The relationship, however, remained strictly medical, and the Ulyanovs scrupulously declined to discuss public affairs with him. Throughout the 1860s Ilya and Maria acted on the assumption that a line of official reforms would be followed permanently in the Russian Empire, and they discouraged their children from showing any sympathy for revolutionary ideas.

If his father and mother were so loyal to their Imperial sovereign, how can they have had much influence upon the development of the world's greatest revolutionary? The question is easily answered. Every substantial memoir points in the same direction. Lenin's parentage and upbringing moulded his personality, and Ilya and Maria had a profound, lasting influence on every single one of their children. They gave them a model of dedication. They worked hard, and put a high value on the life of the mind. To the children they transmitted a burning ambition to succeed. Ilya and Maria were half inside and half outside the Simbirsk provincial elite. At that time plenty of capable, educated individuals rose to membership of the gentry. The Russian Empire was in flux. Large-scale social changes were still going on. It would have been astonishing in such a society if the Ulyanovs had undergone complete assimilation within a single generation. They had made a massive advance, but they had not yet 'arrived'. This transitional status did not matter much to Ilya and Maria at the time. They could cope with the tensions.

It is not social but national and ethnic factors that have stirred controversy. Russian nationalists have always claimed that Lenin's ideology is directly attributable to the fact that he was someone who had little Russian blood coursing through his veins. The Jewish ingredient in his ancestry is the object of particular attention. Such commentary itself is mostly xenophobic. For ethnicity is not an exclusively biological phenomenon; it is also produced and reproduced by the mechanisms of language, education and social and economic relationships. The important thing about Ilya and Maria Ulyanov was that they thought, talked and acted as Russians – and so, too, did their children. Their ethnic origins barely affected them in their daily lives.

Indeed, according to Anna Ilinichna, she learned of the Jewish background of Dr Blank only in 1897, when she was thirty-three. This occurred in the course of a journey to Switzerland. Anna Ilinichna used her mother's surname on foreign trips[38] and the Swiss students she met asked her whether she was Jewish. She was surprised to hear that nearly all the Swiss Blanks were Jews. Anna Ilinichna made enquiries, presumably of her mother, and learned that their grandfather Dr Blank was of Jewish origin. Many years later, indeed after Lenin's death, Anna Ilinichna also learned from a friend that a silver goblet that had once been owned by Dr Blank's parents was of a type used in Jewish religious feasts.[39] Neither Anna nor her siblings were disconcerted by their discovery. But they did not advertise it either. They already knew that their ancestry was not wholly Russian, and perhaps they added the Jewish ingredient to the existing list. It may be that a degree of caution was also at work. Anti-semitism was widespread in the Russian Empire, and the young Ulyanovs may have seen no reason to expose themselves to unnecessary trouble in society.

Yet Lenin, in later life, saw advantage in a cultural admixture having being made to their Russian heritage. He regarded Jews as a specially gifted 'race' (or *plemya* as he put it in the Russian fashion that was then conventional), and he took pride in the Jewish ingredient in his ancestry. As he remarked to his sister Anna, Jewish activists constituted about half the number of revolutionaries in the southern regions of the Russian Empire. According to the novelist Maxim Gorki, Lenin compared the Russians unfavourably with Jews: 'I feel sorry for those persons who are intelligent. We don't have many intelligent persons. We are a predominantly talented people, but we have a lazy mentality. A bright Russian is almost always a Jew or a person with an admixture of Jewish blood.'[40] Nevertheless this was not a matter at the forefront of his attention. He may even have been unaware of it until Anna Ilinichna started to make her enquiries. Lenin primarily thought of himself as a Russian.

In fact it was less the Jewish than the Germanic aspect of Lenin's mother's background that continued to have an influence on the family. Maria Alexandrovna worshipped at the local Lutheran church while her husband attended Orthodox services just as she liked to celebrate Christmas in the German manner by having a fir tree in the house;[41] and Lenin was to mark the season in the same manner whenever he and his wife had children among their guests.

German seasonal customs were not the only lingering element in the family's ethnic ancestry. There was also the strong impetus of German and Jewish culture towards education and public achievement. The Blanks had this aplenty; and Ilya Ulyanov, coming from a non-Russian background and aspiring to a high career in the Russian Empire, reinforced the impetus: he knew that he would succeed on his merits and his qualifications or not at all. Maria and Ilya were alike in seeking fair treatment for those subjects of the Russian Empire who were not Russian. In this they differed from those many people of non-Russian descent who acquired a pronounced antipathy towards non-Russians who would not assimilate themselves to a Russian national identity. Thus Ilya was determined that the non-Russians should receive education in their native language. He was a pragmatist as well as a man of principle. He knew how difficult it would otherwise be to induce the Chuvashes to send their children to his schools. And so he insisted that the Chuvash children in Simbirsk province should be taught not in Russian but in Chuvash. This sensitivity towards other national and ethnic groups was passed on to the Ulyanov children, and was something that exercised Lenin's mind to the very end of his life.

And so the Ulyanovs were Russians of a particular type. They were new Russians in the sense that they were of diverse ethnic ancestry. But Russians they had become. Although Maria Alexandrovna showed traces of her German origins, she had by and large assimilated herself to a Russian identity. Ilya Nikolaevich, too, had put his past aside. Both Ilya

and Maria had about them the ambition that is often found disproportionately among people making a career in the midst of a society with a
different national majority. Living by the Volga among Russians, the
Ulyanovs were a bit like first-generation immigrants. They had a terrific
zeal to succeed, and this zeal was passed on to their progeny. Furthermore, they were selective about the aspects of Russian culture with which
they identified themselves. 'Old' Russia – the Russia of peasants, village
customs, drunkenness, ignorance, arbitrary rule, social deference and
hereditary privilege – held no attraction for them. Ilya and Maria wanted
to get rid of those age-old traditions. They associated themselves with
modernity and wanted Russia to become more akin to the countries of
the West. They were hoping for the reforms of the 1860s to transform
society. The Ulyanovs were believers in Progress, Enlightenment, Order,
Cleanliness, Obedience, Hierarchy and Punctiliousness.

They were therefore attracted to trends in contemporary Russia that
emphasised contact with Europe. All 'progressive' people wanted to learn
French and German. Like other nobles, the Ulyanovs sometimes slipped
out of Russian into French;[42] perhaps, in contrast with an earlier
generation of such Russians, they merely wanted to communicate without the servants knowing what they were saying. But their linguistic
capacity was nevertheless considerable. So, too, were their musical
inclinations. Not every house in Simbirsk took an interest in the operas
of Richard Wagner.[43] The Ulyanovs, moreover, read about the latest
European artistic, philosophical and scientific developments. Ilya and
Maria Ulyanov were 'cultured' Russians; they were patriots. They wanted
to build a 'modern', 'European', 'Western' and 'enlightened' society.
Lenin was the son of his parents.

2

CHILDHOOD IN SIMBIRSK

1870–1885

So what kind of child was Volodya? Until recently there was too little information for anyone to be confident of the answer. It was not that memoirs did not exist. Quite the contrary: Volodya's family left behind a copious record and his sisters Anna and Maria wrote incessantly about him. But only the material published within a year or two of his death in 1924 is frank about anything even mildly critical of him. Censorship was quickly at work in support of the Lenin cult and the memoirs were heavily edited by the central party leadership before appearing in print. Only now can we examine the original drafts. From this material a picture emerges of a little boy who was energetic, brilliant and charming but also bumptious and not always very kind.

Volodya's sister Anna, six years his senior, recorded the impact he made as a baby:[1]

> He was the third child and very noisy – a great bawler with combative, happy little hazel eyes. He started to walk at almost the same time as his sister Olya [that is, Olga], who was a year and a half younger than he. She began to walk very early and without being noticed by those around her. Volodya, by contrast, learned to walk late; and if his sister tumbled inaudibly (or 'shuffled over', as their nanny put it) and raised herself up independently by pressing her hands down on the floor, he inevitably would bang his head and raise a desperate roar throughout the house.

The wooden structure of the house made it into an echo chamber and the floors and walls resounded as the little fellow went on crashing his head on to the carpet – or even on to the floorboards themselves. His mother Maria Alexandrovna wondered whether he might turn out to be mentally retarded. The midwife who had delivered him offered as her opinion: 'He'll turn out either very intelligent or else very stupid.' At the time this was not very reassuring to Maria Alexandrovna, and later she remembered how fearful she had been about her little Volodya.[2]

The family could only make guesses as to why he banged his head, and reached the conclusion that it had something to do with his physical shape. Volodya as a baby had short, weak legs and a large head. He kept falling over, apparently because he was top heavy. Once he had fallen over, they believed, he flailed around to pull himself up and banged his head in sheer frustration.[3]

This did not explain why he continued to be so noisy even when he had learned to walk. He never stopped making a racket and according to Anna, he was boisterous and demanding throughout his childhood.[4] He was much more destructive than the other Ulyanov children. When his parents gave him a small papier-mâché horse for his birthday, his instinct was to creep off with the toy and twist off its legs. Anna watched him as he hid himself behind a door. A few minutes later he was found, perfectly content, with the horse in pieces at his side. What is more, Volodya was not always pleasant to his brothers and sisters. At the age of three, he stamped over the collection of theatre posters which his elder brother Sasha had carefully laid out on the carpet. He ruined several of them before his mother could haul him away. A couple of years later he grabbed Anna's favourite ruler and snapped it in two.[5] By then he was old enough to understand that he had done something seriously wrong in this orderly family. There was a malicious aspect to his behaviour and the rest of the family did not like it.

But he also had much charm and was always forgiven by his nanny Varvara Sarbatova. When he misbehaved, he owned up quickly. This at least reassured his mother to some extent: 'It's good that he never does anything on the sly.'[6] At the age of eight he proved her point. It was then that he was allowed for the first time to travel by paddle steamer to Kazan to visit his Aunt Anna Veretennikova (née Blank) in the company of his sister Anna and brother Alexander. This was a big occasion for him and he had difficulty restraining his tears as he waved his mother goodbye on the Simbirsk quayside. In Kazan he had a rare old time with his Veretennikov cousins and got up to some horseplay. Unfortunately he smashed a glass vase in the process. Aunt Anna heard the commotion, rushed into the room and quizzed everyone about the incident. Volodya, however, kept quiet and did not admit to what he had done. Three months after the event, when he had returned to Simbirsk, his mother found him sobbing into his pillow late at night. When she went upstairs to his bedroom, he blurted out to her: 'I deceived Aunt Anya [Anna's diminutive]. I said that it wasn't me who broke the vase whereas it was me who broke it.'[7]

Volodya was a stocky boy of moderate height with curly light-brown hair which turned ginger in adolescence. He still had shortish legs and a disproportionately large head. Although he was generally in good health, there was concern about the squint in his left eye. His mother took him to Kazan to be examined by the ophthalmologist Professor Adamyuk, who advised that the defect was irremediable and that he would have to manage exclusively with his right eye.[8] Very late in his life, in 1922, Lenin learned he had been misdiagnosed. In fact the left eye was merely short-sighted,[9] and Adamyuk's failure to issue him with spectacles resulted in his habit – much noted when he became a famous politician – of screwing up his eyes when talking to people. His brothers and sister suffered from much greater problems. When Sasha became acutely ill with a stomach inflammation, Maria Alexandrovna fell to her knees before the icon in the sitting-room corner and called over to her daughter Anna: 'Pray for Sasha.'[10] Sasha recovered from his illness, but other Ulyanovs, including Volodya, suffered with their stomachs. There seems to have been a genetic predisposition in the family, possibly one that was inherited from the Blank side.

Yet for most of the time they were fit, active and full of purpose. The children were encouraged to take plenty of exercise. Their father Ilya Nikolaevich went on walks with them along the headland by the river Volga to the north of the town. He also bought season tickets for the family to bathe at one of the nearby beaches.[11] But mainly the children were left to their own devices outside the home. A gap of fourteen years separated the eldest and the youngest of them – Anna and Maria. This meant that the smallest children almost treated the others as adults. But Volodya was different. Sometimes he and the younger children were left in the care of Sasha and Anna, who obeyed and applied the rules set by their parents. Volodya loved and admired Sasha, but still he would avail himself of the opportunity to play up. On occasion he ran into the hall in his muddy galoshes. Floor and carpet were dirtied and Anna and Sasha were horrified. Such antics marked him off from his brothers and sisters.[12]

The children paired off for companionship. Sasha and Anna, the two eldest, got together; then came the boisterous couple, Volodya and Olga; and the third pairing was of Dmitri and Maria. The closeness of Sasha and Anna endured beyond adolescence; they still saw a lot of each other when they became students in St Petersburg. Volodya and Olga were also contented playmates; nobody could remember them ever falling out. Their harmony probably resulted, at least in part, from the fact that

Olga, who had a sweet nature, did as Volodya told her, and as their elder sister Anna recalled, 'he liked to give commands [*komandovat'*].'[13] Volodya and Olga raced about the large garden and played on the trapeze that Ilya Nikolaevich had bought after the family had watched a travelling circus in Simbirsk. On quieter days, Volodya and Olga might get out the croquet set. But always there was some palaver. Their mother's friend Gertruda Nazareva was to write: 'The whole day long you could hear Olga singing, hopping, spinning round or playing with Volodya, who I think caused greater bother than any of the others to his mother and elder sister.'[14]

Again he was hardly a delinquent, just the most mischievous child in a remarkably orderly family. Punishment was rarely thought necessary. Ilya Nikolaevich had a fiery temperament and his sons and daughters feared his disapproval even when his job took him off on lengthy trips around the province of Simbirsk. At such times Maria Alexandrovna punished any misbehaving child by sending them to sit on the chair in Ilya Nikolaevich's study. This was known in the family as 'the black chair'. The family never forgot an episode when Volodya, after a piece of naughtiness, was dispatched to the chair and his mother forgot all about him for hours. Mischievous though he was, he did not dare get down or make a sound until she returned to the study.[15]

And so life went on. Their growing number of children impelled the Ulyanov parents to look for a larger house, and in summer 1878, on Ilya's appointment as Provincial Director of Popular Schools, they moved to 48 Moscow Street. This was the place Volodya was to remember as his Simbirsk home. Moscow Street was near the heart of the town and was one of the larger, more prestigious streets since it contained the official residence of the Simbirsk army garrison commander. (Even so, it was not supplied with a pavement and pedestrians had to walk along wooden duckboards if they wished to avoid the mud and puddles in wet weather.) The Orthodox Cathedral, the Simbirsk Classical Gimnazia and the Karamzin Public Library all lay within a short distance. The location was convenient for the entire family, including Maria Alexandrovna, who could visit the Lutheran Church a few houses away. But the main attraction for the Ulyanovs was the house itself. Ilya had a capacious study on the ground floor; Maria, too, had her own room. Downstairs there were five large rooms and a kitchen and plenty of space existed in the children's bedrooms on the first floor. The garden was substantial; large trees graced the lawn and the family employed a gardener to produce the fruit and vegetables they needed. Like all middle-class professional families, the Ulyanovs had servants.

As they settled into their new home, they were known by their acquaintances as 'the beautiful family'. Ilya was esteemed for his achievements in educational administration and Maria was respected for her musical and linguistic accomplishments. The children without exception were successful at school and were noted for their good behaviour at home and in the town. It was a topic of local amazement that none of them strayed into the horticultural part of the grounds. No flower or vegetable was ever trampled, no tree branch broken. It was a matter of honour that no Ulyanov child, even the disruptive Volodya, should misbehave in public. Any such incident was a cause of local comment. For example, neighbours were surprised in winter when the Ulyanov children, like children in all other Simbirsk families, threw snowballs at passers-by through the wicker fence.[16]

They were not kept apart from other girls and boys because Ilya Nikolaevich and Maria Alexandrovna supplemented their income by taking in lodgers. Among these were the Persiyanov family, who occupied rooms on the mezzanine floor.[17] Vyacheslav Persiyanov was in the same school year as Vladimir Ulyanov. So too was Nikolai Nefedev, whose mother had died and whose father pleaded with the Ulyanov parents to let his son live with them while attending school. The request was granted and space was found for him in a converted bath-house at the bottom of the garden.[18] Vladimir played a lot with Nikolai Nefedev. But generally the Ulyanov children sought their closest companions within the family. The children had been brought up to make something of themselves, and each supported the efforts of the others. Perhaps the close ties of the family made it harder for the children to form deep relationships outside the family. Only four of the six grew to adulthood. Of these, Maria never married and seems to have been celibate; and although both Anna and Dmitri married, the weddings took place in their late twenties: there was no rush to leave the Ulyanov home. Vladimir, despite marrying in his mid-twenties, did so in circumstances that make it unlikely that he did this out of a passionate commitment.

The stable warmth of family life, however, did not stop Vladimir from being antisocial to his sisters and brothers. There was always a touch of malice in his character. Thus, although he got on well with his little brother Dmitri, he sometimes teased him badly. Vladimir used to say that Dmitri could cry 'to order'. Dmitri denied this, but under further baiting from Vladimir he would break down in tears. Then Vladimir would announce that Dmitri indeed cried to order.[19]

Such behaviour annoyed his parents and the older children, particularly Alexander. Yet he was still popular with them and it was not thought that his faults outweighed his virtues, and his sister Olga continued to believe that he could do no wrong. His educational prowess was a source of pride to the family. The best schools in Simbirsk were the Classical Gimnazia for the boys and the Marinskaya Gimnazia for the girls. An entrance examination was obligatory and only very able students secured a place. The Ulyanov children were bright and had been prepared for the examination, and their father's rank in the educational system exempted him from paying the regular thirty rubles per annum for each of them. Maria Alexandrovna had worked on them to get them through the examination. She took each child in turn and used the new-fangled method of phonics and flash-cards to teach them to read.[20] Part-time tutors were also employed, mainly from among the young teachers trained by Ilya Nikolaevich. Several of them came to the Ulyanov home, including Vasili Kalashnikov, Ivan Nikolaev and Vera Prushakevich.[21] The parents' expectation of achievement was intense and an early start in literacy and numeracy was recognised as the most effective means of enhancing the children's eventual educational attainment.

The eldest child Anna sought relief from the pressure of parental expectations:[22]

> It was I who a year later often begged my mother with bitter tears to take me out of the gimnazia, assuring her that I would accomplish more at home; and sometimes I implored her permission to miss school, sitting down to work with considerable zeal. I sensed very painfully that father would look on this as a manifestation of laziness. I felt that this was unjust, but couldn't explain this intelligently and did not dare talk about it to father.

Anna was an intelligent girl who had been promoted to the class a year ahead of her age. But she could not cope with the amount of homework and was suffering badly from headaches and insomnia.

Not daring to mention any of this to her father, she asked her mother to negotiate for her to study alone at home. But her father was implacable.[23] Anna was too loyal to accuse her father of being insensitive; she did the opposite and reproached herself for being a 'fiery, capricious' girl.[24] Yet a sense of resentment persisted. She thought that her father might have been a little more indulgent to his offspring when they did well. If Ilya Nikolaevich liked one of her essays, he used to mention it to her mother but not to Anna herself. Simbirsk's leading educationalist was a poor psychologist. The occasional touch of praise, Anna concluded, would not have gone amiss.[25] Not surprisingly, she grew up with a tendency to panic when faced with educational tests of various sorts. Maria, her younger sister, was the same. Both were intelligent and purposive girls, but Maria spent her early adult years starting course after course and not finishing them. Anna was clear in her own mind that the two of them had been pushed too hard as youngsters and that they had failed to pick up the confidence that seemed to come naturally to her brothers Alexander and Vladimir.

Certainly Vladimir was bright and confident. The succession of personal tutors prepared him for a couple of years and in summer 1879, at the age of nine, he sat the various tests for the Simbirsk Classical Gimnazia. In the autumn he entered the first class, which consisted of thirty boys.[26] In his dark-blue tunic with its upturned, military collar and nine brass buttons he looked just like the others. He was the second Ulyanov boy to enter the school: Alexander was already a pupil there and was the outstanding student of his year.

The kind of education received by Vladimir Ulyanov has not attracted much attention. But in fact it is of great significance for his later development. The Ministry of Popular Enlightenment had laid down statutes for all Russian gimnazii in 1871. The curriculum and timetable were set in St Petersburg. A preparatory class was introduced so that all pupils might start with a roughly equal opportunity of successful completion of their education. Thereafter, from the age of nine, each boy was expected to undergo a further eight years' schooling. In the preparatory class attention was paid to the contemporary educational rudiments. Out of twenty-two hours per week, six were spent on the Russian language, six on handwriting, six on mathematics and science and four on religion. Other subjects were brought into the curriculum as soon as the boys entered the first full gimnazia year. In the first-year timetable of twenty-four hours, eight were given over to Latin, five to maths and physics, four each to Russian and French, three to handwriting, two each to geography and religion. German was introduced in year two, history and ancient Greek in year three. Handwriting was dropped after year one, geography after year four. This balance of subjects was by and large sustained through to the eighth and final year.[27]

Latin and Greek constituted half the timetable in years six to eight. The Ministry of Popular Enlightenment saw Classics as purveying the ideals of belief, truth, endurance and courage; it regarded the ancient authors as promoting loyalty to the interests of the Romanov dynasty. As in the rest of Europe, the norm was to get pupils to translate the works of Homer, Herodotus, Thucydides, Xenophon, Livy, Horace and Cicero. Intellectual curiosity was discouraged. The accurate rendering of the authors into Russian was the requirement and the older classes were taught to transform Greek and Latin hexameters into Russian verse.

Russian literature was hardly studied; nearly all the country's great poets and novelists – Pushkin, Lermontov, Gogol, Turgenev, Lev Tolstoi and Dostoevski – were harassed by the state censorship for supplying ideas subversive of the contemporary political system. But the Russian literary heritage was not entirely ignored. In the restricted time allotted by the Ministry of Popular Enlightenment the pupils were required to learn several poems by heart. The selection included not only politically 'safe' figures such as Krylov, Zhukovski and Koltsov but also even Pushkin and Lermontov. The appreciation of artistry was less important to the schoolteachers than the inculcation of patriotic pride and allegiance to the monarchy. Immense slabs of poetry had to be committed to memory and tested at the end of the school year. It was a tall order. In order to be permitted to move from the fourth to the fifth class in the gimnazia, Vladimir Ulyanov and his fellow pupils had to be able to recite over a hundred poems, including forty-five fables by Krylov and thirty-one of Pushkin's poems. It is hardly astounding that only half the class passed the end-of-year oral test enabling them to proceed to the fifth year. Vladimir was among the successful pupils.[28]

Although the pupils studied French and German, the government strove to stamp out the potential for them to pick up revolutionary ideas. Grammar edged out literature. No Russian gimnazia taught Voltaire, Rousseau or Goethe, and Headmaster Fëdor Kerenski – who by an extraordinary quirk of history was father of Alexander Kerenski, who was to lead the Provisional Government in 1917 which Lenin and the Bolsheviks overthrew – banned his pupils from using the Karamzin Public Library where they might borrow disapproved works of literature. Kerenski was following the government's guidelines. The Ministry of Popular Enlightenment, wishing to insulate gimnazia students from the contemporary world, reduced physics, chemistry and biology to a minimal presence in the curriculum (and the works of the world-famous chemist Mendeleev were withdrawn from libraries). The government also stipulated that gimnazia pupils should attend the Russian Orthodox Church services regularly. Discipline was rigorously enforced. Like other headmasters of the period, Fëdor Kerenski employed beatings, detentions, extra work and heavy moralising, and, as was the fashion in all tsarist schools, teachers encouraged pupils to snitch on their delinquent fellows.[29]

Such schooling was unpleasant for most pupils. The discipline was irksome and sometimes brutal, the workload immense, the curriculum disconnected from everyday life. Although none of the worst disciplinary sanctions was applied to Vladimir, it is difficult to believe that his experience at school left no negative mark on his consciousness. The state's direct, heavy-handed interference in the Simbirsk Classical Gimnazia had a pettifogging aspect and few bright pupils failed to draw the conclusion that if the schools were run in so bureaucratic a fashion, then so were the other state institutions. Vladimir must also have noted the contrast between his studies at home and the regime in the school. Under his mother's tutelage his academic work had been more pleasurable; the fact that many fellow pupils abandoned the gimnazia because of the excessive requirements must surely have given him at least a rudimentary idea that all was not well.[30] Yet, unlike elder brother Sasha at the same age, Vladimir did not rebel. Just once, when he was caught mimicking his incompetent French master Adolf Por, did he get into trouble.[31] But his father made him promise never again to step out of line, and Vladimir reverted to his habits of obedience.

His general attitude, however, was positive and he made exceptional academic progress. Headmaster Kerenski was pleased with the adolescent, awarding him not merely 5s but 5+s in his school reports; he was so impressed that, according to Anna Ilinichna, he 'forgave him certain acts of mischief that he would not so easily have forgiven in respect of others'. She added: 'Of course, an influence here was exerted by his good attitude to Ilya Nikolaevich and the entire family.'[32] The only person to express doubts about Vladimir was indeed his father Ilya Nikolaevich, who worried that academic success was coming to him too easily and that he might not recognise the need to be industrious.[33]

Vladimir's obedience is unsurprising – and not just because of the pressure of parental expectations. The gimnazii were a pathway to the higher echelons of Imperial state and society. Vladimir Ulyanov, once he attained maturity, would automatically obtain noble status. But even the Ulyanovs needed to enhance their opportunities, and an education of this quality secured this. The prior work he had done with his mother and tutors at home meant that the curriculum was already within his reach. He was accustomed to being diligent. Immediately he became the brightest boy of his year. Annual reports gave him the full five marks in subject after subject. Never did he obtain less than this except in the single subject of logic. No doubt it helped a little that he was the son of the Simbirsk Province Director of Popular Schools. In a setting where personal contacts played a large part in everyone's career few teachers would have wanted to offend Ilya Ulyanov. But Headmaster Kerenski did not have to write a fictional account. Vladimir Ulyanov, like his brother Alexander, was a genuinely brilliant pupil. For Vladimir, it was natural to try his hardest at school. Work was a family duty and duty was a pleasure.

He was generally unobtrusive outside lessons but was noted for his sarcasm, and when a fellow pupil broke his pencils, Vladimir grabbed him by the collar and forced him to stop.[34] Not himself a trouble-maker, he met trouble with a direct physical response. No one bullied Vladimir for long. He was strong and stocky, and it did him no harm that he shared his expertise when others could not understand the lessons. But he had no close friends at the gimnazia.[35] Vladimir got on with his work, left people alone and expected to be left alone. He was a bit of a loner.

Meanwhile his education was inculcating an attentiveness to the precise meaning of words; the years of parsing Latin verbs and constru-ing Greek iambics left their mark. The pernicketiness of Lenin the writer–revolutionary owes as much to the literary heritage of Athens and Rome as to Karl Marx and Friedrich Engels. It may even be that he first learned from the orators Demosthenes and Cicero how to discern a crack in the wall of an opponent's arguments and prise it open – and perhaps the stories of heroism in the epic poetry of Homer and the prose of Xenophon and Livy predisposed him to give high value to the potential role of the individual leader. Nor can anyone who has made a close study of the historians Herodotus and Thucydides fail to be influenced by their insistence on delving below the surface of events to their hidden basic causes. But all this is speculation. Vladimir Ulyanov was reluctant to reveal much about his early life. What little we know about his reaction to the Classics comes from his relatives. His sister Anna, for example, wrote that his zest for Latin was such that he provided her – six years his senior – with coaching on the more difficult elements of grammar.[36]

Thus throughout the rest of his life he quoted sentences from the ancient authors even though most of his readers had not had the benefit of his education. This was not just a bit of exhibitionism; it was the unconscious behaviour of former Classicists everywhere in contemporary Europe. In later years he had no time for Latin and Greek. But then suddenly in 1914, at the outbreak of the Great War, he felt a compulsion to resume his philosophical research and (as we shall see) to include Aristotle among the authors he studied.

Yet the gimnazia education was as important in what it failed to do as in what it did to the pupils. In its attempt to avert attention from acute public problems, it vacated space to be filled by ideas that were not to the liking of the official authorities. The fact that a comprehensive training in the humanities was withheld from the pupils exposed them to the attractions of philosophies that incurred the government's official disapproval. Headmaster Kerenski had tried to maintain a monopoly over the ideas available to his pupils by ruling that they needed his permission to use the public libraries. But the effort was counter-productive. Clever boys and girls, when reacting against the contents of their schooling, often identified any proposition opposed to the officially approved notions as being inherently worthy of their commitment. If the tsar thought one way, then the truth must lie in the opposite one. Ilya Nikolaevich, for once, declined to support the headmaster; he had always regarded the gimnazia curriculum as too narrow and had sent his children to gimnazii mainly because they offered an avenue for entrance to universities. While not condoning open subversive reading matter, he allowed his son Alexander to take out a subscription to the weighty *Historical Journal*.[37]

Ilya Nikolaevich himself not only followed the latest discussions of pedagogy but also kept a large general library in his study. He and Maria Alexandrovna were typical of most educated Russians in keeping abreast of the great works of contemporary literature, and Maria Alexandrovna particularly enjoyed the romantic poet Lermontov (who had written in the manner of Lord Byron). Ilya Nikolaevich imparted his cultural enthusiasms by visual as well as academic means. For example, he took Vladimir and a couple of classmates on a trip in the family horse-drawn trap outside Simbirsk to the spot described by the writer Ivan Goncharov in his novel *The Precipice*. There, at Kindyakovka, they gazed up at the precipice described in the novel and clambered about the bottom of it.[38] Other authors, too, were read and discussed in the family. Thus the Ulyanov children read the novels of Nikolai Gogol and Ivan Turgenev. Characteristically they made a competitive game out of what they read. In the evenings, when they had nothing else to do, they would try to guess the name of the author of an excerpt from a poem or a novel. They were a studious lot even when they were having fun.[39]

Politics hardly impinged on Vladimir Ulyanov's early life in any direct fashion. He saw the Turkish prisoners-of-war who were billeted nearby on Moscow Street during the outbreak of the Russo-Turkish War of 1877–8, and his father made a collection for the Red Cross while hostilities were going on. But the Ulyanov parents tended to avoid direct political discussion. At least they did so until 1 March 1881. It was on that day – a fateful one for subsequent Russian history – that terrorists assassinated the Emperor Alexander II. There had been several conspiracies against his life in recent years. But the People's Will organisation, formed in 1879, was more competent than its predecessor and it was partly in response to their violent activity that Alexander II had begun to contemplate granting a consultative national assembly. But the People's Will did not want merely a reformed monarchy. They wanted the Emperor dead, and at last they succeeded with a bomb that was rolled under a carriage bearing him through to the Winter Palace in St Petersburg.

Vladimir Ulyanov was still only ten years old when the family attended the service of commemoration to the deceased emperor in Simbirsk Cathedral on 16 March. All local dignitaries, including the province's governor, did the same. Ilya and Maria were appalled by the killing. They were not revolutionary sympathisers and detested the spilling of blood. Both considered that Alexander II had played a useful role in pushing Russia down the road towards reform, even though he had regressed somewhat in the 1870s. In particular, he had trimmed the rights of the elective provincial administrative bodies (the zemstva); he had also restricted the system of trial by jury after the socialist terrorist Vera Zasulich, who had been caught in the act of trying to assassinate the Governor-General of St Petersburg Fëdor Trepov, failed to be convicted by due process. Yet an agenda of reform remained in place through to the end of Alexander II's life. Indeed, under pressure of the terrorist campaign, he had begun to give thought to sanctioning a consultative national assembly as a means of rallying support for the throne. His assassination had the effect of convincing his son and heir Alexander III to abandon all further reform. He directed intense suspicion at any innovative measures; his emphasis, until his death in 1894, was upon traditional concepts of order.

Vladimir Ulyanov presumably shared the revulsion of his parents from the terrorist act. But, like other children, he can hardly have been preoccupied by thoughts about politics once the anguished excitement about the Emperor's death and funeral had dissipated. His precocity was as a school pupil, not as a revolutionary theorist.

Even so, political themes were not entirely absent from his young life. The Ulyanov children learned from their brother Alexander how to make toy soldiers out of paper and to organise play-battles. Alexander made up his models in the uniforms of Garibaldi's troops of the Italian Risorgimento. Anna and Olga chose the Spanish forces that struggled to free their country from the Napoleonic invasion. Vladimir plumped for the Union Army of Abraham Lincoln that fought against the pro-slavery South in the American Civil War.[40] Their cousin Nikolai Veretennikov was later to object that Vladimir had models of the contemporary 'English' army. But Dmitri Ulyanov, Vladimir's younger brother, repudiated this version. By and large Dmitri was an accurate chronicler and there is all the more reason to believe him because of a second known political element in Vladimir's early life. His favourite book, before he moved on to the Russian literary classics, was none other than Harriet Beecher Stowe's *Uncle Tom's Cabin*. This tale of a Negro slave's attempt to flee the cruelties of a cotton plantation in the American South was given pride of place in his room.[41] Such choices cannot have been coincidental. The Ulyanov children were brought up in a cultural environment that favoured national, political and social freedom.

Yet it is striking that Vladimir's most cherished book described not Russia but the USA. This was in keeping with the desire of his parents to keep themselves and their children away from dangerous discussions of Russian public life. If so, they were a little naive. *Uncle Tom's Cabin* contained ideas of universal significance; its sentimental style communicated ideals of universal human dignity. When we try to trace the origins of Vladimir's political outlook, we often look to what he read in his late adolescence and early manhood. We focus on Chernyshevski, Marx, Plekhanov and Kautsky. But we need to remember that, before these Russian and German male authors imprinted themselves upon his consciousness, an American woman – Harriet Beecher Stowe – had already influenced his young mind.

Vladimir was a lively boy. Once he had completed his school and other academic obligations, he loved to get outside. At the age of nine or ten he gave up playing the piano. His mother was disappointed; she was a serious pianist herself and trained her daughter Anna to a high enough level to play the main classical works as well as the operas of Richard Wagner.[42] But Maria Alexandrovna – for once – complied with

Vladimir's wishes, perhaps because he had so much schoolwork to prepare. Yet the rest of his family did not think this was the reason. His sister Maria guessed that her brother felt that the piano was too girlish an occupation for him.[43] This little event is also noteworthy as an early sign of Vladimir's clinical capacity to decide what was worth doing and to drop everything else. It also reveals the unattractiveness of artistic activity for him. In fact he was an able painter. An extant postcard he made for a friend is executed in vivid colours; and in particular not a drop of paint is spilled where it should not be: Vladimir was already a perfectionist about anything he was intending to show to others. The postcard had one of those coded messages where the painted figures of Red Indians, trees and someone drowning stood for something recognisable to the recipient.[44] He also learned from his mother how to compose a letter in invisible ink with the use of milk – this was to prove specially useful in 1895 when he needed to smuggle messages out of the St Petersburg House of Preliminary Detention.[45]

Vladimir, unlike his brothers and sisters, had no hobbies. Carpentry left him cold. Philately and other kinds of collecting were not for him. In the summertime he was practically never out of the family garden. He and Nikolai Nefedev were always up to pranks. Crouching among the fruit trees and birches, they set cage-traps for blue-tits. They lacked the expertise and were driven to buying birds from a Mr Lapshin, who lived in the Alexander Gardens in Simbirsk. Lapshin also sold them more efficient trapping mechanisms, and in the winter they caught five or six birds. In the following spring, Volodya determined to set them free. Young Nefedev persuaded him to keep a small goldfinch.[46]

On another occasion things took a nasty turn. Nikolai Nefedev and Volodya had the habit of swimming in the shallows of the river Sviyaga in the centre of Simbirsk. Seeing how other youngsters were fishing off the Vodovozny Bridge, they went home to make their own nets with the idea of catching fish of their own. Foolishly they followed another boy's advice to starting fishing in the nearby ditch at a point near the town's distillery. Although the water was not very deep, it was covered in green slime which made it indistinguishable from the quagmire next to it. Volodya lost his footing in search of frogs and tumbled into the quagmire. Both he and Nikolai let out a shriek. A worker ran speedily out of the distillery to their aid, but by then Volodya was enmired to his waist and in grave danger. The unnamed worker waded in after him, dragged him out and settled him on the bank. Knowing that he would be in trouble when his mother found out, Volodya tried to smarten himself up before going home. But to no avail. Inevitably his mother noticed his muddy face and clothes and the upshot was a prohibition on going fishing again.[47]

There was still plenty for Volodya to do outside the house. He liked to skate on the rivers Sviyaga and Volga; this was still allowed. He also enjoyed himself amusing young Dmitri and Maria. His games of hide-and-seek with them were much appreciated. Meanwhile Volodya kept his eyes on his brother Alexander and tried to copy him. There was a family joke that his first question, whenever he was in a quandary about something, was what would Alexander do in similar circumstances. He even ate what he thought would meet Alexander's approval. This was more than a normal wish to imitate. Alexander was the family's pride and joy. It is difficult to avoid the thought that within the sinews of confidence there lurked a streak of diffidence even in young Volodya.

What is clear beyond a shadow of doubt is that his personality had been to a very large extent moulded by his experiences as an adolescent. He had attended, and been successful, at a school where the very highest demands were made in relation to a very restricted curriculum. He emerged – and this would probably have occurred in such a family in any case – as an extraordinarily ambitious and determined young man. His schooling was narrow, but it also had depth, a depth that gave him the lifelong confidence to tackle any intellectual problem that came his way. The mental manoeuvrability required by the study of the Classics was never to leave him. Nor was the belief in the importance of the written word – and especially of the printed word. At the same Vladimir Ulyanov had access to ideas and emotions that predisposed him to question the nature of the society in which he lived. He had this mainly from books. 'The other Russia', the Russia of barge-haulers, peasants, country priests and factory workers, was unknown to him except through reports from his father or the novels of Gogol, Turgenev and Tolstoi.

His intellectual challenge to the status quo had yet to emerge. He was mischievous and sharp-tongued, but these qualities did not express themselves in a political standpoint. For a boy of his age this was not unusual, even though it was not entirely unknown for gimnazia boys to adopt ideas of Revolution. In the eyes of his headmaster, Vladimir was an exemplar of academic devotion. He came from the sort of family that cultivated a spirit of industriousness and hopefulness; and he had gone to a school that gave him the opportunity to proceed to university and then to a career of public distinction. As yet there was no reason to predict that he would adopt an ideology markedly different from that of his father Ilya, who had his disappointments with the regime but flinched from that of any rebellious talk. Vladimir seemed set to achieve all the prizes that his father had achieved and more.

3

DEATHS IN THE FAMILY

1886–1887

Until 1886, the year when Vladimir Ulyanov turned sixteen, he had no outward troubles. His parents had continued to better themselves. They lived in a large town-house on Moscow Street and Ilya had risen to the post of Director of Popular Schools for Simbirsk province. The Ulyanov parents had six children who appeared to be on the threshold of rewarding careers.

Yet the situation was not as congenial as it seemed. Later accounts have neglected evidence in the published memoirs that Ilya Ulyanov was a controversial local figure for the province's more conservative and powerful inhabitants. In 1880 he had completed twenty-five years' service; although he was only forty-nine, his terms of employment compelled him to apply formally for an extension to his contract. In the event he was given an extra year and then a further five years.[1] Matters had been worsened by the stand taken by Ilya in the contemporary Russian debate about schooling. Complaints were being made that, like other educationalists of his generation, he paid scant attention to religious instruction in schools. Ilya in fact complied with the curriculum, which included the teaching of Christian belief. But he did not approve of the Orthodox Church itself being allowed to regulate schools, and he disliked the switch in governmental policy towards the construction of Church schools. Ilya incurred hostility for the stand he took. In 1884 Archpriest A. I. Baratynski attacked him in the local newspaper *Simbirsk Provincial News*.[2] All this cannot have improved his ability to cope with his increasingly frequent bouts of ill health. He was becoming dispirited and had ceased to believe that he would be able to work until the normal age of retirement.[3]

He had always been at his happiest when he could get out and about in Simbirsk province. His last such visit was to the Syzran district, a hundred miles away, in mid-December 1885.[4] His eldest child Anna, who had travelled from St Petersburg where she had been training to be a teacher on the new Higher Women's Courses, joined him in Syzran.

Father and daughter returned to find the rest of the family preparing for Christmas. He had still to write up his annual report on education in the province and much of his time was spent in a feverish attempt to finish this off before the festivities.[5]

It was typical of the family that Alexander, who in 1883 had entered St Petersburg University in the Faculty of Mathematics and Physics, was not compelled to come home for the holiday. Already he was a student of promise. Alexander explained that he had to sit a zoology test in mid-December and a further one in organic chemistry in mid-January. In his letter to his parents he expressed no regret over his absence.[6] He knew that they had hopes of his becoming a university professor[7] and would approve of his wish to avoid disruption to his studies. In truth it would have taken several days for him to reach Simbirsk from St Petersburg. The railway system had still not been extended to Simbirsk, and in winter he could not use the steamship down the ice-bound river Volga.[8] He would not have been able to do much studying on the way. Meanwhile Christmas at the Ulyanovs was organised by Maria Alexandrovna. The four youngest children – Vladimir, Olga, Dmitri and Maria – had finished their school term. A fir tree was erected in the sitting room and cards were painted and dispatched; presents were prepared. On Christmas Day the family went to St Nicholas Cathedral in Simbirsk.

Yet Ilya Ulyanov was not well. On 10 January 1886 he was coughing badly. Next day, when the Ulyanovs had visitors for afternoon tea, he did not join them. The family assumed that he was suffering from some temporary stomach malaise, and Anna Ilinichna talked unconcernedly about her plans to go back to her teacher-training course in St Petersburg. Ilya himself was determined to resume his administrative duties as the holiday came to an end. It was cold outside; snow was on the ground. Ilya refused to let up the pace of his work. On 12 January, although he still felt poorly, he arranged to be visited in Simbirsk by one of his inspectors, V. M. Strzhalkovski. They worked together until two o'clock in the afternoon. Yet Ilya Ulyanov did not come through to eat after Strzhalkovski's departure. He had had another relapse. While the family was eating, he appeared in the doorway and gazed at everybody. They were to remember it as an occasion when he was trying to take his final leave of everybody. He made no direct comment in this vein, but simply went back into his study.[9]

His wife went to find him after lunch, and already he was shivering violently. She called out Dr Legcher and at five o'clock fetched Anna and Vladimir to see their father. By then he was in agony. He shuddered twice and then, just as suddenly, fell silent. Before Dr Legcher could arrive, Ilya Nikolaevich was dead. He was only fifty-three years old. Although there was no post-mortem, Legcher believed that the cause of death was a brain haemorrhage.[10]

Vladimir, in Alexander's absence, performed a role of some responsibility for the family. While his mother and elder sister tended to the dead body and passed the news to relatives and acquaintances, Vladimir was sent out in the family carriage to bring back his brother Dmitri from a friend's house. This was not a sign of Vladimir taking over responsibility for the household. Such a myth was Soviet-inspired, and was always ridiculous; in reality it was his mother and his sister Anna who were in charge of the main domestic arrangements. Vladimir could be spared to do the job of collecting young Dmitri and the fact that he was sent to do this in a carriage was a sign of Vladimir's still rather junior status. The priority was to arrange the funeral, organise the family's finances and generally plan the future for the Ulyanov children. Vladimir had yet to reach the age of sixteen years. His mother and his sister were not deferring to him: they were trying to protect him.

One of Maria Alexandrovna's first needs was to write to the Ministry of Popular Enlightenment on 14 January 1886 requesting the delivery of the due payment of Ilya's pension. According to the terms of her late husband's pension, she could claim one hundred rubles for herself per month and a further twenty-five rubles for each of her children while they remained minors. This excluded Anna and Alexander. Maria Alexandrovna was entitled in total to two hundred rubles a month, a sum that would diminish as her younger four children attained maturity.[11]

The funeral of Ilya Ulyanov was held next day. The sudden death of a much admired local dignitary shocked teachers and educational administrators. Those who had been promoted by him were sometimes referred to as 'Ulyanovites'; he was respected for the cultural benefit he had brought to his post as Director of Popular Schools. Ilya Ulyanov by his activity and his example had made a difference. Wreaths were prepared by schoolchildren and obituary notices appeared in the Simbirsk press. The chief bearer of his coffin, at the age of fifteen, was his second son Vladimir; it was traditional for coffins to be borne by the menfolk. The other bearers were Ilya's closest friends and colleagues. Then the congregation processed to the Pokrovski Monastery in Simbirsk, where the remains of Ilya Ulyanov were buried in the grounds by the south-facing wall. His widow was offered possession of the medal of Stanislav, first class, which her deceased husband had been awarded a few days earlier, but she refused it. She preferred to remember him in a simpler fashion and arranged for a plain tombstone to be erected over his grave.[12]

Anna, her eldest daughter, considered abandoning her teacher's training course in order to assist with the running of the family. Another possibility was for student friends to send on their lecture notes to her in Simbirsk so that she might return to take the exams in the autumn of 1886. Maria Alexandrovna would have none of it. Anna was told to return to St Petersburg to complete her studies. She departed in March.[13] Meanwhile in an effort to stabilise her finances, Maria Alexandrovna rearranged the rooms in the house so that the family occupied only the half of it facing the river Sviyaga. The other half was rented first to a doctor, then to a lawyer.[14]

One of Maria Alexandrovna's problems was the worsening behaviour of Vladimir. Although his father had often worked away from Moscow Street, his very existence had acted as a restraint upon the way Vladimir spoke to his mother. Ilya had not been a parent to be disobeyed and the mere possibility of paternal disapproval had usually been a sufficient deterrent to disrespect. All this changed after Ilya's death. Vladimir became cheeky to his mother. Matters were made worse by his elder brother's residence in St Petersburg: there was no one in the house whose disapproval he feared. When Alexander came home for the summer vacation, Vladimir did not even mind his brother witnessing his misbehaviour. This infuriated Alexander. After a contretemps between Vladimir and their mother while he and Alexander were having a game of chess, Alexander calmly but firmly declared: 'Volodya, either you immediately go and do what Mama is telling you or else I'm not playing with you any more.' Vladimir's resistance crumbled. But he continued, more quietly, to assert himself more than the rest of the family thought seemly.[15]

Anna and Alexander talked about this after their father's death as they tried to sort out their emotions. The pattern of relationships inside the family had been shattered by their bereavement, and the two eldest Ulyanov children – now in their twenties – were also having to come to terms with the fact that their brother Vladimir was entering late adolescence. Anna put the question directly to Alexander: 'How do you take to our Volodya?' His reply was negative: 'Undoubtedly a very able person, but we don't get on.' Indeed when she wrote her memoirs, Anna was not confident that she remembered the exact words, and she wondered whether Alexander had not put it more forcefully, to the effect that 'we absolutely don't get on'.[16]

It was the domineering side of his brother that Alexander could not stand, especially when he was cheeky to their widowed mother. But this judgement on Vladimir, which many historians have eagerly endorsed, is too harsh. He was still a schoolboy. His father had suddenly died and naturally he was badly affected by the experience. Vladimir had not got over the shock. Any youth of fifteen in those circumstances, particularly one accustomed to the direct support of his elder brother and sister, might have been expected to exhibit some degree of uncongenial reaction. The fact that he did not go round maundering about his unhappiness does not mean that he managed to avoid being distraught. On the contrary, Vladimir was profoundly upset and withdrew into himself; the jovial boy of before had disappeared. Books were his consolation and he devoured many classics of Russian literature. His taste moved from Gogol to Turgenev. The wish for Gogolian caricatures of contemporary life had vanished. Now Vladimir Ulyanov preferred the steady and sensitive descriptions of provincial life offered by Turgenev. In Turgenev's novels the public message of the writer was far from being self-evident. His readers assumed that somehow he wanted change in the regime. But was he a liberal, or an impatient conservative, or even a revolutionary?

How Vladimir Ulyanov interpreted the works of his favourite novelist is unknown. His later remarks were not necessarily a truthful reflection of what he had thought in his adolescence. But probably there was some similarity. To be an Ulyanov was to aim at educational improvement, at realistically possible improvement if only the Emperor consented. Vladimir in his adulthood would pick out situations in the novels that corroborated his Marxist interpretation of Russian reality. There were plenty of feckless landed noblemen and well-meaning but ineffectual intellectuals in Turgenev's prose, and Lenin used them in his own writings to denounce Imperial society. Turgenev perhaps also had an influence through his stress that all the talk in the world would not change the world. What was required was action. Few of Turgenev's characters were capable of action, but whereas the novelist pitied them for circumstances which they had little opportunity to alter, Lenin grew up to deride them.

The history of the Ulyanov family until 1886 provides several examples of its members engaging in activities that contributed to the improvement of life in the Russian Empire. Vladimir's most respected forebears were doctors and teachers. They were not doctors and teachers who did little healing and teaching, as was the case in the novels of

Turgenev or in the turn-of-the-century plays of Anton Chekhov. They were practical professionals. It was possible to read Turgenev in other ways. For example, he can appear as an advocate of kindness or the embodiment of Hamlet-like indecisiveness; he may also be regarded as an artist of the word, who was more interested in the manner of exposition than in the substance of his own thought. But, for Vladimir Ulyanov, Turgenev was a brilliant painter of the defects in Imperial society that needed correction.

While Vladimir was starting to ask himself basic questions about life in Russia, his brother Alexander in distant St Petersburg was already an enemy of the Romanov monarchy. The shock of their father's death stayed with him for many weeks, and several people were concerned lest he commit suicide. But they underestimated the young man's determination to continue with his research on the biology of annular worms. His dissertation, once submitted to the university authorities, won the approval of his professors, and he was awarded a gold medal for it. His mother was delighted, though the thought that Ilya Nikolaevich could not share in her joy caused her to burst into tears.

In his letters home Alexander chatted about the cost of lodging, the ghastly food and the unsavoury landladies. Unlike Anna, however, he did not offer to drop his studies out of worry about his mother's widowhood; he intended to consolidate his base for a successful career. But he was troubled by his growing revulsion from the political conditions in the Russian Empire. He had hated the irksome regime in the Simbirsk Classical Gimnazia. He had also lost his religious faith at about the age of sixteen. His purity of purpose was such that his father had made an exception of him and absolved him of the requirement to attend church services on Sundays. His spirit of intellectual challenge persisted in St Petersburg. By 1886 he was coming to agree with those of his generation who called for a root-and-branch transformation of the Russian political and social structure. He had turned into a revolutionary sympathiser. The very outcome feared by Ilya Ulyanov was being realised. Alexander Ulyanov, breaking with his father's example, thought peaceful, evolutionary development of society impossible in Russia.

A large number of university students had the same attitude. In the 1880s there were only eight universities in the Russian Empire and the most prestigious of them was St Petersburg. The others were in Moscow, Kiev, Yurev, Kharkov, Warsaw, Kazan and Novorossiisk. Officials treated students as a necessary evil and suspected them of being extremely prone to subversive notions. The Ministries of the Interior and of Education refused to relax their tight control over them. There were no grants for impecunious students, and many of them barely survived the rigours of their courses by taking paid employment in order to pay for food and shelter. But there were no such worries for Alexander Ulyanov. As long as he reported how he spent his money, he was allocated exactly what he asked for. But more generally Alexander was as irked by the regimentation of academic life as any fellow student. There were regulations about everything from the curriculum and prescribed textbooks to comportment, dress and lodgings. Anything that might bring young men and women into contact with philosophies of liberalism, of socialism, of atheism or indeed of any kind of challenge to the institutional status quo was eradicated.

In reaching his stand as a revolutionary, Alexander mentioned his frustration at the obstacles put in the path of the development of scientific research in Russia. His general hostility to the monarchy, therefore, was induced by personal experience. He felt that the regime was obscurantist about science; he never forgot that science had been discouraged in his gimnazia education. He expanded this particular sensation into a comprehensive rejection of the regime and everything it stood for.

St Petersburg University, like all the great institutions of the Russian Empire, was a vantage-point for observing the power and majesty of the monarchy. Established by the tsars on Vasilevski Island, it was only a short distance from the bridge leading over the river Neva to the Winter Palace. From the university it was possible to glimpse the great statue of the Emperor Peter the Great near St Isaac's Cathedral. Peter's horse seemed about to hurl itself and its rider into the waters. The symbolism of monarchical determination to rule society in his own chosen fashion, to conquer nature and to make Russia into a power respected throughout northern Europe, was unmistakable. Also visible from St Petersburg University was the Winter Palace of the tsars, including the incumbent Emperor Alexander III. The building where he lived and governed stretched along the bank to the south of St Isaac's Cathedral, and was fronted by a vast semi-circular space that gave visitors a view of a neo-Classical frontage with huge, pillared segments. The granite magnificence of the Winter Palace was known across the continent. Opposite it across the Neva stood the Peter-Paul Fortress, where rebels against the Romanovs were traditionally incarcerated.

St Petersburg itself had been created at the behest of Peter the Great; no village had existed on the site before he opted to transfer his seat of government there from Moscow. Marshes were drained. Institutions and dwelling-places were constructed. Moscow lost its status as the capital. Hundreds of thousands of peasants died in the programme of works commanded by Emperor Peter, perishing from exhaustion, malnutrition and disease. It was impossible to live in the central zone of the city, where the university lay, and not be conscious of the power of the Imperial state. And Alexander Ulyanov was an acute observer of his environment.

It was common at this time for the natural science and engineering faculties to attract young men who jibbed against the monarchy. What was different about Alexander and his friends was their willingness to adopt an ideology of violent opposition. Already before his father's death he was taking up with friends who believed in instigating a general revolutionary transformation by assassinating the Emperor Alexander III. Initially he simply talked with them; but steadily they undermined his reluctance to become a participant in their conspiratorial group. The leaders were Orest Govorukhin and Pëtr Shevyrëv. Alexander was a useful recruit for them. His character was such that, once convinced that something was morally desirable, he would stick to his aim through thick and thin; and he had the inestimable advantage of being a scientist with a practical knowledge of chemistry: they wanted him to make up the nitroglycerine for the bomb with which they planned to kill the Emperor. Also important was Alexander's facility with language. They wanted his help with the production of propaganda explaining the political objectives of the group. Late in 1886 he finally threw in his lot with them. The twenty-year-old Alexander Ulyanov intended to be a regicide.

What was the group's rationale? The dominant ideology of Russian revolutionaries had been socialism – or, in some cases, anarchism. They were usually known as *narodniki* (roughly translatable as populists). The leaders and activists in the various clandestine groups had had many disputes, but generally agreed that the peasantry's customs of communal welfare, collective responsibility and co-operation at work and at leisure should be the foundations of the 'good' society. Consequently this generation of revolutionaries can be regarded as advocates of an agrarian ideology; they wanted the transformation of society to begin in the countryside. But they also had a broader agenda. They believed in 'the people' and wished to win the nascent working class as well as the peasants to their cause. They had no time for the idea that Russia would be better off without industry; they were hostile, too, to privileging the

Russians over the other nations of the Russian Empire and would have been enthusiastic supporters of the Socialist International founded in 1889 in Europe. Russian agrarian socialists aimed to enable Russia to avoid capitalism altogether. They wanted to establish a society that embodied socialism and to bring all oppression and exploitation to an end.[17]

The fearful revenge wreaked by Alexander II's son and heir Alexander III had a number of consequences. In particular it discouraged many revolutionaries from persisting with a political strategy that prioritised the campaign to kill the Imperial family. Until Govorukhin's group grew up in 1886, there had been no serious enterprise of the sort for five years.

Another development was of equal importance. This was that many revolutionaries concluded that the agrarian socialists had been deeply misguided in the way they thought about transforming the state and the society of the Russian Empire. A revision of strategy was demanded most notably by Georgi Plekhanov, who maintained that the future of the Revolution did not realistically lie with the peasant, the land commune and the countryside. Plekhanov was a lapsed agrarian socialist. For him, the hunting down of revolutionary activists after Alexander II's death was just one defeat too many. He urged that success could no longer be achieved unless the clandestine groups recognised that Russia was undergoing an economic and social transformation. Railways were being laid to connect all the major cities. Factories were being financed and constructed. Mines were being sunk. Foreign investment was being attracted into the country in pursuit of the quick, high profits available in an economy rich in natural resources and cheap, willing labour. It was no longer feasible, wrote Plekhanov, to dream of transforming Russia into a socialist society without it first undergoing the stage of capitalist development. Capitalism, he declared, had already arrived – and had arrived in force.

This led Plekhanov, who fled to Switzerland in 1880, to proclaim that revolutionaries in Russia should place their faith in the urban working class, in contemporary forms of industrial activity, in large-scale social and economic units. As a former leader of Black Redistribution, he remained an advocate of political change by means of revolution. In 1883 he and his friends Vera Zasulich, Lev Deich and Pavel Axelrod formed the Emancipation of Labour Group – and they announced that only Marxism offered a key to understanding and transforming Russia. Previous revolutionary trends, including their own earlier commitment to agrarian socialism, were rejected by the Emancipation of Labour

Group as being based upon unscientific sentimentality. The future for socialists of the Russian Empire, the Group insisted, lay with Marxism.[18]

These niceties have greater political moment in retrospect than they appeared to have at the time. The differences are more of degree than of kind. For the agrarian socialists did not give themselves this name. They usually designated themselves simply as 'revolutionaries'. Later they became known as *narodniki*; for they always claimed to be acting in the name of 'the people' as distinct from the governing authorities. As often as not, they referred to themselves as adherents of this or that revolutionary group such as Land and Freedom, Black Redistribution and People's Will. Practically all these socialists, while seeing virtues in the ideas and practices of the people, were very far from repudiating the need for Russia's industrialisation. They also found, through bitter experience, that workers were more responsive to revolutionary invocations than were the peasants. When a surge of students went out to effect revolutionary propaganda in the countryside in 1874, many of them had been turned over to the Ministry of the Interior by astonished peasants. Most such socialists regarded Karl Marx and Friedrich Engels as attractive exponents of the economic and social case for socialism. It is no coincidence that the first translation of Marx's *Capital* into any foreign language was made by a Russian populist, Nikolai Danielson, in 1872.

But Plekhanov's Emancipation of Labour Group challenged this eclectic attitude to the definition of the most desirable form of socialism. Plekhanov wanted revolutionaries in Russia to deny, once and for all, that the traditions of the peasantry had anything positive to offer. The remnants of the populist organisations that had survived the police hunts after 1881 were aghast at this, and condemned Plekhanov as an ill-informed betrayer of the revolutionary movement. Bitter polemics were exchanged in 1883–6.

The small organisation joined by Alexander Ulyanov in mid-1886 had as the first of its purposes to kill Emperor Alexander III and as its second to mend the rift between the two rival revolutionary tendencies. For this reason they drew up a statement of objectives which would demonstrably overlap the objectives of the new Russian Marxists – and Alexander Ulyanov was given the task of final literary elaboration. A number of points were primed to appeal to Marxists. Above all, Alexander Ulyanov wrote about scientific 'laws'. He also called for an elective assembly for the whole country – Plekhanov had repeatedly demanded the same thing. He did not mention the peasantry. Alexander Ulyanov insisted that all the oppressed sections of society had an equal interest in the removal of the monarchy. Truth, science, freedom and justice: all were ideals of the revolutionary movement in the Russian Empire. Alexander Ulyanov was well placed to predict which aims would be attractive to Marxists, for he himself had recently used his facility in the German language to translate some of Marx's works into Russian. His organisation's members, poised to exploit a political crisis arising out of the Emperor's annihilation, wished to have as many active supporters on the streets as possible.

Their primitive methods had a trace of theatricality. They kept their activity to anniversaries in revolutionary history. In November, before Alexander Ulyanov joined them, they organised a student demonstration commemorating the life of the anti-monarchy writer Nikolai Dobrolyubov. The group planned that their next venture would involve not a demonstration, which by its nature would mean that other students had to be alerted, but an attempt on the life of the Emperor. The date chosen was gruesomely symbolic: 1 March 1887, the sixth anniversary of the assassination of the Emperor Alexander II.

Nothing, however, went right for the conspirators. One of them was already in the last stages of tuberculosis and another left the country at the last moment. The group's members nonetheless went ahead on the day, but luck played into the hands of the authorities. Two members were picked up in suspicious circumstances and the attempt to blow up the Emperor had to be abandoned. The Okhrana, the government's secret police, interrogated the arrested men and succeeded, one by one, in apprehending virtually all the group's members. Alexander Ulyanov was among them. The Okhrana took friends and relatives of the accused into custody, so Anna Ulyanova too was incarcerated despite having had no part in the conspiracy. The interrogations revealed everything the police needed to know, and when Alexander Ulyanov saw this he took an exceptionally brave decision. First, he determined to take the blame even for aspects of the conspiracy that did not involve him. Second, he made up his mind to use his trial as an opportunity to disseminate the basic ideas of the revolutionaries, an opportunity denied him in the legal press because of the official censorship. This decision, he knew, would probably cost him his life.

Still suffering from the loss of her husband, Maria Alexandrovna was stupefied by what had happened. Even more astonished was Alexander's elder sister Anna. What on earth, she asked, had been going on? Her words expressed the depth of long-unstated emotions: 'There is no one better on earth or more kindly than you. It's not just me who'll say this, as a sister; everyone who knew you will say this, my dear unwatchable little sun in the sky.'[19] Anna was released, but put under police supervision until 1892.

Alexander's mother was not at first convinced that her son had planned regicide. She wrote immediately to the Emperor himself pleading for him to be released. She lied on his behalf, claiming that Alexander had always been 'religious'. But what mother would not have said this and a lot more to save her son from being hanged? In the Ministry of Interior it was recognised that the press might take up her cause unless she herself were to be shown the materials of her son's confession. In a break with precedent she was allowed to come to St Petersburg and talk to the prisoner. Alexander made no pretence. He was guilty of the most heinous crime in Imperial law, and admitted it. His mother's hope was that he would do as others in his group were doing by expressing remorse and begging for mercy. She reasonably thought that he might thereby secure himself a sentence of penal labour. If this happened, she intended to take the younger Ulyanov children – presumably including Vladimir – to Siberia and to assist Alexander in serving out his term. Maria Alexandrovna would stand by her eldest son regardless.

When mother and son met in the Peter-Paul Fortress, Alexander fell to his knees and implored her to forgive him. But he refused to plead for a pardon. The Emperor took note of the trial proceedings and was aware that Alexander Ulyanov was consciously increasing the degree of his responsibility for the assassination attempt, but he saw no reason to commute the court's death sentence. Not only Ulyanov but also V. D. Generalov, P. I. Andreyushkin, V. S. Osipanov and P. Y. Shevyrëv were consigned to the Shlisselburg Prison and at dawn on 8 May 1887 were taken from their cells and hanged.

Alexander's mother had returned to Simbirsk: there was absolutely nothing more she could do for him. After her husband's death and the execution of her eldest son, she was distraught, and contemplated suicide. In her absence in St Petersburg, Anna Veretennikova, the children's aunt, had come from Kazan to look after them. The teacher Vera Kashkadamova also visited the Moscow Street home. All the Ulyanov children were in a condition of deep shock. The two elder daughters were especially distressed. Anna Ilinichna had lost the brother she adored, but managed to keep her emotions from view. Olga Ilinichna, however, threw herself to the ground and sobbed. Then she leaped up and shouted threats against the Emperor who had refused to spare Alexander. Aunt Anna was terrified. But then Olga, too, took herself in hand and strove not to let her mother see her distress. Maria Alexandrovna pulled herself together. She no longer thought of killing herself. When her youngest child, little Maria, climbed on to her lap on her return from St Petersburg, she knew that she had made the right decision. The Ulyanovs were determined to survive.[20]

They endured not only bereavement but also social ostracism. Vera Kashkadamova was one of the very few family friends who would still speak to them. Respectable Simbirsk – its doctors, teachers, administrators and army officers – indicated its abhorrence for any family that could feed and raise a regicide. When Olga went to the gimnazia, her teachers and classmates refused to have anything to do with her. Local society was closing its doors to the family. Most people were aghast at the plot to assassinate the Emperor. In 1881 the Ulyanov family had attended the Cathedral service commemorating the life of Alexander II. But a member of the same family had now been involved in a murderous conspiracy, and the Ulyanovs were treated as pariahs.

This terrible experience has never been accorded its true significance. The point is that the Ulyanovs had never been quite the same as most other noble families of Simbirsk. Ilya Nikolaevich was a newcomer to hereditary titled status. In a single generation, through his own professional efforts, he had clambered up the ladder of society and entered the nobility. The mass of Simbirsk province's noblemen had enjoyed this status for several generations and there was little contact between them and the Ulyanov family. Snobbery was pervasive. Ilya and Maria had tried to surmount the difficulty mainly by ignoring it and getting on with their lives. The pressure on the sons and daughters to do well at school and gain formal qualifications was characteristic of parents who had come from the margins of and wanted to integrate the family into Imperial society. These hopes were shattered by Alexander's rash affiliation to a group of terrorists. They were back in the margins of society, and all the children – from Anna down to little Maria – held the Emperor and his ministers to blame for their social exclusion. They could not think of Alexander without feeling bitter about tsarism.

Vladimir Ulyanov suppressed his emotions more effectively than his sisters Anna and Olga. The hurt was there, but he buried it. There is a story in every account of him that, on hearing of Alexander's execution, he reacted not as a family member but as a revolutionary in the making. According to Maria Ilinichna, he concluded that the strategic bankruptcy of agrarian-socialist terrorism had been proven. 'No,' he allegedly said in her presence, 'we must not take that road.' This has been taken by

Marxist–Leninists – and not just by them – as evidence of Vladimir's principled decision at the age of sixteen to repudiate agrarian socialism. A less plausible story it is hard to imagine, even though generations of scholars have accepted it. Maria Ilinichna wrote her memoir after Lenin's death, when it was obligatory to portray his career as a monolithic piece and Lenin himself as infallible, even as a youth. The usefulness of her testimony is anyway dubious since she was only eight years old when Alexander was hanged. It defies credibility that she would be able to recall the exact wording of a statement whose ideological resonance would have meant nothing to her in childhood.

More believable is the account given by their occasional private tutor Vera Kashkadamova. She was impressed by Vladimir's willingness to play lotto and charades with his young brother and sister in order to distract them from their pain. The topic of Alexander inevitably arose in conversation, and, according to Kashkadamova, Vladimir expressed no opinion that distanced him from his elder brother. On the contrary, she remembered the following comment: 'It must mean that he had to act like this; he couldn't act in any other way.'[21]

This is surely the authentic voice of Vladimir Ulyanov. In the few years after his brother's death, Vladimir joined groups dedicated to the ideas of agrarian-socialist terrorists. This is inexplicable if he had really already opted for Marxism of the kind that rejected what his brother had stood for. Even so, Kashkadamova's account does not demonstrate that Vladimir was so impressed by the precedent of Alexander that he instantly adopted his ideas. There is really no reason to think that Vladimir had fixed thoughts about anything. More likely he was only beginning to know about the world of revolutionary ideas. Probably too he felt an instinctive but still unfocussed sympathy with the choices made by his brother. They had had their disagreements, and had latterly not got along very well, but this was no barrier to Vladimir's surge of posthumous identification with him. It may even have deepened the flood. The phrase remembered by Kashkadamova – 'he couldn't act in any other way' – is probably our best sign that Vladimir felt impelled to discover why his admired elder brother had acted as he did. Alexander's disappearance had the consequence of hardening the thoughts of a brilliant youth into the posture of a revolutionary activist.

4

THE PLOUGHING OF THE MIND

1887–1888

Such was the family's sense of duty that Vladimir and Olga Ulyanov continued to prepare for their gimnazia final-year examinations through the months of Alexander's imprisonment and execution. The tenacity of these two youngsters was extraordinary. Although Simbirsk was not yet on any railway-line, the government ensured that everyone knew of Alexander Ulyanov's crime and its punishment. The town authorities also pasted up posters about the event, and he was the subject of an article in a special issue of *Simbirsk Provincial News* two days after he was hanged.[1]

It was on these very days that Vladimir took the first of his final examinations at the Simbirsk Classical Gimnazia. The examination had begun on 5 May 1887 and lasted a month. Vladimir's concentration was impeccable, even though he and the rest of the family were engulfed by the terrible news from St Petersburg. His academic performance was very impressive; indeed in the circumstances it was almost inhumanly impressive. He had achieved a five, the maximum mark possible, in all ten examined subjects.[2] Vladimir had come out top of his class of twenty-nine examinees and was eligible for the gimnazia's gold medal, just like his brother before him. His sister Olga meanwhile achieved the same result at the Simbirsk Marinskaya Gimnazia.[3] The awarding of these medals had become a delicate matter after the scandal of Alexander Ulyanov's assassination attempt. But the two gimnazii were sufficiently insulated from political pressure for Vladimir and Olga to receive their prizes.

Kerenski wrote a supportive reference for Vladimir:

Extremely talented, consistently keen and accurate, Ulyanov in all classes was the top pupil and at the end of his course was awarded the gold medal as the most deserving pupil in performance, development and behaviour. Neither at the gimnazia nor outside did any occasion come to light when Ulyanov by word or deed attracted a disapproving opinion from the governing authorities or teachers of the gimnazia. His parents always carefully supervised Ulyanov's education and moral development, and from 1886, after his father's death, this involved his mother, who concentrated every concern and care on the upbringing of the children. Religion and rational discipline lay at the foundations of the education.

The good fruits of the domestic upbringing were obvious in Ulyanov's excellent behaviour. Looking more closely at the domestic life and character of Ulyanov, I cannot but remark on his excessive reclusiveness and on his self-distancing from intercourse even with his acquaintances – and outside the gimnazia even with schoolmates who were the great flower of the school – and generally on his unsociability. Ulyanov's mother does not intend to let her son out of her supervision for the entire time of his education at the University.

What was Kerenski's purpose in his last paragraph? Maybe he was guarding himself professionally against the possibility that the boy would become involved in university student disturbances. But probably Kerenski was just telling the truth and his pupil really was rather antisocial. Vladimir had never been very gregarious, and those who knew him while his brother Alexander was in prison observed that he became very depressed and unfriendly.

Maria Alexandrovna needed to think fast. Her first decision was to sell the house on Moscow Street and move to Kazan province. This was sensible. The Ulyanovs faced unending social ostracism in Simbirsk whereas Maria Alexandrovna could count on the family being welcomed in Kokushkino. Dr Blank had added a wing to the Kokushkino mansion house specifically so that his daughters could bring their families on visits, and had bequeathed his estate jointly to his five daughters when he died in 1870. Thus the Ulyanovs had been in receipt of a share of the income derived from the peasants who rented the land. Until 1887 Maria Alexandrovna had left it to Anna Veretennikova and Lyubov Ardasheva, her sisters, to look after her Kokushkino interests.[4] Maria Alexandrovna hurriedly alerted these sisters that she needed to move her place of residence to the estate. As soon as they had responded positively, she sold up the house on Moscow Street – as it happens, the buyer was the then Simbirsk police chief – and did not return to the town until her son Dmitri took a medical post there in 1905.

The children coped with their brother's loss by not mentioning it. This was the way they had been brought up. It was years before the eldest, Anna Ilinichna, could speak about Alexander to anyone, and even then she spoke only to her mother and never to her brothers or her sister.[5] The inner tension was terrible. Her mother asked Anna to give her younger sister Maria some academic coaching. But Maria dreaded the assistance:[6]

> My sister was preparing me at that time for the exams for the gimnazia's second class. Having recently suffered the cruel trauma of the tragic death of a brother she deified, she was very nervous. This was sometimes manifested also in the course of her work with me, bringing torment to both of us. I remember how Vladimir Ilich's face darkened while hearing one of these outbursts, and he said, as if to himself: 'This isn't how to do things.'

Vladimir himself could be abrupt. When little Maria proudly showed him a notebook she had made, he told her that it was unacceptable to sew up white pages with black thread and compelled her to redo the operation.[7] But at least he did not torment her emotionally – and she for her part liked to please him.

He had yet to decide which university to enter and which degree to take. Had it not been for his brother's notoriety, he would have gone to St Petersburg University, but Maria Alexandrovna was told this would not gain official approval. Consequently Vladimir sought admittance to the Imperial Kazan University, where his late father had studied. The choice of degree course caused some surprise. When Vladimir announced that he planned to study jurisprudence, his friends could not understand this. In these years it was the natural sciences which attracted the most able Russian students (such as Alexander Ulyanov). Vladimir's teachers, noting his exceptional proficiency at Latin and Greek, would have preferred him to study in the Philological Faculty. But Vladimir insisted upon studying law. Unlike Alexander, he had never found biology and other sciences attractive. But why, with his interest in literature, did he not enter the Philological Faculty? The answer remains unclear. But perhaps he judged that he would more easily build a career as an independent lawyer than as a higher-education lecturer dependent on a state salary.

His mother Maria Alexandrovna hoped that she had kept him clear of politics and other dangers. She had even got him to stop smoking cigarettes. Her first argument had been that his physical condition would deteriorate if he continued to smoke and that he had not been in the best of health as a child. He ignored her entirely. Then in desperation she argued that, since he had no independent income, he had no right to squander the family's funds on tobacco. He gave way and never put a cigarette to his lips again.[8] Maria Alexandrovna was pleased not only by this but also by the gusto with which Volodya took to the rural sports at Kokushkino. He went shooting in the woods and skiing along the country paths, and often he took Dmitri along with him.[9]

But appearances were misleading. Alexander Ulyanov left behind books and articles that would have shocked his father. Chief among these were works by Nikolai Chernyshevski. When Vladimir talked about this episode later, he acknowledged that Chernyshevski had 'ploughed him over and over again'. Vladimir was at an age when he was susceptible to deep influence from the reading he undertook. He had the technical facility of a rigorous linguistic training, but as yet he did not have beliefs. His Christian faith lapsed when he was sixteen years old. His mind was like an engine without a steering column: it was potentially very powerful, but would remain directionless until he decided what he thought about the world. Neither his father nor his brother was alive to guide him, and he no longer saw his teachers. Vladimir turned to bookcases for inspiration. He extinguished his passion for Latin, wanting no distraction from his political self-education.[10] This was not the last time that he denied himself a pleasure. In future years he would give up chess, Beethoven and skating so as to concentrate on the revolutionary tasks at hand.

Chernyshevski was an odd writer to exercise such an impact. His prose was like a rash of nettles. Sprawling verbiage was covered with densely overgrown constructions, and he seemed immune to the models offered by the great novelists of mid-nineteenth-century Russia. But style was not what drew Vladimir to Chernyshevski. In any case, Chernyshevski's constructions with their elongated sentences and thickets of subsidiary clauses were easily amenable to gimnazia students with their mastery of Latin.

Vladimir's admiration was considerable. In 1864 the Ministry of the Interior banished Chernyshevski as an irreconcilable opponent of the Romanov autocracy to a forced-labour camp in eastern Siberia (and only in 1889, already very ill, was he allowed back to his native Volga city of Saratov). The Russian Empire was so large that it was not necessary to deport subversives from the country: they could be kept in a distant town and prevented from stirring up trouble from abroad. Chernyshevski refused to recant his opinions. In general he is considered to have been a revolutionary agrarian socialist, but nevertheless he was not an idealiser of the peasantry. Nor did he espouse the rural life. He wanted cultural development to be speeded up in his country and advocated industrialisation. He demanded a democratic political system based upon universal-suffrage elections. He supported women's rights. He opposed the discriminatory legislation affecting the non-Russian nations and ethnic groups. He advocated the creation of a classless society. And he depicted the Imperial monarchy as barbaric, parasitic and obsolete.

Indeed, Chernyshevski saw himself as offering a vision of a Russian future congruent with the works of socialist thinkers elsewhere in Europe; he read widely in German and French, and was an enthusiastic reader of Karl Marx. But he was very far from thinking that Russia always had to learn from Germany without teaching something in return. He carried on a patchy correspondence with Marx, who began to learn the Russian language in order to acquaint himself with Chernyshevski's writings on the agrarian question in the Russian Empire. For a young man such as Vladimir Ulyanov, who was at ease with exploring European culture, Chernyshevski embodied an intellectual ideal.

Vladimir Ulyanov was attracted to Chernyshevski emotionally as well as rationally. He was so affected by the heroic example of a man who suffered penal servitude in Siberia for the sake of political ideals that he obtained a photograph of his idol, which he carried around in his wallet. The book that deeply entered his consciousness was the novel *What Is to Be Done?* As a novel it is lamely constructed and unimaginatively written, but it offers a portrait of a group of socialist activists. Their solidarity with each other and their political commitment, dedication to educational self-improvement and irreconcilable hostility to tsarism captivated Vladimir Ulyanov. The main character of the novel was pure of spirit and endowed with the aura of an unchallenged leader. It is a good bet that Vladimir Ulyanov identified himself closely with him. Not all young intellectuals in the making were equally impressed by Chernyshevski's book, and its clumsiness of style and structure made it the object of some mockery. But Vladimir Ulyanov would have none of this. Chernyshevski's *What Is to Be Done?* helped him to define the direction of his life, and he was fiercely protective of Chernyshevski's reputation.

Thus Vladimir Ulyanov was his brother's brother. In the space of a year he had adopted the world-view and aspirations of a revolutionary. Insofar as he aimed to deepen his understanding of politics and society, he would do so at university but not at the feet of his university professors. Even before he entered the Imperial Kazan University, he was looking for trouble.

His mother's guarantee that she would live near her son had been an important factor in getting him enrolled. So, too, were the funds she made available. The surviving Ulyanov children – Anna, Vladimir, Olga, Dmitri and Maria – liked to contend that their entire subsidy from Maria Alexandrovna took the form of the state pension of their late father. This was nonsense. Even the published financial figures reveal the opposite story. The will of Ilya Ulyanov left the 2,000 rubles in the Simbirsk Town Public Bank to his wife and children.[11] This was no insubstantial sum, being a quarter of what the family was to pay in 1889 for the estate bought by the children's mother in Alakaevka. The sale of the Ulyanovs' Moscow Street house in Simbirsk in summer 1887 brought a further 6,000 rubles to the family.[12] There was also Maria Alexandrovna's share of the rent from the Kokushkino estate plus the sums in her bank account left to her by Dr Blank. (Her inherited land at Kokushkino was originally valued at 3,000 rubles.)[13] To top it all, there was the legacy from Vasili, Ilya Ulyanov's brother and benefactor, who had died at the age of sixty in 1878. The Ulyanov family was not bereft of ready cash.

Russian inheritance law entitled Vladimir to a share of his father's capital. There is a record of this in relation to the above-mentioned 2,000 rubles in the Simbirsk Town Public Bank. The District Court ordered the following division of Ilya's legacy. A quarter – only a quarter – was to go to Ilya's widow. An eighth went to each of the two daughters who had not yet reached maturity, Olga and Maria. But a sixth went to each of the three sons, Alexander, Vladimir and Dmitri: the boys had a legal advantage over their sisters.

Lenin was later criticised for living comfortably on private capital while proclaiming himself as capitalism's destroyer. There is something in this. But there is less in the criticism that he had a sumptuous style of life: cautious financial management was Maria Alexandrovna's hallmark. At the end of August 1887 – with the start of the university year – she rented temporary accommodation in Kazan in order to search for a suitable ground-floor apartment. Her sister Lyubov Ardasheva, a widow since 1870, lived on the upper floor of the same house with her sons Alexander and Vladimir. The children of both women had spent previous summers at Kokushkino and enjoyed each other's company. Kazan brought an end to the loneliness suffered in Simbirsk (and indeed in

Kokushkino, since they scarcely saw any neighbours there either).[14] But they could not stay in the apartment for long: they needed a larger place. After a month Maria Alexandrovna had found what she wanted and moved the family to New Commissariat Street.[15] Dmitri and Maria went to the Kazan gimnazii and Vladimir started to attend lectures at the Imperial Kazan University. Meals were taken at home. Maria Alexandrovna hoped to settle the family into something near to the normality that they had enjoyed before 1886.

Yet Kazan was not the quiet city she had fondly imagined. It had been one of the fighting grounds between the Russians and the Tatars in the fifteenth century, and Russia's history textbooks never failed to record that Ivan the Terrible's defeat of the Tatars at Kazan in 1552 and Astrakhan in 1556 opened the way for Russian imperial expansion to the south and east. The city retained a strategic importance in subsequent centuries. Trade was its lifeblood. Perched on an elbow of the river Volga, Kazan was an important entrepôt for goods that required further shipment by railway to Moscow and St Petersburg. Hardly a street existed without its church. Kazan was a gem of Russian architecture. Historical triumphalism was not the only reason for this. The official authorities had also built magnificent churches because they worried about the significance of Kazan as the greatest centre of non-Christian faith in the empire. Moslems constituted a tenth of the city's population. Islam had its various institutions there, including Arabic-script printing presses. The ethnic composition was equally worrisome to St Petersburg. Tatars amounted to 31 per cent of the province's inhabitants – and there were also Bashkirs and Chuvash. The Ministry of the Interior consequently took no chances with the town's affairs. Successive governors were renowned for their abrasive, military approach to civil administration. At times it was as if Kazan was treated like a far-off colony that needed a display of brutality to keep it in order.

The tensions in the city as a whole were evident in its university even though hardly any Tartars belonged to it. In 1884 the central authorities in the capital had tightened the rules for student behaviour, and these were resented as much in Kazan as elsewhere. Demonstrations were held against the rector. Kazan University was constantly on the verge of public disorder, and the rector's response was always to reinforce discipline. But this in turn aggravated the feelings of the students. Compulsory uniforms were introduced in 1885 so as to make the police surveillance easier. Students were prohibited from forming associations not given prior approval by the authorities. Petty regulations about the kind of salutation owed by them to their administrators and pedagogues simply added fuel to the flames. The Ministry of Popular Enlightenment appointed new professors, and anonymous denunciations of delinquent students were encouraged. It had even been proposed that such students should be transferred to military disciplinary battalions. The suggestion was rejected, but the fact that it had been made at all was a sign of the distrust between government and students.

The only associations allowed by the Ministry of Popular Enlightenment were the so-called *zemlyachestva*. These were groups of students based upon geographical origin; they had official approval because they lent a sense of togetherness and stability to young men who were away from home for the first time. They were not a social organism peculiar to students. Travelling traders and workers formed them; they were just one example of the way Russia teemed with local traditions, local accents and dialects, local diets and local religious tenets. The *zemlyachestva* helped Russians to cope with novelty and uncertainty. Immediately upon entering Kazan University, Vladimir Ulyanov joined the Simbirsk– Samara *zemlyachestvo* in order to take advantage of the practical guidance and leisure facilities it provided.

The *zemlyachestva* also functioned as an organisation for students to debate with each other. The academic year was bound to be unsettled. The hanging of Alexander Ulyanov and his fellow students still caused bitterness, and immediately there was discussion of protests that should be made in all universities. Kazan was no exception, and the Simbirsk– Samara *zemlyachestvo* tried to play its part. The disturbances had already begun in Moscow. In each city there were grievances to be aired, and Inspector N. G. Potapov reported to Rector N. A. Kremlëv of Kazan University that his own student informers had warned him to expect trouble.[16] Emotions ran so high that students secretly discussed whether to mount a physical assault on Potapov. On 4 December the outburst took place. It was a sharp winter's day. The snow was on the ground but the sun shone brightly. About midday a crowd of students started to gather in the university buildings. Potapov tried to disperse them: 'Gentlemen, where are you going, where? Don't go!' Yet he was thrust out of the way.[17] among the crowd was the first-year student Vladimir Ulyanov. The students chanted slogans demanding university autonomy from the state and relief from the unpleasant aspects of regulation of the student body. The sacking of Potapov was an immediate aim.

Rector Kremlëv asked professors to mediate on his behalf. But the students were unmoved. At the back of their minds, however, was the knowledge that the rector would ultimately bring in armed troops to disperse the gathering. About ninety of the assembled students were so enraged that on the spot they decided to abandon their special student passes in the room as a sign that they no longer wished to belong to the university. The decision was taken on the spur of the moment. These students knew that, once the administrative staff picked up the passes, the rector would have no choice but to expel them.[18]

Police searches were instigated across the city. Students were stopped in the streets. The university was closed down until further notice, and it reopened only in February 1888. Consultations took place between the Kazan administration and its superior authorities in St Petersburg. A battalion of troops was distributed in units at appropriate points throughout the city. Vladimir returned home to New Commissariat Street and to his distraught mother and his even more distraught former nanny Varvara Sarbatova.[19] What could Maria Alexandrovna do to prevent her second son from sinking still deeper into trouble? The 'beautiful family', as Ilya Ulyanov's obituarist had characterised the Ulyanovs in Simbirsk, was no model for respectable folk. Their potential for brilliant, regular careers would not be fulfilled. In the course of the night of 4–5 December the police came for Vladimir as they came for other Kazan students. Held in custody, they were asked where else they wished to live. They would not be permitted to stay in Kazan. Maria Alexandrovna thought of the obvious solution: she would appeal to the Ministry of Interior for a mandate to return to Kokushkino with her children.

For the moment the family had to await the dispositions of the rector. These were announced on 6 December 1887. Thirty-nine students were expelled from Kazan University and Vladimir Ulyanov was among them. Only two other students were, like him, in their first year.[20] His residence permit for Kazan was withdrawn and on 7 December he was 'exiled' to Kokushkino.

His mother's ability to direct her children was fading. She could still exercise a degree of control over them by dint of their need for her financial support; but usually she gave them whatever they asked for. A more subtle instrument was the fact that the Imperial government granted concessions to Vladimir Ulyanov only if his mother stood as some kind of guarantor of his good behaviour. Thus he was allowed to return to Kokushkino only on condition that she lived there with him. But even this did not give her much leverage over him. She wanted to stay with him more than he wished to be with her. Maria Alexandrovna must have felt let down by Vladimir even if she did not express the sentiment – and there is no evidence that she ever reproached him. The question arises why she was so restrained. Why did she collude in his misbehaviour? One reason would seem to be that Ilya had acted as the family's enforcer of discipline, the usual paternal role in contemporary Russian families. Another reason might well be that she intelligently concluded that nothing could have pulled Alexander back from his self-destructive course – and so why should she assume that curt prohibitions to Vladimir would be more effective?

She had much to put up with. Vladimir's expulsion had disrupted the rest of the family. Dmitri, living in Kazan and going to its Classical Gimnazia, could not return with the family to Kokushkino but would have to lodge at the school. The same was true of her sister Maria; and even Anna, who had been directed to live at Kokushkino, would be affected if the Ministry of the Interior decided to banish her mother's eldest surviving son from Kazan province.

He went home on 4 December 1887 to a mother who no longer controlled him. During his residence in Kazan, he had already got in touch with revolutionary activists. The city was a place of exile used by the central government for the disposal of its enemies – and there were several such persons under police surveillance in this period. It was not unduly difficult for the brother of an executed revolutionary to find out who the local revolutionary sympathisers were and how to join in their discussions. The group that attracted Vladimir Ulyanov was led by Lazar Bogoraz, an agrarian-socialist advocate of terrorism. Bogoraz's precise ideas are somewhat unclear. But he undoubtedly wanted an end to the monarchy and stood for the country's social and economic transformation; and he seems to have hoped, like Alexander Ulyanov, to minimise the incipient divisions within the clandestine revolutionary movement. Vladimir was in the first stage of developing his thoughts about the politics of revolution. It was natural for him to start by learning what he could from people who were akin to his brother, and indeed people who were serious enough about their political commitment that they retained contact with similar groups in St Petersburg and elsewhere.

Indeed, if it had not been for the fracas at Kazan University, Vladimir would have become more deeply implicated in revolutionary conspiracy in the city. His summary expulsion saved him from becoming involved in activities that would have got him a much more severe sentence.[21]

Maria Alexandrovna was willing to support her children regardless of their extra-mural activities, but could not help fretting. Anna Ilinichna wrote to a friend: 'We're now very disturbed by Volodya's fate. It will, of course, be hard for Mama to let him go off anywhere else, but he can't be kept in the countryside.'[22] His mother and elder sister agreed on one thing: he had to acquire a university degree. Somehow permission had to be obtained for him to re-enter the educational system. They spoke to him about it, and he told them of his desire to leave for a foreign university. This was financially possible for the family; but Maria Alexandrovna would not yet hear of it. On 9 May 1888, he therefore wrote to the Minister of Public Enlightenment seeking readmission to the Imperial Kazan University.[23] Concurrently his mother wrote to the Director of the Police Department in similar terms. Both requests were refused. In September he asked permission to leave Russia to study abroad.[24] Again he was turned down. The police objected to his 'active participation in the organisation of revolutionary circles among the student youth of Kazan'.[25] The Ministry of the Interior liked to keep enemies of the regime not only out of St Petersburg and Moscow but out of foreign countries too.

Yet indulgence was shown to the Ulyanovs. The Ministry of the Interior under the tsars was nothing like as systematically oppressive as the police force set up by Lenin at the end of 1917. In September 1888 the family was allowed to resume residence in Kazan. Vladimir had not been tamed by his experience. Full of audacity, he sent a letter to none other than the exiled Nikolai Chernyshevski in Saratov.[26] Once he was back in Kazan, moreover, he searched out the local revolutionary activists. A clandestine circle organised by N. E. Fedoseev was functioning in the city, and Vladimir Ulyanov joined it.[27]

Fedoseev was on the way to declaring himself a Marxist. But such circles were usually still uncertain whether to identify themselves entirely with Georgi Plekhanov's Emancipation of Labour Group in Switzerland. In particular, Fedoseev – very much in contrast with Plekhanov – did not delight in the prospect of the disappearance of the peasantry at the hands of aggressive capitalist development. Fedoseev thought there was a chance that a large class of small-scale farmers might survive – and no doubt his residual sympathy for agrarian socialism meant that he welcomed this possibility on moral grounds.[28] Vladimir Ulyanov was mightily attracted by the sheer intellectual dedication of Fedoseev, who arranged that his circle held frequent discussions on major aspects of economic, social and political trends. This was a period of intense mental effort. Young Vladimir, freed from any obligation to study for a university degree, was reading furiously on his own behalf. Using his brother's

ample library and building up his own, he took account of authors who
were at the centre of European cultural discussion in the 1880s. Among
them were David Ricardo, Charles Darwin, Henry Buckle, Karl Marx
and Friedrich Engels. Marx's *Capital* was a topic of crucial interest.

Vladimir Ulyanov wanted to educate himself on a broader plane
than had been encouraged at Simbirsk Classical Gimnazia or the Imperial
Kazan University. He assumed that he could not take himself seriously
in this project unless there were convincing intellectual foundations to
it. At the same time he was not wholly immersed in politics. Together
with his cousin Alexander Ardashev, he visited a chess club in Kazan. He
also went to opera performances with his sister Olga and his brother
Dmitri. Such was his fascination with chess that he played games by post
with the Samara barrister Andrei Khardin.[29] This was no mean attainment since Khardin was accomplished enough to be taken seriously by
the world-famous player M. I. Chigorin.[30]

The sojourn of the Ulyanov family in Kazan, however, no longer
commended itself to their mother; she was no doubt thinking that she
could better steer Vladimir away from the dangers of politics if she
removed him from his local revolutionary friends. She needed to find
somewhere else to live. There was help at hand. Anna Ilinichna had
acquired a male admirer in Mark Yelizarov, whom she had known as a
friend of Alexander Ilich at St Petersburg University. Yelizarov negotiated
the purchase of a separate estate on the Ulyanovs' behalf. He looked
around not near Kokushkino but in his native Samara province, where
his brother – a successful peasant farmer – farmed 120 acres.[31] Yelizarov
secured an option on a house and land owned by the Siberian goldmine
magnate Konstantin Sibiryakov. Samara province is further south down
the Volga, between Simbirsk and Astrakhan. Sibiryakov had bought up
not just one but several landed estates after making his fortune in the
goldmines in Siberia. But he was an industrialist with a political and
social conscience. He held left-of-centre opinions, and was a sympathiser
with agrarian socialism. But also he believed in up-to-date methods,
and introduced the latest agricultural technology to his land in Samara
province.[32]

Low agricultural prices in the 1880s made it hard for him to make a
profit, and he decided to sell up. His preference was for purchasers who,
like himself, were on the left of the political spectrum. The result was
that Sibiryakov sold his various estates at a cheap rate to owners who
wanted to modernise agriculture without lowering the local peasantry's
standard of living. Some of these owners were agrarian socialists such as

Alexander Preobrazhenski. There were also followers of Tolstoi in the locality, who were Christian and pacifist. The new owners, regardless of their specific orientation, were annoyed that the government had no interest in improving the lot of the peasantry. Sibiryakov welcomed the Ulyanovs as potential buyers of an estate at Alakaevka; and after he had come to terms with Yelizarov, the estate was paid for with the various legacies in the control of Maria Alexandrovna.[33]

But Vladimir's political aspirations remained. He repeatedly visited the Fedoseev group, and also sought out the veteran People's Freedom terrorist M. P. Chetvergova, who was then living in Kazan. In his book-reading and in his various conversations, he imbibed everything he could about the efforts of Russian revolutionaries to get rid of the Romanov dynasty. Chernyshevski had already captivated him. Other revolutionaries, too, endeared themselves to Vladimir. Great agrarian-socialist terrorists such as Stepan Khalturin and Ippolit Myshkin were his lifelong heroes.[34] He was to become no less enamoured of the French novelist Émile Zola, who in 1898 was to make a stirring literary defence of the unfortunate Jewish officer in the French armed forces Alfred Dreyfus. Zola's photograph, too, was kept in Vladimir's wallet. Nor would it be entirely out of order to speculate that Vladimir had his deep hatreds as well as loves. His brother's execution left him an abiding resentment of the Romanov dynasty; and his family's problems after the 1887 assassination attempt must have added to his feeling that the respectable middle and upper social classes – the aristocracy, the landed nobility, the urban merchantry – were deserving of no respect. The conventional picture of Vladimir as a coldly calculating figure is only part of the truth. He was also a young man of intense emotions, and the loves and hatreds in his opinions about politics were passionately felt.

For Vladimir, then, the Russian Empire was not merely too slow in its social transformation. Just as importantly it was oppressive. It was Europe's bastion against the Progress; its troops had intervened directly on the side of the old regimes threatened by revolutions in 1848. Tsarism, insisted Vladimir, had to be overthrown. He could barely contain his anger and, although his revolutionary ideas were as yet unformed, the revolutionary commitment was already firm.

5

PATHS TO REVOLUTION

1889-1893

On 3 May 1889 the Ulyanov family took leave of their Veretennikov and Ardashev relatives in Kazan province and embarked on the paddle steamship that plied the route down the Volga to Samara. The boarding stage lay four miles from Kazan. The Volga flows southward to the Caspian in a slow and winding fashion, and the ferry captain had to avoid the shallows and the islands that lie across the river channel. The steamer needed two whole days to travel the three hundred miles from Kazan to Samara. The Ulyanovs might have enjoyed the trip more had they not been stopping at Simbirsk halfway along the route. Sad memories about Ilya Nikolaevich and Alexander Ilich would be revived. Fortunately the steamer would stop only for two hours, letting off those passengers who had a ticket for Simbirsk and picking up others. Nevertheless the members of the Ulyanov family would inevitably be reminded of their past. They could never forget Simbirsk and many people in Russia would never forget that the Ulyanov family had included a youth who tried to assassinate Emperor Alexander III. That youth's younger brother would one day acquire his own notoriety.

Reaching Samara, the family took carriages to their estate at Alakaevka thirty-five miles to the east of the city. Maria Alexandrovna had made the purchase unseen, relying on Mark Yelizarov's recommendation. She was not disappointed. Alakaevka was truly beautiful with its large wooden house and splendid setting. Forests and hills lay within walking distance; there was also a pond where the most inexpert fisherman could have success.[1] The writer Gleb Uspenski immortalised the district in short stories that were revered by Russian readers, including Vladimir Ulyanov. Indeed Uspenski had lived on one of Sibiryakov's estates in the late 1870s; his wife had taught in a school that Sibiryakov had built there. Sibiryakov was the financial patron of his works;[2] he recognised the author as a brilliant portraitist of the local landscape and inhabitants. He also exposed the difficulties faced by poor peasants in coping with debt, land shortage and policemen. But, unlike many contemporary novelists, he did not idealise the peasantry. He saw how divided each village was by conflicts over land and money. He denounced the peasant proclivity for drunkenness, violence and intolerance of outsiders.[3] All this made him unpopular with many contemporary socialists, but not with Vladimir Ulyanov. In later years Ulyanov and other Russian Marxists were notorious for vituperative attacks on peasant attitudes and practices. Usually their analysis has been traced to Karl Marx and Friedrich Engels. In point of accuracy, the short stories of Gleb Uspenski should be recognised as having contributed to the intellectual development of Vladimir Ulyanov.

It was a time of change for the family. As she settled into Alakaevka, Maria Alexandrovna persuaded her son Vladimir to look after the new property. His Ardashev cousins – Alexander and Vladimir – had supervised the estate at Kokushkino, and Maria Alexandrovna wanted her eldest surviving son to do the same for the newly purchased property.[4]

At first he did as he was asked, going out to meet the peasants and making plans for the estate's management. Meanwhile Anna Ilinichna was studying at home to become a teacher and helping with the running of the household. Olga worked harder than the rest of them. After leaving the gimnazia, she appeared to want to study twenty-four hours a day. Her ambition was to matriculate in medicine at Helsingfors (Helsinki) University, which – unlike the other universities in the Russian Empire – allowed women to take degrees.[5] The younger children Dmitri and Maria went to the gimnazii in Samara. Dmitri, too, hoped to study medicine at university after finishing at school. Their mother was pleased by such purposefulness. She badly wanted to deflect her offspring from political involvement, especially Anna and Vladimir, who had already been in trouble with the authorities.

Yet Vladimir was always an unlikely farm manager. Poor, resentful peasants inhabited Alakaevka; this was the reality across the whole Volga region, especially among the peasantry of Samara province. The local landed nobles had seen the 1861 Emancipation Edict as an opportunity to keep the maximum of land and rid themselves of the slightest obligation to their serfs. The result was 'land hunger' among peasant households. The peasantry had a traditional proverb for their landowners: 'We are yours, but the land is God's.' Russian peasants believed that the social order in the countryside was unnatural. They considered that only those persons who physically worked on the land should have the right to profit from its produce. This attitude prevailed even on the estates that had been owned by the benevolent Konstantin Sibiryakov.

His several successors as landowners were no more likely to assuage peasant bitterness, and within a few years all of them had abandoned farming and sold up. Most of these owners had believed that they could turn their villages into socialist communities. But the peasants were defiantly uncooperative towards them. Resentment of middle-class proprietorship was never eliminated.[6]

There was a single exception to the exodus of the new landowners. This was Alexander Preobrazhenski, who believed until his dying day that socialism could be created in Russian peasant villages. Making the acquaintance of the Ulyanov family, he became a friend of Vladimir Ulyanov. But there was no convergence of minds. Vladimir was already concluding that socialism in Russia would need to base itself on a social class other than the peasantry, and he regarded Preobrazhenski as a companionable but misguided romantic.[7]

As a farmer, Vladimir merely went through the motions of filial obedience. Rather than farm he preferred – if he did anything – to teach, and he advertised his availability as a coach to local schoolchildren;[8] but he did not pursue even this activity as a true priority. Ploughing, sowing, weeding and harvesting were of even smaller interest. He knew next to nothing about agriculture and made no effort to find out. His passion was restricted to revolutionary ideas and he quickly abandoned his activities as estate manager. For their part, the peasants spotted the opportunity offered by the arrival of an urban middle-class professional family. They got up to the usual trickery. They also thieved. The livestock of the Ulyanovs were easy targets: first a horse 'disappeared', then a cow – and when the second cow went missing, Maria Alexandrovna gave up trying to goad her son into taking managerial responsibility. Instead she rented out her Alakaevka property to the peasants, except for the family house.[9] Eventually she sold her land to one of the richer local peasants, a certain Danilin, and thereafter the family took no interest in farming. This may have been the salvation of the Ulyanovs, since in the revolutionary tumult of 1905–6 Danilin was killed by the Alakaevka peasants, who detested him as much as they had hated the noble landowners whom he had replaced.[10] If Vladimir Ulyanov had stayed on as estate manager, he could have suffered the same fate.

All this runs against the widely held notion that his later ideas were based upon his close regular experience of the peasantry of Samara province. Most of the time at Alakaevka he was studying, walking or hunting; he knew no peasant family and the fact did not trouble him. Indeed, Vladimir planned to leave what he called the 'quiet provincial backwater' of Alakaevka just as soon as the Ministry of the Interior's restrictions upon his activities had been lifted. Although he spent five successive summers there, he had no intention of staying longer than he had to.[11] His mother could command him no longer. When he made crude gestures, she might say: 'Ah, Volodya, Volodya, can this be how to behave?'[12] But she had to rely on guile and persuasion; orders were no longer effective.

Meanwhile Vladimir enjoyed himself. He went on long walks in the hills around the estate. He did some fishing in the pond either by himself or in the company of one of his brothers and sisters. Together with Olga Ilinichna he went on reading Gleb Uspenski's stories about the local area; brother and sister spent a lot of time together until her departure to St Petersburg to further her education in the autumn of 1890.[13] But he was also happy to be on his own. His greatest pleasure was to get down to his books. He hated to waste time and could be downright antisocial if he felt that his studies were being unduly disrupted. When his mother was expecting visitors to Alakaevka whom he did not already know, he barricaded himself out of sight and got on with his reading.[14] As an exception he would allow his sister Maria to sit with him while he helped her with her schoolwork.[15] She had transferred her affection from her late father to the eldest surviving Ulyanov male. But Vladimir was a stern taskmaster. He would check next day that she had memorised what he had told her and not simply written it down at his dictation.

He was acting as his own father Ilya had done towards him. By focussing intently upon his self-training he was again copying the paternal example. But Marxism and not pedagogy was Vladimir's preoccupation. It so dominated his life that he began to translate *The Communist Manifesto* into Russian.[16] He also worked to acquire a reading knowledge of English. For many years to come, such labour was a way of diverting himself. His training as a linguist had encouraged him to regard an hour spent in examining a foreign-language dictionary as one of life's treats. Vladimir was trying, like others of his generation, to decide for himself how the revolutionary movement ought to try and reconstruct the Russian Empire. For this purpose it would not be sufficient by itself to read Marx and Engels or to browse through the latest interesting books in German, French and English. His obligation was to study the current trends in the Russian Imperial economy to discern what this revealed about the political and social possibilities.

A less bookish nineteen-year-old might have got acquainted with his peasants. But Vladimir's transformation into a revolutionary came through volumes about the peasantry more than from direct regular experience. He wished to pursue his studies abroad, but in June 1889 the official authorities yet again turned down his request to travel. Yet in the following month he may have reflected upon his good fortune in no longer residing in Kazan when the police arrested the members of Fedoseev's revolutionary circle.

By then Maria Alexandrovna had accepted that Vladimir would never become a farmer and decided to move the family into Samara. They left Alakaevka on 5 September 1889, eventually settling in a rented house on Voskresenskaya Street. Vladimir was delighted; he immediately sought out the public library and the local political dissenters. Critics of the tsarist political and social order used the same libraries, bookshops and coffee-houses. They welcomed a person of Vladimir's intelligence and energy, and he in turn was pleased to get to know Alexei Sklyarenko, who headed one of the most serious discussion circles. Sessions were always held in Sklyarenko's two-room apartment as Ulyanov, who lived with his mother, felt he could not offer his family's residence for such a purpose. The circle was dedicated to the exploration of ideas, and Ulyanov read out the papers he had drafted on Russian economic history.[17] Sklyarenko and Ulyanov set the tone. As former gimnazia students, they insisted that the group studied in a very academic fashion. Only after dealing with culture, history and economics would they allow themselves to proceed to an examination of socialist theory.[18] Thereafter they invited socialists of all persuasions from elsewhere in Russia to address them; and one of the most active contemporary figures in Russian terrorism, M. V. Sabunaev, had visited them in December 1889 (after staying for a while with Bogoraz's group in Kazan).[19]

They wanted to change the world for the benefit of the lower social classes, and yet their group made no attempt to contact industrial workers or peasants. They were students devoting themselves to the study of topics which were absent from the syllabuses of their former schools and universities. Sklyarenko himself was professionally acquainted with the peasantry to the extent that his job as a civil servant required him to make investigative trips to the countryside. But, by and large, the group believed that the official economic statistics provided the most dependable basis for members to decide what to do about contemporary Russia. Ulyanov in particular concentrated on educating himself as a theorist.[20] Books, not people, were thought to supply the answers. And so the group confined itself to going out at night in Samara and sticking up revolutionary proclamations on the walls – and

Sklyarenko impressed Ulyanov with his skill at teasing the authorities verbally. But the main activity was inactivity: collective intellectual self-preparation.

To what ideas did the group adhere? Sklyarenko was an agrarian socialist with respect for the terrorists. Vladimir Ulyanov had been delighted to meet the visiting advocate of terrorism, Sabunaev; and in 1891 he took the opportunity to make the acquaintance of another terrorist sympathiser, Maria Golubeva, who was exiled to Samara in autumn 1891. They met through their friendship with yet another such terrorist, Nikolai Dolgov, who lived in the town and gave her the address of the family of the late Alexander Ulyanov. Already Vladimir Ulyanov, too, had impressed the veteran activist Dolgov with his anti-tsarist attitudes: 'Yes indeed, in everything: both in dress and in behaviour and in conversations – well, in a word, in everything.' Golubeva tried, unsuccessfully, to win him over to the doctrines of agrarian terrorism. She failed; but she noted nevertheless that several doctrines, especially those on 'the seizure of power', never gave him problems. Their basic disagreement was caused by her belief in the revolutionary potential of 'the people'. Vladimir Ulyanov by this time had rejected the possibility of making revolution without a focus on class struggle. He urged the need to rely on specific social classes; and for him this could only mean the primacy of the working class in the making of a socialist society.[21]

He continued to meet former People's Freedom adherents and supporters socially. One of them was Apollon Shukht, ten years his senior, who had come to Samara after serving a term of Siberian exile. Such was the friendship between them that, when their daughter Asya was born in 1893, Mr and Mrs Shukht asked Vladimir Ulyanov to become her godfather.[22] This, by the way, was yet another indication of the way Vladimir Ulyanov maintained many external proprieties of contemporary Russian life while plotting to overturn them in bloody revolution. At any rate the close friendship with a former activist of People's Freedom did not preclude him from seeking a different path to the construction of a socialist society in Russia. Hatred of tsarism was common to them, and Ulyanov was both intrigued and appalled by Anton Chekhov's short story 'Ward No. 6', about a sane public figure incarcerated on the orders of the Okhrana: 'When I finished reading this short story last night, I genuinely felt sick. I couldn't stay in my own room, but got up and left it. I had the kind of feeling as if I'd been locked up in Ward No. 6.'[23]

Both Ulyanov and Sklyarenko went on studying contemporary works on the Russian Imperial economy. Sklyarenko was interested in the significance of small-scale industrial production – in artisanal workshops – for Russian economic growth, and Ulyanov enjoyed their recurrent discussions. But he held back in several other respects. He opposed Sklyarenko's refusal to take a detached view of capitalist economic development. Sklyarenko could not bring himself to accept the 'historical necessity' for the disappearance of the peasantry; and, in line with not a few other revolutionary activists of his generation, he tried to think of ways of preserving a large social class of landed small-holders after the expected revolution against the monarchy. Among Ulyanov's associates, too, there were those who wished to give priority to fostering socialism not so much among the workers as among the peasantry. The prime proponent of this was Alexander Preobrazhenski, who was still trying to build up his socialist agricultural colony near Alakaevka.[24] Ulyanov argued with both Sklyarenko and Preobrazhenski. Capitalism, according to him, would follow the path mapped out by Marx and Engels in Britain and predicted for Russia by Plekhanov. There was no room for sentiment. There were only iron laws of economic development. Russia had stepped on to the capitalist road and could not avoid following the demands of the contemporary market economy.

Thus the peasantry as a class was destined to fracture into two distinct and antagonistic segments: a rural middle class ('bourgeoisie') and a rural working class ('proletariat'). Throughout the winter months Ulyanov strove to expand his knowledge of basic Marxist texts: *Capital* and *The Poverty of Philosophy* by Marx; *Anti-Dühring* and *The Condition of the Working Class in England* by Engels; *Our Disagreements* by Plekhanov. All the while he was confirming his intuition that Russia's future lay with industry, urbanisation and large-scale social organisation. Moral questions, for him, were an irrelevance. From Marx he had already taken a philosophy of history which stressed that the conventional ideas in society were always framed by the ruling classes in their own interest. Morality was consequently a derivative of class struggle. Every political, social and cultural value had only a 'relative' significance. There was no such thing as 'absolute good'; the only guide to action was the criterion: does it facilitate the more rapid and efficient progress through the necessary stages towards the creation of a communist society?[25]

His associates Alexei Sklyarenko and Isaak Lalayants were taken aback by this repudiation of sentiment in politics. They had become revolutionary activists in part because they wanted to serve 'the people'.

They themselves were not workers or peasants, and they thought that the duty of a Russian intellectual was to bring benefit to the oppressed and downtrodden elements in society. They were typical members of the conscience-stricken intelligentsia. What they perceived in their newly arrived comrade was a person who revelled in his rejection of concepts such as conscience, compassion and charity.

It was only later that his harshness acquired an importance in their minds. At the time they were disconcerted, but no more than that. And they were comfortable with him as a comrade. For the first time he was a permanent member of a voluntary group of his contemporaries, and he took to them as well as they did to him. When he produced his reports, with their scrupulously drafted graphs and tables, they were simply pleased that so brilliant a figure was emerging in their midst. He could have shown off academically at their expense, but this was not his style. He participated enthusiastically in their social jaunts. Trips beyond the outskirts of Samara were enjoyed by all of them. They could talk and argue without worrying that they might be surprised by the police, and have fun while they were doing so. They evidently felt that time was on their side. Surely the existing structure of state and society could not last much longer! Whatever else divided them, they agreed about the rottenness of the status quo. They were determined to bring down the Romanov monarchy. Sklyarenko was so fierce in his commitment that he had thrown an inkpot at a gendarme during his last interrogation in Samara prison.

Vladimir Ulyanov restricted his escapades to the occasional sailing trip down the Volga on his own. This would take him miles downstream as far as the river Usa and then back up the Volga. Such a trip might take him away from his family for three or four days at a time, and was not without danger from the unpredictable winds and currents. But he found that the physical exercise and the splendour of the Volga and the countryside removed his feelings of frustration at having to stay with his mother in Samara.

Meanwhile in his relations with the authorities he behaved with a prim civility. This was not just because he held to a gentlemanly code of conduct (except when in dispute with fellow revolutionaries); it was also out of a refusal to put himself at unnecessary risk. Nevertheless the inner fires were as strong in Ulyanov as in Sklyarenko, very probably even stronger. He had a visceral hatred for the slightest sign of illegality or corruption in contemporary Russia, and would never take it lying down, especially when he was personally affected. The existing social hierarchy he could tolerate temporarily. He cheerfully benefited from his own status as a nobleman until such time as the projected revolution inaugurated an entirely new order. Thus when his family vacated their estate at Alakaevka they entrusted their financial affairs to a bailiff by name of Krushvits, whose task was to collect the rents from the local peasants. The Ulyanovs lived off the profits; and Vladimir was unembarrassed, while he lived under a capitalist economic system, about easing his material conditions according to the rules of capitalism.

But any infringement of his legal rights provoked fury to a degree that astounded his friends and relatives. On a jaunt in Syzran, near his native town of Simbirsk, he and his brother-in-law Mark Yelizarov hired a boatman to row them across the river Volga. By doing this, they infringed the unofficial monopoly of a rich Syzran merchant, one Arefev by name, who owned a steam-ferry. As Ulyanov and Yelizarov got to mid-channel, Arefev sent out his ferry to block their passage and take them aboard. Before acceding to force, Ulyanov declared to the ferry captain: 'It makes no difference that Arefev has rented the river crossing; that's his business, not ours, and it doesn't in any way give him or you the right to act lawlessly on the Volga and detain people by force.'[26] Ulyanov punctiliously took down the names of the captain and his fellow employees for further reference while Arefev strutted around in triumph. His brother later recorded that anyone else would have calmed down 'out of inertia and "Russian" indolence'. But Vladimir Ulyanov would not let the matter drop. On his return to Samara, he wrote a formal complaint to the authorities. Samara is sixty miles from Syzran, and Arefev exploited his own standing in Syzran to delay the legal case, and two hearings were held without result.

Maria Alexandrovna tried to get her son to back down: 'Let go of this merchant! They'll postpone the case again and you'll be travelling there in vain. Besides, you should bear in mind that they have it in for you!' With some justification she thought that Vladimir got too worked up about things. But he would not be denied. He took an early-morning train to attend the third hearing and at last got his revenge. Merchant Arefev, to general astonishment, was sentenced to a month's imprisonment.[27]

Vladimir's growing knowledge of Imperial legislation, as well as his character, assisted in this. As soon as the family moved to Samara, he resumed his requests to become a university student. His letter to the Minister of Popular Enlightenment started as follows: 'In the course of two years since I finished my gimnazia course, I have had ample opportunity to become convinced of the enormous difficulty, if not the impossibility, of anyone getting an occupation who has not received a special education.' Despairing of being allowed to study in the normal way inside a Russian Imperial university, he asked to be allowed to take the jurisprudence exams as an external student.[28] His mother reinforced the plea with her own letter; and on 12 June 1890, having at last been granted the necessary permission, he began the process of registration at St Petersburg University.[29] Accustomed to private study, he had no difficulty with this arrangement. He also had the money to order the necessary textbooks. Until such time as he could visit St Petersburg, he could get other family members such as Olga Ilinichna to go round the bookshops on his behalf; and his cousin Vladimir Ardashev advised him on the reading he needed to do for his degree.[30]

Such were the advantages of belonging to a closely knit, affluent family, advantages which were not shared by most contemporary revolutionaries. At last the sons and daughters of Maria Alexandrovna were finding their feet after the disasters of recent years. Olga Ilinichna had been thwarted in her desire to study medicine at Helsingfors University; she had learned Swedish to comply with the entrance qualifications but had recoiled from adding Finnish to her accomplishments and so could not be accepted for the degree.[31] Instead in 1890 she left to take the Higher Women's Courses in St Petersburg and become a teacher. Several of her Veretennikov, Ardashev and Zalezhski cousins were already students in the capital, and she saw them fairly often.[32] There was no sign of Olga getting mixed up in revolutionary activities (although her friends Apollonaria Yakubova and Zinaida Nevzorova were soon to become Marxist activists).[33] Maria Alexandrovna could feel increasingly relaxed as Dmitri and Maria went on working at their gimnazii; and Anna married her fiancé Mark Yelizarov in July 1889, with Vladimir as one of the formal witnesses.[34] As for Vladimir, his mother knew that he would prepare himself properly for his tests at St Petersburg University.

His capacity for fast assimilation of data was so extraordinary that by March 1891 he was ready to go to the capital to take the first stage of his examinations. He rented a quiet room in a building by the river Neva. Vladimir and Olga saw a good deal of each other. Although Olga was his junior, she and their mother corresponded regularly about him. 'It seems to me, Mama,' she wrote on 8 April,

> that you are worrying for no reason that he is ruining his health.
> Firstly Volodya is good sense incarnate and secondly the exams are

very easy. He has already taken two subjects and has received a five for both of them. On Saturday (he had an exam on Friday) he took a break: in the morning he walked to Nevski Prospekt, and after lunch he came over to me and the two of us went for a walk by the banks of the Neva – we watched an icebreaker and then he set off to the Peskovskis.

He's not going to stop sleeping at night since this would be completely unnecessary: a brain cannot work for a full 24 hours, so that rest is needed. He goes and has lunch every day – consequently he's keeping on the go [*progulivaetsya*].[35]

This little excerpt shows the attentiveness given to Vladimir by the rest of the family – or at least by the female members. He was cherished as none other. More was expected of him and more was offered to support him.

He had not been 'spoiled' in the sense of being showered with presents or allowed to behave regularly in an ill-disciplined manner. But, although he was not an only child, he had been surrounded by what might be called an aura of warmly expectant encouragement. His mother was endlessly attentive and sisters Anna, Olga and – later – Maria gave him whatever assistance he required. Vladimir learned how to make use of the emotional interplay in his family. This was a trick that had an influence on his later political life. It was to give him a general presumption that others should indulge his wishes. Thus he appeared a 'natural leader'. But it also limited his awareness of the difficulties he caused. He was so used to getting his way that, if balked in any fashion, he was altogether too likely to throw a fit of anger. He absolutely hated being thwarted. As a young man he belatedly became a sort of a spoiled child nurtured by four women.

One of these women, Olga, was not to be with him much longer. Unfulfilled by her teacher-training course, she was planning to go abroad and study medicine as she had always really wanted.[36] At the end of April 1891 she fell ill in St Petersburg and was taken into the Alexander Hospital. This time it was Vladimir who communicated with his mother. His telegram ran as follows: 'Olya [Olga's diminutive name] has typhoid fever, is in hospital, nursing care is good, doctors hope for a successful outcome.' For the moment he did not feel the need for Maria Alexandrovna to leave Samara. But Olga's condition deteriorated with the onset of a febrile skin infection commonly known as St Anthony's fire. At the beginning of May he sent another telegram to Samara: 'Olya is worse.

Wouldn't it be better for Mama to travel tomorrow?'[37] Maria Alexandrovna got rail-tickets for Moscow and then for St Petersburg. But she arrived too late. Olga died on 8 May 1891, which by a terrible coincidence was the anniversary of her eldest brother Alexander's execution in 1887. She was only nineteen years old, and had been Vladimir's playmate in their childhood. Olga was buried in the Lutheran cemetery in Volkovo on St Petersburg's southern outskirts. After the funeral Maria Alexandrovna hurried back to Simbirsk to look after the rest of the family.

She had broken the law in choosing the Volkovo Cemetery. Anyone baptised as an Orthodox Christian was prohibited from crossing to another faith or denomination, and this applied in death as in life. Olga had been baptised by an Orthodox priest and should have been buried by one. The official state authorities seldom intervened to prevent or punish disobedience; but Maria Alexandrovna's insistence on having her daughter buried by a Lutheran pastor was certainly a sign of the socially marginal status which characterised the Ulyanovs. She no longer worried about what was thought about her in high society. The ostracism confronted by the family since the hanging of Alexander Ulyanov left her no illusions, and she wanted to run her life in the fashion she felt comfortable with. Not that she had particularly strong religious beliefs. It was rather that she aimed to do things her own way. Her son Vladimir had abandoned religion entirely around the age of sixteen and, as a devotee of Russian revolutionary thought, was an atheist. For him, it counted for nothing whether the cemetery was Orthodox or Lutheran. His task as he saw it was simply to make the burial arrangements as unoppressive as possible for his mother.

Although he was considerate towards her, he did not make much display of his feelings. This was the way the Ulyanovs had been brought up. Self-control was a family virtue. Certainly both he and his sister Anna were very volatile; indeed Vladimir had an impulsive, choleric temperament that was notorious in the family. But he displayed it only when he was confronting someone who was challenging him. This was a different situation, which called for him to keep a tight grip on his emotions.

Vladimir accompanied his mother back to Samara and did not return to the capital until the second stage of his examination in September. The two stages involved one written and thirteen oral tests on subjects that included not only judicial proceedings but also ecclesiastical law and police law.[38]

His later hagiographers did not mention these subjects. Presumably it was impolitic to mention that the enemy of the Romanov police-state and founder of the world's first atheist state should have chosen to study ecclesiastical law and police law. Nevertheless Vladimir achieved great success, receiving the highest possible grade in each and every subject. He was the sole student in his year to achieve this. His examiners' recommended that he should receive a first-class diploma from the Imperial St Petersburg University, and he returned to Samara on 12 November 1891 with the qualifications to begin work as a lawyer. It was yet another of the oddities of tsarist public life. The young man whom the state empowered to practise law was himself still the object of the police's secret surveillance on the ground that he was working to subvert the legal order of the state.

He arranged to begin in the barrister's offices of Andrei Khardin, with whom he had played postal chess three years earlier. Since the move to Samara, the Ulyanovs and the Khardins had drawn closer to each other. Olga and one of Andrei Khardin's daughters had been friends, and had written to each other when Olga was in St Petersburg.[39] There was a political tinge to the situation. The authorities in St Petersburg regarded barrister Andrei Khardin as a figure of 'doubtful reliability' in the light of his political opinions, and he too was being kept under surveillance.[40] He was the natural choice for Vladimir Ulyanov while he completed his five years of further training. The term of Ulyanov's status as assistant barrister began on 30 January 1892.

In Samara, he rejoined his comrades in the group of Marxists founded by Alexei Sklyarenko. Work as an assistant barrister was never going to interfere with his revolutionary involvement. This was a moment of horrendous crisis in the society of the Volga region. In 1891–2 a famine afflicted the region, and cholera and typhus followed close behind. The main victims were the rural poor. According to reliable estimates, about 400,000 subjects of Alexander III perished. The assumption of most critics of the Imperial government was that the prime culprits were the ministers in the government. The novelist Lev Tolstoi championed a famine-relief campaign that raised a large sum of money to provide the region with basic foodstuffs. Abroad the reportage on the dying peasants made the Romanov dynasty less popular than ever. It was widely contended that, had it not been for the heavy direct taxation of the peasantry, the famine would never have occurred. In fact this was probably unfair. State revenues relied more upon excise duties than upon direct taxes, and consequently it would have been senseless for the Ministry of Finances to have deliberately impoverished the peasantry in pursuit of industrial growth. On the contrary, the central government's budget depended vitally upon the continued capacity of peasants and others to buy vodka, salt and other taxed products. That there were millions of dreadfully poor peasants is beyond dispute. That the government's fiscal callousness had produced this is a less likely explanation than the freak weather conditions and the backward modes of agriculture.

But most Russian radicals did not give the government the benefit of the doubt. They saw the famine as a ghastly indication of the regime's ineptitude and brutality; they argued, too, that the whole country had been brought into disrepute across Europe. Handuts of food were inadequate. The hospitals were filthy and too few. The civil bureaucracy was extremely slow to react. Marxists, agrarian socialists and liberals concurred that tsarism's rotten heart had been exposed and that, in the short term, opponents of the regime should lend a hand to voluntary organisations seeking to alleviate the famine.

Vladimir Ulyanov stood out against the rest of the intelligentsia; he would not even condone the formation of famine-relief bodies in order to use them for the spreading of revolutionary propaganda.[41] His heart had been hardened. Virtually alone among the revolutionaries of Samara and indeed the whole empire, he argued that the famine was the product of capitalist industrialisation. His emotional detachment astonished even members of his family. His sister Anna Ilinichna went around the town to help the sick, giving them medicine and advice. Vladimir Ilich refused to join her.[42] Maria Ilinichna was confused by all this; she could not reconcile her brother's position with his adherence to an ideology that was meant to serve the poor and the oppressed. In a rare implicit criticism of him, she wrote the following comparison between her brothers Alexander and Vladimir: 'But [Vladimir Ilich], it seems to me, had a different nature from Alexander Ilich, close though they were to each other. Vladimir Ilich did not have the quality of self-sacrifice even though he devoted his whole life indivisibly to the cause of the working class.'[43]

Nothing could shake Vladimir Ulyanov's belief that mass impoverishment was inevitable. The peasantry had always paid a dreadful price for industrial growth – and so it would be in late-nineteenth-century Russia. For Ulyanov, capitalism was bound by its nature to hurt most people and to kill many of them. Humane counter-measures were not merely ineffectual: they would do harm by slowing down the development of capitalism and therefore of the eventual further progress to socialism. Thus the famine, according to Ulyanov, 'played the role of a progressive factor', and he blankly refused to support the efforts to relieve the famine.[44] His hard-heartedness was exceptional. He lived in the very region, the Volga provinces, where the famine raged. Peasants were dragging themselves into the towns pleading for food and for work. Corpses were found lying in the streets. Yet Ulyanov, once he had formed his intellectual analysis, would not be deflected by sentiment. He was not just a witness to the horrors of mass starvation: he was a participant in it. His family derived income from a Samara provincial estate and yet still he insisted that Krushvits, who managed the estate for them, should pay up exactly what had been agreed; and this meant that the peasants would have to pay Krushvits in full regardless of circumstances.[45]

This attitude demonstrates that, much as he was influenced by the ideas of Russian agrarian socialism, he never felt pity for the peasants. In this he was at one with his distant mentor Georgi Plekhanov. Ulyanov was following Plekhanov in his basic interpretation of Marxism, and Plekhanov was becoming an idol for him. For Ulyanov, Plekhanov's interpretation of the works of Karl Marx and Friedrich Engels was unrivalled. In fact there was much controversy among the revolutionaries of the Russian Empire as to whether Plekhanov had got it right. In 1881 Vera Zasulich, the agrarian-socialist terrorist, wrote to Marx himself asking whether he believed that the scheme of social development he had sketched out for the advanced capitalist states was necessarily applicable to agrarian Russia. In many of his works Marx had analysed how the capitalist stage came from the bowels of feudalism. He predicted that the internal processes of capitalism would engender crisis after crisis which in turn would induce the impoverished working class, equipped by capitalism itself with educational and organisational skills, to seize power. Thus the movement from feudalism to capitalism to socialism was not only desirable, it was inevitable. But, asked Vera Zasulich, was this sequence of stages predestined to affect every country? Might there not be a chance for a largely pre-capitalist country such as Russia to avoid capitalism altogether and adopt socialism?

The reply she received from Marx was gratifying. Far from claiming that *Capital* offered a template for all countries, he accepted that Russia's agrarian economy and peasant communal traditions might allow it to have a socialist transformation without capitalist industrialisation. Thus he appeared to condone the strategy of the Russian agrarian socialist. And indeed he and Engels were also known to admire the anti-tsarist terrorists and to dismiss the self-proclaimed Marxists such as Plekhanov as bookish and cowardly.

Thus the Russian controversy over capitalism between the agrarian socialists and the 'Marxists' seemingly encouraged Marx to side with the agrarian socialists. But Marx was not quite so unequivocal as Zasulich claimed. On the possibility of a socialist revolution being based on the egalitarian aspects of the peasant land commune, he had specified that this would not be at all practicable unless there were concurrent seizures of power by socialist parties in the advanced capitalist countries of the West. This was a very large reservation. Moreover, Plekhanov insisted that Marx and Engels should recognise that capitalism had arrived in Russia. The growth of activity in factories, mines and banks was an incontrovertible fact, as all the official statistics testified. Zasulich herself was one of Plekhanov's leading converts and helped him to found the Emancipation of Labour Group in Switzerland. Marx died in 1883, and so Plekhanov's attention was concentrated upon Engels. But Engels did not immediately yield to Plekhanov. Only in 1892, three years before he died, would Engels concede that Plekhanov and the generation of Russian Marxists – including the still obscure Samara writer Vladimir Ulyanov – might be justified in rejecting the agrarian socialism of their forebears. The Emancipation of Labour Group set the precedent for Russian Marxists to treat the Marx–Zasulich letters as a regrettable but temporary episode. The future, insisted Plekhanov, lay in applying *Capital* to Russia.

Vladimir Ulyanov agreed, and dedicated himself to becoming a revolutionary. In 1892 he took on only fourteen cases as a barrister, one of them being the prosecution of his personal tormentor Arefev. This was no heavy workload even if account is taken of his mild bout of typhoid in the course of the year.[46] The burden got even lighter in 1893: from January to August he handled only a half-dozen cases.[47] Most of his clients were from the poorer elements in society,[48] but he was far from being a campaigning humanitarian lawyer. He continued to live off the family legacies; he knew that his mother would never insist that he should earn his own living. His real work, as he saw it, was to understand the economic realities and political opportunities in the Russian Empire and to insert his conclusions into a wider public debate across Russia.

To this end he was already engaged in a lively correspondence with Nikolai Fedoseev, his friend from his days in Kazan. Fedoseev was the first person he had met who could test him intellectually. The topic that engaged them was of acute importance: how to deal with the peasantry once the Romanovs had been overthrown and a democratic republic and a capitalist economy had been established. Fedoseev, unlike Ulyanov, did not recommend that peasants should be surrendered without compunction to the vagaries of the market. Instead he suggested that a very large class of small-holding cultivators was compatible with the medium-term development of capitalism. There were Marxists in Samara, too, who believed that Ulyanov had not taken proper account of the social and economic composition of the Russian Empire. Pëtr Maslov, Ulyanov's senior by three years, built on Fedoseev's analysis by contending that Russian capitalist development was being hobbled by the government's heavy taxation of the peasantry. The result, according to Maslov, was that only the richest peasants could expand their purchasing power and thereby enable Russia to catch up industrially with the advanced capitalist powers. Moral and practical objections coalesced in his objections to the basic orientation of Western capitalism.

But Ulyanov wanted to spread his wings. In summer 1893 his brother Dmitri passed out from the Samara gimnazia. The decision was taken that the family as a whole should move to Moscow. Anna's term of exile had ended in the previous year, and Maria Alexandrovna anyway wished to move to a metropolis. The estate at Alakaevka was still being run by Krushvits at a substantial profit, so the family took up rented accommodation in Moscow. The youngsters Dmitri Ilich and Maria Ilinichna had still to be helped through their higher education, and Maria Alexandrovna wanted to be near them while this occurred. But in the process she was loosening her grip upon Vladimir, who planned to make a name for himself in the intellectual salons of St Petersburg.

6

ST PETERSBURG

1893–1895

Vladimir Ulyanov left home on 20 August 1893, bound for St Petersburg. His journey began with the long steamer trip up the Volga to Nizhni Novgorod, where he stopped at the Nikanorov Hotel. For the first time he could travel around the country without having to explain himself to his mother. He could fill his time as he wanted.

Nizhni Novgorod stands at the confluence of the rivers Volga and Oka. The city experienced a growth in industrial production in the last years of the nineteenth century but was still best known as an important river port, and every year the country's largest fair was held there from mid-July until early September. The Great Fair attracted Russian peasants and merchants as well as the Moslem traders who lived in the Volga provinces. Half a million visitors packed the streets to inspect the booths and stalls that creaked with everything from machine-tools to elaborate daggers and baskets of felt shoes and leather belts. It was all noise and bustle in the summer months. Traders did not bother to bring samples of their wares; they carried their entire stock on their back or by cow, horse or camel. The peasants from deep in the countryside, if they were coming for the first time, could scarcely believe their eyes. To them the large banks, the corn exchange and the railway station were exotic beyond their dreams. At the same time these peasants in bast shoes and rough smocks presented a bizarre spectacle to visitors who had seen only St Petersburg and its inhabitants. Nizhni Novgorod combined Russia ancient and modern.

Yet if Ulyanov walked around the Great Fair, he did not mention it. Admittedly he seldom described such events in his correspondence, preferring to crush the bustle and colour of Russia into a pulp of abstract economic data; but it is quite possible that he passed up the opportunity to inspect the booths and stalls. He looked up fellow Marxists in Nizhni Novgorod. Pavel Skvortsov and Sergei Mickiewicz were among them.[1] Ulyanov had friends in common with them: Skvortsov had taught Fedoseev the rudiments of Marxism in Kazan before Ulyanov had arrived

there[2] – and Ulyanov was cheered by coming into contact with revolutionaries who shared a preoccupation with books and systematic analysis.
They sat up late into the night discussing politics and economics. Next
day he left by train for the town of Vladimir. There his purpose was to
find Nikolai Fedoseev, who had befriended him in Kazan, and seek his
opinion on his writings.[3] Unfortunately Fedoseev was not merely in exile
in Vladimir but in prison, and the meeting could not take place. Ulyanov
set off to Moscow, where he stayed with relatives and worked in the
great library in the Rumyantsev Museum before taking the train to the
north. He arrived in St Petersburg on 31 August.[4]

The capital for him represented New Russia. There was, he thought,
no hope for the country unless industrial and educational progress
could be maintained – and St Petersburg was in the vanguard of that
movement. He hated Old Russia. A few years later he reproached his
sister Anna for choosing Moscow as her place of residence: 'But surely
you agree that Moscow's a foul city? It's a foul place to hang around,
it's a foul place for book publication – and why is it that you stick to it?
I really went mad when Mark informed me that you were opposed to
moving house to St Petersburg.'[5]

What especially attracted him to the capital were not its hundreds of
thousands of factory workers but the little group of young Marxist
authors who published on the Russian economy and society. In previous
decades there had been many political writers who proffered a critique
of tsarism. Among them had been Alexander Herzen, Nikolai Chernyshevski, Mikhail Bakunin, Pëtr Lavrov and Nikolai Mikhailovski. But they
had much difficulty in co-operating with each other and greater difficulty
in publishing their works in the legal press. Not so Vladimir Ulyanov's
generation of authors. Quite a number of them were active in the capital,
most notably Pëtr Struve, Mikhail Tugan-Baranovski (a friend of Sasha
Ulyanov) and Sergei Bulgakov. Others such as Pëtr Maslov were soon to
join them. They were adept at analysing the official statistics on social
and economic trends – and in Russia these records appeared in profu-
sion. Such writers were exercised by the gamut of politics, economics,
sociology and philosophy. They read major contemporary works in
foreign languages and strove to apply the latest ideas to the Russian
Empire; and they were the first intellectual generation without a sense of
inferiority to the great poets and novelists who had emerged in Russia
since the 1820s: Pushkin, Lermontov, Turgenev, Dostoevski and Tolstoi.
The young men of the last decade of the nineteenth century felt that it

had fallen to them to offer the definitive answers to questions about Russia's future.

Ulyanov found a room for rent on Yamskaya Street. He was the sole lodger. The room was clean and the padded door into the hallway meant that the landlady's young family did not disturb him. Yamskaya Street was handily situated, being only a quarter of an hour by foot from the state public library. As soon as he had settled in his lodgings, he went to pay his respects at his sister Olga's grave in the Volkovo Cemetery and assured his mother by letter that the cross and flowers were in place. In a postscript he mentioned that he was running out of money. He had yet to receive his fees in full from Samara. (Not that they amounted to much because he had not been in regular work.) He asked his mother whether his Aunt Anna Veretennikova had sent the Ulyanovs their share of the Kokushkino estate rent and whether Krushvits, too, was paying up on time.[6]

Vladimir Ulyanov aimed to promote Revolution and to be comfortable in the process. On 3 September he took the precaution of registering as assistant to the barrister Mikhail Volkenshtein. A letter of recommendation from Andrei Khardin had preceded Ulyanov, and he made arrangements to establish himself as a metropolitan lawyer. Yet, although he wrote to his mother that his first appearance in court was imminent, no such appearance took place. His legal work went no further than occasional informal advice to friends and associates. Indeed the only time he and Volkenshtein worked together was when Volkenshtein tried to get him bailed in 1896.[7] In reality Ulyanov was preoccupied with Revolution, and saw this as requiring him to read and write about Russian economic development. The bookshops in St Petersburg were better stocked than those in Samara; he also had access to illegally printed political literature. Ulyanov sought out everything available by Marx and Engels. Works he could not obtain in St Petersburg, including the third volume of Marx's *Capital*, he asked his brother Dmitri and sister Maria to find for him in Moscow.[8] Vladimir's appetite for such literature was insatiable.

His own first piece was entitled 'New Economic Trends in Peasant Life' and was devoted to a Marxist interpretation of the quantitative data on the peasantry of southern Russia collated by the economist V. E. Postnikov in a book that was currently the focus of intense public discussion. He sent a copy to Pëtr Maslov in Samara, and asked him to send it on to Fedoseev. Ulyanov's confidence was rising fast. But he was still to prove his talent in the opinion of fellow economic commentators. Fedoseev's reaction to his article was important to him. He wanted Maslov, too, to supply 'as detailed an analysis and critique as possible'. By then he had already had his earliest literary disappointment. The prestigious St Petersburg journal *Russian Thought*, which was noted for its coverage of public affairs, turned him down flat. He thought of issuing it as a separate pamphlet;[9] but this idea, too, came to naught.

On reflection he found his failure unsurprising. The journal had recently published an article by V. P. Vorontsov on the very same book by Postnikov, and Ulyanov reasoned to himself that Vorontsov's liberal political outlook was always likely to appeal to a liberal journal such as *Russian Thought*. He explained to others that he had softened the conclusions in quest of publication, but that this could never be enough to assuage the hostility of the editor.[10] Whether this alone would have prevented publication, however, is doubtful. In any case there were other major journals that he could have approached, including ones which were willing to take articles by Marxists. The Marxist thinkers of the 1890s had an intellectual eminence which was recognised even by their opponents. The problem for Vladimir Ulyanov was not so much the rivalry with Vorontsov as the cogency of the article's arguments. Ulyanov had tried to demonstrate that Postnikov's data confirmed that capitalism was already the dominant feature of the Russian rural economy and that the peasantry was being rapidly dissolved into two contending social classes: namely a landed middle class and an agricultural proletariat. He scoffed at the continuing influence ascribed by Vorontsov to the peasant land commune. For Ulyanov, the commune could no longer practically restrain the economic expansion of the rich peasant households at the expense of the impoverished majority of households.[11]

This was so selective a review of Postnikov's data that *Russian Thought* might reasonably have rejected the article even if the journal had shared Ulyanov's political orientation. But Ulyanov would not hearken to such criticism. He felt that he had compromised enough by toning down his language. His animus against Vorontsov was acute, and it is not difficult to understand why. Vorontsov was a public figure with agrarian-socialist leanings. But even in private he did not call for a revolution against the monarchy; he was resigned to campaigning for the alleviation of economic and social distress within the framework of the existing political order. This was not what most annoyed Ulyanov. His anger was aimed at Vorontsov's contention – and Ulyanov had explained this at clandestine meetings of Marxists in Samara and St Petersburg –

that Russian capitalism would always remain a stunted growth. Vorontsov pointed to the heavy level of taxation on the peasantry as the prime
reason for this. Therefore, he argued, the domestic market would remain
fragile and the peasantry could look forward only to perpetual impoverishment.[12]

Ulyanov was irritated further by the fact that several thoughtful
Marxists shared Vorontsov's economic standpoint on the matter. Maslov,
despite agreeing with Ulyanov in rejecting agrarian socialism and in
believing in the need for revolution, was nevertheless convinced that the
poverty in the countryside was so widespread that capitalist development
would not pass the incipient stage. Such ideas were also to be found
among the St Petersburg Marxists. Ulyanov contacted a group of them
who met in the house of Stepan Radchenko and included students from
the Institute of Technology. A discussion evening was held at the end of
the month, and a bright young engineer called Leonid Krasin gave a
paper on 'The Question of Markets'. Ulyanov was an unforgiving
member of the audience,[13] and had a verbal dexterity which the others
lacked. He was also extraordinarily belligerent. In all such discussions his
fellow Marxists learned to beware of him. In February 1894 another
meeting was held. This time the apartment of the engineer Robert
Klasson was the venue. Ulyanov yet again displayed his revolutionary
fervour. He disliked a discussion if it lacked a sense of practical political
commitment, and he criticised his friends for this. They reeled in the
face of such intemperance. Like him, they were trying to discern the
pattern of current economic development. But Ulyanov wanted more
than this: he demanded that the group examine how best to bring down
the Imperial order.

One of the participants was the Marxist activist Nadezhda Konstantinovna Krupskaya. She detected 'something evil and dry' in his laughter
when someone suggested that the group should form a 'literacy committee' for local industrial workers. Ulyanov asked how such proposals
would aid the revolutionary cause. No one had talked to them in such a
fashion, and Krupskaya was to recall: 'Klasson came up; he was very
upset and said, twitching his beard: "Well, the Devil knows what he's
talking about!" "What do you mean?" responded Korobko, "he's right:
what sort of revolutionaries are we?"'[14] Klasson and Korobko felt
chastened. For the first time someone had pointed out to them that
revolutions did not happen by themselves.

Whether Ulyanov himself was in a legitimate position to criticise
others, however, is a moot point. Although he called for a practical

approach to revolutionary struggle, he had yet to meet factory workers in any number. He saw the factories and commercial offices of St Petersburg only from the outside. He lived as a middle-class *rentier*. And unlike his engineer associates, he lacked any professional training that might put him in touch with the industrial Russia that was coming into existence. Nor did he perceive a need to change his lifestyle. He still thought the most effective way to enhance the prospects of Revolution in his country was to engage in economic and political controversy with other middle-class intellectuals. While he enjoyed trouncing Krasin, Klasson and Korobko, he recognised that they were hardly the outstand-ing thinkers of their generation. He was not arrogant towards them but had no intention of remaining a modest member of their group. Despite his contretemps with *Russian Thought*, he kept up his determination to have a broad impact on informed public debates. This, after all, was why he had come to St Petersburg in the first place.

Luckily for him, Klasson had the connections to attract Pëtr Struve and Mikhail Tugan-Baranovski to his apartment in late February 1894.[15] Ulyanov was at last exchanging ideas with thinkers of his own intellectual calibre. The three of them – Struve, Tugan-Baranovski and Ulyanov – were tackling basic questions of Russia's future. Struve was on the point of making his name with his book *Critical Remarks on the Question of Russia's Economic Development*, and Tugan-Baranovski was to publish *The Russian Factory*. Like Ulyanov, they scrutinised the latest economic data. They had independent means and were converts to Marxism. It was the hope of Ulyanov to get his own works into the legal press.

But their new friend disconcerted Struve and Tugan-Baranovski. Ulyanov had never been abroad and witnessed the higher level of economic development in Britain, France and Belgium. This was not his fault. The Ministry of the Interior had turned down every request he had made to travel to foreign parts. Yet Struve and Tugan-Baranovski felt that Ulyanov had suffered intellectually from his insulation. In particular, they told him, he needed to drop his absurd over-statement of the degree of capitalist development that had occurred in the Russian Empire. His approach was altogether too schematic. To them it also appeared that Ulyanov was excessively keen to prove to Marxists that he was entirely 'orthodox' in his interpretation of Marxism. Struve and Tugan-Baranovski wished to use Marxism as a means of explaining the truth of Russian economic trends but not as an unquestionable creed; they thought Ulyanov was overly exercised by loyalty to Marx regardless of whether Marx was right or wrong. He refused to accept that *Capital* could be faulted in the slightest way. He was a secular 'believer'.

And at the same time they thought he had altogether too much of the Russian terrorist tradition about him. In his own family Alexander had been a practising terrorist and Anna and even young Dmitri sympathised with the terrorists.[16] Vladimir himself went on being friendly with former activists of People's Freedom. He might castigate agrarian socialism, but he did not keep his distance from people who advocated its most extreme practical variant. And so he seemed to them to be an extraordinary mixture of influences – and they assumed that further residence in St Petersburg and a foreign city or two was needed for him to mature in a normal fashion.

There was an obvious paradox. Vladimir Ulyanov had been brought up as a European Russian. He was a fluent reader of German and French and had taught himself to read English. He was a brilliant student of the Classics. His parents, while rearing their family to be proud of Russian culture, had not imparted nationalist ideas. How on earth could such a boy have turned out to be so 'Russian' in comparison with many young Russians who had had much less access to the contemporary currents of European thought? Struve and Tugan-Baranovski were surely correct in saying that Ulyanov's inexperience of Europe was a large part of the answer. But they overestimated the likelihood of him adjusting his ideas in reaction to a trip abroad. He had already made his mind up. From this period onwards, at least until he had held power for a couple of years, he would persist in seeing Russia as more advanced economically and socially than it really was. This was not all. He would also begin to contend that the policies he recommended for his own Russia should be applied to the rest of Europe. His Europeanisation of Russia was a first step on the path towards the Russianisation of Europe.

Another area of division between them was the gap in status between Struve the Petersburg aristocrat and Ulyanov the *parvenu*. When Anna Ilinichna wrote to Struve in 1899, who still professed Marxism, on her brother's behalf, she addressed him formally as 'Gracious Sir';[17] this was not the way that revolutionary activists usually communicated with each other. The Ulyanovs had been rising up the ladder of Imperial society, but they had no friends among the higher hereditary nobility, and after Alexander Ulyanov's execution there was no chance that they ever would. Anna's formal respectfulness towards Struve was just one sign of this. Not that Vladimir minded about his family's position. He had never aimed to ingratiate himself with Old Russia. Unlike his sister, he did not disguise his emotions. He talked to Struve on his own terms, and Struve and Tugan-Baranovski were horrified by what they took to be the crudity of his ideas. But Vladimir Ulyanov did not care. He even disconcerted the Radchenko–Klasson group, whose members were from middle-class backgrounds more akin to his own. Wasn't Ulyanov, they asked, a bit too 'red'?[18] In their eyes, his Marxism retained an excess of the more violent aspects of Russian agrarian-socialist terrorism.

He tried to reassure them that he was committed to 'scientific' Marxism and that he had put his agrarian-socialist phase behind him. But his heroes included precisely the terrorists that the Radchenko– Klasson group objected to. Ulyanov had a penchant for the works of Pëtr Tkachëv, who argued that Engels, after Marx's death, had been insufficiently 'Marxist' inasmuch as his *Anti-Dühring* had offered an excessively deterministic analysis of world history. Tkachëv believed in revolutionary will, conspiratorial organisation and political violence, and thought such tenets congruent with Marxism. Eulogising dictatorship, he declared that if ever the revolutionaries got power they would need to carry out a mass terror against priests, policemen and landlords. More privately he harboured an admiration for Sergei Nechaev. This was an extraordinary hero for him. Nechaev had been the notorious arch-conspirator of Russian agrarian socialism who, in the interests of binding his adherents to their common cause, ordered the murder of one of them. The trial of Nechaev's adherents in 1871 did much to alienate middle-class opinion from the nascent revolutionary movement, and Fëdor Dostoevski put his version of the episode at the centre of his novel *The Devils*. The activists of the People's Freedom organisation disowned Nechaev's criminal and amoral self-aggrandisement.

Yet Vladimir Ulyanov felt that Nechaev's name should be honoured. He reasoned as follows: 'He possessed special talent as an organiser and conspirator as well as the ability to enrobe his thoughts in astonishing formulations.' Nechaev had once been asked who in the ruling house of the Romanovs should be liquidated. The reply was: 'The whole house of the Romanovs!' Ulyanov repeated the phrase, calling it a simple stroke of genius.[19] Thus Ulyanov the Marxist did not exclude non-Marxist idols from his pantheon. The traditions of Russian agrarian socialists, especially the advocates of dictatorship, had a deep and enduring impact upon him.

He shared a visceral hatred of every social prop of the tsarist political order. He detested the whole Romanov family, the aristocracy, the clergy, the police and the high command. He hated the mercantile middle class and the rising industrial and financial middle class. His zeal to smash down these props by violent methods was something he held in common with Zaichnevski, Tkachëv and Nechaev. In fact not all the terrorists he admired had felt this way. Indeed Vladimir Ulyanov's terrorist brother Alexander had not forsworn concepts of morality or the goals of parliamentary elections. So what made Vladimir Ulyanov respond enthusiastically to the rhetoric and rationale of terror and dictatorship? The most obvious answer is the fate of that same elder brother. It had been within the gift of the Emperor Alexander III to commute the death sentence on Alexander Ulyanov. But Alexander Ulyanov was hanged. This would have been enough to turn many a younger brother against 'the house of the Romanovs' even though Alexander Ulyanov's complicity in the assassination conspiracy of 1887 was undeniable. Moreover, the fate of his brother Alexander was bound to incline Vladimir to the bloody invocations of Zaichnevski, Tkachëv and Nechaev.

Yet this is not the whole story. Vladimir's family had always yearned for a transformed Russia. The Ulyanovs felt a certain detachment from the official Imperial culture – and not just because they had non-Russian elements in their genealogy. They wanted a 'cultured', 'civilised' Russia. They wanted an end to privileges. Much in Vladimir's early life had already undermined any inhibition to turning Russia upside down. His education had had a similar effect. The gimnazia curriculum had insisted upon technical linguistic accomplishment dissociated from everyday Russian life. His university training was equally abstract. The purposes of government were transmitted to him in the form of irksome regulations. He saw nothing to lose in destroying his state and society.

At the same time Vladimir Ulyanov was a complex individual who had not abandoned hope of general recognition as a writer on economics and society. Although Struve and Tugan-Baranovski remained uneasy about him, he refused to modify his analyses. He had stood up to his most severe intellectual test to date, and did not feel worsted. His confidence mounted in other ways too. His previous separations from his mother and family had been of short duration so that the move to St Petersburg marked a psychological break. He had all but lost his youthful appearance. Vladimir had inherited his father's looks and one aspect of this gave him some irritation: early baldness. He discussed with his sister Maria Ilinichna whether there might be a way to reverse the process. Probably he was joking. But he kept his beard and what was left of his hair in proper trim. Indeed he hated untidiness – and he admonished family members if they failed to keep their buttons neatly sewn and their shoes repaired.[20]

Yet he was no dandy. While wanting to remain tidy, he did not enjoy shopping for clothes; he got others to do this for him – or rather he wore his clothes until such time as one of his relatives became sufficiently exasperated to buy a new suit or a pair of shoes for him.

The main women in his life were still his mother and sisters, and from St Petersburg he kept in regular contact with them by letter. He visited them in the summerhouse they rented near Lyublino railway station south of Moscow. The members of the Ulyanov family were good at supporting each other. On one of his trips to Lyublino, Volodya learned to ride a bicycle under instruction from Dmitri.[21] He himself encouraged Maria in her educational objectives when she took up a two-year science course in Moscow in 1896. Maria Ilinichna had not had an easy time. She had been refused admission to the St Petersburg Higher Women's Courses taken earlier by Anna Ilinichna.[22] She was not as bright as her exceptional elder brothers, but probably the reason for her rejection was political rather than academic and she was paying a price for being related to brothers and a sister who were troublemakers for the Imperial regime. But she struggled on and Vladimir kept in touch and gave her encouragement to go abroad and finish her education.

Meanwhile his interest in members of the opposite sex was growing; many years later he referred to having chased after one or two of them. The rumour was widely believed that the beautiful Apollonaria Yakubova had caught his eye and become his sweetheart. Certainly he made a trip back to Nizhni Novgorod in January 1894 and met up with her; and in 1897, according to hints dropped by his sister Anna, there continued to be a feeling for him at least on Apollonaria's part. The truth may never be known. By all accounts, however, he did not let affairs of the heart get in the way of public affairs – and this was to remain the case even during his involvement with Inessa Armand before the First World War.

Nor had his childhood quirks vanished. Pencils were still kept (mercilessly) sharp and his desk remained smartly arranged; he cleaned it daily. He also detested waste. When he received letters with blank spaces, he cut off and kept the unused parts. He was careful with his money and warned Dmitri against being diddled by booksellers. Always he drafted articles in his neat longhand. Not for him the 'Bohemian' slackness of his revolutionary associates. There was only one aspect of his personal life, namely his health, where he failed to display due care. He could not be blamed for his typhoid when he was a young man.

But he was less than careful in relation to other problems. Vladimir had terrible, chronic pains in the stomach and the head and could not sleep at night. Doctors diagnosed 'catarrh' of the stomach membrane; nowadays this would be called an ulcer. His brother Sasha had suffered from similar problems as a very small boy; Anna Ilinichna too had the same 'catarrh' at the age of nineteen and their mother had her own difficulty with her stomach.[23]

Apparently there was a genetic susceptibility to severe gastric problems. But the environment, too, had an impact. Nearly always stomach illness occurred in those periods of his life when he was failing to stick to regular meal times and to a well-balanced diet; and any psychological tension arising from political disputes made the problems much worse.[24]

Yet in politics he was less inhibited than any contemporary Marxist in Russia. He was undeterred by his oral disagreements with Struve and Tugan-Baranovski, and in late 1894 wrote a lengthy review of Struve's *Critical Remarks*. This had a print-run of 2,000 copies. Ulyanov looked forward to publishing a work of his own, but the political radicalism of its contents induced him to adopt the pseudonym K. Tulin. He referred to 'Mr Struve' – the use of 'Mr' itself a term of abuse among Marxists – as a 'petit-bourgeois'. Above all, he declared that the 'bourgeois' nature of the contemporary Russian economy had long been established and that capitalism had already been consolidated:[25]

> Is it really only 'over recent years'? Was it not given clear expression in the 1860s? Did it not dominate in the entire course of the 1860s? The petit-bourgeois [Mr Struve] is trying to soften things by representing the bourgeois characteristics of the entire reform epoch [after 1861] as a sort of temporary distraction or fashion.

The contrast between Ulyanov and Struve could only be hinted at in a legal publication. This consisted in Struve's suggestion that the end of capitalism might come about peacefully and even without very much conflict among the various social classes. Ulyanov had objected to this in a pamphlet he had written and had had reproduced on a hectograph machine. Struve, according to Ulyanov, had erroneously overlooked the need for Marxists always to advocate 'class struggle' and violent methods of Revolution.[26] Although he did not say this openly in the new article, he strongly implied it. And the censors in the Ministry of the Interior understood this well enough. They impounded the book before it went on sale. In 1895 all but a hundred of the extant copies were burned. Once again Ulyanov had been thwarted in his attempt to become a widely read author.

Yet he still hoped for a greater future. He had always wanted to travel abroad, and now he had the additional incentive of the possibility of making direct contact with Georgi Plekhanov and his Emancipation of Labour Group. On 15 March 1895, to his surprise, the chance came his way when the Ministry of the Interior at last, for no particular reason, dropped its refusal to grant him a passport.[27] He hurriedly made preparations for a trip to Switzerland, and packed materials about the Russian Imperial economy together with his clothes. On 24 April he set off from St Petersburg to Moscow with his Samara friend Isaak Lalayants, newly released from prison. Next day, alone, he took the train westwards to the Russian frontier across the lands of the Habsburg Monarchy.[28]

Vladimir Ulyanov was under instructions from his mother to write to Moscow as he made his journey, and he dutifully posted a card from Salzburg:[29]

> I've now been travelling 'in foreign parts' for two days and am practising the language: I'm in a bad way; I understand the Germans with the greatest difficulty or, I should say, *I don't understand them at all*. If I go up to the conductor with any question, I don't understand when he replies. He repeats himself more loudly. I still don't understand, and he gets angry and walks off. Despite such a shameful fiasco, I'm not disheartened and am pretty keenly mangling the German language.

Crossing into Switzerland, he was entranced by the Alps and the lakes, and explored the possibility of renting a summerhouse and hiring a maid. He reported, however, that maids received as much as thirty francs per month and had also to be fed – and that they expected to eat well![30] This was the reaction of a man who, whatever his politics, expected to keep expenditure on employees to a minimum. He was more willing to spend money in connection with his own health and, when his stomach continued to give him trouble, he paid for a consultation with an expensive Swiss medical specialist. The advice to Ulyanov was mainly dietary. He was told to eat regularly, avoid oily foods and drink plenty of mineral water.[31]

From Switzerland he made a trip to France, where he rented an apartment in Paris. Returning to Zurich, he found a place outside the city by the lakeside and amid greenery. Then finally on to Berlin, where he swam a lot and visited the Königliche Bibliothek.[32] Whenever he began to run out of money, his mother helped him out. Within the family he was notorious for his reluctance to give presents. He wrote to her just before leaving Berlin offering to bring back a book on anatomy for his brother Dmitri. But what could he bring for his sister Maria? 'I feel', he added, 'that I ought to buy various bits of rubbish.'³³ Hardly the words of a sentimentalist. Yet for once he purchased a present for her. Maria never disclosed what it was, but she adored her brother and was so grateful that she never forgot this uncharacteristic act of generosity. Subsequently the sole presents she got from him were copies of books he had written.

By contrast Vladimir Ulyanov was highly emotional about his politics. Among his purposes in going abroad was to arrange a meeting with his idol, Georgi Plekhanov. His first task in May 1895 had been to track him down in Geneva. The two got on very well. At last Plekhanov had evidence of his growing following in St Petersburg. The tiny Emancipation of Labour Group was encouraged by Ulyanov's visit to consider ways of expanding its influence, and discussed a scheme to establish a journal of socialist theory, *Rabotnik*. Ulyanov had proceeded from Geneva to Zurich in order to discuss further arrangements with Plekhanov's associate Pavel Axelrod. He stayed for a fortnight with Axelrod and his wife at the village of Adoltern. Ulyanov's intelligence, dedication and loyalty impressed Plekhanov and Axelrod. His Marxist faith was unquenchable. While he was in Paris, he looked up Marx's son-in-law Paul Lafargue; and in Berlin he conversed with the prominent German social-democrat Wilhelm Liebknecht. It may reasonably be supposed that he would have paid homage directly to Friedrich Engels if Engels had not died in 1895. Such meetings were not just occasions for mundane political business. Ulyanov, a man who was shy of expressing his feelings, nevertheless confessed to being in love (*vlyublënnost'*) with Karl Marx and Georgi Plekhanov. This young heterosexual revolutionary was more excited by ideology – and its leading exponents – than by women.

He lived for politics. Back in St Petersburg, on 29 September, he brought the good tidings of the contacts he had made. On the way he had stopped over in Vilnius, Moscow and Orekhovo-Zuevo. In each of these places he forged links with local Marxists. He travelled with a yellow, false-bottomed leather suitcase which he had had made for him by a craftsman on Mansteinstrasse in Berlin; and he smuggled in plenty of illegal literature for his comrades.³⁴ But the border crossing had not been as successful as had appeared at the time. The customs officers knew his identity and almost certainly refrained from searching his suitcase in order to enable the Okhrana to follow him back to St Petersburg and discover the names of the rest of his comrades.[35] For Ulyanov personally, however, the trip was a memorable achievement. Organisation on a higher scale than clandestine discussion circles in Kazan, Samara or St Petersburg was in prospect. He expected the linkage with Switzerland to facilitate the construction of a network of political sympathisers across the Russian Empire.

But still the perspective was primarily literary: the co-operation between Ulyanov's comrades and the Emancipation of Labour Group would be focussed upon the production of the *Rabotnik* journal. The Russian word *rabotnik* (or 'worker') signalled the Group's orientation towards the industrial labour movement in Russia. And yet neither Ulyanov nor any of his comrades had plans to meet workers. The St Petersburg Marxists were sincere, hard-studying intellectuals, but they lived in complete isolation from the urban 'proletariat' which they described as the future vanguard of the revolution against the Romanov monarchy. It was only a matter of time before one of the comrades would become frustrated by their political passivity. In fact it was an outsider who provoked them into action. This was the young Marxist Yuli Martov, a newcomer to St Petersburg from Vilnius. Enthusiastic and resourceful, Martov formed his own discussion group before making the acquaintance of Ulyanov and his associates; quickly he pointed out that the business of revolutionaries was not merely to think and to discuss or even to publish, but also to act. Martov laid before them a mode of operation which would give the learned Marxists of St Petersburg the chance to influence the nascent labour movement.

Martov, who was a Jew, argued that Jewish socialists should bind themselves into the general socialist organisations of the Russian Empire. He opposed the idea of forming an exclusively Jewish party. He was very bright and had already acquired a formidable knowledge of the texts of Marx and Engels. His ability to write quickly was rivalled by no one in Ulyanov's circle except Ulyanov himself. The two of them immediately got on well. Their friendship was so close because they agreed on the foundations of their world-view. But another factor was probably the contrast in their personalities. Whereas Ulyanov was neat and self-restrained, Martov – at least in private – had a chaotic, bubbly side. As so often happens with friends, they appreciated each other for their differences.

Martov's experience gave him an edge in the debates held in St

Petersburg after his arrival there in October 1895. The Marxists had a larger number of groups and adherents. More to the point, they had proselytised among the largely Jewish industrial workers and formed further groups of their own. The problem soon arose, however, that the workers whom they attracted tended to move out of the working class once they had received an education at the hands of Marxist activists. Martov's mentor Alexander Kremer had the answer to this. In his pamphlet *On Agitation* Kremer argued the need for Marxists to maintain their study circles but also to include agitation among local factory workers in their immediate tasks. His hypothesis was that Marxism would be spread more widely and quickly by practical leadership of industrial strikes over grievances held by workers than by laborious expositions of *Capital*. While the Radchenko–Klasson–Ulyanov fraternity was investigating agrarian economic statistics, Kremer and Martov had been involved in industrial conflicts between owners and workforces which involved tens of thousands of workers. Martov put the point that the 'Vilnius Programme' should be adopted by the existing Marxist groups of St Petersburg.[36]

Several members of these groups – the so-called Elders (*stariki*) were unconvinced by Martov, and it would seem that Ulyanov was among them. For Ulyanov, a large part of Marxism's attraction had been its emphasis on scholarship and science. He insisted that Marxists had something to teach the working class and that, if Revolution was to be successful, there had to be a widespread dissemination of Marxist doctrines. His intellectual solemnity made him well named as an elder. In fact, as his friend Alexander Potresov was to recall, 'Old Man' was his nickname:[37]

> But he was young only according to his identity document. Face to face you would not be able to give him anything below thirty-five or forty years. The pallid face, the baldness that covered his whole head except for some sparse hair around his temples, the thin, reddish little beard, the screwed-up eyes that looked slyly at people from under his eyebrows, the old and harsh voice ... It was for good reason that in the St Petersburg Union of Struggle of the time, that primary cell of the future party, this young man in years was called 'the Old Man', and we often joked that Lenin even as a child had probably been bald and 'old'.

But Martov and the Youngsters (*molodye*) gained the upper hand at the joint negotiations. A Union of Struggle for the Emancipation of the

Working Class was formed and a five-person committee elected. The burden of Marxist activity was shifted from intellectual discussion-circle debate to economic and political agitation among industrial workers. Vladimir Ulyanov, whatever his early misgivings, moved with the times. In November 1895 he wrote a leaflet appealing to the five hundred striking textile workers of the Thornton Factory in St Petersburg.[38] He visited strike leaders and handed over forty rubles for the relief of workers arrested by the police. In line with the Union of Struggle's fresh policy, he wrote a lengthy booklet on the current legislation about the fines exacted from workers by factory owners. It was printed by an arrangement with St Petersburg supporters of People's Freedom and had a fake announcement about its place of publication (Kherson in southern Ukraine) and about official permission obtained from the censors. Three thousand copies were prepared. Vladimir Ulyanov, the 'red' theorist of action of the most extreme nature, was at last engaging in political activity outside the confines of studious discussion-circles.

7

TO SIBERIAN ITALY

1895–1900

At last the Ministry of the Interior took a hand in the affairs of Russian Marxist organisations. Vladimir Ulyanov and his comrades had stayed out of prison because the Okhrana had thought them too studious to cause much trouble. The rise of the Russian labour movement put an end to this official indulgence. The Union of Struggle for the Emancipation of the Working Class had to be arrested. Ulyanov had no presentiment of the change of policing policy. On 5 December 1895 he wrote chattily to his mother that his cousin Dmitri Ardashev, by now a qualified notary, had asked him to take on a legal case on his firm's behalf. He went to see another cousin Dr Alexander Zalezhski in the city, but Zalezhski was unavailable. Life continued normally; the only trouble Ulyanov experienced was the noise made by his neighbours, who played loudly on their balalaikas: he had never been able to tolerate extraneous sounds when he was trying to read or write.[1]

It was an unpleasant shock for him on 9 December when the police turned up at the apartment and took him into custody. His friend Yuli Martov was detained a month later. By then Ulyanov had been placed in cell no. 193 in the House of Preliminary Detention. Since this was not his first offence, he knew that he was unlikely to be released, as he had been in Kazan in 1887. Ulyanov's first interrogation took place on 21 December. Adjutant Dobrovolski posed the questions scrupulously, avoiding any psychological or physical pressure. Ulyanov, who had trained as a lawyer, easily offered formal compliance to the authorities while divulging no information to them. He phrased himself with precision: 'I do not acknowledge myself guilty of belonging to the party of social-democrats or to any party. Nothing is known to me about the existence at the present time of any anti-governmental party.'[2] In a strict sense he was correct. A social-democratic party had indeed not been created. Ulyanov dearly wished to form just such a party; but he had not yet succeeded. The confrontation between Adjutant Dobrovolski and the prisoner in cell no. 193 was brief and not unpleasant.

Ulyanov treated his stay in the House of Preliminary Detention as a political sabbatical. He got on with his treatise on Russian economic development (which appeared in 1899 as *The Development of Capitalism in Russia*). He could read virtually any legally printed book, and he quipped to his sister Anna Ilinichna: 'I'm in a better position than other citizens of the Russian Empire: I can't be arrested!'[3] He had also taken the precaution of agreeing a code for communication with Nadezhda Krupskaya in the event of arrest He had prepared himself pretty thoroughly.[4]

Anna Ilinichna and their mother moved to St Petersburg from Moscow. Vladimir had a number of demands: good-quality lead pencils, food and linen. Above all, good-quality lead pencils. His family overdid the provision of food and Vladimir complained that a single day's delivery was as large as one of the Easter cakes described in Ivan Goncharov's comic novel *Oblomov*.[5] Vladimir reminded his relatives of the diet prescribed for his stomach problem. They procured bottles of mineral water and even an enema tube for him after the doctor ordered regular bowel clearances.[6] Vladimir got thinner and his complexion turned yellowish;[7] but he also increased his muscular fitness through press-ups and sit-ups. His brother Dmitri recalled:[8]

Vladimir Ilich told that in the preliminary prison he always polished the cell floor himself since this was a good form of gymnastics. And so he acted like a real old floor-polisher – with his hands held behind him, he would begin to dance to and fro across the cell with a brush or a rag under his foot. 'Good gymnastics, and you even get a sweat up . . .'

Physical exertion was uncongenial for most revolutionaries of that generation, but not for Vladimir Ilich.

While he was in the House of Preliminary Detention, he sketched out a Marxist party programme.[9] He wrote it in invisible 'milk ink' which could be read only when the paper was heated and held over a bright lamp. He exclaimed to his sister: 'There's no trickery that can't be out-tricked!'[10] Vladimir Ilich's treatment in prison had its ludicrous side. As he and Anna Ilinichna talked to each other through the cell grille, they used several Russian words of German or French origin. A guard interrupted them on the assumption that they were speaking a foreign language in order to engage in subversive activity.[11] Brother and sister had to adopt a simpler vocabulary in order to avoid further trouble. And much as Vladimir Ilich enjoyed making use of the time to get on with his writing, he was frustrated by his inability to join in the debates among Russian Marxists. He wrote in a political void.

Did he also miss contact with women? In his earlier life there is no sign that he had girlfriends, but this may be the result of the prudery of his relatives when they wrote their memoirs about him. Nevertheless it is remarkable that no woman came forward in the 1920s claiming to have been paid court by Vladimir Ilich in his adolescence. But this absence might have resulted from the official discouragement given to any accounts that described him in terms other than those of political hagiography. Perhaps, however, he was anyway too upset by the deaths of his father and brother to become involved with women outside the family for several years. Perhaps, too, he had to leave home for St Petersburg before he could explore this new side of his emotions. Two female members of the Union of Struggle, certainly, were attracted to him. These were Apollonaria Alexandrovna Yakubova and Nadezhda Konstantinovna Krupskaya, who both planned to catch his eye by standing on the street corner which was observable by prisoners taking their daily walk from the House of Preliminary Detention. Yakubova was unable to be present when the attempt was made, and, although Krupskaya took up position for several hours, she failed to catch sight of Vladimir. Subsequent attempts were no more successful, but Krupskaya and Yakubova at least had tried. They were unable to continue the experiment for very long because both were taken into custody by the Okhrana in August 1896.

On 29 January 1897, the authorities sentenced nearly all the arrested members of the St Petersburg Union of Struggle to three years of 'administrative exile' in eastern Siberia. This was a Russian punishment that involved a convict being sent, without recourse to the courts and their juries, not to prison but to a designated place of banishment. A graded system of banishment had been developed. The more dangerous the convict, the more distant the place of exile. Permission for individual convicts to live in particular houses, to take paid employment and to make trips to nearby towns was granted in accordance with the Ministry of the Interior's assessment of risk. Local officialdom in Siberia had large residual authority. The convicts knew that the conditions of their exile might be worsened if they did not behave themselves.

Another fear was that prisoners were sent in transport supplied by the government or even had to make the trip on foot along with other manacled prisoners. Trudging through the snow and living off inadequate rations, sometimes such convicts died before reaching their destination. The alternative was to get approval to pay privately for the trip to Siberia and travel in comfort. Vladimir Ulyanov successfully made such an application and on 14 February, along with other members of the Union of Struggle, was given three days outside prison to make preparations for the journey. A planning session took place in the house of Martov's family.[12]

They agreed to sit out their term of exile without attempting to escape.[13] Yet political questions divided them. The linkage of the Union of Struggle with anti-tsarist industrial workers was commonly desired; but there was disagreement as to what role should be played in the Marxist political movement by these workers. The experienced Marxist Stepan Radchenko, who was an ex-adherent of People's Freedom and a founder of the Union with definite pro-terrorist proclivities, argued that no worker would be able to do better than a well-read, committed intellectual. His faction became known as the Veterans. Others felt differently. K. M. Takhtarëv and Apollonaria Yakubova – the so-called Youngsters – wanted working-class Marxists to have enhanced opportunities to run the various organisations of Russian Marxism. Vladimir Ulyanov's intellectuality drew him closer to Radchenko than to Takhtarëv and Yakubova. But, unlike Radchenko, he was not absolutely hostile to the working class taking over the Marxist movement. Indeed, he wanted workers to assume such authority, but he insisted that they should have a basic intellectual grounding before they did so. This particular opinion of his, which marked him off from both the Veterans and the Youngsters, was to make an interesting reappearance when 'the worker question' was raised again after the turn of the century.[14]

All this lay in the future. At the time the Department of Police was considering the requests of the mothers of Ulyanov and Martov for their sons to travel to Siberia on their own financial account. Official permission was granted. Maria Alexandrovna could easily afford the train fare and politely declined the offer of a subsidy from the publisher and Marxist sympathiser Alexandra Kalmykova.[15]

Ulyanov was a mite embarrassed that several of his arrested comrades lacked his own family's resources. But he conquered the temptation to travel with them; neither then nor later did he let comradely sentiment get in the way of his material comfort. On 17 February he set out for Moscow on the first stage of his journey. His mother accompanied him and petitioned the authorities that, in view of her ill health, Vladimir should be allowed to stay a few days in the family apartment in Moscow before heading off to Siberia.[16] He finally left Moscow on 23 February, after studying for a few days in the Rumyantsev Museum Library. But he was not in the best mental shape since he was afflicted by the 'nerves' that were to bother him till he died. Like his sisters Anna and Maria as well as his parents,[17] he was highly strung. Bouts of emotional instability frequently occurred when he was stepping into the unknown. Exile was a turning point in his life. For years he had had no serious intention of becoming a full-time lawyer. But his arrest and conviction put him permanently into the bad books of the authorities. Now he could hardly take up the profession even if he wanted to.[18]

He told his mother of his feelings; the act of communication seems to have helped him through his nervous bouts. He signed off letters to his sisters with a perfunctory 'I press your hand. Yours, V.U.'; but when he wrote to his 'dear Mama' he often added: 'I give you a big kiss.'[19] That he genuinely loved his mother there can be no doubt; once he said about her: 'Mama . . . you know, she's simply a saint.'[20] But he deliberately made the most of her saintliness: the constant references to his state of health kept him at the forefront of the family's attention.

The prospect of exile was worse than the eventual reality; but before he left Moscow he had not been informed – indeed the authorities had not yet decided – exactly where in Siberia he would be ordered to stay. Although he was generally calm, there continued to be moments of extreme tension. At Kursk Station in Moscow he bade farewell to his brother Dmitri. His mother, sisters Anna and Maria and brother-in-law Mark boarded the train and accompanied him southwards to Tula.[21] At Tula the Trans-Siberian Railway took an eastward switch of direction, and it was there that he said goodbye to his family and travelled onwards to Krasnoyarsk in central Siberia. Suddenly he again became thoroughly agitated. A problem had arisen on the platform in Tula when it transpired that there were too many passengers for the train. Ulyanov refused to accept this even though he had been lucky in getting permission to use the railway at all. He strode down the platform and angrily upbraided the nearest official. He showed all the confidence of an hereditary nobleman and a practising lawyer by insisting that the authorities fulfil their obligations and attach an additional carriage to the train.[22] The complaint was passed to the station master, and after a flurry of negotiations the convicted revolutionary got his way. The repressive tsarist administration was capable of indulgence in a way that was wholly absent in the Soviet period under Lenin. The passengers proceeded comfortably to Krasnoyarsk.

Some days later they arrived in Krasnoyarsk in mid-Siberia, where

Ulyanov was halted for two whole months because the river Yenisei remained frozen until the spring. Ulyanov took the opportunity to have a tooth pulled out by the town's dentist; he also visited the renowned library of the vodka distiller and bibliophile Gennadi Yudin.[23] It says much about the widening disenchantment of middle-class entrepreneurs with the Romanov monarchy that Yudin gave the young Marxist the run of his library.[24] In the meantime Ulyanov wrote to the Irkutsk Governor-General citing his medical problems and asking to stay in Krasnoyarsk for the three years of his sentence.[25] He did not really expect a positive reply, and proposed Minusinsk district as a second choice. The area was known among revolutionaries as the 'Siberian Italy' because of its congenial climate. If he could go to Minusinsk or some village near by, he would have no great difficulty in seeing out his term in comfort. Camaraderie prevailed among revolutionary sympathisers regardless of their specific political orientation. Thus the doctor and agrarian socialist Vladimir Krutovski, who argued against the Marxists in favour of retaining the peasant land commune, helped Ulyanov the Marxist to acquire certification on his stomach complaint.[26]

By April 1897 Ulyanov had learned that he was to be sent to the lakeside village of Shushenskoe in the Minusinsk district of Yenisei province.[27] Delighted, he tried his hand at writing a poem about 'Shu-shu-shu' or 'Shusha', as he called Shushenskoe, before even seeing the place. The first line went as follows: 'In Shusha, in the foothills of Mount Sayan . . .'[28] But inspiration left him at this early point and he abandoned the attempt. Poetic expressiveness was anyway not his style. He was a passionate man, but his emotions were sublimated in ambitions of class struggle, economic analysis and Marxist ideology and were expressed in heavy, lumpy prose. He still loved literature, and yet increasingly he used it as an empirical source for his political ideas. He did not allow it to take him out of himself. He distrusted effusions of the imagination. He knew what he wanted to do in politics, and refused to be distracted.

But certainly Vladimir Ulyanov was looking forward to 'Shusha'. The journey from Krasnoyarsk would be a pleasant adventure, involving a four-day trip by steamship southward along the river Yenisei to Minusinsk from Krasnoyarsk. Minusinsk was a district capital of 15,000 inhabitants, and it would be from there that the main decisions affecting the conditions of exile for Ulyanov would be taken. He was already far beyond the direct supervision of the St Petersburg ministerial authorities. On 30 April 1897, once navigation became practical after the raging springtime floods had subsided, he set off on the steamship *St Nicholas*.[29]

He was in congenial company. Travelling along with him were Gleb Krzhizhanovski and V. V. Starkov, friends from the St Petersburg Union of Struggle. They, too, petitioned about their ill health and had been allocated a village near to Shushenskoe. They took a cabin on board and, from the middle of the rushing Yenisei, admired the vista of mountains and woods. On reaching Minusinsk, the three comrades formally requested the monthly stipend of eight rubles to which each of them was entitled. This would be enough for an individual's rudimentary needs: food, clothes and rented accommodation. Then they hired a carriage and horses to undertake the last stage of the journey. For Ulyanov, this meant a drive of nearly forty miles to his destination.

The village of Shushenskoe had over a thousand inhabitants and its own administration. The post from Russia was delivered on Thursdays and Mondays, and in an emergency it was possible for the Ulyanov family to send a telegram to Minusinsk.[30] The river Shush ran along the outskirts of the village. There were woods in the vicinity and Ulyanov went bathing in an inlet of the great Yenisei river a mile from his house. He could look out of his window and see the snowy peaks of the Sayan mountain range. The food was cheap and nourishing and Ulyanov ceased to need to drink the bottles of mineral water he had brought with him on doctor's advice. Soon he wrote to his mother: 'Everyone's found that I've grown fat over the summer, got a tan and now look completely like a Siberian. That's hunting and the life of the countryside for you!'[31]

Martov was sent to Turukhansk just south of the Arctic Circle, probably because the authorities knew he was Jewish. Turukhansk would be extremely cold during the long winter and the mail would be delivered to him only nine times a year. Isolation and bickering among comrades were problems that would test Martov's endurance. Ulyanov missed him a lot. Martov had an inspiring levity, and Ulyanov had already decided he wanted to work closely with him – and, apart from anything else, Martov loved to translate and teach others to sing revolutionary songs: in exile they would have had fun together. Instead Martov had to endure the worst conditions of exile with equanimity. Physical hardship was not the only problem for the exiles. Cut off from normal society in Russia, several of them became preoccupied by their own political disagreements and personal jealousies. Bickering sometimes became intolerably intense. Ulyanov's correspondent Nikolai Fedoseev, who had been dispatched from his Vladimir prison to Verkholensk in north-eastern Siberia in 1897, could not endure the slanders heaped on him by some fellow exiles, and shot himself.[32]

The dark side of Siberian banishment did not touch Ulyanov, and it was in Shushenskoe that his skills as a leader were first glimpsed. Although he had striven to get the most comfortable conditions for himself, he did not forget the plight of his comrades, and did what he could for them by writing letters of encouragement to Martov, Fedoseev and others. Ulyanov also regularised his life in relation to women. At least this is how things appeared in his letter to the Police Department in St Petersburg on 8 January 1898, in which he appealed for permission for his 'fiancée' Nadezhda Krupskaya to move to Shushenskoe.[33] Permission was virtually automatic even though Krupskaya had been sentenced to exile in Ufa, a town lying between the river Volga and the Urals mountain range. As Vladimir informed his mother, the plan was to use the projected engagement as a means of getting her transferred to mid-Siberia. The various activists wished to serve out their sentences in proximity.

The question arises whether there was much more to this than political calculation. It was Nadezhda Konstantinovna who had suggested herself as his fiancée when he moved into Siberian exile. According to Anna Ilinichna, Vladimir turned her down.[34] At least at first. Later – perhaps at the end of 1897 – he changed his mind and became engaged to her. Yet she was not the sole woman with whom he was friends. For example, he and Apollonaria Yakubova (or Kubochka as he called her) had had a liking for each other. As he walked from the St Petersburg House of Detention, Yakubova 'ran up and kissed him, laughing and crying at the same time'.[35] Yakubova was a beautiful woman and a committed revolutionary, and Vladimir Ilich may have preferred her to Nadezhda Konstantinovna as his companion. There is a hint of this in an unpublished section of Anna Ilinichna's memoirs. After Yakubova had left him, he declared 'with great tenderness: "Ye-e-es, Kubochka!" '[36] What are we to make of this tantalising passage? Certainly there is no sign whatever in Anna Ilinichna's memoirs that Vladimir Ilich was attracted to Nadezhda Konstantinovna. But Anna Ilinichna was often spiteful about Nadezhda Konstantinovna and she was perhaps distorting the relative appeal of Lenin's two female comrades.

Ulyanov's motives in deciding to get married are not entirely clear. When he wrote to his mother on 10 December 1897, he implied that Nadezhda Konstantinovna had not definitively opted to apply to join him in his place of exile.[37] Maria Ilinichna many years later gave a cool account: 'She made her request to join V.I. [Ulyanov] as his fiancée and they had to get married or else N.K. [Krupskaya] would quickly have been returned to Ufa province, where she had originally been sentenced to stay in exile.'[38] Maria Ilinichna, like her elder sister, played down the mutual attraction of Vladimir and his future bride. Not even Maria, however, denied that affection too was involved.

Several accounts have taken an almost prurient delight in the fact that the relationship was so tepid at the start; they use this to suggest that Lenin was emotionally inert. But recently available evidence shows this to be reflection of the cultural prejudice. The point is that romantic love, where a man and a woman fall passionately in love, was not a condition to which either Vladimir or Nadezhda aspired. Both wrote little about their feelings for each other; but after Vladimir's death Nadezhda wrote a furious letter in 1927 to Bolshevik party historian Vladimir Sorin about the kind of relationships that had enjoyed approval among Marxist revolutionaries of their generation. She strenuously opposed Sorin's suggestion that such revolutionaries fell 'helplessly in love' with each other. They consciously rejected contemporary bourgeois attitudes to matters of the heart and instead aimed to construct a new way of life – and they supposed that their own relationship should be focussed upon working collaboratively for the cause of Revolution. For them, the idea of a permanent marital union had distasteful connotations: tradition, religion, economic self-interest and the subjection of the wife to the husband. Russian Marxists, as Nadezhda pointed out, were keener than their counterparts elsewhere in Europe to form loose partnerships for the greater good of the cause. They were influenced by the revolutionary commune described in Nikolai Chernyshevski's *What Is to Be Done?* and by the anti-bourgeois philosophy of Dmitri Pisarev.[39] Krupskaya did not explicitly describe the feelings that she and Lenin had had for each other, but the hint is unmistakable: the two of them liked and fancied each other enough and thought that for the foreseeable future they could work with each other.

Nadezhda Konstantinovna, furthermore, was physically attractive even though no one could claim she was a beauty. Her face had a good bone structure. She was a couple of inches taller than Vladimir and was a year older. She dressed in rather dull clothes; her hair was plainly combed. She dressed like a typical contemporary schoolmistress (which, if she had not become a Marxist activist, would probably have been her career). Her family had gentry status but was not as comfortably off as the Ulyanovs. Nadezhda Konstantinovna's father had got into trouble as an Imperial army officer: he had been found insufficiently severe on Polish dissenters after the 1863 Rebellion and had been cashiered.

Thereafter he had taken whatever jobs came to hand, including work as an insurance agent. Nadezhda Konstantinovna's mother had written children's books in order to supplement the family's uncertain income.[40] The three of them moved frequently from place to place, but always the parents ensured that the daughter attended the local gimnazia. Nadezhda learned to cope with adverse circumstances and to be cheerful about it. She grew up to be a serious young women; at the age of eighteen she wrote to the novelist Lev Tolstoi asking to be allowed to work on his project for the translation of foreign classics.[41]

On coming to St Petersburg, however, she had become associated with students who rejected Tolstoi for his pacifism and his Christianity, and steadily she too had turned to ideas of Marxist revolution. She had few leisure pursuits outside Russian literature and the learning of foreign languages. She dedicated herself to becoming a revolutionary. More than anything else, this is what attracted Ulyanov to her. 'He could never have loved a woman', she recalled, 'with whose opinions he disagreed and who was not a comrade in his work.'[42] To a much greater extent than he, moreover, she had worked among ordinary labouring people. At Sunday schools and at evening classes she had given courses on reading and writing as well as Marxism, and she had a grasp of contemporary pedagogical theory. She was also a person of tact. Vladimir was moody and volatile and liked to get his way with other people, and anyone who became his wife would need to be patient. Nadezhda, according to nearly everyone who wrote about her, had these qualities in abundance.

Vladimir was not the only Ulyanov to suffer at the hands of the Ministry of the Interior. Dmitri was expelled from Moscow University in 1897 for involvement in the revolutionary movement; he was arrested and banished to Tula. Then the authorities arrested Vladimir's sister Maria for revolutionary activity and banished her to Nizhni Novgorod.[43] Their mother Maria Alexandrovna divided her time between Nizhni Novgorod and Tula. Soon she got permission for Dmitri to serve out his sentence in the family's newly rented house in the little town of Podolsk on the Kursk Railway twenty-five miles south of Moscow, where her daughter Maria eventually joined them.[44]

The move to Podolsk, in spring 1898, was occasioned by the fact that Mark Yelizarov, Anna Ilinichna's husband, had a post in the accountancy department of the Kursk Railway and needed to live locally – and his post had the advantage of offering free travel not only for himself but also for his wife and mother-in-law.[45] Around Podolsk, with its four thousand inhabitants, there were forests and lakes. It was a wonderful spot, where Maria Alexandrovna hoped to stabilise herself mentally. Her 'nerves' were troubling her and she sought help from a medical specialist. She had also been suffering from a stomach ailment. One of the doctor's questions was whether she had suffered recent 'spiritual disturbances'. A more tactless enquiry is hard to imagine. Maria Alexandrovna's husband had died prematurely. Her eldest son had been hanged. Three other children had been arrested, and one of them – Vladimir – was exiled in distant eastern Siberia. She had long since stopped dreaming that her family would continue along the normal paths of their professional careers. Each year seemed to bring a fresh crop of trouble to the Ulyanovs. No wonder Maria Alexandrovna showed signs of strain.

Meanwhile Nadezhda Krupskaya had asked permission to go to Shushenskoe. Before she departed for exile, she was not looking at all well. Her code name among revolutionaries was 'Fish'. This was hardly a flattering designation for anyone, and in her case it probably referred to the incipient bulging of her eyes as a result of a goitre caused by Graves's disease. Among the symptoms is a tendency for the neck to swell and the eyes to protrude. Anna Ilinichna, catching sight of Nadezhda before she departed for Siberia, said with cruel accuracy that she looked a bit like a herring.[46]

Already Nadezhda had negotiated the publication of her fiancé's *Economic Studies and Articles* and acquired a commission for him to translate Sidney and Beatrice Webb on English trade unionism. The publishers, she explained to Maria Alexandrovna, had said that 'even if Volodya has a poor knowledge of English, there is no problem since it's possible to use the German translation and only check it against the [original] English book'. Nadezhda saw that Volodya needed someone near to him who could help to organise him. For example, he required money; but it took Nadezhda to obtain the commission for the Webbs' book's translation. She also made all the arrangements for herself and her mother Yelizaveta Vasilevna Krupskaya to leave Moscow along the Trans-Siberian Railway. Clothes, books, finance, official forms and food had to be put in order before they started. Then they made the long trip by train, steamer and carriage to join up with Volodya. On arrival in Shushenskoe in May 1898, furthermore, she tried to get him to take up new interests. She liked to go hunting for mushrooms; at first Volodya demurred, but soon mushroom-gathering became an obsession for him. 'You can't drag him out of the wood,' Nadezhda reported to his mother. 'We're planning to arrange a garden for next year. Volodya has already contracted to dig out the vegetable beds.'[47]

Yet mainly it was Nadya, as he called her, who had to adjust herself to Volodya. Among her tasks before coming out to Shushenskoe was the purchase of the various books and journals he needed to complete the work. She also needed to get used to his passion for walking. While she liked to stay at her desk on Sundays, he customarily took a stroll. Nadya trained herself to accompany him.[48] And in particular she had to learn how to handle his family. Anna Ilinichna plainly resented the intrusion of another woman into the family; she reproached her sister-in-law for writing frivolous letters and rudely surmised that Nadya was allowing Volodya to edit letters before dispatch. Nadya admitted to showing him such correspondence, but she stated that this was normal between man and wife. When Anna then moaned that he sometimes omitted to say that Nadya had asked him to pass on her respectful best wishes, Nadya replied that this was only because Volodya took it for granted that the Ulyanovs knew that she constantly wished them well.[49] With almost superhuman patience, Nadya declined to comment on Anna's failure to implicate Volodya himself in any breach of good manners.

Thus she was adopting a subordinate role to her husband. Discerning that his equanimity depended on her maintenance of at least half-decent relations with Anna, she bit her tongue. She would bite it again many times in the future since already she shared the reverence shown towards him by Anna Ilinichna and Maria Ilinichna. All three of them thought him a person of unique intellectual and political potential. They wanted to help him and serve him – and he was only too pleased to encourage them in their wish.

At Shushenskoe, Volodya was already living in some comfort and had prepared for the arrival of his prospective wife and mother-in-law by renting a larger house than his first one and employing a fifteen-year-old serving girl. He had allotted himself a study room, where he put his large collection of books as they arrived in packages from Russia. He also kept a photograph album containing pictures of his heroes. Among the heroes were the political prisoners sent out to hard-labour penal colonies in Siberia, a fate that he had escaped. He continued in particular to treasure the memory of Chernyshevski and by now had not one but two photographs of him in his album.[50] Although Volodya Ulyanov professed a dislike for sentimentality in politics, he had a distinctly emotional attachment to certain political figures and to the revolutionary vocation. Not everything about this man conformed to the impression he tried to give. Like many other people, he needed heroes and to have a visual keepsake of them to hand. As yet none of his heroes had let him

The Ulyanov family home on Moscow Street in Simbirsk.

The Ulyanov family in 1879. *From left to right:* (standing)
Olga, Alexander, Anna; (seated) Maria Alexandrovna
with daughter Maria, Dmitri, Ilya Nikolaevich, Vladimir.

Alexander Ilich Ulyanov

Anna Ilinichna Ulyanova

Dmitri Ilich Ulyanov

Maria Ilinichna Ulyanova

Vladimir Ulyanov, aged seventeen

The leaders of the Petersburg Union of Struggle for the Liberation of the Working Class. *From left to right:* V.V. Starkov, G.M. Krzhizhanovski, A.L. Malchenko, V.I. Ulyanov, P.K. Zaporozhets, Y.O. Martov and A.A. Vaneev. Picture taken when they were released from prison before being sent to Siberia.

G.V. Plekhanov

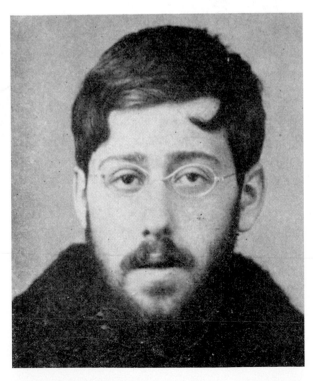

Yuli Martov in 1896

Vladimir Ulyanov in 1895. Picture taken by police photographer.

Nadezhda Krupskaya in 1895

down, but it was to prove traumatic for him in later life when any of them in any way disappointed him.

There were also practical matters on his mind. He had heard from Moscow that his mother wished to sell the Kokushkino estate in Samara province. No one in the Ulyanov family lived there now, and Volodya's arrest and exile made it sensible for Maria Alexandrovna to liquefy her financial assets. She decided to rent a house. Normally she would have turned to her son Volodya for help since he had had legal training. But luckily Mark Yelizarov, Anna Ilinichna's husband, had professional experience as an insurance agent, and he advised on the sale of Kokushkino at an advantageous price. While handling this deal on behalf of his in-laws, Mark showed his solicitude for Volodya's feelings by going through the formality of passing on details of the proposed transaction to him as the eldest male offspring; he also wished to send the Kokushkino estate dog to Volodya when the deal was at last done, but Volodya politely refused: he had already acquired his own Irish setter Zhenka in Siberia – and anyway it would be extravagant to send an unchaperoned dog from the Volga to mid-Siberia.[51]

Yet Volodya did not deny himself the country gentleman's lifestyle. Thus he gladly accepted his brother Dmitri's present of a Belgian two-barrelled rifle.[52] Hunting for hare, rabbit and fox had become a passion; he also went across to the river Yenisei and fished. In the winter he skated and Nadya thought him rather too showy on the ice with his 'Spanish leaps' and his style of 'strutting like a chicken'. But she admired his physical zest. When Vladimir got together with Krzhizhanovski, a much bigger man, they would sometimes have a wrestling contest. Both were among the small number of revolutionary activists who took an interest in bodily fitness. His 'nerves' were relaxed for the duration of his stay in Siberia and his stomach problems vanished. The fresh air and the healthier diet raised the spirits of those Union of Struggle members who had wangled themselves residence in the Minusinsk district. 'Siberian Italy' was everything they had hoped for.

There were, of course, unpleasant sides to exile even in this coveted district. Detainees had to ask permission to visit each other. Occasionally they had to send back to Russia for items of clothing that could not be obtained locally. Thus Volodya asked his mother for a good-quality straw hat for the summer and a leather coat for the winter. Hardmuth No. 6 pencils were the object of another request. (He quickly wore out the first ones sent to him.) Yet material inadequacies were not the main problem. Much more irritating were the local insects. The east Siberian mosquito was amazingly aggressive. After he made a net to cover his head, the mosquitoes simply attacked his hands at night. Volodya asked for kidskin gloves to be sent to him: 'Gleb [Krzhizhanovski] assures me that the local mosquitoes chew through gloves, but I don't believe him. Of course, the appropriate sort of glove needs to be chosen – not for dances but for mosquitoes.'[53] Alas, the historical record does not tell us who was right, Ulyanov or Krzhizhanovski, in their heated discussion about the glove-chewing propensities of the east Siberian mosquito.

Not long after Nadya's arrival in Shushenskoe, preparations for the wedding began. Volodya appreciated the more settled environment that Nadya and her mother brought about and went some way to befriend Yelizaveta Vasilevna and complimented her on her cooking.[54] Ill-advisedly, however, he expressed his satisfaction with a goose she had roasted and remarked on the leanness of the flesh. Yelizaveta Vasilevna was annoyed since the bird on the dish was not a goose but a grouse. But perhaps, on reflection, she recognised that he was trying to be nice to her.

As the wedding day approached, a letter arrived from Anna Ilinichna asking for invitations to be sent to the Ulyanov family. Vladimir was exasperated:[55]

> Anyuta [Anna's diminutive name] is asking when the wedding's going to be and even whom 'are we inviting'!? She's running ahead of things! For a start Nadezhda Konstantinovna must arrive here and then the administration has to give permission for the wedding – we are completely without rights as people. That's what 'invitations' amount to here!

He denied being inhospitable, claiming to want the Ulyanovs to come to Shushenskoe for the ceremony.[56] Although he relayed the concern expressed by Nadya's mother Yelizaveta Vasilevna that the journey might prove too tiring for his mother, for his own part he suggested that this might not be the case if she bought at least a second-class rail ticket.[57] Obviously he was distancing himself from a direct attempt to dissuade his mother from coming. This was in June 1898. In the same month he formally asked permission from the state authorities to wed his fiancée. A pair of copper rings had been hammered out for the couple by a Finnish fellow exile, Oskari Engberg. On 10 July 1898, they were married by Father Orest in the Peter-Paul Church in the village.[58]

Volodya's excuse for haste was that the authorities would otherwise exile Nadya to Ufa province. Really he did not want a grand family wedding, but aimed to set himself up on his own terms. He let his new wife write letters to his family, and her tactful, friendly words relieved him of this obligation. Poor Nadya did not have an easy job. The Ulyanovs made it plain that her duty was to produce an Ulyanov of the next generation. She wrote back to her mother-in-law, barely eight months after the marriage, stating: 'As regards my health, I'm completely healthy, but as regards the arrival of a little bird, there unfortunately things are bad; there is no sign of a little bird planning to come.'[59] The 'little bird' was the hoped-for pregnancy. Nadya and Volodya always wanted to have children and it was Nadya who reported to her relatives about the lack of progress in this aspect of their marital life. She was accepting a submissive role from the start. She was expected to provide a child and Volodya did nothing to assuage her sense of guilt or protect her from the implied demands of the Ulyanov family.

Volodya's pressing wish was to write and publish books. He was drafting *The Development of Capitalism in Russia*. In August 1898 he finished the text with its references to over five hundred books and articles. He asked his Minusinsk co-exiles for their criticisms of the chapters; he did not yet have his later confidence that enabled him to present his books to the world without such consultation.

The snag was that he was not an established author. Indeed he even considered arranging for the book to be printed independently. Pëtr Struve suggested dividing up the text and printing it in the form of journal articles. But Ulyanov wanted to have one last try at getting a contract with a commercial publisher. His thoughts turned to M. I. Vodovozova.[60] Her small St Petersburg press had a tradition of publishing Marxist literature. Volodya asked Anna Ilinichna to explore the possibilities. He laid down conditions for the negotiation, but while encouraging his sister to obtain the maximum of royalties he confessed that 'there's no reason to hurry about the receipt of the money'.[61] His greater concern was that the book should be decently produced with a clear typeface, neat statistical tables and no misprints. He expressed the desire, too, that publication should be swift and the print-run large. An agreement was signed for 2,400 copies to be published for the first edition and for Vodovozova to guarantee royalties sufficient for him to purchase the specialist literature he needed from Alexandra Kalmykova's St Petersburg bookshop.

He published *The Development of Capitalism in Russia*, under the pseudonym of Vladimir Ilin since he was a known revolutionary and wanted to evade problems with the official censorship. The erudition was considerable; the direct political commentary was kept to the barest minimum and the style was austere. But 'Vladimir Ilin' intended the book as a provocation. He had assembled a case that was extreme in its interpretation, and he knew it. But at the same time he expected the book to affirm his status as a major expert on contemporary economic trends. On Marxist philosophical and political theory he confessed his lack of education; and he admitted, for instance, that he had yet to read Immanuel Kant.[62] But on the economy he felt he already knew his stuff.

The contents of the book covered the entire Imperial economy. It is worth looking at his argument not least because he used it to justify much of his later political orientation. Generally he repeated the tenets of Georgi Plekhanov. But he gave them a peculiar twist. Plekhanov had maintained that several trends among the better-off peasants indicated that capitalism was on the rise: the renting and buying of land; the hiring of labour; and the introduction of up-to-date agricultural equipment. Ulyanov went much further. Not only did he assert that capitalism in the countryside was already in an advanced stage of development. He also claimed that the better-off peasants – whom he labelled the rural 'bourgeoisie' – were so effective as farmers that their need for machinery, fertilisers and other such products could and did provide the main market for industrial companies across the Russian Empire. In its turn the manufacturing sector of industry was stimulating output in the mining sector – and this perforce required the support of the financial sector. Transport and communications had to be built up to cope with such demands. According to Ulyanov, the agricultural sector of the economy was not to be regarded as an auxiliary component but as the very motor of Russian capitalist development.

There were social ramifications to his analysis. In particular, the centuries-old category of 'the peasantry' could no longer be applied 'scientifically'. Most peasants had become 'proletarians', who had no land or equipment and who existed by selling their labour in a capitalist market. A small minority of the peasantry was rich – and Ulyanov designated them as 'bourgeois', as rural capitalists, as *kulaki* (or 'fists', because they held their respective villages in their tight grasp). An intermediate group, the *serednyaki*, were about to be distributed between the vast proletariat and the small but dominant *kulaki*. Thus the agrarian-socialist notions of the solidarity and egalitarianism of the peasantry were poppycock. The Russian Empire's immediate prospect was the maturation of an already robust capitalism in town and countryside.

Tucked into this analysis was a side-assault on non-Marxist economic theories current in Russia. Ulyanov felt he had demonstrated, for instance, that the possession of overseas colonies was not a prerequisite of capitalist development. He had also shown that this development was not crucially dependent upon foreign investment and entrepreneurship. Russia, he declared, was generating its own transformation on the basis of its own resources. Furthermore, his exposition dwelt upon the need to take account of the regional concentrations of capitalist development: Petersburg and Warsaw had metallurgy; the Moscow area had textile factories; the Don Basin had coalmines and Baku had oil. Intensive grain cultivation was occurring in Ukraine and southern Russia. Dairy output was growing in western Siberia and in the Baltic region. While backward regions continued to exist, there were many regions of highly effective economic development, development that would soon bring about the transformation of traditional Russia into a country able to rival the advanced capitalist West. Ulyanov derided those economic commentators who argued that Russian material progress was entering a cul-de-sac. Russia, having started upon the capitalist road, would unerringly follow it entirely in accordance with the laws of economic development.

Yet *The Development of Capitalism in Russia*, for all its quirkiness, was a *tour de force*. Ulyanov had the ability to drive an analysis to the most extreme conclusion and to fuel it exclusively with data that corroborated his analysis. To those who thought about politics it was evident what he was up to. If Russia was already a capitalist country, then the time was long overdue for the removal of the Romanov monarchy. A capitalist country needed political democracy and general civic rights. Tsarism was obsolete. Furthermore, the advanced condition of Russian capitalism meant that it would not be long after the 'bourgeois-democratic revolution' against the Romanovs that a second, even deeper revolution could be attempted: socialist revolution. Ulyanov had issued an economic treatise which, he hoped, would attract thousands of converts to the Marxist cause in Russia.

One of his purposes was to demonstrate that Russian Marxists could share in the European socialist dream. What was being done in Germany today, he convinced himself, could be undertaken in Russia tomorrow. Even in exile, therefore, he scanned the available journals for information about Germany. After Engels's death in 1895, Ulyanov's hero in the German Social-Democratic Party was the theorist Karl Kautsky. Like Ulyanov, Kautsky wrote not only on economics but also on politics and philosophy. He took 'theory' seriously. He wanted a socialism with 'scientific foundations'. He wanted systematic knowledge and systematic policy, and he saw himself as the posthumous defender of the legacy of

Marx and Engels. Kautsky was a man after Ulyanov's own heart. Ulyanov warmed in particular to his defence of Marx and Engels against the attempt by Eduard Bernstein, who had been a collaborator of Engels himself, to 'revise' certain key concepts of Marxism. Bernstein denied that advanced capitalist society was divided mainly between two social classes, the bourgeoisie and the proletariat. He disliked revolution, preferring evolution and peaceful reforms, and he believed that socialism would be impossible to construct if it depended upon capitalism bringing the economy to ruin beforehand. For both Kautsky and Ulyanov, Bernstein's revisionism was a betrayal of the tenets of Marxism.[63]

Ulyanov was dismayed that this revisionism was not confined to Germany. It was also happening in Russia. In summer 1899 a document written by two Russian Marxist emigrants, S. N. Prokopovich and Yekaterina Kuskova, was passed on to Minusinsk by Anna Ilinichna for her brother's scrutiny. In a casual aside she referred to it as the 'Credo'. Prokopovich and Kuskova, drawing upon the experience of the labour movement in western Europe, contended that Russian workers – the poor and ill-educated workers of Russia – should not be encouraged to engage in revolutionary politics but should focus their efforts upon the immediate improvement of their working and living conditions. Plekhanov and his Emancipation of Labour Group were appalled by the document, which rejected not only the leading role of the working class in the overthrow of the Romanov monarchy but even politics altogether. Plekhanov denounced Prokopovich and Kuskova as renegades from Marxism. Ulyanov was even more ferocious. Anna Ilinichna's unofficial designation of the document as the 'Credo' made it seem to be more important than it really was – and she regretted the fuss she had inadvertently created.[64] Meanwhile her brother summoned sixteen exiled St Petersburg Union of Struggle members to Shushenskoe, and got their approval for a point-by-point repudiation of everything which the 'Credo' stood for.

Ulyanov's anger over revisionism made even his sister Anna wonder whether he might have lost a sense of proportion. Once he had finished the text of The Development of Capitalism, he longed to return to the active revolutionary fray. The three years of his exile were scheduled to end at the beginning of 1900. In the meantime he published five reviews in 1899 in substantial St Petersburg journals, including one on Kautsky's The Agrarian Question. His attack on Bernstein was also printed. He contributed a learned article on 'The Theory of Realisation' to issue no. 8 of the periodical the Scientific Review. Gradually the Shushenskoe author was becoming a public figure. His years in exile had allowed him to expand his cultural range. He had studied Marx, Engels and Kautsky. He had looked at Western non-socialist economic thinkers such as Hobson, List and Sismondi. He had taken a look at neo-Kantian philosophy (and quickly rejected it, on the ground that it abandoned the materialist standpoint of Marxism). He had gone on reading the writings of the Russian agrarian socialists and gone on ridiculing them on every possible occasion; and he had started to be vituperative about any Marxist who dared to propose major amendments to the version of Marxism elaborated by Plekhanov.

Yet he had to wait upon dispositions of the Ministry of the Interior. Nadya had not served her full term of exile and would have to proceed to Ufa (which was the place originally designated in her case). Nor was it clear what restrictions the Ministry might put upon Ulyanov's freedom of residence. He found the tension difficult to bear; his 'nerves' started to play him up and he stopped eating sensibly.[65] For most of his time in Shushenskoe he had taken plenty of exercise and acquired a ruddy complexion. Latterly, however, he grew pale and thin.

By 19 January 1900 he had at least been informed that he would be leaving Siberia. They loaded their books – all 500 pounds of them – into a trunk. They worried most about the first stage of the trip to Achinsk. The journey from Shushenskoe would have to be undertaken in a roofless carriage in temperatures that could easily be more than 30 degrees below zero. The fact that Nadya's mother was already coughing badly was a cause for concern.[66] But no one thought of delaying until the more clement weather of springtime. On 29 January they set off as best they could. By then Volodya had heard that he was banned from residing in St Petersburg, Moscow or any town with a university or a large industrial area. Nadya and he were going to split up for the duration of her sentence. Whereas she had come to support him in Shushenskoe, he had no intention of reciprocating in Ufa, seven hundred miles east of Moscow. Revolution, not romance, was his preoccupation and he chose Pskov, 170 miles by train from St Petersburg, as his place of exile.[67] He would stay a day or two in Ufa to see that his wife and mother-in-law were settled properly before he moved on.

His destination was Podolsk, in the countryside south of Moscow, where his family awaited him. His mother and his elder sister were shocked by his physical appearance:[68]

First came the impression of disillusionment with his external appearance: thin and with a beard that he had allowed to grow [unacceptably? RS] long, he mounted the staircase. Mother was the most disillusioned. 'How on earth', she exclaimed, 'did you write that you'd sorted yourself out and got fit in exile?'

It turned out that my brother really had sorted himself out in exile but had 'given up' in the last few weeks.

In his thirtieth year he was reaching new heights of achievement and acclaim. The Brockhaus-Efron *Encyclopaedic Dictionary*, which appeared in St Petersburg in 1900, included a brief entry on him as an economist. He was rising fast. He was not yet Lenin in the literal sense because he had not used that particular pseudonym. But in other ways he was Lenin already. He was fiercely Marxist. He retained an enduring respect for the Russian terrorist tradition. He was a man of letters and his revolutionary expectancy was found more upon bookish study than upon direct acquaintance with the working class of Russia. But his confidence in Marxism was total. It stemmed from intellectual conviction. It also conformed to the needs and aspirations that had been created in him before ever he read Marx, Engels and Plekhanov. His parents were committed to Progress, Rationality and Enlightenment and to the making of a new, 'European' Russia. They did not quite fully gain social acceptance; and when Alexander Ulyanov was convicted of terrorism, they were treated as pariahs. Vladimir Ulyanov was deeply imprinted by this experience. Having been rejected by the powers of Old Russia, which he identified with 'Asiatic', 'medieval' and ignorant repressiveness, he yearned to have his revenge by playing his role – increasingly a leading role – in the making of Revolution.

As a child he had striven to get his own way. He needed help, and used his family and his young wife as a crucial means of keeping support. He was not the fittest of men; and although he showed no outward signs of self-doubt, he suffered badly from nerves and other ailments. He was choleric and volatile. He was punctilious, self-disciplined and purposive. He was awesomely unsentimental; his ability to overlook the immediate sufferings of humanity was already highly developed. But at his core he had his own deep emotional attachments. They were attachments not to people he lived with but to people who had moulded his political opinions: Marx, Alexander Ulyanov, Chernyshevski and the Russian socialist terrorists. He had peculiar ideas of his own. But he aggressively presented them as the purest orthodoxy. He had yet to mature as a political leader. But a leader he already was. He was determined to waste no more time in furthering the cause of Revolution.

PART TWO

LENIN AND THE PARTY

What's there to tell you about our life and existence? Nothing special. All of us – that is myself, Nadya and the son-in-law are in good health and up to our eyes in work.

Yekaterina Vasilevna Krupskaya

8

AN ORGANISATION OF REVOLUTIONARIES

1900–1902

After Siberia, Vladimir Ilich Ulyanov's road to Revolution led not through St Petersburg or Pskov but through Zurich, Munich and London. He was a marked man in Russia who knew that the Ministry of the Interior was keeping the Union of Struggle's past leaders under surveillance and that their letters through the regular post were likely to be opened. Ulyanov applied again for permission to go abroad. The ministry obviously decided that he would be less trouble abroad and on 5 May gave him the coveted passport.[1] He left Russia in the second week of July, his aim being to join Plekhanov in Zurich.

Beforehand the police had allowed him to visit Nadya in Ufa. Maria Alexandrovna and his sister Anna accompanied him by train and steamer from Moscow, and it was on this trip that Anna and Volodya had a detailed discussion about their family ancestry, particularly about the fact that the Blanks of earlier generations had been Jews. Quite when Volodya became acquainted with his genealogy is unclear. Probably he already knew of the 'Tatar' elements – as Anna referred to them[2] – on their father's side. But, if it really was not until 1897 that Anna found out about the Jewish elements on their mother's side, it is quite possible that Volodya, who had been in Siberia since that same year, was informed in the course of the steamer journey to Ufa. The true date of his acquaintance with the information may never be known; but about his attitude to the family's ancestry there is no serious doubt. Volodya held the Jews in high esteem and told Anna so. He could think of no finer comrade than Martov. He was sure too that the reason why the southern regions of the Russian Empire experienced more revolutionary activity than Moscow was the presence of a large Jewish population.[3] Perhaps it was also on this occasion that he chastised the 'flabby and lax Russian character' and declared an ethnic mixture to be a distinct asset for a society.[4]

In Ufa, Maria Alexandrovna and Anna Ilinichna, escorted by Volodya, met Nadya's mother for the first time at the flat they occupied on the corner of Prison Street and Police Street. Volodya quipped that this was a suitable location for Nadya. The families did not get on as well as Nadya had hoped. Afterwards Nadya regretted that her in-laws had not stayed longer. She blamed herself for being distracted by her own work in Ufa: she had to take on some tutoring in order to pay the living expenses of herself and her mother – and also she went on writing articles on educational theory for journals.[5]

By then Volodya's mind was focussed upon arrangements to become a political emigrant and it mattered little to him what tensions existed between his wife and his mother and sister. His only worries were of a practical kind. Accompanying his mother back to Podolsk, he needed to satisfy himself that her affairs were in order. She had been ill while he was in Siberia and had recently been plagued by 'nerves'. The sight of her lively, brilliant son cheered her up. In Podolsk he had a wonderful time, going out walking and taking a swim in Pakhra Lake. The long sweep of the fields, the birchwoods and the mushrooms made it a place as beautiful as anywhere he had lived. But he had made his choice, and anyway could not have stayed in Podolsk even if he had wanted; and rather than go back to Pskov, which the official authorities had agreed could be his place of residence, he bought an international rail ticket and boarded a train from Moscow to Smolensk. He looked up the local Marxists along the route before moving on to Warsaw in 'Russian' Poland. At each stop on the way the Okhrana watched him without his knowledge.[6] The various revolutionary groups in the Russian Empire consistently underestimated the efficiency of official surveillance. Vladimir Ulyanov was not inhibited. He wanted, and would make sure he got, revolutionary action.

He was welcomed by the Liberation of Labour Group in Switzerland. On arriving at Hofbahnplatz in Zurich, he met up with Pavel Axelrod. They enjoyed each other's company. But Ulyanov noticed a sticking point whenever he discussed the scheme he had brought out of Russia for a Marxist newspaper. Plekhanov's Liberation of Labour Group had done magnificently, thought Ulyanov, in producing books and pamphlets. But something more was required if the Romanov monarchy was to be overthrown. A newspaper had to be started and a political party had to be formed. Steps in this direction had been taken in Minsk in March 1898, when nine Marxist activists met at what they styled the First Congress of the Russian Social-Democratic Labour Party. Its Manifesto, which had been commissioned from none other than Pëtr Struve, envisaged that a revolution would be led against the Romanov monarchy by the working class and would result in the establishment of a democratic republic. Yet all but one of the Congress participants were arrested within a few weeks. A functioning party had yet to be created.

The First Congress had adhered broadly to the line prescribed for Russian Marxists by Plekhanov. But Marxism in the Russian Empire was extraordinarily variegated. There was no guarantee that Plekhanov, despite his eminence among Marxists, would dominate discussions of policy if and when a Second Congress were to be held. Some Russian Marxists, for example, wanted the immediate resumption of a terrorist campaign. Others wanted Marxists to encourage workers to concentrate on non-political campaigns inside trade unions. Still others wanted the middle class and not the workers to carry out the anti-tsarist revolution in Russia. Russian Marxism had always been in flux. In Ulyanov's urgent opinion, this was a good reason for setting up a newspaper with speed. A newspaper could be used to co-ordinate the convocation of a Second Congress and guarantee the triumph of the Plekhanovite line in the Russian Social-Democratic Labour Party that had yet to be created.

Fresh impetus to this project was given by the emergence around the turn of the century of serious rival political groupings. Through the 1890s the Marxists had been pre-eminent in political and economic debate among critics of the Romanov monarchy. The surviving adherents of People's Freedom ideas were huddled ineffectually in the kind of little circles such as Vladimir Ulyanov had belonged to in Kazan and Samara. They did not have much influence on wider public discussion. Moreover, liberals had next to no formal organisations even though they had opportunities to get themselves published in journals. But the Marxist hegemony was being undermined. Viktor Chernov founded the Party of Socialist-Revolutionaries in 1901, which resuscitated the old agrarian-socialist premise that the future socialist society would most effectively be built if it drew upon the co-operative, egalitarian practices of the peasantry. Even Russia's liberals, while not yet forming a political party, held meetings to propagate their ideas and it would not be long before Pëtr Struve moved across to them and helped to set up the Liberation organisation which was subsequently the basis for the Party of Constitutional Democrats.

Ulyanov argued that time was not on the side of the Marxists and that a properly funded party newspaper was direly needed. It was an obvious case to make, but Lenin saw the urgent need to expound it. Here he could rely upon his new friend Alexander Potresov, who had contacted Alexandra Kalmykova in St Petersburg. Kalmykova was the

bookseller who had supplied Ulyanov with his books in Siberia. She did
not drive a hard commercial bargain with revolutionary activists, and
once Potresov had told her of Ulyanov's plan for a Marxist newspaper,
she readily agreed to subsidise its early issues. Meanwhile Ulyanov had
thought seriously about other practicalities. The newspaper had to be
based in a city with a set of alternative routes of rapid communication
with the main industrial centres in the Russian Empire. Switzerland was
too distant. A better bet would be Munich in southern Germany. There
should be an editorial board. Ulyanov and his young friends Alexander
Potresov and Yuli Martov would have to sit on it. So, too, would the
veteran leaders Georgi Plekhanov, Pavel Axelrod and Vera Zasulich.

Plekhanov saw snags in this. Axelrod was not the best of writers or
editors; he had his work cut out staying alive as an émigré and together
with his wife had set up a little business making *kefir* (which is a Russian
sort of buttermilk). But Axelrod respected Ulyanov's talent. So did
Zasulich. Despite her renowned pugnacity – she had shot the St Petersburg Governor-General F. F. Trepov in 1878 – she was a sweet-minded
person, and behaved maternally towards the younger generation of
Marxists. Even Plekhanov in his calmer moments admitted that the plan
for a Marxist newspaper made a lot of sense. But, if there was to be a
newspaper, Plekhanov wished to dominate it. He sensed that Vladimir
Ulyanov was a leader on the rise who might soon challenge his supremacy among the Marxist émigrés.

Axelrod had warned Ulyanov to deal tactfully with Plekhanov, and
initially Ulyanov complied. He felt a passionate attachment to Plekhanov
from whom, he knew, he had obtained so much. When Nadezhda
Konstantinovna discussed 'love' in her husband's life, she referred as
much to an intellectual partnership as to a broader relationship between
a man and a woman.[7] But Plekhanov's ill-disguised demand for a
personal despotism was insufferable. For a time Ulyanov and Potresov
thought of giving up and returning to Russia to take their chances in
clandestine Marxist organisations. Plekhanov had treated them as careerists. Zasulich proposed a compromise whereby Plekhanov would have
two votes in any disagreement on the editorial board. Ulyanov and
Potresov acceded to this.[8] Going home by ferry across the lake, they
recognised that they had surrendered for no good reason. In their heart
of hearts they – Ulyanov, Martov and Potresov – had expected to be the
real editors while Plekhanov and his participants were meant to be mere
associates. Ulyanov admitted this in the *aide-mémoire* he wrote down
on notepaper acquired from Steindl's Wiener-Grand-Café.[9] So in fact

the invitation to Plekhanov had not been a genuine offer of equal collaboration. Ulyanov and the recently arrived émigrés were his rivals and they knew this.[10]

And so Potresov and Ulyanov decided to locate the newspaper in Munich. Potresov was disgusted at being treated as a 'careerist'. Ulyanov felt the same:[11]

> I supported these accusations in their entirety. At a stroke it also removed my feeling of 'being in love' with Plekhanov, and I resented and was embittered to an incredible extent. Never, never in my life have I related to a particular person with such genuine respect and reverence, *vénération*; I have behaved before no one with such 'meekness' – and never have I felt such a crude kick from behind.

They felt humiliated. Plekhanov had treated them not just as 'careerists' but as 'children', as 'pawns' in a chess-game, 'silly scoundrels' and 'slaves'. The object of his devotion had abused his 'love'. Ulyanov's found the whole saga 'an unworthy thing'.

He confided this to Axelrod (who 'half sympathised' with him) and to Zasulich (whose distress made others think she might commit suicide); and for so prim a man this recounting of his feelings – feelings that were not merely political but deeply emotional with a quasi-sexual undertone – was extraordinary. There is nothing like it in anything else that has come down to us. Not even his surviving love letters to Inessa Armand are so unrestrained. The fact that an encounter with Plekhanov had produced this reaction shows that his life's compass was orientated upon the world of intellectual ideas and revolutionary advance. He could hardly believe that he had fallen out with one of his two living idols. (The other such idol was Kautsky; Lenin did not fall out with him till 1914.) His lengthy account had an unstated subtext: Lenin privately still wondered whether he himself had been the culprit; he did not yet have the full measure of his mature self-confidence. This is why his written version of events continually referred to the similar emotions felt independently by Potresov. Surely, he tried to convince himself, the fault must have been Plekhanov's if Potresov felt the same way.

Ulyanov was not blameless. Reading between the lines of his account, we can detect that he assumed that the younger generation would run the newspaper. Plekhanov was arrogant and vain, but he had some reason to feel that Ulyanov was likely to try to supplant him as the leader of Russian Marxism. Not being introspective, Ulyanov probably had this expressly in his own mind. But his behaviour told the real story. Anyway he learned what he wanted from his experience. The idol had turned out to be the embodiment of insincerity, deviousness and intrigue. Plekhanov had to be rejected as an unchallengeable mentor. Never again would Ulyanov enter a political relationship with unguarded feelings. In a reference to the Bible's story of David and Goliath he wrote down his bitter conclusion: 'And love-inspired youth receives from the object of its love the bitter commandment: it is essential to relate to everyone "without sentimentality", it is essential to keep a stone in one's sling.'[12]

On this disillusioned basis he was willing to go back and treat with Plekhanov on 15 August. Plekhanov again tried to conquer Ulyanov by an hysterical display. At the peak of his performance he shrieked that he was going to retire altogether from public life. Ulyanov and Potresov listened impassively; they had a deal to offer Plekhanov, and he would have to hear them out eventually. When he did, his confidence drained into the sand. The deal was soon done on the terms demanded by Ulyanov and Potresov. Their proposal was for the six prospective editors to publish a collection of their articles as a means of discovering whether they could work together. Only then would they proceed to found the newspaper. Plekhanov agreed. Pitched battle was avoided, and Ulyanov and Potresov had won their war. On 15 August 1900 they left Zurich for Munich.

The trip took several days because they needed to go first to Nuremberg and negotiate with acquaintances in the German Social-Democratic Party. A friendly publishing house had to be found with printers who were literate in the Russian language. A distribution network had to be set up. The financial support promised from Alexandra Kalmykova through the services of Struve had to be secured. At last Ulyanov could concentrate on this great project. He had planned something that would have a practical effect beyond anything dreamed of by the St Petersburg Union of Struggle. The idea had been his, and his too was the responsibility for making it work.

He was also on his own in another way. Correspondence with his family, which had not previously required many precautions, had to be conducted on the premise that any letter might be intercepted at the Russian border. This had not mattered when he had been abroad in 1895. It did in 1900, when he was setting up a newspaper that would have links with clandestine political groups in the Russian Empire. When he wrote from Munich to his mother, he put his address down as Paris and he asked her to send her letters to Herr Franz Modráček at 'Smĕcky,

Prague, Austria [sic]'.[13] He assured her that he had enough bed linen and even enough money. He promised to 'set about taking his waters so as to cure himself in a more correct manner'.[14] The stomach problem had recurred, and he had not been drinking the mineral water prescribed for him. His letters were full of such details. He told Maria Alexandrovna that he had not reached a high enough standard in oral German, and that he swapped conversation lessons with a resident Czech to improve things.[15] For the purposes of conspiracy he also pretended to have moved to Prague: although Franz Modráček was not a fictional character, he certainly lived in Munich.[16]

What did Maria Alexandrovna think about this? She may simply have been relieved that her son was out of the reach of the Okhrana. He was not the most assiduous correspondent, but he did keep in touch. He liked to know what his sisters and brother were doing and to give them advice. The Ulyanovs gave each other advice on each other's lives and problems[17] – and Vladimir was more forthright than the rest of them. Yet he was not homesick, even though he lived a 'pretty solitary' existence in the absence of Nadya.[18]

Munich, to be sure, was not Russia; he could not get used to a winter without deep snow and the temperature reminded him of 'some tawdry autumn'.[19] But otherwise he was contented. The new newspaper – to be called *Iskra* ('The Spark') was efficiently typeset, copy-edited and proofread. In late December the first issue of the journal was printed. (The first printers were based in Leipzig 270 miles away in northern Germany.[20] So much for the need to have everyone in Munich for reasons of geo-communications!) The style was scholastically Marxist. Readers had not only to be highly literate but also to have a sound knowledge of international contemporary socialist debates. Only a few hundred copies were published and it would take weeks to transport them by various couriers across the German, Austrian and Turkish frontiers. There would only be a dozen issues in 1901. The targeted readership was revolutionary activists who already professed Marxism, and *Iskra* in truth was less a newspaper than a journal in newspaper-form that was designed to act in lieu of a party central committee. But a start had been made. The next step was to consolidate *Iskra* and employ it as an organ of propaganda for the holding of a Second Party Congress. Despite the gruelling technical demands of editorial work, Ulyanov addressed this larger task. To his mind there first and foremost had to be a common understanding as to how the party ought to be organised, and he threw himself into composing a booklet on the subject.

On 1 April 1901 his wife Nadya arrived from Russia. By the time they met, she was not best pleased. Although she had sent him a note about her travel plan, he was not at the Munich Hofbahnhof to greet her. After waiting around for a bit, she took a horse cab to the premises of Herr Franz Modráček. Unfortunately Modráček proved to be a Czech with a frail grasp of German. Only after lengthy conversation did she extract sufficient sense from him to discover that her husband was using the alias of a Herr Rittmeyer. She returned to the station to put her baggage in storage and then take a tram to the address, which turned out to be a beer cellar. When she asked in the cellar for Herr Rittmeyer, the owner replied: 'That's me!' Nadya, by now pretty depressed, exclaimed: 'No, that's my husband!' Rittmeyer's wife heard the remark and intervened: 'Ah, this must be Herr Meyer's wife. He's expecting his wife from Siberia.'

Frau Rittmeyer took Nadya to the room of 'Herr Meyer' and left the couple to themselves. Nadya did not hold herself back: 'Bah! Damn it: could you not write and tell me where you were?' Defensively Vladimir explained that he had sent several letters and that they must have been intercepted. Marital peace was resumed. Nadya settled into a role of organising *Iskra*'s correspondence; no doubt her own recent experience convinced Lenin that he needed an expert in these matters. In May 1901, furthermore, Nadya's mother followed her to Germany. This relieved Nadya of much of the burden of housework (and her mother also helped with the preparation of coded letters).[21] Not that Lenin was useless in domestic tasks. He dusted his books. He sewed loose buttons back on to his clothes. He polished his shoes. He dabbed stains off his suit with petroleum. He maintained his bicycle as if it were a 'surgical instrument'.[22] But these were tasks relating to personal neatness. The women, as was normal in those days, did everything else around the house. Not even revolutionaries such as Lenin saw anything unfair about the division of functions; and Nadya, while advocating feminism, did not let it impinge on her marriage.

Yet the two of them also had a lot of fun. They went to the theatre and to musical concerts in Munich and wherever else they were staying. They read Russian literature. They also went to concerts. Lenin was a passionate admirer of Richard Wagner (who was an Ulyanov family favourite). He went to hear renditions of his operas as an active listener; he could not bear to sit passively and let the music wash through him: sometimes the effort disturbed him emotionally to such an extent that he walked out after the first act.[23] The romantic component of his cultural and intellectual personality – a component he tried to hide underneath an exterior of scientific pretension – was revealed on such occasions. But even among Bolsheviks there were few who witnessed this.

During the working day, Ulyanov got on with writing his booklet. The title he chose for it, *What Is to Be Done?*, was plucked from Chernyshevski's novel of the same name. Just as Chernyshevski had described how revolutionary activists could form a revolutionary communal group in the 1860s, Ulyanov intended to sketch the way to organise a clandestine political party in the unpropitious environment of tsarism after the turn of the century. For publishers he turned to J. H. W. Dietz of Stuttgart. The booklet would be sold for one Russian ruble or two German marks. In order to confuse any Okhrana agents the author's name would appear not as Vladimir Ulyanov or even Vladimir Ilin but as N. Lenin. He had recently used this pseudonym in letters to Plekhanov, and it was natural that he should use it again. In Munich at the time he was living in a comfortable flat on Siegfriedstrasse in the middle-class Schwabing district under the alias of a Bulgarian lawyer Iordan K. Iordanov. What's in a name? Much pseudo-psychological speculation has been focussed on Ulyanov's choice of 'Lenin' as a pseudonym. Was he inspired by the Siberian river Lena? Or was Lena the name of an early girlfriend? Or was it that the Slavonic etymological root of Lenin implies laziness and that Vladimir Ulyanov, like a medieval monk in a hairshirt, wanted to remind himself constantly that effort was needed?

At such speculation we can only chuckle and move on. Certainly Vladimir Ulyanov would have been amused. The point is this: Russian revolutionaries used dozens of pseudonyms. What they became known as to the historians depended on many factors. It especially mattered what pseudonym they were using when a major event in their career occurred. Vladimir Ulyanov did not enter the history books for living quietly as Iordan K. Iordanov in Schwabing, or else we should be talking about Marxism–Iordanovism and not Marxism–Leninism.

Nor indeed did he achieve fame as V. Ilin, author of *The Development of Capitalism in Russia*; the few reviews were depressingly flat and negative. He did not accept this with equanimity. One critic was the populist writer M. Engelgardt.[24] The probable reason why Ulyanov did not issue a retort against Engelgardt was simply that he was not a Marxist and Ulyanov did not want to waste his time on him. Less easy to ignore was the review by fellow Marxist Pavel Skvortsov, whom he had got to know in Nizhni Novgorod in 1893. Skvortsov picked apart the book's analysis, especially its fundamental premise that the various sectors of the Imperial economy fitted harmoniously together and that economic crises would not take place.[25] There was something in this criticism. Ulyanov had been so keen to demonstrate the real and potential achievements of Russian capitalist development that he paid little attention to the various obstacles. In other works, of course, he had been only too happy to point to the susceptibility of all capitalist economies, including the one that was developing in Russia, to recurrent crisis. He therefore demanded and received the right of reply,[26] but neither his book nor his defence of it succeeded in catching the imagination of the reading public. Even most Marxists failed to give it much attention.

And so it was *What Is to Be Done?* that thrust Vladimir Ulyanov before the attention of the Marxists of the Russian Empire. He had signed the booklet as N. Lenin and it was as Lenin that everyone mainly knew him from then on. (Not that he stopped inventing and using pseudonyms through to 1917.) *What Is to Be Done?* in the most direct sense made Lenin's name. It did so not because it was a major piece of innovative political theory but rather because it caused huge controversy among its restricted sphere of readers. In Ulyanov's opinion, it was merely a statement of 'orthodox Marxism' on questions of party organisation. He was not wholly straightforward about this. When writing *What Is to Be Done?*, he was in a febrile mood; this was always a sign that he was risking a challenge to strongly entrenched convention. Ulyanov meant to annoy, excite and instigate. But he was not wholly conscious of his purposes. He was therefore caught unawares by the scale of the controversy he stirred up, and the very fact that this controversy led eventually to a communist party and to the October 1917 Revolution means that the booklet has become a twentieth-century political classic.

Ulyanov (or Lenin as we may now call him) offered several obvious postulates about internal party organisation. He wanted a clandestine party. But how could it be otherwise if the Okhrana was to be kept at bay? He wanted a disciplined and centralised party. But how else could any party survive in the Russia of the Romanovs? He wanted a party united on fundamental ideology and strategy. But how could it be otherwise when each party had to demarcate itself from the other parties then emerging? True, these postulates were not universal among Russian Marxists. The so-called 'Economists' among them did not even warm to the project to form a party and to induce the working class to lead the

Revolution against the Romanovs. But most Marxists were already in favour of the postulates. If a party was thought necessary, practically everyone agreed that it ought to operate clandestinely and to recognise the need for discipline, centralism and ideological unity. Lenin sprinkled his chapters with citations from Marx, Engels and Kautsky and argued that his recommendations for the Russian Social-Democratic Labour Party, while taking account of political conditions in the Russian Empire, still lay within the bounds of conventional European Marxism.

So why did the booklet stir up such a storm? One reason was the very preoccupation that Lenin had with 'the organisational question'. For many Marxists it was unpleasantly reminiscent of the traditions of the Russian agrarian socialists of the 1860s and 1870s, who had been obsessed with matters of internal discipline and control – and little good it had done them. Indeed, the failure of those agrarian socialists had supplied a negative example which in the 1880s and 1890s had turned a lot of revolutionary sympathisers towards the kind of Marxism advocated by Plekhanov. Marxists were suspicious of Lenin's insistence on reopening discussion on 'the organisational question'.

Lenin had compounded their worries by several of his *obiter dicta*. For a start he had used the title of a novel by agrarian socialist Nikolai Chernyshevski. Then in the text he proceeded to commend the organisational techniques developed by the Land and Freedom Party founded in 1876. He praised the terrorist leaders of Land and Freedom: P. A. Alexeev, I. N. Myshkin, S. N. Khalturin and A. I. Zhelyabov. Lenin adduced Pëtr Tkachëv too in language of approval, declaring that 'the attempt to seize power as prepared by Tkachëv's sermon and realised by means of a "terrifying", truly terrifying terror was magnificent'.[27] It made matters worse for Lenin's reputation that the remark about Tkachëv came in a section of the booklet where he was arguing against the Marxist L. Nadezhdin, who wanted to resume a campaign of assassinations of individual tsarist functionaries. Lenin contrasted Nadezhdin unfavourably with Tkachëv and glorified the 'mass terror' advocated by Tkachëv to inaugurate a revolutionary state. For *Iskra*'s opponents this was yet another indication that the malignant traditions of the mid-nineteenth century had leached back unnoticed into the body of Russian Marxism. Lenin appeared to them an agrarian-socialist terrorist in Marxist disguise.

Nor did they like the resonance of his remarks about the desirable organisational form of the party. His emphasis on the need for *konspirativnost* seemed to hint not only at clandestine, 'underground' political activity but at outright conspiracies. Marxists conventionally supposed that revolutions happened through class struggle and mass movements, and yet Lenin apparently wished to revert to a clique of highly secretive plotters. This clique, they concluded, would be subjected to a demeaning, ultra-centralist discipline. The booklet's first chapter was a sustained attack on 'freedom of criticism' in the party. Lenin made no secret of the fact that he was not an absolute democrat. The priority was for discipline and unity – and for this purpose he later explained, in his version of the Party Rules, that all who were unwilling to operate actively under the direction of one of the party's officially recognised organisations should have membership denied them.

To the charge that he was little different from the agrarian-socialist terrorists, Lenin had a number of answers. He argued that in Russia's political circumstances it would be suicidal for the party to make a fetish of elections and public discussion. This was not a matter of smuggling non-Marxist contraband into the party. It was simply practical sense. His second point was that he approved of the internal democracy of the German Social-Democratic Party, and when Russia had a freer political environment it was to be expected – at least he implied this – that Russian Marxists would copy their procedures. Nor could anyone deny that Lenin in other aspects of his thought was opposed to agrarian-socialist ideas. He scoffed at notions of building a socialist society upon the model of the peasant commune. He ridiculed the possibility that capitalist economic development was avoidable. He sneered at the moralising of agrarian-socialist figures such as Nikolai Mikhailovski and praised the 'scientific' way of thinking about society practised by Marx and Engels. And Lenin emphasised that the working class should be the vanguard of the revolutionary offensive against the Romanov monarchy. Without the willingness of the industrial workers to take to the streets, he stated, the revolutionary movement could not be successful.

This defence of *What Is to Be Done?* diminished the concerns of some of his *Iskra* associates, including Plekhanov, about its contents. And there have been attempts by historians to assert that Lenin was as orthodox a Marxist as it was possible to find. Such was the line taken by Soviet scholars, but it has also attracted influential support from writers abroad.[28] Yet the whole case is flawed. Marxism did not have a definable orthodoxy. Marx was too elusive a writer to have left a clear-cut legacy behind him. His followers struggled for recognition as authentic interpreters of his 'doctrines', and among them was Lenin. He had assumed that he could openly use certain Russian agrarian-socialist ideas and practices in adapting Marxism to the specific circumstances of the Russian Empire. But when the controversy over *What Is to Be Done?* blew up he stopped acknowledging this debt in public. He needed to exercise caution if he was to assert his 'orthodox' credentials – and he particularly needed to be careful if ever he was to come forward with further controversial proposals for the party.

In any case not all *Iskra*'s admirers worried about such niceties. Many of them felt that the brouhaha had unfairly detracted attention from Lenin's practical impetus and revolutionary commitment. Some of his phrases were especially attractive. For example, he declared: 'Give us an organisation of revolutionaries, and we'll turn all Russia upside down!' On and on he went. He cheered and cajoled his fellow activists. He managed to let them know that, whatever difficulties they might be experiencing, he understood them – and yet he also expected them to produce wonderful results. 'Miracles', he asserted, were within the range of attainment of Russia's Marxists. Too much rationality was no great thing: 'We've got to dream!'

This was a language of exhortation that no Marxist before him in the Russian Empire had spoken. It came forth not from a great stylist and his language was never to become mellifluous. But this did not matter to him or his followers. His angular grammar and syntax made activists feel that he was akin to them. For them, his abrasive rhetoric was the manifestation of a necessary, down-to-earth belligerence. Fine words and elegant arguments were hardly the most important requirements for the overthrow of the Romanov monarchy. Lenin and his followers wanted policy to be based on sound intellectual ground; but, while intellect was important to them, action – uncompromising revolutionary action – was of equal significance. And Lenin's crude verbal formulation rather appealed to them. If he called democratic procedures a 'harmful toy', so what? He had worked in clandestine political organisations in the Russian Empire and he knew what he was about. If his polemical approach involved the unfair presentation of arguments put forward by his more moderate opponents, what did this matter? Lenin could touch the parts of their ideology, propaganda and especially their hopes and fears that no other leading Marxist had yet reached.

The magnificence of the booklet, for readers who were not hostile to him, was his hymn to leadership. *What Is to Be Done?* is widely misunderstood as having offered a detailed practical blueprint of techniques for running a clandestine political party. Far from it: there is scarcely any practical advice from beginning to end (and even in his follow-up work, 'Letter to a Comrade about our Organisational Tasks', the level of detail is surprisingly low). But he had tapped a deeper need among many of those Marxists working away in the Russian Empire with his insistence that the great duty in politics was to lead the way. The central party leaders should lead the local groups. The local groups should lead the working class. The working class should lead the other discontented and oppressed groups in Imperial society. If all this could be achieved, nothing could save the Romanov monarchy. No wonder Lenin's booklet had so formative an influence on the contours of Leninism and outlasted the peculiar environment of its writing in 1901–2. It was a work of its time, but its fundamental assumptions and attitudes had an impact upon the decisions taken by the Russian Communist Party in that very different time after the October Revolution of 1917.

What Is to Be Done? was written between April 1901 and February 1902 and published by Dietz in March. Lenin was usually rapid in composing his works; not often did it take him so many months to write fifty thousand words. He knew the controversial nature of his work. He kept clear of Martov, his closest friend, while he was composing it. Lenin's sense of urgency was readily observable. He could hardly have a conversation without tightening his fists as he gripped his waistcoat. His associates picked up the mannerism and adopted it as their own.[29]

Increasingly he was attracting not so much associates as followers. He took counsel with them individually. Indeed there were the beginnings of competition for his attention among them, and Nadezhda Konstantinovna prevented him from being bothered by people he did not want to see. Lenin wished to keep his discussions confidential. When pressed to reveal whom he had been talking to and how he had gained some piece of information, he had a fixed response: 'Who did I hear this news from? A swallow brought it to me on its tail!'[30] These followers had to put up with a certain elusiveness on Lenin's part. At any time they might turn up at his flat and be told that he was not at home even when he really was. Usually he was merely talking to someone else. Nadezhda Konstantinovna was adept at mollifying the feelings of disappointed visitors by stressing that 'Vladimir Ilich very much wishes you well.'[31] Lenin had a busy life and expected his followers to respect his need to curtail their access to them. He was friendly, but only up to a point. He was not like the rest of the émigrés. He was not the sort of fellow whom his comrades slapped on the shoulder in friendship: he always kept a distance between himself and his followers.[32]

Another reason for his slowness in finishing What Is to Be Done? was his involvement in other political tasks. He was helping to edit *Iskra*; he was also engaged in co-writing a draft party programme in readiness for the Second Party Congress. The work was time-consuming and irksome. Once he had made peace with Plekhanov in 1900, he encouraged him to write a draft programme, but Plekhanov kept on demurring. Lenin was frustrated. He himself had drafted such a document in Shushenskoe, and every *Iskra* follower desired the newspaper to adopt a draft of some kind since there was bound to be a debate on the matter at the forthcoming Congress. But Plekhanov concentrated his energy on works aimed at refuting the economic and philosophical opinions of Struve, who was moving away from Marxism to liberalism. There was no clearer proof of Plekhanov's incapacity, concluded Lenin, to lead the party. But still it had to be Plekhanov, the founder of Russian Marxism, who made the first main draft and thereby gave it his seal of legitimacy.

Worn down by Lenin, Plekhanov turned up with his attempt on New Year's Day 1900. The six editors of *Iskra* agreed to give themselves a week to study it and propose modifications. They would convene in Lenin's Schwabing apartment. Plekhanov was getting agitated not merely because he had to travel from Switzerland but also, surely, because he saw that the moment was approaching when he would be made to pay for his haughty treatment of his juniors. If so, he was right. Ulyanov had spent days finding holes to pick in Plekhanov's draft. Plekhanov had implied that the working class constituted the majority of the Imperial population. Plekhanov's language was weak: he said 'discontent' when he could have said 'indignation'. This just would not do, and Lenin sent Plekhanov back to Switzerland with the task of doing better next time. The teacher–pupil relationship was being tilted in the opposite direction.[33] By agreement they went on amending the draft by post. Lenin wrote out material of his own, making himself responsible for new sections on industrial workers and the agrarian question. Between Munich and Geneva they fired angry letters at each other like bullets.

The whole business took a lot out of Lenin. He had reproved Plekhanov for producing a mere declaration of principles and not the programme suitable for a fighting political party.[34] Plekhanov got his own back when Lenin put forward his own amendments and additions. Lenin objected to 'the deliberately offensive tone of the comments':[35]

> The author of the comments reminds me of a coach-driver who thinks that good driving requires the more frequent and robust jerking at the horses' reins. I, of course, am no more than 'a horse',

just one of several horses being handled by driver Plekhanov; but it can happen that even the most heavily bridled horse can throw an excessively zealous driver.

But the destination was eventually reached. On 1 June 1902 *Iskra* was at last able to print the agreed draft Party Programme in issue no. 21.

Several of Lenin's demands were incorporated in the draft. The most decisive was his insistence that direct mention should be made of 'the dictatorship of the proletariat'. This term, invented by Marx, referred to the beginning of the second stage of the forthcoming revolutionary process. The first stage would be the overthrow of the Romanov monarchy and the inception of a 'bourgeois-democratic republic'. The workers would play the leading role at this stage but would not benefit from the capitalist economy, which would concurrently be strengthened. The second stage would involve the seizure of power by the 'proletariat' – and this would inaugurate the socialist order in Russia. Following Marx, Plekhanov had included the term in his earliest draft, but because of a misunderstanding with Lenin, he had then excised it. Lenin belligerently demanded its reinstatement, Plekhanov acceded; this was one of his rival's demands that he could willingly accept. Both agreed that when the time came to establish socialism there should be no guaranteed civic rights for the old ruling classes. Subsequent events were to show that Lenin's concept of dictatorship was considerably more violent and arbitrary than Plekhanov could imagine in 1902. But for a while they had agreement – or thought they had.

Other changes were also significant. Lenin got Plekhanov to state, against his better judgement, that capitalism was 'already the dominant mode of production in the Russian Imperial economy'.[36] This was a minor concession in words; but the practical implication was that Lenin, by urging that Russia had an advanced capitalist economy, was opening the door to a faster possible movement towards socialism than others such as Plekhanov would approve. Lenin was to use this recognition for precisely that purpose in 1917. Ideology counts.

Nor was this the sole example of a significant insertion by Lenin. Another was his proposal that the party should campaign for the restoration of the land lost from the peasantry's cultivation through the 1861 Emancipation Edict. This was to occur as soon as the Romanov monarchy was overthrown. He was not calling for all the land to go to the peasants, only the lost parts, amounting to 4 per cent of what they had had before being emancipated. Lenin's purpose was to increase the party's attractiveness to the peasantry. He could not, according to conventional Marxist wisdom, propose to turn over all the land to the peasants, whose agricultural methods were thought too backward. Consequently he wanted to offer them a titbit that would draw them to the side of the Russian Social-Democratic Labour Party. He was laughed at for this. Chernov's Party of Socialist Revolutionaries wanted all the land to be expropriated from traditional gentry and the not-so-traditional farmers. Marxists could hardly compete with the Socialist Revolutionaries. But Lenin wished to lay down at least a bid for peasant support. He was an improviser; he worked by instinct as well as by doctrine. His agrarian project was unconvincing in its own terms, but his intuitive searching was understandable. He wanted the party, when finally it came into existence, to take account of the fact that 85 per cent of subjects of the Russian Empire were peasants.

He suffered a hailstorm of abuse for this manoeuvre. Why, he was asked, was Lenin the doctrinaire so facile about the agrarian question? And how many peasants, knowing that Chernov's Party of Socialist Revolutionaries wanted all the land to revert to them, would opt for Lenin's promise of the cut-off strips? At the same time was not Lenin's wish to indulge peasant opinion yet another sign that the man was not really a Marxist but essentially an agrarian socialist? Thus it came about that, as the *Iskra* group prepared the ground for the Second Party Congress, it was not Plekhanov but Lenin who attracted most of the attention. In the small world of organised Russian Marxism he became the figure whom everyone either loved or detested. He left hardly anyone neutral towards him.

His manipulation of the arrangements for the Congress intensified this dual attitude. *Iskra* 'agents' – he liked to use this word – were not known for their fairness in handling the selection of delegates to the Congress; his sister Maria, his brother Dmitri and his old friend Gleb Krzhizhanovski were among them: Lenin liked to use activists of proven personal loyalty.[37] In trying to ensure that the *Iskra* group's projects dominated the proceedings, he strove to keep the number of non-supporters of the newspapers to a minimum. As agents travelled back to Russia, furthermore, they carried *What Is to Be Done?* and the draft Party Programme. This activity reinforced the impression that the *Iskra* group were worthy party leaders. Plekhanov, Lenin and Martov – whatever their weaknesses as known to their close associates – seemed to be in a class of their own. Their agents were ruthless organisers, but all of them were willing to lay down their liberty in the defence of the party and its campaign to win over the working 'masses' to the cause of Marxism and social revolution. Many of them already looked upon Lenin as their leader. With him, they thought, the spark would light the fire.

9

'HOLY FIRE'

1902–1904

Lenin and his friends on the editorial board were becoming anxious about the attentions of the Bavarian police and decided to transfer *Iskra*'s base from Munich. They needed a place where no one would worry about foreign Marxists. The obvious alternative was Switzerland, but the altercations with Plekhanov were fresh in everyone's mind and the younger editors searched out other options. The decision was taken to try out things in London. The Metropolitan Police were famously unbothered about revolutionaries, even about the few British ones who came to their attention. The postal network was efficient and the cultural facilities – libraries, museums and art galleries – were as good as in any other European city.

And so Lenin and Nadezhda Konstantinovna packed up and left Munich, and, after brief stays in Cologne and Liège, arrived by ferry and train at London's Victoria Station in April 1902. According to a prepared plan, they took a hansom cab to the St Pancras district where a set of rooms had been rented for them by the Russian emigrant and *Iskra* supporter Nikolai Alexeev. The apartment was at 30 Holford Square to the south of Pentonville Road. Martov, Potresov and Zasulich meanwhile took up the occupancy of rooms across the Gray's Inn Road in Sidmouth Street. Alexeev himself lived down the hill from Holford Square in Frederick Street. All were within a few hundred yards of each other. It was a convenient arrangement since Alexeev had negotiated for *Iskra* to use the flat-bed printing machine of the Twentieth Century Press in 37a Clerkenwell Green at the end of Farringdon Road. Near by, too, was the British Museum on Great Russell Street. Lenin's British contacts provided him with a letter of recommendation from I. H. Mitchell, Secretary of the General Federation of Trade Unions, which enabled him to register as a reader under the alias of Dr Jacob Richter. On most working days he popped into the Sidmouth Street flat to conduct any necessary business with Martov and then proceeded to the British Museum to conduct his researches beneath the vast glass dome of the Reading Room at desk L13. Whenever publishing day was approaching, he would also visit the printing facilities on Clerkenwell Green.

Lenin's political activity lay within the Georgian-terraced triangle of Holford Square, Great Russell Street and Clerkenwell Green. He and his fellow editors were satisfied with their environment; they had moved to England not to work with the British labour movement but to concentrate on their own propaganda. For this purpose the St Pancras and Bloomsbury areas were ideal. Lenin grew to like London, ranking it alongside Geneva as his favourite European city. (By contrast, he thought Moscow 'a foul' place.)[1] In London he was safe from the Okhrana. He had ready access to great libraries, to a reliable printing press and to an efficient communications network. And he could also enjoy his leisure time. Lenin and Nadya visited Hyde Park Corner on Sunday mornings to listen to the open-air speakers. They also amused themselves by jumping on board buses to view the outer districts from the top deck and admire the greenery.

But not everything was to Lenin's liking. He was affronted by the ménage at Sidmouth Street, which he disparaged as a 'commune'. This was a revealing use of language. Lenin the Marxist – a believer in the desirability and inevitability of a communist society – was repelled by the idea of a collectivist style of life. 'Commune' was a dirty word for him; he preferred the lexicon of order, neatness and obedience. The Bohemian manners of his fellow *Iskra* editors, he thought, displayed the worst features of the east European intelligentsia:[2]

> Above all, he loved order, which always reigned in his office and his room – and these were in sharp contrast to Martov's room, for example. There was always the most chaotic disorder at Martov's: cigarette ends and ash lay all over the place and sugar was mixed up with tobacco so that visitors whom Martov served with tea were squeamish about taking the sugar. It was the same situation in Vera Zasulich's room.

Loose practices of this sort were prohibited up the hill at 30 Holford Square. Lenin did not exactly ban cigarettes from the premises, but if visitors lit up he frowned meaningfully and opened the windows regardless of the day's weather. Snow was no deterrent to him.

While Lenin sat in judgement on Martov and Zasulich, his own lifestyle was put under question by his landlady in Holford Square. The redoubtable Mrs Yeo expected him to conform to local custom by putting up curtains, and remonstrated with 'Dr and Mrs Richter' until they complied.[3] Vladimir and Nadya were not amused. They already felt miffed at the need to go down to the cellar to fetch coal for the fire and water for cooking.[4] They disliked English food. Oxtail stew, that culinary delight, so disgusted Lenin that he put his diet into the hands of Nadya – by her own admission, not the best of cooks – and her mother. English stew, English cakes and English deep-fried fish were not the only things to annoy them. Visiting the Seven Sisters Church seven miles north-east of Holford Square, they found English socialists praying to the Lord. Lenin considered that genuine socialism absolutely had to involve atheism. When he became a Marxist, Lenin felt that he had chosen the path of Science and Progress and that Christian socialism was a contradiction in terms. He could hardly find a good word to say about the socialists of England – or indeed about the English in general.

He found an Englishman called Mr Henry Rayment to help him master the country's language. Despite having translated a book by the Webbs, Lenin had not acquired written or oral fluency in English – and he found Londoners harder to follow than resident Irishmen.[5] (There is an unconfirmed suggestion that Lenin spoke with an Irish accent.) In Rayment's company, he attended political meetings in the East End, where they came across Jewish immigrants from the Russian Empire. When Rayment was disconcerted by their exotic habits, Lenin thought that his language tutor's surprise was yet further proof that the English were a 'closed-in people'.[6] Possibly his contact with the East End's Russian Jews, many of whom were open to ideas of international socialism, restored his faith in 'European socialist revolution'; and in March 1902 he gave a speech to the Jewish Branch of the Social-Democratic Federation in the New Alexandra Hall.[7]

Yet in his own way he was just as 'closed-in'.[8] He built a little Russia around himself in St Pancras and Bloomsbury. Early one morning in autumn 1902 there was a knock on his door in Holford Square. The visitor was Lev Trotski, who had escaped from Siberia and wanted to join the *Iskra* editors in England. Trotski would become as famous as Lenin would in the October 1917 Revolution, but had yet to establish himself as a Marxist leader. He was dying to meet Lenin, but Lenin was still in bed and, being a creature of fixed habits, refused to come into the sitting room until he had finished his ablutions and got himself prepared for the day. It was Nadezhda Konstantinovna who had to pay off the Cockney cab driver and make Trotski a cup of coffee – and not the tea that Mrs Yeo, the English traditionalist, would have prepared for a guest.[9] Lenin got up at his usual hour and introduced himself. He and

Trotski quickly became friends and Lenin spent time taking him around the tourist spots. The two became so close that Lenin proposed to appoint Trotski, who had literary gifts, as the seventh member of the *Iskra* editorial board. Plekhanov objected to this. In his eyes, Trotski's was 'Lenin's disciple' and his co-optation to the board would be tantamount to allocating an additional voting place to Lenin.[10]

Bad temper returned to the *Iskra* board meetings as the Second Party Congress drew nearer. In April 1903 it had been decided to shift *Iskra*'s base from London to Geneva; this meant that Lenin and Plekhanov were seeing each other again. The move was initiated by Martov, who recognised the damage being done by the distance at which Plekhanov had been held. Martov believed that Geneva would offer an opportunity to resume a more comradely approach to affairs.[11]

Lenin alone voted against the move. He reminded them that Plekhanov had always caused trouble and that this was why *Iskra* had had to be established outside Switzerland. But nobody would listen, perhaps because the kettle was calling the pot black. Lenin was in despair. 'The Devil knows', he exclaimed to Nadya, 'that nobody has the courage to contradict Plekhanov.'[12] His 'nerves' started playing him up once more as the arrangements were finalised for the transfer. Then physical symptoms appeared in the form of inflamed chest and spinal nerve-ends; he fell into a fever. Nadya consulted a medical textbook and decided that he must have sciatica. Then she consulted fellow Russian Marxist and St Pancras resident K. M. Takhtarëv, who had trained for some years as a doctor. Takhtarëv agreed with the diagnosis and Nadya bought some iodine and applied it to her husband's body. The diagnosis was completely wrong and the iodine plunged Lenin into 'tormenting pain'. In later years it was officially claimed that Lenin could not afford the guinea fee for a consultation with an English doctor.[13] But he never stinted in payment for medical attention. The likeliest explanation is that Lenin and his wife were panicking and did not have the presence of mind to question Takhtarëv's competence.

In late April 1903 they left London for Switzerland, where Lenin had to lie in bed for a further fortnight. By then a correct diagnosis had been obtained. Lenin was suffering from 'holy fire', also known as St Anthony's fire or erysipelas. 'Holy fire' is a severe contagious infection of the skin and its underlying tissue, and can prove fatal. Nowadays it is curable by antibiotics. But doctors at the turn of the century could only advise their patients to rest for several weeks until the disease disappeared. This was what happened to Lenin.[14]

Meanwhile Plekhanov and Lenin had to find ways of working together. The Congress arrangements had been in the hands of Lenin and the various *Iskra* agents travelling to and from Russia, and one of the things that Lenin hated about leaving London was the resumed oversight over his own activity. An Organisational Committee for the Congress had been set up in March 1902. It was this committee that gave rulings about which bodies in the Russian Empire and in Europe had the right to send delegates to the Congress. Lenin had already been busy marshalling opinion in the Organisational Committee to secure a preponderance of *Iskra* supporters at the Congress. Plekhanov examined his activity at close range. Fortunately, however, he concluded that Lenin had done a good job for *Iskra*. Plekhanov and Lenin concurred on the need to curb any influence that might be wielded at the Congress by either the large Jewish Bund (which disliked the idea of a highly centralised party) or the Geneva newspaper *Worker's Cause* (which did not approve of intellectuals deciding everything in the name of the working class). Lenin was ruthless in discovering pretexts to give Congress places to *Iskra*'s supporters while limiting those given to its opponents. Steadily Plekhanov gave Lenin the freedom of operation he wanted.

Lenin's methods can be savoured in a letter to an *Iskra* agent:[15]

> I'm really, really delighted to know that you've moved the matter of the Organisational Committee quickly forward and have composed it with a membership of six ... Take a stricter approach with the Bund! Abroad write as strictly as possible, too (to the Bund and to 'Worker's Cause'), reducing the function of the foreign operation to such a minimum as will mean that it can in no way have any significance. The technical side of the Congress you surely can leave to special delegates on your behalf or to your own special *agents*: don't entrust this task to *anyone else* and don't forget that the average émigré membership is hopeless at conspiracy.

Here was a consummate manipulator passing on the tricks of the trade to his apprentice.

The venue chosen for the Congress was the Belgian capital Brussels. Before going there, Lenin took a holiday in Brittany with his mother and his sister Anna. Oddly he did not take Nadezhda Konstantinovna with him. Quite why she stayed in London is unclear. She had made an effort with his family despite the frostiness of Anna Ilinichna in particular. Probably she had too many practical arrangements to make before the

Congress met; her time was consumed by the daily arrival of letters from
the Russian Empire that needed decoding. Lenin's mother, however, did
not think this an adequate explanation and referred to the 'various
pretexts' proposed by her daughter-in-law.[16] His family retained its
frostiness towards his wife and he declined to take sides. As usual he was
doing what he wanted to do. On this occasion it suited him to see his
mother in Brittany, and he did not mind abandoning his wife in London.
By his actions he was making it clear that, if she wanted to live with
him, she had to cope with his relatives even when they were not being
especially nice to her. He was the dominant partner in the marriage and
knew that Nadezhda Krupskaya would continue to fulfil her political
duties despite such behaviour on his part.

From Brittany, Lenin anyway wished to see his mother. He filled his letters to her
with advice about trains, hotels and luggage, and told her how much he
missed his native region: 'It would be good to be on the Volga in the
summer. How splendidly we travelled along it with you and Anyuta
[Anna] in the spring of 1900! Well, if I can't come to the Volga, the
Volga folk have to come here. And there are good places here, albeit of
a different kind.' Lenin genuinely loved his mother. But in going to
Brittany he was also trying to escape the disputes in the party that were
wrecking his nerves.[17] He confessed as much to the unsympathetic
Plekhanov. He badly needed a break before the expected rigours of the
Congress.

From Brittany, Lenin went by train directly to Belgium (where he
was joined by Nadezhda Konstantinovna). Switzerland was thought
unsuitable because the large Marxist émigré colony did not want to draw
the attention of the official authorities upon itself. Apartments were
found in Brussels where the delegates could stay for what were likely to
be lengthy proceedings. The Congress began on 17 July. Yet the Organisational Committee immediately had trouble from the Belgian police
after the Okhrana in St Petersburg passed on information about the
violent revolutionary purposes of several of the participants. Hurriedly
the Congress transferred itself across the English Channel back to
London. There the local personal contacts of the *Iskra* board helped in
the search for new premises. When the Congress was reopened five days
later on 29 July, the delegates met in the unlikely surroundings of the
Brotherhood Church, a Congregationalist chapel run by a committed
socialist – the Rev. F. R. Swann – on Southgate Road in north London.[18]
Lenin had to conquer his distaste at socialists holding their gatherings
on a Christian site. In any case the delegates remained edgy about

security and adjourned some of the remaining sessions to the English Club on Charlotte Street.

Angry speeches beset the Congress. Lenin's manipulations were picked out for censure, and Plekhanov was asked by the Bundist Vladimir Akimov to disown him. But Plekhanov refused. 'Napoleon', he declared, 'had a passion for making his marshals divorce their wives; some gave in to him in the matter even though they loved their wives. Comrade Akimov resembles Napoleon in this respect: he desires at any price to divorce me from Lenin.'[19] Just as Lenin had once professed that he had been in love with Plekhanov, so Plekhanov now suggested that a kind of marriage existed between them. Both were expressing themselves in innocence of the oeuvre of Sigmund Freud. Unconsciously they were giving a signal of the phenomena that, for most of the time, brought out the greatest passion in them. They lived for their ideas and their political fulfilment.

Plekhanov, of course, had been disingenuous about his commitment to the 'marriage'. Before the Congress he had been regularly infuriated by his young consort. But the Congress was not alerted to this, and the record of the Congress organisers – Lenin included – was approved. The proceedings continued to be highly disputatious. Except to aficionados the details were arcane in the extreme. Lenin was not alone in picking apart every practical question as if it were a bomb of great doctrinal significance waiting to explode. Nothing was too trivial for Marxists to examine from the standpoint of its philosophical principles. But the Devil really was in the detail. Even the apparently mundane matter of the position of the Jewish Bund within the Russian Social-Democratic Labour Party was dynamite. One reason for this was obvious. The Bund's delegates represented thousands of members in the western borderlands and no region of the Russian Empire could match this. The Bund contended that the allocation of only five places out of forty-three at the Congress was grossly unfair. But the other delegates turned the argument down flat. The Bund then demanded broad autonomy for itself in the party as a whole. But this, too, was controversial. The Bund recruited members on a specifically ethnic basis, and the Congress did not wish to make an exception for any particular ethnic group.

The second reason was that several of the *Iskra* group had a Jewish background: Axelrod, Martov and Trotski. Lenin's Jewish great-grandfather, old Moshko Blank, had lived in the region where the Bund was now active. Axelrod and the others had turned against everything Jewish. They had become Marxists to escape their religious and ethnic origins and disliked the whole idea of Jewish Marxists such as those of the Bund giving priority to work exclusively among Jews. The Bundists for their part sniffed a degree of anti-semitism at the Congress, and they thought the renegade Jews to be the worst offenders. But the Bund was on a hiding to nothing and its organisational demands were supported by no delegates but its own.

There followed a discussion of the Party Programme. Lenin was to the fore, and to general surprise – but they didn't know him yet – he showed finesse in winning the doubters to his side. He made an admission of his polemical excesses. Referring to his booklet, *What Is to Be Done?*, he stated: 'Nowadays all of us know that the "Economists" bent the stick in one direction. To straighten the stick it had to be bent in the opposite direction, and this is what I did.' This was not quite an apology, but it was not the unmitigated arrogance that *Iskra*'s critics had been led to anticipate. Everything went sweetly for Lenin and Plekhanov: the draft Party Programme with its emphasis on 'the dictatorship of the proletariat' was accepted. The main disagreement was over Lenin's ideas on the agrarian question. But the *Iskra* group held firm and the draft was ratified. It must have been tempting for Plekhanov to let Lenin be defeated on those clauses in the Party Programme that had previously divided them. But a deal was a deal. If the Congress was to be controlled, the *Iskra* group had to stick together. For most of the sessions it did precisely that.

One difficulty was caused by the Party Rules. Rival proposals were put forward by fellow *Iskra* editors, Lenin and Martov. Martov had bridled at Lenin's imperiousness in Munich, London and Geneva. For his own self-respect he had to face up to him at the Congress. Martov wanted a set of Party Rules to restrain the ruthlessness of Lenin and his like.

The specific rule that brought things to a head related to the qualifications for party membership. The verbal distinctions between Lenin and Martov were microscopic. Lenin wanted a party member to be someone 'who recognises the Party Programme and supports it by material means and by personal participation in one of the party's organisations'. For Martov, this was authoritarian excess. Gentler qualifications were needed, and Martov suggested that a party member should be someone 'who recognises the Party Programme and supports it by material means and by regular personal assistance under the direction of one of the party's organisations'.[20] Martov's phrase about operating 'under direction' was by most criteria more bossy than Lenin's original.

But the subtleties of language were of no concern to Martov and Lenin, and historians have wasted their ink on the semantic contrast. What mattered for both of them was the essence of the matter. Martov wanted a party with members who had scope to express themselves independently of the central leadership; for Lenin, the need was for leadership, leadership and more leadership – and everything else, at least for the present, was to be subordinate to this need.

Lenin was defeated, by twenty-eight votes to twenty-two. He was disconcerted, but he recovered. Combativeness was second nature to him and his section of the *Iskra* group. They revelled in being described as the 'hards'. The barracking of their opponents at the Congress was becoming normal, and some of them took their machismo still further. Alexander Shotman threatened to beat up a fellow 'hard' who had defected to Martov's section. Lenin pulled back Shotman and told him that only 'fools use fists in a polemic'.[21] Nevertheless the Russian Social-Democratic Labour Party had acquired a gangsterish aspect. To one of his supporters around this time Lenin put the matter bluntly, although he had his usual difficulty in enunciating his consonants: 'Politiggs is a diggty business!' Dirty or not, politics was his profession and he was adept at it already.

Lenin was admired by his fellow 'hards' for the very unpleasantness and harshness of his behaviour at the Congress. Yet the internal division of the *Iskra* group threw its plans for the future leadership of the party into disarray. Already Lenin had an agenda of his own, and he had revealed it confidentially to Martov. Lenin's scheme had been to reduce the board of *Iskra*, which was to become the official central party newspaper, from six members to three. The casualties of the change would be Axelrod, Potresov and Zasulich. Such a manoeuvre, as Martov must have foreseen, would give him and Lenin the whip hand over Plekhanov in any board dispute. But the sight of Lenin behaving with such belligerence at the Congress shook Martov's faith in him. The snag was that Martov, who was always a defective tactician, had left it too late. Lenin had taken the precaution of assuring Plekhanov that the reason for dropping the others was their scant usefulness in the past. When the Congress discussed the central party bodies, Lenin had his allies lined up to denounce Martov as a hypocrite for trying to carp at his proposals: 'He knew! He didn't protest!'[22]

Martov had misplayed his hand. By the time all this was being discussed, the composition of the Congress had undergone alteration. The five Bundists and the 'Economists' had walked out in protest. These delegates, if they had remained, would have supported Martov against Lenin. If Lenin had been in such a situation, he would have struck a deal to keep potential supporters in the hall. Martov was not so sly. Lenin could argue his case in a Congress whose political balance had been tipped in his favour. The sheep was left in an unguarded fold and the wolf was at the gate.

Next the 'hards' pushed to realise concepts of centralism, discipline and activism. At the apex of the party there was to be a party council. The Council would control a three-person *Iskra* board and a three-person central committee. The vote on this structure and its personal composition resulted in victory for Lenin and Plekhanov. Acting together, they would run the party; and neither of them worried that the cost of their triumph had been the exodus of the Jewish Bund as well as other groupings. For this reason Lenin redesignated his 'hards' as the 'majoritarians' (*bol'sheviki* or Bolsheviks). Always he was a step ahead of his adversaries. When there was a crucial political matter in dispute, he was everyone's superior in tactical and linguistic inventiveness. He had lost to Martov on the Party Rules: in such a situation, if he had been Martov, he would have dreamed up a triumphal name for his supporters. Martov passed up the chance. Worse than this followed. Martov proceeded to accept the Leninists' self-description as Bolsheviks and to call his own group the 'minoritarians' (*men'sheviki* or Mensheviks). When the Congress filled the places on the Central Committee and the *Iskra* board, Martov's tactical ineptitude became manifest.

The majority was now held by the supporters of Lenin and Plekhanov. The Central Committee was initially composed of Gleb Krzhizhanovski, V. A. Noskov and F. V. Lengnik; the *Iskra* board kept only Lenin, Plekhanov and Martov from its previous composition. The ostensible result was the definitive creation of the Russian Social-Democratic Labour Party with a fixed Party Programme and Party Rules.

Yet this situation did not long prevail. Plekhanov, reverting to his previous suspicion of Lenin, came to regret that he had supported him at the Congress. The Russian Social-Democratic Labour Party, whose creation he had dreamed about for two decades, was being born as Siamese twins who needed to be divided. His depression – one might say, post-natal depression – was such that he confessed to suicidal thoughts. He and Lenin had not stopped arguing since Lenin had come abroad in 1900, and Plekhanov was pushed over the brink at the assembly of the Foreign League of Russian Revolutionary Social-Democracy in Geneva in October 1903. The League had been recognised by the

Congress as the official co-ordinating body of all the dozens of émigré party members in Switzerland, France and England. Its sessions in Geneva were the first occasion for the emigrants to draw breath after the schism at the Congress. Martov seized the bull by the horns by making a personal attack on Lenin. In the course of a lengthy speech he revealed that Lenin was disingenuous in forming an alliance with Plekhanov. Before the Congress, Lenin had said to Martov: 'Don't you see that, if you and I stick together, we'll keep Plekhanov permanently in a minority and there'll be nothing he'll be able to do about it?'

Lenin made for the door, slamming it after him. Plekhanov, who had been listening impassively, announced he was willing to step down from *Iskra* in order to put an end to factional strife. Lenin felt so disarmed that he sent in his own resignation from *Iskra* and the Party Council. Lenin, the party's king in the making, banished himself from court. His Bolsheviks became the minority. He had forgotten to 'keep a stone in his sling'. For the first and last time he had retired from a position of strength. He soon repented his action, and remorse turned to anger as Plekhanov increasingly sided with Martov and the Mensheviks.[23]

Yet there was still a stone left at the bottom of the sling. Lenin worked feverishly to inform the *Iskra* agents about how, in his opinion, he had been tricked into defeat. He wrote his one-sided history of the internal party dispute and published it in May 1904 in the booklet *One Step Forward, Two Steps Back*. His old companion in the St Petersburg Union of Struggle and in Siberian exile, Gleb Krzhizhanovski, was a member of the newly elected Central Committee. When Krzhizhanovski arrived from Russia in November 1903, Lenin made the simple request that he should co-opt him to membership of the Central Committee. Krzhizhanovski was delighted to agree. Neither he nor Lenin nor any of their close comrades had any time for democratic procedures. If Lenin had been cheated, the swindle had to be turned on its head. Lenin had got his second wind. From this time onwards he turned his cantankerous, dishonest methods into a political art. He never ceased to be interested in perfecting it. Having walked out directly from the Party Council, he would insist on re-entering it as one of the Central Committee's representatives.

He wrote up his self-defence in obsessive detail in *One Step Forward*. His gimnazia training as a collator of data came in handy; so too did his lawyer's understanding of the opportunities offered by the Party Rules. He did not care a fig for democracy, but he was determined to show

how his adversaries had infringed democratic procedures. Once he felt wronged, he assembled every available argument that he had been done down. Lenin, the critic of moral sensitivity in economic and social analysis, put his own sense of moral outrage on display.

Nevertheless his style in politics placed him under intense strain and, with the opening of the archives on his medical condition, we can now see just how near he came to collapse. As he insisted to friends, he was not 'a machine'.[24] Already in spring 1903 he had suffered from St Anthony's fire and, although his mental tensions had not produced the illness, they did not help him to recover very quickly. As Nadezhda Konstantinovna witnessed, his 'nerves' had been tightened to snapping point before the Second Party Congress. Afterwards they finally burst and Lenin had terrible nights with insomnia and terrible days with migraine. The Russian Social-Democratic Labour Party's man of iron sometimes returned home to 10 Chemin du Foyer in Geneva, after a day's work at the Bibliothèque Publique et Universitaire or the Société de Lecture, in a state of collapse. If his recurrent ill health had started to affect him only in 1903–4, there might be reason to think that the party's factional troubles had caused them. But the medical problems had been evident for years. The sole difference was that they were more acute and more frequent than previously. Lenin was determined to sort things out and consulted the latest textbooks. He also sought out the best Swiss doctors. His stomach problem was investigated by a leading specialist and he received a prescription that was somewhat effective, at least for a while.[25]

He later told his sister Maria Ilinichna that he lost the prescription.[26] This is a curious thing for so meticulous a person. Perhaps he did not want to worry Maria about his general condition, especially if he had told the specialist about his other physical malaises – insomnia, migraine and tiredness – and about his father's death through a heart attack brought on by cerebral arteriosclerosis. Lenin came out of the consultation a very concerned man. The specialist had told him that his stomach was not the main problem. When Lenin asked him to explain, the answer was curt: 'It's the brain.'[27] Lenin told no one what the specialist meant. But medical wisdom at that time is likely to have put forward two diagnoses: one would be that Lenin was suffering from 'neurasthenia'; the other that he had inherited the physical characteristics which had killed his father.

Neurasthenia had been a fashionable diagnosis since the late nineteenth century for patients complaining of headaches, ulcers, insomnia and tiredness. These symptoms, it was thought, stemmed from the hectic pace of contemporary urban society. Their radical cause was thought to be an exhaustion of the nervous system. The conventional remedy, ever since neurasthenia had been 'invented' as an illness, was complete withdrawal from heavy mental work. This was believed to be still more important than the adoption of a particular diet. In later life, too, some of his doctors diagnosed Lenin as suffering from neurasthenia, and always they asked him to slow down his schedule of political commitment. Few specialists nowadays would accept that a specific illness of neurasthenia exists or that Lenin's various symptoms resulted from a problem with his central nervous system. But neurasthenia was in fashion at the turn of the century, and Lenin appeared to fit the paradigm of the textbooks. But, even if his specialist had ignored this possibility and instead suggested that Lenin had a cerebrovascular weakness, the treatment regime would have been the same: the permanent, drastic lowering of his workload.

Unfortunately it would have driven him to distraction to decrease his involvement in public affairs. Politics was his life. He acceded to the desirability of taking lengthy holidays, but this called for no change in lifestyle since he had been accustomed to spending the summer in Kokushkino. Otherwise he made no serious adjustment to the way he lived his life. He was the despair of his doctors.

A connection apparently existed between periods of political controversy and bouts of stomach illness, insomnia and headache. But what was the nature of the connection? His health made him agitated; his politics made him agitated. His political style and his medical condition worsened each other. The situation was exacerbated by his growing conviction that he was a man of destiny. The Revolution had to be made fast and deep and Lenin aimed to be its leader. He thought that he was the person who had been called to indoctrinate and guide the anti-tsarist political movement. After his spat with Plekhanov, he regarded no Russian Marxist as being his equal in intellectual and political potential. All this added to his inner tension. He had not yet got used to being isolated and the fact that a friend like Gleb Krzhizhanovski had turned his back on him in 1904 depressed him. If he had not had an unshakeable belief in the righteousness of his cause, he might even have cracked in the early years of emigration while establishing himself in the party leadership. He 'knew' he was correct and he would not back down in the face of criticism.

Even his self-belief might not have been enough for him to survive, however, if he had not been able to rely on his family, whose support for him was constant. His mother, sisters and brother gave him the impression that he could do no wrong, and it was rare for Nadezhda Konstantinovna to contradict him in the course of their long marriage. He had a secure framework of daily life. Most of his years as an emigrant were spent in places he found congenial. Paris, where he lived in 1908–12, was the exception; he never took to the French capital. Munich, London and Geneva were the cities that he loved to stay in.

Lenin lived life on his own terms. The golden boy at home and in the gimnazia retained this status in adulthood. His bookishness; his demands on the attention of others; his regimen of regular exercise; his willingness to give advice on subjects from politics through philosophy to medical care: these features were treated as evidence of his genius. Lenin insisted on absolute silence when he was working, and such was his intolerance of distraction that he would not let even himself emit a noise while he worked. Nadezhda Konstantinovna records that he used to move about his study on tiptoe in case he interrupted his train of thought: the cat, when left on its own, was a mouse.[28] Lenin just had to have everything in order – whether it was the array of pencils on his desk or the political and economic policies of the Russian Social-Democratic Labour Party – before he could feel at ease. There was no one else to whom he answered. This may seem strange for a politician who referred to Marx and Engels as figures of authority, but the paradox is only apparent: Lenin felt that only he could read their works aright, even though he did not say or write this expressly until the Great War.

The family took part in politics on his side. As soon as Nadezhda Konstantinovna proved an efficient organiser, Lenin delegated crucial tasks of party correspondence to her. His blood relatives were also important. Dmitri Ilich Ulyanov had been working as an agent of *Iskra* in 1900–2 and was a delegate to the Second Party Congress. Anna Ilinichna carried messages between Europe and Russia; and both she and her younger sister Maria did the same in later years. The version of Marxism favoured by Anna, Dmitri and Maria was a reflection of his. All of them were arrested together with Dmitri's wife Antonina in January 1904;[29] and when any of them got into trouble with the Russian Ministry of the Interior, their mother uncomplainingly accompanied them into administrative exile.

The emotional and political assistance that Lenin received from his relatives during his personal isolation in 1903–4 was of crucial importance. He never doubted the rightness of his cause. But his touch as a campaigner was still being brought to maturity, and his 'nerves' were a chronic irritation. If he had not been able to retreat into this milieu of encouragement, his career would not have prospered quite as it did. To men such as Nikolai Valentinov it did not matter whether Lenin's behaviour in internal party disputes had been fair by the Party Rules. Valentinov looked up to him as an active, irrepressible leader. He and others liked Lenin's punchy phrases about turning Russia upside down. They had no worry about his agrarian-socialist affinities. They knew that he admired the notorious Pëtr Tkachëv's journal *Alarm* and the proclamations of the still more notorious Sergei Nechaev (whose complicity in murder had caused the Swiss authorities to make a legal exception in 1872 and extradite him to St Petersburg). Lenin recommended his associates to read these materials and learn lessons from them.[30] Practically every early Russian Marxist had admired the older generation of agrarian socialists to some degree. They had also had much respect for the Jacobins in the French Revolution. Indeed all the younger members of the *Iskra* editorial board had once approved of terrorism.

What is more, Lenin's Marxist admirers could not fail to appreciate his devotion to making a revolution and his practicality as a party chief. And he was a chief with the common touch. When Valentinov arrived penniless in Geneva, Lenin helped him with his part-time job as a barrow-pusher. Valentinov got a commission, but could not fulfil it by himself. Lenin leaned a shoulder to the barrow – and Valentinov never forgot the favour. Nor did other Marxists who arrived from the Russian Empire. Very often it was Lenin who, acting on information coming through to Nadezhda Konstantinovna, met them off the train in Geneva. Lenin took the trouble to interview them, acquainting himself with their personal circumstances and the political situation at home. Lenin had been brought up surrounded by books in large, easeful households, but he was also growing 'outwards' as a person and was not too haughty to carry out laborious tasks. Overt pride had been anathematised in the Ulyanov family and, when things needed to be done, they had to be done without fuss. Lenin had not been brought up to manual labour. But he had been educated by his parents to do whatever needed to be done in pursuit of any great cause. For his father, the cause had been Enlightenment, for Lenin it was Revolution, and Enlightenment through Revolution.

Lenin had fewer adherents than he had expected after his victory at the Second Party Congress. When the emigrants of the Russian Social-Democratic Labour Party split into two factions, the Bolsheviks and the

Mensheviks, the activists in the Russian Empire were horrified by the news: few committees and groups were willing to take the road towards schism. The theory of Marxism as expounded by Marx and Engels was that a single class – the proletariat – would undertake the task of introducing communism. It stupefied Russian Marxists that the Marxist movement should be split into two separate organisations. Only a few groups – such as the far-left Marxists in St Petersburg – went along with Lenin's divisive methods and policies.

He had even forfeited the sympathy of old friends. He had always been thought unusually hot-headed, but now several associates felt that he had lost all sense of proportion. Among them was Gleb Krzhizhanovski, who hated the prolonged factional struggle. Days after co-opting Lenin to the Central Committee, Krzhizhanovski tried against Lenin's wishes to reconcile the two factions. He offered to withdraw Lenin's supporter L. Galperin from the Party Council and to co-opt some of Martov's Mensheviks to the Central Committee. Lenin was furious, but Krzhizhanovski put it to him bluntly: how could he conceivably be right to hold out for unconditional factional triumph when practically everyone, including his own supporters, thought him incorrect? Krzhizhanovski had said everything short of calling him egocentric and irreconcilable – and Krzhizhanovski continued to bristle with indignation about the conversation after the October 1917 Revolution.[31] Ceaseless imprecations were made against Lenin. Krzhizhanovski and Noskov were losing patience, and in February 1904 wrote to him formally in the Central Committee's name: 'We implore the Old Man to drop his quarrel and start working. We await leaflets, pamphlets and all kinds of advice – which is the best way of calming the nerves and responding to slander.'[32]

These two sentences show how the relationship between Lenin and his notional equals on the Central Committee had evolved. He was the Old Man, the senior organiser. He was the vital provider of advice. He was the peerless writer–activist. And he had to be treated tactfully: he could not be instructed but only implored: his position of superiority was beyond dispute. But this did not prevent the Central Committee members from drawing his attention to his excessive absorption in questions of internal party authority at the expense of carrying out his vital roles on the party's behalf. Lenin was taking things too personally, and they were not surprised to hear that he was suffering again from bad 'nerves'. According to Krzhizhanovski and Noskov, the solution to the party's problems lay in Lenin agreeing to take himself in hand.

But Lenin pitifully reminded the Central Committee that he was 'not a machine' and could not forget the insults from Plekhanov and Martov.[33] Yet the Central Committee showed him no sympathy. Although all its eight members were Bolsheviks by spring 1904, only a couple of these stood by Lenin. The rest of the Central Committee felt that the best place for Lenin was not Switzerland but Russia, where they themselves were operating. In May 1904, Noskov arrived in Geneva and, speaking on the Central Committee's behalf, ordered Lenin to submit to party discipline. Noskov particularly forbade him to campaign for the convocation of a Third Party Congress. The Central Committee wanted to mend the party split and a Congress, if held in the near future, would only deepen animosities. Noskov aimed to halt publication of the savage anti-Menshevik tract *One Step Forward, Two Steps Back*. But he did not quite have the confidence to carry out his mandate. A compromise was reached allowing the tract to be published and recognising Lenin and Noskov as joint representatives of the Central Committee abroad. Lenin in person had proved a tough negotiator. In formal terms Noskov had surrendered and Lenin was able to go on as before.

This took a great deal out of Lenin. He found it demeaning to have to deal with Noskov; the fact that Noskov thought he was doing the party a favour only made the situation more difficult. Lenin had convinced himself that the entire revolutionary cause was being mishandled:[34]

> The party in reality had been torn apart, the rule-book had been turned into paper rubbish, the organisation had been spat upon. Only naive bumpkins can yet fail to see this. But to whomever has grasped this it must be clear that the pressure exerted by the Martovites needs to be answered with real pressure (and not with tawdry whimpering about peace and so on). And the application of pressure requires the use of all forces.

From this analysis he would not budge. His willpower was extraordinary, and he deployed it to surmount his own intellectual doubts (few as they were) and the political criticisms of others (which were plentiful).

In the first half of June 1904 Lenin and Nadya decided to take a rest from the internal party warfare. Earlier in the year he had been cycling in Geneva and had run into the back of a tramcar. He badly gashed his face and for weeks had to walk around with it bandaged up. His other ailments of stomach and head were also intensifying, and the after-effects of the St Anthony's fire lingered. He very badly needed a holiday. And so he and Nadya gave up their rented Geneva quarters and headed for the mountains with rucksacks on their backs and a copy of the Switzerland *Baedeker* in hand. They took with them Maria Essen, one of only two Central Committee members still supporting Lenin. The Bolshevik threesome swore to avoid talking about politics 'so far as was possible'. It was the perfect trip for them. Switzerland was well organised for mountain walkers. The Hotelkeepers' Association had developed a system whereby a visitor could send a telegram in advance to book a room for the next night, and the *Baedeker* stated that a really bad hotel or inn was 'rarely met with'. The telegraph network was the densest in the world. Thus the three of them would be able to have plenty of restorative exercise while being certain that their food and shelter would be of good quality.

First they headed by steamboat for Montreux and visited the castle of Chillon. They did a lot of walking. Lenin's zeal to push himself to his limits was focussed, for just a while, upon recreation; and he encouraged his companions – his wife and Maria Essen – to keep up with him as they scrambled along the mountain trails. In late July they settled for a while in a *pension* by the Lac de Bré. It was a very long vacation.

Not until 2 September did they return to Geneva.[35] There they rented an apartment a few days later at 91 Rue de Carouge. This was a street of tall, plain tenement buildings with shops and cafés on the ground floor and layers of private residences above them; and it lay at the heart of the area favoured by the city's political emigrants. The streets around the Rue de Carouge were a little, middle-class Russia. For Lenin it was like coming home. He had returned refreshed for the fray after the longest holiday of his adult life. Without it, quite possibly he would have had a nervous collapse. Only this explains the risk he now took with his political position. He had gone away in the knowledge that Noskov, in his absence, might undermine him further in the Central Committee. He had taken the precaution of transferring his own powers to trusted friends; but none of these had his talent to resist the irresistible. Noskov, moreover, regarded his agreement with Lenin with regret. In July 1904, he got to work in Russia and, by a mixture of persuasion and co-optation, converted the Central Committee to his policy of reuniting the Bolsheviks and Mensheviks. A declaration was drawn up to this effect, and Lenin was reprimanded for failing to supply a stream of pamphlets. The Bolshevik-led Central Committee confronted the Bolshevik leader.

When informed of this, Lenin – his physical and mental well-being restored – called a meeting of his few remaining émigré supporters and arranged for them to travel round Russia and put together a so-called Bureau of Committees of the Majority with the purpose of convoking a Third Party Congress. Finance became available through the efforts of the brilliant young Marxist writer Alexander Bogdanov. To put it gently, Lenin was not always very charming towards Bogdanov. If Bogdanov omitted to write a letter on time, Lenin felt free to curse him for his 'swinishness'. But Lenin kept himself in check, or just about. He could see that a friendly relationship with Bogdanov was necessary if he was to have access to the money and personal support he would need in order to reassert himself. Together with Bogdanov and Anatoli Lunacharski, therefore, he arranged to publish a rival newspaper to *Iskra*. Its name would be *Vperëd* ('Forward'). The first issue appeared on 22 December 1904. To Noskov's consternation, furthermore, Lenin's section of the Bolsheviks were able to recruit many adherents in the Russian Empire. There were plenty of Marxists who had read *What Is To be Done?* and were still keen to back Lenin as potential party leader.

Thus the civil war in the party raged on. Lenin had put together a parallel organisation which would act as his fighting force against the Mensheviks and indeed against any Bolsheviks who opposed him on the battlefield. It was in this mood that the émigré leadership of the Russian Social-Democratic Labour Party greeted the New Year in 1905.

10

RUSSIA FROM FAR AND NEAR

1905–1907

There are not always extraordinary people around to take advantage of an extraordinary political situation. Many observers had long predicted a revolutionary crisis in the Russian Empire. Clandestine parties were working for a change of regime and all of them hated the Romanovs; and Lenin had plenty of reason in both ideology and family history to want to overturn the Romanov dynasty.

Huge resentments existed in Imperial society. The Okhrana patrolled the trouble with the limited financial and human resources available to it; the Russian Empire was indeed a police-state in the making. But it was not a state that found it easy to keep its people in check. Poor harvests in the new century had made the peasants restive. The workers as ever resented the absence of organisations through which they might represent their case to employers. Several national groups, especially the Poles, had underground organisations looking for a chance to confront the Russian Imperial government. And a whole range of clandestine political groupings were operating. Not only the Russian Social-Democratic Labour Party but also the Party of Socialist Revolutionaries were working to undermine the regime. The Socialist Revolutionaries managed to assassinate the Minister of the Interior, V. K. Pleve, in summer 1904. Even the liberals were becoming active. A Union of Liberation had been formed under the leadership of Pëtr Struve, who by then had broken with Marxism; its main mode of challenge was to hold public banquets and to facilitate the delivery of speeches that obliquely attacked the monarchy. Emperor Nicholas II, who had acceded to the Imperial throne in 1894, was under assault from virtually all sides.

What made matters worse was the fact that Russia unwisely went to war with Japan in 1904 in pursuance of its interests in the Pacific region. Large land forces were sent along the Trans-Siberian Railway, and the Baltic Sea fleet had to circumnavigate the globe to take on the Japanese navy. Through the later months of the year there were reports of a gathering catastrophe. Troops were penned into Port Arthur in the Far

East. Supplies were scarce, discipline poor and political and military leadership execrable. Meanwhile the Baltic Sea fleet crossing the North Sea had opened fire on an English trawler, mistaking it for a Japanese warship and nearly starting a war with the United Kingdom. Disaster and farce were blended in equal proportions. The Emperor and his court were declining into universal public disrepute.

But then on 9 January 1905 a peaceful procession of men, women and children took place in St Petersburg. Its destination was the Winter Palace of the tsars and its object was to present a petition to Nicholas II for the granting of universal civil rights, including a degree of democratic political representation. It was a Sunday. The marchers were dressed in their best clothes. The mood was firm but jovial. At the head of the procession walked an Orthodox Church priest, Father Georgi Gapon. The petition-campaign had been organised by him through the Assembly of Russian Factory and Mill Workers of the City of St Petersburg; his idea on that fateful Sunday was to present a set of loyally phrased requests to the Emperor Nicholas II in person. The Assembly was a trade union operated under the strict supervision of the Ministry of the Interior in a scheme begun in the Russian Empire at the instigation of Moscow police chief Sergei Zubatov. Gapon acted as intermediary, but increasingly he took the workers' side against the authorities.

As they drew near to the Winter Palace, the marchers were ordered to disperse but they ignored the instruction and walked on. The troops in front of the building, in the Emperor's absence, were beginning to panic and their commanding officers decided to fire upon the crowd. Scores of innocent demonstrators were killed. Instead of suppression, the result was mayhem. Everywhere in Russia there were strikes and demonstrations, and everywhere the blame was put upon the dynasty.

The news of the Russian revolutionary crisis reached Geneva within twenty-four hours of 'Bloody Sunday'. Among the first Bolsheviks in the city to read the papers were Anatoli Lunacharski and his wife, who hurried to Lenin's apartment on Rue David Dufour on 10 January. There was jubilation despite the information that innocent people had been shot outside the Winter Palace. The point for Lenin was that tsarism stood on the edge of a precipice; the throne of Ivan the Terrible and Peter the Great was beginning to totter. Together the Lenins and the Lunacharskis walked over to the café run by Panteleimon and Olga Lepeshinski at 93 Rue de Carouge. This was the main social centre for Russian Marxists, a place where they could eat cheaply and talk about politics and party organisation for as long as they liked. The Lepeshinskis were Marxist veterans who ran their business without expectation of great profit. They offered a service as much as a commercial operation. The tables were always cluttered with coffee cups, porridge bowls and plates of stuffed-cabbage pastries and salami, and there were always several groups of revolutionaries chatting to each other. On that particular day, however, the café had become packed very quickly. The emigrants scented the possibility of Revolution.

But what was to be done? Indeed what were the emigrants, who depended on Swiss journalists for information on Russia, in any position to do? They had been caught out by the events in St Petersburg and could not easily gauge how best to proceed. Nearly all of them decided to wait on events. Rather than return immediately to Russia, they tried to plan strategy for their followers. Without direct experience of the fast-changing circumstances in St Petersburg, they analysed and predicted things in the light of their previous doctrinal ruminations. They were unembarrassed by this. The working assumption of these revolutionary intellectuals was that their previous doctrines would supply the backbone of practical strategy for their followers in the Russian Empire.

Certainly Lenin took time to recognise the need for a fundamental strategic reconsideration. His initial reaction to 'Bloody Sunday' was to affirm again and again that the priority for Bolsheviks was to maintain a separate organisational identity from the Mensheviks. In December 1904 he had ranted to every member of the Bureau of Committees of the Majority that reconciliation with the present editorial board of *Iskra* was impossible – and he railed that fellow Bolshevik Noskov had tricked him while he and Nadya had been on holiday. Indeed he had done what any contemporary gentleman, be he a squire or an army officer, would have done in such circumstances: he formally cut off all personal relations with Noskov.[1] The problem was that the Central Committee, including some of Lenin's close supporters, did not accept his judgement and calmly made arrangements for a Third Party Congress that would bring Bolsheviks and Mensheviks back together. Surely, thought Lenin, 'Bloody Sunday' would put an end to such stupidity and Bolsheviks would recognise their duty to stand up for Bolshevism as the only genuine revolutionary trend? But even his friend Sergei Gusev, a Central Committee member, turned against him. Lenin raged at all of them by letter. They were 'wretched formalists'. He didn't care if they all went over to Martov. They were a disgrace to Bolshevism! No compromise!

Nadezhda Konstantinovna had to encode such correspondence, and perhaps it was she who pointed out the counter-productive effects of

Lenin's tone. Or maybe Lenin came to his senses by himself and saw that, if he ditched his Bolsheviks, no revolutionary group would be left to him. His only supporters, unless he could hold on to Sergei Gusev and other such comrades, would be his wife, his brother and his two sisters; and even Lenin knew that the Ulyanovs, however pertinacious they proved, were too few to turn Russia upside down.

Even so, he continued to claim that a permanent split with the Mensheviks was crucial:[2]

> Either by truly iron discipline we'll bind together all who wanted to wage war, and through this small but strong party smash the crumbling monster of the new *Iskra* and its ill-assorted elements; or else we'll demonstrate by our behaviour that we deserve to perish as contemptible formalists.

This was still offensive but not to the point that Bolshevik leaders would seriously take umbrage. More likely was that they marvelled at the surreal inappropriateness of his words. At a time when hundreds of thousands of Russians and Japanese were dying in the conflict in the Far East, Lenin talked blithely about 'war' in the party. They must surely have thought him outrageous in describing the Mensheviks, a tiny and committed group, as monstrous. They might also have been perplexed by his insisting that revolutionary duty demanded that they support the Japanese cause politically. This was an early version of the stand he was to take in the Great War; for Lenin, any foreign power attacking Russia deserved the support of Russian Marxists (and he habitually portrayed such a power as being less reactionary than the tsarist state). Anything to pull down the Romanovs! And was it not odd that, when every other Marxist was putting his mind to overturning the Romanov dynasty, Lenin thought that the most urgent task was the closure of *Iskra* in far-off Switzerland? What could anyone think about his behaviour but that he had finally gone somewhat mad? Perhaps they began to wonder whether they had made a mistake when they had taken his side against Martov in 1903.

And so the Central Committee, led by Bolsheviks, went ahead with a unifying Party Congress. Invitations were carried to practically all the important committees in the Russian Empire. The venue was to be London, and Lenin in high dudgeon got Nadya to buy tickets for the rail trip on the overnight train across France from Geneva. Days later, after arriving at Charing Cross Station, they took up lodgings at 16 Percy Circus in St Pancras. The Congress was to be held in April, and Lenin's anger steadily dissipated. Plekhanov, Martov and other *Iskra* leaders were refusing to come to London at all. They argued with some justification that the Central Committee had not been even-handed in its scrutiny of the validity of delegates' mandates and called upon Mensheviks to attend their own gathering in Geneva. Consequently, for most purposes, the so-called Third Party Congress in London was a Bolshevik Congress even though the Central Committee had managed to tempt at least a handful of Mensheviks to come to London and participate. Lenin, did he but know it, was a lucky man; he was like a man rescued from a chronic disease by a brilliant but invisible physician. He had wanted a Bolshevik Congress. A Bolshevik Congress was what he got. And he no longer felt the need to go around Bloomsbury in a foul temper about the *Iskra* group.

Instead he had the chance to explain his ideas on strategy to activists who had come over from Russia and to learn directly what was going on in St Petersburg and the provinces. Here he came into his own. One of his strengths was his ability to set down his thoughts clearly and pungently, at least to people who shared most of his basic assumptions. Few Bolsheviks had this talent to his extent; perhaps only his rival Bolshevik leader Alexander Bogdanov was in the same class as an expositor. Lenin loved Congresses. He liked to meet delegates. He liked the chance to exchange ideas with the working-class delegates. Along with Nikolai Alexeev, he assisted delegates with addresses of cheap temporary lodgings and with tips on English pronunciation.[3] (The fact that, to the British ear, he enunciated his rs like a Frenchman did not deter him.) And of an evening he would walk along with delegates to the little German pub at the top of Gray's Inn Road to have a beer and talk over the proceedings – and several of them were to recall how much inspiration Lenin drew in this period from the ideas of the Russian nineteenth-century agrarian-socialist terrorists and from the terrorist practice of the Jacobins in the French Revolution in 1792–4.

An affordable hall was found for the Congress, which began on 12 April 1905; the desire for secrecy was such that we still do not know the hall's name. Lenin, whose reputation among Bolsheviks in Russia and abroad had been in tatters in the previous months, suddenly reasserted his dominance. He chaired most of the sessions and manipulated the agenda for his own purposes. At last endeavouring to specify how to make Revolution, he presented a set of slogans that electrified the audience: 'armed insurrection', 'a provisional revolutionary government', 'mass terror', 'the expropriation of gentry land'.[4] Each slogan secured rapturous assent. The proceedings were not published at the time; otherwise, probably, he would not have spoken so enthusiastically about dictatorship and terror. But among his own Bolsheviks he felt no inhibition, and it is striking how his audience found nothing objectionable in his remarks. Bolsheviks were a ruthless bunch. They expected to make a revolution and to have to fight against counter-revolutionary forces, and did not see why they should eschew the violent methods developed by Robespierre and his confederates in the French Revolution. Bolsheviks were hard-headed and confident. If they played their anticipated vital role in overthrowing the Russian Imperial government, they assumed, they would be indispensable to the task of securing the political and economic gains; their aim had to be to join the subsequent revolutionary administration. Lenin had ventilated ideas that had expressed their innermost inclinations.

But not everyone could understand how the new slogans fitted the earlier common understandings of Russian Marxism. Some asked how a Marxist party could aspire to join a government whose purpose was to consolidate a capitalist economy. And if the landed nobility was to be expropriated, where should the agrarian reform stop? Delegate M. K. Vladimirov enquired whether the party should stop short of specifically socialist measures – such as the introduction of collective farms. Lenin was unruffled. He came back instantly with his injunction: 'Never stop!'[5]

When the Mensheviks heard of Lenin's contributions, they declared him a proven renegade from Marxism. He admired Tkachëv and praised terror. He wanted to give the entire land to the peasantry. Violence and dictatorship fixated him. Lenin tried to prevent the criticisms getting out of hand by writing yet another booklet, *Two Tactics of Russian Social-Democracy in the Democratic Revolution*, which he was still writing during the Congress. Its purpose was not only to justify his new radical slogans but also to drum some organisational sense into fellow Bolsheviks. He noted, for example, that they were slow in Russia to found trade unions and other organisations for the working class. Lenin was furious with them, urging an end to the preoccupation with clandestine methods of running the party. He tried to make them a bit less 'Leninist'! Now, to general amazement, he aimed to form a large, open-entrance party. For him, no somersault was involved here. *What Is to Be Done?* was a tract for its time and situation; its universal theme was the need for leadership but it offered no permanent detailed prescription for the modalities of party organisation. Now, said Lenin, there was a real revolutionary opportunity – and the party had to change the way it operated. Otherwise the Revolution would leave the party far behind.

Lenin was not changing his assumptions, just his practical proposals in the light of the changed political situation. A revolutionary opportunity existed and the party absolutely had to exploit it. The Russian Social-Democratic Labour Party had been created precisely for this purpose. He was readying his party – or rather his section of it – to recognise and exploit this opportunity. He was a pressure-cooker on the stove waiting to blow off its lid.

His campaign shows both how much and how little he had come along the road towards becoming a leader of Revolution. The Congress understood his defects. This was why, against his objections, it decided to limit the emigrants' influence upon the party. In particular, the Central Committee and the central party newspaper, now to be known as *Proletari*, were to be switched to the Russian Empire. Lenin was being put on notice that if he wished to lead the Bolsheviks he would have to operate not in Geneva but in St Petersburg. For over six months he had ignored this warning. Nothing – not even a decision by Congress – would induce him to return to Russia until his freedom from arrest seemed secure. Thus Lenin was a theorist and rhetorician of Revolution more than a leader. He retained his wholly unrealistic belief that he could direct Bolshevik activity in Russia by means of letters sent from the Switzerland. He failed to comprehend the volcanic unpredictability of the forces that were being released. He had read about the French Revolution, about the Revolutions of 1848 and about the Paris Commune of 1871. But what he had learned from his books had been about the 'class interests' of the contending political forces. Like Marx, he had striven to focus on the internal logic of developments. But at the same time he had overlooked the chaos of each of those great historical events as experienced by the people who took part in them.

Yet Lenin was not complacent. In Geneva he sensed the need to acquire a more lively sense of what was happening in St Petersburg even though he refused to go there. Weeks after 'Bloody Sunday' he met the fleeing Father Gapon. Other Marxists were cold-shouldering the Russian Orthodox priest, but Lenin talked with him at length. They even exchanged copies of books they had written; this was not Lenin's usual reaction unless he was impressed with someone. From the beginning there was a rapport between the two men.

And so Lenin welcomed him to the Rue de Carouge. As they

discussed current developments, peasants' son Gapon – charismatic, gruff, bearded and hostile to both the Emperor and the Orthodox Church hierarchy – captivated him as someone who had a deep understanding of the feelings of ordinary Russians.[6] The fact that Gapon was neither a theorist nor a party member was all to the good; he knew things that were elusive to emigrants. A former tsarist loyalist, Gapon had turned to Revolution only after the massacre outside the Winter Palace. He could speak about haymaking, slums and Sunday schools – all subjects in which Lenin's knowledge was deficient. Lenin was also intrigued by Gapon's slogan 'All the Land to the People'. Obviously this went far beyond Lenin's demand that the cut-off strips should be restored to the peasants. But Gapon insisted that his own radicalism was justified. God alone, said the priest, was the land's sole owner and peasants should be helped to rent it. Needless to add, Lenin rejected the proposal in its religious encasement.[7] But Lenin drew inspiration from it in political terms. Lenin was even more impressed when Gapon showed him his open letter to Russia's socialist parties, calling on them to come to an agreement and prepare the armed overthrow of tsarism. Here was a man of the cloth who understood the practical tasks of the Revolution. Lenin the militant atheist referred approvingly to Gapon's proposal in the Bolshevik newspaper *Vperëd*.[8]

Lenin was developing as a politician. He was a Marxist, albeit a Marxist who had been inspired by earlier generations of Russian socialist thinkers. He was a scholar–revolutionary with a deep commitment to the perfectibility of mankind inherited from Enlightenment philosophy. But he was also increasingly capable of assimilating ideas from other sources. Although he expressed himself in the lexicon of Marxism, he needed to go outside the Marxist fraternity for help to think through his strategy.

His policies, despite pointing away from conventional Marxist policies, held to the axiom that the great march to socialism would occur in two distinct stages: first a 'bourgeois-democratic' revolution and then a socialist one. But there were also distinct oddities in his argument. *Two Tactics of Russian Social-Democracy*, for example, insisted that liberals and other middle-class parties were incapable of being trusted even to bring about that first revolution. Even stranger was the project for a 'provisional revolutionary democratic dictatorship of the proletariat and the peasantry'. Lenin announced that such a dictatorship would exercise a powerful appeal to the lower social classes. But the Mensheviks retorted that Lenin had thrown out the two-stages concept. They rightly suggested that, if the dictatorship was going to be enormously popular, the bourgeoisie would never be able to supplant it. They also challenged Lenin's case that a dictatorial regime was the most effective way to introduce universal civic rights and a market economy. His whole project was a contradictory mishmash. Yet Lenin did not deign to respond to these attacks; he had convinced his Bolshevik followers and was unwilling to expose the flaws in his case in a general public debate. This also carried the advantage of allowing him to go on believing that he had stayed within the perimeter of conventional Marxism.

In fact Lenin was tempted to expound a one-stage strategy and drafted an article called 'Picture of the Provisional Revolutionary Government' in which he sketched ideas for 'a revolution uninterrupted'. But then he had second thoughts and withheld his piece from the press. Not all Marxists were worried about flouting convention. Inspired by the ideas of the German Marxist Alexander Helphand-Parvus, Trotski proposed unequivocally that the socialist parties should seize power, establish a 'workers' government' and not open themselves to replacement by liberals. Trotski wanted not just to preach but also to practise revolutionary leadership. Returning to Russia in summer, he joined the striking workers of St Petersburg.

Across the summer the troubles of the Imperial government became acute. The news from the Far East was terrible. Russian land forces had been overwhelmed at the battle of Mukden in February, and the navy, having circumnavigated the globe, was annihilated at Tsushima in May. Count Witte, brought out of retirement by the Emperor, managed to negotiate surprisingly gentle terms of peace from the Japanese, but the sense of national humiliation was widespread. So too was the spirit of revolt. In city after city there were industrial strikes and in May there was a novel phenomenon: the soviet. The word, meaning council in Russian, came to stand for an elected body of the lower social classes that assumed the power of local government. It happened first in Ivanovo-Voznesensk but quickly spread elsewhere. Workers without much prior deliberation had set up embryonic alternative administrations. Trotski became Deputy Chairman of the Petersburg Soviet in September. The clandestine political parties came into the open, and even the liberals formed a political party at last: the Party of Constitutional Democrats (or Kadets). Unions proliferated. Censorship almost collapsed. The police were too timid to intervene. Peasants began to take timber from the landlords' woods and to pasture their cattle on gentry land. Poles and Georgians made their countries ungovernable from the Russian capital. Tsarism was in mortal danger.

This entire crisis occurred in Lenin's absence. Other Bolsheviks nagged him about this and in September he was firmly requested by his comrade Alexander Bogdanov to return home immediately. Bogdanov was also an intellectual; he too was a prolific author and a theorist. But he was also restless for action. Indeed it was Lenin's plea for action in *What Is to Be Done?* that had turned Bogdanov into a Bolshevik. He simply could not understand why Lenin would not take the risk of going back to Russia, and he told him this in plain language. But still Lenin would not budge. He had never gambled with his personal safety or engaged in mere revolutionary gestures. His activity in emigration with its intellectual debates, its publications and its library research continued to fulfil him. No one meeting him on the Rue de Carouge would suspect that this neatly dressed, scholarly type intended, as a basic purpose in his life, to transform the politics and society of the world. He believed that revolutionary leaders were meant to supply doctrinal guidance and practical policies, and to keep themselves free from arrest. He therefore had no trouble in brushing Alexander Bogdanov's complaint aside.

What changed his stance was the news from St Petersburg that the regime was at last making serious reforms. On 17 October 1905 Emperor Nicholas II issued a Manifesto, promising to realise universal civil rights as well as convoke a State Duma. Immediately Lenin felt reassured. The Okhrana, he thought, would no longer be hunting for him on the streets. Or at least he could hope so. In the first week of November he boarded the train in Geneva and began the journey that led him across Germany. Nadezhda Konstantinovna's preparations were meticulous. From Germany she and Lenin crossed to the Swedish capital Stockholm, where Bolshevik associates had false papers ready for them. Ferry tickets had been bought for both of them and they took the steamer from Stockholm across the Baltic to Helsinki. For the first time in five years Lenin set his feet on ground ruled by the Russian Emperor. Leaving Helsinki, Lenin and Nadya took another train to St Petersburg. It was a journey of 280 miles and they crossed the Russo-Finnish administrative border at Beloostrov. When they alighted at the Finland Station on 8 November, they were discreetly met by the Bolshevik Nikolai Burënin, who showed them to the first of several apartments where they were to stay over the next few weeks.[9]

Initially Lenin and Nadezhda Konstantinovna registered legally as residents; they expected to operate in the open. But they dropped this delusion the very next day when the Okhrana surrounded the area with agents who had no talent for disguising themselves. From then onwards they were looked after by fellow Bolsheviks in a succession of safe-houses. Nevertheless Lenin was confident enough to visit his mother and his sister Anna, who were living at the little village and railway-stop of Sablino outside St Petersburg. He also kept up regular contacts with Bolsheviks who were working in the soviets, trade unions and other organisations. All the while he was gulping down impressions about Russia in revolution. But most of his working time was spent in his traditional fashion. He wrote newspaper articles and booklets and sat through the endless discussions of party committees. Occasionally, more-over, he gave speeches to party congresses, conferences and other such gatherings. From November 1905 through to summer 1906 he resided in St Petersburg with the odd visit to Finland, to Moscow and – in April 1906 – to Stockholm for the Fourth Party Congress. His purpose as ever was to guide and control his Bolshevik faction and maximise its influence in the Russian Social-Democratic Labour Party. He was not, and did not aim to be, the tribune of the people.

Not for him, then, the delivery of fiery speeches to public meetings in the fashion that was making Trotski famous. He attempted only one such oration in 1905–6. This was to an all-party meeting in May 1906 in the People's House. It was a testing experience for him. He was unusually nervous before getting up on to the platform and being introduced to the audience as 'comrade Karpov'. He need not have worried. Once he was on the platform, he handled the situation well. Screwing up his eyes and grasping the lapel of his jacket, he leaned forward and fixed his gaze on the audience. Then he rapped out his slogans. Everyone went away impressed with his utmost belief that these slogans were the sole means to accelerate progress to socialism in Russia. Slowly Lenin was acquiring the skills of twentieth-century open politics.

The comparison with Trotski is not wholly fair. The rise and fall of the Petersburg Soviet, where Trotski made his declamations, had largely happened before Lenin's arrival. Thereafter all revolutionary politicians, not just Lenin, concentrated on sorting out the affairs of their respective parties. This was a mammoth task for Lenin because his Bolsheviks continued to despise the soviets and to exaggerate the advantages of political conspiracy. Lenin argued that the time was overdue for Bolshe-viks to form a mass party, to participate in the various other public organisations and to organise Revolution. When his recommendations were accepted but only with reluctance, he responded by suggesting the need for the Russian Social-Democratic Labour Party to be infused with young blood. Lenin cared little whether the recruits were already Marxists. The priority was to attract radical, working-class activists, activists who raged to be active. And Lenin wanted them to have complete freedom to express their impatience; indeed he tried to strengthen their impatience. Industrial workers inside and outside the party, he declared, should take the Revolution into their own hands. They should not be restrained by their parties. The working class should act as the vanguard of all the forces hostile to the Russian Imperial state.

He was apt to get carried away about such matters. Repeatedly he had deplored the failure of the 1871 Paris Commune to resort to repression; in 1905, however, he not only confirmed his commitment to violent methods but gave them a specificity that was more bloodthirsty than anyone thought imaginable. He displayed a virtual lust for violence. While he personally had no ambition to kill or to maim or even to witness any butchery, he took a cruel delight in recommending such mayhem.

This delight was intense shortly before his return to Russia. Thus he wrote the following summons to members of the Combat Committee attached to the Bolshevik Central Committee: 'Here what is needed is frenzied energy upon energy. I see with horror, for God's sake with real horror, that there has been talk about bombs *for more than a year* and yet not a single bomb has been made!' Lenin's solution was to give arms to detachments of workers and students and let them get on with revolutionary activity regardless of whether they belonged to the Russian Social-Democratic Labour Party. The detachments should kill spies, blow up police stations, rob banks and confiscate the resources they need for an armed insurrection.[10] His imagination ran wild. When it came to street conflicts, he suggested, the detachments should pull up paving stones or prepare hot kettles and run to the tops of buildings in order to attack troops sent against them. Another proposal was to keep a store of acid to hurl at policemen.[11] These tactics were not only alarming but also impractical. If used, they would have stiffened the will of troops and policemen to suppress rebellion. Lenin was expressing a rage deep inside himself. He himself did not have to handle bombs, kettles and acids. But unconsciously he got satisfaction from putting his thoughts about them on paper.

He did not worry that others might be appalled by his approach:

Of course, any extreme is bad; everything good and useful taken to an extreme can become and even, beyond a certain limit, cannot help but become a harmful evil. Uncoordinated, unplanned petty terror, when taken to an extreme, can only disintegrate forces and waste them. This is true, and naturally cannot be forgotten. But on the other hand it absolutely mustn't be forgotten that the slogan of insurrection *has already been given*, the insurrection has already *been started*.

The breakdown in logic here was significant. Having begun with a justification for not going to an 'extreme', Lenin ended abruptly with an assertion that the armed uprising was under way.

Within a month, however, he had calmed down. His Bolshevik associates in Moscow were acting with precisely the zeal he had wanted. And yet the Moscow Rising, which they had organised together with the other political parties in the City Soviet, was a disaster. The fighting commenced in mid-December 1905. It was concentrated in the Presnya industrial district and the valour of the rebels was beyond dispute. But they were no match for the same troops who had recently closed down the Petersburg Soviet in the Technological Institute. The Rising was ruthlessly put down. Over-optimistic attempts at insurrection, concluded Lenin, should no longer be indulged. He also wished to persuade the Bolsheviks to take full advantage of the Emperor's October Manifesto. Elections were to take place in early 1906 for an elected, representative assembly: the State Duma. There were severe limits upon the new Russian parliamentarianism. In particular, the Emperor retained the right to disperse the Duma and to rule by decree. But Lenin argued that the Russian Social-Democratic Labour Party should put up its own candidates and use the Duma as an opportunity for the dissemination of party propaganda.

This was a battle he could not win. In mid-December 1905 he was defeated at the Bolshevik Conference held in the Finnish town of Tampere, three hundred miles north-west of St Petersburg. But he persisted with his strategic shift even though it broke sharply with everything he had been saying since the Second Party Congress in 1903. He even condoned reconciliation with the Mensheviks. For two years it had been an article of his crusading faith that Menshevism was a heresy, a set of organisational and strategic proposals that flew in the face of Marxist principles. When his followers had queried his hostility to compromise, he had shown them his utter contempt. In Lenin's eyes, the 'Conciliator Bolsheviks' had been hardly better than the Mensheviks.

And yet now Lenin wished to reunify with the Mensheviks. His calculations were not difficult to decipher: he could not control Bolshevik policy. To balance the zealots in his own faction, he therefore needed Mensheviks, most of whom wanted the party to participate in the soviets and to campaign in the State Duma elections. He contemplated this despite the chasm that separated him from Menshevism. Lenin stood for a 'provisional revolutionary democratic dictatorship of the proletariat and the peasantry', for a class alliance of workers and peasants, for the repudiation of the middle classes and for mass terror. The Mensheviks by contrast urged that the 'bourgeois-democratic' revolution should be led by the middle classes and that this revolution should immediately implement universal civil rights. It would take all his charm and persuasiveness to bring the Bolsheviks and the Mensheviks back together. But Lenin always had abundant self-belief. Without expressly announcing his change of stance, he did all he could to enable the two factions to join each other at the Fourth Party Congress. His highest immediate priority was to get the Congress to sanction participation in the legal political activities that the Imperial government had been compelled to concede. For Lenin, a sinuous manoeuvrer, this was not a tall order.

The Congress was arranged for Stockholm. As the Congress delegates set off across the Baltic Sea to the Swedish capital in April, Lenin opened negotiations with Menshevik leaders. The Mensheviks had a slight majority over the Bolsheviks among the Congress delegates and would undoubtedly win the main debates. This had the effect of freeing Lenin to say what he wanted about a wide range of policies, including those which were diametrically opposed to Menshevism. Lenin enjoyed being aggressive. Refining his project for expropriation of the landed gentry in favour of the peasantry, he called for 'land nationalisation' by the 'provisional revolutionary dictatorship'. The Mensheviks too had widened their demands on the agrarian question and called for 'land municipalisation'; they contended they would thereby avoid the centralised bureaucracy that Lenin's scheme would involve. Lenin had casually assumed that it would be a simple administrative task for the revolutionary regime to ensure that the peasants, who would gain use of the land at a very low rent, would adopt efficient farming techniques. But both the Mensheviks and many of Lenin's critics among the Bolsheviks replied that this would be a task of gigantic complexity. In truth Lenin woefully underestimated the dangers of bureaucratic degeneration.

Lenin was defeated on agrarian policy at the Congress and his other initiatives also met with reverses. The Mensheviks brought up the very embarrassing matter of the Bolshevik factional leadership's complicity in the organisation of bank robberies in the Russian Empire. This was a growing scandal in the Russian Social-Democratic Labour Party. For Mensheviks, such robberies were an intolerable method of financing the party and Lenin's secret sanction for them was a disgrace. Plekhanov added his weight to the criticism, repeating that Lenin's strategy of Revolution – especially his wish for a class alliance with the peasantry – was reminiscent of the Russian agrarian socialists. It was an uncomfortable moment for Lenin. His self-control was strained to the limit because the Bolshevik factional leadership had simultaneously invited him, the advocate of participation in Duma elections, to put the case for boycotting them. He phrased his speech on the subject with uncharacteristic vagueness, which was the most he could do to signal his disquiet with the policy of the Bolshevik faction. But when at the end of the Congress the Mensheviks unexpectedly tabled a proposal to enter the electoral campaign still in progress in one region of the Russian Empire, namely the Caucasus, he broke cover and voted against most of his fellow Bolsheviks. The Menshevik proposal was accepted. At least on this matter he had obtained a degree of pleasure.

The new Central Committee of the reunited party included seven Mensheviks and only three Bolsheviks. Lenin was not among them. He was being warned by fellow Bolshevik delegates that his ideas were not to their liking: his policies on the Duma and on land nationalisation were especially unappealing to them. As a consequence his mood had darkened by the time he took the ferry back from Stockholm. His nerves were frayed.

But the mood quickly lightened. The Bolshevik faction aimed to keep its organisational apparatus separate from the rest of the party and established a secret Bolshevik Centre. Lenin was readmitted to the leadership alongside Bogdanov and Leonid Krasin. From this position he would be able to undo those decisions at the Congress which he did not like, and on this he had Bogdanov's warm collaboration. The two of them got on better than for years and decided that they and their wives should set up house together. They feared the attentions of the Okhrana as the Imperial regime sought to assert control. Their enquiries led them to Vaasa, a large two-storey dacha at Kuokkala in the Grand Duchy of Finland. Kuokkala lies less than forty miles from St Petersburg; it was only five miles from the existing Russo-Finnish administrative border at Beloostrov and had a station on the railway between St Petersburg and Helsinki. Lenin and his friends were opting for safety. Finland was not as secure as Switzerland but had limited self-government even under the tsars. Its border was not just of a formal significance. Travellers had to show their passports and allow the police to inspect their baggage. The Finns had their own currency and postage stamps and were so different from the Russians that they forbade people from buying alcohol on public premises unless it was accompanied by a meal. Finnish ports received ferries regularly from Hull, Lübeck, Stettin and Stockholm; it was possible, in an emergency, to leave for central and western Europe without going back to Russia.

Thus Finland, which had been subjected to Russian Imperial control since 1809, was almost a foreign country without quite being abroad – and the Finnish socialists so detested tsarism that they were willing to lend a hand to almost any of its victims. It was there that the Bolshevik Centre decided to set up its base. Lenin, Nadya, Bogdanov and his wife Natalya would be able to get on with their writing, their organising and their observation of politics from a safe distance. Shortly before he left for Finland, Lenin visited the Sablino dacha rented by his mother. From 20 August 1906 he was at Kuokkala and there he stayed until late November 1907. Otherwise he ventured forth only briefly for important conferences and congresses. He attended meetings in the Finnish towns of Tampere, Terijoki and Viipuri; he also travelled to the Fifth Party Congress in London and to the Congress of the Socialist International in Stuttgart. But he did not venture back into Russia. Little did he know that he would not see St Petersburg again for nearly a decade.

From beginning to end the Fifth Party Congress was disrupted by rows. Lenin no longer had need of decent relations with the Mensheviks since they had already fulfilled the function of helping him to get the Bolsheviks to put up candidates in the State Duma elections. He repaid them by stating, before the Congress opened in April 1907, that they had prostituted their Marxist principles. They came back at him with denunciations of insincerity. He had talked in favour of the party's reunification but had created a separate Bolshevik Centre and kept funds out of the hands of the Mensheviks. Disputes exploded throughout the Congress between the two factions: about the peasantry, about Russian liberalism and even about philosophy. But Lenin had a successful Congress. He was assisted by the fact that the various Marxist parties of the borderlands of the Russian Empire attended. The Poles led by Rosa Luxemburg and Leo Jogiches had considerable significance and were inclined to favour Lenin's strategic judgement that the party ought to prefer the other socialist parties, including those of the peasantry, to the Kadets as allies. Menshevism was thwarted. So too were the Bolsheviks such as Bogdanov who continued to resent participation in the State Duma. By parleying with Latvians and Lithuanians as well as Poles, Lenin was able to secure several positions that were to stand him in good stead in future years.

Even so, he was not elected to the Central Committee. On several counts he had been criticised by the Congress. The question of Bolshevik complicity in armed robberies came up again. Lenin and the Bolsheviks were condemned for their 'anarchist tendencies', and it was stated that no further bank raids should take place. But by then Lenin did not care. He was no longer as interested in manoeuvring between the Bolsheviks and Mensheviks as in securing hegemony over the Bolshevik faction. And he looked forward to the Stuttgart Congress of the Second Socialist International in good spirits. His delight was unbounded when, partly as a result of his efforts, the International toughened its declaration of hostility to militarism and imperialism with the support of the German Social-Democratic Party. When Rosa Luxemburg advised him that the German Social-Democratic Party would be less committed in practice to anti-militarism and anti-imperialism than he believed, Lenin dismissed her as an obsessive factionalist. He was to regret this in 1914.

The fifteen months in the rambling wooden rooms of Vaasa were a period of crisis for Russian revolutionaries. Lenin watched the situation from afar as tsarism tightened its grip. To his chagrin, the First State Duma elections were ignored by the Bolsheviks. Nevertheless the peasants voted for candidates who stood for the transfer of agricultural land to the peasantry. The liberals, led by the Kadets, continued to object to the limitations placed by the Basic Law upon the powers of the Duma. The First State Duma had turned out to be a hotbed of opposition to the Romanov monarchy. By then Nicholas II judged that he had the better of the new political parties; he dispersed the Duma and called fresh elections. The Kadets decamped to Viipuri in Finland and called upon Russians to withhold taxes and conscripts until such time as the Imperial government showed respect for the elected representatives of the people.

Yet the Second Duma too produced an assembly that refused to do a deal with the Emperor. Nicholas II for his part never had respect for the liberals again; he had some lingering hopes for the conservative party of Alexander Guchkov and the so-called Octobrists, who had always wanted to make the limited constitutional reforms work as well as they could, but he soon distrusted Guchkov as well. The man he most relied upon was his Minister of the Interior, Pëtr Stolypin, who used the noose to suppress rural rebellion. Stolypin's 'necktie', as it became known, reduced the countryside to quiescence. Order returned to town and village. Stolypin knew that state coercion would not save the dynasty, and he introduced a series of measures to conserve the tsarist state. Becoming Chairman of the Council of Ministers, he was determined to refashion the Duma by redrawing the electoral law and giving greater parliamentary weight to the gentry. He also began to introduce an agrarian reform aimed at a phasing out of the village land commune and its replacement by a large class of sturdy, independent farmers. For Lenin, this was proof that the Imperial regime was incapable of coming to terms with contemporary capitalism. Stolypin's measures in the countryside were taking the 'Prussian path' instead of the 'American' one. What he meant by this was that the gentry landlords remained in positions of authority and dominated the countryside as they did in Prussia. The chance to open up agriculture to those who simply wanted to farm the land – as had happened in the American West in the nineteenth century – had been lost. Now only Revolution could modernise the Russian economy.

Lenin discussed all this with his fellow lodger in Vaasa. Bogdanov was easily the most brilliant intellectual force inside Bolshevism. He was the only thinker in the faction whose mental capacities outmatched Lenin's. Bogdanov had never taken to the authoritarianism embodied in Lenin's ideas. At Vaasa they talked a lot. They could hardly avoid each other: Bogdanov lived on the top floor and passed by the Ulyanovs' quarters every time he went out into the garden. Increasingly they found themselves at odds about political theory, culture and philosophy. And they disputed immediate policy: Lenin wanted participation in Duma elections, Bogdanov vehemently opposed this. From having been boon comrades in the struggle against the Mensheviks, they became rivals for the leadership of Bolshevism.

11

THE SECOND EMIGRATION

1908–1911

Lenin hoped to go on sheltering in the Grand Duchy of Finland. Although he thought that the political 'reaction' would endure several years, he did not intend to move from Kuokkala.[1] But the situation was becoming volatile. Pëtr Stolypin, Chairman of the Council of Ministers, carried out a constitutional coup on behalf of Nicholas II in June 1907. This involved the disbandment of the Second Duma and the introduction of new electoral rules so as to produce a Third Duma, later in the year, with more places and greater influence for the landed gentry. Meanwhile the Okhrana redoubled its efforts to catch the revolutionary leaders. Far too many Bolshevik activists had taken a trip to Kuokkala for the Imperial police to be unaware of the general whereabouts of the Bolshevik Centre.

One day in late November a message came to the Centre's members that policemen were searching the vicinity. Immediately Lenin packed and headed in the direction of Helsinki, 240 miles away. His attitude was that the commander had to survive even if the officers were captured. Dutifully Nadya remained behind at the dacha with Alexander and Natalya Bogdanov and Iosif Dubrovinski. They spent their time preparing to move the Bolshevik Centre abroad and burned those party files that could not be transported. Nadya, worrying that the police might be suspicious of the fresh pile of ash, organised its hurried burial. Other files were passed for safe-keeping to Finnish Marxists. Then the dacha's owner rushed round to alert the tenants to the imminence of a police search. In fact the Okhrana was preoccupied by its hunt for a group of Socialist-Revolutionary terrorists and was unaware of the identity of the Vaasa tenants. But the Kuokkala tenants feared the worst. Meanwhile Lenin went to ground at the village of Olgbu outside Helsinki. Party organisers had arranged for him to be given a room at the back of a house belonging to two Finnish sisters, where he settled down to write articles on the agrarian question. Some days later he was joined there by Nadya. By then it was clear that they had to move abroad if they were to avoid arrest.[2]

The Bolshevik Centre decided to make for Switzerland; but this was easier said than done. A permanent system of contact with Russia had to be put in place. Nadya was entrusted with such pieces of party business, and she returned to St Petersburg to make the final agreements with activists. Lenin waited in Olgbu as she went about her tasks. Nadya was under great pressure. In particular, she had to secure the efficient transfer of *Proletari*, the main newspaper published by the Bolsheviks, from Finland to Switzerland; she also had to visit her sick mother Yelizaveta Vasilevna, who at that time was refusing to re-emigrate with her daughter and son-in-law.[3]

Lenin had faith in her abilities and feared for his personal security. In her absence in St Petersburg, he decided to re-emigrate and left instructions as to how she could catch him up in Stockholm. Nadya accepted her abandonment with stoicism. Little did she imagine that Lenin, through his insistence on a rapid escape, was putting himself in great danger. The plan was for him to take the ferry from Turku to Stockholm. An ice-cutting ferry steamship plied this route, but Okhrana agents were known to keep watch at the Helsinki rail station and the Turku ferry terminal. Police on the boarding stage were looking out for fleeing Bolsheviks, Mensheviks and Socialist-Revolutionaries. The advice to Lenin from Finnish comrades was that he should avoid Turku and travel to the second stage of the ferry's journey at Nauvo Island twenty miles to the south-west in the Gulf of Bothnia.[4] Lenin complied. From Turku he set off by carriage and then made his way by boat to Kuustö Island. Secrecy remained essential and he moved from shelter to shelter by night. From Kuustö he was accompanied not only by a local co-op chairman but also by a friendly Finnish police officer to Lille Meljo Island. This was the penultimate section of the trip. From Lille Meljo he intended to reach Nauvo, where he would board the Stockholm ferry on 12 December.

The problem was that Lenin would have to go on foot to Nauvo Island and the Finnish comrades for some reason had failed to explain that the ice was not reliably continuous. Indeed the 'walk' to Nauvo would necessitate a lot of leaping across the small gaps between ice floes. Nor had Lenin, usually a cautious man, bargained for the fact that his guides across the ice from Lille Meljo to Nauvo would be a pair of local peasants not noted for their sobriety. On the appointed day, as the three walkers set out from Lille Meljo to Nauvo, Lenin was the only one who was not the worse for drink. Midway across the ice, there was a heaving and cracking of the surface, and only by means of a last, desperate lunge did Lenin manage to clamber up on to a solid glacial fragment. 'Ach,' he thought, 'what a stupid way to perish!'[5] Death by drowning, for most people, would be tragic and not merely stupid. Only someone who had a glorious future in mind for himself could see the threat as something frivolous.

Napoleon's main demand of his marshals was that they should be lucky — and Lenin was extremely lucky in 1907. He boarded the ferry as planned on Nauvo Island and next day arrived in Sweden. Not long afterwards he was joined by Nadya, who by then had cleared up the Bolshevik faction's business. From there they travelled first to Berlin and then to Geneva. Lenin and Nadya had been suffering from influenza, and Lenin wrote to the writer Maxim Gorki with an oblique request to be invited to stay with him on the island of Capri off the Italian coast near Naples.[6] The wish for physical rest was not his sole concern. The return to Geneva, where once he had confidently plotted Revolution in Russia, was too much for him. He groaned to Nadya: 'I've got the feeling that I've come here to lie in my grave.'[7] He was speaking from the heart: Lenin the revolutionary optimist felt defeated. Would he ever, he must have wondered, get another chance to play a leading role in his native land? Since leaving Switzerland in late 1905 he had spent more time in Finland than in Russia; and in the short time he spent in St Petersburg he had often been in hiding. How was he ever to lead his country to Revolution? To a friend he blurted out his confession: 'I know Russia so little. Simbirsk, Kazan, Petersburg and that's about it.'[8]

This pool of self-awareness quickly evaporated. Within weeks Lenin was again laying down the policies for Bolsheviks as if his alone was the analysis of Russian state and society that counted. In emigration he revised little in his strategic planning. His conclusion about the revolution of 1905–6 was that the Bolsheviks had had the correct policies. Quite why the Revolution had not succeeded, he did not explain. Lenin stuck to his certainties. The Bolsheviks needed to keep the faith so that they might be ready to improve their political performance for that inevitable future occasion when a revolutionary situation recurred in Russia.

For a few months Lenin and Nadya stayed in Geneva, first at 17 Rue des Deux Ponts and then at 61 Rue des Maraîchers. Gradually their health improved and their spirits rose. But Bogdanov and the other Bolshevik leaders found Switzerland uncongenial. Lenin disagreed, but he was in no position to prevent the Bolshevik Centre's decision to decamp to Paris. Dolefully he and Nadya paid their Swiss landlord and journeyed to France in December 1908. Arriving in Paris, Lenin, Nadya and her mother Yelizaveta Vasilevna were joined by Lenin's sister Maria Ilinichna. The four of them lived together with a fair degree of harmony. It is true that Yelizaveta Vasilevna, while respecting the 'scientific work of Nadya and the son-in-law',[9] told Lenin what she thought of him, and that she was not always complimentary. Lenin responded in kind. He declared, for example, that the worst punishment for a bigamist was that he acquired two mothers-in-law.[10] Yet any tiffs were short lived. Yelizaveta Vasilevna and Vladimir Ilich respected each other and a certain rueful fondness existed between them. One Sunday when she was feeling particularly fed up, Lenin discovered that she had nothing to smoke and went out to buy her a packet of cigarettes despite his aversion to tobacco smoke.[11]

For a while the women did the housework without a maid. Lenin as a Central Committee member had a regular income from the party and derived money from his book royalties; and the Bolsheviks had their own separate fund built up from the armed robberies and from legacies. Yekaterina Vasilevna, too, contributed a little to the finances of the ménage. But, hard though they tried, they could not persuade any Frenchwoman to work for them because Russians had the reputation of being demanding and undependable employers. When Mark Yelizarov, Anna Ilinichna's husband and Lenin's brother-in-law, visited them after a trip to Japan, he criticised them for doing their own cooking and cleaning; he also could not stand Nadya's cooking. A bluff, straightforward man, he announced that they simply had to get hold of a maid. Usually his wife Anna objected to his habit of saying the first thing that came into his head.[12] But not on this occasion: she had always been tactless in respect of Nadya and did not mind Mark's snipe at her. Anyway the Ulyanovs accepted his advice and made another attempt to secure domestic assistance. This time they overcame the local Russophobia; the new housekeeper moved in and Nadezhda Konstantinovna's siege on the stomachs of the Ulyanovs was lifted.[13]

Lenin stayed out of any quibbling of this sort. He himself did no cooking in the normal run of things and took no interest in the quality of his food beyond asking whether the ingredients conformed to his medical regimen. Nadya noted, with unintended humour, that 'he pretty submissively ate everything given to him'.[14] This compliance, so rare in Lenin the politician, induced the women in his life to go on 'mothering' him. Boyishly he would ask them: 'Am I allowed to eat this?' Indeed, several other of his habits were also endearing to them. Yelizaveta

Vasilevna was impressed that, each day before starting to write, he took out a duster and buffed up his desk.[15]

Not that he ceased being the family's dominant figure. Lenin had for years been a cycling enthusiast, and from Geneva he had frequently taken Nadezhda Konstantinovna and Maria Ilinichna on mountain rides at weekends. Lenin was the fittest of the three. If the women flagged, he would ride in turn alongside each of them and cajole them to keep going. Cycling in the Alps was a growing pastime for tourists, especially the British, Germans and French. His *Baedeker* for Switzerland noted that the Germans and French took things easy when the gradient became steep and that the custom was to hire a horse, tether the bicycles behind and ride gently uphill by means of equine power. The British would have nothing to do with this namby-pamby method, and it would seem that Lenin, usually a Germanophile, sided with the British on this. Holidays were not holidays for him unless he could push himself hard. Better still if he could push others too, as Nadezhda Konstantinovna and Maria Ilinichna ruefully noted. At night in the village *pensions*, too, he was still in charge. He refused to let Maria leave anything on her plate, explaining that if she did not eat the entirety of the supper, the innkeeper would halve the portions next evening without reducing the fee.[16]

Lenin hated to be done down in the slightest way and bicycles were a matter of persistent concern. When they lived in Paris, he rode daily to the Bibliothèque Nationale. He disliked this library because of the lengthy time he had to wait for the books he ordered, and he was irked further by the need to pay the concierge ten centimes for parking his bike outside. But one day something still worse happened when his beloved bike – that 'surgical instrument' of his – was stolen. When Lenin remonstrated with the concierge, however, she boldly retorted that his ten centimes covered only the permission to park and did not constitute a guarantee of security.[17]

For once, Lenin had met his match and did not get his money back. On another occasion his protest was more successful. Not long after he had bought a new bike, a nasty incident occurred. In December 1909, while returning from an aeroplane show a dozen miles from central Paris at Juvisy-sur-Orge, he was knocked from the saddle by a motor car and badly bruised. The bike lay in a mangled mess by the roadside. Fortunately there were witnesses and Lenin sought redress through a lawyer. In this he showed the same persistence that he had shown in Syzran in 1892 when prosecuting Arefev the merchant. Marxist zeal also came into play when Lenin found out that the Parisian motorist was a viscount. Lenin, himself a hereditary nobleman, showed no sense of class solidarity and sued for financial compensation.[18]

Lenin had never taken to Paris and went around describing it as 'a foul hole'.[19] Politics were part of the reason. During his French sojourn he was annoyed with the Mensheviks. He was annoyed, too, with anti-Duma Bolsheviks such as Bogdanov. Indeed, he was equally annoyed with those Bolsheviks who, despite agreeing with Lenin about Bogdanov, did not show the degree of annoyance that Lenin required of true Bolsheviks. About the other parties Lenin cared hardly at all, and when he met up with Socialist-Revolutionaries in the Parisian cafés frequented by the Russian revolutionary émigré 'community', he could be quite affable. Nevertheless his jokes took a combative form, as Viktor Chernov recalled:[20]

> I said to him: 'Vladimir Ilich, if you come to power, you'll start hanging the Mensheviks the very next day.' And he glanced at me and said: 'It will be after we've hanged the last Socialist-Revolutionary that the first Menshevik will get hanged by us.' Then he frowned and gave a laugh.

Quite apart from his gallows humour, Lenin was exhibiting an unceasing obsession with factional disputes inside the Russian Social-Democratic Labour Party. Bolsheviks had entered the Third State Duma and Lenin did not need Martov and Dan to help him to compel the Bolshevik faction to put up candidates in the Duma elections. Thus the need to keep the Mensheviks sweet had passed. Without delay Lenin resumed polemics against Menshevism, and his jokes reflected this.

Lenin's struggle against Bogdanov was even fiercer. The detestation of the Duma among Bogdanov and his sympathisers retained the capacity to destabilise Bolshevik factional policy. Some went so far as to advocate that Bolshevik elected deputies should immediately be withdrawn from the Third State Duma. Others, and Bogdanov was one of these, wished to deliver an ultimatum to the deputies to withdraw on pain of expulsion from the faction. The first group were called the Otzovists ('Recallists'), the second the Ultimatumists. Both groups also argued that the party should concentrate on preparing for and organising armed insurrection. For Lenin, they were living in a mental pressure chamber that had rendered them incapable of appreciating current political realities.

Lenin also brought up disagreements of an even more fundamental nature. Whereas Bogdanov gave priority to encouraging the working class to undertake its cultural self-development, Lenin stressed the guiding role of intellectuals. Admittedly Lenin did not insist that the intelligentsia should come from a middle-class background. But Bogdanov remained appalled by the Leninist idea that socialism had to be introduced to the workers by intellectuals; indeed he stipulated that the general culture of society had to be transformed so that socialist ideas might mature. The dominant present-day culture, according to Bogdanov, was 'bourgeois' since it was focussed upon individualism, authoritarian commands, formality, hypocrisy. A new culture – a 'proletarian culture' – had to be introduced, and Bogdanov suggested that it would be beyond the capacity of intellectuals to invent it because they themselves were the product of the culture of the bourgeoisie. All this and more infuriated Lenin. Bogdanov even suggested that Lenin's notions about absolute truth, about eternal categories of thought and about the demonstrable reality of the external world were old-fashioned poppycock. Lenin, unlike Bogdanov, refused to involve himself in the broad philosophical debates in Europe of the time. Bogdanov had read Immanuel Kant and neo-Kantians such as Richard Avenarius and Ernst Mach. He admired but refused to idolise Marx. At the Vaasa dacha he had been writing a book, *Empiriomonism*, which recapitulated his exploratory ideas. He simply fizzed with intellectual vitality. Lenin thought the time had come to mount a frontal attack on him and his world-view.

Lenin had nothing to lose. The anti-Leninist Bolsheviks were highly influential inside the Bolshevik faction at home and abroad; they may even have been a majority. Equally pertinent was Lenin's recognition that there was little immediate chance of another revolutionary crisis in the Russian Empire. It therefore felt opportune to resume the old schismatic tactics. If the second period of emigration was to be made endurable, Lenin believed, he had to recruit and mobilise a reliable Bolshevik faction in the image of himself.

Thus when Maxim Gorki had invited Bogdanov and Lenin together to his villa on Capri, Lenin at first refused, even though he had asked to come and stay. Lenin eventually went in April 1908 and suppressed his feelings to the extent that he played chess with his old partner in chess and politics. A degree of joviality was obtained. The problem was that Lenin's competitive side got the better of him; Gorki was astounded at how angry and 'childish' he became when he lost a game.[21] This happened even when Lenin and Bogdanov were avoiding conversations about politics. Only when he went fishing did Lenin relax. The local fishermen took him and Gorki out in their boats and taught them how to use a line without a rod. The trick was to wrap the end of the line over the forefinger of one hand and wait for the vibration signalling that a fish was biting. The fishermen told him what it would sound like: 'Così: drin, drin. Capisce?' Their Italian charm captivated Lenin, and as soon as he got a nibble, he cried out: 'Drin, drin!' Afterwards the fishermen called him Signor Drin-Drin – the only one of his nicknames not chosen with the Revolution in mind. They missed him when he left the island, asking Gorki: 'How is Drin-Drin getting on? The tsar hasn't caught him yet?'[22]

Lenin had stayed just for a week. He did not understand much Italian, far less could he make sense of the thick Neapolitan dialect. He had been a busy visitor, managing to squeeze into it a walk up Mount Vesuvius on the mainland as well as a visit to the museums of Naples. But he felt restored by his trip. He had loved the villa, the azure sea, the freshly caught fish, the operatic ballads, the generous, lively inhabitants. The trip to the Italian south had raised his spirits; he was ready again for the political fray.

Taking the ferry over to Naples, Lenin made the long ride north by train through Rome back across the Alps to Switzerland. His mind was made up: once he had reached Geneva, he would break definitively with Alexander Bogdanov and his sympathisers and open a campaign to rid the Bolshevik faction of them. It was a fast-changing situation. Bogdanov was nowhere near as obsessed as Lenin with the minutiae of political organisation. He was tired out by the endless scheming that engaged the leading Bolsheviks; he dearly wanted to have more time for his writing. In short, Bogdanov had had enough of Lenin and, after their Capri meeting, he resigned from the editorial board of the Bolshevik newspaper *Proletari* rather than put up with personal vilification. But because Bogdanov retained his place in the Bolshevik Centre it was by no means clear that Lenin would succeed in holding Bolsheviks as a faction to the line of supporting participation in the State Duma and legal public organisations in Russia. Gorki went on trying to convince himself and his friends that Lenin would not take his disagreement with Bogdanov to the point of splitting the Bolshevik faction.[23] But Gorki was wrong: Lenin was firmly resolved upon a break with Bogdanov.

What made this feasible was that Lenin's group had recently attained a degree of financial independence from Bogdanov. It had come about in a most peculiar way. A young revolutionary sympathiser N. P. Shmidt, nephew of the wealthy Moscow industrialist Savva Morozov, had died suddenly in 1907, and his will left many hundreds of thousands of rubles to his two sisters. Lenin helped to devise a scheme to lay his hands on this legacy by contriving to get two Leninist Bolsheviks, V. K. Taratuta and A. M. Andrikanis, to woo the sisters, marry them and obtain funds for the faction. This was a morally shabby scheme. But for Lenin the criterion was whether a particular action aided the Revolution, and the emotional deception of two heiresses fell well within the zone of acceptability. It had been a theme of Lenin's since adolescence that 'sentimentality' had no place in politics. Now he refined this point in a paradoxical fashion by exploiting sentiment for political gain.

Lenin confessed to friends that he would not have had the nerve to carry out the scheme himself. He had been brought up to behave well in personal relations, and everything about the scheme was distasteful to him. But he also had a weakness for rough working-class Bolsheviks like Taratuta, whose bravado appealed to him: 'He's good inasmuch as he'll stop at nothing. Here, tell me directly, could you go after a rich merchant lady for her money? No. And I wouldn't either, I couldn't conquer myself. But Viktor [Taratuta] could ... That's what makes him an irreplaceable person.'[24] Amazingly the scheme worked. Taratuta and Andrikanis were two highly disingenuous charmers, and they managed to entice the Shmidt sisters into marriage with them. The problem for Lenin was that he depended on the Bolshevik suitors sticking to their factional obligations. After the dual weddings he waited nervously to see what would happen. In fact Andrikanis double-crossed him and apparently not even Taratuta handed over everything as agreed. But a substantial sum eventually came his way and placed him in a position of financial independence from the Bolshevik Centre. At last he did not depend on Bogdanov and his friends.

First, in February 1909, he broke off personal relations with Bogdanov. Lenin had done this once before, in 1904, when he felt traduced by V. A. Noskov; and he persuaded himself that Bogdanov had also put himself beyond the pale. By June 1909 the scene was set for a final confrontation at the *Proletari* editorial board meeting held in Paris's Caput café and attended by members of the Bolshevik Centre. Lenin had prepared carefully, and a majority of the participants were willing to support him. Bogdanov's policies were criticised; he was declared, by virtue of his 'deviations from the path of revolutionary Marxism', to have automatically broken away from the Bolsheviks.

Lenin challenged Bogdanov even on philosophical ground. For Lenin, like all Marxists, believed that a political and economic vision needed to be directed through a sound epistemological prism. Lenin used the opportunity of his trip to London for the duration of May 1908 to complete his researches on his book *Materialism and Empiriocriticism*. Based at 21 Tavistock Place in Bloomsbury, he lived close by the British Museum, which he visited daily.[25] Quickly – too quickly – he read the major texts of the philosophers admired by Bogdanov. The book was produced in fast order, and Lenin intended it as a weapon in the struggle for supremacy in the Bolshevik faction. Its chapters became a philosophical bible for official Soviet intellectuals after 1917 even though much private derision was showered on it. The intrinsic ideological reasons why Lenin was angry enough to write it are clear. He was a grandson of the European Enlightenment. He believed in the kind of science advocated by philosophers in the eighteenth century. For him, there were such things as absolute truth and the independent reality of the external world. Persons who dissented from this, even if they claimed to be Marxists, belonged to the 'camp' of political reaction.

Bogdanov, in his eyes, was a dangerous relativist. Bogdanov believed in nothing. Bogdanov could not see that some things had been discovered and proved once and for all; indeed Bogdanov did not believe that 'seeing' was a reliable mode of cognition at all. Lenin had a profound faith in Marx, in the eighteenth-century ideals of the natural sciences, in the capacity of the human mind to register a wholly accurate picture of the universe around itself. He thought of the mind as a camera and of the camera as an infallible guide to cognition. By repudiating this way of understanding the world, Bogdanov was siding with priests and mystics. Lenin accused Bogdanov not only of having given up on Marxism but also of having given up on the Russian labour movement and on genuinely practicable revolutionary ideas.

Although the timing of the attack was politically motivated, Lenin truly considered Bogdanov had abandoned key precepts of Marxism. But there has to be a question about the substratum of his assumptions. Lenin was saying that epistemology begat social analysis which begat economics which begat political strategy. Thus Bogdanov, being wrong about epistemology, was bound to be wrong about politics. Lenin liked to give the impression that his own thought by contrast followed a logical pattern. But he protested too much. When we consider his several abrupt shifts in policy in the course of his career, the suspicion surely arises that he needed to entertain this image of his thought in order to gratify his part-political, part-instinctive desire to do whatever would put him and his faction into a position of power in Russia. The protestations of ideological purity were but a mask; and when he donned the mask and looked in the mirror, he was not necessarily aware that his face was occluded from view. This was a source of strength for him as a politician; too much self-awareness would have turned him into a self-questioning politician like Martov or Chernov. Lenin wanted to conquer, and he let nothing complicate his quest for victory.

From 1908 he had nothing good to say about Bogdanov. The help he had received from him in 1904, when Lenin's fortunes were frail, receded into oblivion. The comradeship of the Lenins and Bogdanovs in Kuokkala in 1906–7 faded from his memory. Expecting the same forgetfulness to be shown by his associates, he took it amiss that his sister Anna thought that *Materialism and Empiriocriticism* overdid the polemical crudity.[26] He would have been even angrier if he had known that his sisters Anna and Maria were reading and enjoying Bogdanov's novel *Engineer Menni*.[27]

Lenin had concentrated his energy on attacking Bogdanov and assumed that any concession to his factional enemies would dissipate his effectiveness. This was a militancy he practised throughout his career. Every time he split his party or faction, Lenin believed he was ridding himself of unreliable elements and consolidating the core of the Bolshevik organisation under his control. He was unwise in this because each split left him with supporters who objected to aspects of his policies, and a smaller organisation did not result in a more cohesive compound. Indeed this was the case at the very same meeting at which he defeated Bogdanov. The Bolshevik Centre, while agreeing with Lenin on the need to reject Bogdanov, insisted against Lenin's wishes on seeking to found a legal large-circulation newspaper in St Petersburg. It even contemplated closing down the émigré weekly *Proletari*, and although Lenin managed to avoid this, he had to agree to its being published only on a monthly basis. Worse for Lenin was the Bolshevik Centre's desire to negotiate with Trotski in Vienna with the idea of offering Bolshevik collaboration and funds for the running of Trotski's popular newspaper *Pravda*.

What Lenin had not bargained for was that, in getting rid of Bogdanov and the anti-Duma Bolsheviks, he was tipping the balance of opinion inside the Bolshevik faction in favour of those who sought to co-operate with the Mensheviks. Prominent among them was the otherwise inconsequential figure of A. I. Lyubimov. The Bolshevik Centre rubbed home its message by choosing Lyubimov as its secretary. Yet Lenin refused to listen; instead he threw himself into a hysterical, vain effort to get Lyubimov to toughen the Bolshevik Centre's terms for collaboration with Trotski. Lenin's family life did not lighten his mood. For once, it was he who had to look after his relatives rather than they who had to tend to him. Maria Ilinichna had fallen ill first with typhus and then with appendicitis, and Lenin had to play an active part in securing proper treatment for her. (Always his adoring and overawed sister, she appreciated his endeavours on her behalf.)[28] But he had been driving himself too hard on too many fronts. After the Bolshevik Centre meeting he could take it no longer, and, together with Nadya, her mother and Maria, he moved off to the village of Bombon in Seine-et-Marne. Meekly he agreed to terms that, for him, were stiff indeed: he was to avoid talking and writing about politics.[29]

He did not keep his word and nobody seriously expected him to. Among his supporters there were still those who queried why one man could so easily reduce the party to a shambles. The Menshevik Fëdor Dan had often heard the question. His answer was straightforward: 'Oh, it's because there's no such person who is so preoccupied twenty-four hours a day with revolution, who thinks no other thoughts except those about revolution and who even dreams in his sleep about revolution. So just you try and cope with him!'[30] Dan had put it in a nutshell. Lenin was difficult because he was a factionalist and he was a factionalist because he thought only his ideas would genuinely advance the cause of the Revolution.

It was Bolsheviks and their sympathisers, however, who criticised him most severely. They could no longer give him the benefit of the doubt. Gorki could not abide his 'hooligan tone'. When *Materialism and Empiriocriticism* appeared under the imprint of St Petersburg publishers L. Krumbyugel, he read only a few pages before throwing the book across the room:[31]

All these people shouting to all and sundry – 'I'm a Marxist' and 'I'm a proletarian' – and then immediately sitting on the heads of their neighbours and barking in their face – are repugnant to me like all philistines; each of them is for me 'misanthrope entertaining his own fantasy' as [the short-story writer] Leskov called them. A person is rubbish if a vivid consciousness of his linkage with people isn't beating inside him and if he's willing to sacrifice comradely feeling on the altar of his vanity.

Lenin is like that in his book. His dispute about 'truth' is conducted not so that truth might be victorious but so as to prove: 'I'm a Marxist! The world's best Marxist is me!'

These were words that would have wounded Lenin if Gorki had said them openly rather than expressed them in a private letter to the

Bogdanovs. Whereas the Mensheviks accused Lenin of megalomania, Gorki – a Bolshevik sympathiser – suggested that his was a personality driven by vainglory.

Lenin's fortunes went on dipping. On their return from Seine-et-Marne, after a five-week sojourn, he and Nadya took a flat in the quiet Rue Marie-Rose. Lenin was immediately angered by the news that other Bolshevik Centre members had gone beyond their overtures to Trotski and were contacting Martov. Even his closest associate Grigori Zinoviev refrained from supporting him.

In a rage Lenin withdrew from the editorial board of the Central Committee's newspaper *Social-Democrat*. His political obsessiveness usually permitted him to recognise the advantages of emotional restraint, but not always. Lenin sometimes failed to hold the lid on himself and, in these instances, no one else could press it down either. No sooner had he resigned than he regretted his action, and on calm reflection he withdrew his resignation. But then in January 1910 came the long-awaited Central Committee plenum in Paris. This was a real ordeal. The united Central Committee, which included more Bolsheviks than Mensheviks, ordered the Bolshevik Centre to be closed down and the Bolshevik factional monthly *Proletari* to cease publication. It demanded a switch of the central party leadership's centre of gravity from Paris to Russia. A Russian Board was created and given the right to act in the Central Committee's name. The Shmidt monies, obtained by the Bolsheviks without any Menshevik assistance, were to be handed over to the Central Committee and to a group of trustees consisting of the German Marxists Karl Kautsky, Franz Mehring and Clara Zetkin. The defeat of Bogdanov in June 1909 had been undone on a broader level by the Central Committee plenum.

Yet Lenin had recovered his grip; by 1910 he was his ebullient old self. The Marxist leaders in the Russian Empire who criticised him and other émigrés were themselves in disarray. The Okhrana was breaking the local committees with ease. Some Marxists, most of them Mensheviks, were so dispirited that they campaigned for the party to be disbanded and for activists to operate entirely in the legal workers' movement. These 'Liquidators' as Lenin dubbed them were not a majority of the party, but their existence allowed the Bolsheviks to claim that only they could keep up the spirit of Revolution. The Bolshevik leftists, whether they were Recallists or Ultimatumists, had a diminishing appeal to politically inclined factory workers. Lenin sensed that his time might soon come around again.

In an emotional sense his second chance had already arrived. His marriage to Nadya had never involved deep romantic feelings on his part, or indeed hers, and there must have been occasions when other Bolshevik women had a strong appeal for him. Over the years, too, the Graves's disease had taken its toll on Nadya's looks. Poor woman! Her eyes protruded and her neck bulged as it tightened its grip. Her weight increased and she had heart palpitations, and both she and Lenin had given up thinking that they would be able to have children. One of the widespread features of Graves's disease is the infrequency of menstrual periods for female sufferers. Whether this was a problem for Nadezhda Krupskaya is unclear, but it is a distinct possibility. Lenin sympathised and urged her to undergo a surgical operation to try and eliminate the condition. But she refused, no doubt being aware that the operation was neither guaranteed to succeed nor even very safe. She was no longer the vigorous young woman that Lenin had married. She had become dowdy and at forty-one years, in 1910, she looked her age. She had never been vivacious but now she was ponderous and ailing.

Until then, apparently, Lenin resisted sexual temptation. This restraint, if indeed it had been holding since his marriage in Siberia, seems to have broken down in Paris when he became acquainted with Inessa Armand. Everyone knew her simply as Inessa. She was a widow. Her father had been French, her mother English. Inessa had lived in Russia as a child; on growing up, she married Alexander Armand, in whose parents' family she was training to become a domestic tutor. She had five children, but her marriage became a sham after she started sleeping with her brother-in-law Vladimir Armand. This liaison, however, was short lived: Vladimir died of tuberculosis in 1909. Inessa then moved to western Europe with three of her children (and her husband Alexander continued to support her there financially). She had already been involved in revolutionary activity and been exiled by the Ministry of the Interior to Archangel in the Russian far north, and in Paris she aligned herself with the Bolshevik faction in the Russian Social-Democratic Labour Party. Her fluency in Russian, French and English ensured her a warm welcome.

Inessa Armand was a fine-looking woman in her mid-thirties with long, wavy auburn hair. The pictures in the archives show that she had a beautiful face. When reproduced in Soviet history books, they never did her justice[32] – and the thought occurs that the authorities, wishing to downplay speculation about a relationship between her and Lenin, tried to make her seem visually less appealing than she was. She had high, well-defined cheekbones. Her nose was slightly curved and her nostrils were wonderfully flared; her upper lip was slightly protrusive. Her teeth were white and even. She had lustrous, dark eyebrows. And she had kept her figure after having her children. In pictures taken with them as adolescents she looks more like an elder sister than a mother; her appearance was such that the Okhrana agents underestimated her age by several years. Inessa was also vivacious. She liked to ride side-saddle when she could, and to play Beethoven on the piano. She adored her children, but did not let them get in the way of her wish to enjoy herself. In particular, she had an uninhibited attitude to extramarital relationships.

The relationship between Lenin and Inessa Armand began slowly, and the passion originated on her side. She later wrote eloquently about this to him:[33]

> At that time I was terribly scared of you. The desire existed to see you, but it seemed better to drop dead on the spot than to come into your presence; and when for some reason you popped into N. K. [Krupskaya]'s room, I instantly lost control and behaved like a fool. Only in Longjumeau and in the following autumn in connection with translations and so on did I somewhat get used to you. I so much loved not only to listen to you but also to look at you as you spoke. Firstly, your face is so enlivened and, secondly, it was convenient to watch because you didn't notice at that time.

In the same letter she added: 'At that time I definitely wasn't in love with you, but even then I loved you very much.'[34] Soon she fell in love with him. No letter survives to demonstrate that he in his turn fell equally for her, and this has led some writers to conclude that there was no affair.[35] But Lenin's epistolary silence is not surprising. In mid-1914, when the relationship had waned, he asked her to return the correspondence he had sent her;[36] it is difficult to imagine that his purpose was other than to destroy the evidence of what had taken place between them.

The associates and acquaintances of the Bolshevik leader took it for granted that the two were having an affair in 1910–12. When the French Marxist Charles Rappoport came upon them talking in a café on the Avenue d'Orléans, he reported that Lenin 'could not take his Mongolian eyes off this little Frenchwoman'.[37] A hint was dropped also by Lidia Fotieva, one of Lenin's secretaries after the October Revolution, who recalled from her own visits to Lenin's apartment that Nadya no longer slept in the marital bedroom but in the bedroom of her mother.[38] In September 1911, Inessa moved into the Rue Marie-Rose and lived next door to the Lenins at no. 2.

Admittedly, the evidence is circumstantial. But the intensity of the letters they subsequently sent each other makes it unlikely that Lenin was just flirting with Inessa; the probability is that they had had an extramarital affair. A reciprocal passion had obviously existed even if Lenin, unlike Inessa, did not explicitly refer to it in the correspondence. What, though, was the attraction between the two of them? For Lenin, it was probably crucial that Inessa was someone who, as she confided to her last diary, thought that life ought to be lived in the service of some great cause. The Bolshevik vision of revolutionary strategy was exactly such a cause for her. And, of course, she was lively, beautiful and 'cultured' in the broadest sense. No wonder Lenin took to her. She in turn left a record as to why she was attracted by him. She adored his lively eyes, his self-belief and his intimidating presence. Even his initial unawareness of her intense interest in him had an appeal to her, but she found him irresistibly fascinating, and she absolutely had to have him.

For a time she surely succeeded. The victim of this process was Nadya, who had dedicated her life to Lenin's career since their marriage in 1898. She was an enduring soul. Yet she understandably drew the line at participating in a permanent *ménage à trois*. The detail of their disagreement was carried to their deaths with them, and rumours sprang up to fill the void. It is said that Nadya wanted to walk out and leave the lovers to their relationship. Lenin was aghast that his marriage might end. A sense of indebtedness to Nadya may have influenced him, and he perhaps also was sorry for her difficulties with Graves's disease. Possibly, too, his happiness depended on having Inessa without losing Nadya. In Nadya he had a personal secretary and household organiser. Inessa would never be as competent as Nadya at this dual role. She might not even agree to fulfil it at all. And so, according to the rumours, Lenin urged Nadya to change her mind: 'Stay!'[39] And Nadya did as requested, but only after being assured that his passion for Inessa did not exclude Nadezhda from his affections.

Nadya and Inessa felt no hostility for each other, and worked together in the party school a dozen miles to the south of Paris at Longjumeau in late 1911 where the Ulyanovs rented an apartment at 140 La Grande Rue.[40] Furthermore, it was a lasting sadness to both Lenin and Nadya that their marriage had produced no children. The presence of Inessa's offspring in the neighbouring house on Rue Marie-Rose

brought delight to the Ulyanov couple, who acted like uncle and aunt to
the youngsters not only in Paris but years later in Moscow.

In other ways, too, Lenin enjoyed life to the full. He had been
accustomed as an emigrant to swapping apartments pretty frequently as
well as moving from country to country. But in the three years after
escaping from Finland at the end of 1907 he was a political gypsy,
travelling across the middle of Europe from top to bottom giving talks
and attending meetings – and, of course, having holidays. Among the
major European cities he visited were Berlin, Bern, Brussels, Copenhagen, Geneva, Leipzig, Liège, Lucerne, London, Naples, Nice, Paris,
Stuttgart and Zurich. He had plenty of time for relaxation, too, in Breton
villages and on Capri. He was learning the knack of balancing his
political preoccupation with enjoying a more private lifestyle. He derived
great pleasure in August 1910 when he arranged to meet his mother in
Stockholm and live together with her for a fortnight (and he cherished
the Swedish chequered blanket she bought for him there). The party
school he established at Longjumeau also lightened his spirits. He
relished the opportunity to give lectures and see the keen Russian
working-class pupils whom he could turn into Bolsheviks.

He never eliminated his tendency to fret. There was plenty to push
him over the edge: the Shmidt legacy, the bicycle accident and the (not
very) philosophical polemic with Bogdanov. But he managed to keep
calmer than was usual for him. He travelled, he wrote, he studied, he
biked, he listened to music, and especially he enjoyed the company of
Inessa Armand.

And he could see a way out of the organisational impasse that had
cornered him inside his faction. The Central Committee of the entire
Russian Social-Democratic Labour Party met in Paris on 28 May 1911.
Lenin attended with some trepidation: he could not expect to exercise
any kind of control over its proceedings while Menshevik-conciliating
Bolsheviks like A. I. Lyubimov held authority. But the Paris decisions
played into his hands. Three bodies were created: the Foreign Organisa-
tional Commission, the Russian Organisational Commission and the
Technical Commission. The first two were instructed to convoke a party
conference. The Mensheviks were reluctant to take part even before
Sergo Ordzhonikidze, Lenin's supporter in the Russian Organisational
Commission, presented an ultimatum to the Foreign Organisational
Commission to submit itself to the Russian Organisational Commission.
At this Leo Jogiches, the Polish representative from the Central Com-
mittee, gave up on the party and withdrew. This gave Ordzhonikidze

and Lenin a wonderful opportunity. A Bolshevik gathering took place in Paris in December 1911 masquerading as a meeting of representatives of the entire party. The participants, led by Lenin, decided to replace the Foreign Organisational Commission with a Committee of the Foreign Organisation and to empower this new body to hold a party conference.

This émigré flurry taxed the understanding of all but the most obsessive factionalists. What really mattered were not the organisational changes in themselves. No one but a Lenin loyalist could say that he had acted within the spirit of the regulatory framework. But he had got his way. Against every expectation he had suddenly leaped from a lowly position where he was little more than the controversial leader of a sub-faction in the party to a new peak: he was about to hold a party conference at which he would be able to declare that his sub-faction was equivalent to the party as a whole. Then, he anticipated, it would not count for much that other factions continued to exist. Lenin would have the aura of constitutional legitimacy. He would be able to select a new Central Committee and the editorial board of a new party newspaper. Bolshevism would at last become a party. The three years of the second emigration had started in humiliation and were about to culminate in success. Only a factional recidivist such as Lenin could delude himself with such optimism.

12

ALMOST RUSSIA!

1912–1914

Most of the great social theorists in the nineteenth century – Herbert Spencer, Auguste Comte, John Stuart Mill, Jeremy Bentham, Karl Marx and Friedrich Engels – were inheritors of the eighteenth-century Enlightenment. Their understanding of human culture, organisation and behaviour was linked to assumptions about the basic rationality and predictability of people. But they had not had everything their way. Thomas Carlyle had proposed that most people in most societies were capable of rational, purposeful activity only when guided by charismatic leaders. The theologian Søren Kierkegaard and the novelist Fëdor Dostoevski pointed to dark recesses in the motivations of human conduct. By the end of the nineteenth century, Sigmund Freud and other psychologists proposed that the mind has a subconscious capacity inducing people to do things which they do not deliberately contrive. The philosopher Friedrich Nietzsche rejected the Enlightenment's commitment to Progress. Like Carlyle, he contended that problems of the human condition could be alleviated, if it was at all possible, only when great men lead their societies and offer themselves as heroic models. Other thinkers, too, highlighted the virtues of individual leadership in counteracting the less attractive features of contemporary industrial society. Among them were the outstanding social theorists Max Weber, Robert Michels, Gaetano Mosca and Gustave Le Bon.

But were their ideas a source for Lenin's kind of politics? Certainly *What Is to Be Done?* picked out the crucial role of leadership and Lenin behaved as if the revolutionary cause would be ruined unless he was in charge. He passionately believed his own guidance of the party and the party's guidance of 'the masses' to be indispensable if the Russian labour movement was to adopt the correct political ideas. Lenin gave the impression of sensing a special destiny for himself; Grigori Zinoviev confided that Lenin felt '*he* had been "called"'.[1]

There is little direct evidence that Lenin paid attention to those contemporary intellectual trends. He hated the way other Marxists such as Alexander Bogdanov, Nikolai Bukharin and Anatoli Lunacharski took up ideas from the fashionable books on philosophy, culture, sociology and economics regardless of whether the contents were congruent with Marxism. Lenin had formed his world-view in the final two decades of the nineteenth century, and no thinker emerged after 1900 whom he admired. He was comfortable about his own fundamental assumptions and did not itch to re-examine them. He had yet to settle his practical policies, and went on changing them nearly until the day he died. But he had a settled intellectual physiognomy. Carlyle, Freud, Kierkegaard, Le Bon, Michels, Nietzsche and Weber were ignored, totally or very nearly, in his works (although he was to keep Nietzsche's *Thus Spake Zarathustra* in his Kremlin book cabinet).[2] His preoccupation was to widen and deepen his knowledge of Marx, Engels, Plekhanov and Kautsky. Equipped with references to the works of these admired figures, Lenin could contrive to appear orthodox even while asserting the most unorthodox analysis. He was a brilliant, ruthless disputant, and could always find some justification in the Marxist classics – classics that were far from being homogeneous – for the policies of his party. Lenin believed in leadership and was pleased when he was exercising it; and engagement with the general intellectual problems posed by the critics of Marxism would only have distracted him.

But the very fact that he stressed his claim to Marxist orthodoxy gives rise to the suspicion that he lived a secret intellectual life. About his admiration for the Russian agrarian-socialist terrorists there can be no doubt, even though, after the uproar over *What Is to Be Done?*, he had ceased to mention this in public. But was this secretiveness confined to his fondness for these Russian terrorists?

The answer, probably, is no. After 1917 he was to refer admiringly in correspondence to Machiavelli; the Florentine writer's justification of the uses of brutality in governance especially appealed to him. Then there was the little bronze statue that he was to keep on his desk in the Kremlin. This was a representation of a monkey examining a human skull and was an obvious sign of Lenin's fascination with the ideas of Charles Darwin.[3] Nothing is more implausible than the notion that when Lenin entered a library he examined only the works of Marxism and economic statistics. In the Great War we know for certain that he picked up and devoured the German philosopher Hegel and the German military theorist Clausewitz – and it can be shown that they left an imprint on his thought. He also returned to his Classical authors, especially Aristotle. From his notebooks we can see that Hegel,

Clausewitz and Aristotle helped him to sharpen his interpretation of Marxism and his strategy for Revolution. Perhaps Machiavelli and Darwin did the same for him. Darwin in particular was popular among Marxists, and it would be astonishing if Lenin was unfamiliar with his argument about 'the survival of the fittest'. Both Machiavelli and Darwin would anyway have been congenial to him, who had detested 'sentimentality' in politics and who relished struggle almost as a way of life. If anyone ever was, Lenin was a fighter by nature.

Outside his family no one got close to him without eventually querying his combative style. But for a while he kept the admiration of the Bolshevik organisers of the next Party Conference. Chief among these was Sergo Ordzhonikidze, who was in charge of the arrangements for the next Party Conference. Ordzhonikidze was a fiery, hard-drinking and industrious Georgian devoted to the cause of Revolution; he despised what he saw as the half-heartedness of the Menshevik revolutionary strategy. No intellectual, he was impatient about establishing clandestine party groups in Russia, overturning tsarism and making the advance towards a socialist society. Lenin was Ordzhonikidze's hero and Lenin for his part welcomed his admirer as precisely the kind of practical, ruthless organiser that the Bolsheviks needed.

Journeying out from Russia to make contact with the Bolshevik emigrants, Ordzhonikidze agreed with Lenin that something ought to be done to pull the faction together. They proposed to hold a party conference for this purpose. But for a location they decided to avoid cities such as Paris and Geneva where the Russian Marxists lived in colonies. Instead they would seek to hold it in Prague, capital of the Bohemian lands in the east of the Habsburg Empire. The choice was a cunning one. Prague was an awkward destination for travellers from both Russia and France. It was also a place without a colony of Russian Marxists. At the same time it was a place where the police could be relied upon to leave the delegates alone; indeed the Habsburg Empire welcomed almost every kind of revolutionary who wanted to strike tsarism down. Furthermore, the Czech Marxists would definitely give assistance to any conference organised by their Russian comrades. Lenin and Ordzhonikidze would be able to exploit this situation to the advantage of the Bolshevik faction. The few delegates who might arrive in Prague would, with hardly an exception, be Bolsheviks. The proceedings would be secret and would be dominated by Lenin and Ordzhonikidze, who could argue that the Bolsheviks had been the largest of the factions at the Fifth Congress of the Russian Social-Democratic Labour

Party and therefore had the right to guide party policies with the minimum of concessions to Menshevism.

This calculation proved correct as the Conference delegates assembled in Prague, were greeted warmly by the Czech socialist leadership and were put up in houses around the centre. Proceedings were held in the centre of city. The venue was the Workers' House in the middle of Hybernska Street, which stretches from the medieval Powder Tower down to a railway station. The Workers' House, owned by the Czech Social-Democratic Party, was a three-storey building with a large internal courtyard; originally it had been the Kinsky Palace.

Lenin and his comrades made their arrangements for the Conference undisturbed. Although they had sent invitations to a few Mensheviks who sided with Plekhanov, they avoided contact with those other Mensheviks – the great majority of them – who refused to break off relations with the so-called Liquidàtors. Trotski was infuriated by this and organised a rival party conference in Vienna, and practically all Mensheviks felt that Trotski's was the meeting that they should attend. The result was that the Prague Conference had only eighteen participants and sixteen of them were Bolsheviks. On reaching Prague, some of these were offended by the discovery that other factions had no representation, and tried to rectify the imbalance by sending out last-minute invitations of their own. Ordzhonikidze saw nothing wrong with their initiative; presumably he calculated that the opponents of the Bolsheviks would be unable reach the Conference in time and in a number sufficient to gain a majority. But Lenin would take no chances and threatened to walk out if the invitations were accepted. This was stupidly excessive even for Lenin. Ordzhonikidze already thought that the fractiousness of 'the damned emigration' was ruining the party. Now he discovered that Lenin was the worst offender and joined the other Bolshevik delegates in criticising him personally.

There had been no Bolshevik gathering where Lenin was given so hard a time. The delegates were perplexed by a basic question: if Leninist Bolsheviks agreed with Mensheviks about the importance of legal political activity, why was Lenin still using a megaphone to announce the iniquity of Martov and his fellow Mensheviks? Lenin ducked the question. In truth there was no intellectually respectable answer available.

The Prague Conference at any rate went ahead without additional arrivals and claimed the right to elect a new Central Committee and ordain policies for the entire party. To this large extent Lenin got exactly what he had been after. The new Central Committee was a Bolshevik

Central Committee, with the exception of the Menshevik David Shvartsman. As Lenin wished, the Conference also approved the party's enhanced commitment to taking part in the State Duma and other Russian legal organisations. But Lenin lost a lot of the personal authority he had held. Ordzhonikidze and others wanted power to belong to the leading activists operating in Russia and not in the emigration. This was to be achieved firstly by withdrawing the official recognition of the Committee of the Foreign Organisation as the Central Committee's adjunct abroad – and it had been through the Committee of the Foreign Organisation, with Inessa Armand as its secretary, that Lenin had exerted heavy influence over both his fellow emigrants and the party as a whole. Secondly, the Conference ruled that the Central Committee's seven members would include only two émigrés: Lenin and Zinoviev. The centre of gravity in the leadership was about to be shifted away from émigré factional disputes to organisation and propaganda in the Russian Empire.

Yet Ordzhonikidze could not know of other forces at work that would undermine any decisions taken by the Bolsheviks in Prague. The Okhrana saw Lenin as a brilliant potential executor of the task demanded by the Emperor: the disintegration of the Russian Social-Democratic Labour Party. The enhancement of Lenin's career was the Okhrana's confidential priority.

The instruments lay easily to hand after the Prague Conference. One of the members of the new Central Committee was the St Petersburg trade union organiser Roman Malinovski. Malinovski was a Bolshevik of working-class origin and was a spell-binding speaker in front of a crowd; he was one of the candidates successfully put up for election to the Fourth State Duma later in 1912. And he was highly regarded by Lenin. The problem was that, unbeknown to Lenin, Malinovski had fallen on hard times and had secretly become a paid agent of the Okhrana. His main task was to remove any obstacles to the schismatic measures proposed by Lenin. Malinovski's authority among Bolsheviks in Russia rose as the Okhrana arrested the other members of the Central Committee when they returned to Russia. With each arrest, Lenin's position was likewise enhanced. Co-optation of new members gave him a chance to choose activists whom he had reason to trust. He had not been cowed by Ordzhonikidze at the Conference, and had even managed a laugh when the emigrants' contribution to the party had been disparaged. 'I have no fear'. he declared, 'of factional struggle being condemned.' He had suffered and surmounted greater setbacks in the past.

Leaving Prague for Paris, Lenin continued his tirades. He had no intention of abiding by the letter or spirit of Ordzhonikidze's reform of the Bolshevik leadership. Soon, he thought, political life would go on as before, and he wrote to his mother that he was staying put in Paris. Lenin would not be ruled by Conference; he would work to set himself up more solidly as the faction's dominant figure.

Inside the Russian Social-Democratic Labour Party he already had a substantial reputation; indeed he was its most notorious figure. The leaderships of the other Russian political parties, too, were aware of his ideas and activity. All the socialist emigrants were acquainted with him in the Russian colonies of Zurich, Geneva and Paris. German and Polish Marxist leaders were painfully conscious of what he got up to. For them, Lenin was the single greatest obstacle to unity among Russian Marxists. His general significance was also recognised in the form of fifteen biographical entries on him in various Russian encyclopaedias by the time he returned to Russia in 1917.[4] But this fame was restricted to a tiny world and certainly did not extend to much of the serious reading public in his country. One of Lenin's followers in St Petersburg, Mikhail Kedrov, valiantly tried to put out a three-volume edition of his collected works, but collected only two hundred subscriptions. Kedrov had a print-run of three thousand but managed to sell only half of the copies by 1912. Disappointed, he sold the remainder as waste paper.[5]

This is important information that is overlooked by the dozens of scholars who have seen his volumes, examined his 'texts' and concluded that Lenin attracted widespread notice in the Russian Empire before the Great War. Most subjects of Nicholas II knew nothing about Lenin. He had made only a little headway since he started to come to public notice in St Petersburg with his writings in the late 1890s. His name, physical appearance and policies were obscure. His writings were little discussed – and were thought unintelligible or excessively intemperate by those who bought his books.

Lenin kept faith in himself because he saw nothing to shake his assumptions. The Russian Empire and the rest of Europe, he thought, were on the brink of Revolution. Another assumption was that social classes, even if they were quiescent for lengthy periods, could quickly rise to the tasks of carrying out Revolution. A third was that it did not matter how small the party of Revolution was before it seized power. The most important thing in Lenin's eyes was to have a party, however minuscule, of indoctrinated revolutionaries who could spread the word. A fourth assumption was not stated expressly, but indisputably he believed that the cleanest test of a revolutionary was simply whether he or she stuck by Lenin in factional disputes. He was fixed in his ways. He also knew that even the most anti-emigrant Bolsheviks recognised his individual talent and accepted that the emigrants gave continuity to the party despite the Okhrana's efforts. Emigrants had the intellectual sweep and could write and organise. They maintained the party records; they constituted the party's collective memory. Despite the exposure of his faults in Prague, few Bolsheviks seriously wanted rid of Lenin.

In spring 1912 he wrote to his mother:[6]

We're planning to go off for the summer to Fontenay, outside Paris, and are thinking about a complete move there for the entire year. It's expensive in Paris: the price for the apartment has been raised, and anyway it will definitely be healthier and quieter in the outskirts. In the next few days I'll undertake a trip and do a search.

Lenin never wrote about politics to his mother. But in a separate letter to Anna Ilinichna, who was staying with her in Saratov, he noted how much criticism had been aimed at the Conference organisers by the other 'groups and sub-groups' in the party. Even fist-fights, he added, had taken place. But by and large he was pleased with the Russian revolutionary scene in France.[7]

Yet the move to Fontenay was not realised. The main reason was that the Bolshevik Central Committee, despite its depletion by arrests, was carrying out the plan to focus its energies on work in the Russian Empire. An early objective was to found a legal newspaper in St Petersburg. Since 1906 it had been lawful for political parties to operate in Russia and run their own press; the Basic Law, much as it was manipulated by Nicholas II, was never repealed. Of course, the Okhrana closed down newspapers when editors strayed beyond the fixed limits of public expression. It was not allowed, for example, to call for the downfall of the Romanov dynasty or to recommend 'the dictatorship of the proletariat'. But within the limits it was possible to print much that was subversive of the government and its policies. And so revolutionary groups such as the Bolsheviks and Mensheviks were able to conduct propaganda in the open. Lenin had campaigned for Bolsheviks to stand in the Duma elections but had been reluctant to advocate the foundation of a legal daily newspaper. Although he did not explain this, he surely disliked any Bolshevik editor other than himself controlling what appeared in the press under the faction's imprimatur. Yet the new

Central Committee had made up its mind and Lenin had to deal with this reality.

On 22 April 1912 the first issue of *Pravda* appeared. Lenin knew that if he stayed in France he would lose all influence over the Bolsheviks in Russia. If he himself moved back clandestinely to St Petersburg, however, he would eventually be arrested. Sensibly he decided to move as near to the Russian Empire as he could without actually crossing the frontier. Nadezhda Konstantinovna made enquiries about the Austrian-ruled part of Poland, Galicia. The replies were positive. The choice fell upon Kraków. Tensions between the governments in Vienna and St Petersburg meant that Lenin would be safe from extradition. Kraków had 150,000 inhabitants, and of these it is reckoned that as many as 12,000 were political refugees from the Russian Empire. Nearly all the refugees were Polish, but Russians too were among them. The Union of Assistance for Political Prisoners, founded in Kraków, gave material help to new arrivals. Lenin and his associates would also be well placed for communications with St Petersburg. A rail route ran from the Russian capital through to Warsaw and from Warsaw there was a regular service to Kraków. Postal communications were quick. Lenin would be able to provide a foreign base for the Central Committee, receiving visitors and mail from St Petersburg. He had not wanted this transfer but could foresee some practical advantages.

Lenin, Nadya, her mother, Zinoviev, his wife Zinaida Lilina and their little boy Stepan travelled together. Leaving Paris on 4 June, they arrived in Kraków after stopping in Leipzig for a few days. There was no attempt at secretiveness. Lenin's stay at the Hotel Victoria was announced in the local newspaper *Czas*; and when Inessa wrote from Paris, she openly addressed her postcards to the Ulyanovs.[8] The only difficulty was contact with local socialists. Sergei Bagotski, who belonged to the Russian Social-Democratic Labour Party, had arranged to meet them on a particular bench in the leafy Planty promenade outside the Jagellonian University's main building. There were many such benches; the promenade stretched for miles and the Jagellonian University had not one but several principal buildings. In fact Lenin and Nadezhda Konstantinovna sat themselves down punctually on the correct bench and Bagotski was there too. But they failed to recognise each other, and they sat for half an hour before Nadya importuned her neighbour by asking whether his name was Bagotski.[9]

Had Nadya, perhaps, been even more assertive just a few weeks earlier? There have been suggestions that the move from Paris occurred

at her insistence in order to break Lenin's contact with Inessa. This is
scarcely credible. Otherwise it is hard to explain why in summer 1912
Nadya considered sending her own mother to Arcachon, the little holiday
resort on the Atlantic coast ten miles south-west of Bordeaux which was
favoured by Russian revolutionary emigrants, even though Inessa was
likely to be there. Probably there were political reasons why neither
Lenin nor Inessa wanted to stay in Paris. The focal point of the Central
Committee's activity had been moved to the Russian Empire at the
behest of the Party Conference. Lenin had to have closer contact with St
Petersburg and Inessa's role as secretary to the Committee of the Foreign
Organisation was redundant after the abolition of the Committee itself.
Inessa and Lenin continued to see each other, moreover, after he moved
the main Bolshevik foreign base to Kraków; indeed she stayed with Lenin
and Nadya in Kraków before slipping over the frontier to conduct
clandestine revolutionary work in Russia in July 1912.

But undoubtedly the close relationship between Inessa and Lenin
collapsed around this time. It is clear that it was Lenin who decided
to end the relationship and that Inessa was exceedingly distraught.
She implored Lenin to reconsider. She told him that the relationship
was harming no one; presumably by this she meant Nadya. She was
entranced with him and remained so until her death in 1920. But Lenin
stayed firm. Things could not go on as before. Even if the rumours
about Nadya's ultimatum are untrue, Lenin must have wondered
whether the current emotional complication was permanently sustain-
able; and after so many years living and working with Nadya, he probably
felt that he could humiliate her no longer. Just possibly, and here we are
guessing, he may have judged that only one of his two potential partners
was a dependable political assistant. Nadya was solid, reliable and
hardworking; she had proved her worth. And so the temptation of Inessa
had to be rejected and all her pleadings ignored.

The change of location must have helped a bit: Lenin greatly enjoyed
Kraków. Although it was only the provincial capital of Galicia in the east
of the Hapsburg Empire, its history as the royal seat of Poland until 1597
impressed every visitor. Kraków is situated by the river Vistula. Rising
high above the river is the Royal Castle, which contains the sarcophagi
of the Polish kings and queens. Latin Christianity had been brought
to the region by missionaries such as St Adalbert, whose little church
stands on the edge of the Market Square at the centre of the city. The
Market Square's dominant feature is the Cloth Hall with its long, double
line of archways. Grain, garments and cattle were the primary objects of

commerce for the region around Kraków; but there was also a religious and intellectual effervescence. Also on the Market Square is St Mary's Church with its magnificent altarpiece by the painter Veit Stoss. Every hour a bugler leans out of the bell-tower and blows a musical phrase to commemorate the unfortunate bugler who was hit by an enemy archer when trying to warn the city of the sudden arrival of the Mongol Horde in 1241. To the north of the square – and very important for Lenin – was the Jagellonian University. Founded in 1364, it was the *alma mater* of Copernicus. The university had a decent reading room and the cafés and cultural societies near by were lively centres of intellectual discussion.

By summer 1912 they had found an apartment at 218 Zwierzyniecka Street down the hill and across the river Vistula from the centre of Kraków. One of the helpful Polish comrades, Jakub Hanecki, lived along the road. The house was on the outskirts and Lenin could take walks in the neighbouring fields and hills and go swimming in the Vistula. In the first winter he bought a pair of skates and started skimming around as he had done in his youth in Simbirsk. He frequently also took the train from Kraków to the nearby Tatra Mountains and went scrambling up the rock faces with Sergei Bagotski.

Culture and recreation were not the sole attraction of Kraków: Lenin also liked the way it reminded him of home. The peasants who swarmed into the city on market days were recognisable types. And the large Jewish quarter, Kazimierz, could just as easily have been a shetl in the western region of the Russian Empire, as he indicated to his mother:[10]

> I must also give you my new address exactly. This summer I've travelled a very long way from Paris, to Kraków. Almost Russia! The Jews here are like the Russians and the Russian frontier is eight versts [five miles] away (it's two hours by train from Granica, nine hours from Warsaw); there are bent-nosed women in colourful dresses – it's just like Russia!

Nadya did the shopping in Kazimierz because the Jewish butchers' meat was half the price of their Polish rivals'. She took time to get accustomed to the need to haggle. When she was being overcharged, she had to walk away and wait until the trader called her back. She was also taken aback by the response to her request for meat fillets: 'The Lord God made the cow with bones, so how can I sell meat without bones.'[11]

Lenin did not bother to learn Polish; in emergencies he relied upon gestures and simple Russian phrases. When he spoke to Polish socialists, he used German as the common language. He could find most of the books he needed in the Jagellonian University reading room and correspondence with Russia was easily handled. The flat on Zwierzyniecka Street was just a few minutes by foot from the post office and half an hour from the main railway station. If he felt that he needed to send a particularly secret message to St Petersburg, he could usually arrange for it to be posted across the Russian Imperial border in Lublin. Peasants living within a zone of ten miles on either side of the border could freely travel backwards and forwards so long as they had an identity document, and the Bolsheviks employed individuals to carry the mail for them in this way.[12]

Not that Lenin and his friends were the most acute threat to the tsarist monarchy posed from Kraków. The fact that Roman Malinovski was a leading member of the Bolshevik Central Committee meant that the Okhrana knew its most intimate secrets. Subterfuge with coded messages, invisible ink or even the post office in Lublin could not prevent Lenin's plans from being known. Lenin was unaware of this. But he was also a realist about émigré politics in Kraków. Much the greatest menace to tsarism came not from Russians but from Poles. Józef Piłsudski's Left Polish Socialist Party had a substantial presence in the city. His members aimed at the restoration of an independent Polish state. Obviously this objective would have meant the loss to Austria Hungary of its Polish lands, but Viennese confidence at the time was so high that the destabilisation of 'Russian' Poland was thought desirable. Piłsudski was accorded immense freedom of action. More or less openly he armed and trained troops in the fields outside Kraków for eventual use against the forces of the Russian Empire. Such was Piłsudski's hatred of the Romanov monarchy that he was willing to assist virtually any other enemy of tsarism. Thus his men helped with the dispatch of messages to Russia on behalf of the Bolsheviks.

Meanwhile Lenin and Nadya frequently received visitors from Russia and put them up for the night in their flat. They greeted not only *Pravda* editorial staff but also the six Bolshevik members of the Fourth State Duma, who took their seats in November 1912. Lenin gave advice on political manoeuvres, on the editorial line and on the contents of Duma speeches. By the end of the year he, Zinoviev and Malinovski were the only three of the Central Committee members elected at the Prague Conference who remained at liberty. Their authority rose accordingly and some of the resentment of Lenin's factionalist excesses faded.

So what else did he get up to in these years? One of his regrets was that, although he lived close to the Russian Imperial frontier, he was unable to see any of his relatives. His mother was in fading health and was preoccupied by the twists and turns in the life of her eldest daughter Anna. In 1911 Anna Ilinichna and her husband Mark Yelizarov were staying in Saratov in the Volga region and had read in the papers about Georgi Lozgachëv, a 'child prodigy' living in the same town who had precociously taught himself to read Russian and was presently trying to master Church-Slavonic and Hebrew.[13] Freckle-faced Georgi, aged six, was from a poor family and there was little prospect that he would receive a decent formal education. When Anna and Mark offered to adopt him, his parents agreed. Georgi (or Gora, as everyone knew him) and his Uncle Volodya were to become chums in 1917. But it was Maria Ilinichna rather than Volodya with whom Anna discussed the desirability of the adoption.[14] In truth he might have tried to dissuade her from adopting Gora Lozgachev. For within months she was arrested for revolutionary activity and kept in Saratov Prison. Meanwhile Maria Ilinichna had qualified as a domestic teacher of French, which was her latest attempt to establish herself in a professional career. Dmitri Ilich was working as a doctor in Crimea and enduring the gradual breakdown of his marriage to Antonina. All these dramas were happening not so very distant from Kraków, but Lenin had no influence over them.

In fact Lenin and Nadya shared Anna Ilinichna's wish for children. Like many childless couples, they made a fuss of their friends' children. In Kraków they liked to entertain Stepan Zinoviev (or Stepa, as he was nicknamed) after Lenin had finished work for the day. The two of them ran about the house, clambering over furniture and crawling under the beds. When Stepa's father or mother complained about the noise, Lenin would have none of it: 'Stop interfering: we're playing!' On another occasion he confided to the Zinovievs: 'Eh, it's a pity that we don't have such a Stepa.'

But of course Lenin did not let emotional disappointments get in the way of his politics. As soon as he reached Kraków, he strove to assert control over the Bolshevik faction in Russia. Central Committee meetings were held in Galicia; they occurred seven times between November 1912 and the end of 1913.[15] There were also consultations with the editorial board of *Pravda* and with the Bolshevik deputies to the State Duma. But he was now under greater supervision. The Central Committee after the Prague Conference divided its membership between a Russian Bureau and a Foreign Bureau. Lenin and Zinoviev constituted the entirety of the Foreign Bureau, and Nadezhda Konstantinovna served as its secretary. But the Foreign Bureau was not allowed to take over the Central

Committee simply by way of regular contact by post and through personal trips from the Russian Empire. Lenin had to behave himself. Policy had to be formulated with the consent of Russian Bureau members. He also had to obtain the consent of the Bolshevik Duma deputies if he was to get them to do what he wanted done in the Duma and outside. Their public prominence in Russian politics outside the party made them an invaluable asset.

Lenin wanted the six Bolshevik deputies to form a Duma fraction separate from the seven Menshevik deputies. Yet although he saw them from time to time in Kraków, this was not the same as collaborating with them on a daily basis and understanding their problems. Iosif Stalin – a talented Bolshevik organiser from Georgia – was not a man known for his patience, but even he urged that Lenin should ease off and try to win the Bolshevik deputies to his 'hard policy' by steady persuasion.[16] Initially just one Bolshevik deputy took Lenin's side and this was Malinovski the Okhrana agent. The *Pravda* editorial board, too, angered Lenin by turning down forty-seven of the 331 articles he submitted to the newspaper before the outbreak of the Great War.[17] He wrote as follows to the editors in St Petersburg: 'Why did you spike my article on the Italian Congress? It would generally do no damage to give notification about unaccepted articles. This is not at all an excessive request. To write "for the wastepaper basket", i.e. to write articles that are rejected, is very disagreeable.' As a young activist in St Petersburg in the mid-1890s Lenin had written some excellent short pieces useful for Marxist propaganda in the factories. But in later years he had ignored the regular requests to write such pieces again. He insisted on writing the lengthy 'theoretical' articles and booklets that maintained the polemics with the other fractions of the party; and, to be fair to him, he composed articles for *Pravda* and speeches for the Duma deputies. But he did not like other people setting his work-agenda for him.

Lenin would have had a harder time if the Okhrana had not been efficient in arresting so many awkward Central Committee members and *Pravda* editors. One such editor was Iosif Stalin. After the Prague Conference, Stalin had been co-opted to the Central Committee and in autumn 1912 was appointed as *Pravda*'s chief editor. Lenin had referred to him as 'the marvellous Georgian'. But, like other leading Bolsheviks, Stalin disliked the harsh and repetitious baiting of the Mensheviks demanded by Lenin for *Pravda*. Quickly the Okhrana seized Stalin. Then in May 1913, after Stalin's successor Yakov Sverdlov was also arrested, Miron Chernomazov took over. Chernomazov acted as an obedient

Pencil sketch by William Ansell of
Clerkenwell Green before World War I.
In the foreground note the premises of
the Twentieth Century Press, now the
Marx Memorial Library.

Number 21 (now 36) Tavistock
Place in Bloomsbury, where Lenin
stayed while writing *Materialism
and Empiriocriticism* in 1908.

Panteleimon Lepeshinski, Geneva café-owner and amateur cartoonist, drew a scene from émigré disputes after the Second Party Congress. In the first he depicts Lenin as the cat attacked and persecuted by the Menshevik mice. In the second Lenin is shown on the counterattack.

Georgi Gapon

Alexander Bogdanov takes
on Lenin at chess on the
island of Capri, 1908.

To The Director
of the British Museum

I am writer by profession. I have sent
to the British Museum from Geneva,
where I am usually living, two of my
russian books (my pen-name is Iljin).
I came now in London in order to
study comparatively new english and
new german philosophy. I enclose
a written recommendation from a
London householder, and I should
be very much obliged if You would
give me admission ticket to the
Reading Room of the British Museum.

N. Oulianoff

21. Tavistock Place. 21.
London. W. C.
18-th may 08.

Lenin's not entirely correct
English letter of re-application
for a British Museum
reader's ticket.

Inessa Armand

Lenin in 1914. Photograph taken before his departure for Switzerland.

Country house rented by Lenin and Krupskaya in Poronin in 1914.

Herr Titus Kammerer outside his shop on Spiegelgasse in Geneva.
Lenin and Krupskaya rented rooms on an upper floor.

Grigori Zinoviev

Karl Radek

Leninist. The reason for this, however, was that Chernomazov was an Okhrana agent and the Okhrana wished *Pravda* to become more violent in its editorials so that the authorities would have the necessary pretext to close the newspaper down. The result was the recurrent disruption of *Pravda's* publication. Lenin, of course, did not know about the Okhrana's role. The signs were there if only he had been alert, and no doubt he was disabled by not being able to see Chernomazov at work in St Petersburg. Even so, he had been remarkably naive.

Lenin gained the internal factional policy he craved, but at the price of workers in St Petersburg not being able to read the newspaper regularly. Things were not much better in the State Duma. In November 1913 the Bolshevik deputies at last submitted to Lenin's arguments in favour of breaking up the joint Bolshevik–Menshevik Duma fraction. They came over to his side mainly because the labour movement was becoming more militant, and yet the Menshevik newspaper *Luch* was remarkably reticent in its support of strikes. But the split in the Duma had the consequence of involving the Bolshevik deputies in factional disputes that baffled ordinary workers – and to this extent Lenin was responsible for the Bolsheviks in Russia failing to make the fullest political gain from the situation in the factories. He was too much the factional conspirator, too little the national leader.

Furthermore, he had not abandoned all of his obsessions when he left Paris. He went on pestering the three German trustees of the Shmidt legacy – Karl Kautsky, Franz Mehring and Clara Zetkin – for the transfer of all the moneys to the Central Committee. Kautsky was exasperated by the whole business. Lenin's intransigence fitted the nineteenth-century stereotype of Russian socialists spending all their time wrangling. It was poppycock for Lenin to claim that the Central Committee was the unchallengeable embodiment of the leadership of the Russian Social-Democratic Labour Party; and Kautsky and Mehring, after trying to get the Bolsheviks and Mensheviks to compromise with each other, washed their hands of the business. Pleading ill health, they resigned their trusteeship. Thereafter the third trustee Clara Zetkin was given no peace. Lenin wrote a formal letter indicating that unless she restored the monies, she would be subjected to legal proceedings. Having taken expert advice from the Swiss advocate Karl Zraggen, he came to a deal with French socialist activist and Court of Appeal advocate Georges Ducos de la Haille whereby Ducos de la Haille would be paid 5,000 francs if he could conclude the case quickly and satisfactorily for the Bolsheviks.[18]

But Monsieur Ducos de la Haille could not work miracles and so Lenin turned to a German advocate, Alfred Kahn. It was all getting out of hand; and Kautsky decided in December 1913 that the International Socialist Bureau in Brussels should take an interest in the extraordinary bitterness of factional conflict in the Russian Social-Democratic Labour Party. Kautsky wanted not only financial but also political disputes to be considered. All this sent Lenin into a frenzy. Any such discussion in the International Socialist Bureau might lead to the loss of the Shmidt monies and to a campaign by European socialists, encouraged by the International Socialist Bureau, for Russian Marxists to reunify their party. Lenin could only play for time. He agreed to Bolshevik participation in a meeting of all the factions in the Russian Social-Democratic Labour Party with the objective of a 'mutual exchange of opinions'.

The person he selected to represent the Bolsheviks in Brussels was none other than Inessa Armand. Inessa had left Kraków in July 1912 to carry out party activity in the Russian Empire. But she was arrested by the Okhrana, and developed tuberculosis after some months in prison. Released on bail, she made a dash to the frontier in August 1913 and looked up Lenin in Galicia.[19] By then he was no longer in Kraków. He and Nadya had moved sixty miles southwards to Biały Dunajec on the railway that winds its way towards the winter sports resort Zakopane. Lenin and Nadya rented a large wooden country-house there because Nadya had been advised that her health would benefit from the fresh air of the countryside. They were anyway fed up with urban life and Lenin in particular looked forward to going climbing. Communication with Russia was not going to be drastically slower in Biały Dunajec. The post train from Kraków stopped twice a day at the nearby village of Poronin and usually a letter took only two days to arrive from St Petersburg; and Lenin positively enjoyed walking or cycling to pick up their letters from Poronin. The Lenins signed for an occupancy through to early October, when they returned to Kraków for the winter. They had had so pleasant a time that they repeated the experience in 1914 and took an apartment in Poronin itself.

Biały Dunajec and Poronin lay in a peaceful area and a very exotic one after the years spent in Switzerland, Italy and France. The residents were not like the Poles of Kraków. Most of them were so-called Guraly. The men wore black, flat-rimmed hats, white shirts and beige trousers. The women had long dresses of the brightest colours. They had dark complexions and a fierce demeanour when approached by strangers. The style of agriculture had been the same for centuries. They kept cows and, in the less hilly areas, grew rye. Their houses had thick, wooden walls. There was no factory for miles, and such handicrafts as existed were devoted to domestic use. Further up the road lay Zakopane, where the thousands of holidaymakers and TB patients who made their way there were providing employment for a number of villagers. There was a growing commercial demand for wooden carvings and lace; the recent completion of the Kraków–Zakopane railway began the process of eroding the area's isolation – a process that was noticeably incomplete at the end of the twentieth century. 'It's a wonderful spot here,' Lenin wrote to his sister Maria. 'The air is excellent, at a height of around 700 metres.'[20]

Nadya did not immediately take to the area. She found it distasteful to have to bargain with the landlady over the rent. Then they employed a maid who turned out to be incompetent and not very bright. There was also much more rain than in Kraków. The worst thing of all was the decline in her physical condition: the problem with her thyroid gland had led to heart palpitations. Indeed Poronin and the surrounding mountains may have contributed to this. Although she benefited from the wonderfully clean air, Biały Dunajec was so high above sea level that the low atmospheric pressure was bound to affect her weak heart. Evidently the medical advice they had been receiving was not of the best. Anyway, Lenin became convinced that Nadya could not go on as before. In his opinion, she needed to undergo a surgical operation on her goitre, and after a lot of persuasion he obtained her consent to this. In June 1913, he accompanied her to Bern in Switzerland to seek treatment from Professor Theodor Kocher.

Nadya had previously objected to surgery on the reasonable ground that one in five patients died under the knife from that specific operation. Lenin, however, discovered Kocher, who was the world's leading researcher and practitioner in the field of thyroid treatment and had reduced the mortality rate to one in two hundred. Then in his early seventies, he was famous around the world after being awarded the Nobel Prize for Medicine in 1909. His innovative method was to remove a particular portion of the gland; by 1913 he had performed over five thousand excisions and had effected a complete or partial cure of the condition in many cases. Nowadays doctors would administer effective drugs to such patients, but before the Great War Kocher's method was the best technique available. Unfortunately he was also expensive. Lenin wrote to the *Pravda* editorial board requesting a subsidy, but there is no record of his having received one. He had arranged the trip regardless;

Lenin and Nadya lived modestly in most ways, but never stinted in expenditure on holidays, books or health-care. The money could always be found, even though Lenin habitually pleaded poverty in negotiations inside the party.

In order to reach Bern the Lenins took the train from Kraków from east to west across the empire of the Habsburgs. This was a trip of over seven hundred miles and Vladimir Ilich was angry that Kocher declined to treat his wife immediately. A dispute took place, but Kocher would not yield and Nadya had to wait her turn. She was not looking forward to the operation since Kocher performed it without anaesthetic and was not the most communicative of doctors. But Nadya was stoical. The decision had been taken to have the operation and she had to hope for the best. Lenin was fearful about her prospects, but somehow he managed to keep this from her; he commented that Kocher might have a 'capricious' personality but was 'a wonderful surgeon'. The operation went ahead and, although Nadya ran a high fever, she recovered quickly and there were grounds for thinking that Kocher had cured her. Lenin dutifully spent several days visiting her, but his patience was running out. Kocher gave instructions that Nadya should go off for a fortnight's recuperation in the nearby Alps. The Lenins rejected this advice, and as soon as she was judged fit for the journey Vladimir Ilich brought his wife back from Switzerland.

On their return, Nadya got on better with Inessa than she had in Paris. The two women together accompanied Lenin on his walks and fellow Bolsheviks referred to the threesome as 'the hikers' party'. An alternative soubriquet was 'the anti-cinema-ists' party'. This was a reference to Lenin's disapproval of the passion of his comrades Kamenev and Zinoviev for going to the cinema and avoiding physical exertion. Since Kamenev and Zinoviev were of Jewish parentage, Lenin jokingly adjusted the name to 'the anti-semitic party'. (This banter, by the way, indicates what little mind Lenin usually gave to the Jewish ingredient in his own ancestry.) Inessa had lively cultural interests and encouraged Lenin and Nadya to attend Beethoven piano concerts. For Lenin, Beethoven was a treat, for Nadya less so. But this did not matter. The three of them enjoyed their discussions with each other. Lenin read voraciously in the Russian literary classics; a dog-eared copy of Tolstoi's *War and Peace* was especially well thumbed. The only snag was that the local bookshops were poorly stocked with Russian books. But this was a quibble. Generally Lenin and his friends were content with the diversions available in Galicia.

But by November Inessa had gone. In a poignant letter from Paris she wrote to him:[21]

> You and I have split up, we've split up, my dear one! I know it, I feel it: you'll never come here! Looking at the very familiar places, I clearly recognised – as I never did before – what a large place you occupied in my life here in Paris, so that almost all activity here in Paris was tied up by a thousand threads to thoughts of you. At that time I definitely wasn't in love with you but even then I loved you very much. At the moment I could manage without the kisses: just to see you and to talk with you sometimes would be a pleasure – and this could do no one any harm. What was the reason for depriving me of that? You ask whether I'm angry with you for 'carrying through' the break. No, I think that you didn't do it for your own sake.

These words must surely have referred to an affair of some kind and to Inessa's judgement that he had finished with her because of his concern for the feelings of Nadya. This was the letter of a rejected lover who believed that her man still felt more deeply for her than for his wife.

Inessa was getting desperate. Playing her last card, she stressed that she cherished Nadya. Her implicit plea to Lenin was that the three of them could live without discomfort or guilt. He turned her down, and in subsequent letters Inessa became more combative towards him as he persisted in staying away from her. In one letter he had remarked that he was on close terms of friendship and respect with very few women. Inessa's reply accused him of arrogance, alleging that he had stated that only two or three women in his life deserved his respect.

In July 1914, Lenin retorted that she had misconstrued what he had written:

> Never, never have I written that I value only three women. Never!!! What I wrote was that my *unconditional* friendship, *absolute* respect and trust are dedicated to only two or three women. This is a completely different, utterly and completely different thing.
>
> I hope that we'll see each other here after the Congress and talk about this.

He was walking a tightrope. He wanted to stay on friendly terms with Inessa and to persuade her that he had behaved properly by her. But this was not all. Lenin also wished to continue to deploy Inessa on important party missions. He had to strike a balance between the emotional and political considerations. While indicating that he had not condescended to her at the end of their affair, Lenin aimed to use her as a subordinate in politics. Having secured her assent to represent the Bolsheviks at the 'mutual exchange of opinions' meeting of Russian Marxist factions in Brussels, he deluged her with advice on how to handle the occasion.

A complex of dilemmas faced him in his political life. As Lenin was negotiating with Inessa about the Brussels meeting, he learned that the Bolshevik Duma deputies had fallen into disarray. Roman Malinovski was the cause of it all. In summer 1914 he had cracked under the pressure of his dual allegiance to Bolshevism and the Okhrana, and secretly fled St Petersburg. A few days later he turned up in Galicia. By this time there was public speculation in Russia that Malinovski was a police agent. This would have been an embarrassment at any time for the Bolsheviks. But Lenin, who was only beginning to stabilise his private life and was preoccupied with the financial and political developments in the International Socialist Bureau, reeled from this latest blow.

Malinovski belonged to both the Duma and to the Bolshevik Central Committee; he was the most famous Bolshevik active in the Russian Empire. Malinovski and Lenin had been hand in glove. Lenin's enemies had always said that he was much too complacent about the kind of people he surrounded himself with. There had been several notorious examples. Taratuta and Andrikanis had deceived young women into marriage for the faction's pecuniary gain; Kamo had robbed banks for the faction. Lenin had defended them all from criticism, as well he might since he had instigated their shady activity. His criterion of approval was whether or not a person adhered to current Bolshevik policies. He scoffed at anti-Bolsheviks who were horrified by his refusal to assess the moral character of members of his faction. He had often been warned about Malinovski. But he took no precautions. To Lenin, Malinovski appeared to behave exactly as a Lenin-style Bolshevik should. And he was a better organiser and speaker than all the other Duma deputies put together. He could talk the language of ordinary Russian workers. Why, then, distrust him? Weren't the faction's enemies just out to cause mischief for Bolshevism?

Even so, Lenin felt obliged to put together a Central Committee commission of enquiry. Although Lenin and Zinoviev were the dominant figures on it, they themselves were subject to scrutiny. In judging Malinovski, they were judging themselves and their past behaviour. In the nature of such situations it was difficult to be sure about the evidence, and Malinovski was adept at turning any evidence inside out.

Lenin anyway sympathised with Malinovski, even though the other Bolshevik deputies to the Duma remonstrated that Lenin was treating him far too softly. In a similar unofficial trial in 1906, the Socialist-Revolutionaries had decided that Father Georgi Gapon was a police agent and had hanged him. But Lenin and Zinoviev gave Malinovski the benefit of the doubt. No charge against him could be totally proved and, they concluded, he had to be considered an innocent man.

While this confidential commission was sitting in June, Lenin was losing any vestigial sense of proportion. His distraction from Russian revolutionary possibilities was total. His political intuition – sharp as a razor in 1917 – was extremely blunt in mid-1914. He had no excuse. Living in Habsburg Poland he was in daily receipt of the Russian news. Through June and July there were strikes in St Petersburg against the government as well as against factory owners. Barricades were briefly put up in industrial quarters. There seemed a strong possibility that the Romanov monarchy was about to face a test equal to its experiences in 1905–6. But no guidance was forthcoming from Lenin in Galicia. Nor did he give much attention to the gathering diplomatic crisis among the European great powers that was about to engulf the continent in the catastrophic Great War. Lenin had other things on his mind: Brussels, Kautsky, the Shmidt legacy, Inessa and Malinovski. His priority at the time was to score points in discussions with other leading socialists in the parties of Russia and the rest of Europe. Real war, real famine, real impoverishment were not things of his direct experience – and until he was thrust into daily Russian politics in 1917, he failed to rise to the level of the kind of politician that he aspired to be.

13

FIGHTING FOR DEFEAT

1914–1915

Then it happened: in August 1914 Germany declared war on Russia. This came at the end of weeks of diplomatic threats in Europe following the assassination of the Austrian Archduke Franz Ferdinand by a Serbian nationalist in the Bosnian capital Sarajevo. On 23 July the Habsburg government in Vienna had delivered an ultimatum whose terms were so humiliating as to make it politically impossible for Serbia to comply. When the Russian Imperial government declared support for Serbia, the German government stated that, unless the Russians stood down their forces, Germany would go to war against Russia on the Austrian side. But Russia would not budge. It had endured a series of disputes with Germany and Austria–Hungary in the past half-decade, and Nicholas II's sense of dynastic and imperial honour induced him to conclude that the time had come to make a stand. Within days, Britain and France announced that they would fight alongside Russia. These three powerful states formed a coalition against three other such states – Germany, Austria–Hungary and the Ottoman Empire. The Great War was under way. Diplomats were staggered by the speed with which international relations had spun out of their expert hands.

In every country, including Russia, several political parties and newspapers were ready to condemn their government for any sign of weakness against the national enemies. Yet most rulers were untroubled by this and in the early stages of the diplomatic crisis had expected that a general military conflict would be avoided. This hope was wrecked in August. Two great coalitions were ranged against each other. Austria–Hungary and Germany faced enemies on two fronts. In the west there were the combined forces of France and Britain, in the east there was Russia.

Lenin's inattention to the intensifying crisis is unmistakable. His understanding of politics outside his party had always been of a very general kind. He had always disdained to scrutinise the twists and turns of Russian Imperial government policy; in the same fashion he took little interest in international diplomacy's vicissitudes in summer 1914. His Marxist approach accustomed him to concentrate on the economic and political foundations of regimes, and as a result he had simply become complacent about the personal security he enjoyed in the Habsburg Empire. He was not the only person in Europe to be taken by surprise. But this is the best that may be said of him. Really it did not require much foresight to guess that any war between Russia and Austria would place him in jeopardy. Living in Galicia, he might well be arrested as a Russian agent at the outset of hostilities; and if the Russian Imperial forces were to occupy the region, he would certainly be treated as a traitor.

He saw his mistake when it was already too late. As Russia started to mobilise, the Habsburg police initiated enquiries about foreign residents. Lenin was living only a few miles from the Russian border and had visited the frontier posts. He had written frequently to St Petersburg and opened his home to Russian politicians. He had roamed the mountains near Zakopane and had quizzed the inhabitants of the area about rent-levels, climate, ethnic variety and the best routes from one village to another. He possessed a Browning pistol. Lenin lacked only a swarthy countenance and a black cape to complete the caricature of a Russian spy.

War hysteria affected every Polish city and village, and the Catholic priests in Galicia were preaching that resident Russians were at work poisoning the wells. The fact that Lenin had hitherto been an honoured anti-tsarist emigrant made no difference. The maid employed by Lenin and Nadezhda Konstantinovna invented stories about them which she told to peasant women in Biały Dunajec. It all could easily have ended in violence, perhaps a lynching. Nadezhda Konstantinovna sensibly bribed the maid by paying her off and giving her a free one-way rail ticket to Kraków.[1] Yet the local hostility to Russian emigrants was unabated. Things would have been easier for Lenin if he had stayed in Kraków, where the police were more sophisticated than in Biały Dunajec. The problem facing the officer who arrived in the village from Nowy Targ on 7 August (NS) was that he knew that he would be reprimanded if he failed to arrest someone who subsequently proved to be the agent of the Romanovs. A display of bureaucratic zeal was predictable and the officer was bound to see everything in the worst possible light.

A brief search confirmed the officer's expectations. Among Lenin's possessions he found extensive notes on contemporary agriculture, including statistical tables. The officer deduced that such material was a coded message for the suspect's espionage superiors in St Petersburg. The discovery of the Browning pistol further incriminated Lenin. Even the pot of glue was thought peculiar. To the officer it seemed likely that the pot was a bomb. Retrospectively – but only retrospectively – the situation had its amusing side. At the time Lenin and Nadezhda Konstantinovna were scared that the man's nerves might get the better of him.

In the end it was agreed by the three of them that only Lenin needed to be subjected to further interrogation. Polish courtesy towards women saved Nadezhda Konstantinovna (even though she, a promoter of female emancipation, asked for no favours). The officer planned to take Lenin back to Nowy Targ, nine miles away, but relented after Lenin gave his solemn word that he would not abscond. Lenin would take the train to Nowy Targ next day. As soon as the officer had departed, Lenin hurried to Poronin to look up Sergei Bagotski and Jakub Hanecki, who volunteered to obtain affidavits from fellow Marxists elsewhere in Austria–Hungary to the effect that he was not a spy.[2] Meanwhile Lenin sent a telegram asking the Kraków Director of Police to confirm to the Nowy Targ authorities that he had been living in Galicia as a political emigrant, and the Director quickly did as requested. Then Lenin returned to make the final arrangements in Biały Dunajec. By a stroke of luck a Bolshevik, a certain V. A. Tikhomirnov, had just arrived in the village. Lenin offered him accommodation in return for Tikhomirnov giving manly protection to Nadezhda Konstantinovna and her mother.[3]

On 8 August he went to Nowy Targ, where he was put in prison. While he was being held in cell no. 5, his friends outside were working hard on his behalf. Bagotski and Hanecki were not alone. By some oversight, Grigori Zinoviev had been left alone by the police. This left him free to cycle around the whole area campaigning for Lenin's release. Sigmund Marek, a Marxist, quickly wrote to the authorities on behalf of Lenin. Telegrams were dispatched by Nadezhda Konstantinovna. Viktor Adler in Vienna and Herman Diamand in Lwów rapidly responded as requested.[4] 'Are you sure', an Austrian minister asked Adler, 'that Ulyanov is an enemy of the tsarist government?' Adler replied: 'Oh yes, a more sworn enemy than your Excellency!'[5] Hanecki and Nadezhda Konstantinovna visited the prisoner regularly in Nowy Targ to cheer him up. They need not have worried unduly. Lenin busied himself talking to fellow prisoners – most of whom were being held for acts of petty criminality – and used his legal training to assist them in preparing their defences. He was a popular figure despite his slender grasp of Polish, being known in the prison as a 'real bull of a fellow'.

On 19 August Lenin was released and allowed to return to Biały Dunajec. By then it was urgent for him and his associates to leave Galicia. Russian Imperial armies were advancing fast and there was a possibility that Galicia would be occupied. In such a contingency the mercy shown by the Austrians to the leader of Bolshevism would not be repeated. Lenin and Nadezhda Konstantinovna determined to make for neutral Switzerland and they wrote to fellow Marxist Herman Greulich asking him to support their application to resettle there. On 26 August, accompanied by the Zinovievs, they left for Kraków. Permission was obtained for their further trip to Vienna, where Viktor Adler helped them get the necessary documentation for the journey to Switzerland on 3 September (NS).

There had been quite an influx of Russian revolutionaries from the belligerent countries. Lenin wrote to Vladimir Karpinski in September:

> It's said that a new French emigration has now set off for Geneva from Paris, Brussels, etc. Isn't there an extraordinary price inflation, especially for apartments? And so we'll have to set ourselves up temporarily: is it possible to find rented rooms (two small ones) on a monthly basis, with use of the kitchen?

Bolshevik associates lent a hand and the Lenins occupied an apartment at 11a Donnerbühlweg in Bern. By then he was extremely angry. Before leaving Galicia he had read in the newspapers that the German Social-Democratic Party's representatives in the Reichstag had voted war credits to the German government. Lenin was astounded and appalled. To Bagotski he had exclaimed: 'This is the end of the Second International.' He was referring to the failure of the German Social-Democratic Party to stick by the resolution of the Stuttgart Congress of the Second Socialist International that socialist parties should do all in their power to prevent their governments from waging war in Europe or elsewhere. Militarism and imperialism had been condemned by the Congress. At the time Lenin had had to exert pressure upon the German Marxists to accede to the resolution during the Congress; but he had never imagined that they would renege on it. Now the German Social-Democratic Party, the most authoritative party of the Second International, had done precisely that.

Lenin's mood was choleric not least because he had shared the almost universal respect in which the German Social-Democratic Party was held by European Marxists. For all his pride in Russia and in

Bolshevism, he had expected 'the socialist revolution' in Europe to be led not by Russians like himself but by Germans. He had esteemed Karl Kautsky despite the financial altercations he had had with him. And yet Kautsky, the arbiter of Marxist orthodoxy for Vladimir Lenin, had refused to break with the German Social-Democratic Party over the vote on war credits. For Lenin, this was tantamount to supporting militarism and imperialism. Kautsky had therefore to be denounced.

The wartime phenomenon of socialist parties supporting their governments became the norm. Across Germany, Austria, France and the United Kingdom the majority of them took the line that national independence was under threat. Only a few parties held to the Socialist International's policy of active opposition to war, and Russian parties were prominent among them. Not that all their leaders refused to back the Russian war effort. Several prominent Bolsheviks, Mensheviks and Socialist-Revolutionaries regarded Germany as being bent upon an imperialist aggression that required them to support their Imperial forces even though they detested the Romanov monarchy. Most notably Georgi Plekhanov dropped his struggle against the government and called on patriotic Russian socialists to follow his example. Hundreds of political emigrants in Paris volunteered to fight in the armies of the Allies, and others moved to France to join them. But most of the Bolshevik, Menshevik and Socialist-Revolutionary leaders stuck to anti-war positions of one sort or another. Some were pacifists. Others did not reject war as such but wished to end this military conflict by means of pressure exerted by socialists of all belligerent countries – and many of these, including the Menshevik Yuli Martov, felt that in Russia's case this would still have to involve the wartime overthrow of the Romanovs.

Lenin's position was at the extremity of Russian Marxism. Before reaching Switzerland he had drafted a brief article, 'The Tasks of Revolutionary Social-Democracy in the European War'. He agreed with Martov that the military conflict in Europe was 'bourgeois, imperialist, dynastic', and both he and Martov contended that the German Social-Democratic Party had behaved disgustingly. But Lenin had a preoccupation of his own: 'From the viewpoint of the working class and the toiling masses of all the peoples of Russia, the lesser evil would be the defeat of the tsarist monarchy.'[6] Martov condemned the 'imperialist' governments indiscriminately. For Lenin, this was not enough. However conditionally, he wanted Marxists to welcome German success at war with Russia. This was extraordinary for a man who was under no intellectual compulsion to prefer one set of 'imperialists' over another.

His language was intemperate. In a notorious phrase he referred to the Russian Imperial armies as 'Black Hundred gangs'. The Black Hundreds were groups of reactionary thugs who organised pogroms of Jews in the Russian Empire before the war. Now Lenin was casually describing the workers and peasants conscripted into the armed forces as anti-semites. Bolshevism's strategy of revolution, as formulated by Lenin since 1905, called for a 'class alliance' of the working class and the peasantry. Yet from wartime Switzerland he was dismissing both groups in blistering terms. He did not get away with this in meetings he held with fellow Bolshevik emigrants. The first occurred in woods outside Bern so as to avoid giving annoyance to the Swiss authorities, who wanted to keep the country distant from the politics of the war. One of the Bolshevik State Duma deputies, F. N. Samoilov, was present; and when he went back to Russia, he carried with him news of the Bolshevik discussion. Lenin then travelled to address other Bolshevik groups in Geneva and Zurich. When Karpinski encountered him, a row ensued about the contents and language of 'The Tasks of Revolutionary Social-Democracy in the European War'.

Lenin had to back down, at least a little. He continued to express a preference for Russia to be defeated, but concurrently he insisted that socialists of other countries should likewise campaign for their own respective governments to lose the war. Thereby he displayed a negligible understanding of how wars are fought. Despite claiming to be putting forward 'scientific', 'practical' policies, he never explained how it would be possible for all the belligerent states simultaneously to go down to defeat. Unconsciously he had omitted to remove the national ingredient of his recommendations. He had always asserted that his ideas had a European nucleus, but he had always been a very Russian European. Whatever was happening in Europe, he wanted Nicholas II and his regime to be trampled down.

Instead he concentrated on urging that the onset of war in Europe had brought the era of European socialist revolution nearer. He had always taken a European perspective on revolutionary strategy. While being bitterly disappointed with the German Social-Democratic Party since August 1914, he did not lose faith in the imminence of capitalism's demise. The duty of socialist parties was to rally support among the working class for revolutionary political struggle. The fact that most socialist leaders in most countries had ceased to oppose 'chauvinism' was neither here nor there: Lenin contended that the conditions were ripe for workers to be turned towards revolution by even quite small groups of determined, experienced revolutionaries such as the Bolsheviks. The European socialist revolution could therefore be brought about in wartime. He introduced a new slogan: European Civil War! Lenin proposed – again without elaborating his idea in any detail – that the urgent assignment was to turn the 'imperialist war' into a 'civil war' across the continent. The working classes of all European countries should unite in the fight against the concert of the continent's middle classes. Class struggle, not peace among the classes, was what was needed in that time of war.

His confidence proceeded from calculations he had expressed in a letter to Maxim Gorki in 1913: 'War between Austria and Russia would be a very useful thing for the revolution (in the whole of eastern Europe), but it's scarcely likely that Franz Joseph [the Hapsburg Emperor] and Nikolasha [Lenin's nickname for the Russian Emperor] would grant us this pleasure.'[7] The governments of the European great powers had done the improbable: Lenin's joy was unbounded.

His indifference to the scale of the human suffering was colossal. In this he was not totally unusual; one of the reasons why the war took so long to evoke popular resentment in the combatant counties was that there was little knowledge of conditions on the western and eastern fronts. Not only the generals of both the Allies and the Central Powers but also most ordinary people were unaware that so much carnage was occurring in the name of national defence. Lenin, too, was not closely acquainted with the military situation. But being in neutral Switzerland, where newspaper reports were freer than elsewhere in Europe, he surely understood that this was a war grossly more destructive than others in recent European history. On the trip from Biały Dunajec he had witnessed the Kraków hospitals crammed with soldier casualties. But he did not refer to the subject. Such commentary would have seemed unnecessarily sentimental to him. Nevertheless it is striking that when he talked about 'war', 'struggle' and 'conflict' he was usually referring to factional campaign inside his party rather than to the Great War. Internal Marxist politics remained his obsession.

It is not as if he had no access to writings by fellow Marxists who emphasised the ghastliness of conditions on the two fronts. Many such as Martov and Axelrod understood that the war was like industrialised slaughter and that the moral and political imperative of socialism was to stop it. But Lenin had been unmoved by the Volga famine of 1891–2. He had cared little when the number of casualties had soared in the Russo-Japanese War in 1904–5. Eventually he met a couple of Russian soldiers in Switzerland who told him of their experiences; and he resumed contact by letter with Roman Malinovski after his capture as a soldier in the Russian Imperial armies by the Germans. He had the information. But he ignored it: he was impervious to the wreckage of lives at the front and at home that was being reported.

Lenin maintained this frigidity throughout the Great War; he hated letting what he called 'sentimentality' interfere with his political judgement. But this does not mean that he was happy with himself in broader ways. His internal life was frenetic as never before – and he had never been known as a calm fellow. He found it increasingly difficult to stay tranquil when challenged on the logic and practicality of his opinions. He was nervous and bad-tempered days before he was scheduled to give speeches to meetings that would be attended by people who were not Bolsheviks, and was not much more comfortable among members of the Bolshevik faction. The violence of his language shocked even his sister Anna: 'I'm being terrorised by you: I have a fear of making any incautious sort of expression.'[8] Alexander Shlyapnikov, the leader of the Russian Bureau of the Central Committee, told everyone in the faction that Lenin's treatment of Bolshevik colleagues had gone beyond acceptable bounds.[9] Anna Ulyanova agreed. This served only to infuriate Lenin, who brutally retorted that 'she had never made sense in politics'.[10] Anna, usually her brother's admirer, drew the obvious conclusion that he was no longer entirely in control of himself. Lenin was becoming a little unhinged.

The years of traipsing from one European city to another were taking their toll. After years of declining health, Nadya's mother died in Bern in March 1915. She had inherited a large sum of money on the death of her sister, and – as Nadya noted – had thereby become a 'capitalist'.[11] Yelizaveta Vasilevna had been one of the few people who had been willing to speak frankly to her son-in-law. But they had got along pretty well and naturally Nadya was stricken with grief.

But what was wearing down Lenin to an even greater extent was the ceaseless writing and organising against every Marxist leader on the face of the continent:[12]

> This, then, is my destiny. One fighting campaign after another – against political imbecilities, vulgarities, opportunism, etc. This has been going on since 1893. And this is the reason for the hatred shown by the philistines. Ah well, I still wouldn't swap this destiny for 'peace' with the philistines.

It was a revealing comment. (Significantly, he made it in a private letter to Inessa, the person before whom he had the habit of trying to justify himself.) Even iron Vladimir was capable of self-pity. But this extraordinary outburst must not overshadow the other important aspect: namely that, however much he felt sorry for himself, he still believed he was right in his struggle against what he saw – without a glimmer of doubt – as idiotic, vulgar and opportunist opponents. Yet photographs of him in the Great War show a man who looked older than his age. His haggard features and uncharacteristically puffed-out physique were signs of the turmoil within him. Lenin, the indefatigable pre-war factionalist, was becoming an exhausted force.

But that sense of his correctness saw him through. The moods of depression, bad as they were, were turned inside out as soon as he pondered the political ideas of his rivals; immediately he again became confident and militant. Lenin never questioned his own judgement or motives. He had ascertained the proper revolutionary line for the war. It was the only proper line, and that – in his estimation – ought to be the end of the matter: Marxists of Russia and the rest of Europe were at best misguided if they refused to follow his lead.

Apart from politics, his emotions were engaged only with the few people who were close to him. One was his mother. Her health had been poor for years, and he had been solicitous about her in letters both to her and to his sisters and brother. Her support for his career had been unfailing even though she did not display sympathy with his politics. For her, he and her other children were simply that: her children. Maria Alexandrovna believed they could do no wrong. When they ran into trouble with the authorities, she took their part and, whenever possible, went to live with them in exile. She would have done this for Vladimir if he had let her, but he wanted his freedom. He declined to enable her to accompany him into Siberia in 1897 and to attend his marriage in the following year, and there was never any question of her joining him in emigration. She had enjoyed taking a holiday with him in Brittany in 1903 and journeying across the Baltic to see him in Stockholm in 1910. Unlike his sister Maria, she had not 'shrieked with pleasure' on seeing him at last, but she loved him. Her way of showing this was to buy him a blanket and to urge him to eat more: he was much too thin for her liking.[13]

The warmth between mother and son lasted through to her death at the age of eighty-one in July 1916. When he wrote to Inessa Armand in July 1914 about the 'two or three women' to whom he was dedicated,

Maria Alexandrovna must have been one of those he had in mind. Naturally the news of her death made him distraught. Yet the Ulyanovs were reluctant to display emotions about personal matters and there is no record that Vladimir was any different on this occasion. But his mother was one of the props he used to cope with all the pressures on him. He could not even attend her funeral. Instead it was her son-in-law Mark Yelizarov and family friend Vladimir Bonch-Bruevich who carried her coffin to her grave in the Lutheran Cemetery in the Volkovo Cemetery in St Petersburg.

In the same years he was also trying to deal with the emotional debris of his relationship with Inessa Armand. Letters continued to pass between them and she helped the Lenins with the arrangements for their trip from Galicia. In the course of the war she had moved from Paris to Switzerland, eventually settling in Les Avants in the mountains above Montreux. Soon, at Lenin's insistence, she herself shifted house to Bern to be near him. The threesome of previous years – Lenin, Nadya and Inessa – resumed their habit of going for long walks in the countryside together. In Nadya's recollection, they each had an idiosyncratic way of passing the time when they sat down. While Lenin buffed up the language of his speeches, Nadya taught herself Italian and Inessa did some sewing and read works on feminism.[14] Inessa's mind was exercised in particular by the question of women's rights. In January 1915 she went off by herself to the mountains, and jotted down the outline of a booklet which she sent to Lenin. Only one aspect prompted a reaction. This was Inessa's demand for 'freedom of love'. Lenin sputtered back that such a demand was not a 'proletarian' but a 'bourgeois' one. He called on her to take note of *the objective logic* of class relations in matters of love', and then he signed off in his improbable English: 'Friendly shake hands!'[15]

Lenin's comment took some beating for sheer pomposity. Inessa sensed that the subtext of his criticism was his hostility to the idea that women should be given *carte blanche* to have affairs any time they wanted. She threw his words back at him, denying any such purpose and claiming that he was confusing 'freedom of love' with 'freedom of adultery'. This stung Lenin into retorting: 'And so it turns out that *I* am doing the identifying and that you are setting about scattering and destroying *me*.'[16] It served him right. Lenin had been tactless in his first letter about her draft, and now she was paying him back. Surely she was also avenging herself for his decision to break off their relationship in mid-1912.

But he put up a fight. Inessa had written that 'even a fleeting passion' was 'more poetic and cleaner' than 'kisses without love' between man and wife. Lenin had a biting reply:[17]

Kisses without love between vulgar spouses are *filthy*. I agree. These need to be contrasted . . . with what? . . . It would seem: kisses *with love*. But you contrast 'a fleeting (why a fleeting?) passion (why not love?) – and it comes out logically as if kisses without love (fleeting) are contrasted to marital kisses without love . . . This is odd.

It would have been odd if indeed Inessa had written about 'freedom of love' within the narrow framework of debate described by Lenin. By then, however, Lenin was out to defend himself not only in terms of social principles but also out of loyalty to Nadya. Implicitly he was denying that his marriage had anything 'filthy' about it. Nadya and he meant something to each other even though the marriage had gone through rough patches. In arguing against casual sexual pairings, moreover, Lenin was getting a bit of his own back. Inessa had not been known to deprive herself of intimate male companionship in her earlier life. By contrast Lenin was suggesting that a durable commitment was required.

He mastered his feelings to such an extent that he increased the amount of purely practical advice and instruction he felt able to give to Inessa. He no longer addressed her familiarly as *ty* but more formally as *vy*. He told her to get a house nearer to other faction members and to stop being such a recluse. It was almost a parental interest that he took in her condition. What, however, should we make of this? Inessa was still in love with him. But we can only guess at his feeling for her. A residue of their relationship must have lingered with him. Otherwise it is hard to understand his pained attempt to justify himself to her and to persuade her that his ideas were believable and honourable. But he also worked to keep her in his faction. In wartime, he was concentrating again on politics. He even wrote dreamily to Inessa herself about how he felt that he was 'in love' with Karl Marx. What more could he have done to shake her off emotionally?

Meanwhile he went on trying to win the support of the Bolshevik faction. His two policies on the preferability of Russia's military defeat and on the need for 'European Civil War' lost him plenty of friends abroad. Only Nadezhda Konstantinovna and a few other Bolsheviks, including Zinoviev, stood by him; no one else among the émigrés felt really convinced by him. Often there were scandalous outbursts when he spoke in Swiss cities. On one occasion he took the opportunity to make an attack on Plekhanov in Lausanne in October 1914 by hiding his face at the back of the hall during Plekhanov's address and then making a blistering attack on him as a 'chauvinist' who had parted for ever with Marxism.[18] Many of Lenin's associates were too much in awe of him to reject him entirely. But he was certainly short of friends. What irked him was his negligible influence in the Russian Empire. Galicia had offered him the regular conduit of letters and personal visits, and meetings of central party bodies were frequent. Nothing like this happened in Bern. The average letter took several weeks. The eastern front in the Great War cut a line along the north–south axis of the continent. In order to keep the faction abroad in contact with the faction in Russia, a tenuous linkage across Germany and Scandinavia was arranged – and Lenin had to give encouragement to all Bolsheviks so that they might go on working for the revolution.

Bolshevism was not exactly flourishing back in the Russian Empire. One of the reasons for this was that the Okhrana no longer protected leading Bolsheviks from arrest. Bolsheviks were the most bitter enemies not only of the Romanov dynasty but even of the state as a whole. The round-ups of Bolsheviks through the war was relentless. It was also effective. First of all the Bolshevik Duma deputies and their advisers were put on trial. Among the advisers was Lev Kamenev, who angered Lenin by disowning the policy of 'defeatism' he had prescribed. Then there were the recurrent arrests of Bolshevik committees and groups in Petrograd (as the capital was renamed because St Petersburg sounded too German) and the provinces. There was the complete prohibition of legal Bolshevik newspapers; difficulties existed for Bolsheviks in getting their articles published in journals and magazines even when oblique critical language was employed. Strikes broke out in large industrial cities in late 1915, but the Okhrana quickly repressed the trouble and pulled a further cohort of Bolshevik activists into prison before dispatching them to Siberia. The Russian Bureau re-established itself in September 1915 under Alexander Shlyapnikov; the other members were G. I. Osipov, E. A. Dunaev and Anna Ulyanova: none of them had previous experience of factional leadership.

There was only one positive side for Lenin in this crumbling of the faction in Russia: he and Zinoviev were left to develop their ideas and pursue their activity unhindered by fellow leaders in the Russian Empire. They revived the émigré central factional newspaper *Social-Democrat* and could print their own articles without referring to others. *Social-*

Democrat could then be carried by courier for dissemination in Russia. A journal of Marxist theory was also set up in conjunction with a group of young Russian writers led by Nikolai Bukharin and Georgi Pyatakov at Baugy-sur-Clarens in the suburbs of Montreux in Switzerland.

Yet these successes meant little in the face of further setbacks experienced by Lenin. Not only did the post take weeks between Russia and Switzerland, but also Lenin had fewer contacts in Russia than at any time since he had first become an emigrant in 1900. The confidential political address-book maintained by Nadezhda Konstantinovna contained only twenty-six persons who lived not in emigration but in the Russian Empire, and sixteen of these were no longer active by the end of 1916. The Okhrana had success in trimming back the already slim size of the faction. Of the ten addresses that remained operational through the war, only three were outside Petrograd, Moscow and Siberian exile.[19] Nadezhda Konstantinovna was getting desperate. 'We need direct relations', she wrote, 'with other towns.'[20] But she was crying into the wind. Most of the correspondence – indeed virtually all of it – had to be passed through the conduit of Shlyapnikov and Anna Ulyanova if it was to reach the rest of the disparate faction; and Shlyapnikov had to keep travelling to Alexandra Kollontai in Oslo in order to pick up what Lenin had written. It was a frail apparatus with which to try to make revolution in Russia.

14

LASTING OUT

1915–1916

In January 1917, Lenin gave his most pessimistic speech ever to a meeting of young Swiss socialists at the Volkshaus in Zurich:[1]

> We, the old people, perhaps won't survive until the decisive battles of this forthcoming revolution. But it occurs to me that it's with a large amount of confidence that I can articulate the hope that the young people who work so wonderfully in the socialist movement of Switzerland and the entire world will have the happiness of not only fighting but also of winning victory in the forthcoming proletarian revolution.

Since the 1890s his premise had been that socialist revolution across Europe was imminent. Now he was saying he might not live to witness it.

Whenever he had got moody before the Great War, he had been worrying not about European socialist revolution but about internal factional politics. This he confided in a letter to Inessa Armand:

> Oh, how those 'little matters of business' are mere fakes of the real business, surrogates of the business, a real obstacle to the business in the way that I see the fuss, the trouble, the little matters – and how I'm tied up with them inextricably and forever!! That's a sign more [*sic.* This sentence and the next one were written by Lenin in English] that I am lazy and tired and in a poor humour. Generally I like my profession and yet often I almost hate it.

Lenin did not bother about the criticisms aimed at him by persons who were not Marxists, but he was depressed by the wartime disputes among Bolsheviks. He became so edgy that he did not trust himself to speak in public. After New Year 1917 he wrote privately: 'I *wouldn't* want to travel to Geneva: (1) I'm not well; my nerves are no good. I'm *scared* of giving lectures; (2) I'm booked here for 22 January, and I've got to prepare for a speech *in German*. For this reason I don't promise to come.'[2]

Nor was Lenin living in his customary comfort. His mother's death on 14 July 1916 terminated the pension she shared with her children whenever they fell on hard times. The Bolshevik factional treasury had also fallen away. The Bolsheviks were no longer operating openly in Russia and *Pravda* had been closed down by the Imperial government. The number of active Bolshevik adherents had collapsed. Most of them anyway no longer shared Lenin's opinions. Anna Ilinichna, working for the Russian Bureau of the Central Committee, did what she could and asked him for a statement of his basic monthly requirements.[3] But the money coming from Petrograd was never going to be enough; other sources of income had to be found. Lenin and Nadya tried to obtain commissions as freelance authors; the snag was that they wrote in Russian and had to find their publishers in distant, wartime Russia. Yet Nadya devised a project for a *Pedagogical Encyclopaedia* whose potential readership would not be confined to Marxist activists. Lenin, too, sought to write little pieces for money. It was a difficult task for both of them.

They economised by starting to eat horsemeat rather than beef and chicken. They bought no new clothes even though Lenin, a stickler for looking tidy, began to seem rather grubby in his old suit and walking boots. In February 1916 they moved to cheaper lodgings at Spiegelgasse no. 14 in Zurich, where the cobbler Titus Kammerer sublet rooms to them.[4] Spiegelgasse was a neat, leafy street; it had been there, at no. 12, that the German dramatist Georg Büchner wrote his play *Woyzeck* eighty years before. But Lenin and Nadya felt rather sorry for themselves. Next door to the house lay the shop of Herr Ruff, a butcher who made his own sausages.[5] Lenin, who avoided oily products because of his delicate stomach, was disgusted by the smell and dropped his ritual of aerating a room even in cold weather. The windows were kept constantly closed.[6]

Yet the Ulyanovs enjoyed the acquaintance of fellow inhabitants of the building. Among them were a German conscript's family, an Italian man and a couple of Austrian actors with a beautiful ginger kitten. Kammerer's wife Luisa captivated Lenin, who admired and shared her belief that soldiers should turn their rifles against their own governments. Luisa also taught Nadya some of the tricks needed to buy food cheaply and cook it quickly. Nadya rather overdid things by going out and buying meat on one of the two days per week when the Swiss government had appealed to citizens not to buy meat because of wartime shortages in supply. Whether Nadya made a mistake or had flouted the regulations is uncertain, but on returning from the shops she asked Frau Kammerer how on earth the federal authorities of Switzerland could ensure that its proclamation would be obeyed. Did it send investigators round to people's homes? Frau Kammerer laughed, saying that only the middle class would refuse to show a sense of civic responsibility. The working class, she exclaimed, were very different. Then she added, to ease Nadya's conscience, that the proclamation 'didn't apply to foreigners'.[7]

Lenin admired the Kammerers as exemplary proletarians, ignoring the fact that they were not workers but a 'petit-bourgeois' couple who ran a shop and sublet apartments. Really they were little capitalists and Lenin was seeing and hearing what he wanted. Having found a family who shared many of his political assumptions, he persuaded himself that they belonged to a social class of which he approved: the proletariat. The Kammerers' respect for the public good encouraged him in his basic assumptions. Lenin in 1917 was to stress the need for the state and the workers to 'check and supervise' the fulfilment of revolutionary objectives. The ideas for the October Revolution came from many sources. Marx supplied many of them in his voluminous writings. Frau Luisa Kammerer was unknowingly reinforcing one or two others.

Thus Lenin felt sustained in his Marxist faith. Through Marx and Engels he 'knew' that the future would bring about a final and wonderful stage in world history. His life had purpose. Lenin clung to a rock of attitudes and assumptions, and on it he was able to construct almost any notions about politics and economics he wanted. Overtly he claimed that Marxism had a readily identifiable logic that permitted the development of one single policy for any given situation. But this was pretence. What he really assumed by this was that his own version of Marxism was the sole authentic one. He held to this assumption even though his version of Marxism and, to an even greater extent, his practical policies changed a great deal over his long career. His faith had survived many years of emigration. Only a few of the Marxists of the 1880s were still alive and active by the Great War. Lenin was one of them, and such was his inner confidence that he felt no pressure to question the way he operated as a politician. And so whenever the current situation looked bleak – in the faction, in the international socialist movement, in the family, in his marriage, even in his physical and mental well-being – he could do something about it. He could look forward to the radiant future.

History, he trusted, was on his side. Or rather he thought that he was on the side of History. Lenin's bouts of depression were serious but temporary. That a European socialist revolution would eventually occur, with or without him, he had not the slightest doubt. Despite the concerns expressed in his address to the Swiss young socialists, he more usually believed that it would not take long for this revolution to break out. For most of the war, he had gone round predicting a general revolutionary explosion. This indeed was the bone of contention between him and so many socialist writers. Kautsky, Martov and others refused to accept that he had proved his case that Europe's working classes could easily be brought into revolutionary activity against their national governments. Nor did they believe it sensible to concentrate on splitting the socialist movement in each country. How, they asked, could socialists lead a united European working class if they were themselves divided? Lenin's other critics, notably Plekhanov, went further and suggested that most German workers were so patriotic that they would drop lip-service to the 'internationalist' principles of the Second International in the event of Germany's military defeat of Russia.

To those few persons who followed Lenin's professional activities, then, he seemed a cantankerous, somewhat unhinged utopian. But this did not trouble him. He continued to declare that the Romanov monarchy was a likely casualty of the war. He repeated that Nicholas II had done the Bolsheviks a favour by engaging in armed conflict with Germany. Revolution in Russia was on the immediate agenda. Indeed Lenin argued that the overthrow of tsarism was not merely desirable for its own sake but was one of the prerequisites for revolution in the rest of Europe. Tsarism, according to Lenin, was '1,000 times worse than [German] Kaiserism'.[8] The regime in Petrograd was allegedly so powerful and reactionary that its removal was crucial for socialists to be able to make revolutions elsewhere in Europe. Lenin put it as follows: 'The bourgeois-democratic revolution in Russia is now already not merely a prologue but an inalienable, integral part of the socialist revolution in the West.'[9]

During the wartime years, moreover, Lenin dabbled with strategic ideas to compress the schedule of Revolution. He had last done this in 1905, and now again he pondered whether the Bolsheviks were right to accept the idea that socialism in any country had to be introduced in two stages. Contemporary conventional Marxism held that there would first occur a 'bourgeois-democratic revolution' which would consolidate democracy and capitalism and that only subsequently would there take place a socialist revolution putting the working class into power. Lenin came back to this in the Great War and urged left-wing Marxists to abandon 'the theory of stages'.[10] Thus he was showing a willingness to consider the possibility of making a socialist revolution without the need for an intermediate bourgeois-democratic revolution. His own version of the two-stage revolutionary process in any case had always been controversial. In particular, the proposal for a 'provisional revolutionary democratic dictatorship of the proletariat and the peasantry' had seemed to most people – apart from fellow Bolsheviks – a scheme for instant socialism. In 1916 his sense of urgency about strategy and schedule returned to him: no chance should be lost by Marxists to seize and keep power in Petrograd.

Lenin's impatience was sharpened by his perception of the alternative scenarios. On the one hand, he did not think it unfeasible that Russia might defeat Germany; on the other hand, he did not discount the possibility that Nicholas II, if his armies continued to be defeated, would sign a separate peace on the eastern front with Germany and Austria–Hungary. If Nicholas proved too inflexible, furthermore, he might be pushed aside by the anti-socialist parties in the State Duma. According to Lenin, this might happen in several ways. Perhaps the moderate conservative groups led by Alexander Guchkov and the liberals under Pavel Milyukov might form a political coalition and somehow force Nicholas II to give way to them. Another option might be that Milyukov would ally with the right-wing Social-Revolutionary Alexander Kerenski. Lenin urged that all such scenarios could and should be pre-empted by revolutionary action led by Bolsheviks.

But what would his socialist government look like? Lenin addressed this question in notebooks he started to fill in 1916. He did not do this on his own. The small group of leading young Bolsheviks based in Baugy-sur-Clarens in Switzerland had ideas on this and were equally impatient to make a revolution. Nikolai Bukharin, in particular, did not think that the administrative and coercive agencies of advanced capitalist states should simply be taken over and reformed by socialists. Instead he argued that the entire capitalist state ought to be destroyed. In justification, he pointed to the extraordinary growth of state power within the advanced capitalist countries. Such states had developed unprecedentedly efficient and ruthless methods of political, social and economic control. They had even proved capable of suborning their respective socialist parties and using them to maintain the loyalty of the working class. Consequently it would be naive for Marxists to leave intact the existing state institutions – the civil service, the army and the economic regulatory bodies – once they had overturned the *ancien régime*. Bukharin asserted that this was the fundamental mistake of Karl Kautsky. Socialism had to build a revolutionary state anew.

At first Lenin attacked Bukharin's thought as anarchistic. The older man resented the intrusion of the bright younger writer into his domain of Marxist theory. But Lenin steadily changed his stance. Bukharin had identified a principal difficulty that would be encountered in the establishment of a socialist administration; he had also very commendably exposed a further weakness in Kautsky's thought. What Bukharin had failed to do was to explain how a socialist administration might ever be established. Lenin turned this over in his mind and came to the conclusion that the Russian workers' movement of 1905 provided the solution. In his notebooks he explored the idea that the workers' soviets could be the instrument for introducing socialism. Helped along by Bukharin, Lenin had arrived at a position that would have a decisive impact on later events. The seeds of strategy for the October Revolution of 1917 were germinating in Switzerland even before the Romanov monarchy's downfall. As yet Lenin was not quite sure of himself. He needed time to elaborate his notions, but he was committed to them in their outline form.

Neither Lenin nor Bukharin was the first Bolshevik to try to work out in detail how the 'bourgeois state' could most effectively be eradicated. Before the Great War his rival Alexander Bogdanov had argued that the prerequisite for the introduction of socialism was the development of a wholly 'proletarian culture'. 'Bourgeois culture' had to be eliminated because of its adherence to concepts of individualism, absoluteness and authoritarianism. Bogdanov felt that no socialist revolution could succeed unless a cultural as well as a political and economic transformation accompanied it.

Even in 1916 Lenin declined to go this far, and the reasons for his reluctance tell us a lot about his kind of socialism. He continued to believe that there was such a thing as an absolute truth and that such truth was discoverable by the individual intellectual acting in adherence to Marx's doctrines. The contrast with Bogdanov could not have been greater. Bogdanov wanted to encourage the workers to dispense with supervision by middle-class intellectuals and to formulate their own collectivist culture and explore new forms of social experience. Lenin concurred that there was a need for cultural development among the working class. But the need, he argued, was of a restricted nature. Workers needed to be taught to be literate, numerate and punctilious. Lenin thought that Bogdanov was just a dreamer and that the working class, in order to carry through a revolution, needed to have the technical accomplishments which 'bourgeois culture' alone could provide. Thus the 'bourgeois state' but not 'bourgeois culture' had to be extirpated. Consequently no *rapprochement* was feasible. As always, Lenin had his own agenda. He thought politically. The soviets, he surmised, would offer the means whereby the socialist revolution would be prevented from taking the path of compromise and betrayal already followed by Europe's greatest Marxist party, the German Social-Democratic Party.

He trusted as strongly as ever in the correctness of Marxism, in the vanguard party, in the predictability of 'historical development', in the virtues of urbanism and industrialism, in capitalism's inevitable collapse, in class struggle, in the imminence of the European socialist revolution. And about the need for dictatorship he also did not waver. He did not mind being the solitary factional fighter: he preferred this to any option that would involve him in compromising deeply felt convictions. He stuck to his polemical style unrepentantly. Again and again he claimed that he was merely defending and elaborating the precepts of Marxist orthodoxy.

Yet he recognised that Kautsky had shared several precepts of this orthodoxy. Kautsky had been among his heroes. There must therefore have been something wrong, thought Lenin, about the way Kautsky had arrived at the precepts. Lenin set himself the task of examining the roots of Kautsky's Marxism. By digging down in this way, he was inevitably engaged not only in looking at Kautskyanism but also in self-investigation. He did not say this openly. Indeed he did not say this to anyone at all. He confided his researches to his notebooks; and although he tried to produce a philosophical article on the subject, he did not have the time to finish it before events in Russia called him away from Switzerland in 1917. But he read avidly in the Bern Public Library and quickly came to a startling conclusion, which he put as follows in his notebooks:[11]

> *Aphorism*: It is impossible to obtain a complete understanding of Marx's *Das Kapital* and especially its first chapter without first having made a thorough study and acquired an understanding of the *whole* of Hegel's *Logic*. Consequently not one Marxist in the past half-century has completely understood Marx.

Lenin was monumentally pleased with himself. He felt that he had done something that had foiled all other successors of Marx and Engels. Implicitly he set himself up as the only true expounder of the Marxist tradition. From Marx and Engels a straight genealogical line could now be drawn to Lenin.

Lenin belonged to a community of socialist intellectuals in which it was thought very bad form to make personal boasts: he therefore did not use the aphorism in public. But he meant it seriously nonetheless. He had come to his revised understanding of Marxism by means of intensive philosophical study. He picked up particular texts by Marx and Engels, especially Marx's *Theses on Feuerbach*. But he also took up an examination of Hegel, who had had an impact upon the formation of the ideology of Marx and Engels. Hegel's vast *History of Philosophy* was the object of his detailed attention. Feuerbach, too, attracted his scrutiny.

Nor did he stop at that. He went, too, to the works of Aristotle. For the first time since adolescence he took an opportunity to search out some significance in the Classical heritage he had learned in the Simbirsk gimnazia. Until then he had confined himself to proverbs and phrases he remembered from his youth. In the Great War, Lenin wanted to draw intellectual sustenance of a more substantial kind from ancient Greek philosophy. Marxist scholars had always known in principle of Hegel's influence on Marx, and Hegel openly alluded to Aristotle as his own precursor in many fundamental aspects of epistemology and ontology. This was enough for Lenin to go back and explore Aristotle's work. He had to do this from scratch since Aristotle had not been an author on the gimnazia curriculum. Perhaps if Lenin had known more about Marx's other intellectual influences (which was not possible for anyone in the early years of the century), he would probably have been drawn to the works of the pre-Socratic philosophers. Marx had written a brilliant dissertation on one of them, Heraclitus, when he was a postgraduate. But Lenin anyway found plenty of things of interest in Aristotle.

This was not an endeavour lightly undertaken. The dense German prose of Hegel's *History of Philosophy* involved labour enough, but Aristotle's *Metaphysics* were even more onerous as Lenin had not kept up his Greek since the gimnazia, and he made use of a parallel-text edition in German and Greek. His school training had given him an ability to understand any text very quickly. Although he could speak German and French (and English rather less satisfactorily), he read things much more fluently. He had few rivals in picking up books and filleting their contents for quick information.

In returning to the Classics, Lenin was looking for justification as a Marxist theorist. More generally – and less consciously – he sought to examine and shore up his own intellectual foundations. He had been brought up not only as a Russian but also as a European. He was the child of parents and teachers who believed in Science, Enlightenment and Progress. Within that cultural milieu it had been customary to trace a line of human achievement back to the great writers of Athens and Rome. The Classics were at the origins of European civilisation and were a resource of invaluable intellectual refreshment. His Marxism discouraged him from using terms such as civilisation positively except in unguarded moments; for Marx had taught that all 'civilised' societies in history had been characterised by exploitation and oppression. But under the surface of his ideology Lenin was a typical late-nineteenth-century middle-class European. The good life was a European one. Civilisation was European. The rest of the world, like the USA in the recent past, had to be Europeanised. When he wanted to refer in shorthand to people who had yet to attain a reasonably high level of culture, he referred breezily to 'Hottentots'. Lenin was not devoid of the prejudices of a privileged, educated member of an imperial nation.

So what did he discover in Aristotle? The unfinished language of Lenin's notebooks conveys his excitement. Essentially he was dropping large parts of the epistemology of his 1908 book, *Materialism and Empiriocriticism*. He was not frank about this. When he criticised past Marxist expositions, his targets were Kautsky and other leading Marxists, not himself. In fact his own theory of knowledge had been cruder than any offered by any leading Marxist theorist; *Materialism and Empiriocriticism* had suggested that the human mind was akin to a camera and that 'external reality' was always accurately registered and reproduced by the mind's camera-like processes. Not so in the notebooks written in the Great War:[12]

> Cognition is nature's reflection by man. But it's not a simple and not an unmediated, complete reflection but the process of a series of abstractions, of the formation or construction of concepts, laws, etc.; and these concepts, laws, etc. (thought, science = 'the logical idea') also comprehend in a conditional, approximate fashion the universal pattern of an eternally moving and developing nature.

This statement would have been unimaginable in any of Lenin's writings before 1914.

What had happened was that he had at last found a rationale for the risky, exploratory approach to politics for which he was well known. Earlier he had claimed that his policies were based on predetermined scientific principles. Now he asserted that 'practice' was the only true test of whether any policy was the right one. Flexibility was essential. Ideas had to be 'hewn, chopped, supple, mobile, relative, reciprocally linked, united in opposites in order to embrace the world'. This, he held, was the truth available from the philosophy of Aristotle, Hegel and Marx. Nothing was permanent or absolutely definite; everything was interactive: it was in the nature of material and social relationships that factors clashed with each other and – by virtue of this 'dialectical' process – produced complex, changeable results. Politics required experimentation and Marxists should accept that they would involve 'leaps', 'breaks' and 'interruptions of gradualness'. All this, for Lenin, was a philosophical antidote to Kautsky.

The pleasure he took in this particular result gives a hint that Lenin had not been studying epistemology and ontology with anything like an open mind. His research in the Bern Public Library had not been undertaken out of simple intellectual inquisitiveness; he was devouring Hegel, Feuerbach and Aristotle with a specific end in view. If his research had corroborated Kautsky's position, he would simply have looked to other authors for support. Lenin, as had been obvious since his economic works of the 1890s, was a reader with a political mission. Another point deserves emphasis. This is that Lenin did not manage to arrive remotely near to a coherent philosophical standpoint. His notebooks were full of contradictions. While asserting the 'conditional, approximate' nature of cognition, he still believed in the attainability of absolute truth and in the independent existence of the external world. The notebooks were the part-time jottings of a man who would not have passed a first-year philosophy examination. They were muddled. They were also ungenerous: Lenin did not have it within him to acknowledge that essentially he had reversed his position in regard to several basic criticisms he had made of Bogdanov in 1908. Admission of error was something he did only very rarely.

Yet he had readied himself intellectually for the kind of revolutionary process that occurred in 1917. Even in 1905 he had altered policy at his whim. But now he had a rationale. He had justification, as he saw it, for splitting with any Marxist in Europe who irked him. This became evident when far-left socialists opposing their respective governments in the war began to co-ordinate their activity. Lenin wanted such co-ordination. But he was not the leading light of such efforts. This indeed was part of the problem: the Swiss socialist Robert Grimm and the Italian Odino Morgari had campaigned for some time to organise an international meeting of socialists who wished to end the war. Yuli Martov, too, had played a prominent role. All were appalled at the way their fellow socialists had given up campaigning against governments for the duration of the war. The point, they argued, was to stop the fighting. They attributed the war's outbreak to a variety of causes. Personal, dynastic, diplomatic, economic and imperial factors were adduced in their many pamphlets on the subject; and not a few of the pamphleteers were simply pacifists. Lenin, advocate of 'European Civil War', stuck out like a sore thumb.

But at least they agreed that neither military coalition was blameless. Everyone contacted by Grimm believed that the Allies and the Central Powers were as bad as each other. The solution, they argued, had to be based on internationalist principles. Military victory for either the Allies or the Central Powers would involve annexations and indemnities. It would be the triumph of one imperialism over another. It would be no peace worthy of the word. Lenin could therefore accept Grimm's invitation to join him in the Swiss village of Zimmerwald for a conference of anti-war left-wing socialists from the combatant countries in Europe.

He worked hard to develop the arguments to strengthen his political case. This led him to conduct research on the global capitalist economy; his notebooks contained references to 148 books and 232 articles. Already Lenin had endorsed a book by Bukharin on the same topic, but he wanted to put things his own way. Privately he thought Bukharin to have exaggerated the smoothness of present economic developments. Lenin considered it wholly wrong to predict that capitalism would eventually form a 'world economic trust'. Bukharin, he thought, had forgotten the Marxist axiom that capitalist economies were inherently unstable and incapable of harmonious co-operation with each other. The result was a book, *Imperialism as the Highest Stage of Capitalism*, which he asked his sister Anna to get published legally in Petrograd. Anna duly complied, and secured a contract for him. But she sensibly noted that Lenin had filled his draft with bilious remarks about Kautsky. On her own initiative she excised them in order to render the book more appealing to the publishers. Lenin had either to accept her action or forgo the contract. For once, albeit with bad grace, he backed down – and publication was scheduled for 1917: only the outbreak of the February Revolution meant that it failed to appear under tsarism.

There was already a large Marxist literature on imperialism. Karl Radek, Rosa Luxemburg, I. I. Skvortsov-Stepanov, Nikolai Bukharin and Karl Kautsky himself had worked upon the ideas of Rudolph Hilferding. All agreed that capitalism had entered a mature period of dominance by 'finance capital' and that national economies were being thrust by the very nature of capitalism into economic rivalries that made them seek external markets, grab colonies and fight other imperial powers for theirs. Lenin, too, was influenced by this literature. He was also impressed, like Hilferding, by the efficiency of the German war economy. The wartime regulatory framework for production and consumption was ironically known as *Kriegsozialismus* ('War Socialism'), which Hilferding thought could be turned to good account by the socialists. The high level of co-ordination within the capitalist economy, he argued, provided one of the preconditions for a total social revolution. But Lenin disagreed utterly with Hilferding beyond this point. Whereas Hilferding felt that violent revolution could and should be avoided, Lenin was unable to see any other way of making a revolution. 'It is necessary for us *ourselves*', he wrote, 'to seize *power* in the first instance, and not chatter in vain about "power".'[13]

Hilferding and Kautsky had put forward the possibility that capitalist countries might eventually resolve their political disputes in such a fashion as to be able to exploit their colonies in common. Lenin was aghast. To advocate such a plan was to accept that capitalism could endlessly survive. Lenin by contrast urged that the various empires could not help but clash with each other. He described a hierarchy of imperialisms in order of economic progressiveness. The USA was at the top. Germany and Japan came next, followed by Britain and France. Portugal was last of the imperial powers, being only marginally ahead of Russia. This world of imperialisms would not settle down at the end of the Great War. According to Lenin, either there would be socialist Revolution or else there would be recurrent wars until such time as Revolution took place. Lenin was out to show that any dreams of softening the conflict of world capitalism were illusory. Only Revolution would do.

And so to the international socialist movement organised by Morgari and Grimm and attended by Lenin. Two little Alpine conferences were held. The first took place in the holiday village of Zimmerwald, up the mountains behind Bern, in September 1915; the second occurred in Kiental in the same vicinity in April 1916. Both conferences were sparsely attended. Trotski remarked that half a century after the foundation of Marx's First Socialist International it was still possible for all of Europe's internationalists to be accommodated in four charabancs.[14]

Whereas everyone else regretted the paucity of delegates, Lenin was delighted. He knew that the smaller the number was, the greater would be the proportion of those who advocated policies near to his own. Still, however, he was angry. He raged at the invitations sent to Karl Kautsky and Hugo Haase, who refused to break openly with the German Social-Democratic Party, and was even more annoyed when Haase promised to come. At first Lenin let Zinoviev conduct negotiations with like-minded delegates from other countries. But he did not fully trust even Zinoviev and took to discussing matters directly with Karl Radek, the Polish Jew who had once held membership of the German Social-Democratic Party. Radek was not easy to cajole. Lenin had to drop his formula that socialists should campaign for the military defeat of their national governments. He was also compelled to stop demanding a complete break with the official socialist parties that had voted war credits for their governments. Radek's more judicious line prevailed. He knew Lenin's history, and resolved that the Zimmerwald Conference would not be turned into an assembly of polemical doctrinairism. Nevertheless the group of delegates put together by Radek and Lenin never amounted to more than eight, including both Radek and Lenin.

Having made his compromise with Radek, Lenin decided to be a good fellow and not rock the boat (or rather the charabanc). Only once did he cause trouble. This was when Georg Lebedour objected to Radek's call for street demonstrations. Lenin exclaimed: 'The German movement is faced with a decision. If we are indeed on the threshold of a revolutionary epoch in which the masses will go over to revolutionary struggle, we must also make mention of the means necessary for this struggle.'[15] These were words of a believer and a logician. The Zimmerwald Conference was being asked to spell out the things that many delegates who were anxious about the reception that might await them back home aimed to obfuscate. Yet the leftist speakers got some of what they wanted. The Conference declared the Great War to have been caused and prolonged by 'imperialist' rivalries. It castigated the socialist parties that had voted war credits (without naming them directly). The Conference agreed that military hostilities could be ended only by engagement in 'irreconcilable proletarian class struggle'.[16]

But it was the convenors of the Conference, especially Robert Grimm, who gained most satisfaction from Zimmerwald. They had good reason. In December 1915 Hugo Haase, having returned from Switzerland, led a faction of German social-democratic deputies in the Reichstag in open criticism of war credits. Haase and Kautsky called for socialists everywhere to put all pressure on their government to compose a 'peace without annexations'. Here was proof, argued Grimm against Lenin, that persuasion could have a positive effect. He looked forward to enhancing this atmosphere at the next Conference, to be held in Kiental from 26 April 1916.

Grimm, however, was disappointed. The Kiental Conference, attended by forty delegates, was noisy and bad-tempered from the start. The mandates of some delegates were challenged. Delegations fell into internal altercations. Several invited delegates found reason not to come; in particular, Haase and Kautsky took exception to the fact that the Zimmerwald Conference had set up an International Socialist Commission. For them, this was an infringement of the rights of the International Socialist Bureau; and they held to this opinion even though the International Socialist Bureau had barely operated in wartime. Of course, Lenin was delighted by their absence, having convinced himself that Kautsky was the incarnation of political betrayal. Kautsky, he asserted, was a *Mädchen für Alle* – a political prostitute who would go to bed with virtually anyone in public life if he could avoid a clash with the German government. Having come to this conclusion in August 1914, Lenin would not budge. It had become an indissoluble ingredient not only in his politics but also in his emotional life that Kautsky was a renegade. The last thing Lenin wanted was for Kautsky to have a chance to resume his doctrinal sway over European Marxism.

At Kiental, Lenin shone no more brightly than at Zimmerwald. The difficulty was that the far-left delegates (who now called themselves the Zimmerwald Left) were few and all of them suspicious of Lenin. Nonetheless he had some grounds for cheer. The Kiental Conference condemned pacifism even though many delegates wanted an end to the war at any price; it also called for 'vigorous action directed at the capitalist class's overthrow'. This was close to Lenin's idea that revolution was the way to end the war, and at the end of the proceedings he was happier than he had thought he would be.

He was lucky that the German Marxists whom he criticised for indulging their government did not know that he had some unusual contacts of his own with the same government. At first this had taken the form of sending political literature to Bolsheviks in German POW camps. Chief among these was none other than Roman Malinovski, who had enlisted in the Russian Imperial forces and had been taken captive. Lenin, who still refused to believe that Malinovski had worked for the Okhrana, spread Bolshevik propaganda among Russian POWs through lectures given by Malinovski.[17] The German high command facilitated this since Lenin advocated Russia's defeat. Baron Gisbert von Romberg, the German minister in Bern, had been made aware of Lenin's activities through an Estonian nationalist, Alexander Keskuela, who also sought the overthrow of the Romanovs. Another adviser to the Germans was Alexander Helphand-Parvus, who had influenced the thinking of Lev Trotski in 1905. Parvus was a German left-wing critic of the German Social-Democratic Party; he was also a wealthy businessman whose murky deals in Scandinavia, the Balkans and Turkey had involved errands on behalf of the German government. One of Lenin's associates, Jakub Hanecki, was an employee of Parvus in Stockholm. Although Lenin's direct meetings with Keskuela and Parvus were rare, there is strong circumstantial evidence that the Germans made finance available to the Bolsheviks as a result.

Thus Lenin was trying to foment the 'European socialist revolution' with a secret financial allowance from people he publicly denounced as German imperialists. The relationship was perfectly logical for him. His aim was to bring about capitalism's overthrow and the sole criterion for any action was whether it would strengthen the cause of Revolution. The spreading of Bolshevik ideas in Russia and in German POW camps fell into this category. The only snag was that his machinations had to be kept strictly confidential. Indeed any breach of secrecy would have finished him off politically just months before the February 1917 Revolution – and twentieth-century history would have been very different.

Through the rest of 1916 and the beginning of the following year he repeated his song that Revolution was 'ripe'. It was 'imminent'; it was 'growing'. Time was on the side of those who held to 'orthodox' Marxist precepts and put them into practice by subverting capitalist governments. Lenin did not think that 'European socialist revolution', whenever it occurred, would happen overnight. He stressed that there might be countries whose capitalists would fend off the revolutionary assault. There might be a Second World War and even a Third. This was an unusual idea among his far-left socialists; indeed there was no one else in European politics who expressed it. But Lenin, despite being a firebrand, took Revolution very seriously. He felt in his bones that he lived in a revolutionary epoch. Epochs could be very lengthy. Epochs could involve a tangled sequence of events. Epochs could include setbacks as well as advances. Lenin was preparing himself for the long struggle. He knew that the future, both for him and for his party, would require adaptability, perceptiveness and endurance. Above all, endurance. But about the correctness of his fundamental strategy Lenin had not the slightest doubt.

His firmness of purpose was surprising to acquaintances who did not know his granite-like character. As the year 1916 drew to a close, Lenin was forty-six. He was a man of intellectual and practical talent, and yet he had never had the impact on his country's affairs that his talent could have facilitated. He was a leading Russian Marxist and was known in the Second Socialist International in Europe as well as in the Okhrana offices in Petrograd. He had written books and pamphlets and was a prolific journalist; Russian encyclopaedias contained brief entries on him. But his followers in the Russian Empire were a dwindling group in the Great War. Even his sister Anna questioned his political judgement. His contact with Bolsheviks in the Russian local committees was getting ever more slender; and the man who had preached Revolution to Marxists at home and abroad was reduced to seeking consolation in Hegel and Aristotle. There was hardly a Russian worker outside the narrow confines of the party who even knew his name. For such a man to emerge as the ruler of Russia the situation had to undergo fundamental change. He needed not only his firmness of purpose and his talent but also an access of good fortune. And this is precisely what occurred in the following year.

PART THREE

SEIZING POWER

Entre nous: if they bump me off, I would ask you to publish my notebook, 'Marxism on the State' (it's held up in Stockholm). A navy-blue bound folder. There's a collection of all the citations from Marx and Engels as well as from Kautsky against Pannekoek.

Lenin in summer 1917

15

ANOTHER COUNTRY

February to April 1917

At the end of February 1917 the political eruption took place that Lenin had long predicted. Revolution came to Petrograd. Industrial strikes had been occurring for some days, starting with action by women textile workers. The trouble had quickly spread to the labour-force of the Putilov metallurgical plant and the police proved incapable of keeping control. When the guards regiments were called out, the revolutionary groups in the capital – Mensheviks, Bolsheviks and Socialist-Revolutionaries – were reluctant to organise street demonstrations. The Okhrana had crushed strikes in late 1915 and late 1916, and there seemed no reason why this would not happen again.

But the popular mood was implacable. Workers were aggrieved by the deteriorating conditions in the factories and by the food shortages. The strikers, moreover, could no longer rely upon the troops in the capital's garrisons to suppress political protest. Gradually the revolutionaries regained their confidence. Down the Nevski Prospekt in the centre of Petrograd marched the demonstrators: no one any longer dared to oppose them. Out of the shadows came the leaders of the Fourth State Duma, which had recently been prorogued by Nicholas II; they formed a confidential committee and hoped to be able to exploit events before they ran out of control. Nicholas II was not in Petrograd but at military headquarters in Mogilëv and all this information threw him into panic. The Mensheviks meanwhile re-formed a Petrograd Soviet and campaigned for a republic. By then the socialist parties sensed that the moment of Revolution had arrived. The Emperor tried to abdicate in favour of his haemophiliac son Alexei; but it was not to be. On 2 March he saw that the game was up and abdicated in favour first of his son and then of his brother Mikhail. This concession was inadequate for the rebels and power passed to the leaders of the dispersed State Duma. The Romanov dynasty which had ruled Russia since 1613 had been overthrown.

When the news about the seriousness of the situation came through to Zurich, it took the Russian emigrants by surprise. The reports from Petrograd had been turning a spotlight upon the troubles in their country, yet it was impossible for revolutionaries abroad to judge whether the final crisis of tsarism had arrived. Lenin was no different from his fellow émigrés; he waited patiently to see what would happen. Thus it came about that he was prepring to set off for the library in the normal fashion after lunch, leaving Nadya behind to clear the table and do the washing up.[1]

Hotfoot to 14 Spiegelgasse came a comrade, M. G. Bronski, who had read in the Swiss newspapers that Revolution – *the* Revolution, the long-awaited Revolution, the glorious Revolution against the Romanovs – was occurring. The telegrams had arrived that morning. Bronski was astonished that the Lenins had not yet heard: 'Don't you know anything?!' Lenin and Nadya hastened to the side of the lake where they would be able to check Bronski's story against the contents of newspapers pasted on boards for public display. Perhaps, they surmised, Bronski had been exaggerating. All the emigrants wanted a revolutionary eruption so badly that they guarded themselves against casually believing that it was occurring. But this time the story was true. Both the Swiss newspapers and the telegrams from Petrograd had the same message. Stunned and delighted, Lenin and Nadya read the reports several times to themselves.[2] There really could be no doubt: Revolution had occurred. This time there were not merely the signs of a monarchy under pressure; the monarchy had been blown away. Nicholas II, whose father had shown no clemency towards Lenin's brother Alexander and whose whole family was detested by Lenin, had become citizen Romanov.

The rest of the day was spent in a hubbub of meetings with fellow emigrants in Zurich. Hands were shaken, congratulations were exchanged, revolutionary songs were sung – and Lenin loved to exercise his baritone voice on such occasions. Nadezhda Konstantinovna lost herself in the celebrations to such an extent that she could remember nothing about them.

Sharing in the delight, Lenin wanted to supply what leadership he could to the Bolsheviks at work in Russia. This could not be done directly: he had to dispatch messages through Alexandra Kollontai in Oslo, who maintained links with the Central Committee in Petrograd. On 3 March 1917 he composed a telegram affirming the need for Bolsheviks to stick by their old slogans. Lenin warned against any change of party policy on the war. On no account should socialists allow themselves to approve of 'the defence of the fatherland'. Reunification with the Mensheviks should be rejected. The Bolsheviks needed their own separate party. The objective should be '*international* proletarian revolution and the conquest of power by "Soviets of workers' deputies"'. He did not fail to mention that no compromise was tolerable with Kautsky.[3] This was quite a political summons; it was a gauntlet thrown at the feet of the Provisional Government. Lenin was not going to accept the right of Milyukov, Guchkov and Kerenski (who he had predicted a year previously would try to form a governmental coalition) to govern Russia. His language was unmistakably insurrectionary. Let the soviets assume power! Let the Revolution spread beyond Russia! Let every true socialist promote the revolutionary cause across Europe!

Lenin did not bother to consult with the other Bolshevik emigrants. More than that: he wrote without any detailed knowledge of what was happening in Russia. Quite wrongly, he thought that Nicholas II was organising a counter-revolution; and his preoccupation with Kautsky showed how out of touch he was with the wishes of Petrograd workers. But Lenin was a leader. He offered whatever guidance he could, and Kollontai telegraphed by return of post with a request for further directives. Steadily he clarified his intentions in his messages to her and to the Bureau of the Central Committee, even though he had no idea how they were being received in Russia.

He did not intend to repeat the mistake of 1905, when he had returned to Russia months after the revolutionary turmoil began. But this time a war cut through the central zone of Europe. He could not cross to Russia through France and the North Sea without the permission of the Allies, and this would never be forthcoming. To have tried to enter Russia via the Mediterranean was similarly unfeasible. The Turks were unpredictable and Russian revolutionaries might not have been allowed free transit. And so Lenin had to contemplate alternatives. His most imaginative thought was to dress up as a deaf-and-dumb Swede and take the train across Germany to Denmark and then make his way to Finland and eventually to Petrograd. Nadya dissuaded him, pointing out that he would inevitably blabber about the Mensheviks in his sleep and be discovered. His other ideas were equally madcap. At one point, for example, he proposed to charter a plane – then an unreliable mode of transport – to the other side of the eastern front. But he would not drop the plan until someone mentioned that no flying machine could yet travel such a distance and that anyway the artillery of the Central Powers would shoot him down.

Yet sound alternatives were few, and indeed there was only one that was worth exploring. This was the idea put forward by Martov that the Russian socialists in Switzerland should seek permission from the German government for their passage across Germany in return for the Russian Provisional Government releasing an equal number of German nationals interned in Russia. Robert Grimm negotiated with the German consul in Bern, Gisbert von Romberg, on behalf of the Russians. Quickly Grimm gained a positive response from Berlin. The only further requirement was the Provisional Government's formal approval, but the problem was that Russian Foreign Minister Pavel Milyukov objected. Martov declined to implement the plan until such time as the Petrograd Soviet had pressed Milyukov into conceding permission.

But Lenin would not be put off. Quite unfairly blaming Grimm for incompetence, he turned to one of Grimm's Swiss far-left socialist opponents, Fritz Platten, for help. Platten agreed to go and see Romberg with a proposal formulated by Lenin and Zinoviev. Romberg immediately secured his Foreign Ministry's sanction for any number of Russian political emigrants to cross Germany by train and for such a train to have extraterritorial status during the journey; he also confirmed that his government would make no demand for the release of German prisoners-of-war in exchange.[4] Lenin was ecstatic and immediately planned the details with Zinoviev. Thirty-two travellers would make the trip and Lenin and Zinoviev stipulated that all of them should pay their own fares: no subsidy from the Germans would be allowed. The trip would not be restricted to Bolsheviks. For example, a female leading member of the Jewish Bund was welcomed as a passenger with her four-year-old son Robert. The schedule called for the travellers to make their way to Zurich and assemble at the Zähringerhof Hotel on 27 March. From there they would take a local train up to the border. Such was Lenin's appreciation of Platten's intervention with Romberg that he asked him to act as the travelling party's intermediary for the entire journey. Thus Lenin would have no need to talk to a single German between Switzerland and Denmark.

Nadezhda Konstantinovna argued that he would have to travel ahead of her. How, she asked, could she possibly do everything in time? She knew that it would be her responsibility to pack the Bolshevik correspondence archive, gather their suitcases of belongings, organise their bank accounts and make arrangements for people to keep in touch with them in Russia. She was also upset at having to leave her mother's ashes, and wanted to wait until she had collected them.[5] But Lenin would have none of this. Nadezhda Konstantinovna, he insisted, should come along with him. The Revolution awaited them. The main thing was to get on to the train with their basic possessions as well as pillows and blankets for the journey in the traditional Russian fashion. In the meantime the travellers should ignore the jibes made at them by other emigrants.

The day came, and Lenin and the rest of the travellers walked from the Zähringerhof Hotel to Zurich railway station. Then followed the trip to Schaffhausen on the Swiss side of the border. The German train already stood there for them. After getting on board, they travelled on to the customs point at the hamlet of Thayngen. There they were deprived of some of the food they had brought with them since the amount was greater than the legal limit; the Swiss officials allowed them to send the confiscated chocolate and sugar to relatives and friends. Thereafter they moved across the Alps and over the border to Gottmadingen in Germany. The train halted there and an order was given for the Russian emigrants to be isolated from the rest of the travelling public and escorted to a waiting room. Two German army officers introduced themselves before instructing the Russian emigrants to form separate groups of men and women. The emigrants panicked at this, thinking that something awful was about to happen to the men. A protective ring was formed around Lenin as the Bolshevik leader. But German officers explained that they simply wished to accelerate the business of form-filling before the train could leave the station.[6] The travellers then boarded the train and took their reserved places in the II–III-class carriage, and the train left Gottmadingen on its momentous journey.

The protocol for the journey had been drawn up beforehand. The two German officers were instructed to stay in the rear of the carriage behind a line drawn in chalk dividing 'German' from 'Russian' territory. Seals were affixed to three of the doors to the carriage; but the fourth, which was adjacent to the sleeping compartment of the German officers, was left unlocked. Thus the passengers were not really barred off from the world as they travelled and the famous 'sealed train' is a misnomer. Indeed they spoke to people who came into the train *en route*. This happened because Platten got off in Frankfurt to buy beer and news-papers and asked some soldiers to take them on board for him. Several railway workers joined the soldiers, and the irrepressible Radek had a rare old time inciting them to make a revolution in Germany. What was less acceptable to Lenin was the permission given by the German government for the German trade union leader Wilhelm Janson to get on board in Stuttgart. The emigrants held a brief discussion and told Platten to tell Janson that they would not meet him. They had taken quite enough risks already and did not want reports to reach Russia that they had spoken to enemy citizens on enemy territory.[7]

All this increased the tension. Lenin's nerves – never very relaxed at the best of times – were tautened by the behaviour of his fellow passengers. He and Nadya had been prevailed upon to take a separate coupé so that he could get on with his writing. The problem was that the neighbouring coupé was occupied by Radek, Grigori Safarov, Olga Ravich (Safarov's young wife) and Inessa Armand. The din they made was incessant. When they were not singing, they were laughing at Radek's jokes. Lenin could bear it no longer and, late into the night, burst into their coupé and hauled out Olga Ravich.[8] This was the first case of Bolshevik revolutionary injustice in 1917, for the real noise-maker was not Ravich but Radek. But Lenin could pick on her with greater licence because of her youth, gender and lack of political influence; and it is no surprise that he refrained from laying hands on Inessa: too many deep waters of emotion would have been disturbed. Anyway, Lenin had overstepped the mark: the coupé's occupants defended Ravich and Lenin had to back off.

Lenin refused to retreat, however, on the question of toilet usage. Radek and the other cigarette smokers avoided lighting up in their compartments out of consideration for fellow passengers who did not smoke. They smoked instead in the toilet. This had the effect of creating a queue down the corridor and, to put it delicately, induced considerable physical discomfort. On Lenin's initiative a system of rationing was introduced for toilet access. For this purpose he cut up some paper and issued them as tickets on his authority. There were two types of ticket, one for the normal use of the toilet and the other for a discreet puff on a cigarette. This compelled smokers to limit the number of times they smoked, and quickly the disputes in the queue subsided. It was a comic little episode. Yet, without overdoing the point, we might note that Lenin's intervention was typical of his operational assumptions. He thought that the socialist way of organising society required above all a centrally co-ordinated system of assessing needs, allocating products and services and regulating implementation. Lenin after the October Revolution went further and banned those activities of which he disapproved. But on the journey across Germany he reined himself back. Smokers could indulge themselves so long as they did it rarely and confined themselves to the toilet.

Another feature of the episode was Lenin's imposition of order on his colleagues. Radek drew attention to this, suggesting that it proved that Lenin had it in him to 'assume leadership of the revolutionary government'.[9] As the train rolled on to Berlin and halted in sidings for a whole day, this prognosis seemed far-fetched.[10] Then on 30 March, six days after leaving Switzerland, the emigrants reached the northern port of Sassnitz. Yet another set of forms had to be filled in. As a precaution and on Lenin's suggestion, the travellers should invent fresh pseudonyms for themselves. This was an absurd overreaction since the Germans already had detailed information about the Russians in their care. The German authorities accepted the forms without making a fuss. This had the comical result that, when Lenin's trusted helpmate Hanecki telegraphed from Trelleborg in Sweden with an enquiry as to whether a Mr Ulyanov was present among the passengers, he at first received a negative reply from the Germans.

Eventually the Bolshevik leader admitted his true identity and tickets were purchased for the ferry *Queen Victoria* to convey them from Sassnitz to Trelleborg; they all set sail the same day. The crossing was a rough one and most of the Russians were violently seasick. According to Radek and Zinoviev, only three passengers – Lenin, Radek and Zinoviev – endured the journey without vomiting. They may have been boasting. Or perhaps the story is true because the three of them spent their time on deck arguing furiously about politics, which may well have distracted them from feeling sick. Hanecki treated them to a celebratory banquet on their arrival in Trelleborg. The passengers threw themselves upon the several courses – all the passengers save for Lenin, who concentrated on eliciting information about Russia from Hanecki. Next day the travellers took the train to Stockholm. Again they were fêted. Indeed this was the first occasion in Lenin's career he was given recognition by official foreign leaders. The mayor of Stockholm, Karl Lindhagen, laid on a breakfast to welcome the Russians. The newspaper *Politiken* carried a piece on the returning émigrés and – yet again for the first time – a photograph of Lenin was published. This brief Swedish sojourn marked a stage in the Bolshevik party's transition to prominence.

Radek understood that this required Lenin to present himself rather differently. He put this with typical tartness:[11]

Probably it was the decent appearance of our stolid Swedish comrades that was evoking in us a passionate desire for Ilich to resemble a human being. We cajoled him at least to buy new shoes. He was travelling in mountain boots with huge nails. We pointed out to him that if the plan had been to ruin the pavements of the disgusting cities of bourgeois Switzerland, his conscience should prevent him from travelling with such instruments of destruction to Petrograd, where perhaps there anyway were now no pavements at all.

Lenin was marched off to a department store where clothes were bought for him. Thus refitted, he was judged appropriately dressed to lead the struggle against the Russian Provisional Government.

On 31 March, the passengers boarded the evening train from Stockholm northwards to Finland while Hanecki, Radek and V. V. Vorovski stayed behind to look after Bolshevik affairs abroad. This time Lenin and Nadya had no compartment to themselves. Georgian Bolshevik David Suliashvili, who took the bunk opposite Lenin, watched as he 'rapidly devoured the newspapers with his eyes'. While reading the Russian press, Lenin could not contain his annoyance with the Mensheviks: 'Ach, the scoundrels! ... Ach, the traitors!'[12] Several hours and dozens of ill-tempered exclamations later, the train reached the border with Finland at Harapanda. There the passengers got off and hired sleighs across the road bridge into the town of Tornio. They were briefly searched by Russian border guards before getting on yet another train for Helsinki. In Tornio Lenin had picked up recent copies of *Pravda*. He took himself off to a corner of the waiting room and studied the contents. This gave him two unpleasant shocks. The first was that Malinovski had been proved beyond peradventure to have been an Okhrana agent. Lenin went white with astonishment. Zinoviev sketched the scene: 'Several times Ilich, staring eyeball to eyeball, returned to this theme. In short sentences. More in a whisper. He looked straight in my face. "What a scoundrel! He tricked the lot of us. Traitor! Shooting's too good for him!"'[13] The second shock was the news that the Bolshevik Central Committee, led by Lev Kamenev and Iosif Stalin since their release from Siberian exile, had adopted a policy of conditional support for the Russian Provisional Government. Already disgusted with the Mensheviks, Lenin was infuriated by leading Bolsheviks.

From Helsinki the émigrés took the Finland Railway to Petrograd. The train went at a steady speed, never reaching forty miles per hour, and the passengers grew impatient. At Beloostrov, twenty miles north of the capital, their train halted at the Russo-Finnish administrative border for the regular passport and customs checks. The Bolshevik Central Committee had sent ahead none other than Lev Kamenev to greet the returning leader and discuss the reception awaiting him. Lenin received him with something less than hospitality: 'What have you been writing in *Pravda*? We've seen a few copies and have called you all sorts of names!'

Lenin was also getting nervous again. As the train drew near to the capital late into the night on 3 April, he fretted lest he should be arrested on arrival despite the reassurances of Kamenev. In fact Kamenev was right. The Bolshevik leadership had arranged a welcome at the Finland Station in the Russian capital. Mensheviks and Socialist-Revolutionaries from the Petrograd Soviet also turned out. Twenty minutes before the train's arrival, two sailors' units assembled on the platform as a guard of honour for Lenin. The naval officer expected him to say a few words of greeting to them. It was almost midnight. Nikolai Chkheidze, a Menshevik leader and Petrograd Soviet chairman, turned up to greet the returning Bolshevik leader. Outside the station building a crowd of workers and soldiers had gathered, just as had happened at the Kursk Station when leaders of the various socialist parties had arrived from Siberian exile. Eyes were fixed on the railway line to the north, and at last the lights of the train were glimpsed in the darkness. The locomotive wound its way towards the station like a fiery snake. Steam hissed from the pistons. The crowd, most of whom had never previously seen Lenin, started to push towards the building. The train rumbled to the side of the platform. He had arrived. After a decade abroad Lenin stepped down from the carriage on to Russian soil.

Then the celebrations started to go awry as Lenin refused to join in the spirit of comradeship. Improvising a speech to the sailors of the guard of honour, he told them that they had been deceived by the Provisional Government.[14] He was starting as he meant to go on. Followed by Nadezhda Konstantinovna and Kamenev, he strode through to the reception rooms formerly reserved for the Imperial family. Chkheidze greeted him as a respected emigrant and appealed for co-operation among all socialists, but Lenin barely looked at him and replied with a summons for 'world socialist revolution'. He then walked out of the station and clambered on top of an armoured car brought to the Finland Station by local Bolsheviks. From this position he could survey the crowd of thousands. His message to them was that capitalism had to be brought down in Russia and the rest of Europe, and that genuine socialists should withhold all support for the Provisional Government.

Lenin's words disconcerted practically everyone who heard them that night; many listeners — or at least those who were close enough to hear him – thought he had gone off his head. Kamenev and other leading Bolsheviks were baffled, and hoped that once he had got over his long separation from Russia in Switzerland he would come to his senses. Even Nadezhda Konstantinovna seems to have doubted his sanity.[15] Just a few colleagues were pleased by what he had said at the Finland Station. Among these were Alexandra Kollontai and Alexander Shlyapnikov. A lot of Bolsheviks of a lesser standing in the faction agreed, having been appalled by the agreement of most Mensheviks and Socialist-Revolution-aries and indeed many Bolsheviks to lend conditional support to the Provisional Government. Lenin had returned to a fluid situation. There was a chance – a chance that was bound to grow larger with time – to build a separate anti-governmental party. The man who had stood high on the armoured car in dead of night had not been a lone wolf; he was part of a pack that would get noisier and stronger. Bolshevism was finding its confidence again. A leader had returned to Petrograd who would give clarity to Bolshevik ideas and add resolve to Bolshevik practical campaigns.

In the trains between Switzerland and Russia he had busied himself by sketching his proposed strategy. These he was to call his *April Theses*. He gave them a polish between Beloostrov and Petrograd, keeping his phraseology short and punchy. There were ten theses. Some were chiselled with attention to detail, others were offered in lapidary slabs. Lenin wrote his *April Theses* deliberately so as to appeal to all far-left socialists who were uneasy with the Provisional Government's stance. He wanted to convince his own Bolsheviks; his desire was also to attract recruits from the other parties.

There is much confusion in scholarly writings about the *April Theses*. Most of it results from the assumption that Lenin was a politician averse to verbal fudging. This is quite wrong. Lenin had to operate in a specific legal environment and, although he wanted the Bolsheviks to seize power, it would have been dangerous to say this directly. He had not travelled to Petrograd to offer himself as a martyr. His purposes were evident even though they were couched in oblique terms. Essentially he was taking his wartime thought a little further and explicitly redefining Bolshevism. And this constituted a rejection of the traditional Russian Marxist notion that a 'bourgeois-democratic' revolution should be con-solidated in Russia before any attempt at a further revolution, involving a social and economic eradication of capitalism, should be made. In April 1917 he demanded the abandonment of 'the old Bolshevism' and the reduction of the two stages of the revolutionary process to one. Even so, Lenin's demand was not made explicitly. He may have disliked acknowledging a strategic change of mind; or perhaps he did not want to get involved in a doctrinal dispute at a moment when his priority was to secure assent to a practical policy. Above all, the Provisional Government had to be replaced. Lenin in his *April Theses* argued that only by this means would there be a fundamental solution for the Russian Empire's political, economic and social problems and an end to the Great War with a peace that would be unoppressive for all the belligerent peoples.

There had been grave questions about Lenin's strategy since 1905 when he had aimed to make a 'bourgeois-democratic revolution' by setting up a 'provisional revolutionary democratic dictatorship of the proletariat and the peasantry'. He had never successfully countered the charge that his ideas, if implemented, would establish an oppressive, arbitrary regime and very probably set off a civil war. His *April Theses* were even less capable of addressing these questions. And yet, although an oppressive, arbitrary regime was built into his new strategy, he refused to recognise the fact. He used logical flourishes but did not bother with consistent logic; he would not be fussed about niceties. The time had come, he stated boldly, to begin the advance on power.

Few Bolsheviks could believe their ears when he addressed them at a couple of meetings on 4 April. The first meeting occurred in the premises of the Bolshevik Petersburg Committee in the early hours of the morning. This was the large town-mansion on Kronverski Boulevard previously occupied by the ballerina Matilda Kseshinskaya, Nicholas II's former mistress. Showing no tiredness, Lenin delivered a diatribe against the Bolshevik Central Committee's caution. He raged like a bull. Everything about him reflected impatience and determination. There was a clarity of intent that no one else in his party possessed. Indeed very few politicians in the other parties had quite the self-belief of Vladimir Lenin. Politics in Russia were turbulent and unpredictable, and most leaders had a degree of doubt about their policies; they naturally tended to seek support for the actions and to have their close colleagues tell them that what they were doing was right. There were exceptions to this. Kadet leader Pavel Milyukov had no need for his party members to bolster his commitment to basic liberal concepts; and Socialist-Revolutionary Alexander Kerenski's confident understanding of the political possibilities inured him to criticisms by his fellow party leaders. Milyukov and Kerenski felt they could, if permitted by circumstances, act as the embodiment of the Revolution in Russia. Lenin felt the same, but, unlike these rivals, he did not see it as his task to modify the policies of the Provisional Government. Lenin aimed to make another Revolution.

He had yet to settle himself into the extraordinary environment. Arriving in Petrograd, he had no idea where he and Nadya would stay the night. But his family had thought about this on his behalf. Anna Ilinichna and her husband Mark Yelizarov were then living at 48 Broad Street, a multi-storey tenement built at the turn of the century in the Petrograd Side district to the north-east of the city's centre. Younger sister Maria lived in the same apartment. After the Bolshevik Petersburg Committee meeting, Volodya and Nadya proceeded to Broad Street.

As they tried to make sense of developments, they were certain about one thing: the days of emigration were over for good. Nadya put this into her memoirs:[16]

> When we were left alone, Ilich scanned the room: it was a typical room in a Petersburg apartment; there was an instant sense of the reality of the fact that we were now in Piter [Petrograd's popular nickname] and that all those Parises, Genevas, Berns and Zurichs were already something genuinely in the past. We exchanged a couple of words on this subject.

There was no time for a longer conversation since it was late into the night and an important day awaited them. Lenin and Nadya slept separately. Gora Lozgachëv, the adoptive son of Anna and Mark, had pinned a notice over the two beds: 'Proletarians of all countries, unite!'[17] It was a fitting scene. Lenin and Nadya were not paying heed to their marriage; their minds were fixated on the political tasks ahead. The opportunity to have a daily influence on Russian politics had been snatched from them in 1907. Now it had been restored and each was going to grasp it.

Lenin had one private duty to perform before he could dive into the political torrent. After breakfast, he asked Vladimir Bonch-Bruevich – friend of the Ulyanov family and a fellow Bolshevik – to obtain a car for his use. Together with Bonch-Bruevich, he visited the graves of his mother and his sister Olga in the Volkovo Cemetery. Lenin controlled his emotions at the graveside. Bonch-Bruevich, who was more typically Russian than Lenin in his emotional reactions, had expected him to weep, but this was not how the Ulyanovs had been brought up to behave.

Lenin enjoyed living again with his sisters. Dmitri Ilich was still serving as a doctor in Crimea and Lenin did not meet him for another two years. Lenin liked to play with young Gora. Anna Ilinichna ran the domestic regime according to strict rules and frightened any children who displeased her; she also stopped her husband from indulging their adoptive son.[18] But she never dared to order Vladimir Ilich about and had only to leave the room and the noise would start. Gora and he engaged in every sort of horseplay. It was nothing for them to set the chairs flying in the sitting room. Lenin also played tricks on Gora. This involved a considerable amount of teasing at poor Gora's expense. Nadya objected to the 'inquisitorial' aspect of Lenin's behaviour: 'Volodya! Well, now that you've completely tormented him, leave the child in peace! Look what you've done – you've broken the table.'[19] On this occasion Lenin had lunged so suddenly at Gora that the two went tumbling over the table. A horrified Anna Ilinichna returned to ascertain what was happening.[20] If her husband Mark had been responsible, he would have earned the lash of his wife's tongue. But Lenin was different. Lenin could be forgiven everything. He was the family's darling; he could be gently reproved, very gently; but no one was allowed to thwart him. It was all right to 'spoil' Lenin.

Anna Ilinichna had transferred her sisterly affection from Alexander to Vladimir after Alexander's execution. Vladimir the writer and public figure embodied her ideal. But she idolised him also because the traumas of the family's past could somehow be salved by Vladimir's career. Her brother Vladimir was bent on eradicating the old regime which, in her opinion, had treated the Ulyanovs brutally. He was a fighter in a noble cause.

We do not really know how much Lenin thought about Sasha's execution, and certainly he had a propensity for clinical political judgement. But beneath the cool, analytical surface he was also a man of passion. Whatever his precise feelings about the Romanovs, he raged against the entire social order of tsarism. He detested the nobility, the industrialists, bankers. For Lenin, moreover, liberals were as bad as conservatives and outright reactionaries. Unlike other political leaders, he saw the Provisional Government not as the embodiment of a new regime but as a newer form of the old. His version of Marxist theory propelled him in the direction of denouncing the 'capitalist ministers' and their supporters. But so, too, did his family's experience. He recalled – and no doubt the visit to the Volkovoe Cemetery reminded him forcibly – how his family had been ostracised in Simbirsk after Alexander's execution. He felt no impulse to forgive and forget. Lenin had spent his adult life denouncing non-socialists as being no better than the regime they purported to oppose. Lenin, without saying this explicitly, wanted to settle some scores. He wanted revenge, and the surviving members of his family – as well as others in his own party (and in the general population) – felt the same.

It was in this spirit that he returned from the cemetery and went to his second political meeting of 4 April. This took place in room no. 13 of the Tauride Palace. This was the building which had formerly housed the State Duma and which, since the February Revolution, had contained both the Provisional Government and the Petrograd Soviet. The large parties were allowed to hold meetings there. A gathering of Bolsheviks from all over the country was held there in advance of a conference of the country's soviets of workers' and soldiers' deputies. Lenin astounded practically everyone who had not yet heard his proposals. Without naming names, he attacked those who offered reconciliation with the Mensheviks. The contents of the *April Theses* were revealed and explained. Most Bolsheviks could hardly believe their ears. Notable exceptions were Alexandra Kollontai and Alexander Shlyapnikov. The rest were aghast. Kamenev in particular believed Lenin to have taken leave of his senses. Most of Lenin's friends hoped that he would calm down once he had had a chance to acquaint himself with the realities of the contemporary situation in Russia. Surely, they asked, this madness could not long continue?

Lengthy debate was impossible, however, because Lenin had already spoken for an hour and a half and his presence was awaited at a third meeting downstairs where the State Duma had once held its proceedings. This was to be a unificatory session of all Marxist delegates to the conference of the country's soviets of workers' and soldiers' deputies. Mensheviks went up to room 13 to press the Bolsheviks to bring their leader along with them.

The chairman of the session was Nikolai Chkheidze, and Lenin was again given the platform. His lengthy journey had left no mark on him. Pacing up and down, he was like a liberated animal. Having rehearsed his ideas twice already, he had a clear head – and he made a stormy declaration of revolutionary intent. But this time the response was critical. First of all, Irakli Tsereteli as Menshevik leader of the Petrograd Soviet made a plea for a unified Marxist party and argued that an early seizure of state power would lead to disaster. Mildly he suggested that eventually he would be able to co-operate with Lenin. Getting to his feet, Lenin instantly disillusioned him: 'Never!'[21] Former Bolshevik I. P. Goldenberg compared Lenin with the mid-nineteenth-century anarchist leader Mikhail Bakunin, who had polemicised with Marx himself:[22]

> The throne is now occupied which has been empty for thirty years since the death of Bakunin. From this seat the banner of civil war has been unfurled in the midst of revolutionary democracy. Lenin's programme is sheer insurrectionism, which will lead us into the pit of anarchy. These are the tactics of the universal apostle of destruction.

After such a denunciation there was no chance of a rapid reconciliation between Bolshevik and Menshevik leaders. Other speakers continued the attack on Lenin. As the rowdy session broke up, the chairman Chkheidze permitted himself the jibe that 'Lenin will remain a solitary figure outside the revolution and we'll all go our own way.'[23]

Yet Lenin did not remain alone. He was pleased with his first day's work in Petrograd and wished to consolidate it over the following weeks. On every possible occasion he harangued the Provisional Government, harangued the Mensheviks and Socialist-Revolutionaries for supporting the Provisional Government, harangued Bolsheviks who sympathised with the Mensheviks and Socialist-Revolutionaries. He spoke at open mass meetings. He wrote for *Pravda*. He attended and guided the Bolshevik Central Committee. He talked with visitors to Petrograd in order to get information about the provinces. He scoured the non-Bolshevik press for further news. He kept in touch with Radek in Stockholm and stayed abreast of the military and political situation elsewhere in Europe. He was aflame with zeal. Everything he did was undertaken so that the *April Theses* might become the foundation of Bolshevik revolutionary strategy.

But he was not inflexible. In the *April Theses* he had had the tact to recognise that not all the people who supported the Provisional Government were out-and-out imperialists. He knew that most workers and soldiers retained a patriotic will to defeat Germany. He had to persuade them carefully to come over to Bolshevism. For this to happen, moreover, the Bolsheviks had to obtain majorities in the soviets and other mass organisations: there could be no lasting possession of power unless the party had secured widespread popular support. The Bolsheviks therefore had to secure their opportunity to operate legally. Propaganda in the press and at open meetings would be crucial, and Lenin did not wish to create difficulties for the party by the open advocacy of activity that would invite repression by the Ministry of the Interior. On arrival in Petrograd he also learned that his own slogans were problematic.

Most listeners were deeply disturbed by his talk of the need to turn the 'imperialist war into a European civil war'. Nor did workers, soldiers and peasants in general warm to the prospect of a 'revolutionary war' or a 'dictatorship'. As for his demand for Europe's socialists to campaign for the defeat of their respective governments, this was a notion which simply offended Russian public opinion at all levels.

Lenin quickly dropped such slogans in his articles for *Pravda* and his speeches to heavily attended open meetings. He did not cease to believe in the slogans; he remained convinced that they alone were adequate to the epoch of socialist transformation which, according to him, had already arrived. But he was adjusting himself to practical needs and was sensible enough, for the present, to hearken to the warnings given to him by Kamenev. And even when modified, his slogans offered a massive contrast with the programme of the Provisional Government. He called for rule by the soviets. He demanded the nationalisation of large-scale industry and the banks. He urged the governmental expropriation of agricultural land. He advocated the cause of peace throughout Europe and argued that only a socialist administration, constituted by the soviets, could achieve this.

Constantly he declared that the Mensheviks and Socialist-Revolutionaries were at best fools and at worst renegades in espousing co-operation between the Petrograd Soviet and the Provisional Government. He rejected their entire argument, which once he had shared, that Russia was at altogether too low a point of industrial and cultural development for the beginning of 'the transition to socialism' to be feasible. He denied that the country was best protected against military conquest by a political alliance of all social classes, and he scoffed at the suggestion that the primary task of the moment was to protect the gains of the February 1917 Revolution (even though he acknowledged that Russia had become 'the freest country in the world'). His refrain was that the Mensheviks and Socialist-Revolutionaries were the subordinate partners of the Kadets and that an 'imperialist' government had been established. Lenin pointed to the fact the Pavel Milyukov, who espoused the expansion of Russian territory at the expense of the Ottoman Empire, was Foreign Affairs Minister. This, he said, was proof that the replacement of Nicholas II by the Provisional Government had changed nothing essential in the orientation of official policy in Petrograd.

Events ran in his favour when it became known that Milyukov had notified the Allies that the government stood by Nicholas II's war aims. On 20–21 April there was a protest demonstration in the capital against this. Bolsheviks joined in enthusiastically. Milyukov and Guchkov were compelled to resign from the cabinet and Prince Lvov had to put together a new coalition, including Mensheviks and Socialist-Revolutionaries as ministers. Ostensibly the Mensheviks and Socialist-Revolutionaries acquired great influence at the apex of the state. In reality they became tarred with the brush of the Provisional Government's continued failures to deal with the multiplicity of crises in the country.

At the Party Conference held by the Bolsheviks in the Kseshinskaya mansion from 24 April, Lenin seized his chance. The 'Milyukov Note', he declared, had proved that the Provisional Government was not to be trusted. Vacillating Bolshevik organisations had come over to his side. Few Bolsheviks who had disapproved of the *April Theses* were elected as delegates to the Conference. Many of the anti-Leninists, indeed, had already deserted the Bolsheviks. By moderating his language in public, furthermore, he allayed the doubts of leaders such as Kamenev who had attacked him in the Central Committee; and he agreed that, for the moment, the emphasis should be on propaganda rather than insurrection. Then, behind the closed doors of the Conference in the Kseshinskaya mansion, Lenin demanded the establishment of a socialist dictatorship. This alone, he maintained, would give land to the peasants, bread and employment to the workers, national self-determination to the non-Russians and peace to everyone. Objections were made that he had scrapped Marxist orthodoxy about stages in historical development. But most delegates had no patience with such niceties and Lenin's call for Bolsheviks to play their part in the imminent revolution in Russia and the rest of Europe carried the day. On the 'national question' and on 'the agrarian question' too he was victorious. Bolshevism was back in his firm grasp once again.[24]

His rhetoric and imposing presence had made the best of a situation in the party that was already propitious. And both he and the Conference as a whole saw that the situation in the country was also turning in favour of the socialist far left. The difficulties facing the new government were almost intractable in current conditions. The dislocation of industry and commerce was worsening. The food-supplies crisis was becoming acute. On the war fronts there was no good news. The framework of state administration, already somewhat creaky, was tottering dangerously. The abolition of the monarchy had opened politics to open public discussion and organisation, and the workers, soldiers and peasants expected much from the Provisional Government. Its ministers would find it extremely hard to satisfy them.

16

THE RUSSIAN COCKPIT

May to July 1917

Lenin had won over his party; his task now was to convince those of his fellow citizens to whom his party wished to appeal. It had not been difficult to convince the leaders and activists who attended the Party Conference. Much trickier would be the task of tossing the net of propaganda and organisation beyond the ranks of committed Bolsheviks. There was no certainty of success. If 'Soviet power' was to become a reality, very large sections of the Imperial population had to be brought over to Bolshevism.

Lenin aimed his slogans at workers, soldiers, sailors and peasants and he also tried to win over the non-Russian nationalities. The principal culprits for the country's woes, he stated, were the industrialists, the bankers and the agricultural landlords. According to this analysis, on one side were 'the people', the exploited majority; on the other were the parasitical few. Although Lenin claimed to be offering policies based on unsentimental, scientific premises, his language was highly emotive and moralistic. It was also remarkably selective. Throughout these months Lenin strove to avoid giving offence to elements in the population that might otherwise have rallied to an anti-Bolshevik cause. Thus he made no overt threat to small-scale entrepreneurs, shopkeepers and self-employed artisans. He said nothing untoward about priests, mullahs and rabbis. He did not criticise officials and clerks in the various administrations of government, public services and business. Lenin wanted a clear field for the main political struggle, which he saw as being a contest between the 'proletariat' and the 'bourgeoisie'. Whenever he wrote or spoke, he declared that the bourgeoisie was already on the offensive; he put forward his party as the only possible defender of the working class.

Lenin insisted that the Provisional Government was imperialist in intent and obedient to the interests of Russia's robber capitalists. The people, he declared, were being tricked:[1]

Ruin is imminent. Catastrophe is on its way. The capitalists have brought and are bringing all countries to destruction. The sole salvation is revolutionary discipline, revolutionary measures taken by *the revolutionary class*, the proletarians and semi-proletarians, the transition of all state power into the hands of this class that will be able in reality to introduce such control, in reality to carry through victoriously 'the struggle against the parasites'.

Lenin's language was a curious mixture. His Marxist jargon was uncompromising: 'proletarian' was unusual enough, 'semi-proletarian' even more so to most of his fellow citizens. Yet there was also a punchy thrust in his writings. Ruin, catastrophe and destruction ran like a red thread through his vocabulary. When he got up on a platform, the audience was transfixed. He paced up and down. He fixed the crowd with a piercing gaze. He pinned his thumbs in his waistcoat like a schoolteacher, which added to the impression he gave of purveying genuine knowledge. He was not a conventionally brilliant orator. His enunciation was imperfect since he still failed to say his *r*s properly. He also took time to settle into a rhythm in the course of his speeches. But this did not matter to his audiences. The very opposite was the case: the awkwardness of his stocky, unprepossessing figure on the platform conveyed the impression of passion and willpower. In any case, it was often difficult to hear exactly what he was saying at the open public meetings, and the audiences were attracted as much by what they saw – an uncompromising militant leader speaking for the people's cause – as by the precise verbal content of his oratory.

Also of some significance was the fact that Lenin began to dress differently from before 1917. Since leaving Sweden he had a new suit, shoes and cap, which had been bought at Karl Radek's insistence. Consequently he no longer traipsed aroung in heavy, worn-down mountain boots. But it was the cap that his audiences remembered (and which has gone down in sartorial history as a 'Lenin cap'). Commentators have usually contended that his new headwear was typical of the Russian working man of the period. Really his cap, bought in Stockholm, was the floppy sort worn around the turn of the century by painters.[2] The result was to lend a touch of raffishness to Lenin's appearance. Although he wore a smart suit like other politicians, his cap distinguished him from them and their solemn Homburg hats. his devil-may-care policies added to the effect. Lenin, in contrast with rival politicians in other parties, was visibly enjoying the Revolution. He relished every moment, and wished Russians to do the same. Lenin wanted them to abandon their inhibitions and seize the opportunities for self-emancipation with enthusiasm.

Thus Lenin rubbed shoulders comfortably with the factory labourers and garrison soldiers attending his meetings. He loved frequenting such a milieu; he was finding fulfilment as a Marxist in company with the working class and was in a mood of constant excitement. He confided to Nadya, when he joined her in the Ulyanov apartment at 48 Broad Street, that he had found himself politically at last.[3] This adaptation required much effort. At one of his early meetings he sat on the platform with Alexandra Kollontai. At the last moment he panicked and asked her to deliver the speech on his behalf. Kollontai was astounded. She thought of Lenin as a confident party leader. She herself liked holding forth to large audiences, and persuaded Lenin that there was nothing very much to oratory. Lenin took heart and repaid her faith in his ability. He never again needed his inner belief to be enhanced by her or anyone else.[4]

Lots of people who disliked his policies confessed to being enthralled by his speeches. Many readers of his newspaper articles registered the same effect. He had an unrivalled ability to set out his arguments and lay out a militant case. His aggressive descriptions of his enemies and their policies gave everyone the feeling that here was a man who could wield governmental power. Provisional Government ministers were tame by comparison. Kadets, Mensheviks and Socialist-Revolutionaries had to compromise with each other; but Lenin treated compromise as a dirty word. He wanted dynamic, ruthless, correct measures to be taken, and contended that only a standpoint based upon 'class struggle' would suffice. He wrote a great deal: forty-eight pieces appeared in *Pravda* in May 1917 alone. As the Bolshevik central newspaper, *Pravda* was the main conduit of his ideas to the party, and no one's name appeared in its pages more often than Lenin's. He was in his element. He thought, wrote and acted as if he and the party were interchangeable. The country's other newspapers had the same opinion that Lenin embodied the sole alternative to the political status quo.

He made public appearances too, delivering twenty-one speeches in May and June. Some of his speeches were short contributions to closed party meetings; others were disquisitions that included a couple of tirades to the First All-Russia Congress of Soviets. But he reserved most of his energy for *Pravda*. Lenin was a politician of the printed word; he was the brilliant gimnazia student who had turned into a Marxist scholar – and it had been he who developed the theory for Russian Marxists that the best instrument to establish a clandestine party was a newspaper, *Iskra*. He could adapt his style, but only up to a point. Words in print were still his revolutionary touchstone and he badgered colleagues who spent their time speaking at mass meetings rather than writing.[5] The conventional wisdom that he was the master of all the political skills between the February and October Revolutions is unconvincing.

Yet Lenin enjoyed his politics. Petrograd was a place of great cultural effervescence in 1917. The world-famous bass Fëdor Shalyapin was giving concerts. There were shows of paintings. Previously banned books were appearing. Street carnivals were organised. Symphony concerts were frequent. But Lenin kept his distance from them. Later he explained himself to Maxim Gorki:[6]

> But often I can't listen to music. It acts on my nerves. It makes one want to say a lot of sweet nonsense and stroke the heads of people who live in a filthy hell-hole and yet can create such beauty. But you can't stroke anyone's head today – you'll get your hands cut off. The need is to beat them over the head, beat them mercilessly even though we, as an ideal, are against any coercion of people. Hm, hm . . . it's a hellishly difficult necessity.

These words came from a man who knew he could not trust his emotions if he was to succeed at Revolution – a man who was willing to contemplate merciless violence not only against the party's enemies but against just about anyone. Not that he had to try very hard to suppress his more generous impulses. He did it very easily, and did it with ever greater facility over the course of his career. The political task at hand was all that mattered.

But, before any heads could be beaten, Lenin had to have power. The Bolshevik party needed to overthrow the Provisional Government and set up a new revolutionary administration. The soviets and other 'mass' organisations, in Lenin's vision, ought to become the basis of governmental authority. Thus would the 'transition to socialism' be undertaken.

With this purpose in mind it was vital for the Bolshevik party to enter the soviets without delay. Bolsheviks should campaign in elections and get themselves into leading soviet posts at the expense of the Mensheviks and the Socialist-Revolutionaries. Accused of wanting to lead his small party into a *coup d'état*, he replied in *Pravda*: 'We shall be for the transition of power into the hands of the proletarians and semi-proletarians at such a time when the soviets of workers' and soldiers' deputies come over to the side of our politics and want to take this power into their own hands.'[7] Thus he affirmed that he would not seize power regardless of popular opinion and that the priority for the Bolsheviks was to obtain a majority in the soviets. The Provisional Government had come into existence only through the acquiescence of the Petrograd Soviet, and ministers ignored the policies of the soviets at their peril. Furthermore, an All-Russia Congress of Soviets of Workers' and Soldiers' Deputies was scheduled for June. The soviets were about to set up a national administrative framework parallel to the Provisional Government, and Lenin urged his party to get ready to use this framework as an instrument to rule the country.

He himself was willing to modify policies further in the light of popular demands. In the *April Theses* he had called for 'land nationalisation'. But, after a survey of peasant opinion undertaken by the Socialist-Revolutionaries indicated hostility to any such nationalisation, Lenin dropped the slogan. Several of his Bolshevik adjutants, notably Stalin, had long argued that it would be hopeless to try to take agricultural land into state property once the peasantry had launched a violent campaign against their landlords. Lenin by August was willing to alter his stance. He would need the consent of the peasantry if he was to consolidate a revolutionary regime. The Bolshevik Central Committee announced a new slogan, 'land socialisation', which gave the peasants virtually a free hand to dispose of the land. He preferred nationalisation, but the greater good – from his standpoint – was served by the acquisition of the peasantry's support.

Another change of policy occurred when he learned that workforces in Petrograd were beginning to institute 'workers' control' in their factories. Just as previously he had objected to peasant communes being allowed to control the villages, so he had never liked the idea of workers taking over their respective factories without direction from the party. But this was a revolutionary situation and, Lenin urged, workers had to be encouraged to make revolution. Their 'creativity' and 'initiative' had to be fostered. The Bolshevik party leadership would do what it could to guide the revolution from above, but 'the masses' had to participate; they had to undertake their revolution from below. And so the Bolshevik leaders had to learn to listen to the voices of workers, soldiers and peasants. Bolshevism in 1905–6 had been too doctrinaire, and Lenin had been exasperated at his fellow activists' distaste for becoming involved in the soviets, trade unions and other mass organisations. There should be no repetition of this blunder in 1917. The Bolshevik party had to be dynamic and flexible within the broad lines of its policies. Consequently it was to be welcomed if workers in Petrograd aspired to institute supervision over factory managements in order to keep their factories in operation.

In May and June 1917 most of the policies were fairly clear. The Bolshevik Central Committee and *Pravda* stood for the revolutionary transfer of governmental power to the soviets. They advocated a general peace in Europe, preceded by an armistice on the eastern front. They called for the nationalisation of large-scale industry and banking, for workers' control in the factories, for the transfer of agricultural land to the peasantry, for national self-determination and for intensified cultural development. The vanguard of this political movement would be the Bolshevik party, which would guide the lower social orders to their destiny: socialist Revolution. Revolution in Russia would quickly be followed by fraternal revolutionary seizures of power elsewhere in Europe. What Russian workers could easily do, he asserted, would be accomplished with still greater ease by the workers of the more advanced industrial powers.

Such a prospect appealed to his party, and over the same months the joint organisations of Bolsheviks and Mensheviks went their separate ways. The Bolsheviks became a genuinely separate political party for the first time. Nor was there any doubt about who led the Bolshevik party. It was Lenin. Initially he was able to keep Nadezhda Konstantinovna working at his side. But she was the first to recognise that the arrangement could not last:[8]

> In the meantime I did not entirely succeed in handling matters in the Secretariat. Of course, it was more difficult by far for Ilich to work without a personal secretary such as I had previously been for him; but now it caused inconvenience since I had to attend both the [*Pravda*] editorial board and Central Committee meetings. Ilich and I talked it over and decided that I should give up the secretaryship and go off and do educational work.

Her self-description as Lenin's personal secretary was too embarrassing to be printed until the late 1980s: Lenin was officially meant to have no particular privileges at home or at work. At any rate the other Bolshevik leaders evidently resented the additional influence accruing to Lenin from her presence at his side, and formal respect for the equal rights of Central Committee members was restored. First Yelena Stasova, then Yakov Sverdlov ran the Secretariat. Lenin did not approve. But he backed down and to his relief he found that both Stasova and Sverdlov were his political admirers no less than was his wife.

Nadezhda Konstantinovna was not telling the full story. While she worked briefly in the Central Committee Secretariat, her sister-in-law Maria Ilinichna was the editorial secretary of *Pravda*. Rivalry for his attention had often arisen among Lenin's women and Nadezhda Konstantinovna's culinary incompetence continued to provoke ribaldry. She did not mind too much since she never claimed to be a chef. But she could have done without Maria Ilinichna making such a song and dance about Lenin's enthusiasm for her chicken dishes. It was hardly surprising that Lenin enjoyed the change of diet since he and Nadya had had to eat horsemeat too often for their liking in Switzerland. (Russians, like the British, tend to be squeamish about eating the horse.) In any case Maria knew how to needle her sister-in-law. Refusing to continue this domestic competition in the central party offices, Nadya took herself off and settled down to political work as party organiser and educator in the Vyborg industrial district.

She was still bothered by Graves's disease, and her cardiac instability was still troubling her, but she was determined to play a part to her fullest ability in the Revolution. She was also the daily provider of emotional succour to the Bolshevik leader. The frantic political pace put him under unrelieved pressure. Headaches and insomnia returned. Maria Ilinichna said that his lifestyle abroad had caused his problems because he had never had a regular, healthy diet. But the disruption of routine got worse in Petrograd; and the fact that he had to attend Central Committee and *Pravda* editorial sessions at which most of his colleagues chainsmoked was an additional irritation. He was constantly exhausted. It is possible that he was already suffering the minor heart attacks that certainly took place within the next two years. But, if attacks occurred, he kept quiet about them. He had lived for the Revolution, and the historic moment of Revolution had arrived. Lenin needed no second thoughts: he could not allow the moment to pass him by – and he had the arrogance to assume that the Revolution might crash if left to itself.

Nadya did what she could to help, but this was difficult. At party meetings and in front of the crowds Lenin had to perform:[9]

On 1 May, Vladimir Ilich gave a speech at the Field of Mars. This was the first May holiday since the overthrow of tsarist power. All the parties turned out. May Day was a *festival* of hopes and aspirations connected with the history of the world-wide labour movement. On that day I lay flat on my back and did not hear

Vladimir Ilich's contribution; but when he arrived home he was not happily excited but rather tired out.

He used to get very tired at that time, and consequently I held back from quizzing him about work. Things turned out badly with our walks too. Once we went out to Yelagin Island, but it turned out to be so crowded and bustling there. We strolled over to sit by the Karpovka embankment. Then we took up the habit of walking around the empty streets of Petrograd Side.

No Alpine air. No vigorous striding up mountain paths. No trips on his bicycle. Just a quick little stroll around the block from Broad Street.

But increasingly Lenin could leave important party functions to others in the Bolshevik Central Committee. Sverdlov was a brilliant administrator in the Secretariat. Kamenev did regular work in the Petrograd Soviet. Stalin was adept at handling most jobs given to him. Zinoviev was a captivating orator. The party also started to attract other Marxists who had previously not accepted Bolshevism. One such was Felix Dzierżyński, a Polish leader who had worked closely with Rosa Luxemburg. But perhaps the most surprising new Bolshevik adherent was none other than Trotski. Lenin courted him once Trotski had made his way back from North America in May 1917. For his part Trotski thought Lenin's decision to go for immediate socialist revolution to be a tacit espousal of Trotskyism. Trotski was therefore keen to enter the only large party that was unconditionally hostile to the Provisional Government: he gave up entirely on the Mensheviks. But years of vituperation between Trotski and the Bolshevik faction were not easily expunged from the minds of other leading Bolsheviks, and Lenin had his work cut out persuading his less calculating comrades to welcome the dazzling literary, oratorical and organisational skills of their former enemy. But Lenin succeeded, and Trotski joined.

It was as well for Lenin that he could depend on such a team since there were limits to his influence inside and outside his party. Few people knew what he looked like. Contemporary Russian newspapers carried no pictures of him; and unlike Alexander Kerenski, the real master of the modern technology of politics in 1917, Lenin had no opportunity to have newsreels taken of him. Moreover, *Pravda* was a dour newspaper and commissioned no cartoons of him, and posters of Lenin were not made until after the October Revolution. Contrary to the conventional impression about them, the propaganda techniques of the Bolsheviks in 1917 were not very imaginative, and it was the newspapers of the other political trends that pioneered pictorial representation. Even so, such newspapers did not popularise Lenin's image with anything near to accuracy. For example, the caricaturists in the Kadet newspaper *Rech* portrayed him as a great bear of a man rather than the squat, stocky fellow that he was – and, as often as not, without his moustache and with more hair than he had since his early twenties.

Lenin did not stray from Petrograd on political campaigns; he turned down every invitation to visit the rest of Russia after his long journey from Zurich. What he knew about the country came through visitors to Petrograd and from the newspapers. There was obvious irony in this. He was credited by the Provisional Government and the anti-Bolshevik parties with almost miraculous power (and this reputation has not vanished in our day). Yet the Bolshevik party was not the well-oiled machine of command that would have made this possible. Its committees in the provinces were reluctant automatically to toe the line drawn by the Central Committee. Organisationally the party was as anarchic as any other contemporary political party. It was also equally subject to the vagaries of the post and telegraph services. Messages from Petrograd arrived slowly or not at all. And the party's central newspaper *Pravda* had a typical print-run of only ninety thousand copies for a population of 160 million people,[10] and half of these copies were kept for distribution in the capital. The link that Lenin wanted between himself and the general populace was pretty weak in practice.

Yet the enemies of the Bolshevik party identified him as the greatest single threat to political stability. Liberals and conservatives treated his trip by special train across Germany as proof that he was a German spy. Less respectable newspapers played the anti-semitic card, claiming that Lenin was pursuing the interests of the Jews. The press campaign against him stirred up passions that threatened his personal safety. On one occasion a couple of upper-class Russian women burst into the *Pravda* offices and announced: 'We have come to beat up Lenin!' Luckily for him, this was an isolated episode; it might have been different if, instead of two ladies, a group of Cossacks had come to get him. Nevertheless the Bolshevik Central Committee took the precaution of assigning several party members to go round with him.

His recurrent concern was to keep probing the defences of the Provisional Government. For this purpose there was no better method than a large political demonstration, preferably involving armed soldiers and sailors. He had no elaborate plan for insurrection, or any plan whatsoever; but he was constantly on the look-out for any weaknesses that might be exploited. He had tried this in the protest demonstration against the Milyukov Note in April. He tried the same again in June, when the Central Committee organised a demonstration to coincide with the opening of the First Congress of Soviets. The demonstration was to be an armed affair, and unsurprisingly the Provisional Government foresaw trouble. Ministers consulted the Mensheviks and Socialist-Revolutionaries in the Petrograd Soviet, who were equally worried. The Provisional Government and the Petrograd Soviet decided to ban the Bolshevik-led demonstration and the Petrograd Soviet held its own demonstration in support of the First Congress of Soviets, a demonstration that would include Mensheviks, Socialist-Revolutionaries and Bolsheviks. Mensheviks and Socialist-Revolutionaries prided themselves on a bomb deftly defused. At the Congress of Soviets, lasting from 3 to 24 June 1917, they celebrated victory and proceeded to establish a Central Executive Committee to co-ordinate all the country's soviets until the next Congress.

The great leaders of the Petrograd Soviet – Tsereteli, Chkheidze, Dan and Liber – paraded their achievements since the February Revolution. They highlighted the concordat between the Petrograd Soviet and the Provisional Government on civil freedoms and national defence. They boasted that, when Foreign Minister Milyukov tried to wriggle out of this, the Petrograd Soviet had forced his resignation and the creation of a government coalition involving several Mensheviks and Socialist-Revolutionaries. The Menshevik and Socialist-Revolutionary leaders claimed that all this had been beneficial for the socialist cause in Russia.

Lenin spent his energies denouncing this co-operation as a fundamental betrayal of socialism. His words were aimed at people who were very well known to him: Chernov, Dan, Tsereteli and Martov. He had polemicised with them over many years. This had not stopped him from having coffee with one or other of them if he happened upon them in a foreign coffee-house; mutual political exasperation had not prevented social contact. This changed irreversibly in 1917. For Lenin, the behaviour of his Mensheviks and Socialist-Revolutionaries after the February Revolution put them beyond the pale. He did not engage them with a detailed refutation of their policies. In some measure this was because he was so disgusted with them. But it was also because he did not want to draw unnecessary attention to the strength of their case. For a start, it was entirely reasonable for them to deny that conclusive evidence existed that Europe was on the brink of a general socialist revolution. They worked hard to convoke a conference of Europe's anti-war socialists in

Stockholm; but they argued, too, that it would be irresponsible to forget that Russia should be defended against the Central Powers. They also touched a raw nerve when they mentioned that Lenin himself had until recently scoffed at the idea that the Russian Empire was yet industrially and culturally equipped to progress towards socialism.

As ministers, too, they were having an impact. Viktor Chernov as Agriculture Minister gave peasant-led 'land committees' the right to take uncultivated land into their control despite the protests of gentry farmers. Mikhail Skobelev, overriding the protests of employers, used the Ministry of Labour to introduce schemes for compulsory health insurance, for safety at the work-place and for the arbitration of industrial conflict. Tsereteli's post as Minister of Posts and Telegraphs did not inhibit him from insisting that greater autonomy should be accorded to non-Russian regions such as Finland and Ukraine.

Yet the clock was ticking against the Mensheviks and the Socialist-Revolutionaries. Every concession they wrenched from the hands of the Kadets was small alongside the problems bearing down on the Provisional Government. Monetary inflation was meteoric and industrial production plummeted. Wages, which had risen after the fall of the Romanov monarchy, failed to maintain their real value. Food supplies to the towns ran short. The central state administration steadily disintegrated. Regions, provinces and cities ran their affairs without regard for the Provisional Government. Elective sectional organisations, especially the soviets, began to act as if they wielded formal state power. The workers' control movement began to spread beyond Petrograd. Peasants in Russia and Ukraine were illegally pasturing their cattle and chopping down landlords' timber – and there was an increase in expropriations of landed estates. Soldiers were deserting the eastern front in their thousands. Refugees in their millions roamed Russia's cities. The Provisional Government was seen to support the interests of the propertied elites, for it refused to undertake basic reforms until after the end of the Great War – and the end of the Great War was not in sight. Such a situation was primed for Lenin and the Bolshevik party to exploit.

This is not to say that the Provisional Government acted with consummate skill. Alexander Kerenski, its Military Affairs Minister, opted to abide by Nicholas II's commitment to resuming a Russian offensive on the eastern front. No doubt the Provisional Government felt that it needed to show the Allies that it was not a broken reed. It also wanted to deflect Russian public criticism by means of a swift victory against the Austrians.

Yet ministers had been confident as they accounted for their activities to the First Congress of Soviets. In their view there was no realistic alternative. Tsereteli at the inaugural session on 3 June had asked whether his audience could imagine any party 'taking the risk' of taking power alone in revolutionary Russia. Lenin sat impassively. But Tsereteli had offered him the opening he craved. Next day he was given the platform for fifteen minutes:

> At the moment a whole range of countries are on the brink of destruction, and those practical measures that are said to be so complicated that they'd be hard to introduce and are in need of special elaboration – as was stated by the previous speaker, the citizen Minister of Posts and Telegraphs – those same measures are entirely clear. He said that that no political party exists in Russia that would express a readiness to take power wholly upon itself. My answer is: 'There is! No single party can refuse this, and our party doesn't refuse this: at any moment it is ready to take power in its entirety.'

His Bolsheviks applauded on cue. The greater part of the audience, however, could not take seriously this severe little politician with the rasping voice and the schoolmasterly gesticulations. A wave of laughter swept through the Congress hall.

But it was not long before mockery gave way to fear. Two self-inflicted problems confronted the Provisional Government. The first was military. The long-awaited offensive was started on 18 June. It was a frightful gamble. For, after initial success, the Russian forces were held up by a spirited defence bolstered by German reinforcements. Kerenski handed propaganda material to Lenin on a plate. The worse the military situation, the better for the Bolshevik party. The second problem was political: the Kadet ministers were so incensed by the Menshevik and Socialist-Revolutionary plan to confer regional autonomy upon Ukraine that the last fortnight of June was spent in intense dispute. The governmental coalition was about to break apart.

Lenin and the Bolshevik Central Committee itched to put the Provisional Government to a further test. A grand political demonstration was the most obvious technique. Prevented from organising an armed demonstration of their own during the First Congress of Soviets, they aimed to try again at the end of the month. The idea for this did not originate with Lenin. By then the Bolshevik party had plenty of radical far-left activists who wondered impatiently whether the Central

Committee would ever let them take on the Provisional Government on the streets. The main central body in the party where such activists were to be found was the Bolshevik Military Organisation, which co-ordinated the propaganda and organisation of the party in the armed forces. Outside the party there was a growing amount of support for violent mass action. The sailors of the naval garrison on Kronstadt Island, not far from Petrograd, seethed with hostility to the Provisional Government. Soldiers in Petrograd, too, were turning towards the Bolsheviks. More and more factory workers were doing the same. Their calls were frequent for the Bolshevik Central Committee to put its slogan 'All Power to the Soviets' into action.

Lenin hearkened to this mood. He talked with such ordinary workers, soldiers, sailors and peasants as came his way. In contrast with 1905, he was not marooned in Switzerland. He could see things for himself, and combine his observations with his capacity for intuitive judgement. He had a knack for weighing up the pros and cons of a political gamble. Unlike his party's enemies, Lenin was incapable of being indecisive. He well understood, moreover, the need to keep a close eye on events as they abruptly developed. It was in this spirit that he came to the Bolshevik Central Committee and upheld the proposal to organise an armed political demonstration. His precise rationale was not committed to paper. Mensheviks, Socialist-Revolutionaries and Kadets nevertheless heard of what he had sanctioned and concluded that his thoughts were focussed on nothing less than a violent seizure of central state power. Such a rationale cannot be excluded. But there is no need to assume that a clear-cut set of plans existed in Lenin's head. More likely by far is that he was improvising and that he was testing the waters with the aim of discovering the strength of force and determination that the Provisional Government retained.

This is not to say that he would have been hostile to trying to overthrow the cabinet if sufficient popular support was forthcoming on the streets of Petrograd. Some Bolsheviks felt this unambiguously. Sergo Ordzhonikidze referred to the demonstration as 'the first serious attempt to finish with the power of the coalition government';[11] and the Military Organisation was behaving like a law unto itself in the Bolshevik party. A conference of the Military Organisation had taken place on 16–23 June. Lenin gave a speech urging that risky adventures should be avoided.[12] 'We must', he stated, 'be specially attentive and careful not to succumb to provocation ... One false step on our part can bring the whole cause to perdition.'[13] But he knew that his words were not taken completely to heart. It was an extremely tense political situation. Anything could have happened.

Yet it was precisely then that Lenin, for the first time since he had arrived at the Finland Station in April, took himself away from Petrograd. He was exhausted, and looked forward to having a break in the countryside. For this purpose he accepted the long-standing invitation of Vladimir Bonch-Bruevich to join him and his wife at their dacha in the Finnish village of Neivola near to the Finland Railway a dozen miles north-west of Terijoki. Lenin had been complaining of ill health for weeks. At the First Congress of Soviets he was designated by the Bolshevik fraction to reply on its behalf to Chernov's report on the agrarian question. Two hours before Lenin was scheduled to speak, he was phoned by Nikolai Muralov to remind him. In breach of party etiquette Lenin advised Muralov to do the job himself, and put down the phone.[14] On 29 June he set off from the Finland Station with his sister Maria and the Bolshevik poet Demyan Bedny, who led the way from the little country railway stop to Neivola village. Nadya did not come along; she no longer operated at Lenin's elbow and was enjoying her involvement in the politics of the Vyborg district.[15] Their marriage had been loosened by his relationship with Inessa, and Nadya did not need the holiday – and the fact that the terrier-like Maria would be accompanying him was not exactly an attraction for her. Having walked to Neivola and surprised the Bonch-Brueviches with the sudden visit, Lenin spent the following days relaxing. They walked, took saunas and swam. Steadily Lenin's health was being restored.

His decision to take a holiday has led to the accusation that he was trying to cover himself in the event of a failed uprising.[16] This is not impossible, but it was not in Lenin's personality to let important things happen without his guidance, and Neivola was only a couple of hours from Petrograd by train. Yet no evidence has been produced to demonstrate that he went there with such a conspiracy in hand. Perhaps he should have conquered his lassitude and pain for the duration of the growing crisis. But he did not do this. Probably he was genuinely exhausted. This had happened before, in summer 1904, when Lenin went on vacation despite the probability that his rival V. A. Noskov would take political advantage; he needed above all to put his mental and physical faculties back in order.

He was all the more astounded early on Tuesday morning, 4 July, when awoken by an emissary from the Bolshevik Central Committee. Out to Neivola by train had come Maximilian Savelev, who worked on the *Pravda* editorial board and was closely linked to the Bolshevik radicals of the Military Organisation. Savelev broke the news that the demonstrations against the Provisional Government were about to get out of hand and that ministers were planning stern counter-measures. Whatever his state of health, Lenin would have to terminate his holiday and return to Petrograd. There might well be an insurrection, and it might well be a fiasco. Bloodshed was almost inevitable. Lenin's place was not in Finland but alongside his Bolshevik Central Committee comrades. Bags were quickly packed and the little group – Lenin, Maria Ilinichna, Savelev and Bonch-Bruevich – took the first train back across the Russo-Finnish administrative border at Beloostrov and on to the Finland Station. They were travelling on legal passports and Bonch-Bruevich worried lest they run into trouble with fellow passengers; but there was no incident. From the Finland Station they hurried to the Kseshinskaya mansion to join the Central Committee around midday.

The strikes and demonstrations had been taking place for a couple of days; a crowd of workers, soldiers and sailors had frequently gathered outside the mansion in expectation that the Central Committee would instigate a decisive push against the Provisional Government. The same happened shortly after Lenin's return. He was asked to come out on to the balcony to address the crowd. At first he demurred, but local Bolshevik leaders from Kronstadt prevailed upon him. By then he was in no doubt that the crisis was becoming overheated and that the Military Organisation leaders had been acting irresponsibly. Turning to those of them who were in the Kseshinskaya mansion, he exclaimed: 'You ought to be given a good hiding for this!'[17] Out on to the balcony he went, and told the crowd to stay calm. He asserted that the anti-governmental demonstration should above all be peaceful. This did not go down well. The crowd had assumed that Lenin, who had written powerfully about the necessity of removing the Provisional Government, would be on the side of immediate, violent action. But his judgement held sway, and in the early hours of 5 July the Bolshevik Central Committee completed its retreat by calling off the demonstration that had been planned for later in the day.

Yet the crisis was not over. The Provisional Government had sanctioned lengthy enquiries into the sources of the Bolshevik party's finances, and the Counter-Espionage Bureau had reason to believe that the Bolsheviks were in receipt of a subsidy from the German government. Some of the Bureau's materials were passed to newspapers despite the wish of most ministers to wait for conclusive proof. The Petrograd garrisons were also informed. On 5 July the newspaper *Zhivoe slovo* duly denounced Lenin as a German spy.[18] The offensive against Bolshevism was in full spate. A raid on *Pravda*'s offices took place the same morning. A similar action against the Kseshinskaya mansion was carried out next day. The Bolsheviks had to lie low throughout the capital.

Through all these days, fortuitously, the Provisional Government had been buffeted by internal dispute over Ukrainian regional autonomy. Prince Lvov had resigned as premier, and on 7 July his place was taken by the Socialist-Revolutionary Alexander Kerenski. An official investigation was ordered into the events of 3–4 July and into the degree of responsibility for the trouble to be assigned to members of the Bolshevik Central Committee and its Military Organisation. Arrest warrants had been issued for Lenin, Zinoviev and Kamenev on 6 July, and a detachment of troops had gone in quest of Lenin at the apartment of Mark and Anna Yelizarov. Although he had already fled, the apartment was thoroughly searched. Nadezhda Konstantinovna, Maria Ilinichna and Mark Yelizarov were at home at the time and were asked about Lenin's whereabouts. Krupskaya let slip that he had been staying at Neivola.[19] But this did not matter since by then he was hiding in Petrograd: first he stayed with M. L. Sulimova, then with N. G. Poletaev. The search was anyway pretty incompetent. The soldiers mistook Yelizarov for Lenin and took him and Krupskaya into custody. Yelizarov was tall and bulky; his brief detention was yet another sign that Lenin was not visually familiar to the general public.

There was every reason for Lenin to keep things this way. He and his comrades decided that he should not give himself up to the authorities. Initially he had not been unwilling to sit in prison, and Bolshevik leaders negotiated with the Central Executive Committee of the Congress of Soviets about the terms under which he might surrender himself.[20] Several party figures felt that a trial was the sole means whereby the party could clear its name. The personal danger to Lenin should not in their opinion take precedence. This horrified Maria Ilinichna, who thought that no risk should be taken with the party's leader and that he should be spirited away to Sweden.[21]

Opinion then turned against Lenin's surrender since the Central Executive Committee gave only weak assurances. Moreover, the atmosphere of vengefulness thickened as most newspapers picked up the allegation that the Bolshevik party had carried out the commands of the German government. The possibility arose that Lenin might be assassinated, and he resolved to stay in hiding and to damn the consequences.

Poletaev's flat was thought inappropriate: too many visitors came to the building.[22] Another safe-house had to be found with urgency. Lenin and Grigori Zinoviev, accompanied by Zinoviev's wife Zinaida Lilina but not by Nadezhda Konstantinovna, moved secretly again on 7 July. This time their haven was provided by the veteran Bolsheviks Sergei and Olga Alliluev in their comfortable apartment on Tenth Rozhdestvenka Street – it even had a smartly dressed concierge. The Alliluevs had only just rented the place and so the police were unlikely to look for Lenin there. Lenin moved into the room being readied for their regular lodger Stalin; he stayed in contact with the Central Committee members by scribbling notes that Sergei Alliluev and others conveyed. Most of the time he worked in his own room. The Alliluev children remembered the noise of a 'scraping of the pen day and night' behind his door.[23]

But Lenin and Zinoviev wanted to get out of Petrograd, if only temporarily; to both of them it seemed best to leave for the countryside and wait on events. They had to let others decide where they might best find refuge. No longer were Lenin and his companion the makers of a revolutionary situation.

17

POWER FOR THE TAKING

July to October 1917

Lenin and Zinoviev were secretly escorted out of Petrograd on 9 July by Bolshevik activists supplied by the Central Committee. For reasons of security they travelled without their wives. Just before the trip, Lenin decided that he needed to change his appearance. Olga Allilueva, who had recently qualified as a nurse, wrapped his face and forehead in a bandage. But when Lenin looked in the mirror, he knew that he would attract rather than evade attention. He might not even get past the concierge of the apartment block.

His own idea was simpler: he would shave off his moustache and beard. For some reason he decided that he would not do this himself. Instead Stalin, who was visiting the flat, lathered up the soap and performed the task.[1] 'It's very good now,' said Lenin, 'I look like a Finnish peasant, and there's hardly anyone who'd recognise me.'[2] Just to make sure, however, he borrowed Sergei Alliluev's coat and cap instead of his own.[3] And so people who had seen him in the suit and headwear that he had bought in Stockholm at Radek's instigation would have no clues to who he was. Then, leaving the Alliluev flat, Lenin made his way on foot to the Sestroretsk Station together with Zinoviev and the Bolshevik metalworker Nikolai Yemelyanov. This station was the terminus of the little coastline railway running along the Gulf of Finland from Petrograd to Sestroretsk. It was the peak of the summer season and the trains were packed with middle-class passengers leaving the capital and going off to enjoy the seaside and the fresh air. Lenin, Zinoviev and Yemelyanov planned to get off the train before Sestroretsk and stay at the village of Razliv, where Yemelyanov owned a house and land and could offer his roomy and comfortable hayloft as a hiding place.

The three Bolsheviks arrived at Razliv late at night and went straight to bed. Next day Lenin got back to work; his first task was to expound his strategic ideas for the benefit of the Central Committee. The armed demonstration in Petrograd had been suppressed. Kerenski had become the Minister–Chairman of the Provisional Government and, although he was trying to include socialists in his cabinet, his police were rounding up leading Bolsheviks. Already Trotski, Kollontai and Kamenev were behind bars. Since the party's acceptance of the *April Theses*, Lenin had suggested that his comrades should be engaged mainly in getting Bolsheviks elected to the soviets and in denouncing the Provisional Government and the Mensheviks and Socialist–Revolutionaries who had served in it. But what now? What precisely should the Bolshevik Central Committee adopt as its strategy of survival and advance?

Obviously Lenin's flight from the capital was not going to stop him from trying to impose his ideas upon comrades in the Central Committee. Absence made him still more strident than usual. Sketching out his strategic notions, he stated: 'All hopes for the peaceful development of the Russian revolution have definitively disappeared.' Kerenski, according to Lenin, had established a 'military dictatorship' and the soviets had become 'the figleaf of the counter-revolution'. Lenin urged Bolsheviks to withdraw the slogan 'All Power to the Soviets' and dedicate themselves to the organisation of an 'armed uprising' and the formation of a revolutionary government.[4] The problem was that he was asking for the overturning of a policy that had been at the core of party strategy since April 1917. Lenin had insisted on this and Bolsheviks had got used to the notion that when they seized power, they would rule through the agency of the soviets. The Central Committee was aghast at his latest thinking. Lenin had not even taken the trouble to explain how the party's activists could set about justifying the change in policy in their propaganda to workers and soldiers.

A lengthy meeting of the Central Committee started in Lenin's absence on 13 July and was resumed next day. The Bolshevik leaders had much to sort out. The 'July Days' in Petrograd had brought the party near to disaster and a debate on strategy was urgently required. But the result was never in serious doubt: Lenin's July theses were firmly rejected.[5] Lenin responded furiously with an article 'On Slogans', but the Central Committee would not budge. Stalin summarised its position as follows: 'We are unambiguously in favour of those soviets in which we have a majority, and we shall try to establish such soviets.' The slogan 'All Power to the Soviets' was retained. Absence from Petrograd was already weakening Lenin's influence on the central leadership of his party.

The hayloft was safe only as a temporary refuge and Lenin and Zinoviev took up Yemelyanov's idea of moving two miles to the far side of the lake from the village. There he had a hayfield and a thatched, wooden hut. Couriers could still reach them regularly from the capital, bringing the daily Petrograd newspapers and Central Committee business; indeed leading Bolsheviks also visited the fugitives in the hours of darkness. Lenin tried to make the best he could of things. In particular, he resumed his work on Marxist political theory, later to be published as *The State and Revolution*. He had always been able to calm himself by reading and writing, and he had plenty of material with him in the hut. For relaxation, Lenin and Zinoviev helped Yemelyanov to mow the hay. They also went swimming. Life near Razliv was quite uneventful until Zinoviev foolishly went hunting in a prohibited area and bumped into Mr Axënov the gamekeeper, who ordered him to hand over his rifle. Zinoviev pretended to be a Finn and to be unable to understand Russian. Mr Axënov was taken in by this act and, luckily for Zinoviev, relented. Afterwards Zinoviev sensibly refrained from shooting expeditions.[6]

Meanwhile the insects were making conditions unbearable in the hut, as Yemelyanov was to remember:[7]

> A kitchen was erected alongside: a pot was hung from stakes and tea was boiled in it. But at night things were insufferable; the insatiable mosquitoes gave absolutely no respite. It didn't matter how you hid from them, they would always get to where they wanted and they would frequently eat you. But there was nothing that could be done about it: you simply had to submit.

Relief came only when it rained, and the summer of 1917 was a very wet one. But the storms also brought hardship because the water poured through the roof. Lenin and Zinoviev could not promote Revolution while they were sodden and cold, and decided to change plans.[8] Zinoviev was less worried than Lenin about being arrested and chose to risk returning incognito to Petrograd. Lenin, however, still thought he might be hanged if ever he was put on trial; he therefore asked the Central Committee to arrange for him to travel to a safe-house in Finland. The two refugees, Lenin and Zinoviev, would leave Razliv together.

They were provided with wigs. Kerenski's Ministry of the Interior had hoped to prevent this kind of subterfuge by banning the hire and sale of wigs without proof of special need. But the Petrograd Bolshevik Dmitri Leshchenko pretended to need wigs for a railwaymen's amateur theatrical troupe to which he belonged. The next step was to obtain formal travel papers. It was necessary to have these when crossing the Russian–Finnish administrative border.[9] Lenin and Zinoviev had to be photographed in this new disguise and Leshchenko trudged out with the

bulky equipment from the rail-stop to the hut on the other side of
the lake. The job had to be done soon after dawn so as to minimise the
danger of Lenin and Zinoviev being seen and recognised by passers-by.
The whole process was a palaver. Having no tripod, Leshchenko had to
crouch so as to hold the mirror-chamber while taking the picture. This
meant that Lenin and Zinoviev too had to kneel. Only after taking
several pictures did Leshchenko feel confident that he had a satisfactory
image. Then he travelled back to Petrograd to print the negatives and fix
the photograph to the forged papers.[10]

Several of the negatives came out badly, but one of them was good
enough and a scheme was devised for Lenin and Zinoviev to leave in the
first week of August. Accompanied by Yemelyanov and the Finnish
Bolsheviks Eino Rahja and Alexander Shotman, they were to make for
Levashevo, a small station situated halfway between Petrograd and Beloostrov on the Finland Railway. From there it was intended for them to take
a train back in the direction of Petrograd, to Udelnaya, where they would
stay overnight in the flat of the Finnish factory worker Emil Kalske.
Thereafter Zinoviev would make his way back to Petrograd and take his
chances there in safe-houses provided by the Bolshevik Central Committee. Lenin, who was still the Ministry of the Interior's most wanted
man, would not take the risk; instead he would head north for Finland.

From Razliv, Lenin and Zinoviev were committing themselves to an
expedition of seven miles through the woods in an easterly direction
from the lake. On their way they would have to cross a large peat bog
and a bridgeless river. Lenin soon regretted that he had not supervised
the planning. The expedition was a farce. The first thing to happen was
that Yemelyanov got them lost in the woods. Then they had to cross a
large area of peat which the owner had set on fire and which was still
smouldering. Worse was to follow. Shotman had packed only three baby
cucumbers; he had not even brought a bread-roll. Hours later, the
walkers, hungry and tired, heard a distant train-whistle. Their pleasure
melted away when they discovered that they had reached not Levashevo
but Dibuny. Lenin was furious with Shotman:[11]

> Vladimir Ilich must be given his due: he cursed us with extreme
> savagery for the bad organisation. Surely it had been necessary to
> obtain a detailed local map? Why hadn't we studied the route in
> advance, and so on? We also caught it over the 'reconnoitring': why
> did it only 'seem' to be the right station? Why didn't we know
> precisely?

But at least Dibuny had a railway station and was situated on the Finland Railway. Things, hoped Lenin, might be about to get better.

Unfortunately, things got worse. Yemelyanov and Shotman stood around at the station while Lenin, Zinoviev and Rahja loitered in hiding. As they waited for the next train to Udelnaya, an army officer grew suspicious of Yemelyanov and took him into custody. Then a youth armed with a rifle spoke to Shotman, who distracted attention by getting on the train without Lenin, Zinoviev and Rahja. Shotman planned to warn the Bolsheviks in Udelnaya about the difficulties that had arisen at Dibuny. But he was such a bundle of nerves that he alighted three miles down the track at Ozerki instead of at Udelnaya. It was three o'clock in the morning when he finally reached Kalske's flat in Udelnaya.

But the luck of the other travellers had begun to change some hours earlier. From Levashevo they took a train to Udelnaya and stayed overnight in the home of Finnish factory worker Emil Kalske, who lived half a mile from the station. Next day Lenin was given a stoker's clothes to put on, and in the evening he joined train no. 293 driven by Hugo Jalava across the Russo-Finnish border bound for Terijoki. Accompanying him were Shotman, Rahja and a third Finn, Pekka Parviainen. Jalava played out a charade with Rahja:

> 'Where are you going at such a time?' I exclaimed so as to distract attention. Comrade Rahja replied: 'Home to my dacha, to Terijoki.'
>
> And then, pointing to Ilich, he asked me to take a comrade on board the steam engine, explaining that he was a journalist wanting to acquaint himself with steam engine travel. I agreed. Ilich grabbed hold of the handrail and clambered up into the engine while comrade Rahja went into the empty wagon. I explained to my assistant that they were local dacha owners. So as not to get in the way of work during the stoking of the fuel, Ilich retreated to the tender and loaded timber into the box.

The trick worked. At Terijoki, after a journey of twenty-five miles from Udelnaya, they left the train and took a carriage to Jalkala, nine miles into the Finnish interior.

In the morning they moved on by train to Lahti. This journey, too, proved hectic. The problem was the disguise adopted by Lenin in Jalkala. Its main feature was an adhesive face-mask. The glue started to melt before the travellers reached Lahti and Lenin hurriedly had to remove the mask without the aid of Vaseline or water before getting off the train.[12] Lenin wrote about the 'art of revolution'. Demonstrably he himself was no master of revolutionary cosmetics.

On the platform at Lahti he and his companions were worried that station employees might take an interest in him because of his face, which was still smarting from the glue's removal. But no one was so inquisitive, and Lenin's party calmed down. Shotman went ahead to organise Lenin's secret arrival in Helsinki (Helsingfors). For many years Finnish Marxists had warmly co-operated with the Bolshevik faction because of its appreciation of 'the national question'.[13] They were past masters at deceiving the Russian governmental authorities and, unlike Yemelyanov, did not need maps to get around their own country. Lenin reached Helsinki on 10 August, and over the ensuing weeks he stayed at various safe-houses. One of them belonged to Gustav Rovio. Lenin could hardly have been more securely looked after since Rovio was the Finnish capital's elected police chief. It was an astonishing situation. While the Russian Minister of the Interior in Petrograd was offering a reward of 200,000 rubles for the apprehension of Lenin, his formal subordinate in Helsinki was hiding Lenin from arrest.[14]

Lenin settled himself to a rhythm of work while couriers established a line of contact with both Petrograd and Stockholm. There were two differences from his years as an emigrant. The first was that Lenin was physically distant from the central party apparatus. The second was the absence of Nadya. It is true that she visited him twice after obtaining a passport from 'the old woman Atamanova' and disguising herself as a worker. Yet he could not encourage her to stay; considerations of security even stopped him chaperoning her back to Helsinki railway station.[15]

Meanwhile Lenin remained angry with the Central Committee for rejecting his proposals on slogans. Literary activity offered a little consolation. He had plenty of books and got down properly to the treatise on *The State and Revolution*. He had already been filling a dark-blue notebook on the subject before he left Switzerland. This contained his jottings from the works by Marx and Engels he had read there. Indeed his notes already contained a preliminary sketch of the book he wanted to write, and he believed that his ideas, if only he could get them into print, would be recognised as his masterpiece. He wrote to Kamenev about this, asking him to take responsibility for this if ever it should happen that he was arrested and executed: '*Entre nous*: if they bump me off, I would ask you to publish my notebook, "Marxism on the State" (it's held up in Stockholm). A navy-blue bound folder. There's a collection of all the citations from Marx and Engels as well as from

Kautsky against Pannekoek.'[16] With rising excitement he wrote up the chapters in Helsinki. He looked forward to publishing them and demonstrating that his idiosyncratic general interpretation of Marxism was the only authentic one.

So why has Lenin been charged with monumental insincerity in relation to the book? The main reason lies in the contrast between the predictions made in *The State and Revolution* and the reality of Bolshevism in power. *The State and Revolution* described an imminent future when the working class would become the ruling class and ordinary workers themselves take the crucial decisions of state and society. Things turned out very differently after October 1917, when the Soviet state quickly became a one-party dictatorship that used force against industrial strikes and political protests by workers. A long shadow of doubt was cast over his intentions when he wrote *The State and Revolution*.

Now it must be conceded that Lenin, a power-hungry politician, was often disingenuous and deceptive. His criterion of morality was simple: does a certain action advance or hinder the cause of the Revolution? Although he seldom lied through his teeth in politics, he had unrivalled proficiency in evasion of truthfulness. He was notorious for manufacturing statements that deliberately misled his enemies. But in 1917 he was attacked for going far beyond this. Not only was he charged with having always known that Roman Malinovski was an Okhrana agent but he himself was accused of operating as a paid German agent. In the liberal and conservative newspapers he was accused of treason to his country. Until the February 1917 Revolution it had been possible for him to deny that Malinovski had belonged to the Okhrana service; but the opening of the Ministry of the Interior's files destroyed this illusion. Lenin had a case to answer and had had to attend the official hearing in the early summer. In self-defence he had simply argued that the Okhrana and Malinovski had fooled everyone. And he succeeded in persuading the hearing that the Bolsheviks before 1917 had never knowingly acted in concert with the tsarist monarchy's secret police.

Less easy to shrug off was the charge that the Bolshevik Central Committee since the February Revolution had acted as Germany's conscious puppets. There was much circumstantial evidence that the Bolsheviks were in receipt of money from Berlin. The Russian Counter-Espionage Bureau released the story to Petrograd newspaper editors on 4 July when the government was dealing with the trouble being caused by the Bolshevik party and its supporters in the centre of Petrograd.

The Counter-Espionage Bureau's investigators believed it plausible –

but could not quite prove – that the money was transmitted to the Bolshevik Central Committee by Jakub Hanecki, who received it from the German intermediary Alexander Helphand-Parvus. Apparently Hanecki, an official of the Foreign Bureau of the Bolshevik Central Committee in Stockholm, secretly moved the funds by bank credits and by courier. It is now known that the German authorities made millions of marks available for the purpose of enabling Russians to conduct pro-peace propaganda. It can scarcely be a coincidence that the Bolsheviks, despite having only a minority of places in the soviets and other mass organisations after the February Revolution, rapidly set up a large number of newspapers. How much Lenin knew in detail about the German subsidy is unlikely ever to be discovered; but he was a politician who liked to be in control. It stretches credulity that he did not know what was going on. It so happened that the investigators were close to catching Hanecki himself red-handed on the frontier at Tornio. They were frustrated, however, by the premature disclosure of some of their findings by Petrograd daily newspapers.

Lenin took a lawyerly approach to the accusation. He could easily repudiate the slur that he was acting on the instructions of the German government. He was also safe in denying that he had talked to Helphand-Parvus, and he could ridicule the suggestion that he had taken money into his personal possession from Hanecki. In this way he did not have to tell the direct lie that, under his general supervision, the Bolshevik leadership had accepted no money from Russia's wartime enemy. Lenin's evasiveness would have been explored aggressively if he had been in the Provisional Government's custody. But he was living in Helsinki police chief Rovio's house and he could wait for the storm about 'the German gold' to blow itself out.

As he pressed forward with *The State and Revolution*, the task took longer than he had imagined – and he had not completed the final chapter before the October Revolution. He had very practical motives for wanting to write fast. He saw the book as a vital contribution to his party's ability to deal with the current political situation in Russia. More generally, he aimed to explain the most appropriate strategy for Bolsheviks in Russia and far-left socialists elsewhere to establish a socialist state. He enjoyed asserting himself as a theorist. The argument of *State and Revolution* was that the other socialist parties, notably the Mensheviks and Socialist-Revolutionaries in Russia and the German Social-Democratic Party, had an inadequate strategy for the achieve-ment of socialism. Lenin heaped the blame on Karl Kautsky, whom he treated as the originator of the basic ideas of Mensheviks and Socialist-Revolutionaries; and he dedicated half the book to an examination of the political transformation predicted by Marx and Engels and already realised to some extent by the Russian soviets of workers' and soldiers' deputies in the direction of European socialist revolution.

Lenin made several fundamental assertions. Marx, he said, had assumed that usually it would take a campaign of violence for socialists to come to power. The middle classes held all the advantages under capitalism; they would use their education, money and any maleficent methods that came to hand in order to ward off Revolution. Socialists should therefore recognise violence as the necessary midwife to historical change. Furthermore, the revolutionary socialist regime would not long survive unless it continued to deploy violent methods. It should therefore fight to set up a 'dictatorship of the proletariat'. In the early period of the socialist Revolution there should be an administration based unequivocally on principles of 'class struggle'. The former upper and middle classes should lose their civic rights. Rule would be imposed by the working class, which steadily would infuse society – not just in Russia but in the entire industrialised world – with socialist reforms.

Laboriously Lenin adduced the legacy of Marx and Engels and tried to show that they had invented a specific series of stages whereby the perfect community – known as communism – would be attained around the world. This series, he proposed, would develop as follows. Capitalism would be overthrown by a violent revolution that would be consolidated by the 'dictatorship of the proletariat'. Such a dictatorship, at first ruthless, would steadily impregnate the institutions, practices and ideals of socialism. The need for class-based discrimination would gradually diminish as the remnants of the old upper and middle classes ceased to constitute a threat. Socialism, as it matured, would facilitate enormous progress beyond capitalism. The lower social orders would get accustomed to running the administration, and the economy, liberated from the constraints of capitalism, would be expanded in those sectors bringing benefit to people's general objective needs. Nevertheless socialism would still involve a degree of political and social inequality and would still necessitate the existence of a state. Lenin stressed that the *raison d'être* of states was to use coercion to favour the interests of the ruling classes as they sought to dominate the other classes. Under socialism it would be the 'proletariat' that ruled.

Yet Marxism's ultimate goal, as Lenin emphasised, had always been to achieve a society without oppression and exploitation. This would be the very last stage of historical development. Under communism the principle would at last be realised: from each according to his abilities, to each according to his needs. There would be no distinction of material reward. Each individual in society would have the fullest opportunity to develop potential talent. A person could do both manual and mental labour. The whole people would engage in its own administration; and the need for a professional political stratum, professional bureaucracy and professional armed forces would lapse. According to Lenin, a kitchen maid would be entrustable with decisions previously undertaken by ministers. The need for the state would disappear. As communism approached, there would be a 'withering away' of the state.

Lenin represented himself as the humble excavator of the foundations of Marxism buried by a generation of interpreters, especially Kautsky, who had rejected not only the need for violent socialist Revolution but also the commitment to the ultimate communist goal of a stateless society. But Kautsky and Martov quickly raised questions about the cogency of Lenin's case. They pointed out that Marx had used the term 'dictatorship of the proletariat' only infrequently and had not discounted the possibility of a peaceful socialist transformation. They also indicated that Marx in his later years had acknowledged that advanced capitalist societies were not polarised between a tiny capitalist class and a vast impoverished working class but increasingly included intermediate groups of experts: engineers, teachers, scientists and administrators. Kautsky and Martov criticised his sociology. Did he not understand that any proletarian dictatorship would inevitably involve oppression by a class that was itself a demographic minority? Did he not comprehend that advanced capitalist societies stood in permanent need of training and expertise? Was Lenin not more akin to the nineteenth-century authoritarian revolutionaries opposed by Marx and Engels: Wilhelm Weitling, Louise-Auguste Blanqui and Pëtr Tkachëv?

All such revolutionaries had espoused terrorist campaigns, and yet in *The State and Revolution* Lenin had avoided a discussion of state terror. Indeed he wrote only glancingly about it in the rest of the year. Thus he compared Russia in 1917 with France in 1793:[17]

The Jacobins declared as enemies of the people those who 'assisted the schemes of the united tyrants against the republic'.

The example of the Jacobins is instructive. Even today it has not become outdated, but we need to apply it to the revolutionary class of the 20th century, to the workers and the semi-proletarians.

The enemies of the people for this class in the 20th century are not the monarchs but the landlords and capitalists as a class . . .

The 'Jacobins' of the 20th century would not set about guillotining the capitalists: following a good model is not the same as copying it. It would be enough to arrest 50–100 magnates and queens of bank capital, the main knights of treasury-fraud and bank-pillage; it would be enough to arrest them for a few weeks *so as to uncover their dirty deals*, so as to show to all the exploited people exactly 'who needs the war'.

There must be scepticism as to whether he really expected his projected government's use of terror to be as soft and short-lived as he was claiming in *Pravda*. Lenin was capable not only of lying and deceiving: he could also produce phrases of egregious political fudge.

From this it is clear that Lenin in 1917 did not, as is widely supposed, offer a libertarian vision of socialism.[18] He used words such as 'freedom' and 'democracy' pejoratively. He ridiculed concepts such as the division of power among legislative, executive and judicial authorities. Even the public life as such is despised: Lenin expected the socialist Revolution to move society away from 'politicking' towards 'the administration of things'. 'Parliamentarism' for him was a tainted objective. He had no time, therefore, for inter-party competition, for cultural pluralism or for the defence of the interests of various social minorities. Individual citizens' rights were of no concern to him; he wanted his dictatorship to judge everything by criteria of 'class struggle'. Civil war held no dread for him. He regarded such conflict as a natural and desirable outcome of the advance of the socialist cause. *The State and Revolution* has been described as dispiriting because of its failure to recognise the benefits of liberal-democratic values of government. This is true as far as it goes. But the analysis can go further: we have also to recognise that the book contains not merely a failure to propound universal civic freedom but in fact a definite, deliberate campaign against such freedoms.

It was experienced Marxists in Russia and Europe whom he was trying to rally to his side. *The State and Revolution* was an impenetrable forest of citation and argument for most of the reading public, and anyway the book was not published until 1918. But it reflected his basic strategic assumptions in the making of Revolution. These were assumptions that he shared to a greater or lesser extent with his comrades in the Central Committee, and *The State and Revolution* helped to narrow the discrepancies between one leading Bolshevik and another and to reinforce the primacy of Lenin's ideas in the definition of Bolshevism.

While writing the book, he also contributed to the party press. Thus his influence reached beyond the Central Committee, and his fellow Bolsheviks across the country were kept aware that Lenin remained active. In July and August he went on demanding that policies should be changed. He based his analysis on a French historical analogy; allegedly Alexander Kerenski, Prince Lvov's successor as prime minister, was trying to become the Bonaparte of the Russian Revolution, playing off one class against another and rising above the fray to establish a personal despotism. Kerenski's cabinet, set up on 25 July, had a majority of socialist members; but Lenin argued that there was nothing socialist about the policies. The Provisional Government was a bourgeois class dictatorship. In fact Lenin overstated the cohesion and 'counter-revolutionary' nature of the Russian state as run by Kerenski. Nevertheless the cabinet undoubtedly wished to prevent another such outbreak as had occurred on 3–4 July, and among its priorities was the restoration of law and order in the armed forces and in civilian public life. Capital punishment was reintroduced for desertion and other serious military disobedience. The new Commander-in-Chief, Lavr Kornilov, arranged with Kerenski for the imposition of the government's authority over the soviets, trade unions and factory-workshop committees.

When the Bolshevik party secretly held its Sixth Congress from 26 July to 2 August, Lenin could not attend. There was too great a chance that the Provisional Government might have caught him. It was a chance for the party to take stock of the situation. Several leading Bolsheviks pondered whether European socialist Revolution was imminent, whether a revolutionary war was practicable and whether the economic decline was quickly reversible. Nevertheless Lenin's insistent optimism had not faded, and his specific current recommendations of policy were starting to have an impact. In particular, the Congress agreed to drop the slogan 'All Power to the Soviets'. After a lengthy debate about slogans, it was decided to replace it with 'All Power to the Proletariat Supported by the Poorest Peasantry and the Revolutionary Democracy Organised into Soviets of Workers', Soldiers' and Peasants' Deputies'. A clumsier slogan can hardly be imagined. Perhaps his Bolsheviks needed the absent Lenin more than they recognised.

His advice to them in August was angry and impatient. The Kerenski cabinet, he expostulated, had acted as he had always predicted. It was fighting the war to the bitter end. It was silencing opposition in the armed forces and threatening disruptive urban soviets with dissolution. It was keener to rally support from the Kadets and the high command than to make concessions to the socialist parties (and Viktor Chernov resigned in disgust over this). And yet still the Mensheviks and Socialist-Revolutionaries refused to throw Kerenski out on his heels. The left-wing Menshevik Yuli Martov had the idea of calling for a socialist administration, based on the parties represented in the soviets, to take power, but his colleagues ignored him. The collusion of the Mensheviks and Socialist-Revolutionaries with Kerenski's 'military dictatorship' was complete. Lenin made further progress as the difficulties for Kerenski mounted. Peasants were seizing land, soldiers were deserting the eastern front, workers were taking over factories. Industrial production was dislocated and food supplies sharply declined. And on 21 August the German armies advanced along the northern sector and took the city of Riga. Repeatedly Lenin asked the Bolshevik Central Committee why it was allowing the Provisional Government to survive.

Then came the 'Kornilov Affair'. Kerenski and his Commander-in-Chief Kornilov had an agreement for Kornilov to move troops into Petrograd to impose order on the soviets. But Kerenski, noting Kornilov's popularity in right-wing political and military circles at the State Conference held by Kerenski himself in Moscow on 12 August, became wary of him. Relations between the two men were made worse by the meddling of their aides. On 28 August Kornilov was ordered to put off the agreed movement of frontline troops to Petrograd. Kerenski feared a *coup d'état*. In the increasing confusion Kornilov concluded that Kerenski was not fit to govern and decided to disobey him. The Provisional Government was at Kornilov's mercy. Kerenski turned in panic to the parties of the soviets, including the Bolsheviks, to support him by sending out agitators to persuade Kornilov's troops to obey the Provisional Government and allow Kornilov to be detained in custody. This was duly accomplished, but at the price of the readmittance of the Bolshevik party to the open political arena.

Lenin was delighted. On 1 September he began an article, 'On Compromises', reinstating the slogan 'All Power to the Soviets' and suggesting that a peaceful transition to a socialist government was possible. Kerenski was having to be more considerate towards the Mensheviks and Socialist-Revolutionaries, especially as the full extent of secret Kadet encouragement to Kornilov became public knowledge.[19]

> It is only in the name of this peaceful development of the revolution
> – in the name of a possibility that is *extremely* rare in history and
> *extremely* valuable, an exceptionally rare possibility – it is only in its
> name that the Bolsheviks, supporters of world-wide socialist revo-
> lution and supporters of revolutionary methods, can and must in
> my opinion proceed to this compromise.

The 'compromise' he had in mind was that the Bolsheviks would stick
to non-violent political procedures so long as the Mensheviks and
Socialist-Revolutionaries formed a government 'wholly and exclusively
responsible to the soviets' and permitted the soviets in the provinces to
constitute the official administration while the Bolsheviks would be
guaranteed 'freedom of agitation'.[20] These conditions were hardly likely
to be fulfilled, and probably he knew this. He wrote an addendum on 3
September in which he stated that recent events meant that the historic
compromise was impracticable.[21] He was referring to Kerenski's formation of a five-person Directory and to the reluctance of the Mensheviks
and Socialist-Revolutionaries to break ties with the Kadets. The Directory
was obviously counterposed to 'All Power to the Soviets'.[22]

He did not cease justifying his case in subsequent articles, but this
changed abruptly on 12 September when he started a letter to the Bolshevik
Central Committee, the Petersburg Committee and the Moscow Committee. By then the Bolsheviks had majorities in both the Petrograd and
Moscow Soviets, and Lenin urged: 'Taking power *immediately* both in
Moscow and in Piter [Petrograd] (it doesn't matter who goes first: perhaps
even Moscow can do it), we will *absolutely and undoubtedly* be victorious.'[23] Central Committee members had a right to feel that he was being
irresponsible about the party's security. On 13 September, before receiving
this letter, they decided to put the basic notions of Lenin's article 'On
Compromises' into the party's general declaration to be read out at the
so-called Democratic Conference of all parties to the left of the Kadets on
14 September. His strategic somersaults were becoming insufferable. He
was evidently out of touch with possibilities in Russia and ought to be
ignored. But this time Lenin kept undeviatingly to his line. On 13
September he began a second and longer letter, headed 'Marxism and
Insurrection', in order to drive home his argument. He contrasted the
situation of 3–4 July with the current circumstances. The working class
was at last on the party's side. The popular mood was in favour of
revolution and the political enemies of the Bolshevik party were trapped
by their indecision. Insurrection was crucial.[24]

The Central Committee considered Lenin's letters on 15 September in the presence of Trotski and Kamenev, who had been released from prison. Most members were appalled by what they read. There was no telling what Kerenski might do if he learned of the contents of the letters. The Central Committee agreed to burn all but one copy of the letters.[25] Little doubt can exist that the Bolsheviks would have met with disaster if they had complied with Lenin's demand for an immediate insurrection. Most soviets remained in the hands of the Mensheviks and Socialist-Revolutionaries, and there would have been intense armed strife if the Bolsheviks had taken to the streets. An attempted seizure of power by the Petrograd Soviet would have provided Kerenski with a marvellous pretext for the elimination of the Bolshevik party from public life.

But Lenin would not be thwarted, and he knew that there were elements in the party, among garrison soldiers and among the working class, that he would be able to call upon. Maria Ilinichna, ever loyal to him, flouted the Central Committee's orders and conveyed Lenin's letters to the Petersburg Committee.[26] Lenin wanted to be directly involved, and asked Shotman to get the Central Committee to permit his return to Petrograd. The Central Committee overruled the request. Lenin furiously retorted: 'I will not leave it at that, I will not leave it at that!'[27] Shotman found his utopian political thought almost as unacceptable as his insurrectionary impatience, and argued that socialist Revolution was a complex business. Lenin flared up at him:[28]

> Rubbish! Any workers will master any ministry within a few days; no special skill is required here and it isn't necessary to know the techniques of the work since this is the job of the bureaucrats whom we'll compel to work just as they make the worker–specialists work at present.

Throughout 1917 he implied that the coming socialist Revolution would be an easy one, and he stressed that most workers, peasants and soldiers would support the party. Shotman experienced this directly. Leaning towards to him and squinting with his left eye, Lenin asked: 'Who will be against us then?'[29]

Although he exaggerated for effect, he probably meant what he said at least in a general fashion. We cannot be absolutely sure about this since he seldom confided his innermost calculations to anyone. And obviously he wanted to reassure his party that all would be well after power had been seized. Perhaps, furthermore, other possibilities were already taking shape in his mind. Like other Bolshevik leaders, he had read a lot about the French Revolution and was always looking for French precedents for contemporary Russian developments. He admired Robespierre, the Jacobins and their forceful efforts to consolidate the revolutionary regime even though they were ultimately unsuccessful. It is hard to believe that it never crossed his mind that, if his own party seized power, the international and domestic resistance might result in protracted carnage. Indeed there is documentary evidence that he deliberately downplayed this admiration in public for fear of weakening the party's popularity. For example, he was furious with Trotski for threatening the opponents of Bolshevism with the guillotine. But he did not object to terror as such. His notion instead was that 'the guillotine should not be joked about'.[30] And yet simultaneously he reassured himself that a Bolshevik-led socialist revolution would be unlike any previous revolution. The mass of the people would be on its side, at first in Russia and then in Europe as a whole. Repression, then, would not have to last so long or cut so deep.

Undoubtedly Lenin did not care that the middle classes would oppose the Bolshevik party. He thought that Russia faced a choice between two extremes: a bourgeois dictatorship and a proletarian dictatorship. For the first period since his return from Switzerland he wrote openly of his dictatorial intentions in the central party press. The country, he declared, was simply ungovernable by the Mensheviks, Socialist-Revolutionaries and Kadets. Their strategy had been exposed as irremediably frail by the *putsch* attempted by Kornilov. Now it was time to agree on the supreme priority: the insurrection against the Provisional Government.

Disregarding party discipline and bypassing Alexander Shotman, Lenin turned to Gustav Rovio for help with arranging a safe-house for him in Vyborg, the Finnish town near the Russo-Finnish administrative border. A farce took place with the fitting of a new wig. Rovio took him to a theatrical specialist, who required several weeks to make up an item for any customer. Lenin asked for a ready-made item that would fit his head even approximately. The only such wig was silvery grey and the wigmaker was reluctant to sell it since it made his customer look to be in his sixties. Lenin, naturally, did not reveal that he wanted a wig not to adorn but precisely to disguise his appearance.[31] At last the transaction was made, and Rovio produced a false passport and found him a place to stay in Vyborg with yet another Finnish comrade.[32] Arriving there at the beginning of the last week in September, he immediately sought ways to proceed to Petrograd. Within a few days he was off. Again he bypassed Shotman. Again he commissioned a wig, this time adopting the disguise of a Finnish pastor of the Lutheran Church.[33] Lenin the militant atheist returned to Petrograd as a man of God. His travelling companion was the metalworker Eino Rahja; the train driver was the same Hugo Jalava who had carried him in the opposite direction across the Russo-Finnish border in August.[34]

He stayed in Petrograd with a young Bolshevik agronomist Margarita Vasilevna Fofanova, who lived in Serdobolskaya Street overlooking the Finland Railway in the Vyborg district. Fofanova had to comply with 'his firm regime':[35]

> He told me to obtain on a daily basis, no later than at half-past eight each morning, all the newspapers appearing in Petrograd, including the bourgeois ones. Times were laid down for breakfast and lunch. Then Vladimir Ilich added: 'It will be difficult for you, Margarita Vasilevna, in the first week. Everything will fall on you.'

Rahja helped with the errands; the only other visitors to the apartment were Nadezhda Konstantinovna and Maria Ilinichna. Lenin spent most days locked inside while Fofanova was out.

But he still needed to argue his case directly at the Central Committee if he was to secure its assent to an immediate armed uprising. On 10 October a session was organised, in the Petersburg Side flat of Galina Flaxerman, who was married to the left-wing Menshevik Nikolai Sukhanov. Sukhanov discreetly spent the night in his office: such were the inter-party *politesses* of the period. Flaxerman brewed up tea in the samovar and kept the participants supplied with biscuits. The meeting began around ten o'clock in the evening. In the chaotic revolutionary conditions, when communications and transport were unreliable, only twelve Central Committee members managed to be present. What they heard was to have a gigantic influence over events. The main item on the agenda was the question of the party's seizure of power. It took the rather obscure form of a 'report on the current moment' by Lenin. The room was softly lit. For most participants this was the first occasion they had seen Lenin for months. It was quite a surprise for them since he was still dressed as a Lutheran pastor. Unfortunately he had not learned the knack of stopping the wig from falling off, and had developed the nervous habit of smoothing it down with both hands. His fellow leaders found his mannerisms comic.

Yet their hilarity was of short duration. After Sverdlov had given a survey of current developments, Lenin spoke passionately for a whole hour in favour of insurrection. Every listener witnessed his anger and impatience. He declared that the Central Committee had shown 'a kind of indifference to the question of insurrection'. Now the moment for decision had arrived. If the 'masses' were apathetic, it was because they were 'tired of words and resolutions'. According to Lenin, 'the majority are now behind us'. The peasants might not be voting Bolshevik, but they were seizing the land and this was disrupting the authority of the Provisional Government, which he accused of scheming to surrender Petrograd to the Germans. The debate was lengthy and spirited. No one could fail to recognise the danger of following Lenin's line. But he won over the Central Committee. As dawn broke on 11 October, his motion was ratified by ten votes to two.[36]

This meant that the Central Committee had committed itself to focusing its energies on 'the technical side' of planning insurrection.[37] Lenin was pleased with the result and returned in triumph to Fofanova's apartment. He had not got everything his own way. In particular he had argued that the Northern Congress of Soviets, scheduled to meet in Minsk on 11 October, should be 'used for the start of decisive actions'.[38] This proposal did not appear in the final resolution. The Central Committee, on the proposal of Trotski and others, strove to make the future insurrection look less like the seizure of power by a single party. For this purpose they were coming to the conclusion that the transfer of power should be delayed until the All-Russia Congress of Soviets in Petrograd later in the month.[39] Lenin's idea was completely impracticable; he had left things far too late. If his urgings had been hearkened to, moreover, the party might have put itself at risk by exposing its intentions before it had a chance to organise action in the capital. Although he had spoken eloquently on the need to treat the making of insurrection as an art, he had not practised what he preached. And yet the strength of his conviction was huge. He had proved himself a leader.

The problem for Lenin was that his two main opponents during the night had been Kamenev and Zinoviev, who were in the front rank of the party leadership. Disinclined to let Lenin's victory stand, they sent a jointly written letter to the party's various major committees. Their argument was that popular opinion would shortly compel the Mensheviks and Socialist-Revolutionaries to form a government and include the Bolsheviks in the coalition. They denied that workers would support a violent assumption of power by the Bolsheviks. They pointed out, too, that Lenin's faith in an imminent European socialist revolution was empirically unverifiable.[40]

Another Central Committee meeting was held on 16 October to settle the dispute. Members gathered on the northernmost outskirts of the capital. The venue was the picturesque wooden building of Lesnoi district Duma, which by then was under the leadership of the Bolsheviks. As a precaution, the meeting took place at night. Representatives from the Petersburg Committee, the Military Organisation, the Moscow Committees and other major party bodies attended. Potential supporters of Kamenev and Zinoviev who had been absent at the earlier session had arrived. Lenin was in combative mood. He was late in getting to the building since he had had to take the usual conspiratorial precautions. By the time he started speaking, he was angry and impatient:[41]

> The situation is plain: either a Kornilovite dictatorship or a dictatorship of the proletariat and the poorest strata of the peasantry. It's impossible to be guided by the mood of the masses. For it's changeable and can't accurately be gauged; we must be guided by an objective analysis and evaluation of the revolution. The masses have put their trust in the Bolsheviks and are demanding from them not words but deeds . . .

And as the debate ensued, he had to listen to many local speakers, who otherwise would love to have supported him, explaining that workers and soldiers did not wish to take part in an uprising. Kamenev and Zinoviev re-expressed their doubts and Lenin pulled off his wig in frustration.[42] But support for his critics ebbed in the night. When the vote was taken, nineteen members were with him and only two were against – with four abstentions.

The only remaining question for most participants was whether the Bolsheviks should go out of their way to instigate a clash with the Provisional Government. Nothing specific was decided. Instead Lenin's successful motion affirmed 'complete confidence that the Central Committee and the [Petrograd] Soviet would at the right time indicate the propitious moment and the appropriate methods of the offensive'.[43]

This vagueness gave Lenin what he needed to sanction rapid action. Back to Fofanova's apartment he went. Politically he was pleased, but he was still in a grumpy mood. The problem was tiredness. Although the meeting had broken up at 3.00 a.m., it took him a couple of hours to trudge home. According to Lenin, his escort was incompetent. Moreover, it had been windy as well as rainy; both his hat and wig had been blown off and become muddy.[44] Fofanova had to wash them in hot, soapy water. But she failed to calm him down. Lenin felt he could not assume that the Bolshevik Central Committee would do as agreed. Through the following days he bombarded its members with notes. Yet the Central Committee did not see fit to invite him to its three sessions between 20 and 24 October. It is reasonable to conclude that his fellow members thought he lacked the close knowledge and temperamental stability required for the necessary planning to be undertaken. They would organise the insurrection, but they would do it in their own fashion through the Military-Revolutionary Committee of the Petrograd Soviet; they would time the armed action to coincide with the opening of the All-Russia Congress of Soviets.

By 24 October 1917 Lenin was at fever pitch. Fofanova spent the whole day running errands for him; each time she got back to the apartment, he had another message for her to deliver. He begged permission from the Central Committee to come and join his leading comrades. He extracted what information he could from Fofanova about the situation on Petrograd's streets. What he heard was highly agitating. The bridges in the city were being raised: evidently the Provisional Government still had some fight left in it. The Central Committee infuriated Lenin: 'I don't understand them. What are they afraid of?'[45]

He wrote a letter to its members in the evening and upbraided them as follows:[46]

> There can be no delay!! Everything may be lost!! . . .
> Who must seize power?
> This is now unimportant: let it be seized by the Military-Revolutionary Committee or 'another institution' that will announce that it will hand over power only to the genuine representatives of the people's interests, the army's interests (the immediate proposal of peace), the peasants' interests (the land must be seized immediately and private property abolished), the interests of the starving.

He promised Fofanova that he would wait until 11.00 p.m. for her return. But Rahja arrived at the flat in the meantime and Lenin could no longer contain himself: 'Yes, it must begin today.'[47] They drank a cup of tea and took something to eat. Then Lenin fixed his wig and wrapped a bandage around his head for additional disguise. He left a brief note for Fofanova: 'I've gone where you wanted me not to go. Goodbye, Ilich.'[48] They slipped out at 8.00 p.m. to catch a tram. On the way to the Smolny Institute, where the Petrograd Soviet had been based since the beginning of August, Lenin could not resist enquiring of the conductress what had been happening in the centre that day. Alighting at the tram stop, they picked their way through Kerenski's army patrols.

Rahja's presence was crucial since he had no fear when confronted by inquisitive, boisterous soldiers. Lenin did not need to do much talking. On they walked towards the Smolny Institute. The leaders of the Bolshevik Central Committee and the Military-Revolutionary Committee were unaware that he was coming; they were busily preparing themselves for the agreed coup against the Provisional Government. Reaching the building, Rahja pulled out two forged admittance tickets. Throughout the building the lights were on. At about the same time Fofanova was travelling back to her apartment in accordance with what she and Lenin had agreed. She was going to be late, so she took a horse cab. She arrived on time at 11.00 p.m. to find the brief note from Lenin explaining his absence. By then Vladimir Ilich Lenin was in room no. 71 of the Smolny Institute and was persuading, convincing, prodding, urging and haranguing his comrades to accelerate the locomotive of Revolution. Power – state power – was in sight of attainment. This was the moment, the historic moment, to which he had dedicated the three decades of his adult life. The moment of socialist Revolution had arrived.

18

THE OCTOBER REVOLUTION

October to December 1917

Sporadic violence took place on Petrograd streets on the night of 24–25 October. The Military-Revolutionary Committee ordered its loyal garrison soldiers and the armed worker-volunteers known as the Red Guards to control a list of places. When Kerenski had closed down Bolshevik newspapers and raised the bridges over the river Neva, Trotski was able to claim to be defending the soviets against harassment. The Military-Revolutionary Committee was intent on ensuring that the Second Congress, when it met on 25 October, could declare the overthrow of the Provisional Government as a *fait accompli*.

Lenin exerted pressure for an uprising as soon as he arrived at the Smolny Institute. Not a few observers felt it to be an incongruous scene. Before 1917 the building had been a secondary school belonging to the Society for the Upbringing of Well-Born Girls. It had been constructed to a plan by the Italian architect Quarenghi. The façade of Grecian pillars and the generously proportioned main hall were symbols of an age of privilege, tradition and power. Now it was the workshop of Revolution as Lenin arrived to play his part. On arrival, he was spirited into room no. 71, where he perched himself on the edge of a table. The situation was chaotic in anticipation of the Second Congress of Soviets. Congress delegates were coming and going through the night and the place was a bustling, noisy, ill-kempt and smoke-filled hive of activity. Everyone knew that the decisions taken at the Congress would be decisive for the course of the Revolution and that the Provisional Government's fate hung on what happened in the Institute. The Bolsheviks, at the very time they were seizing power, operated in the same building as Mensheviks and Socialist Revolutionaries, who wished to prevent this. As Lenin sat with his comrades, into the room wandered the Menshevik Fëdor Dan, the Socialist Revolutionary Abram Gots and the Bundist Mark Liber, all of them major figures in their parties. One of the three had left his overcoat hanging there and had come to retrieve a bag of bread, sausage and cheese to share with his companions. Lenin sat tight, thinking that his wig and facial bandage would disguise him. But Dan and his friend were no fools; they recognised him immediately. And they quickly fled the room.[1]

Dan, Gots and Liber had a sense of what might be called revolutionary decorum: they wanted to confront adversaries across a Congress hall and not in a private verbal brawl. Lenin split his sides laughing. Already his presence was having its effect on his Bolshevik comrades; he could afford a moment of jollity. At 2.35 p.m. there was an emergency meeting of the Petrograd Soviet in the main hall of the Institute. The introductory speaker was Trotski, the soviet chairman. There was, unusually, total silence. Trotski's announcement was historic: 'Kerenski's power has been overthrown. Some of the ministers have been arrested. Those who remain unarrested will soon be arrested.'[2]

To applause from the Petrograd Soviet, Trotski went on to explain that a socialist administration would be assuming power. Then he announced that a speech would be given by none other than Lenin. The ovation lasted several minutes.[3] Once it had died down, Lenin spoke triumphantly:[4]

> Comrades! The workers' and peasants' revolution, which the Bolsheviks have all this time been talking about the need for, has been accomplished.
>
> What is the significance of this workers' and peasants' revolution? Above all, the significance of this coup [perevorot] consists in the fact that we'll have a Soviet government as our own organ of power without any participation whatever by the bourgeoisie. The oppressed masses themselves will create their power. The old state apparatus will be destroyed at its roots and a new apparatus of administration will be created in the form of the soviet organisations.

Lenin was exaggerating. In fact the Provisional Government had not yet been eliminated and the struggle in Petrograd had only just begun. But yet another stage in Lenin's advance on power had been attained: the caution of the Bolshevik Central Committee and the Military-Revolutionary Committee had been surmounted and the Petrograd Soviet had been convinced that the decisive struggles of the socialist seizure of power had already largely been won.

The left-wing Menshevik Nikolai Sukhanov entered the hall halfway through Lenin's speech, and was stupefied:[5]

As I entered, there was on the platform a bald, shaved man who was unknown to me. But he spoke with a strangely familiar hoarse, loud voice, with a throaty quality and very characteristic stresses on the end of his sentences ... Bah! It was Lenin. He made his appearance that day after four months of an underground existence.

The Bolshevik leader had taken hold of his party and of the Revolution.

Power could now be presented as a *fait accompli* to the Congress of Soviets. The Mensheviks and Socialist Revolutionaries might object to the Provisional Government's overthrow, but they could not reverse what had happened. This was a first concern that could now be forgotten. A second had also become less acute. This was the possibility – feared especially by Lenin – that the Mensheviks and Socialist-Revolutionaries themselves might turn against the Provisional Government and demand Kerenski's removal. The Pre-Parliament had passed a vote of no confidence in him late on 24 October and called for peace to be concluded immediately on the eastern front and for the landed estates of the gentry to be distributed to the peasantry. Lenin had no intention of sharing power with the Mensheviks and Socialist-Revolutionaries. He had cunningly refrained from spelling this out to the Bolshevik Central Committee before the insurrection had started. If he had done so, the Central Committee would probably have refused to support armed action altogether. Consequently it remained a priority for him on the night of 24–25 October to keep the Mensheviks and Socialist Revolutionaries at arm's length, and he strove to manufacture a situation in which the Bolsheviks would have the dominant role in forming the next government. Thus power had to be seized without the slightest delay.

Lenin knew much needed to be done to establish his government. The battleship *Aurora*, loyal to the Bolsheviks, moved up the river Neva towards the Winter Palace. The State Bank, the post and telegraph offices and the rail terminals were occupied by the insurgents. Kerenski arranged his escape through the cordon around the Winter Palace in order to rally forces outside the capital.

The Bolshevik Central Committee met in the early hours and took decisions about the general complexion of the government. This was done on the initiative of V. P. Milyutin and not Lenin. The fact that Milyutin, who had not slept for several nights and was also associated normally with the right wing of Bolshevism, had instigated such a discussion indicates that not everything done in the early hours of 25 October was the work of Lenin's hands. He was back among a group of

Photo of Lenin and his fellow travellers in Stockholm, days after disembarking from the 'sealed train' across Germany. The woman in the large bonnet following Lenin is his wife Nadya. Behind her walks Inessa.

Lenin's prized notes on 'Marxism and the State' which he brought from Switzerland in 1917 and worked up into *The State and Revolution*.

Picture taken of Lenin by Dmitri Leshchenko for his official documents with which to escape to Finland. Lenin had to pose seated on his knees.

The Smolny Institute, where the Bolsheviks planned and carried out their seizure of power in October 1917.

Lev Trotski addressing Red Army troops in the Civil War.

Lenin and (to the right) Yakov Sverdlov at the unveiling of a statue of Marx and Engels on the first anniversary of the October Revolution.

M.S. Nappelbaum's official portrait of Lenin, January 1918. This was the first such photo taken of him after the seizure of power and the regrowth of his beard.

Lenin's Kremlin office.

Above: The Kremlin kitchen of
Lenin and Krupskaya. Some of the
pots and pans were patched.

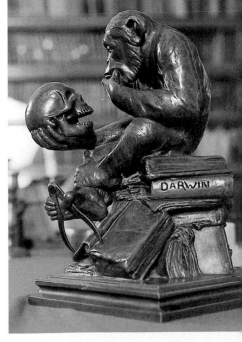

Right: The 'Darwin' statue
Lenin kept on his desk.

Nadezhda Konstantinovna Krupskaya in 1919

revolutionaries who knew that they had gone too far to turn back. If there was going to be a revolution, then let it be undertaken efficiently. But, of all the participants in the Bolshevik Central Committee in room no. 36, Lenin was the least exhausted, and it was he who was asked to write a proclamation on behalf of the Military-Revolutionary Committee. He passed it to one of its leading officials, Vladimir Bonch-Bruevich, for publication at 10 a.m. It ran as follows:[6]

> To the Citizens of Russia:
> The Provisional Government has been overthrown. State power has passed into the hands of the organ of the Petrograd Soviet of Workers' and Soldiers' Deputies, the Military-Revolutionary Committee, which stands at the head of the Petrograd proletariat and garrison.
> The cause for which the people has struggled: the immediate proposal of a democratic peace, the abolition of the gentry's landed property, workers' control over production, the creation of a Soviet Government – victory for this cause has been secured.
> Long live the revolution of the workers, soldiers and peasants!

By asserting that the Military-Revolutionary Committee was acting as the government, Lenin knew that he would infuriate the Mensheviks and Socialist-Revolutionaries when he came to address the Congress of Soviets.

The Congress was scheduled to start at 2 p.m., but the Bolshevik central leadership wanted to achieve the occupation of the Winter Palace beforehand. This took longer than expected by the Military-Revolutionary Committee. Lenin gave vent to his anger: 'Why so long? What are our military commanders doing? They've set up a real war! What's it all for? Encirclement, transfers, linkages, expanded deployment ... Is this really a war with a worthy enemy? Get on with it! On to the attack!'[7] But the Military-Revolutionary Committee refused to commit its forces to an unconditional offensive. Kerenski had escaped and there was no significant military threat. The siege continued throughout the day around the last remaining stronghold of the Provisional Government in the capital.

At 10.35 p.m. the organisers of the Congress could wait no longer. On behalf of the Central Executive Committee, Fëdor Dan rang the bell in the assembly hall for proceedings to be started. There were 670 delegates. Three hundred Bolsheviks constituted the largest group. They would have to rely on the other delegates in order to make up a majority.

Fortunately there were plenty of these to hand. The left wing of the Socialist-Revolutionary Party had already decided to form a separate party, and this new party – like the Bolsheviks – wanted to transfer land to the peasantry. There were also dozens of delegates to no party what-soever who wished for a government based on the soviets. The other hope for Lenin was that the Mensheviks and Socialist-Revolutionaries, offended by the events of the previous night, would walk out of the Congress. To this end he had bent his efforts. But he did this quietly and avoided making any public appearance or signing any public declarations in the course of the day. Nor did he turn up to the first session of the Congress. Trotski rather than Lenin headed the group of Bolsheviks and Left Socialist-Revolutionaries who took the leading position on the platform in reflection of the strength of their Congress delegations.

Martov from the floor cried out for negotiations to be started for a peaceful end to the current crisis. The Congress overwhelmingly en-dorsed his proposal. But there followed Menshevik, Socialist-Revolutionary and Bundist criticisms of the violence elsewhere in Petrograd – and to the delight of Lenin, who still held himself in the background, the large anti-Bolshevik socialist parties stalked out. At this point it became harder for Martov to proceed, and he and his group of Menshevik-Internationalists also walked out. Trotski condemned them. Lenin was delighted that events were so strongly running his way and that he could rely upon Trotski in this matter.

He continued to handle himself carefully. In the eyes of his party's enemies he embodied the most extreme political intransigence and destructiveness – and even many Bolsheviks retained reservations about his combative style of comportment. Furthermore, there was a strong body of opinion in the Bolshevik party as a whole and especially in the Central Committee that welcomed the formation of a government coalition of all socialist parties. Kamenev had returned to the Central Committee once the uprising had begun and Lenin ignored the attempt by Kamenev and Zinoviev to forestall the October Revolution. And so Kamenev became useful as the moderate face of Bolshevism while the Bolshevik leaders tried to present themselves as the people's defenders against the oppressive Provisional Government. Most Bolshevik delegates had acquired mandates from their local constituencies on this same assumption. It is consequently possible that Lenin's Central Committee colleagues judged it impolitic to let him loose as its main spokesman on 25 October 1917. Or perhaps he made this assessment for himself without pressure being brought to bear. At any rate he focussed his energies upon cajoling his associates in the Military-Revolutionary Committee and the Bolshevik Central Committee and to discussing what kind of government and policies should be announced next day.

Films were made of the October Revolution, novels written, songs sung and even ballets danced. In practically all of them a misleading image of Lenin was disseminated. There he is, with his fist raised, mouth tensed and a bearded chin. In fact, on that historic day of 25 October 1917 he spoke only briefly. He was not the Revolution's great orator. He did not even look like his normal self because it took several further weeks before his moustache and beard grew back to their normal appearance – and indeed he would not agree to being photographed until January 1918. Contrary to conventional accounts, then, Lenin's importance was not as a speaker in the Congress hall but rather as a strategist and inspirer behind the scenes – and in this role his contribution to the Revolution's success was crucial.

At any rate he could afford to leave the Smolny Institute by the evening of 25 October. The management of the insurrection, he could at last concede, was in secure hands. His job next day would be to present not just slogans but actual decrees. At that time it would no longer be sufficient to castigate Kerenski: the new government would have to offer something different of its own. Lenin had snatched only the odd hour of sleep on 25 October. He badly needed some rest, and Bonch-Bruevich suggested that he should come home and sleep at his nearby flat. (He also gently pointed out that Lenin no longer needed his wig.) The Winter Palace was evidently on the brink of capture by the besiegers some time after midnight – and this duly came to pass. Accompanied by a large bodyguard, Lenin left the Institute for Bonch-Bruevich's flat. He became drowsy in the car; he was obviously exhausted. Bonch-Bruevich gave Lenin the bedroom while he himself slept on the sofa in the living room. Even so, Lenin could not get to sleep. Once Bonch-Bruevich seemed to have drifted off into unconsciousness, Lenin crept back into the living room and drafted the decrees he had to present to the Congress of Soviets on 26 October.[8]

He did not mind how hard he drove himself so long as he was serving a higher purpose. But there was another impulse at work too. The Central Committee had asked him, at the meeting of 21 October which its members had banned him from attending, to prepare various 'theses' for use at the Congress of Soviets. He had done nothing to comply with this injunction until that night in Bonch-Bruevich's flat. He had been suffused by the fear that the insurrection might not take place at all; perhaps he even suspected that the Central Committee's request for theses had been a way of keeping him busy – and keeping him out of the way in Fofanova's flat. Now he could at last concentrate properly on the theses and have them ready in rough form for the morning.

Both his Decree on Peace and his Decree on Land were of large significance for twentieth-century world history. Lenin knew this. The proclamation of a new government and a socialist revolution were only part of his brief. He needed also to propound a set of policies that contrasted entirely with those of Nicholas II, Prince Lvov and Alexander Kerenski. He did not want merely to take office. He wanted to wield power in Russia on different principles from those espoused by his predecessors. And he was determined that the message would go quickly beyond the Congress of Soviets in Petrograd. He told his host Bonch-Bruevich not only to publish little booklets of the decrees but also to go and buy up the remaindered copies of 1917 calendars on sale at a discount at the Sytin bookshop on the Nevski Prospekt. This strange request disconcerted Bonch-Bruevich. But Lenin explained that workers and soldiers lacked wrapping paper for their cigarettes. If booklets of decrees were handed out, people would simply roll them around twists of tobacco. Lenin's scheme was meant to provide the Bolshevik party's supporters with paper sufficient to allow them to avoid the need to do anything other than use the booklets for their intended political purpose.[9]

Although Bonch-Bruevich and Lenin had not had the rest they needed, they hastened back next morning to the Smolny Institute. Lenin greeted everyone he met with words of congratulation on the birth of the socialist Revolution. Already a manifesto had been released in the name of the Congress of Soviets. Anatoli Lunacharski had read it out to the Congress, but it was Lenin who had composed it. Inside the Institute he completed his work on the Decree on Peace, the Resolution on the Formation of a Workers' and Peasants' Government and the Decree of Land. Interspersed in his editorial work were meetings, both with particular delegates to the Congress and with the entre Bolshevik fraction and the Bolshevik Central Committee. An appeal was issued to the Left Socialist Revolutionaries to join a governmental coalition with the Bolsheviks. They refused, and Lenin without further ado resolved on a one-party government. He at last came before the Congress of Soviets, to tumultuous applause, at 9 p.m. By then it had been decided that he would be the government's leader and that he would be described as the

Chairman of the Council of People's Commissars (which was known by its acronym, Sovnarkom).

The session of the Congress of Soviets continued through the night of 26–27 October. Lenin went on consulting with his central party colleagues – Vladimir Bonch-Bruevich, Vladimir Milyutin and Lev Trotski – about his wording. He drafted a Decree on Workers' Control, which was not published for several days. He also drafted a Decree on the Press, accepted and printed on 27 October. The point was that he gave literary expression to the October Revolution and that his various decrees were the clearest statement of his purposes. Lenin announced his government's intention to be unlike any other in world history. Supposedly the people would know in full about its government's internal discussions, and transparency of deliberation and decision would be complete.

Not once did Lenin mention Marxism in his various speeches of 25–27 October. He referred to 'socialism' only very fleetingly. Nor did he explain that his immediate objective was the establishment of a class-based dictatorship and that ultimately he aimed at the realisation of a communist, stateless society as described in his *The State and Revolution*. He was keeping his political cards close to his chest. He was a party boss, and wanted Bolshevism to be attractive to those workers, soldiers, peasants and intellectuals who had not yet supported it. And so terms such as dictatorship, terror, civil war and revolutionary war were yet again quietly shelved. He also continued to leave aside his lifelong imprecations against priests, mullahs and rabbis, against industrialists, the landed gentry and kulaks, against liberal, conservative and reactionary intellectuals. His emphasis was skewed more sharply in favour of a revolution 'from below' even than in *The State and Revolution*. His every pronouncement was directed towards encouraging the 'masses' to exercise initiative and engage in 'autonomous activity' (*samodeyatel'nost'*). His wish was for the Bolsheviks to appear as a party that would facilitate the making of Revolution by and for the people.

Sovnarkom, the new Soviet government, was announced to acclaim at the Congress on 26 October. Lenin was Chairman: he eschewed a title such as Premier or President. His People's Commissar for External Affairs was Trotski. Stalin was the People's Commissar for Nationalities Affairs. Bolshevik Central Committee members accepted governmental posts with enthusiasm and turned up in the next few days at the old ministries to implement the policies of the October Revolution. They thought – and they fended off every Menshevik and Socialist-

Revolutionary criticism of their naivety – that the Russian revolutionary example would be followed within hours by working classes elsewhere in Europe. If not within hours, then within a few days. If by some extraordinary mishap not within days, then certainly within months.

The person who had given the most vivid expression to this way of thinking was Lenin. His speeches and decrees were rousing by any standards. The Decree on Peace, which he personally presented to the Congress on 26 October, was carefully formulated inasmuch as it did not overtly demand 'European socialist revolution'; Lenin appealed not only to the peoples of the belligerent states but also to their governments (even though he had been condemning these governments as irredeemably 'imperialist'). But the Decree's gist was a practical summons to revolution:

> The [Soviet] government proposes to all the governments and peoples of all the warring countries to conclude a truce immediately, while for its own part it considers it desirable that this truce should be concluded for no less than three months, i.e. for such a time that would entirely facilitate the completion of negotiations on peace with the participation of representatives of all peoples and nations without exception that have been dragged into the war or compelled to take part in it, as well as the convocation of plenipotentiary assemblies of popular representatives of all countries for the definitive confirmation of peace conditions.

These words were astonishing after three years of war. Hostilities on the eastern front were instantly suspended.

The Decree on Land was the other great reform of policy Lenin personally introduced to the Congress. Dismay at his dilatory approach to producing it had led the Central Committee to ask Vladimir Milyutin – the leading Bolshevik economist after Lenin and the newly appointed People's Commissar of Agriculture – to get together with Yuri Larin to draft a decree. But Lenin took over and finished the job. He also took over the list of peasant demands as compiled in June by the Party of Socialist Revolutionaries as the detailed clauses of his decree. But the lengthy preamble was Lenin's. It was not written in his most exciting language. Dryly he announced the abolition of landed property of the gentry, the Imperial family and the Church. Nor was it a work of legislative coherence. There was uncertainty about which institute was to dispose of the expropriated land: land committees, peasant communes or peasants' soviets. The terminology, too, was vague. It was specified that the land of 'rank-and-file peasants' should be inviolable. But no definition was given of such peasants. And it was simultaneously laid down that private property in land, presumably including land owned by peasants, should be abolished in perpetuity.

Yet legal niceties were of no interest to Lenin. He wanted the Decree to have a 'demonstrative' effect and to foster the advance of Revolution. His general intent was anyway clear enough: the peasantry was invoked to take collective action to seize and cultivate all land not currently owned by peasants. Only in cases where large-scale advanced agriculture was practised did Lenin aspire to preventing a break-up of landed estates. He expressed unbounded faith in the peasantry. His speech to the Congress of Soviets spelled out his rationale:[10]

> A crime was committed by the government that has been over-thrown and by the conciliationist parties of the Mensheviks and SRs when on various pretexts they postponed the resolution of the land question and thereby brought the country to ruin and to a peasant uprising. Their words about pillage and anarchy in the countryside echo with falsehood and cowardly deceit. Where and when have pillage and anarchy been provoked by sensible measures?

Lenin, of course, was not genuinely the peasants' champion. He thought that, if they took over the land, they would soon start competing with each other within the framework of a capitalist market economy – and eventually, he hoped, the Soviet government would be able to intervene on behalf of the 'rural proletariat' and nationalise the land. And so his ultimate objective remained to set up socialist collective farms.

He did not intend to let the October Revolution stand or fall by virtue of democratic consent. In those very first days at the Smolny Institute he tried to browbeat Sverdlov and other Central Committee members into announcing the postponement of the Constituent Assembly elections. Sverdlov refused. Bolsheviks had been saying that only they could be trusted to convoke the Constituent Assembly on time: they could not immediately postpone the elections. Lenin's cynicism was rejected, at least initially.

Less controversial in the Bolshevik Central Committee was Lenin's requirement that the resistance to the Soviet government should be ruthlessly quashed. Troops were sent out to oppose the Cossack detachments assembled by Kerenski; and the units of the Military-Revolutionary Committee continued to patrol the city. On 27 October, furthermore, a Decree on the Press was issued with Lenin's signature. This was the first governmental instruction enabling the establishment of censorship. Any 'organ of the press' was liable to closure for inciting resistance to Sovnarkom. Indeed a newspaper could be put out of operation simply for being deemed to have 'sown confusion by means of an obviously defamatory distortion of the facts'. Despite having campaigned in earlier months for the principle of 'freedom of the press', the Bolsheviks were not slow to arrogate to themselves powers enabling them to monopolise the information available through the media of public communication. The Decree mentioned that Sovnarkom regarded this as a temporary measure. But again it is open to doubt whether Lenin truly believed in this provisionality; he had said repeatedly in 1917 that 'freedom of the press' was a principle that played into the hands of the bourgeoisie. He was unlikely to alter this assumption in the heat of revolutionary struggle.

The immediate threat, however, came not from conservative and liberal newspapers but from Kerenski; and this situation widened the scope for sympathisers of the Mensheviks and Socialist-Revolutionaries to put political pressure on Sovnarkom to establish a broad socialist coalition. Kamenev and other right-wing Bolsheviks thereby also acquired a leverage on Lenin and Trotski. The All-Russia Executive Committee of the Railwaymen's Union (Vikzhel) warned that it would go on strike unless a coalition was formed. Kamenev was empowered by the Bolshevik Central Committee to negotiate with Vikzhel and Menshevik and Socialist-Revolutionary representatives. Lenin had to stay out of the way. He recognised this, but he did not trust Kamenev. In the circumstances it is remarkable that he kept the lid on his impatience and intransigence. For Kamenev on 30 October consented to a plan for an all-socialist governmental coalition that would exclude Lenin and Trotski.[11]

But by then Lenin was uninhibited by questions of internal party diplomacy. Sovnarkom's security had increased. It had become improbable that the railwaymen would obey a call for a strike and the Cossacks of General Krasnov were defeated on the Pulkovo Heights. Lenin could safely attack Kamenev again. At the Bolshevik Central Committee on 1 November there was a decisive confrontation. Lenin and Trotski held to the opinion that an ultimatum should be delivered to the other parties declaring that a coalition would be entertained only if Bolshevik policies were pre-agreed as the basis of the government's. This was really a way of breaking off negotiations without appearing to do so. The Menshevik and Socialist-Revolutionary leaders with their long experience of Lenin had never been optimistic about the possibility of collaborating with him. His ideas on dictatorship and terror as well as his despotic personal behaviour were anathema to them. Nor did they approve of his closure of Kadet newspapers – and they saw signs of even greater trouble ahead when it became clear that Sovnarkom had prohibited right-wing Menshevik newspapers from operating. Lenin struck at Kamenev in the Bolshevik Central Committee on 2 November, and the policy of no compromise with the Mensheviks and Socialist-Revolutionaries was resumed.

There was a further tremor on 4 November when Kamenev and four colleagues resigned from the Bolshevik Central Committee and several People's Commissars announced either their resignation from Sovnarkom or their disapproval of Lenin's refusal to negotiate sincerely in pursuit of an all-socialist coalition. But Lenin did not yield and Trotski stood by him. Together with Central Committee Secretary Sverdlov and People's Commissar for Nationalities Affairs Iosif Stalin they were determined to proceed with revolutionary political consolidation. The inner core of the Bolshevik Central Committee was rock-hard. Its members were aware that their infant regime had not yet faced its greatest trials. Every day that Sovnarkom lasted, they thought, was a major accomplishment. But at the very least they wanted to leave a mark on the history of Russia and Europe in the event that they were forced to flee from Petrograd in defeat. Decrees, proclamations, instructions and summonses flowed out from the Smolny Institute. Nerve and faith were required. Lenin and his associates had taken a vast gamble with the politics of their party and their country, and it was by no means certain that they had laid a sound bet.

After that first fortnight of political insurrection, armed defence and inter-party negotiation there was a need for them to consolidate their position. This required three main achievements. Firstly, they had to spread their administrative authority to other parts of the country. Secondly, they had to complete the promulgation of their revolutionary decrees. Thirdly, they had to deal with the Central Powers on the eastern front. It was an awesome task – and most of their enemies in the country were already convinced that they would fail. Surely they had already made too many grievous errors of anticipation? Their assumptions had been infantile. They thought that the armies of the Central Powers would be dissolved by the corrosive effects of fraternisation with Russian soldiers. They believed, too, that workers in Russia who had voted for the Bolsheviks would constantly support them. They trusted that the rushing decline of the economy could quickly be reversed by means of governmental restrictions on capitalism. They had little sense of the grip of age-old traditions upon popular consciousness, traditions of religion, social deference and political indifference. Their enemies depicted Lenin and his associates as ill-educated, reckless semi-intellectuals at best. Among the most reactionary political elements there was another dimension: they asserted that Lenin was a Jew, a cosmopolitan and an anti-Russian in league with Russia's national enemies.

But few people in Russia at the time had a presentiment that Lenin's regime might last for years, far less that it might stretch to seven decades of existence. The supreme Bolshevik leaders were not entirely convinced either. They had a phrase for their condition: they lived by 'sitting on their suitcases'. How long could they last out? In such a situation it was natural for the very highest stratum of the party to try and find succour in leadership. Increasingly it seemed to the metropolitan provincial party leaders that Lenin, despite his occasional strategic and tactical lapses, was a reliable guide. He was, furthermore, a willing leader. Even if they survived the current political crisis, they would need a leader. Lenin was such a leader.

He did not experience any impulse to question what he was up to. He knew, at least in broad terms, his purposes. Bolsheviks, he repeatedly argued, had to face up to the consequences of the October seizure of power. He had told them – even if he had kept it secret from the workers who voted for the Bolsheviks – that a government of firm, even authoritarian purposes was crucial. In April, Lenin had told his Bolsheviks to prepare themselves to take power. Most observers had mocked him. But he had ignored the ribaldry and steeled his party to hold its nerve, and against widely expressed expectations the Bolsheviks had succeeded in taking power. Now the party's critics laughed at him on the ground that he expected that the October Revolution would succeed in fulfilling his strategic analysis. But he no longer took Kadets, Mensheviks and Socialist-Revolutionaries seriously. He had not done so for a dozen years; and unlike other revolutionaries, he did not experience second thoughts about his analysis when others considered it eccentric. He had never minded singing as a soloist. Now that he was in power there was still less of a temptation to cramp his vocal cords, and he hymned the Revolution with all his passion.

Lenin liked to explain his strategy in dualistic terms. He wanted a revolution from above and a revolution from below; he wanted both dictatorship and democracy. He aimed at authoritarian imposition and liberation. His writings in 1917 had combined these polarities. And yet, however much he toyed with such dualism, he raged to impose Sovnarkom's authority and would let nothing get in his way. Coercion steadily assumed prominence at the expense of persuasion. Lenin instructed and commanded and he sanctioned violence, including outright state terror.

In the first few days he wrote up or edited the various decrees he had not yet submitted. Among them, on 29 October, was a Decree on the Eight-Hour Day. At last the founder of the working-class dictatorship took up the specific interests of the working class. On the same day a Decree on Popular Education committed Sovnarkom to the provision of universal, free, secular schooling for children. Then on 2 November came the Declaration of the Rights of the Peoples of Russia, which assured every citizen that Sovnarkom opposed every vestige of national and religious privilege. National self-determination, even to the point of secession, was offered to the nations of the former Russian Empire. The Declaration was co-signed by Lenin and Stalin. On 14 November, the Decree on Workers' Control – which Lenin was meant to have written earlier – was issued. This was the scheme whereby the workers of a given enterprise should be given the right through an elected committee to supervise the enterprise's management. Still the decrees kept coming. On 1 December, Sovnarkom established a Supreme Council of the National Economy to take proprietorial and regulatory authority over industry, banking, agriculture and trade. All banks were nationalised on 14 December and steadily in the ensuing weeks a number of large-scale factories were taken into the hands of the state. Sovnarkom was carrying through the programme it had promised in the months when the Bolsheviks were advancing on power.

Not every decree had been adumbrated in public before the October Revolution. Lenin had tried to strike a jovial tone in saying how the Bolsheviks might try to emulate the Jacobin Terror in the French Revolution. But, as soon as he took power and had seen off the prospect of an all-socialist coalition, his true harshness was displayed again. He it was who came to Sovnarkom to make the case for the re-establishment of a secret political police. The October Revolution, he argued, had to be efficiently protected. Thus there would be created an Extraordinary Commission. Its head, on Lenin's recommendation, would be Felix Dzierżyński, and its powers in 'the struggle against counter-revolution and sabotage' were left deliberately vague and were kept free of interference even from Sovnarkom. It was called the Extraordinary Commission

mainly because even Lenin believed that the need for such an organisation would be only temporary; and it must be mentioned, too, that
Lenin did not at this stage call for a campaign of extensive mass terror.

But it was a fateful step. Not being someone who believed in legality,
Lenin felt comfortable with a political police untrammelled by niceties
of written procedure – and the Extraordinary Commission's charter
allowed him and Dzierżyński to expand its range of functions at will. He
was forever talking and writing about bourgeois bloodsuckers. Class war
was congenial to him. A conversation took place about the Bolsheviks'
intentions between Lenin and the Left Socialist-Revolutionary Isaak
Shteinberg. 'In that case,' asked Shteinberg, why should we bother with
a People's Commissariat of Justice? Let's honestly call it the Commissariat for Social Annihilation and we'll get involved in that!' Lenin
responded as follows: 'Well said! . . . That's exactly how it's got to be . . .
but it can't be stated by us.'[12] It cannot be proved that Lenin held the
total physical liquidation of the middle classes as a party objective. But
cases of abuse towards the rich, the aristocratic and the privileged
certainly failed to arouse pity. His resentment against the old ruling
elites, which he had felt acutely after the hanging of his brother
Alexander in 1887, was never far from the surface of his thinking.

He thought back to the political writings of the Russian radicals of
the previous century. Talking to an old acquaintance, he said: 'We are
engaged in annihilation, but don't you recall what Pisarev said? "Break,
beat up everything, beat and destroy! Everything that is being broken is
rubbish with no right to life. What survives is good . . ."'[13] Although the
conversation cannot be independently verified, it has the ring of plausibility. Lenin wished to annihilate every vestige of the old regime and to
use every available weapon in the struggle.

It remained unclear how far he would go in assuaging his wish for
revenge, a wish that was given an intellectual veneer in the form of his
version of Marxism. The three first months of the October Revolution
had solved nothing as yet. Soviets in industrial towns had gone over to
Sovnarkom's side and had declared themselves the local governmental
authority. The peasantry of Russia and Ukraine were taking up the
injunctions of the Decree on Land. Non-Russians, especially the Finns,
were welcoming the scope provided for national self-expression. And
German and Austrian diplomats were sitting down with representatives
of the Bolsheviks to discuss what should happen after the truce on the
eastern front came to an end. The Bolsheviks even managed to entice
the Left Socialist-Revolutionaries into becoming junior partners in a

Sovnarkom coalition, and they began to take their places on 9 December. All this was to the good. But could it last? Could it lead to the general popular socialist Revolution in Russia, Europe and the rest of the world that Lenin had believed when he wrote out his *April Theses* and his *State and Revolution*?

19

DICTATORSHIP UNDER SIEGE

Winter 1917–1918

Questions about the spread and survival of the Revolution were bothering Lenin. Although other members of Sovnarkom and the Bolshevik Central Committee were thinking about them, most of them concentrated on their institutional functions. Only Trotski gave as much attention to general policy as Lenin did. Lenin did not particularly welcome Trotski's contributions since they sometimes contradicted his own thoughts. He preferred to do the thinking himself and to encourage his leading comrades to get on with the business of running their People's Commissariats. The Bolsheviks lacked prior experience of large-scale administration, and several of them were embarrassed about this. Lenin's reply was emphatic: 'But do you think that any of us has that?'[1]

The mood among Bolsheviks and Left Socialist-Revolutionaries remained utopian. They were confident that European socialist Revolution was imminent and that Russia's revolutionary transformation would be swift and easy. Trotski was as hard-headed as any other Bolshevik leader, but on arrival at the old Ministry of Foreign Affairs to take over as People's Commissar he thought that his job would be strictly ephemeral. He would enter the building, publish the secret treaties between Nicholas II and the Allies and then simply 'shut up shop'. Thus Trotski underestimated the will of the Central Powers to crush the Russian forces on the eastern front. Other Bolshevik governmental officials were equally intoxicated. Nikolai Osinski, Chairman of the Supreme Council of the National Economy, spent days elaborating charts and statistics for the perfection of the structures of industry and agriculture while the economy itself went to rack and ruin. Nikolai Podvoiski was absorbed in his plans to reorganise the armed forces at a time when most soldiers were jumping on trains and returning to their villages. Yuri Larin, it seemed to Lenin, constituted the most absurd case. Hardly a week passed without Larin composing a proposal for fundamental reconstruction of this or that People's Commissariat.

Lenin too was a utopian thinker, but he was able to adjust his policies in the interests of political survival. It is true that he did not always use this capacity and that he had often stuck to doctrinal positions when his party might have helped itself by being more flexible. But he had revised many policies in pursuit of power in 1917, and afterwards it became axiomatic for him that the October Revolution had to be protected at all costs. Indeed Lenin felt in his element. He derived pleasure from his historic responsibility to work out a programme of measures that would save the October Revolution and enhance its achievements.

Several things worried him. Even while seizing power in October 1917, he had anticipated that the Bolsheviks and their allies would not win the Constituent Assembly elections. He was also alarmed about economic conditions. He began to query whether the urban working class had the discipline and commitment necessary for a proper socialist revolution. He was equally concerned about the progress made among the non-Russians. The promise of national self-determination had failed to give rise to a socialist seizure of power in Ukraine and Finland. Worse still, there were no insurrections in Germany, Austria, France and the United Kingdom. The 'European socialist Revolution' had stalled, and Lenin learned from Trotski on his trips back to Petrograd from Brest-Litovsk that the Central Powers were bent on invasion if Russia rejected their terms. Lenin had argued, in the teeth of opposition among Bolsheviks in April 1917, that socialist Revolution would be an easy business. He had scoffed at the dire predictions about Bolshevism made by Mensheviks and Socialist-Revolutionaries. Now his job was to persuade Bolsheviks that the tasks of Revolution would be harder than he had convinced them it would be.

Lenin could at last take the measure of things on the streets of Petrograd by going for walks near the Smolny Institute. From 10 November 1917 he and Nadezhda Konstantinovna had a two-room flat on the first floor. The period of separation was over, at least for the next few months. The flat itself was small but comfortable, and Nadezhda Konstantinovna remembered it fondly:[2]

At last Ilich and I settled down in the Smolny [Institute]. We were allocated a room there that had once been occupied by an upper-class lady. It was a room with a partitioning screen on the other side of which stood the bed. One had to enter via the washroom. No one could get along to the couple's flat without a special permit signed by Lenin.

Not that Lenin and Krupskaya spent much time there. His office was room no. 81 on the second floor in the north wing, and when Lenin was not in his office he was usually in the reception room opposite the office where officials waited to have a word with him. There was always a queue of them and the reception room got packed out. He loved to talk with them and often took the chance to deliver a short speech on current issues.[3] The flat of Lenin and Krupskaya was not a genuine domestic sanctuary. The neighbouring large room was used for Sovnarkom sessions; and Trotski and his family lived in the flat opposite to that of the Lenins. People's Commissars and their various deputies and assistants bustled up and down the corridor. In the English phrase, Lenin and Krupskaya 'lived over the shop'. Krupskaya had been appointed as Deputy Commissar of Popular Enlightenment and had to get out and about; she could not, and was not asked to, attend to her husband. It was not just his Revolution: it was also hers; and in any case his colleagues in the Central Committee had firmly refused to have her back in a secretarial capacity. Lenin and Krupskaya were political colleagues, but colleagues in separate institutions; they no longer had an intimate working relationship.

Lacking a woman to organise his domestic affairs, Lenin – according to Krupskaya's memoirs – lived from hand to mouth:[4]

Ilich was in a pretty neglected condition. [His bodyguard] Zhëltyshev fetched Ilich his lunch, bread, that which was laid down as his ration. Sometimes Maria Ilinichna brought him food of some sort from her home; but I wasn't at home and there was no regular concern for his diet.

Perhaps Krupskaya was trying to stress her importance to Lenin's wellbeing and his sister Maria's inadequacy. Be that as it may, his women had their own political commitments and left him largely to his own devices. The result was that he forgot to eat at the normal times of day and sauntered along to the communal cafeteria to grab a piece of pickled herring and some bread.[5] His health deteriorated; headaches and insomnia returned.[6]

When Lenin and Krupskaya did have time together, they took a walk – usually unaccompanied by Zhëltyshev. On one occasion a dozen housewives standing outside the Institute screamed at them. In fact the women had not recognised Lenin: they were abusing everyone they spotted coming out of the building.[7] Thus Lenin and Krupskaya could go around incognito even though his name was in the newspapers every day.

In fact denunciations of his dictatorial regime were frequent. The tone was strident and direct, but occasionally there was an attempt at satire. The most notable occurred in the Socialist Revolutionary newspaper *Delo Naroda*, when the writer Yevgeni Zamyatin wrote a sequence of short pieces ridiculing Lenin in the guise of a certain Theta. In case the reader missed the point, Zamyatin mentioned that Theta was treated as a son by Ulyan Petrovich – a verbal glance at Lenin's family name. Theta is a person without a home. He is a pathetic, bald little man whose usefulness to Ulyan Petrovich is that he can fill in forms for him at the local police station. He has odd habits such as drinking ink while at work. But Theta is also casually unpleasant; in particular when he visits the countryside to investigate reports of cholera, he simply bans the disease and orders corporal punishment of a villager who catches it. The villager, however, 'antigovernmentally died'. In the end Theta's powers wane to such an extent that he turns into an ink stain and passes away.[8]

Zamyatin had put his finger on the harmful dottiness of much governmental activity and language. But such satirical exposures became increasingly rare as the Bolsheviks closed down the critical political press. Lenin was not personally offended; he simply wanted to put a stop to criticism of all types outside the Bolshevik party. He was a cheerful repressor and his regime grew much more severe than Zamyatin could have imagined it would.

Even so, Lenin was already showing signs of physical and mental strain. The workload in Sovnarkom and the Bolshevik Central Committee was enormous and evidently was unlikely to diminish in the foreseeable future. After all, a government had seized power which was committed to comprehensive penetration of every aspect of political, social and cultural life. Nadezhda Konstantinovna could see the effects and on his health and, whereas in earlier years they would have chatted about politics on their walks, now she sought to enable him to get relief from the tensions of the Smolny Institute. If they spoke about politics, it would usually be in connection with her work in the People's Commissariat of Enlightenment – and even then it would be at Lenin's instigation rather than hers. Their marriage had become a coupling of comfort, and the comfort was unidirectional: Krupskaya supported her husband and coped with her own difficulties without telling him.[9] Her role was of considerable importance to him because his sisters Anna and Maria paid only fleeting visits to the flat; and Krupskaya, like every Bolshevik, sensed that the party and its leader were lighting up a dawn in the history of humanity.

Gradually their routines at home and at work became more settled. Lenin took on Vladimir Bonch-Bruevich and Nikolai Gorbunov as his personal assistants. He also acquired a personal chauffeur, Stepan Gil, who drove him around the city in a limousine. He had Margarita Fofanova and other young Bolshevik women as secretaries. He and Krupskaya had their own maid, paid for by the state, and Lenin began to eat much better than in Finland when he had cooked on a little kerosene stove.

It was their physical security that drew Lenin and Krupskaya to live in the Smolny Institute. They genuinely wanted to stay there because the Institute was the heart of the great Revolution and they had no plan to return to a flat in the city's tenements. Apart from their occasional strolls near the Institute they spent little time in the city. Naturally Lenin gave speeches to large meetings at the Putilov Works and other principal locations of the Bolshevik party's activity, but he did not venture out very often. Politics had always dominated his social life; even when he took summer holidays, he talked, read and wrote about party affairs – and Krupskaya suggested that he dreamed about them when asleep. And so it was a true delight for him, at least in the first weeks after the October Revolution, to live, work and rest in the Institute. Here Lenin met visitors from 'the localities', which meant anyone who was not living in Petrograd. One of the defining moments in his career had occurred in 1905 when he and Father Gapon had closeted themselves together day after day. Now Lenin could see and chat with any worker, soldier or peasant in the capital. And all the great revolutionary institutions were based within its walls. Here was the Bolshevik Central Committee, the Military-Revolutionary Committee, Sovnarkom, the Petrograd Soviet and the Central Executive Committee of the Congress of Soviets.

On each of these institutions he had a direct, steady influence. It was a welcome change after those months in hiding in Razliv and Helsinki, when he was dependent upon others to carry his written messages to fellow party leaders. And what a relief after the émigré years of faulty postal links, factional strife and police infiltration!

High politics were concentrated in a single building and never more than a short stroll away from Lenin. He felt that he had been made for this moment, for this Revolution, for this beginning of an epoch in the world history. He communicated his contentment to his comrades in the Institute. When events turned out not quite as predicted by him, he would dredge one of his learned proverbs from memory. Quoting Goethe, he said: 'Theory is grey but life is green.' For a man who had chronically divided his party on questions of Marxist dogma this was not a little paradoxical. But Lenin had never been a one-dimensional politician; intuition and improvisation had always been his characteristics. He put this, in his portentous fashion, at the Central Executive Committee of the Congress of Soviets: 'Socialism is not brought into existence by commands from above. State-bureaucratism is alien to it; socialism that is living and creative is the creation of the popular masses themselves.'[10] But he was not going to leave everything to those 'popular masses'. Moving from room to room in the Smolny Institute, he ensured that the central state and party institutions imposed whatever degree of authority they could in the turbulent conditions of revolutionary Russia.

As he quickly discovered, this required that a degree of authority should be imposed on the institutions. He had plenty to do. The Bolshevik Central Committee was fairly orderly, but its members had only the task of setting down general guidelines and were anyway subject to party discipline. The new state institutions were a different matter. The Central Executive Committee of the Congress of Soviets held noisy meetings that sprawled over days and was rarely able to get on rapidly with its legislative work. Although a Presidium was formed under the chairmanship of Sverdlov, the chaotic conditions were not eliminated. Sovnarkom was little better. Long, self-indulgent speeches and endless discussion of trivial practical matters were the norm.

Lenin introduced a set of formal procedures. In particular, he gave People's Commissars a maximum of ten minutes to present their reports.[11] He interrupted them whenever a report looked likely to be extended into a doctrinal exposition: he wanted practical policy, not oratory. He reprimanded and even fined those of them who were late for meetings; he simply could not stand it if they chatted during the proceedings. He himself stuck to the rules and expected others to do the same. A problem for him was that People's Commissars were often so laden by duties that they had to send one of their deputies to put the Commissariat's case for them. Sovnarkom was becoming a social entertainment for many participants. Several of them were not even Bolsheviks but Left Socialist-Revolutionaries or their various sympathisers. And yet Sovnarkom had to take decisions swiftly and imposingly, and few but Lenin had an appropriate sense of responsibility to deal with the situation. Even if he had not seen colleagues for months, he refrained from holding up proceedings but instead would pass them a written note of greeting. Always he was trying to hurry things up. And to delineate policy and check that it was being carried out.

Among the regular troublemakers was Cheka Chairman Felix Dzier-żyński. Although Dzierżyński was an enforcer of discipline throughout the revolutionary regime, he defied the ban on smoking at Sovnarkom meetings. Most of the People's Commissars smoked and found it difficult to get through a meeting without a puff or two. Dzierżyński made up any number of excuses to wander away from the long green-baize table and when he thought he was out of Lenin's sight he lit up a cigarette next to the chimney-breast.

It was in this disorderly environment that Lenin was trying to sort out his thoughts. As a communist he wanted a transformation of state and society throughout the world, but increasingly he concluded that some of the party's policies were hindering the advance towards communism. Everything on his short, peripatetic outings near the Smolny Institute suggested to him that changes needed to be made. In 1918 he reversed many policies. The transformation was so rapid and so drastic that there was talk at the time and subsequently that everything Lenin did was the result of a long-laid plan to deceive his way to power by disguising his true intentions. This would mean that the maker of the October Revolution was a world-historical cynic. According to such an interpretation, Lenin had always intended much harsher measures in government than he had espoused in opposition. Some of his critics attributed this to his megalomania. Others traced it to the secret subsidy forwarded to the Bolshevik Central Committee by the German Imperial government; their contention was that it was the Germans who dictated the party's foreign policy, in particular after the October seizure of power.

And yet, while Lenin was cunning and untrustworthy, he was also dedicated to the ultimate goal of communism. He enjoyed power; he lusted after it. He yearned to keep his party in power. But he wanted power for a purpose. He was determined that the Bolsheviks should initiate the achievement of a world without exploitation and oppression. In 1917, while his party received money from Berlin, he did not regard himself as a German agent any more than the German authorities felt that they had bought him on a permanent basis. Each side was confident that it had tricked the other.

Lenin was ready to contemplate a lengthy period for the consolidation of the European socialist Revolution. There might be civil war – in fact there almost certainly would be such wars. There might be wars between socialist and capitalist states. Indeed there might even be a Second World War if the European socialist Revolution did not occur and inter-imperial capitalist rivalries persisted. Lenin could not stand it when his fellow Bolsheviks failed to understand that such setbacks were only to be expected. Unlike him, they could not grasp that politics was always messier than the prescriptions of doctrine. The few who had this understanding had caused him problems in the recent past. Kamenev and Zinoviev had warned that the October seizure of power would be followed by political catastrophe, and several of the People's Commissars who resigned their posts were of similar mind. Stalin, despite sticking by Lenin throughout the crisis, had never believed that the European socialist Revolution was imminent. It was crucial for Lenin to bring these figures back to his side and let bygones be bygones. He needed their help to face down the other party leaders – by far the largest number – who resented his proposed reversals in Bolshevik policy; they had agreed to the *April Theses* because they had accepted Lenin's argument that Revolution would be easy in Russia and easier still in Germany.

One proposal by Lenin, however, had become uncontroversial among Bolsheviks. Since the first day of the October Revolution he had urged them in vain to postpone the Constituent Assembly elections for fear that the party would not win them. His prediction was fulfilled in November, when the Bolsheviks achieved only a quarter of the votes. Opinion started to turn in favour of ignoring the result of the elections. Even Bolsheviks who had wanted an all-socialist governmental coalition agreed on this. The same was true of the Left Socialist-Revolutionaries. Thus Lenin secured Sovnarkom's agreement to breaking up the Constituent Assembly after it met in Petrograd in January 1918.

Bolsheviks and Left Socialist-Revolutionaries would not let the revolutionary transformation in Russia and Europe be jeopardised by a Constituent Assembly election. Neither the Bolsheviks nor the Left Socialist-Revolutionaries had a basic commitment to electoral procedures, and, having seized power, they did not intend to relinquish it. They were revolutionaries first and democrats only insofar as democracy strengthened the revolutionary cause. The also argued that the arrangements for the Constituent Assembly elections, inherited from the Provisional Government, put them at an unfair disadvantage. The list of the Party of Left Socialist Revolutionaries had been drawn up before the split with the Party of Socialist-Revolutionaries in November. The result was that the peasants who supported the Left Socialist-Revolutionaries'

approval of Lenin's Decree on Land could not vote specifically for
the Left Socialist-Revolutionaries. Equally irksome was the fact that the
elections took place in mid-November, long before most people in
the country had had time to become acquainted with Lenin's innovations
in policy. The Sovnarkom coalition thought that it could have pulled off
a victory in the Constituent Assembly elections if only the arrangement
had been delayed a few months.

Lenin made this point while plotting the destruction of the Constituent Assembly. His plan was insidiously clever. The Assembly's elected
members would be allowed to meet at the Tauride Palace, where
Sovnarkom's representatives would demand that the Assembly's main
party – the Socialist-Revolutionaries – accede to the basic policies
decreed by Sovnarkom and to the form of government provided by
the soviets. If the Constituent Assembly refused, its members should
be locked out of the building next day. The beauty of the plan would be
that it would involve little bloodshed.

The other great change of policy contemplated by Lenin was a lot
more contentious within the Sovnarkom coalition. This was his suggestion that a separate peace should be signed with the Central Powers. The
Bolsheviks had always argued that the Great War was imperialist in
motivation and that there was only one way to end it: socialist revolutions across Europe. They thought that propaganda and fraternisation
among soldiers would do the trick. If such an outcome did not occur,
the Bolsheviks expected to instigate a 'revolutionary war' to carry
socialism into Europe on the points of their bayonets. But they were
optimists and assumed that 'revolutionary war' would not be necessary.
The notion of a separate peace on the eastern front was inconceivable to
them, as indeed it was to every other Russian political party. It was
against this logic, which he himself had helped to establish, that Lenin
began to make a stand. Signs appeared on 17 December, when he ordered
the issuing of a questionnaire on Russian military preparedness. His
questions were brutally searching. Was it really possible for a German
attack to be repelled? Was it wise to continue to put the case for
'revolutionary war'? Would soldiers in fact prefer the signature of a
separate peace? The replies confirmed whatever worries he already
possessed: the Russian armed forces barely existed in strength on the
eastern front and such soldiers who remained were largely in favour of
peace at almost any price.[12]

There has always been speculation that Lenin's questionnaire was a
feint to disguise the fact that he was complying with the instructions of

his paymasters in Berlin. Those who believe 'German gold' paid for the October Revolution contend that the separate peace on the eastern front was the price exacted in exchange.[13] This is pretty implausible stuff. Whatever promises or intimations Lenin gave to German diplomats, he was not a man to stick to his word, a word given to a rapacious, imperialist government. Indeed perhaps the greatest work he did for the German military cause had already been accomplished on 26 October when he published his Decree on Land and his Decree on Peace. He would have introduced these measure regardless of his financial relationship with Berlin. Their result, anyway, was the degradation of the ability of the Russian forces to wage war because the soldiers on the eastern front flooded back to their villages in order to get their share of the land that was being redistributed. But the Central Powers wanted more: they demanded that Sovnarkom should formally disclaim any sovereignty over Poland, Latvia and Belorussia. They demanded the signature of a treaty. Lenin's willingness to come to terms was dictated not by financial indebtedness but by the fear that, if Sovnarkom did not give way, the demands of the Central Powers might become still more grievous – as in fact happened in January 1918.

As his worries about the eastern front became acute, Lenin was also troubled by the gamut of Soviet economic and social policies. The easy Revolution predicted by him for Russia had not been realised, and he had to reformulate strategy in order to maintain the regime's impetus. But for this he also needed a break from the daily routine of Sovnarkom and the Bolshevik Central Committee. Ill health and overwork were dragging him down. Apart from his brief walks around the Smolny Institute, he had no chance to relax. Just two months after re-entering the public gaze at the Second Congress of Soviets, he decided to slip away from the Smolny Institute for a brief holiday.

On 24 December he set off with his wife Nadya and his sister Maria for the Finland Station to meet Eino Rahja, whose train would take them along the familiar track to the north. Their destination was the tuberculosis sanatorium at Halila near the Finnish village of Uusikirkko, forty-five miles north of the Russian capital. Lenin badly needed to restore himself. Central Committee member Jan Berzins and his family were already convalescing there. The snow was crisp and deep, the air was fresh and Lenin was able to go out for walks in the countryside. It was one of those odd moments in his life. Lenin was the premier of the Russian state and had recently granted independence to Finland. By going to Uusikirkko, he was from a legal standpoint crossing a state border without permission. But he thought less about the implications of his own legislation than about his earlier experiences as a fugitive in the Finnish countryside in 1907 and 1917. Unconsciously he started to talk in a low voice so as not to be overheard by potential agents of the Ministry of the Interior! He forgot that it was now he who controlled the secret police. Another problem was that the daylight hours were even shorter, that far north, than in Petrograd. He spent most of his time stuck indoors writing – writing and fretting.

Even in Halila he had no peace from his colleagues in Sovnarkom. Hardly had he got there than Stalin wrote asking him to return to the Smolny Institute by midday on 28 December. Stalin needed his advice on relations with Ukraine.[14] Lenin held on until 29 December, but not surprisingly he hardly felt he had had a proper holiday. He brought back several draft articles with him, but their contents were so pessimistic that he did not hand them to *Pravda*. The reason for this was not the dark midwinter in Uusikirkko but his own presentiment that, unless Sovnarkom became firmer in its imposition of order in Russia, the days of the October Revolution were numbered.

In those drafts, preserved in Lenin's archive, he called for soviets and other popular organisations to hold fewer open meetings. Too much time was being wasted. According to Lenin, moreover, workers had become excessively self-indulgent. The striking printworkers should be treated as hooligans and, if their withdrawal of labour continued, put under arrest. The Soviet regime had been altogether too soft. Lenin expostulated that comprehensive 'registration and supervision' were urgently overdue, explaining:

> The objective of this registration and supervision is clear and universally understandable: that everyone should have bread, go about in sturdy footwear and decent clothing, should have a warm dwelling and should work conscientiously; that no scoundrel (including anyone who shirks doing any work) should be free to roam about but should be held in prison or should work off his sentence in forced labour of the heaviest kind; and that none of the wealthy, evading the rules and laws of socialism, should be able to evade the same fate as the scoundrel – the fate that in justice ought to become the fate of wealthy people.

From this it was clear that Lenin intended to give no mercy even to the sections of society that had once supported the Bolsheviks enthusiastically.

What he was doing, without being properly aware of it, was facing up to the consequences of the October Revolution in the light of the political and economic setbacks. Authoritarianism had always pervaded his thought; it now became more evident and extreme. Writing in Uusikirkko, he jotted down the theme of another article he wanted to write soon: 'First vanquish the bourgeoisie and then fight the bourgeoisie abroad.'[15] This implied a will to prioritise political consolidation in Russia and to wait awhile before spreading revolution to other industrial countries. And his various drafts show that the struggle to vanquish the Russian bourgeoisie would be accompanied by massive intimidation of 'the masses'. Lenin's hard heart was hardened further.

Inside the Smolny Institute, he conferred with Sverdlov to finalise preparations for the reversal of the first (and until 1993 the last) remotely free universal-suffrage elections in Russia's history. Lenin and Trotski had not made a secret of their hostility to the Constituent Assembly. All through December they had argued that such elections were not a true gauge of the people's interests, and they had the entire membership of the Bolshevik and Left Socialist-Revolutionary Central Committees on their side. Violent suppression was openly contemplated, if not in *Pravda* then certainly on the streets. Sverdlov made the necessary military dispositions. Sovnarkom could rely upon having several units including both the Latvian Riflemen and the Red Guard on its side. The socialist opponents of the Sovnarkom coalition – Mensheviks, Socialist-Revolutionaries and Bundists – had no serious counter-force. Lenin made a show of nonchalance and on 1 January 1918 he took a two-mile trip in his official limousine from the Smolny Institute to the Mikhailovski Manège in central Petrograd. With him were Maria Ilinichna, Fritz Platten and Nikolai Podvoiski. Lenin had made many such trips to meetings in November and December. Security precautions were few: Lenin wanted to show that he was a popular politician at the head of a popular revolution. In any case he was enjoying himself.

Having delivered a rousing speech at the Mikhailovski Manège, he started back around seven o'clock in the evening with his companions. His speech had been well received by party members and by the workers they had brought with them. The little group were looking forward to having supper in the Smolny Institute. It was already very dark but they were being carefully watched by two armed men. The car had barely left the Manège and reached the Simeon Bridge when the men stepped off the pavement, took aim and fired at the limousine. At the sound of shots, Platten instinctively threw himself across Lenin's body. It was an incompetent attempt at assassination, but it had very nearly succeeded. Platten suffered worst. His act of courage left him with a hand wound. The limousine carried on to the Smolny Institute and Dzierżyński began a search for the attackers. A few days later it became clear that they had been monarchists. But in the interim a pretext was given to Sovnarkom to charge the socialist parties outside the governmental coalition with complicity in terrorism. The aim was to tar the majority parties in the forthcoming Constituent Assembly with the brush of anti-popular violence.

Lenin had often been accused of physical cowardice. He had gone out of his way to evade the police forces of both Nicholas II and the Provisional Government at times when others in his party took personal risks. But from 25 October 1917 his approach had changed. He had led a revolution. He knew that he would go down as a figure in the history books. Every day that the Soviet regime lasted was another page added to the annals of Lenin and Bolshevism. He joined other Bolsheviks in facing further danger, knowing that he had already survived for the event that meant most to him in his life: the Revolution.

But he did not seek martyrdom, and while he was alive, he knew that much needed to be done to enhance the prospects of Revolution. For him, this always meant that things had to be done rapidly and ruthlessly. His ideology and his temperament pushed him in the same direction. Probably his ill health did too: he felt that he had no time to waste. Lenin wanted to get on with the Revolution. Nothing was to stand as an obstacle. Over the next few days, he concentrated on the arrangements for the Constituent Assembly in the Tauride Palace. He could barely begin to discuss the subject temperately. The first session was scheduled for 5 January 1918 and he was already very tense when he arrived at the Tauride Palace. He knew that his intended action – the Assembly's forcible closure – was of historic importance. As the proceedings began, Lenin was white as a sheet. Lacking armed support, the Socialist-Revolutionaries under Viktor Chernov could not resist the Bolsheviks. Chernov was subjected to catcalls and threatening gestures. But it was Sverdlov who spoke for the Bolsheviks. Lenin confined his contribution to permitting himself to be seen scoffing at the proceedings. By putting up Sverdlov instead of himself, Lenin was showing contempt for more than his old adversary Chernov. He was despising free and universal-suffrage elections as a mode of political struggle.

Quite how to stop the first session of the Constituent Assembly had not been worked out by Sovnarkom. Chernov looked as if he would keep open the proceedings indefinitely. Yet again Lenin urged direct action upon his party and after some dispute his line was accepted. The Assembly would be closed and would not be permitted to resume work next day. Lenin's plan nevertheless involved a degree of finesse. On his orders, the Assembly guard under the anarchist–communist Anatoli Zheleznyakov announced to the flabbergasted Chernov that the 'guard was tired' and that the building ought to be cleared. Chernov had no option but to comply and the Tauride Palace was emptied.

Since the Constituent Assembly had not approved all the Sovnarkom decrees, Lenin felt that he had acquired more than enough excuse to go to the Congress of Soviets of Workers', Soldiers' and Peasants' Deputies to secure agreement that the Assembly had outlived its usefulness. Subsequently the fount of legitimacy for the regime would be the Congress itself, and the Cheka – the new political police established in December – could freely hunt down the enemies of the Sovnarkom coalition. Lenin had got what he wanted. He had done this without having to harangue either the Constituent Assembly or the Congress of Soviets. He was the acknowledged leader of the October Revolution but he did not act alone. His Bolsheviks and the Left Socialist-Revolutionaries in the Sovnarkom coalition had been moving in the same direction. The point was becoming obvious. Once Sovnarkom had taken power, it needed to use force to maintain itself. Not every party leader had recognised this before the October Revolution; but all of them did by 5 January 1918. It was a fateful process of learning. If they had known this in advance, they might not have sanctioned the seizure of power. But they had acceded to Lenin's insistence on the Provisional Government's overthrow in the fashion and at the time he demanded. Now they were getting used to living with the consequences, and to living with them without blaming him.

20

BREST-LITOVSK

January to May 1918

The huge task facing Lenin after the Constituent Assembly's dispersal was to get Bolsheviks and the Left Socialist-Revolutionaries to accept the separate peace pushed under their noses by the Central Powers. It was the fiercest struggle of his career. On his return from Switzerland, his *April Theses* had tipped the balance of Bolshevik party opinion. In October 1917 he had thrust the party towards overturning the Provisional Government. But on the question of war and peace Lenin faced a massive impediment. His Bolshevik party, having carried out the October Revolution and issued the Decree on Peace, would not accede to the signature of a peace with the imperialist governments of Berlin and Vienna.

Steadily the scale of the military threat on the eastern front was disclosing itself. In the last weeks of 1917, Trotski as People's Commissar for External Affairs returned from the negotiations at Brest-Litovsk, the town nearest to the trenches, still believing that he could endlessly prolong the truce. At any time, he thought, Revolution could erupt across Europe. On 7 January 1918 he returned in a more sombre mood, bringing news that the Central Powers had presented an ultimatum. Lenin instantly argued for agreeing to the German demands for fear that the terms of the ultimatum might soon get even worse, but Trotski demurred and proposed that the negotiations be dragged out by means of a tactic of 'neither war nor peace'. At that point Lenin took his case to the central and local leaderships of the Bolshevik party. At the Third Congress of Soviets on 8 January, he presented his 'Theses on the Question of a Separate and Annexationist Peace'. Members of the Bolshevik fraction, after getting over their astonishment at his volte-face, turned him down flat even though most of them recognised that 'revolutionary war' was impracticable; they gave preference to Trotski's policy of 'neither war nor peace'. Lenin remained defiant: 'In any event I stand for the immediate signature of peace; it is more secure.'

At the Central Committee next day, he made no secret of the distaste he felt for his own policy:[1]

> Undoubtedly the peace that we are currently compelled to conclude is an obscene peace; but, if war begins, our government will be swept aside and peace will be concluded by another government ... Those who stand on the side of revolutionary war point out that by this very step we will be engaged in a civil war with German imperialism and that thereby we'll awaken revolution in Germany. But look! Germany is only pregnant with revolution, and a completely healthy baby has been born to us: the baby that is the socialist republic, which we shall be killing if we begin a war.

Lenin argued that the 'socialist fatherland' had to be protected in the short term but that nevertheless the Bolsheviks had to stay in readiness to spread revolution to Europe.

His chances of convincing his party with such thoughts were small and the Left Socialist-Revolutionaries would not even listen to them. He had been in such situations in the past, before 1917; but in those years he could afford to take the risk of isolating himself: in 1918 he was leader of a governing party and the state was going to stand or fall in consequence of the decision taken about the separate peace proposal. It was not entirely helpful that among his main supporters in the Bolshevik Central Committee were figures who had had their doubts about his revolutionary strategy in 1917: Stalin, Kamenev and Zinoviev. Stalin went about asserting that 'there is no revolutionary movement in the West'. Lenin genuinely believed that the 'European socialist Revolution' would eventually take place, and had to distance himself from Stalin's position. And steadily Lenin began to exert an influence on the Bolshevik Central Committee. He worked to undermine the confidence of his opponents and focussed upon Bukharin. This was astute. Bukharin had never thought it possible for Russia to wage a successful war on German capitalism; he simply assumed that 'revolutionary war', if ever Trotski's policy of 'neither war nor peace' should prove ineffective, would be the party's sole alternative with ideological justification. This was the opinion of most leading Bolsheviks.

Already some of Lenin's opponents could no longer assent to 'revolutionary war' as a practical option. Lenin himself, speaking at the Central Committee and at open public meetings in Petrograd, stressed his commitment to 'European socialist Revolution'. He got his supporters in the Secretariat, Sverdlov and Stasova, to disseminate information on his behalf to the party in the provinces. As the arrangements were laid for the Seventh Party Congress, he reverted to his old method of providing mandates to activists known to be loyal to his policies. He also let it be known that, if the decision went against him, he would resign from the Central Committee and campaign throughout the party for the signature of a separate peace.

As he had predicted, the Central Powers grew impatient. On 10 February 1918, Trotski was given another ultimatum at Brest-Litovsk; he was told that an invasion would take place unless the Soviet authorities did as demanded by the governments in Berlin and Austria. The weakness of Trotski's policy of 'neither war nor peace' was exposed. Trotski made the best of a bad job by announcing to the negotiators of both sides that Russia was simply withdrawing from the war. But by 16 February the patience of the Central Powers was exhausted. Unless peace was signed, they warned, their offensive on the eastern front would be resumed within two days. The Central Committee met on 17 February in Trotski's presence; and Lenin issued a questionnaire to fellow members to discover what each of them would do in certain contingencies:[2] he wanted to ensure that they, like he, felt personally responsible for whatever decision was taken. Decisiveness was his supreme quality and he aimed to make his colleagues understand that they should expect to live by the consequences of their recommendations. And yet he could not get his way in the Central Committee: a narrow majority yet again accepted Trotski's policy of calling the bluff of the Central Powers.

Lenin was becoming frantic, and so were all his comrades: any option they chose would have repercussions on the eastern front and on the Great War as a whole. Political life was lived on a knife-edge. On 18 February, the day of the threatened invasion, the Central Committee met again. Lenin implored fellow members:

> Yesterday there was an especially characteristic vote when everyone recognised the need for peace if a [revolutionary] movement in Germany weren't to supervene and an offensive were to occur. Doubt exists whether the Germans want an offensive with a view to overthrowing the Soviet government. We stand before a situation where we must act!

But his plea was turned down. This time the German high command organised a vast advance along the Baltic littoral. By the afternoon its troops had travelled virtually unopposed through to Dvinsk. They were within four hundred miles of Petrograd. The Central Committee reconvened in haste and Lenin declaimed: 'History will say that you gave away the Revolution.'

At last his argument hit home and by a slim margin of seven votes to five, he defeated Bukharin. Lenin gained the support of Trotski, who later said that he did not wish to opt for war unless he could do so with a united Bolshevik party. Even so, Trotski had hardly left the Central Committee before he set about enquiring whether the Soviet government might get emergency aid from the Allies if it refused to sign the peace treaty with Germany and Austria–Hungary. He won favour for this idea in the Central Committee on 22 February. Again the Central Powers were intransigent and demanded that Sovnarkom should disclaim sovereignty not only over Poland and the various Baltic provinces but also over Ukraine. This was the final ultimatum; failure to comply would result in a massive military invasion. On 23 February the weary members of the Bolshevik Central Committee hauled themselves along to hear Sverdlov's report on the German ultimatum to the effect that Sovnarkom was given until seven o'clock next morning to confirm its acceptance of the Central Powers' terms. This was the crucial meeting and Lenin spelled out its significance: 'These terms must be signed. If you don't sign them, you are signing the death warrant of Soviet power within three weeks.'[3]

Lenin kept nagging his antagonists. Among those who announced his continued opposition was Karl Radek. Lenin was furious and retorted that Radek was deluding himself:[4]

> You're worse than a hen. A hen can't decide to cross the line of a circle drawn in chalk around it, but at least the hen can say in self-justification that someone else's hand had drawn that circle. But you drew your formula around yourself with your own hand and now you're gazing at the formula and not at reality.

Lenin's imagery was always richer when he was trying to intimidate an opponent.

Still the dispute was not at an end. Lenin's critics in his presence considered excluding him from Sovnarkom and starting a revolutionary war. Even Stalin wondered whether it was yet right to come to terms with the Central Powers. But most Central Committee members had no stomach for such a fight. And Lenin was like a rock and held firm while others in the room trembled. Yet again he indicated that, if his opponents won the day, he would resign from Sovnarkom – he would not need to be forced out – and resume his campaign for a separate peace treaty. And he got what he wanted; by a vote of seven to four with another four abstentions, the Bolshevik Central Committee resolved that the treaty should be signed. This decision had been taken in the nick of time to forestall the German invasion. If Lenin had not won the debate, there is little doubt that the Central Powers would have concluded that the Bolsheviks were no longer of any use to them. The result would have been the occupation of the Russian heartland and the collapse of the October Revolution.

The Treaty of Brest-Litovsk was signed on 3 March. The Central Powers by and large stood by its contents and refrained from invading Russia once Sovnarkom had delivered up Poland, the Baltic provinces and Ukraine to their armies. Half of the industrial and agricultural resources of the Russian Empire were situated in this vast area as well as a third of the population. Furthermore, the German high command was enabled to transfer army divisions from the east to the west in order to attempt a final concentrated campaign against the French and the British forces. The decision taken in the Smolny Institute in the presence of fifteen Bolsheviks on 23 February had consequences that were quickly appreciated around the world.

In Russia the broader picture of international relations was ignored in the Bolshevik party press, and the party's control over the press meant that the other parties knew little directly about what was happening elsewhere in Europe. But Lenin was sure that he had done the right thing. Immediately he set about persuading his party that it could exploit the 'breathing space' given by the peace Treaty. There was a tussle in the Bolshevik Central Committee about who should be deputed to go out to Brest-Litovsk to put his pen to the document. The obvious person would have been Lenin; but he arranged things so that his candidacy was not discussed. Members of the group who had carried out the negotiations refused to carry out the task, and it was obviously senseless to ask anyone who had supported Trotski or Bukharin. Grigori Sokolnikov therefore performed the unenviable role. This was not the last time that Lenin stayed aloof from decisions that might pollute his future reputation. No party in Russia, apart from the Bolsheviks, approved of the Brest-Litovsk Treaty. If things did not work out, Lenin might pay dearly for his gamble in international relations. His instincts told him to minimise the personal damage.

Yet the political struggle in Petrograd was not over. The Bolshevik

Party Congress, too, had to be persuaded to sanction the turnabout; and it was not definitively clear that the Congress would agree. Worse still, the Left Socialist-Revolutionaries had no internal strife about 'revolutionary war': all of them were intensely opposed to Lenin's policy. For this reason Lenin adopted a step-by-step approach. First he dealt with his own party's Congress. Proceedings began on 6 March and were introduced by Lenin:[5]

> A country that is petit-bourgeois by nature, disorganised by war and dragged down by it to an unbelievable condition has been placed in extraordinarily heavy circumstances: we have no army and yet we have to live side by side with a robber who is armed to the teeth. He still remains and will remain a robber, whom it was impossible, of course, to get at through agitation about peace without annexations and indemnities. A peaceful domestic pet has been lying side by side with a tiger and trying to convince him of the need for peace without annexations and indemnities while such a peace was obtainable only by attacking the tiger.

Lenin's sarcasm contrasted with the performance of the other side led by Bukharin. On point after point Bukharin gave ground. He admitted that a revolutionary war was impossible and that he had no principled objection to a separate peace with the Central Powers.

And so the clash between Lenin and the Bolshevik left was one-sided. Lenin knew that he would triumph and was willing to let Bukharin's supporters vilify him uncontested on the Congress floor. He could remain calm while Zinoviev and Trotski had a tiff about the usefulness of the previous policy of 'neither war nor peace'. Indeed he proceeded to a debate with Bukharin on the contents of the Party Programme, and politely entreated his opponent not to carry out his threat to refuse to serve in the next Bolshevik Central Committee. In short, he could show magnanimity in victory.

Lenin had succeeded through his skills and determination. He was also helped by the fact that the internal party opposition lacked both tactical confidence and cunning. The Bolshevik left – or the Left Communists as they called themselves – did not really believe that a 'revolutionary war' would be feasible. Wherever they tried to rally mass support among workers likely to be conscripted in the event of such a war, they encountered hostility, and they were aware that the peasants who had filled the ranks of the Imperial Army had already voted with their feet on the question of war or peace: most of them either had deserted or had been demobilised. Yet they did not consciously recognise this, and they went on grumbling about the separate peace. Initially they withdrew from the Bolshevik Central Committee and Sovnarkom. So, too, did the Left Socialist-Revolutionaries. Lenin railed against what he saw as their political puerility; but he tried to be diplomatic. He needed all the People's Commissars he could get his hands on, and they for their part were prevailed upon to give support to the revolution of the workers and peasants. One by one they returned to their posts on an unofficial basis.

The danger from the German forces had not been expunged. Having signed the Treaty, Sovnarkom could not be confident that the Germans would not keep moving on Petrograd. Lenin and his fellow People's Commissars reluctantly accepted the need for them to shift the seat of government to Moscow. The decision had a practical motive. The Central Powers were conquering areas virtually unopposed; and although it had been Sovnarkom's intention since the previous month to form a Workers' and Peasants' Red Army, the units were small in number and primitive in training: they were plainly no match for the troops of Germany and Austria–Hungary. And so on 10 March the government's main personnel embarked on the night train from Petrograd to Moscow.

Initially most of the personnel were lodged in the Hotel National on Okhotny Ryad three hundred yards from the northern wall of the Kremlin. Lenin shared a makeshift apartment with his wife Nadezhda and his sister Maria. There were just two rooms together with a bathroom, and the hotel staff cleaned his shoes and generally looked after all of them.[6] In later years there was a suggestion that he did not avail himself of the services of the staff; but Nadezhda Konstantinovna remonstrated against such saccharine idealisations: she liked to idealise him, but not in regard to his personal habits.[7] Outside the Hotel National there was always noise. Okhotny Ryad was full of market stallkeepers throughout daytime hours. Students and other revolutionary enthusiasts were constantly arguing, canvassing and pasting up posters. The Bolshevik party leadership positioned loyal military units throughout the area. The Latvian Riflemen were especially welcome to Sovnarkom. But Lenin was a person who liked his settled routines. Ignoring the noise, he rose from his bed in mid-morning as he had always done in London, Zurich and Paris. He was going to make Revolution on his personal terms.[8]

It is true that Lenin saw people of all sorts every time he left the

Hotel National, and increasingly received visitors from the provinces. Thus he was never without information about the condition of ordinary people in Soviet Russia. But he did not live the lives of those people. Eating and sleeping in the Hotel National and working in the Kremlin, he always had a refuge from the harsh realities of misrule, hunger and war; and when people talked about such things, he pressed their information through the filter of his own ideas and only altered policies when the very existence of the Soviet regime was menaced.

The stay in the sumptuous Hotel National was meant to last only until such time as the Kremlin had been got ready for Sovnarkom. It was not a task that Lenin relished. He had never liked Moscow because it was so much less Westernised than Petrograd. Physically and culturally Moscow embodied traditional Russian values. For Lenin, this was no recommendation at all. He wanted a Russia that abandoned all tsarist nostalgia, Orthodox Christianity and peasant aspirations. He had never retracted his remark of 1898 that Moscow was 'a foul city'.[9]

Indeed Moscow was more like a great conglomeration of villages than a metropolis. Foreigners – and Lenin was a bit like a foreigner himself – noted that lots of inhabitants still wore traditional peasant smocks and shoes made out of straw rather than leather. Few streets had pavements. The thoroughfares were extremely muddy in spring 1918, shortly after Sovnarkom arrived. In contrast with Petrograd's rectilinear design, Moscow stretched out in a higgledy-piggledy sprawl, and Muscovites were proud of the difference. Each resident social stratum, from industrialists and bankers down to street-hawkers, felt that the unplanned, exuberant diversity of Moscow, which had been the capital of the country until Peter the Great started to build St Petersburg at the beginning of the eighteenth century, expressed something essential about Russia. Moscow's factory owners were the foremost advocates of Russian nationalism. They had built magnificently in the past twenty years in a style that mixed traditionalism and explorative modernity. They had textile factories aplenty. They had strong connections with the countryside, and some of them were Old Believers. They thought that Petrograd's elites had betrayed the national interest to foreign capitalist powers, and they judged Moscow to be the genuine capital of Mother Russia.

Perhaps it served Lenin right, then, that he encountered a number of practical problems in the Kremlin. When trying to enter by the Trinity Gate with Bonch-Bruevich a day after the train trip from Petrograd, he was refused admission by a guard who did not recognise him.

The guard was a Bolshevik supporter, but took some minutes before convincing himself of Lenin's identity and allowing him admittance.

Once inside the walls of the Kremlin, even Lenin was struck by the magnificence of the buildings. The inner precinct left a lasting impression. The Kremlin is a great triangular fortress in the city's centre, standing 130 feet above the river Moskva. The walled perimeter is a mile and a quarter long and inside it there is a dazzling collection of ancient buildings. Chief among them was the Great Kremlin Palace. Next to the Palace was the Uspenski Cathedral; it was there that the tsars had been crowned until Peter the Great's construction of St Petersburg. There was the Senate built by Catherine the Great. There were bells, bell-towers, golden cupolas, gigantic cannons, barracks, an armoury and spacious squares. On each tower there was a two-headed eagle, symbol of the glory and power of tsarism. From the top of the highest bell-tower it was possible to see across to a horizon twenty miles away. Everywhere he looked, Lenin saw the physical embodiment of a history that he had come to power in order to eliminate.

But the Kremlin was in a mess. The neglect had set in with the monarchy's downfall in February 1917 and fighting had occurred between Red Guards and monarchist officers at the end of the year. A dispiriting scene confronted Lenin and Bonch-Bruevich. The Senate Building, where it was proposed to base Sovnarkom and to assign Lenin an apartment, remained a shambles. The horse manure lay uncollected. There was hay, filthy bandages, broken paving and – when the spring came – the mud, mud, mud. Temporarily Lenin, Trotski and other Bolshevik leaders were put up in the Cavalry Corpus of the Great Kremlin Palace. Some of Nicholas II's servants had remained at their posts. One elderly waiter, a certain Stupishin, was a stickler for traditional propriety. When Lenin and Trotski dined together in the evenings, Stupishin served their suppers on Imperial crockery. Stupishin would not allow them to start eating until he had ensured that the double-headed eagle symbol on the plates faced each person at the table. Lenin endured the fuss with amusement. In truth, not all the meals were fit for a tsar. Sometimes the diners had only buckwheat porridge and thin vegetable soup.

Yet Lenin did not obtain permanent accommodation for Sovnarkom and for himself and his family until the end of the month, and then only after demanding to know the names of those 'guilty' for the delay.[10] Bonch-Bruevich had put aside a comfortable apartment for Lenin, Nadya and Maria Ilinichna on the first floor of the old Senate

Building. There were three main rooms and a hallway, a kitchen, bath-room and a maid's room. Next door were the administrative bureaux of Sovnarkom, and from Lenin's office a door led directly to the hall in which the meetings of Sovnarkom were held.

The Senate Building apartment became his home. He had wandered around for so much of his life that it is doubtful whether he was capable of feeling at home anywhere by 1918. The fact that he lived in his place of work can hardly have produced an atmosphere of homeli-ness. Both Nadya and Maria, furthermore, were nearly as busy as he was with political affairs. All three of them lived on the run, grabbing food and sleep as and where they could. They could not care less about money and Lenin formally reprimanded Bonch-Bruevich for raising his salary as Sovnarkom Chairman without his sanction.[11] What he wanted was a clean and quiet flat and an office well stocked with books. One of his first actions on occupying the premises was to demand a set of Vladimir Dal's Russian dictionary and a map of the former Russian Empire. He put up a portrait of Karl Marx on the wall, and later added a bulky picture of the populist terrorist Stepan Khalturin. His daily needs no longer detained either his wife or his sister. A maid had been hired, and the chauffeuring was done by Stepan Gil. Meals were cooked for the inhabitants. Lenin and Nadya acquired a cat. They adored the animal, and Lenin was often seen carrying it along the corridor to the Sovnarkom meeting room. The cat knew how to look after itself. In the meeting room, it would snuggle down in Lenin's armchair in the knowledge that no one would dare to disturb it. Nadya and the maid fed the cat, and, whenever the maid had a day off, Nadya asked a Sovnarkom secretary to take over the duty. She did not trust Lenin to lay out the food as was necessary.

In fact Lenin was dependable in his care of their cat even if he was not always punctual in putting a plate in front of it.[12] Most of the time both he and Nadya were preoccupied by their political tasks. The apartment was a place where they slept and ate. From the Kremlin, Lenin could order books from any library in Russia. He was able to phone any political functionary in the capital or the provinces, and meet the visitors who thronged to the Kremlin to meet him. He could buttonhole People's Commissars as they emerged from their own apart-ments into the precinct and most of his main Bolshevik comrades – Trotski, Sverdlov, Kamenev and Stalin – were within easy reach together with their families. And he was able to organise receptions for party officials or for groups of peasants petitioning him on some matter.

From the great walled precinct Lenin set out on trips to meetings at factory gates elsewhere in the city. He also visited Nadezhda Konstantinovna when she convalesced in the Sokolniki district on the north-eastern outskirts. But, except when he himself spent periods of recuperation at the village of Gorki twenty miles from Moscow, he stayed in the central parts of the new capital. He had every opportunity to go to other towns and cities, but his only brief forays were to Petrograd in 1919 and 1920. Not even his frequently expressed nostalgia for the Volga region drew him back there. His place remained at the centre of revolutionary politics.

While he demanded orderliness as Sovnarkom sought to consolidate the regime and its policies, his comrades exasperated him. Late at night he would switch off his office light in the full knowledge that his economical attitude to electricity was not a defining characteristic of other Bolsheviks. Sovnarkom's Chairman paced down the corridors switching off the lights left on by his comrades.[13] None of them would ever be quite like him. No doubt they left their pencils unsharpened, their buttons unsewn, their books unreturned to libraries. How could you make the Revolution with such people? But, whatever the irritation he experienced, he got over it. He was cheered by the thought that the October 1917 Revolution had already lasted longer than the eleven weeks of the 1871 Paris Commune. This was the nearest he came to overt sentimentality unless we take into account his enthusiasm for the working class. Nadezhda Konstantinovna was uncomfortable about this. As they rode by car through Moscow, she noted the rising amount of vandalism: windows smashed, wooden walls and roofs broken up and stolen. To her it was obvious that delinquent workers should be punished for such behaviour; and she told her husband severely that he should smarten up his thinking. There could be no socialism while such behaviour remained condoned by default.

This marital dissension, which was kept from view by the Soviet censorship authorities, failed to induce Lenin to change his stance. It never did. He had fixed his mind on a strategic orientation that included the need for the working class to establish its dictatorship. He painted with a broad brush. He wanted to encourage revolutionary initiative and toss aside any considerations of 'bourgeois morality' for some years ahead. Yet there was much that had changed in his thought since the October Revolution. At every point of tension between elitist authoritarianism and mass self-liberation, Lenin's priority was to secure his regime's position – and this usually meant an increase in authoritarianism.

Indeed his measures began to cause consternation among the Left Socialist-Revolutionaries. Initially the Sovnarkom coalition partners had got on reasonably well. The Left Socialist-Revolutionaries, who were already delighted with Lenin's Decree on Land, were equally pleased in February 1918 when he signed the Basic Law on the Socialisation of the Land which – with the vigorous support of the Left Socialist-Revolutionaries – ratified the transfer of agricultural land to the peasants. But he also wanted local soviets to get the necessary food supplies into the towns. He repeatedly asserted that there was an abundance of grain in the countryside and that the greed of the better-off peasants, or kulaks as he called them, was responsible for the low rations provided by central and local government. There was no time for shilly-shallying. Even before the Brest-Litovsk Treaty Lenin had believed that ruthless measures ought to be taken. He was committed to the maintenance of the state monopoly of the grain trade and in the longer term he wanted to take land ownership away from private persons, including peasants, and to give it to the state. All this complicated the already difficult relations with the Left Socialist-Revolutionaries, who had joined the Sovnarkom on the specific premise that they would be able to look after the interests of the peasantry.

Lenin's way of consolidating the regime, however, was no longer subject to compromise. Already on 14 January 1918 he had drafted a Sovnarkom decree that minced no words:[14]

> [Sovnarkom] proposes to the All-Russia Food Supplies Committee and the Commissariat of Food Supplies to intensify the dispatch not only of commissars but also of numerically strong, armed detachments for the most revolutionary measures for the movement of loads, the collection and distribution of grain, etc., and also for a merciless struggle with speculators right through to the proposal for local soviets to shoot discovered speculators and saboteurs on the spot.

His bleak inclinations of the past few weeks were taking shape as policy. Although it was not yet an open theme in his speeches, the movement towards ever greater severity was unmistakable.

Sovnarkom had no compunction in spring 1918 about suppressing the many soviets in the provinces that elected Menshevik majorities. The Cheka and the new Red Army contingents were deployed to prevent effective resistance. The regime no longer limited itself to hunting down its declared enemies: the Kadets, Mensheviks and Socialist-

Revolutionaries; it was starting also to persecute those groups in society on whose support it had relied in order to come to power. Lenin had assumed that, once the working class had begun to favour the Bolsheviks, it would never return to the enemies of Bolshevism. But his faith in 'the proletariat' had always been conditional even in 1917; and in 1902 his booklet *What Is to Be Done?* had asserted the total inadequacy of the workers to adopt revolutionary policies unless firmly and correctly guided by the Marxist intelligentsia. At best he had been an ideological paternalist. Now he felt uninhibited about overturning the civic rights of the working class: the supremacy of the regime was not permitted to be challenged. Even at the work-place there should be no concession to indiscipline, and Lenin indicated that he wanted to introduce the time-and-motion principles of the same American theorist, F. W. Taylor, whom he had once excoriated as an advocate of capitalist interests.

Dictatorship, he thought, was crucially desirable. Reviewing the party's strategy in April 1918 in his booklet *The Current Tasks of Soviet Power*, he acknowledged that external threats to the country's security persisted and that there were massive and growing internal difficulties increased in food supplies, transport, industrial production and administrative efficiency; and he insisted: 'But dictatorship is a big word. And big words should not simply be thrown up into the wind. Dictatorship is iron authority, authority that is revolutionarily audacious as well as rapid and merciless in its suppression of both exploiters and hooligans.'[15] He followed this assertion with an analysis that shocked many of his closest associates of earlier months. Lenin declared that '*guilt* for the torments of hunger and unemployment is borne by *all* who break labour discipline in any factory, on any farm, in any enterprise'. The solution was the application of truly dictatorial methods. He explained that it was 'necessary to learn how to discover those guilty of this and to hand them over to the courts and punish them pitilessly'.[16]

The Constituent Assembly's dispersal and the signature of the Treaty of Brest-Litovsk's confirmed Lenin's will to stay in power even if every other political party, group and individual in the country remained opposed. The Bolshevik party under his leadership had driven even the Left Socialist-Revolutionaries away. This was not the only result. The movements and clarifications of governmental policy had done much to alienate broad sections of opinion in society. Workers and, when they heard about the October Revolution, peasants had welcomed Sovnarkom's decrees; but, as Lenin and the Bolshevik Central Committee developed policy, they encountered hostility in many quarters. Equally importantly, they met with apathy. The Bolsheviks were ruling what was left of the Russian Empire, which was mainly the Russian-inhabited regions, as a beleaguered political minority. And their awareness of this led them to harden their attitudes. They felt that the best way to deal with trouble was to get tougher rather than offer compromises. This common attitude brought Lenin and the Bolshevik Left Communists back together even though, after Brest-Litovsk, they could not flaunt their growing collaboration.

Their *rapprochement* was assisted by the way Lenin stiffened the element of state ownership and regulation in industry and agriculture. An increasing segment of public opinion called on Sovnarkom to scrap the state grain-trade monopoly and allow the peasants to sell their produce on the open markets. There was plenty of evidence that the peasantry was hoarding grain. In order to resuscitate economic exchange between town and countryside it was widely proposed that concessions to private trade were vital. The Kadets, Mensheviks and Socialist-Revolutionaries in the Provisional Government had approved and maintained the state grain-trade monopoly. Out of office, as the economic collapse reached the abyss, they urged that a drastic reversal of policy was required.

But the Bolshevik leaders would not contemplate this; they had made a 'socialist revolution' and would not countenance removing the anti-capitalist elements in policy that even a 'government of capitalists' – the Provisional Government – had consolidated. Indeed the internal differences of Bolsheviks on the measures needed to stave off utter economic disintegration were steadily disappearing. For some months after Bukharin, Osinski and their associates had criticised Lenin for his caution in organising the rapid transformation of the entire economy along socialist lines; they demanded the total nationalisation of industry, agriculture, trade, finance, transport and communication. Some of them believed that this was also Lenin's requirement; but if they had carefully read his work between the February and October Revolutions, they would not have misled themselves. Certainly Lenin had argued that Russia was ready for and indeed badly needed a 'transition to socialism', and he postulated that all power should be transferred to class-based mass organisations such as the soviets. But, despite wanting a complete immediate transformation of politics, he urged that the economy should be handled more cautiously. According to Lenin, only those enterprises ought to be nationalised which were already run on large-scale capitalist lines.

In Russia this would mean the banks, the railways, the biggest factories and mines and some of the landed estates; but it should not involve the rest of the economy – and, although he had not spelled this out, the rest of the economy in fact involved most of the country's working population. Russia was a country of peasants, artisans and stall-holders. The bank, the large factory and the intensively cultivated estate were still the exceptions among the tens of thousands of enterprises in the general economy.

Consequently Lenin wanted Sovnarkom to expropriate only the most 'advanced' enterprises. The remainder needed to be organised into larger units and equipped with up-to-date technology before they were to be nationalised; and Lenin believed that this task would best be undertaken by capitalism. The revolutionary socialist state would have to protect private sectors in industry and agriculture and foster their growth. He referred to this symbiotic relationship of Bolshevik politics and capitalist economics as 'state capitalism'. It was a phrase that satisfied his wish to stay within conventional Marxist notions about the necessary stages of economic development (even though he had abandoned those notions as regards political development). But of course it offended those many Bolsheviks – probably most of them – who had made the October Revolution with a view towards turning the world upside down. Lenin's stipulation that capitalism should be widely maintained was simply incomprehensible to them. Nor was their anger mollified by his insist-ence that his scheme was a method of exploiting capitalism. They wanted a more direct and uncompromising revolutionary strategy. Bukharin and his friends wanted to take not only banks and metallurgical plants but also workshops, market stalls and peasant plots into governmental ownership.

They put their arguments against Lenin in terms of doctrine: in their opinion, he was offering a strategy that made too many compromises with capitalism. What they omitted to mention was that his strategy was simply unworkable. Lenin had announced that his intention was to exploit capitalists and then get rid of capitalism. Already he had nationalised banks and many factories and mines; he had introduced a system of heavy state regulation of foreign trade; he had repudiated his government's obligation to pay its debtors at home and abroad. He had abrogated the civic rights of the wealthier citizens and estab-lished the Cheka. He had established a class dictatorship. In such circumstances it is surprising that he was able to find any industrialists who would agree to have dealings with him. One such man of business,

V. P. Meshcherski, was discovered. But negotiations quickly broke down; the terms of Leninist 'state capitalism' proved altogether too socialistic for Meshcherski.

By then all Lenin's instincts were pointing him away from compromise. As he came to appreciate the enormity of the difficulties ahead, he was already inclined to tip the balance in his thought ever more heavily on the side of state command and control. He had not come to power in order to lessen the degree of intervention by the public authorities in the economy or any other aspect of social life. If difficulties existed, they had to be tackled by increasing the intensity of regulation. His theory of Revolution before 1917 had been marked by inconsistencies and contradictions. In power, he had to resolve this tension by practical means: he had to make his abstract formulae operational. This entailed an ever greater accentuation of the themes of dictatorship and violence. Also important, as his thought became clarified, was his commitment to centralism, hierarchy and discipline. Lenin essentially wanted the state to act, under the Bolshevik party's control, as an engine of co-ordination and indoctrination. He still saw it as being important to release popular initiative; but the increasingly unpopularity of his party had jolted him into assuming that, if it came to a choice, he preferred to prescribe and impose policy rather than to let others – whether the entire people or a section such as the working class – take a course of action that annoyed him.

Not that the social bias in Lenin's thought had disappeared. Far from it. He continued to stress the need to build up a state that gave favour to the working class. Enhanced opportunities for workers to be promoted to administrative office had to be guaranteed – and the assumption remained that the prime task facing the regime was the establishment of an efficient administration. His socialism was also avowedly and unashamedly urban in orientation. Villages had to be industrialised, peasants had to be turned into labourers and managers of collective farms. Small organisational units, furthermore, had to be phased out generally in society. Activity on a large scale with a huge number was regarded as inherently superior. Big was thought indisputably beautiful.

The essence of socialism, Lenin repeated *ad nauseam*, was 'account-keeping and supervision'. For this purpose it was essential to concentrate on raising much higher the general standards of literacy, numeracy and punctuality. Absent from this vision, however, was a will to nurture altruism, kindliness, tolerance or patience. More fundamental to Leninist ideology was the emphasis on class struggle and civil war. Mercy was adjudged an inexcusable sign of sentimentality. The ruthless pursuit of the party's aims was thought the supreme task. This had to be carried out dynamically. Leninism placed a high value upon the need for pressure to be exerted on institutions, groups and individuals to achieve its aims. Lenin accepted a great deal intellectually from the heritage of capitalism. Unlike the Left Communists, he thought that it would be helpful to maintain the old 'specialists' in their posts in factory, farm, bank and army regiment. 'Bourgeois' expertise had to be emulated before the 'bourgeois' experts themselves could be sacked. Lenin also accepted that the principle of competition, basic to capitalism, ought to be retained during the 'transition to socialism'. Ways had to be found to put institution against institution in the fulfilment of the central state organs' objectives.

Lenin was far from suggesting that the socialist Revolution would succeed merely through functionaries acting according to books of carefully framed rules. He demanded action, frenetic action. Procedural regularity was scoffed at. The ends justified the means in his thought, and there need be no moral criterion but whether a particular action helped or hindered the Revolution; and it was asserted that the Bolsheviks were equipped with scientific knowledge of what needed to be done. And so Lenin claimed unrivalled correctness for his ideology and was uninhibited in aspiring to indoctrinate the whole society with his prescriptions. He had no concept for arbitrariness because his mode of rule was itself essentially arbitrary by nature. His formal philosophy expressed contempt for any absolute commitment to universal goals such as democracy, social fairness and justice.

For many observers, then and later, this was a strange sort of socialism. Initially there were few books analysing the Soviet regime, since the potential writers were too active in political life. But soon they caught their breath and responded studiedly to the October Revolution. Most of the classical works of socialist theory not only in Russia but throughout Europe had started from the premise that socialism's introduction would involve an immediate expansion of political participation, mass creativity, democratic and legal rights and practices, popular consultation and industrial democracy. Before 1917 there was already plenty of reason to question whether Lenin, the eulogist for dictatorship, was properly categorised as a socialist. He was not the only self-styled socialist who evoked such objections; similar criticism had been made of the whole tradition of advocates of dictatorship: Louis-Auguste Blanqui in France, Wilhelm Weitling in Germany and Pëtr Tkachëv in Russia. But, unlike them, Lenin had come to power; and the castigation of him was all the fiercer. In the eyes of Mensheviks and Socialist-Revolutionaries at home and most socialists abroad, his Sovnarkom had unjustly called itself a 'socialist' government and had besmirched the name of 'socialism'.

Lenin had also introduced huge confusion into general understandings about politics. Whereas his enemies tried to deny his membership of the fraternity of world socialism, he refused to accept that they were genuine socialists; and in order to demarcate himself from them he got the Bolshevik Seventh Congress in March 1918 to rename the Bolsheviks as the Russian Communist Party. Thus he hoped to point out to everybody that Bolshevism was aiming to achieve the ultimate goal: a communist society. But this had the effect of baffling most people. They noted that this 'communist' leader continued to call himself a socialist and to refer to the need to promote the 'European socialist Revolution'. For those who were willing to read *The State and Revolution*, which had finally appeared (albeit in unfinished form since Lenin did not have time to write the last chapter before the October Revolution), a solution to this perplexing matter was available. Lenin had argued that socialism was the first great stage in the post-capitalist advance towards communism. It was possible, according to Lenin, to be both a socialist and a communist simultaneously. Such a conflation mortified non-Leninist socialists since it resulted in conservatives and liberals everywhere claiming that the inevitable consequence of any conceivable socialist government would be the sort of political, social and economic oppression that characterised Lenin's Russia.

21

AT GUNPOINT

May to August 1918

In 1918 Lenin liked to remind people of the Bolshevik party's achievements:[1]

> And so this policy, this slogan of 'All Power to the Soviets!' implanted by us in the consciousness of the broadest popular masses, gave us the opportunity in October [1917] to win so easily in Petersburg [and] turned the last months of the Russian Revolution into a single total triumphal procession.
>
> The civil war has become a fact. What we predicted at the start of the revolution and even at the start of the war was greeted by a significant segment of socialist circles with distrust and even ridicule: the transformation of the imperialist war into civil war. On 25 October 1917 it became a fact for one of the largest and most backward countries taking part in the war. In this civil war the overwhelming majority of the population proved to be on our side and consequently victory came to us extremely easily.

In his estimation, the ideas inspiring the Petrograd seizure of power had been vindicated.

Once the party entered government, Lenin ceased to be as coy about those aspects of his thought that might annoy workers, soldiers and peasants – and indeed his party members. He publicly rehearsed his favourite topics: dictatorship, terror, civil war and imperialist war. He was still confident; it remained his premise that the amount of armed violence needed to protect the Revolution at home would be small. This assumption strikes us as peculiar only because we know what was about to occur: the Civil War. But Lenin's mistake has to be understood in relation to his assumptions about socialist Revolution. Like other revolutionaries, he had read about the civil wars in Britain in the mid-seventeenth century and in France at the end of the eighteenth; but his interest was always in how the armies represented the interests of contemporary social classes. Civil war, for Lenin, was a more or less intensive class struggle. The 'civil war' he most studied was the large political struggle initiated in 1871 by the Paris Commune. In Lenin's opinion, the Commune offered a rudimentary model for popular self-administration; repeatedly he expressed admiration for what it had achieved before being suppressed by the government forces of Adolphe Thiers.

Lenin in his simplistic way judged that the Paris Commune had come to grief mainly because it failed to impose a tight internal regime and to organise adequate military contingents. From this he drew the cheering conclusion that, if the 'toiling classes' of Russia avoided the Commune's error, their numerical and organisational superiority would guarantee victory. And he persuaded himself that the period of 'civil war' that followed the October Revolution was coming to an end.

The odd little trouble spot survived. 'But, in the main,' he suggested:[2]

> The task of suppressing the resistance of the exploiters was already resolved in the period from 25 October 1917 to (approximately) February 1918 or to the surrender of Bogaevski.
>
> Next on to the agenda there comes . . . the task – the task that is urgent and constitutes the peculiarity of the current moment – to organise the *administering* of Russia.

Who was this Bogaevski? His name is recorded only in recondite accounts of the military actions in southern Russia in 1918–19. Afrikan Bogaevski was a Cossack commander who fought the Bolshevik-led forces, was captured after a minor engagement, but was allowed his freedom on condition that he refrained from further military activity. Lenin's assessment was hugely amiss. He utterly failed to anticipate the intensity of the fighting about to engulf Russia. Even in southern Russia the Civil War was not ending but beginning as a Volunteer Army was being readied for action by Generals Alexeev and Kornilov, and this Volunteer Army was just one of three large forces being assembled by self-designated White officers pledged to overthrow the government in Moscow.

These were not the only groups aiming at the overthrow of Bolshevism. The Socialist-Revolutionaries, after the dispersal of the Constituent Assembly, had reconvened in the city of Samara in the river Volga region and had founded an administration claiming to be the rightful government of all Russia. This administration called itself Komuch (which was the acronym of the Committee of Members of the Constituent Assembly), and was socialist in orientation. Elsewhere even the Left

Socialist-Revolutionaries were contemplating uprisings against Sovnar-
kom. Massive armed conflict was on the point of exploding across
Russia. Lenin was famous for his strategic intuition in advance of the
October Revolution. He had no such instincts about the Civil War.

In May 1918 he went on applying his general policies to the shattered
economy. Chief among these was the imposition of what he called a
Food Dictatorship, which rationalised the various local measures already
being taken to procure food supplies for the towns. At Sovnarkom
sessions he pressed his plans with urgency. When the Presidium of the
Supreme Council of the National Economy seemed to hinder a co-
ordinated approach by the Soviet state to industry and agriculture, Lenin
was furious with Presidium leader V. P. Milyutin. Going home in a
condition of shock, Milyutin confided to his diary:[3]

> Sovnarkom issued a reprimand to the Presidium. Ilich even declared
> that 'it would be worth putting the Presidium in prison on bread
> and water for a week, but because of our weakness let's limit
> ourselves to a reprimand . . .'; and that while it was possible to put
> us on to water and even to plunge us into water, it was sheer utopia
> to put us on bread and that even the People's Commissariat of
> Food Supplies wouldn't permit such a luxury.

The fact that Milyutin was one of the few leading Bolsheviks who had
supported Lenin in the Brest-Litovsk dispute gained him no relief. Lenin
was on the rampage.

Lenin's economic priority was the collection of grain from the
countryside. Civil war was the last thing on his mind. He told Trotski,
who was assembling a Workers' and Peasants' Red Army in his new role
as People's Commissar of Military Affairs, to devote nine-tenths of the
Army's efforts to the procurement of food supplies. He told Sovnarkom
that the secreting of grain should become the most heinous crime. He
urged that hoarders be treated as 'enemies of the people' and that the
state should 'wage and carry through a merciless and terrorist defence
and war against the peasant bourgeoisie and any other bourgeoisie
holding on to grain surpluses'.[4] The clumsy phrasing gives a sense of the
forceful emotions powering Lenin. Sovnarkom preferred a more temper-
ate formulation, but on the substance of policy he easily got his way:
most Bolshevik leaders were itching to augment state control. As the
Food Dictatorship was inaugurated, Lenin secured the establishment of
a new institution: committees of village poor (kombedy). When the
government's commissars reached the countryside, they were empowered

to liaise with these committees so as to discover the identities of the better-off peasants engaged in the hoarding of grain. Any hoarded grain was to be weighed out on the spot and a portion was to be distributed to the village's poorer members before the remainder was taken on to the towns.

Lenin had much greater difficulty with a further economic priority. By summer 1918 it was obvious that his proposal for collaboration with Russian industrialists such as Meshcherski would not work. Instead, to his colleagues' amazement, he urged the conclusion of commercial deals with German businessmen. This second proposal was so contentious in later years that it was kept secret in the Sovnarkom archives. And it is easy to understand why. The Bolsheviks were critics of other socialists who failed to struggle for the overthrow of the 'European bourgeoisie'. Lenin had spent the Great War denouncing Kautsky for avoiding a confrontation with Germany's Imperial government and the magnates of German financial and industrial might. Now he wanted to deal commercially with those same magnates.

But then again Lenin had made the October Revolution on the premise that Russia would make its 'transition to socialism' with help from capitalists. He had hoped to get this from Russian capitalists. If this proved impracticable, why not try to appeal to German capitalists? Ever the tactician, Lenin could not see why his party was not capable of being as flexible as himself.

Yet his desire to make overtures to the capitalists of Germany did not signify a permanent accommodation to 'German imperialism'. Lenin was still Lenin. He wished to exploit capitalist Germany while he could; but he still expected that such a Germany would not long endure. 'European socialist Revolution' remained high on his agenda. He had no doubt that far-left socialists abroad would triumph sooner or later. Justifying the Brest-Litovsk Treaty to the Fourth Congress of Soviets in March 1918 he had asserted: 'We know that [Karl] Liebknecht will be victorious one way or another: this is inevitable in the workers' movement.' Lenin acknowledged that the Treaty gave no absolute guarantee of a 'breathing space' in Russia until such time as Liebknecht got going:[5]

> Yes, the peace we have come to is unstable in the highest degree and the breathing space we've received can be broken any day from both east and west: there's no doubt about it; our international situation is so critical that we must strain every nerve to survive as long as possible until the Western revolution matures, a revolution

that is maturing much more slowly than we expected and wanted; it is feeding and covering ever more and more combustible material.

There were terrible moments for him. The worst was the declaration by Central Committee member Sokolnikov, the very man who signed the Treaty at Brest-Litovsk, that the Germans were no longer to be trusted and that the Treaty had been a mistake. He attacked the Treaty at the Central Committee on 10 May, and it was only Lenin's fierce counter-offensive that saved Russia from going to war again.

Worse was to follow. At the end of the month there was one of those small military incidents that were occurring all over Russia: a group of soldiers rebelled against Soviet authority. But this incident was not easily dealt with. It involved Czech former prisoners-of-war captured by the Russian Imperial Army who, under an agreement with the Allies, were travelling across Siberia to North America so that they could fight on the western front against the Central Powers. The mutual distrust of the Soviet authorities and this Czech Legion was profound; and when Trotski tried to have them disarmed, a confrontation took place in May. The 35,000 Czechs, stronger than any military force that Sovnarkom could put against them, turned their trains back towards central Russia and indicated their readiness to fight on behalf of Komuch in Samara for the overthrow of Lenin and his fellow People's Commissars.

Responsibility for dealing with the crisis was left to Trotski: even at this point Lenin did not sense the vital threat posed by the Czech Legion. He was preoccupied with the Fifth Congress of Soviets, which was scheduled to meet within the next few weeks. The two former partners in the Sovnarkom coalition, the Bolsheviks and the Left Socialist-Revolutionaries, eyed each other nervously throughout June 1918. The Congress opened on 4 July and such was the tension that each party placed a guard over its delegations. The Left Socialist-Revolutionaries were the first to act. On 6 July, while the Congress was debating, one of their leaders Yakov Blyumkin mounted an operation designed to blast the Treaty of Brest-Litovsk into oblivion. Blyumkin worked for the Cheka and had obtained a pass to visit the German embassy in Moscow. Once inside the building, he asked for a meeting with Ambassador Wilhelm von Mirbach, in the course of which he pulled out a revolver and shot him before dashing outside. Mirbach was mortally wounded, and it was Blyumkin's hope to provoke a diplomatic incident that would end with the Bolsheviks starting a revolutionary war with Imperial Germany.

The news was relayed to Lenin and Dzierżyński. Lenin perceived what Blyumkin had been calculating and sought to forestall a German invasion by suppressing the entire Left Socialist-Revolutionary Party. He also paid a visit to the German embassy to express condolence on behalf of Sovnarkom. The government in Berlin had to be reassured that the Soviet authorities desired to maintain friendly relations. Dzierżyński was instructed to take reliable Cheka units to the Left Socialist-Revolutionary headquarters on Trëkhsvyatitelski Lane and arrest the Left Socialist-Revolutionary Central Committee.

The operation was carried with Bolshevik military ineptitude. Arriving at the Left Socialist-Revolutionary headquarters, Dzierżyński was himself taken into custody. Lenin was at his wits' end. If he could not rely on Dzierżyński, who could he turn to? (One answer might have been Trotski. But he was busy with the Czech Legion, and anyway he did not inspire total confidence at this stage.) The only thing for it was to assume personal control. Now he had two major tasks: the arrest of the Left Socialist-Revolutionary Central Committee and the liberation of Dzierżyński. For this he would still need a further agency of enforcement. His only option was to approach the leader of the Latvian Riflemen, General I. I. Vacietis, to head the attack. Lenin told him that Sovnarkom might not survive till morning. He may have been exaggerating in order to raise Vacietis's feeling of pride. More probably, he had an acute sense of the danger to the regime in the capital. If a poorly organised group had been able to seize power in October 1917, another such group might repeat the feat. To Lenin's relief, Vacietis agreed to the assignment.

Things began to improve. The visit to the German embassy went as well as could be expected, and Vacietis's troops did their violent job with efficiency. The Left Socialist-Revolutionary headquarters was captured on 7 July. Their leaders were arrested and Dzierżyński was found unharmed. Lenin and Dzierżyński decided that, although proof was not available of the Left Socialist-Revolutionary Central Committee's complicity in the assassination, a member of their Central Committee should be executed. Thus the Germans would be shown that the Bolsheviks meant business in protecting the Brest-Litovsk Treaty. Bolsheviks were not discomfited by the thought of killing other socialists. On 9 July 1918, Dzierżyński in person undertook the task and shot Left Socialist-Revolutionary Central Committee member V. A. Alexandrovich.

The Cheka's inefficiency during the Mirbach crisis continued to rankle with Lenin. He was also intrigued by how the Left Socialist-Revolutionaries had organised their armed action against the Bolsheviks, and on 7 July he decided on the spur of the moment to pay a visit to their former headquarters in Trëkhsvyatitelski Lane. Stepan Gil as usual was the chauffeur. As they made their way, a group of armed men sprang on to the road and shouted at them to stop. Lenin instructed Gil to comply, but the armed men started to fire at them before they stopped. Luckily the men turned out to be Bolshevik supporters, and Lenin let them off with a rather schoolmasterly admonishment: 'Comrades, you mustn't casually fire at people from behind corners without seeing who you're firing at!'[6] This was the least he might have said in the circumstances. But the travails of that day were not yet over. Lenin's car was stopped again after the visit to Trëkhsvyatitelski Lane. A semiofficial patrol of youths demanded to see his identity papers and decided that the document indicating that he was Sovnarkom Chairman was invalid. He was arrested and taken to the nearest police station. At least on this occasion he was not threatened with gunfire, and the police officer and he felt able to laugh about the incident.[7]

Even then his day's tutorial in life's dangers in the Soviet republic had not been brought to a close. Shots were fired at their car on the journey back from the police station.[8] The shots missed. Gil put his foot down hard on the accelerator and the two men arrived more exhausted than infuriated at the Kremlin. Their little trip around Moscow had several times brought them close to death.

Lenin had not obtained much additional knowledge about the affair. Nor did he have an opportunity to acquire it in subsequent weeks. A still more serious military emergency was taking place in the Volga region. Komuch, having acquired a military force in the form of the Czech Legion, was ready to mount an offensive into the central region of Russia. From Samara they marched unopposed on Kazan before any defence could be assembled. Trotski as People's Commissar for Military Affairs rushed to the Volga and, to general astonishment, the new Red Army succeeded in holding off the Komuch troops at the battle of Sviyazhk. As the Bolsheviks consolidated themselves in south-eastern Russia, there were growing problems in the north. The British had landed troops at Archangel and Lenin was concerned lest this be followed by a march on Petrograd. Recognising Sovnarkom's military weakness, he secretly appealed to Germany for assistance. It was a highly sensitive option since Lenin could not be sure that the German forces themselves would not occupy Petrograd *en route* to Archangel. In fact the crisis faded and military collaboration between Sovnarkom and Ludendorff was not needed. But it had been a close-run thing. 'Soviet power' and the Bolshevik one-party state were under constant threat of collapse.[9]

All the while Lenin was in a rage. Nothing could quite satiate his appetite for revenge against those elements from Imperial Russian society that he despised. Some he simply hated. He had a personal score to settle with the descendants of Alexander III, the emperor who had refused to spare the life of his elder brother Alexander. Nicholas II, his wife Alexandra and their family had been held since 30 April in the Ipatev House in Yekaterinburg. There was a constant possibility that anti-Bolshevik forces might break through to the Urals and rescue the Imperial family. For months the Bolshevik Central Committee had secretly pondered what to do with Nicholas II.

A line of communication was in place for the Bolshevik regional leadership in the Urals to give information and receive orders. Nicholas II, at the time of his abdication in the previous year, had been the object of nearly universal contempt. Sympathy began to grow for him when he became simply citizen Nikolai Romanov. But Lenin and the Bolshevik Central Committee were implacable. The Romanovs had at the very least to be neutralised as a force in public life, and Trotski recommended that Nicholas should be brought back to Moscow and put on trial for the abuses committed by him and in his name before 1917. For a while Lenin demurred. Probably he did not like to associate himself directly with the judicial killing of Sovnarkom's enemies. The Left Socialist-Revolutionary Central Committee member V. A. Alexandrovich had been executed in secret and Lenin kept his distance from the event. But as the military encirclement of the Soviet-held territory continued, he hearkened to the argument for drastic steps to be taken. Nothing was more drastic than the event in the early hours of 18 July 1918. The former Emperor and his family were woken from their beds, taken down to the Ipatev House cellar, lined up against the wall and shot.

It was among the most gruesome massacres of the Revolution. The victims included not only Nicholas and his wife but also their four daughters and their haemophiliac son together with several servants. In captivity, Nicholas had spent his time reading the Old Testament and Russian nineteenth-century classic novels. He and his family diverted themselves by putting on playlets for each other. Nicholas acted nobly as the paterfamilias and Alexandra proved herself an able manager of the family's very restricted domestic budget. The Bolshevik leaders hardly appear in the last records they left behind. Alexandra's diary in 1918 mentions Lenin only once. The Imperial couple's main worry was that Nicholas should be put under duress to co-sign the Treaty of Brest-Litovsk. How little they knew their Lenin. Neither Lenin nor any other Bolshevik leader would have dreamed of using the Romanovs in order to lend legitimacy to the Soviet regime. But about one thing they were absolutely right: that Lenin had the power of life or death over them. Empress Alexandra wrote on 4 June 1918: 'I had a bath at 10. Lenin gave the order that the clocks have to be put 2 hours ahead (economy of electricity) so that at 10 they told us it was 12. At 10 strong thunderstorm.'[10] Like most Russians, the Romanovs were disoriented by the changes made by the Bolsheviks. They were devout, perplexed and very middle-class in their habits. For them, Lenin was the Antichrist.

He exterminated the Romanovs because they had misruled Russia. But he also turned to such measures because he enjoyed – really enjoyed – letting himself loose against people in general from the *ancien régime*. He hated not only the Imperial family but also the middling people who had administered and controlled Russia before 1917. He had never forgotten the ostracism undergone by the Ulyanovs after the conviction of Alexander Ilich. Landlords, priests, teachers, engineers and civil servants had treated them as pariahs. Why should he protect them now?

There was a contradiction here. In *The State and Revolution*, at the height of his optimism about the working class, Lenin had argued that middle-class 'specialists' in the various professions would need to be kept in employment until such time as ordinary workers could be trained to take their place. But by mid-1918 he was fomenting the maltreatment of 'the bourgeoisie'; and, if he had given even the slightest attention to what this meant in practice, he would have known that this would have grievous consequences for those much needed 'specialists'. And yet this does not mean that he definitely and positively wanted scientists, teachers, accountants and writers to suffer. It is more likely that he allowed his angry zeal for class struggle, including terror, to dominate everything in his thought. Politics had become viciously violent. Bolsheviks were not only purveyors of terrorism: they also were the targets of terrorist actions. Lenin indeed had nearly been assassinated in January 1918, and a leading member of the Party City Committee in Petrograd, V. Volodarski, was killed in June. The violence in Russia was largely the product of the October Revolution, and was to a considerable extent the fault of Lenin. But once the cycle of violence had started rolling he was no longer the only person responsible for applying it. He was transfixed by his concern to terrorise every conceivable opponent of Sovnarkom.

The old problems with his health – headaches and insomnia – agitated him throughout spring and summer. From April to August his distraction was such that he published no lengthy piece on Marxist theory or Bolshevik party strategy. This was hardly odd behaviour in the case of most politicians. But it was highly uncharacteristic of Lenin. Nadezhda Konstantinovna noticed that his illness was stopping him from writing.[11] His inability to sleep at nights must have left him in an acutely agitated condition; he never had the chance of calm consideration of public policy. Everything was done in panic. Everything was done angrily.

Lenin's choleric intensity is obvious from a letter he sent to the Bolsheviks of Penza on 11 August 1918:[12]

> Comrades! The insurrection of five kulak districts should be *pitilessly* suppressed. The interests of the *whole* revolution require this because 'the last decisive battle' with the kulaks is now under way *everywhere*. An example must be demonstrated.
> 1. Hang (and make sure that the hanging takes place *in full view of the people*) *no fewer than one hundred* known kulaks, rich men, bloodsuckers.
> 2. Publish their names.
> 3. Seize *all* their grain from them.
> 4. Designate hostages in accordance with yesterday's telegram.
> Do it in such a fashion that for hundreds of kilometres around the people might see, tremble, know, shout: *they are strangling* and will strangle to death the bloodsucking kulaks.
> Telegraph receipt and *implementation*.
> Yours, Lenin.
> Find some truly hard people.

These words were so shocking in tone and content that they were kept secret during the Soviet period. The lax definition of victims – 'kulaks, rich men, bloodsuckers' – was a virtual guarantee that abuse would occur. The entire message invited such abuse. Persons were to be judicially murdered simply for belonging to a social category.

Indeed Lenin was treating whole areas of Penza province as 'kulak districts'. By his extravagant language he increased the hazard of armed units marching into villages and treating everyone as kulaks. He wanted to intimidate the whole rural population, not just the rich minority –

and he was reckless of the negative impact this might have on his own policy of creating 'committees of the village poor'. It is the vicious relish in exemplary terror that is so disgusting. Not even just a firing squad and a quick death. No, Lenin demanded a public hanging. Knowing that not all Bolsheviks would have the stomach for this, he told the Penza comrades to go out and find some sufficiently hard types to carry out the measures. This kind of message was not the exception but the rule. Throughout summer 1918 and the rest of the Civil War, Lenin ranted in the same manner. He urged that the city of Baku should be razed to the ground in the event of its being attacked and that public announcement of this should be posted around Baku so that collaborators might be discouraged.[13] He reverted the practices of twentieth-century European war to the Middle Ages. No moral threshold was sacred.

And whenever he heard about Komuch and the Volga region his rage was awesome. Was this a geographical coincidence? Possibly Lenin in some subconscious fashion was taking revenge on the Volga region for the ostracism of the Ulyanovs after his brother's arrest. What is clear is that he was taking a very detached approach to his regime's murderous imposition. His first cousin Vladimir Ardashev, with whom he had spent summers on the family estate of Kokushkino, had worked as a lawyer. Lenin as a youth had spent much time with the Ardashevs and there had been visits to him abroad by members of the Ardashev family. In summer 1918 the news came through to Lenin in Moscow: Vladimir Ardashev, an innocent professional person, had been shot by Bolsheviks in Yekaterinburg as belonging to the undesirable category of the 'bourgeoisie'.

But Lenin was barely disconcerted. Cousin Ardashev had been caught on the wrong side of the growing Civil War. He had been inactive in politics, and he had done nothing to deserve his execution; he was a decent human being, but the logic of events forced a choice upon all Russians: for or against the 'proletarian dictatorship'. Family ties were subordinate to politics. It never occurred to Lenin to ask what kind of Revolution was worth while that condoned the physical elimination of well-meaning, competent and honest people like his cousin. Lenin kept himself out of range of the Revolution's carnage. This was the behaviour of a bookish fanatic who felt no need to witness the violent actuality of his Revolution. He knew what he wanted in abstract political terms, and treated the death of innocent individuals as part of the unavoidable messiness of historical progress. And so he did not mind having blood on his hands. When he made those disgusting demands for mass terror along the river Volga, many of the victims would inevitably include people such as his deceased cousin. But this did not bother Lenin.

Meanwhile the emergencies of the Moscow summer had not come to an end. Lenin had been caught unawares by the Mirbach assassination on 6 July and been shocked by the Left Socialist-Revolutionary rising. He had been put in danger when he travelled around the capital with Stepan Gil on 7 July. Even worse was to befall Lenin in the following month.

It happened on 30 August 1918. Lenin's sister Maria Ilinichna pleaded with him not to leave the Kremlin that day. There had already been reports of the assassination of the Petrograd Cheka chief. But neither Maria Ilinichna nor Bukharin could adduce anything concrete to put him off his programme.[14] Lenin laughed and announced he would go ahead with things as he had agreed several days ago. This was set to include two short open-air speeches. The first was to be at the Corn Exchange two miles to the east of the Kremlin, in Basmanny district, before he swept down to the south. Lenin was on good form; he did not take his bodyguard, but set off alone with his chauffeur Stepan Gil.[15] He was acting true to the party's ethos. The Bolsheviks as a party downplayed the political importance of individuals and discouraged leaders from acting as if they were indispensable. Lenin's foolhardiness at least disproves the allegation that he was a physical coward. There had been a suspicion of this in July 1917 when he had fled Petrograd rather than defend himself before the law against charges of being a German agent. But his activity in 1918 had been very different. Daily he was taking his chances along with fellow Bolshevik leaders in open public view in Moscow.

At the Corn Exchange he roused the audience: 'Let every worker and peasant who is still wavering on the question of power just take a look at the Volga, Siberia and Ukraine, and the reply will come back on its own, clear and definite!'[16] He gave another such speech at the Mikhelson Factory. He told his second audience that 'democracy' was an abused term in contemporary political parlance. Like a religious zealot trying to cleanse the lexicon of faith, Lenin declared: 'The place where the "democrats" rule is where you'll find genuine, unvarnished robbery!' All agreed that Sovnarkom's Chairman had been on good form.

As he made his way back to the car by the Mikhelson Factory yard, Lenin was approached by a couple of women complaining about the official barrier detachments that prevented peasants from coming into Moscow to trade their grain. He agreed with them that the detachments were not operating as they should.[17] Gil revved up the engine in anticipation of the trip back to the Kremlin. Lenin had reached just three paces from the car when several shots were fired. The target was Lenin; and on this occasion the assassins were more accurate than their predecessors in January 1918. Lenin was hit twice and was bleeding profusely. Uproar ensued in the yard and the Bolshevik party activists tried to surround their leader and grab the suspects. The priority, however, was to bundle Lenin into the car. When Lenin began questioning him about what was happening, Gil told him abruptly to keep quiet. Gil took control. He decided not to drive to a hospital in case a further group of killers lay in wait but to make straight for the Kremlin. Medically this could have been disastrous since at this stage no one knew the nature of Lenin's wounds. But, in the light of the summer's events in Moscow, Gil was correct that the Kremlin was the only safe refuge.[18]

On arrival at the Kremlin, Lenin himself acted with complete disregard for common sense. He had been hit twice. One bullet had pierced his left shoulder-blade and gone through to near the collar-bone on his right side. The other was lodged on the left at the base of his neck. Although the blood was pouring from him, he rejected Gil's offer to carry him upstairs to his apartment. (It would have been sounder to avoid any movement whatsoever.) Lenin stumbled upstairs. He lurched into his bedroom and slumped on to a chair. Maria Ilinichna got up to see what was happening, and was horrified. There was no surgeon on duty. The Kremlin precinct was restricted to Bolshevik leaders, their families, servants and security personnel.

And so an urgent word was put out for Bolsheviks in the Kremlin who had some medical training. Two were found: these were Vera Velichkina (wife of Lenin's personal assistant Bonch-Bruevich) and Vera Krestinskaya (wife of Bolshevik Central Committee member Nikolai Krestinski). Maria looked around for some food for Lenin while Bonch-Bruevich and Krestinskaya examined him. There was in fact no food in the apartment. So much for Maria's greater skill at housekeeping! Then Nadezhda Konstantinovna, arriving back from a meeting at Moscow University, was told by Alexei Rykov what had happened.[19] Her first thought was that he might be about to die. It had already been discovered that he had a punctured lung. What else might be found out? Nobody said much to reassure her. The Latvian maid was so terrified that she locked herself away. Panic was growing. Meanwhile Maria Ilinichna wanted to send someone out to the nearest grocer's shop for a lemon. But she stopped herself when the thought occurred to her that the grocer, too, might be a collaborator of the assassins and might be plotting to purvey poison to the Kremlin. Lenin's four female carers – Maria, Nadya and the two Veras – limited themselves to sending out to the nearest pharmacy for medicine.[20] Why chemists should have been politically more reliable than grocers was not considered.

Things calmed down as prominent hospital surgeons were summoned to attend, and Professors Vladimir Rozanov and V. M. Mints arrived in the early hours of 31 August.[21] A pot was already on the boil in the next room for the sterilising of the bandages. Rozanov and Mints disrobed the patient and staunched his wounds. Lenin's arm was raised on a hoist.[22] At last Lenin recognised the seriousness of his injury: 'Is the end near? If it's near, tell me straight so that I don't leave matters pending.'[23] The doctors reassured him that his condition would soon be stabilised.

By 1 September he was fit enough to be X-rayed.[24] Lenin told his doctors that he felt no great discomfort from the puncture wounds and it was thought best to leave the bullets alone.[25] Rozanov and Mints wanted to prevent their patient from exerting himself too quickly. The arm-hoist was invaluable for this purpose. Lenin was immobilised for as long as it was in place. He was also persuaded to take a lengthy period of convalescence outside Moscow: anything was better than the hoist in the Kremlin. By chance a large mansion house had come into the hands of the government in the previous week. It lay outside the village of Gorki, twenty-two miles to the capital's south.[26] It could be reached by road or by train to the little rail-stop of Gerasimovka. The house already had electricity, a telephone and central heating. It was also conveniently empty; the previous owners General and Mrs Reinbot had not lived there for years. It was readily convertible to use as a sanatorium. Lenin was passed fit for the journey and driven by road to Gorki on 25 September 1918.

Few Russians and even fewer foreigners had predicted that Lenin's party would get its hands on power in the first place. Had it not been for the Great War, there would have been no October Revolution. Lenin had been given his chance because of the wartime economic dislocation, administrative breakdown and political disarray. And he had adjusted his thought and behaviour to the opportunities on offer. In particular, he had handled his party with perceptiveness, determination and daring. Without Lenin there would still have been problems for the Provisional Government. Almost certainly the Provisional Government would have fallen. But Lenin's activity ensured that the manner of its collapse led to a political order of extreme authoritarianism. It also made civil war inevitable. Lenin had blustered, bullied and gambled. He had made extraordinary mistakes. He had pretended to a scientific attitude belying his intuitive approach to politics. He had tugged Marxism round to the kind of revolution he desired. He had split socialism in Russia and Europe into antagonistic camps and had set about building a world with the instruments of ideological polemic, political struggle and civil war. He had yet to show that his general prognosis was realistic. In the heat of armed conflict, as a variety of forces were concentrating their efforts to overthrow Sovnarkom, Lenin hoped and expected to justify himself.

PART FOUR

DEFENCE OF THE REVOLUTION

There's nothing else I have.

Lenin in 1922

22

WAR LEADER

1918–1919

By most criteria there were few politicians less suited to fighting the Civil War than Lenin. As the eldest son of a widow, he had not been liable for service in the Imperial armed forces; and he made no secret of his military inexperience.[1] Certainly he had read Clausewitz's classic work *On War*. But the notes he took were peculiar. The conclusion Lenin drew from Clausewitz about the waging of war was that it was becoming an ever simpler technical matter. He did not expect complication. After his party assumed power, he left the practical details to others and did not go near the Red Army. Lenin carried his black Browning revolver with him for considerations of personal security. But he did not fire it. The closest he came to soldierly activity was on his hunting expeditions with his rifle outside Moscow, when he shot ducks and foxes. But this was the extent of his personal direct violence. His experience of large-scale armed conflict between one set of human beings and another had always been at second hand; and he had next to no foresight about the intensity of the Civil War that was exploding across the former Russian Empire.

Yet in at least one sense he was prepared for war. Quiet and inexperienced though he was, Lenin felt no inhibition about giving orders to use military force and the resultant bloodshed gave him no sleepless nights. The writer Maxim Gorki asked him how he knew how much force to use. Lenin, in Gorki's opinion, was too ready to deploy the Cheka and the Red Army. But Lenin was unrepentant: 'By what measure are you to gauge how many blows are necessary and how many are superfluous in the course of a particular fight?'[2] For Lenin, the winning of the fight was the important thing. Only pedants were concerned about the careful calibration of violence. Lenin preferred to overdo the blows than to risk letting an opponent survive assault.

As a war leader, moreover, he developed very quickly even though he was distant from the military campaigns. By all accounts, he was the linchpin of the Bolshevik central party machine. Trotski as People's

Commissar for Military Affairs won the public plaudits as the party leader in closest contact with the Red Army. He had his own vehicle, which quickly came to be known as the Trotski Train, for travel to the war fronts. He addressed commissars and commanders and rank-and-file troops with panache. There were others who had wonderful talents. Bukharin was an expeditious editor for *Pravda*. Kamenev could handle the municipal administration for Moscow, Zinoviev for Petrograd. Stalin could run the People's Commissariat for Nationalities Affairs and any other organisation requiring a firm, decisive hand. Sverdlov, Lenin's right-hand man in the Kremlin, had the capacity to co-ordinate not only the Party Secretariat but also the Central Executive Committee of the Congress of Soviets. They all of them could exercise power with competence. They had sharp intelligence and an abundance of confidence.

Indeed they raged to amplify their power and to change the world around them in accordance with their doctrines. The year after the October Revolution had been a terrible lesson to them. Persuaded by Lenin in 1917 that the soviets could constitute the core of the 'dictatorship of the proletariat', they had found the experience of government less than totally satisfactory. In doctrine they were Marxists of Lenin's type. They worshipped orderliness, discipline, centralism, hierarchy and monolithic unity. They wanted their commands to be executed without attenuation. They aimed to impose their will mercilessly. Each of them let his subordinates know that results were expected to arrive fast. The Bolshevik central leadership had taken power so as to hasten a transformation of the political and economic world. The reality of power, however, was different. The Russian Empire had broken asunder. The economy and the administration had fallen apart. Politics had given way to chronic, indecisive military struggle. Impoverishment, hunger and disease were becoming normal. And in this situation the Bolsheviks knew that a fully centralised system of order was required. Practical as well as doctrinal exigency was at work.

The Bolshevik central and local leaders were themselves in part to blame for the disorderliness. Each of them wanted the Revolution on his or her terms. The vertical line of command was a shambles in soviets, trade unions and other public bodies. When Lenin wrote to the Astrakhan communists, he had to threaten (or at least he felt he had to threaten) to kill them in order to secure compliance. The central public bodies were in constant disagreement with each other. Lenin could usually get his way with any of them. But he was the October Revolution's leader: it would have been a pretty poor job if his personal authority had not carried some weight. Others in the Central Committee and Sovnarkom had a harder time. Personal jealousies and institutional rivalries were acute. Nor was the situation improved by the Bolshevik proclivity for establishing new bodies whenever an existing state body could not surmount a specific difficulty. Functional demarcation between institutions had been ridiculed by Lenin in *The State and Revolution* as a middle-class trick to disguise the reality of the 'bourgeois dictatorship' established under capitalism; and he and his party were staggered by the chaotic nature of administration after 1917.

Lenin called on his associates to work harder and, in some cases, to set a better example. The disputes between Trotski and Stalin infuriated him. Each of them wrote to him putting his case; the mutual hatred was naked. Lenin alone could effect an accommodation of sorts. He was not averse to playing the stern father to the party. When the sailors' leader Pavel Dybenko was put under arrest for insubordination, Lenin took his wife Alexandra Kollontai aside: 'It's precisely you and Dybenko who should be setting an example to the broad masses who are still so far from understanding the new Soviet power – you who enjoy such popularity.'[3] He released Dybenko only if Kollontai stood as the personal guarantor of his future good behaviour. No one but Lenin could have succeeded with Kollontai like this.

But the solutions he proposed to Bolsheviks were expressed very abstractly. He called for centralism, order, discipline and – increasingly – punishment. The theorist of organisation had never been very good at precise organisational advice. Even in *What Is to Be Done?* he had been loath to get down to details; and when he did, as in his 'Letter to a Comrade about our Organisational Tasks', he had tended towards a rather schematic set of recommendations. At any rate in late 1918, as he convalesced, he did not give much attention to pressing organisational matters. Instead he wrote a booklet to counteract what the party's enemies had written about him. He had one enemy especially in mind: Karl Kautsky. Out at the sanatorium he composed *Proletarian Revolution and Kautsky the Renegade*. For the first time in his career he did not write in longhand. His recuperation took some weeks, and even Lenin had to content himself with dictating his thought to a Sovnarkom secretary, Maria Volodicheva. The inner Lenin revealed himself. Despite his personal and political woes, what did he think it most important to do? To refute Kautsky, a theorist whose existence was completely unknown to the vast majority of the citizens of the Soviet republic, and who was not even the major Marxist leader in Germany.

His words were unexceptional by Lenin's standards, except for their bluntness. The various verbal evasions of 1917 were put behind him. He mocked Kautsky's rejection of the desirability of 'dictatorship', and declared:[4]

> It's natural for a liberal to talk generally about 'democracy'. A Marxist will never forget to pose the question: 'for which class?' Everyone knows – and the 'historian' Kautsky knows it too – that the uprisings and even the strong cases of unrest among slaves in antiquity instantly exposed the essence of the ancient state as a *dictatorship of slave-owners*. Did this dictatorship eliminate democracy *among* slave-owners, *for* them? Everyone knows this not to be true.

And so Lenin reaffirmed the precept that his socialism, which he thought to be the sole genuine form thereof, could be introduced only though dictatorship. He pressed the argument directly: 'Dictatorship is the power relying directly upon force unbound by any laws.'[5]

Yet he continued to be coy about the influences upon his thought. He mentioned Marx, Engels and Plekhanov, but practically no one else. Not once did he mention his admiration for the agrarian-socialist terrorists. Nor did he advertise another influential figure for him: the fifteenth-century writer Niccolò Machiavelli. Whereas Marx had written about the need for dictatorial repression, Machiavelli spelled out how to repress effectively. But having got himself into trouble in 1902 by praising the Russian *narodniki*, Lenin did not wish to associate himself with a thinker who for centuries had been notorious for promoting amoral techniques of rule; and when Lenin mentioned him in confidential correspondence, as in a letter to Molotov in 1922, he did not refer to Machiavelli by name but as 'one wise writer on matters of statecraft'.[6] Machiavelli, he confided to Molotov, 'correctly said that if it is necessary to resort to certain brutalities for the sake of realising a certain political goal, they must be carried out in the most energetic fashion and in the briefest possible time because the masses will not tolerate the prolonged application of brutality'. So much for the idea that Lenin was always trying to limit the brutal nature of his regime. In fact he wanted the brutality to be as intense as possible in the short term so that it might not need to be unduly extended in time.

Although we do not know when Lenin read Machiavelli, it is clear that that he was an admirer. There were several other authors he studied after the October Revolution. A few of them are known to us. Among them was John Maynard Keynes, whose treatise on *The Economic Consequences of the Peace* denounced the Treaty of Versailles. In this case Lenin was open about the influence; for Keynes castigated the territorial and economic dispositions made by the Allies in 1919. He also read Osvald Spengler's *Decline of the West*. Spengler wrote that Western capitalism was doomed because of the natural cycle of civilisation from birth to life and then death. Lenin did not like the book, preferring an economic and political explanation for the doom that he too anticipated for the principal market economies; he said that Spengler was a bourgeois whinger.[7] Evidently when Lenin read for pleasure, it could frequently be the pleasure of caustic contempt.

In general, though, his intellect was engaged by concerns nearer to home. He focussed his efforts on sustaining the Soviet dictatorship against the attacks of White armies and foreign expeditionary forces. The solution chosen by the Central Committee and supported by the local party bodies was that a single supreme organ should head the Soviet state, decide policies and regulate their implementation. This, they believed, would eliminate the chaos and indiscipline. The organ they selected was their own party.

There is controversy as to why this happened. All Soviet and most Western historians have suggested that it resulted from a deeply laid scheme stretching back to *What Is to Be Done?* in 1902.[8] Yet it strains credulity – now that we can get at archival sources and scholars have looked for 'dirt' on Lenin wherever it may be found – that if the Bolsheviks had been planning a specific institutional form of state they would not have left evidence in their letters and memoirs. But such evidence has not come to light. Certainly Lenin was the founder of the one-party, mono-ideological state, but his sketches had been vague on crucial practicalities. What he had articulated was really a set of basic assumptions. He praised leadership and professed a capacity for infallible policies; he also believed in the need for a vanguard party. This was not yet a prescription for the Bolshevik party to become the supreme organ of the Soviet state. But the pressure of events pushed Lenin and his comrades to elaborate their assumptions and move towards this institutional invention within a year or so of the October Revolution. Those assumptions about revolutionary strategy started to count seriously in 1918–19. Policies changed; assumptions were modified in details, but not fundamentally.

Not only Lenin and the Central Committee but the local party leaders were content with the transformation of politics. In January 1919 the Central Committee, most of whose members were frequently absent from Moscow in fulfilment of military or political duties, set up two small inner subcommittees: the Political Bureau (Politburo) and Organisational Bureau (Orgburo). The Central Committee, the Politburo and the Orgburo were empowered to take charge of the highest affairs of state. Despite being party bodies, they were really the supreme agencies of state and their decisions were mandatory for Sovnarkom, the Council of Labour and Defence and the People's Commissariats.

Lenin belonged to the Central Committee and Politburo and retained his post as Chairman of Sovnarkom and the Council of Labour and Defence. No one else had quite so steady a presence in the Kremlin. The only possible exception was Sverdlov, who was both Central Committee Secretary and Chairman of the Soviet Central Executive Committee, and it was Sverdlov who directed state affairs when Lenin was shot on 30 August 1918. As soon as Lenin recovered, Sverdlov resumed his position as Lenin's right-hand man in Moscow. The dominance of Lenin and Sverdlov was such that their critics – and even some of their friends – described their rule as a duumvirate. Sverdlov was an imperious little man with an improbably deep voice and a penchant for dressing from head to toe in black leather; his energy seemed boundless. But on 16 March 1919 he died suddenly after a brief attack of 'Spanish' influenza. Deprived of a loyal adjutant, Lenin gave an impassioned eulogy at his graveside. Lenin and Sverdlov had not been friends. They spent no time relaxing in each other's company, and Lenin did not show much regard for Sverdlov's intellectual capacity or political understanding. But as an organiser, Sverdlov had been outstanding. He was irreplaceable and Lenin knew how much he was going to miss him.

In ensuing years he tried out a series of substitutes for Sverdlov in the Central Committee: Stasova in 1919, Krestinski, Serebryakov and Preobrazhenski in 1920, Molotov and others in 1921 and – most fatefully – Stalin in 1922. All except Stalin were more subordinate to Lenin than Sverdlov had been. In the frequent absences of Trotski, Stalin and Zinoviev, there was great latitude for Lenin as an individual to grasp the main levers of the central party and governmental machines.

His confident manipulation of the levers is remarkable against the background of a private life that had entered an unsettled phase. After recuperating from the assassination attempt, he returned to full-time political work in the Kremlin on 14 October 1918. In fact he was not in good health. He was suffering from his old problems of headaches and insomnia. He had coped by taking walks around the Kremlin's pathways at midday and midnight. His personal guards, who had no knowledge of his medical history, found this rather maddening since he could easily have been targeted by another gunman. Worse still, he disliked being surrounded by them and sometimes deliberately broke away from them.[9] Often he invited either Nadya or his sister Maria to join him. He needed to talk to people he could trust – and neither Maria nor Nadya pressed their ideas on him. His other form of exercise was his hunting trips, which he undertook with Bolshevik associates. The People's Commissars set off to slaughter the wildlife of the Moscow countryside. Lenin had last gone hunting when he was in Siberian exile and he was delighted to have a regular opportunity to go out with his rifle over his shoulder.

Yet the trips were dangerous from a medical viewpoint. On several occasions he felt a tightening round his chest and an acute pain in his legs. His reaction was to think up some excuse to sit down; he mentioned nothing to his shooting partners. Almost certainly he was suffering what are designated as transient ischaemic attacks (or mild heart attacks). Lenin must have been aware of their seriousness since he consulted medical textbooks whenever he had physical problems. The shadow of mortality grew longer. Lenin became ever more impatient to do what he could for the Revolution before he died.

His health was not the sole thing disturbing him. Although Nadezhda Konstantinovna's memoirs refer to no tension between husband and wife, the external signs suggest a different story. When Lenin moved out to the Gorki sanatorium, she did not go with him.[10] This would be explicable as feminist self-assertiveness if other things had not pointed to Nadezhda Konstantinovna's disgruntlement. It must be of some significance that among the first visitors to Lenin's bedside after the assassination attempt in August 1918 had been Inessa Armand.[11] Inessa was then working in Moscow as a state functionary for the province's economy and lived not far from the Kremlin. Her arrival in the Kremlin can hardly have been wonderful news to Nadezhda Konstantinovna. In late 1918 only a few persons could visit him and always they had to have an invitation or his prior permission. Lenin and Inessa had seen something of each other after the October Revolution since he had specifically asked that she should be invited to attend Sovnarkom sessions. Yet there is no evidence that Lenin resumed his affair with her (although this cannot be excluded). His days had been packed with work. What is more, he and Inessa were not in accord over politics; like most leading Bolsheviks, she had been thoroughly hostile to Lenin's campaign for the signing of the Treaty of Brest-Litovsk. But their friendship transcended politics, and, when Lenin lay prostrate with bullet wounds, he wanted her by his bedside.

Meanwhile Nadya's Graves's disease and her heart palpitations were bothering her, and soon after Lenin returned to the Kremlin she departed for the park in the Sokolniki district on the city's north-eastern edge; she stayed at her own request in a school where she was allocated a small first-floor room.[12] Her treatment remained in the hands of Professor Gete, the family doctor for both the Lenins and the Trotskis.[13] She stayed there through December and January. It was an odd move from a medical standpoint since the doctors could have more conveniently treated her if she had not left the apartment she shared with her husband and sister-in-law. Why, then, did she go? It may be that she needed a break from the busy routines of the Kremlin and that Professor Gete did not mind travelling out to examine her. But there are other possibilities. If indeed Nadya was shaken by Lenin's request to see Inessa after the shooting, perhaps Nadya simply decided to find some tranquillity by herself. She may have thought that by isolating herself she would provoke Lenin into some deeper appreciation of her as his wife and lifelong companion-in-arms.

This is as far as reasonable speculation can take us. Lenin, Nadya and Inessa did not leave further clues about their feelings at that time. Or, if they did, such clues have been lost to history. Nor should it be forgotten that, whatever the nature of Lenin's relationship with Inessa Armand in 1918–19, his preoccupation in life was still with politics. Making and consolidating the Revolution remained his supreme passion.

In any case, he kept a sense of marital obligation to Nadya and she in turn was gratified by his visits to her in Sokolniki. Usually he would arrive in the evening after work, accompanied by his sister Maria and driven by Stepan Gil.[14] On Sunday, 19 January 1919 this was very nearly the cause of his death. Lenin, who had had been asked by the children of the Sokolniki school to attend a fir-tree party, set out from the Kremlin with Maria, Gil and his current bodyguard I. V. Chebanov. When they reached the Sokolniki Chaussée, they heard a sharp whistle. It was already dark; into the snow-laden road leaped three armed men who commanded Gil to halt the car. Gil thought them to be policemen and he obeyed the order. (In mid-1918 he had ignored such an order and the police had fired at the car!) Quickly Lenin showed them his documents. But the men forced him and the other passengers out of the vehicle, put a gun to Lenin's temples and searched his pockets. Lenin remonstrated: 'My name is Lenin.' But they took no notice. The passengers still did not understand that the men were not policemen, and Maria asked to see their documents. The reply came back: 'Criminals don't need documents!' The thieves stole Lenin's Browning revolver and sped off in the car. Chebanov's only positive accomplishment was to save the can of milk they were bringing for Nadezhda Konstantinovna.

They trudged to the offices of the Sokolniki District Soviet, where Lenin had difficulty in convincing the clerk that he really was Lenin. Eventually the Soviet's chairman and his deputy appeared, and recognised Lenin. Thus Lenin and his group arrived late at the children's fir-tree party. On the same evening Dzierżyński organised a police hunt. The car was found after the robbers ran it into a snowdrift. A Red Army soldier and a policeman lay dead by the side of the vehicle: this could easily have been the fate of Lenin and his partners. Dzierżyński intensified the hunt. The robbers were detected and interrogated. They argued that they had misunderstood what Lenin had said to them. Instead of 'Lenin', they had heard 'Levin'. But, having made their escape, they re-examined the documents and recognised who their victim really was. Their audacity was extraordinary. One of them, Yakov Koshelnikov, wanted to return immediately and kill Lenin. He calculated that the blame would be placed on counter-revolutionaries. There might even, Koshelnikov fantasised, be a *coup d'état* and he argued that in such a situation there would be no manhunt for the robbers. His fellow gang members, however, rejected his advice. Lenin was luckier than he knew at the time.[15]

Yet Lenin and the other central Bolshevik leaders could not help but recognise the fragility of the state's rule over Russia. Biographies in the past have tended to overlook this. If a gang of three desperadoes in the capital could casually ponder whether to go back and assassinate the head of the government, things had come to a pretty pass. Indeed they had always been at a pretty pass and were not to undergo improvement until after the Civil War. Chaos and confusion in the meantime was the norm.

Over the winter of 1918–19 there were several attempts to straighten out the crooked corners of the state's institutions. By and large, Lenin had the support of officialdom of his party in this process. Soviets, party committees, trade unions and factory-workshop committees were brought to account by a central party and government apparatus that no longer felt inhibited by the need to consult with 'the localities'. The Party Central Committee and Sovnarkom pressed for all institutions to behave in a more obedient, orderly, military-style fashion. The need for this had become acute in November 1918. Until then the Red Army had been fighting against forces assembled by the Socialist-Revolutionary ministers of Komuch in Samara, and Trotski had been able to report several successes. Kazan was retaken on 10 September. The Komuch army, despite having been strengthened by the Czechoslovak Legion, was no match for the Reds. But in the meantime other armies had been formed to invade central Russia. These were led not by socialists but by former Imperial Army officers who detested not only Bolshevism but also socialism in general, as well as most kinds of liberalism. In southern Russia a Volunteer Army had gathered under the leadership of Generals Alexeev and Kornilov. In mid-Siberia there was another anti-Bolshevik contingent led by Admiral Kolchak. In Estonia, General Yudenich was putting together yet another. The military threat that had been posed by Komuch was about to be intensified.

Once again, neither Lenin nor the rest of the Central Committee had any presentiment of this. Until then one anti-Bolshevik force seemed much like any other. But on 18 November 1918 Admiral Kolchak's high command arrested the Socialist-Revolutionaries in Omsk and proclaimed Kolchak as Supreme Ruler of All Russia. The objective of this White Army was to move rapidly through to the Urals and then into central Russia. As they came to the strategically important Urals city of Perm in December, a desperate defence was expected. Instead the Bolshevik party and the local Soviet regime fell apart. In the ensuing winter months a triumphant Kolchak looked close to taking Lenin's place in the Kremlin.

Lenin's reaction to the Perm disaster showed up his weaknesses in this initial period of the Civil War. He had a matchless knowledge of the mechanisms of the supreme state agencies. He saw to it, too, that he stayed in touch with popular feelings by means of his trips around Moscow and his audiences with peasant petitioners from the provinces (even though he ruthlessly trampled on such feelings whenever he felt that considerations of either Marxist ideology or *Realpolitik* should take precedence). But Lenin had little appreciation of the enormous chaos of the regime lower down the administrative hierarchy from the Kremlin. Sitting in his office, he could rely on the phones working. He could order books from libraries and read the day's papers on the morning of publication. He could count on personal assistants and secretaries to do whatever he wanted of them, and he never wanted for food, clothing and shelter. He did not live sumptuously in the Kremlin; but by the standards of party, government and army officials outside Moscow he was a pretty protected, not to say pampered, leader. His isolation from provincial reality dissuaded him from blaming any setbacks on his own policies or upon the inherent difficulties of politics in the regions. Instead he chastised individuals. Always they were judged too weak, too stupid or too dissolute. In the case of the military *débâcle* at Perm, Lenin simply concluded that one of the main local officials, M. M. Lashevich, had been drunk on the job.[16]

But Lenin himself was coming in for fierce criticism by lower party and governmental officials. They wanted a tighter hierarchy inside the Soviet state than currently existed, and accused Lenin of tardiness in imposing it. In short, they demanded that the central political leadership should properly centralise the state administration. Some insisted that this process should be accompanied by provisions for democratic accountability within both the party and the soviets. These critics became known as the Democratic Centralists and were led by N. Osinski and T. D. Sapronov. Another group of disgruntled local officials could not care less whether democratic accountability – even in the extremely limited form proposed by the Democratic Centralists – was secured. They simply wanted the state machinery to function reliably. Among such critics was Lazar Kaganovich. Osinski, Sapronov and Kaganovich went on carping at Lenin and Sverdlov from their different standpoints.

These were not the only criticisms of policy. Trotski, with Lenin's consent, had introduced Imperial Army officers into the Red Army. To each of them he attached a political commissar to keep watch over their loyalty; and for good measure he took hostages from their families who would pay with their lives for any acts of treachery. But Trotski did not stop at that. He shot political commissars, too, if they disobeyed orders. He lined up regiments of deserters and carried out the Roman punishment of decimation. He scorned the notion that long-standing Bolshevik party officials should have no special treatment in the Red Army. For many Bolsheviks in the armed forces, this was insufferable and they demanded military reform. Some of them even argued that Trotski, who had not been a Bolshevik before 1917, might emerge from the armed forces like Napoleon Bonaparte in the French Revolution and become dictator. Lenin tried to avoid the controversy for as long as possible. But inside the party a so-called Military Opposition – inspired behind the scenes by Stalin, Trotski's bitter enemy – demanded the sacking of the former Imperial Army officers. Only when it came to a definitive choice between the continuation of the policy and Trotski's resignation did Lenin agree to arbitrate; and by and large he backed Trotski rather than lose him as People's Commissar of Military Affairs.

Other changes of policy were made in that terrible winter. On 2 December the committees of the village poor were scrapped after it was found that they caused more harm than benefit to the party in the countryside. Peasants basically disliked the divisiveness introduced by the committees. Moreover, it frequently occurred that the committees harassed not just the richer households but the 'middle peasantry' that, as Lenin had repeatedly declared, the party wanted to keep on its side. The abolition of the committees was notable in a couple of ways. The first was that Lenin dropped the policy without acknowledging that the mistake in introducing it had been principally his own. He did not often admit to past error, and this occasion was no exception. Secondly, it was evident that the committees of the village poor, despite being unpopular with the peasantry, remained congenial to party officials. Lenin had to convince his party of the practical need to avoid alienating popular opinion by too rapid and coercive a movement in the direction of socialist measures. Not for the last time.

The need for him to react speedily to situations was at a premium. Abroad the Great War drew abruptly to a close on the western front on 11 November when the Central Powers were compelled, after the failure of their massive summer offensive, to sue for an armistice. Britain, France, Italy and the USA had triumphed. Lenin's instant reaction was to abrogate the Treaty of Brest-Litovsk. The eight months of the 'obscene peace' were at an end. Lenin could at last demonstrate to his critics in the party that he was genuinely committed to 'European socialist Revolution'. Finance, political propaganda (including a German translation of *The State and Revolution*) and envoys were rushed from Moscow to Berlin. The assumption was that military defeat had brought about a revolutionary situation; neither Lenin nor the rest of the Central Committee were concerned about the potential response of the Western Allies. The priority had to be the promotion of a far-left socialist seizure of power in Germany. Such an achievement would, thought Lenin, make for a political 'block' between Russia and Germany that no army in the world could overthrow. The main problem was that no communist party yet existed in Germany. Instead Lenin would have to work through the Spartacus League headed by Karl Liebknecht and Rosa Luxemburg, and with this in mind he initiated moves to convoke a founding meeting of a Communist International. The European revolutionary political offensive would require careful preparation.

Yet the German government after Wilhelm II's abdication was constituted by leaders of the German Social-Democratic Party who utterly disapproved not only of Lenin and the October Revolution but also of Liebknecht and Luxemburg. The Spartacus League had long ago abandoned hope in the German Social-Democratic Party. Liebknecht and Luxemburg went their own way and planned insurrection. Yet even this could not bring unconditional comfort to Lenin. For Liebknecht and Luxemburg were not exactly admirers of Lenin. In particular, Luxemburg had written criticising Leninist agrarian policy (too easy upon 'petit-bourgeois' peasants), national policy (too indulgent to the non-Russians) and policy on government (disgracefully anti-democratic). If the Spartacus League succeeded, then the Bolsheviks in Russia might well encounter problems both in the rest of Europe and in Russia. But if it failed, what would be left of the strategic prognosis of Bolshevism?

Things turned out badly for the Spartacists. On 6 January 1919 they attempted to overturn the socialist government in Berlin. The Defence Minister Gustav Noske mobilised every available anti-communist unit, including troops recently demobilised from the western and eastern fronts. The Spartacus League was hopelessly outgunned. Liebknecht and Luxemburg were captured and butchered and their bodies were deposited outside the Zoological Gardens. This was a disaster for international communism, but Lenin lost no sleep over it. At least, he foresaw, there would be greater freedom than he had expected in the organisation of the Third International; and since he continued to assume that the German working class was culturally superior to Russian workers he had no doubt that a successful socialist revolution would anyway soon occur in Berlin. The practical snag was that communist parties did not exist outside Russia. Lenin would have to draw delegates from far-left organisations that had yet to align themselves with the policies of the October Revolution. He would also have to surmount the travel problems that many such delegates would encounter at a time when Soviet Russia had no diplomatic relations with the outside world.

The end of the Great War also had consequences in Russia's borderlands. Since the signature of the Brest-Litovsk Treaty a great western swathe of the former Russian Empire had lain outside the proclaimed sovereignty of Sovnarkom. The withdrawal of the German forces gave Lenin his opportunity to invade this region and set up organs of 'Soviet power'. The Red Army, aided by local volunteers, made rapid progress; and, at Lenin's insistence, it did not incorporate the region into the Russian Socialist Federal Soviet Republic but established independent Soviet republics in Estonia, Lithuania and Belorussia, Latvia and Ukraine.

The Russian Socialist Federal Soviet Republic would have ties with each of them on a bilateral and equal basis.

The establishment of a growing number of independent Soviet republics was not welcomed by many leading Bolsheviks, especially those who had been brought up in the borderlands and who had been drawn towards Bolshevism precisely because of its commitment to eradicating nationalism. Independent Soviet republics appeared to them – and several of the most articulate among them were Jews who felt especially vulnerable to the anti-semitism of the region's nationalists – as yet another dereliction of universal socialist values. Lenin, of course, was partly Jewish by ancestry. But he had not had a youth scarred by negative national discrimination. He had been brought up as a Russian European and had campaigned on this platform as a politician, and he hated any manifestations of what he called Great Russian chauvinism. His background enabled him to take a more detached standpoint on 'the national question' than most of his colleagues. National and ethnic sensitivities in the borderlands, he insisted, had to be respected. His party was aghast at this; but he tried to explain that he was taking precautions against the independent Soviet republics being able to behave independently. The communist parties in the republics would be treated as mere regional organisations of the Russian communist party and its Central Committee. Real power would thus be held not in the 'independent' Soviet republics but in Moscow.

Over the winter of 1918–19 the mood in the Bolshevik Central Committee was schizophrenic. Europe was again on the boil, and the possibility of a European socialist revolution was in the thoughts of all central party leaders. Yet to the east there was cause for intense worry. Kolchak was rampaging further towards Moscow from Perm. There might well soon be Soviet republics in Warsaw, Prague and Berlin. But would socialism survive in the cities of the October 1917 Revolution?

As the First Congress of the Third International (Comintern) opened in the Kremlin precinct on 2 March 1919, Lenin stressed the imminence of Revolution in Europe. It was an unprepossessing gathering for an organisation that was aimed at changing the face of world politics. There were thirty-four delegates, yet all but four of them were already resident in Russia. Lenin and his associates had picked people who came from other countries and then given them a mandate to speak on behalf of the entire far left. The French revolutionary grouping represented in Moscow anyway had only twelve members across all France. Lenin had got up to this sort of trick often enough before the Great War at

Bolshevik meetings that he defined as meetings of the entire party. But the First Comintern Congress was even more brazenly organised under Bolshevik auspices. The German representative Hugo Eberlein protested against manipulation, but was cajoled into accepting a *fait accompli*; he was made to feel that otherwise he would spoil the general mood of enthusiasm. Lenin added to the embarrassment by reading out a letter purporting to come from the Soviet of Workers' Deputies in the English Midlands. This was poppycock, and it is quite likely that Lenin knew it. But it had the necessary effect: the Comintern Congress applauded the magnificent 'news' and looked forward to the expansion of the socialist Revolution to the west of Russia.

Once the pleasantries had been completed, the Bolshevik leadership stepped forward with a series of draft resolutions that confirmed their dominance of the proceedings. Lenin spoke on 'bourgeois democracy and the dictatorship of the proletariat'. His argument was that the civic freedoms that existed in capitalist countries were enjoyed exclusively by the middle classes; and Lenin and succeeding Bolshevik speakers – Bukharin, Zinoviev, Osinski and Trotski reinforced the message that Kautskyite hopes of effecting a socialist transformation in Europe by largely parliamentary methods were doomed to failure. Not even Lenin pushed his luck too hard. He barely referred to Marx, Engels and Marxism, to communism, to civil war or to the role and internal organisation of the party. This omission was no coincidence. The Bolshevik leadership's objective at the First Comintern Congress was to obtain consent to the founding of the new organisation and to secure control over it in the immediate future. Having got agreement to a generally anti-parliamentary strategy, Lenin and his fellow leaders would later be able to impose further details of ideology and tactics. The Comintern's foundation may have been organisationally ramshackle, but the consequences for the world over the next couple of decades were immense. A body with pretensions to undermining global capitalism had been created, and every political trend to the right of communism learned to recognise the threat posed from Moscow.

Quite how the threat would be realised was as yet unclear. Not even Lenin had accurate information or instincts about the current developments in world politics. Some of his prognoses were so awry that they were kept permanently out of the various editions of his collected speeches. A striking example is the funeral oration he delivered at the Volkovo Cemetery in Petrograd on 13 March 1919 after the death of his brother-in-law Mark Yelizarov:[17]

France is preparing to hurl herself upon Italy, they haven't shared the booty [from the Great War]. Japan is arming herself against America ... The working masses of Paris, London and New York have translated the word 'soviets' into their own languages ... We'll soon see the birth of the World Federal Soviet Republic.

Few things were more unlikely than a Franco-Italian war. Japan was distrustful of the USA, but hardly in belligerent mood. Nor in truth did French, British and American workers translate Russian vocabulary; instead they kept words like 'soviets' in their transliterated form as if wishing to emphasise the exotic nature of what they were reading about Russia in their newspapers. Lenin was not just trying to cheer his supporters. He was in a genuinely elevated mood, and let his imagination and ideology take over from cool judgement.

He was brought down to earth in the same month at his own party's Eighth Congress. There was hardly a policy that was not controversial among leading Bolsheviks. Lenin and the Central Committee were applauded for convoking the Comintern Congress, but for precious little else. The opening report was given by Lenin himself, who was greeted by shouts of 'Long live Ilich!' He gave no opening to any critic past or present. The Brest-Litovsk Treaty had been right. The establishment of the 'committees of the village poor' had been right (even though they had had to be abolished). The use of Imperial Army officers had been right. The creation of independent Soviet republics had been right. The Central Committee had done its bit and any faults were to be attributed to those who carried out the policies, not the policy-makers. If there were problems, they had not arisen in Moscow: 'Organisational activity has never been a strong side of Russians in general and the Bolsheviks in particular, and in the meantime the main task of the proletarian revolution is precisely an *organisational task.*' Lenin was attempting to throw back all the problems in the face of his critics. Either they failed, out of ignorance, to understand the wisdom of the policies or they fell short as implementers of the wise measures. The Central Committee could not be faulted.

This was quite a claim. The Bolsheviks had traditionally been seen as the most ideological and most tightly organised of Russian political bodies. They had come into existence in 1903 precisely because of their rejection of amateurism in the organisational life of the party in the Russian Empire, and Lenin's *What Is to Be Done?* had been their cardinal factional text. The reality had always been different: the Bolsheviks had usually been as chaotic and ill-disciplined as any other Russian political party until the last few months. Yes, Lenin was trying to obviate criticism of the Central Committee. But also he was blurting out what he genuinely felt in general terms. He adhered to an ethnic hierarchy in his revolutionary politics. For him, Germans were culturally superior to Britons and French, who in turn were superior to Finns; and, of course, Finns had a distinct edge over the Russians. Lenin was experiencing constant frustration from the country he now found himself in. It did not help that a civil war was raging; but he knew that, even without the fighting, he would find Russia a terrible place in which to make a revolution.

Thus the young Lenin who wanted to turn Russia into a 'European', 'Western' country had not faded away. At the Comintern Congress he had played up the Russian theme: the Bolsheviks had started a socialist revolution and the other Europeans had to agree to model themselves on the Russians. At the Eighth Party Congress he chastised the Bolsheviks for being too Russian. The result was a wrangle: several of his critics were fellow leaders who had been his co-speakers at the Comintern Congress. Lenin in his turn was attacked by Osinski for running the party and government on the principles of an amateur; he was also accused by Bukharin of insufficient radicalism in drafting the Party Programme. On and on it went. The granting of state independence to Finland was described as a fiasco since Lenin's expectation had been thwarted that a Finnish Soviet republic would result. By then Lenin was having such a hard time that he opted to let others defend Trotski on the matter of the Red Army's organisation. Yet he could not entirely avoid debate, and when the discussion began in a secret Congress, Lenin not only defended Trotski but also chastised Stalin for the excessive military losses on the southern front. As party leader he would impose himself.

On nearly every main policy he got his way. He had to compromise a little on the 'military question'; he also had to find an equivocal set of words on the 'national question': his slogan of 'the freedom of secession for nations in reality' was too much for most delegates. But he got his way more successfully on the 'agrarian question'. The Congress agreed that the middling sections of the peasantry should be indulged. Possibly it helped, too, that news of the outbreak of a Hungarian socialist revolution was delivered towards the end of the proceedings. Lenin rose to the occasion. Raising his fist, he strutted forward to the edge of the platform and – with all the force of his lungs – he assured the audience:

'We are convinced that *this will be the last heavy half-year.*' He noted that international imperialism had not yet been defeated. But he was unworried. 'This wild beast', he affirmed, 'will perish and socialism will conquer throughout the world.'

23

EXPANDING THE REVOLUTION

April 1919 to April 1920

In the year and a half after the October Revolution the Bolsheviks had laid the foundations for a unique state that lasted in Russia for seven decades and was the model for communist regimes covering a third of the inhabited world after the Second World War. There was a single ruling party. There was a politically subordinate legislature, executive and judiciary. The party in reality was the supreme state agency and Lenin in all but name was the supreme leader of that agency.

Not everything was yet in place. The party had not thoroughly subordinated the other state agencies. In some respects it did not try to. Once the Politburo had fixed the personnel appointments and the strategy, the Red Army operated without interference; and the Cheka, which had been protected by Lenin since its creation, was criticised but never seriously punished for its frequent 'excesses'. Thus the state was not as tightly co-ordinated as Leninist political doctrines demanded. Furthermore, there were several aspects of the later one-party state that had not been introduced. As yet there was no decision on the permanent constitutional interrelationship of the various Soviet republics. There was no comprehensive plan for dealing with the former upper social classes once the Civil War had been won. Nor had the party's strategy been fixed for the creation of a new socialist culture, for conditions of work, remuneration and recreation and even for the long-term role of the party in the one-party state. Wide gaps existed in Leninist theory about dictatorship, democracy, social justice and human rights. Even though the general architecture of the state had already been established, much about the Soviet order had yet to be elaborated.

It was unclear in spring 1919 that the building would stand much longer. The Whites were still confident that their cause would prevail in Russia and that they would soon drive the Reds from the Kremlin. This was not the only civil war at the time. There was another Russian civil war, waged on a local basis, between the Russian peasantry on one side and any army – whether Red or White – in the vicinity. In each borderland of the former Russian Empire there were also civil and ethnic wars. But Lenin was preoccupied by one of these wars: the war waged by his Red Army on three great, moving fronts against the White forces of Kolchak, Denikin and Yudenich. The Red commanders assumed that, if and when this war had been won, they would easily proceed to victory in the others; and the Politburo under Lenin added that such a victory would constitute only the preface to chapters of further revolutionary expansion in central and western Europe.

But could they win the Civil War in Russia? Lenin's prophecy in March 1919 that Bolsheviks would have only one 'last heavy half-year' was only a little over-optimistic. The military campaigns went in favour of the Reds. Admiral Kolchak's advance into central Russia was held up in April, and Ufa in the southern Urals fell back into the Red Army's hands in June. Lenin goaded his leading political commissars and generals relentlessly. Always he demanded greater effort and ruthlessness. He predicted doom unless instant success could be obtained. To the Revolutionary-Military Soviet preparing an offensive against Kolchak from its temporary base in Lenin's native town Simbirsk, he telegraphed: 'If we don't conquer the Urals before the winter, I consider the death of the Revolution inevitable. Concentrate all the forces.'[1] From a strategic standpoint this was nonsense: there was no conclusive reason to believe that Kolchak had to be defeated by late autumn. But Lenin wanted to incite his subordinates. He so much liked the phrase about the death of the Revolution that he used it in another telegram on the same day to leading commissars on an entirely different front, in Kiev over five hundred miles to the south-west of Moscow.[2]

The city of Perm, where the Reds had been ignominiously defeated in December 1918, was retrieved in July 1919, and Kolchak fled into mid-Siberia, never to return. Kolchak's primacy among the White commanders had been recognised by Anton Denikin in southern Russia. Denikin was ready to begin his own assault on the Red heartland in July 1919. He did this by splitting his forces. One wing was sent across the Don Basin, the other northwards up the river Volga. Denikin's strategy was uncomplicated. He issued a Moscow Directive to move in a straight line as fast as possible towards the capital. The recent defeat of Kolchak freed the Reds to strengthen their defence. In summer 1919 they drove Denikin back into Ukraine. The news was greeted with huge acclaim in the Kremlin. Until the battles in northern Russia there had been a distinct possibility that Denikin would succeed where Kolchak had failed. But Lenin's delight was given no public display. The Bolshevik Central

Committee and Sovnarkom held no celebration. He devoted no speech or article to the event. War was not like Marxist theory or economic policy. War was something to be won, but not theorised – and perhaps theorising anyway would have made winning less likely.

Winning, for Lenin, was everything. After his recovery from the August 1918 assassination attempt, his personal assistant Bonch-Bruevich persuaded him to have a short film made in the Kremlin precinct. The aim was to prove that he was still alive. It was not all that interesting a performance by Lenin and Bonch-Bruevich:

The scene: Lenin and Bonch-Bruevich stand near a tree inside the Kremlin precinct.

The paraphernalia: Lenin appears wearing his three-piece suit while Bonch-Bruevich, obviously a softy, appears in a raincoat.

The action: Lenin and Bonch-Bruevich talk together, and Bonch puts him at his ease so that Lenin is seen offering a lively reaction to something said by Bonch.

The conversation: The contents of the conversation are not known.

The film had a negligible impact. Everyone who might have attended the cinema in the Civil War was scrabbling after food and fuel, and Russian cinemas were short of the equipment they needed to put the Sovnarkom Chairman on screen. Lenin anyway could not relax in front of the moving-action camera; the conversation with Bonch-Bruevich was nowhere near as gripping for an audience as films taken of Kerenski boarding trains and waving at crowds in 1917. Lenin had no such inhibition about photographs, to which he was more accustomed. After seizing power, he had initially forbidden these to be taken of him, a prohibition resulting not from shyness but from a pragmatic judgement about propaganda. In July 1917 he had had to shave off his beard, and only began to grow it again on 25 October 1917. Not till January 1918, when he again felt happy about the way he looked, did he allow an official photographer to get near him. Although he did this in the interests of publicising his party and its policies, he took no expert advice. The whole business of propaganda remained amateurish for several years and each party leader did things his own way.

Nevertheless there was an appreciation of Lenin's unique importance as party leader and increasingly he was singled out for special attention in *Pravda*. The campaign to erect a political cult of him began in earnest after the attempt on his life in August 1918. Zinoviev wrote a biography of him. Articles appeared in party and government newspapers. Posters were pasted up. No Bolshevik – apart from Trotski in the Red Army – was accorded such individual acclaim as Lenin.

The image was of a selfless leader brought low by humanity's enemies. The party's writers described him as an authentic son of Russia and a fighter for material improvements, for enlightenment and for peace. Lenin appeared as a Soviet Christ: superhuman powers were attributed to him. His survival was ascribed to a miracle; the writers did not bother to explain how to reconcile this with their militant atheism. All manner of nastiness was attributed to his assassins. There was a story that the bullets had been tipped with a deadly poison used on the arrows of South American Indians. Another tale suggested that the Allies had been the instigators of the attack. Ludicrous as this was, the counter-propaganda of the anti-Red forces was no nearer to the truth. The posters and printed handouts of the Whites were forerunners of German Nazism. In them, Lenin appeared as a demonic entity. Usually he was represented alongside Trotski as co-leader of an international Jewish conspiracy pernicious to both country and world civilisation. Strife, blood, vengeance: these were the inevitable results of Russia's having fallen victim to Leninism.

Of course, Lenin was indeed of part-Jewish 'ethnic' descent. He was also truly an internationalist. He really did initiate and aggravate mayhem in Russia and detested most forms of Russian patriotism. And yet the White notion that he was leading a Judaeo-Masonic crusade against Mother Russia was just as preposterous as the Red notion that he was the secular Christ of the Great Socialist Revolution. Whether demonised or sanctified, he was the object of political propaganda. But he did not mind. He took no heed of what the Whites said of him, and although he apparently felt distaste for adulatory remarks made about him in his presence, he was not unduly disconcerted by the Lenin cult in general and did not seek to terminate it.

He must have calculated that the cult would help to consolidate the regime and his position within it. He understood the need to adapt his political message to his surroundings and knew that most Russians, being either peasants or people who had left the villages only recently, were not well informed about public life. The party's message had to fit the lineaments of the country's popular culture, as he explained to Maxim Gorki:[3]

> Well, in your opinion, millions of peasants with rifles in their hands: they're a threat to culture, aren't they? Do you really think

that the Constituent Assembly would have been able to cope with [their] anarchism? You who make such a noise about the anarchism in the countryside ought to understand our work better than anyone. We've got to show the mass of Russians something very simple, very accessible to their way of reasoning. Soviets and communism are a simple thing.

Gorki was rather shocked by the revelation that Lenin obviously had a deep suspicion of ordinary Russians. For Lenin, they were like promising children who had yet to go to school. He thought this not just about the party's enemies – kulaks, priests, merchants, bankers and nobles – but about those whom the party supposedly cherished: the lower social classes.

Although peasants incurred his special ire, even workers could irritate him by sticking to the traditions of the religious calendar. In advance of the summertime feast day of St Nicholas he exclaimed: 'It's stupid to be reconciled to the "Nikola" festival. We must get all the Chekas up on their feet and shoot people who don't turn up for work because of the "Nikola" festival.'[4] Lenin explained that similar preventive violence should be prepared for the festivals at Christmas and New Year. Some workers' friend!

He was at his angriest, needless to say, about the middle and upper classes. For example, he upbraided Zinoviev for trying to prevent Petrograd workers from rampaging around the city's affluent districts. Another correspondent received the following telegram, and there is hardly anything like it as a justification of repression:[5]

> There can be no avoiding the arrest of the *entire* Kadet party and its near-Kadet supporters so as to pre-empt conspiracies. They're capable – the whole bunch – of giving assistance to the conspirators. It's criminal not to arrest them. It's better for dozens and hundreds of intellectuals to serve days and weeks in prison than that 10,000 should take a beating. Eh, eh! Better!

There was also an element of sheer pleasure in the terror he wanted to inflict:[6]

> It is *devilishly* important to finish off Yudenich (precisely to finish him off: give him a *thorough* beating). If the offensive [by him] has started, isn't it possible to mobilise 20 thousand Petrograd workers plus 10 thousand bourgeois, place artillery behind them, shoot several hundred and achieve a real mass impact on Yudenich?

This statement was so outrageous that it was kept secret until after the collapse of the Soviet Union.

How on earth were his commanders meant to line up the contingent of victims as Yudenich's troops bore down on them? Anyway the Red Army high command took the view that what mattered to Lenin were fast military victories and that the armed forces knew best how to obtain these. (Not that this was any excuse for his sadistic self-indulgence.) For a short while, in October 1919, there was panic in Petrograd when Yudenich marched from Estonia. Zinoviev's nerves were shattered. Even Lenin, despite his suggestion on tactics, queried whether the city could be defended. Trotski enjoyed a rare moment of being able to press for a more confident attitude. The Revolution had to be defended and Petrograd saved. The old capital was the symbol of the Revolution. And so the defences were reinforced. The Red Army, albeit without being proceeded by a screen of middle-class prisoners, dispersed the forces of Yudenich; and as Denikin was simultaneously preparing to evacuate his army from Kiev, it was clear that the Civil War's crucial battles were over. The Reds had conquered the Russian Empire's core. Moscow, Petrograd and Kiev were run by Bolshevik administrations.

Foreign military powers were stronger than the Reds, but faced internal obstacles to their armed intervention in Russia. Unrest among their socialist parties was a factor. Although Lenin was by no means popular except with groups on the far left, a reluctance prevailed among socialists to castigate the Bolsheviks unequivocally. The soldiers who had fought and won the Great War did not relish the prospect of fighting the Red Army. The victorious Allies – France, the United Kingdom, the USA and Italy – decided to end their economic blockade of Soviet Russia. Kiev, occupied by Denikin in summer 1919, was taken again by the Reds in December. Where Soviet republics had been established in the winter of 1918–19, they began again to be installed. Lenin searched Europe for a sign that 'socialist Revolution' might be expanded west-wards. He thought of northern Italy. He looked at the Czech lands, hoped that these might be a bridge across which the Red Army might march into Germany. Temporarily he had to give up hope for Hungary since Béla Kun's communist state in Budapest had been overrun by counter-revolutionaries in August 1919. But still he wanted to launch a 'revolutionary war'. He could not imagine that his Soviet republic would survive unless a fraternal socialist party elsewhere seized power and overturned capitalism. Revolution had to be consolidated in Russia and initiated in Europe – the two processes would reinforce each other.

Already Lenin was considering how his party and government might promote post-war reconstruction. Since the October Revolution, and especially since mid-1918, the movement of policy had been unilinear. Less room was left for other parties in which to operate. The Left Socialist-Revolutionaries were hunted. The Socialist-Revolutionaries who had set up the Komuch administration were treated as counter-revolutionaries even though individual members were allowed to join civilian bodies as well as the Red armed forces. The Mensheviks kept a few newspapers going, but were frequently harassed and none of their leaders could count on remaining free. Sovnarkom was running a one-party state in all but name. It operated a virtual monopoly over what could be printed. It declared the fundamental correctness of Marxism. It had formally nationalised the industrial, transport and banking sectors of the economy and introduced massive legal restrictions on private activity in commerce and agriculture. It was starting to offer national and ethnic autonomy to the non-Russians it ruled over, but was intent upon maintaining the old multinational state of the Romanovs intact whatever the opinions of the populace. Such an outcome pleased Lenin. Even when he had not done the drafting, he agreed with the plans.

But how on earth could a case be made for the communist economics of wartime? In fact Lenin, Sovnarkom's principal theorist, made no attempt at a fundamental defence. In trying to explain his policies in the Civil War, some writers have postulated that he was pushed towards them solely by the unexpected and unpredictable circumstances after October 1917.[7] The more traditional Western idea is that they were always his intended policies but had been kept secret until he had power. The likelihood is that neither is true. He had often been warned by the Mensheviks and Socialist-Revolutionaries about the circumstances that would result from a seizure of power by his party. He chose to ignore the predictions. But in doing so, he operated not so much on the basis of a secret grand plan as upon his general assumptions about Revolution. This enabled him to formulate policies as the situation changed with immense rapidity. When he hugely increased state economic ownership even beyond his specifications before October 1917, he could draw upon a range of operational assumptions. He approved of centralism, governmental control, coercion and class struggle; he hated private profit and longed to crush the social groups which benefited from it. And having witnessed the increase in state powers in the capitalist countries in the Great War, he assumed that the socialist dictatorship should aim at an even greater increase in Russia.

Thus he spoke of the iniquity of kulaks (killing was too good for them) and factory owners and bankers (why shouldn't they lose their factories and banks to the state?). He argued for the eradication of envy, greed and theft. He argued for a fully socialist economy to be established; and he implied that the current policies would put industry, agriculture, transport and commerce back on their feet. As time went on, moreover, he found the policies more and more congenial. He hoped to prolong them after the Civil War was over.

In this he was a typical Bolshevik of the time. A consensus had been reached about how best to run the party and the state, to transform society and spread the Revolution abroad. Of course, several factions, groupings and individuals breached this consensus. The Democratic Centralists continued to demand that the lower party bodies should be enabled to influence the Central Committee and, increasingly, that the soviets should obtain a degree of autonomy from the party. Another faction, the Workers' Opposition, went much further. Led by Alexander Shlyapnikov and Alexandra Kollontai, the critics attacked Lenin for failing to abide by his own precepts of 1917. They wanted workers and peasants to exercise greater authority over economic and social life. They called for trade unions and soviets as well as the party to be engaged in politics, and urged a democratisation of political structures. This was an awful affront to Lenin's Bolshevism as it had developed after the October Revolution. He dealt with it ruthlessly. The factionalists found themselves asked by the Secretariat of the Central Committee to move to jobs outside the main industrial cities of Russia. Democratic Centralist leaders were sent in disproportionate numbers to Ukraine, where they would be unable to unsettle policies in the party as a whole.

There were divergences among the Central Committee members themselves. The trouble came from the factions of the Democratic Centralists and Workers' Opposition. But there were other less predictable spats. Kamenev and Bukharin complained about the arbitrariness of conduct allowed to the Cheka by Lenin. But by and large Lenin prevented reform; the Cheka proceeded with its Red Terror unimpeded by the need to hand over its victims to the People's Commissariat of Justice.

Neither Kamenev nor Bukharin believed strongly enough in procedures of jurisprudence to take their arguments further, and Lenin offered Bukharin a small concession: he was given the function of liaising with Dzierżyński, the Cheka Chairman, on the Central Committee's behalf. But in another dispute in the Central Committee there was, in

Lenin's opinion, no room for compromise. In this instance his adversary was none other than Trotski, whose tour of the military front in the Urals had convinced him that the party's economic policy had to be changed. In February 1920 Trotski called for a partial repeal of the grain-requisitioning measures. His reasoning was that the campaigns of expropriation by the state created a vicious circle of hoarding by peasants, state violence, reduction of the sown area and peasant rebellions. Instead he proposed that in certain agricultural regions there should be a restriction on the amount of seizable grain. Peasant households, Trotski declared, should be allowed to trade their grain surplus. The circle had to be broken if there was to be an end to the famine, ruin and chaos in the country.

This proposal was phrased in pragmatic terms. Trotski was no more moved to moral indignation on the peasants' behalf than was any other Bolshevik leader. He was exercised by the threat of agrarian dissolution. Usually Lenin was alive to the need to adjust policy for practical reasons. But not on this occasion. In 1918–19, reacting to the emergency in food supplies, he favoured state monopolies in official economic policy. Throughout the Civil War he claimed that there was no genuine scarcity of grain. Kulak hoarders, he claimed, were the beginning and end of the problem. For this reason he rejected Trotski's diagnosis. It was a heated meeting of the Central Committee, and Lenin and Trotski criticised each other ferociously. Lenin got so worked up that he accused Trotski of supporting 'Free Trade'.[8] Since this was a policy of nineteenth-century British capitalists, the charge was wounding to Trotski, who did not like being compared to Richard Cobden, Robert Peel and John Bright. Lenin's words were indeed unjustified, for Trotski was not proposing unrestricted or permanent agrarian reform; he did not even want it to be applied to the whole country. But Lenin was pretty sure of a majority, and triumphed by eleven votes to four.

Usually when Lenin argued in the Central Committee, he kept control of himself. His anger on this occasion may have stemmed from resentment at Trotski's attempt to prescribe economic policy from his post as People's Commissar of Military Affairs. Lenin had become accustomed to dominating the civilian agenda. But also he was sure that the party, once it had ascended the summit of state economic ownership, should not climb down. He was in fiery, confident mood. Trotski was not going to be permitted to disturb him or unsettle his policies.

Even Lenin, whose ability to take pragmatic decisions in order to save his party from disaster was legendary, had his own lapses when ideology occluded his vision. Trotski had the advantage of being able to observe provincial Russia on his trips to the war fronts. By contrast Lenin's experience of the country after the October Revolution was restricted to Moscow, Petrograd and a handful of villages outside Moscow – and he also depended on the letters he received and the oral reports made to him in the Kremlin. But this will not do as an explanation of Lenin's foolishness in rejecting Trotski's proposal. Lenin had greater knowledge of Russia's situation than is usually suspected. Daily he walked in the streets around the Kremlin; when his bodyguards complained about his casual attitude, he chastised them for denying the civil rights of each Soviet citizen to the Chairman of Sovnarkom.[9] The streets of the capital were not very different from streets elsewhere. Lenin had frequently observed the beggars, the poor and the hungry. He saw the chaos and disorder. Lenin himself had been shot at. He had been robbed by bandits. He could not even depend on the honesty of the bodyguards assigned to him: on one unforgettable occasion he briefly left his jacket behind in his office and returned to discover that one of his bodyguards had filched his Browning revolver.[10]

It was a fine dictatorship when the supreme leader was treated contemptuously by his underlings! Lenin had to explode with anger before the revolver was given back. There was a long way to be travelled before most ordinary workers and peasants would learn Marxist tenets and start to act like disciplined socialists. In the Kremlin itself a woman cleaner told Lenin to his face that she did not mind who was in power so long as she got paid.[11] But Nadezhda Konstantinovna had a still more dispiriting tale to tell him. A female worker in the People's Commissariat of Enlightenment informed her that she was not going to work that day for no other reason than that workers were the masters now and she personally did not want to work.[12] Then there was the time when Lenin and Nadezhda Konstantinovna were crossing a bridge in Moscow. The bridge was in poor repair, and a peasant passer-by remarked that it was a 'Soviet-style [sovetskii] bridge, if you'll pardon the expression'.[13] Soon Lenin started using 'Soviet-style' as a pejorative epithet.[14] The lack of conscientiousness in institutions and in daily life annoyed him intensely, and it was a mass phenomenon that he had not predicted before the October Revolution.

His general attitude was not to the liking of Nadezhda Konstantinovna, who was appalled by his refusal to criticise workers for thieving wood from the structure of a state-owned house: 'You, Vladimir Ilich, think in terms of broad plans. These little matters don't get to you.' She used the polite Russian form of 'you' – and it is probable that this verbal formality was meant to signal her anger at his complacency.

But Lenin would not yield and reminded her that the workers needed wood for fuel: cold, ignorant men and women were not to be blamed. If workers froze, they would die. But Nadezhda Konstantinovna had had a glimpse of a deeper malaise than he would ever acknowledge. Indeed he had persistently aroused the working class into taking crude, violent action. When fellow Central Committee member Zinoviev tried to restrain attacks on middle-class people in Petrograd, Lenin was incandescent. From Moscow he dispatched a telegram threatening all manner of unpleasantness unless the mayhem were given political sanction again. Lenin the class warrior had an intuition that he needed to keep on supporting the mass expression of social revenge, and he sensed that he needed to maintain the pressure in the Civil War. No class enemy, he suggested, should be allowed to feel safe under Soviet rule. The Cheka by itself could not do everything. Workers, too, had to be let loose. The problem was that he had no plan for staunching the flow of their angry bitterness if ever the Russian Communist Party and the Red Army were to emerge victorious over the Whites.

Lenin assumed that the best way to handle the workers was to keep them under tight control. He thought the same about soldiers, sailors and peasants. According to him, the crucial objective in internal social policy was to secure the prerequisites of economic reconstruction. For this purpose he was willing to postpone the immediate satisfaction of the consumer needs of society. The state's priority, he declared, was to raise productivity in town and countryside.[15] Hunger, disease and homelessness would continue for some time before Sovnarkom would tackle them. First and foremost for Lenin was the need to augment output in agriculture and industry. He was acting entirely within character. As a young man in the 1890s he had looked away when the other revolutionaries, including his elder sister Anna, had drawn attention to the plight of starving Volga peasants. At that time he had argued that the greater good was served by the peasantry's impoverishment, namely Russia's industrial development. Now in 1920 he sought macro-economic reconstruction before attempting to feed, cure and shelter the mass of society. And no one in the central party leadership felt differently.

And yet on particular matters he would yield. When, for example, Kollontai approached him with some story of abuse, he would often grant her demand. Then, meeting her at some official assembly, he would enquire: 'Now what? Are you satisfied? Now that we've done such and such.' Kollontai was not easily quietened. As often as not she would reply along the following lines: 'Yes, but things are bad for us in that area over there. We've let things slip there.'[16]

It was in this spirit that he supported another of Trotski's proposals. In January 1920 there seemed to be a serious possibility that military campaigns were about to come to an end. The Reds had beaten the Whites in Russia, and the last White Army – led after Denikin's resignation in April 1920 by General Vrangel – was organising a last-ditch stand in Crimea. The Red Army's task in reconquering the other non-Russian regions was not regarded as likely to present undue difficulties. The sole imponderable factor was the international situation. But, so long as the great powers did not intervene, the Politburo could expect to reconstitute the Russian Empire in its preferred socialist form within a short time.

As discussions about military demobilisation were started, Trotski made an unusual suggestion. This was that Red Army conscripts should be transferred into 'labour armies' and deployed in the service of economic reconstruction. Under army discipline, they would be more effective than the existing urban workforce in restoring roads, buildings, mines and industrial enterprises to operational efficiency. When Trotski spoke, he gave the impression that the 'militarisation of labour' might even become a long-term phenomenon. Lenin endorsed the suggestion. But he did so in more cautious terms, and he took care about his public image. Labour armies were going to be unpopular with the conscripts and their families. They would also be unpopular with existing urban workers, who would perceive that official labour policy was becoming very authoritarian. While agreeing with Trotski that the labour armies would at least help in the short term with vital economic tasks, he took care that his speech on the subject to the Moscow province Party Conference was reported only very sketchily in *Pravda*. He was aware that both he and his regime were suspect in the eyes of the working class, the conscripts and the peasantry without unnecessarily antagonising them with the disciplinary rhetoric used by Trotski.

Lenin was an ideologue, but he was also a sinuous politician in pursuit of his ideological goals. His handling of the 'national question' is a case in point. As Denikin was driven out of Ukraine, Lenin insisted that the Ukrainian Soviet Republic should be re-established. He knew that the Bolsheviks had frail support there. The peasantry hated Reds and Whites equally, and few ethnic Ukrainians had joined the Bolshevik faction before 1917. In order to govern Ukraine it was crucial, as Lenin discerned, to attract political groups that had once been hostile to the Bolsheviks. For this purpose he persuaded the central party leadership to sanction the incorporation of the Borotbists in the Communist Party. This was an extraordinary step. The Borotbists were Socialist-Revolutionaries, and in Russia the Socialist-Revolutionaries were being persecuted by the Bolsheviks. But Lenin did not mind being inconsistent. The Borotbists were mainly ethnic Ukrainians; they were also socialists. They would be able to provide a contingent of Soviet administrators congenial to Ukrainians. Simultaneously Lenin ensured that Jews, who were highly uncongenial to Ukrainian peasants, should be prevented from filling administrative posts in any great number. Ukrainian sensitivities were not to be offended.

Lenin put things as follows to Kamenev: 'Let us, the Great Russians, display caution, patience, etc., and gradually we'll get back into our hands all these Ukrainians, Latvians . . .'[17] Thus he wanted to enable the Bolsheviks to continue to pretend that the Ukrainian Soviet Republic was truly independent of Russia and that the bilateral treaty was founded upon equality between the two states. In reality Ukraine's government would remain strictly under the control of the Russian Communist Party and its central party bodies in Moscow, and the Ukrainian Communist Party would operate as a subordinate and regional party organisation.

These were clever, ruthless politics and Lenin was pleased with the result. He had not been so clever in his reaction to Trotski's proposal for a reduction in the amount of grain requisitioning, but as yet he did not have to pay the price for his obstinacy. What appeared important to Lenin was that the Reds had survived and triumphed in the Civil War. Their institutions, practices and attitudes had been elaborated in the heat of the military conflict and he assumed that they could be used to win the peace. He was a happy man, and enjoyed himself in the spare moments he had for relaxation. Such moments were very few. The burden of office was immense. Lenin remained at the fulcrum of political business. He chaired the Politburo and the Central Committee. He chaired Sovnarkom. He chaired the Council of Labour and Defence. He kept a watch over the Orgburo and the Secretariat. He was living the Revolution in the most intense way. He was fulfilled. There was no physical threat to the regime that he felt his party, his government and its armed forces could not handle – and the Communist International was building communist parties elsewhere in Europe. The cause to which he had devoted his adult life was being advanced with success.

Just one part of his life was less successful than it might have been.

This was the personal corner. His health was no better and the head-aches, the insomnia and the heart attacks continued to give him problems. He tried to ignore all this and to get on with his work. But his family was not giving him the support to which he was accustomed. Anna Ilinichna was distracted by grief for her husband Mark Yelizarov, who had died in March 1919. Maria Ilinichna was hard at work as *Pravda*'s 'responsible secretary'. Nadezhda Konstantinovna, who had her own room in the Kremlin flat,[18] went on a trip to the Volga region for a couple of months from July. Dmitri Ilich arrived from the Crimea just after Nadezhda Konstantinovna's departure. The brothers had not seen each other for a decade, and went off swimming together in Pakhra Lake near Podolsk. There was a nostalgic aspect to this: in 1897 the Ulyanov family had rented a house in the vicinity while Lenin was in Siberian exile. In 1919, he showed off to Dmitri by refusing to use a towel.[19] It was as if they were lads again by the river Sviyaga in Simbirsk. Lenin also relaxed by playing skittles with Nikolai Bukharin even though he habitually lost;[20] and he enjoyed riding around Moscow with Anna Ilinichna's adoptive son Gora Lozgachëv.

But these interludes did not change the basic situation: Lenin was not feeling in the best of sorts either physically or emotionally. And it served him right. Nadya's trip down the river Volga on the paddle steamer *Red Star* meant her running the risk of either typhoid or capture by anti-Bolshevik armies or bandits. It would not be a holiday, not by any stretch of the imagination. (Alexandra Kollontai, an adventurous person, had taken the same journey in the previous year and was in no doubt that she had taken an immense risk.)[21] Nadya's purpose was to give speeches to workers and peasants at each port on the way. She could not have given clearer indication that she wanted to get away from Moscow, from the Kremlin and from Lenin. The marriage was almost certainly entering one of its less happy phases. Lenin's attitude to Inessa Armand was quite possibly among the causes of the malaise. When a terrorist explosion occurred in the Moscow city party headquarters it was Inessa who ran to alert Lenin in person in the Kremlin.[22] Inessa remained devoted to him. Perhaps he responded in kind; perhaps not. Yet there may well have been sufficient brusqueness in his attitude to Nadezhda Konstantinovna that she thought she had nothing to lose by leaving for the Volga.

Possibly, too, she thought that he might appreciate her more if she was away from him. If this was her purpose, it was successful. He wrote frequently and affectionately to her and these messages are the only ones that Nadezhda Konstantinovna kept from their long partnership. A few phrases exemplify the tone:[23]

> Dear Nadyushka,
>
> I was very glad to get news from you. I've already sent a telegram to Kazan and, not having a reply to it, sent another to Nizhni [Novgorod], and there was a reply from there today ... I give you a big hug and ask you to write and telegraph more often.
>
> Yours [*Tvoi*],
>
> V. Ulyanov
>
> NB: Listen to the doctor: eat and sleep more, then you'll be *completely* fit for work by the winter.

Local party officials kept him informed about her progress.[24] The news was not good: she was bothered by the heat and mosquitoes and was careless about her recuperation. Out of Lenin's sight, she was not going to be told how to behave.

Their personal relationship in any case was not the main thing in their lives and never had been. They lived for the Revolution; and when Lenin laid emphasis on her returning to fitness for work, he was expressing a priority that they shared. Both of them were feeling optimistic in general political terms. Yet it would have done Lenin good to join his wife on the *Red Star* steamship and witness the devastation alongside the river Volga. Moscow, despite its shabbiness, was untouched by military action. This helps to explain why Lenin in the winter of 1918–19 remained so full of confidence. In fact he and his party were facing a number of problems in the time ahead. Power at home was not as secure as he thought. The economy was a shambles. Rebellions by peasants and soldiers were in prospect. Workers' strikes were already taking place. The spread of the Revolution westwards would not be simple even if an opportunity arose. In April 1920 Lenin agreed to attend a Bolshevik party celebration of his fiftieth birthday. Eulogies were delivered, and he made his embarrassment plain. But obviously he was pleased that the birthday was attended by such joy on the part of his close colleagues. He was about to discover that the general situation of his regime was worse than his eulogists – or indeed he himself – imagined.

24

DEFEAT IN THE WEST

1920

Lenin was acquiring the reputation of a politician whose main aim was to rule Russia rather than make the 'European socialist Revolution'. Perhaps, it was thought, he was just a modern sort of Russian nationalist leader and his commitment to internationalist socialism had lapsed. This was a profound misperception and it is surprising that it is still widely shared to this day.[1]

For the newer evidence from archives bolsters the old argument that Lenin's zeal for spreading the October Revolution was undiminished. Only the vastly superior power of Germany had stopped him in 1918 and the Civil War had prevented him from sending the Red Army abroad when the Germans withdrew at the end of the Great War. Yet it remained Lenin's fundamental belief that Europe was in need of a revolutionary transformation. He was ready to gamble on offending the victor powers in the Great War – the Allies – by stirring up trouble to the west of Russia. His reasoning had been given in years past and he repeated it in 1920: 'We've always emphasised that a thing such as a socialist revolution in a single country can't be completed.'[2] Lenin, like practically every Bolshevik leader, assumed that fraternal socialist states needed to be established elsewhere in Europe in order that Soviet Russia could bring its socialism to maturity. The prospects for an isolated Russia were pathetic. Territorial integrity and post-war economic enhancement would remain insecure until such time as Europe as a whole joined the side of the Revolution.

Lenin did not mind how this was achieved. As in 1917, he hoped that revolutions would occur without the need for Russian assistance; but he was willing to supply finance, propaganda and political instruction to hasten and strengthen the process. He was still expecting, too, to commit the forces of the Red Army. In confidential discussions he let himself go. 'As soon as we're strong enough to cut capitalism down as a whole, we'll quickly seize it by the throat.'[3] Europe remained the key to Lenin's strategic calculations.

The opportunity for action came unexpectedly. Clashes between Russian and Polish military forces had taken place since the end of the Great War. As the Civil War ended in Russia, the question arose whether the Red Army would be able to control the Russian Imperial borderlands. The Poles had no intention of losing their statehood. Their Commander-in-Chief Josef Piłsudski made an incursion into Ukraine with a plan to annex Ukrainian territory to a federal state based in Warsaw, and he took Kiev on 7 May 1920. Piłsudski was not unknown to Lenin. In 1887 the Okhrana had arrested and exiled him in the course of suppressing revolutionaries after the attempted assassination of the Emperor Alexander III by the terrorist group to which Lenin's brother Alexander had belonged. Piłsudski indeed had links with the friends of Alexander Ulyanov. After five years in Siberia, Piłsudski returned to lead the Polish Socialist Party. Like Lenin, he announced support for Japan in the Russo-Japanese War of 1904–5. Like Lenin, too, he had sanctioned armed robbery in order to acquire a treasury for his party (and Piłsudski, a real man of action, led his team in person). Piłsudski and Lenin had lived in the same region of Austrian Poland before 1914. They took coffee in the same café, and Lenin's Bolshevik faction received help from Piłsudski's Union of Riflemen in strengthening its security against the Okhrana.

Lenin and Piłsudski had believed that one's enemy's enemy could be one's friend. Both had hated the Romanov dynasty while disagreeing about practically everything else. They surely recognised that they shared a temperamental hardness; they were leaders incarnate. But after assuming power they ignored each other. For Lenin, Piłsudski had become a pawn of Anglo-French imperialism. For Piłsudski, Lenin was no different from the tsars of old. Poland had to be defended, and Piłsudski believed that the federal amalgamation of Poland and Ukraine was the key to Polish security.

In Moscow there was panic. Imperial Army officers who had lain low during the Russian Civil War were summoned by former General Alexei Brusilov to enlist in the Red Army and assist in the liberation of the 'Motherland'. Steadily the Red Army regrouped itself. Trotski and Stalin were dispatched to the western front to bolster the Bolshevik party's control, and Piłsudski was forced back into the Polish lands. By then the Polish–Soviet War had become a focus of international diplomatic attention. Negotiations were under way to establish a permanent territorial demarcation and peace. The British Foreign Secretary was involved in drawing up a map satisfactory to both sides.

But then Lenin had a change of mind and decided that the time had come, as Piłsudski retreated, to launch the 'revolutionary war' that the Left Communists had demanded of him in 1918. Quite what had convinced him of the attainability of victory is not known. But he had always believed in the 'ripeness' of Europe for Revolution and in the efficacy of military means to achieve that result. His immediate scheme was breathtaking in its scope. Poland was meant to be just the first revolutionary prize of war. Then moves should be made to 'sovietise' nearby countries, perhaps Czechoslovakia, Hungary and Romania. As if by afterthought, he suggested that Lithuania might be sovietised in the same campaign. He dreamed, too, that Italian far-left socialists might organise their own revolution in the northern cities of the country.[4] The great prize, Germany, should be grasped in the same campaign. Once Warsaw had fallen, the Red Army should burst through into East Prussia and race for Berlin. Lenin anticipated that the Polish and German 'proletariats' would welcome the Reds from Russia and rise against their national 'bourgeois' governments. As the delegates assembled in Petrograd's Smolny Institute from all over the world for the Second Congress of the Communist International in summer 1920, Lenin hoped that he would soon be seeing them again as the people's commissars in their own Soviet-style governments.

Lenin's colleagues shared his vision, but not his judgement. Unlike him, they had direct experience of the difficulties faced by the Red Army: the overstretched lines of communication and supply, the shoddy equipment, the inadequate rations and the absence of a popular will to prolong the war. Not even Trotski, who had caused him trouble over the Treaty of Brest-Litovsk, was in favour of invading Poland; and Bolsheviks of Polish origin warned Lenin that he underestimated the distrust felt by Poles for Russian armies, even armies sent into their country with professed internationalist objectives. But Lenin insisted. The fact that most other leading members of the central party leadership were outside Moscow gave him his chance. No formal session of Sovnarkom, the Central Committee or the Politburo discussed the question of war or peace. There was no repetition of the laborious, disputatious deliberations over Brest-Litovsk in early 1918. Lenin was helped by the fact that there was at least a consensus that Piłsudski had to be taught a lesson. The Red Army was already committed to the pursuit of the Polish armed forces. The borders of Soviet Russia and Poland were as yet unfixed. The reaction of foreign governments remained unclear and Lenin wanted to make the most of the confusion. He prodded his comrades into letting him have his way. Poland ought to be sovietised.

And once the decision was taken, it was given full support by his fellow Bolshevik leaders. There was no repetition of the kind of disputes about 'revolutionary war' that had divided the party in 1918. Trotski and Stalin were in the armed forces as they pressed into Poland.

The Second Comintern Congress went ahead while all this was going on. Proceedings began on 19 July 1920 in the Smolny Institute, where Lenin and the Bolshevik Central Committee had been based during the October Revolution. It was the first time Lenin had returned to the city since March 1919 (and it was the last occasion when he visited a Russian city outside Moscow). Lenin's delegation had travelled there from Moscow's Nicholas Station on 18 July 1920. The proceedings were heavy with symbolism. The Congress was taking place in the birthplace of the October Revolution. Foreign delegates were shown around the revolutionary sights: the Finland Station, the Kseshinskaya mansion, the Winter Palace and the corridors and hall of the Smolny Institute itself. Naturally it was not beyond the wit of Lenin to think that, if he based the Comintern Congress in Petrograd, he would find it easier to impose Bolshevik party policies on the Communist International. Awed by the surroundings of revolutionary history, the foreign communists would accede to the demands of the only communists who had yet undertaken a successful seizure of state power.

Lenin gave several major speeches and thoroughly enjoyed himself. Strutting up and down on the platform, he repeated his belief that the October Revolution offered a model to the rest of the world's socialists. Between speeches he squatted on the stairs underneath the aspidistras, drafting his contributions to the Congress. He was fêted whenever he appeared, but he also tried to meet delegates privately. The Congress, he convinced himself, would be the last such assembly to be held in Russia. During the Congress a map of Europe was hung to enable delegates to follow the advance of the Red Army from Ukraine into Poland. Little red flags were pinned to it. There was about to be a 'European socialist revolution'. The Politburo reinforced the morale of everyone as the Red Army raced towards Warsaw. Lenin suggested that the Italian comrades should return to Milan and Turin and organise revolution.

The Congress was a watershed in communist history. Nearly all the debates were inaugurated by leaders of the Russian Communist Party, and on no point were they blown off course by the foreigners. Lenin and his associates wanted to make Soviet Russia into the model for far-left socialist movements abroad. Communist parties should be formed. Their organisational principles should be centralism, hierarchy, member-ship selectivity, activism and discipline. The best chance for 'European socialist revolution' was for Germans, French and British to copy the methods of Bolshevism. Lenin and his associates had evidently calculated that the establishment of highly centralised parties elsewhere would enable the Politburo, through the Executive Committee of the Comintern, to dominate the new communist parties throughout Europe and the rest of the world.

The proceedings occurred at a hectic pace and in an atmosphere of intense expectancy, and for several days they had to be suspended because of military developments in the Polish–Soviet War. But when the Congress was resumed Lenin stepped forward to offer a trenchant defence of his version of socialism with its reliance on dictatorship and terror. In other ways, however, he suggested that communists had to rethink how socialism might be achieved. In the past he had argued, like all Marxists since the 1890s, that socialism could not be constructed except on the foundations of an existing capitalist society. For Lenin, the Russian economy was already predominantly capitalist before the turn of the twentieth century. In 1920 he quietly dropped this tenet and stated that non-capitalist countries, despite their 'backwardness', might be able to bypass capitalism altogether and proceed towards socialism. He introduced these novel ideas in order to encourage communists in colonial countries around the world to throw off the chains of European imperialism. He attempted no detailed justification of his intellectual somersault and did not deign to explain why he had always opposed the Russian *narodniki*, who had argued that capitalism could be bypassed.

Why should this matter? The main significance lies in the casual fashion in which Lenin treated his Marxism whenever a goal of practical politics was in his sights. Although he thought seriously about social and economic theory and liked to stick by his basic ideas, his adherence was not absolute. In mid-1920 the priority for him was the global release of revolutionary energy. Ideas about the unavoidable stages of social devel-opment faded for him. Better to make Revolution, however roughly, than to fashion a sophisticated but unrealised theory. If intellectual sleight of hand was sometimes necessary, then so be it. Even when he stayed close to his previously declared policies, Lenin was mercurially difficult to comprehend. Parties belonging to the Comintern, he declared, should break with 'opportunistic' kinds of socialism which rejected the need for the 'dictatorship of the proletariat'; but simultaneously he demanded that British communists should affiliate themselves to the British Labour Party: Lenin's argument was that communism in the United Kingdom was as yet too frail to set up an independent party.

He got his way at the expense of mystifying the Comintern Congress and irritating the British delegate Sylvia Pankhurst, communist and feminist. Pankhurst might have raised a fuss if all eyes had not been on the map of the war front. Everyone at the Congress concentrated upon the question of how to aid the process of Revolution presently being advanced on the bayonet tips of the Red Army. A Polish Revolutionary Committee was selected by the Politburo from Polish communists known to be implicitly loyal to directives from Moscow. The same was not done with German communists, but this was essentially only a matter of time. The Red Army was the advancing front-line of the Comintern. Socialist governments were expected to dominate the map of the European mainland very soon, and world imperialism supposedly could hardly be much longer in collapsing. Back to Moscow travelled Lenin and his fellow commissars, eager to receive news of further Red successes when they disembarked from the train. He felt that he was on the brink of achieving a lifetime's ambition. Russia had fallen to him in 1917–18. Europe, country after country, was surely about to succumb to a multinational communist assault, by the Red Army and by 'local' communist parties, upon the bastions of continental capitalism.

If Lenin dreamed of heading a European socialist federal regime, he refrained from giving vent to the notion. In general he was very reticent. But among his associates he could not contain himself. All the time he wanted action on the front, action in the rear and even action beyond the lines. His intemperance was extraordinary, as was obvious in a note he scribbled to Trotski's deputy E. M. Sklyanski: 'A beautiful plan. Finish it off *together* with Dzierżyński. Disguised as "Greens" (we'll heap the blame on them afterwards) we'll advance 10–20 versts and hang the kulaks, priests, landed gentry. 100,000 rubles prize for each one of them that is hanged.'[5] Here was Lenin the class warrior as well as Lenin the excited political schemer: he had listened to the generals long enough, and wanted to add his own ideas. And yet these ideas were not only extremely nasty; they were also not very practical. The Red Army, if it was going to win the war, would conquer Poland by moving its great regiments forward and crushing Piłsudski – and surreptitious viciousness of the kind proposed by Lenin would not make a difference in practice. If anything, the hanging of priests would have turned most Polish citizens against the Reds.

Meanwhile Piłsudski had retreated to Warsaw with the intention of reorganising Polish defences. Trotski, Stalin and the high command had split the Red Army into two great prongs, and Piłsudski had a chance to tackle the invaders outside the Polish capital. Trotski had grave difficulties in co-ordinating his forces, and certainly he could not count on the southern prong – whose commissar was Stalin – being as co-operative as it might have been. In mid-August 1920, Piłsudski offered battle by the river Vistula outside Warsaw. Quite against Lenin's prediction, the worst happened. The Red Army was severely defeated. As the Poles exploited their advantage, the Soviet forces retreated headlong along the Smolensk road towards Moscow. Lenin had no choice but to sue for peace. One summer day's battle had ruined everything. No more grandiose predictions about the federal Union of Europe. No more advice on unholy political alliances of far right and far left. No more expression of pride in the invincibility of the Red Army. All that came forth from Moscow was a recognition of the military disaster and the dire necessity of signing a peace on whatever terms were made available.

Lenin had been forcing the pace. He had urged his Politburo colleagues to start thinking how Europe would be organised. If 'European socialist Revolution' was about to become a reality, they had to have serious plans. Lenin and Stalin had an exchange of opinions about this, and Stalin never forgot the vehemence with which Lenin argued his case. For Lenin, this would be a simple process. He wanted to form a federal Union of Russia and the various Soviet republics of the former Russian Empire. Whenever a state in central and western Europe acquired a Soviet-style government, it could be admitted to this great, expanding Union. In such a Union there was no scheme for Russian political pre-eminence and Stalin objected to this as being unrealistic. For him, it was self-evident that neither a Soviet Poland nor a Soviet Germany would enter into a Union founded by Russia. Old national pride would not quickly be erased. And so Stalin proposed that the RSFSR should constitute the core of one great federation while Germany formed another federation. Lenin was shocked by Stalin's position and accused him of chauvinism.[6] The October Revolution had been undertaken with the purpose of ending the division of Europe into separate state blocs. Stalin appeared to wish to maintain the blocs – and Lenin could scarcely believe what he heard from him.

Stalin did not even accept that Russia and Ukraine should enter their own Union on equal terms. Now that the Civil War was nearly over, he wished to scrap the various bilateral treaties and simply incorporate the other Soviet republics into the RSFSR. Of course, not even Lenin wished to provide Ukraine with freedom from control by Moscow; but he felt it politic to preserve the outward trappings of such freedom. Thus the planning for Revolution in Europe became enmeshed in a discussion of the future constitutional arrangements in Russia. Lenin and Stalin wanted to get things straight in advance of the anticipated European socialist Revolution. Their anger with each other in June 1920 only seems comic now because the Red Army was halted outside Warsaw and the socialist revolutions elsewhere either did not happen or soon petered out. But at the time they were in deadly earnest. They saw themselves as not only social engineers in Russia but also master planners for the entire continent. Their acquaintance with foreign leaders in the Communist International inclined them to think that no one could discharge the task as competently.

Yet, while Lenin was castigating Stalin for a betrayal of internationalist principles, he was quietly being criticised by prominent German communists for the same sin. The history of Germany in the past couple of years had taught Lenin not to exaggerate the independent potential of the German political far left. The German Communist Party had been formed at the very end of 1918, and its hold on the German working class was weak. For this reason it could not be assumed that the Red Army's arrival in Berlin would be sufficient to touch off a successful socialist insurrection. Lenin had a cunning strategic ploy to hand. According to him, Germany had been reduced to colonial status in all but name by the Treaty of Versailles. It was therefore appropriate for the German Communist Party to seek allies for a war of national liberation from the Anglo-French yoke. Among such allies, none would be more effective than the Freikorps and other military units on the political far right. Such an unholy partnership would have as its objective to overturn Versailles. This would in turn disturb the political equilibrium in the states of the victorious Allies. In the ensuing chaos the German Communist Party would seize its chance to take on the German far right in the continent's supreme political struggle.

For Lenin, this recommendation was mere common sense. Politicians had to be flexible in pursuit of their strategic objectives. He failed to comprehend the negative response he obtained from the German comrades. He should have done. They had become communists in part because they were copying him. He had turned intransigence into an art form. He had defied all public opinion in his country – conservative and liberal as well as socialist – in his preparations for seizing power in 1917. He had discerned that questions of ideological principle were at stake when his adversaries saw only minor practical matters. He had taught that Marxists should hold fast to Marxist orthodoxy. Now this same Lenin, their revolutionary model, was telling them to link arms not even with fellow socialists but with the proponents of the darkest political reaction.

While all this was happening, a terrible event occurred in Lenin's personal life. Inessa Armand had returned from her Red Cross mission to France and had fallen ill. Lenin wrote her a note:[7]

> Dear Friend,
> Please write a note to say what's up with you. These are foul times: typhoid, influenza, Spanish 'flu, cholera.
> I've only just got out of bed and am not going out. Nadya has a temperature of 39° and she's asked to see you.
> What's your temperature?
> Don't you need something to make yourself better? I really ask you to write frankly.
> Get better!
> Yours,
> Lenin

Despite the chatty style, he preserved an emotional distance by addressing her with the polite Russian *vy* rather than the familiar *ty*; and he can hardly have been trying to conduct a secret affair with her because he mentioned that his wife Nadya wanted Inessa to visit her. The ties between Lenin and Inessa were close, but they were not of the same nature as in Paris in 1912. Nadya by contrast seemed to have gained in influence over him. Alexandra Kollontai, whose novel *The Love of Worker Bees* was an allegory of the Lenin–Nadya–Inessa triangle in Paris in 1911–12, noted in her 1920 diary how 'he takes great notice of her'.[8]

As for Lenin, he was bossy towards Inessa but there was an endearing ineffectuality about his efforts. When he wrote again to her, he tried to stop her venturing outside in the cold. He knew that she would ignore his instructions and directed her to tell her children to command her not to go outside in the freezing cold. It was Lenin's habit to supervise the medical treatment of his associates, but there is no parallel to his detailed intervention in the case of Inessa.

She recovered from this bout of ill health and agreed to act as interpreter at the Second Comintern Congress in July. This was very intensive work and – coming on top of disputes with colleagues such as Alexandra Kollontai – induced a relapse. In truth Inessa was exhausted, and Lenin advised her to go to a sanatorium. He suggested that, if she insisted on going abroad, she should avoid France for fear she might be arrested. In Lenin's opinion it would be better if she made for Norway or Holland. Better still, he suggested, she might try the Caucasus, and he promised to make dispositions for a pleasant period of care for her there. To cheer her up he mentioned that he had been hunting in the woods near the old Armand estate outside Moscow, and that the peasants had talked nostalgically about the days before 1917 when there had been real 'order'. Inessa agreed to go to the spa town Kislovodsk in the mountains of the north Caucasus. Lenin gave orders that she and her son Andrei – then a lad of sixteen – should be well looked after. But the area was affected by a cholera epidemic; it also had not yet been pacified by the Red Army. Inadvertently Lenin had sent his former lover into mortal danger. First she caught cholera. Then the order was given for people to be evacuated to Nalchik. Inessa's health was finally broken, and she perished on 24 September 1920.

Knowing she was dying, she had put down her last thoughts in a presentational notebook given to her at the Comintern Congress. They make for poignant reading. Inessa wrote on 1 September:[9]

> Will this feeling of inner death ever pass away? I've reached the point where I find it strange that other people laugh so easily and that they obviously get pleasure from talking. I now laugh and smile almost never because an inner joy induces this in me but because it's sometimes necessary to smile. I'm also struck by my present indifference to nature. And yet it used to make me tremble so strongly. And how little I've now begun to love people. Previously I would approach each person with warm feelings. Now I'm indifferent to everyone. But the main thing is that I'm bored with almost everyone. Hot feelings have remained only for my children and for V.I.

There was only one person she could have referred to as 'V.I.', and that was Vladimir Ilich Lenin. Inessa continued:[10]

> It's as if my heart has died in all other respects. As if, having devoted all my strength and all my passion to V.I. and to the cause of our [political] work, all sources of love and sympathy for people

– to whom it once was so rich – have been exhausted. With the exception of V.I. and my children I no longer have any personal relationships with people except purely practical relationships.

Inessa called herself a 'living corpse'; it was not only cholera but also a broken heart that did for her. Ten days later she contemplated the meaning of her life:[11]

> For romantics, love holds the first place in a person's life. It's higher than anything else. And until recently I was far nearer to such a notion than I am now. True, for me love was never the only thing. Alongside love there was public activity. And both in my life and in the past there have been not a few instances where I've sacrificed my happiness and my love for the good of the cause. But previously it used to seem that love had a significance equal to that of public activity. Now it's not like that. The significance of love in comparison with public activity becomes quite small and cannot bear comparison with public activity.

On the point of death, she tried to persuade herself that her work for the Revolution meant more to her than the man she loved.

The matter-of-fact official telegram to Lenin cut him to the quick: 'It has been impossible to save Comrade Inessa Armand who was ill with cholera. She died on 24 September. We are accompanying the body to Moscow.'[12] Lenin had been responsible for her convalescing in the chaotic Caucasus rather than in France, and now she had perished there. It took a fortnight before her body was brought back in a leaden coffin to Moscow. The train arrived in the early hours of 11 October, and the cortège made its way from the railway station after dawn. Lenin and Nadezhda Konstantinovna had been waiting at the station. As the cortège neared the capital's centre, Lenin was obviously overcome with grief. Nadezhda Konstantinovna understood, and gripped him by the arm to hold him up. No one could forget the pitiful condition of the man. The young Bolshevik Yelizaveta Drabkina watched the horse-drawn hearse and the draped black flag: 'There was something inexpressibly sad about his drooping shoulders and lowly bent head.'[13] Angelica Balabanova had the same impression at the funeral: 'I never saw such torment; I never saw any human being so completely absorbed by sorrow, by the effort to keep it for himself, to guard it against the attention of others, as if that awareness could have diminished the intensity of his feeling.'[14]

Lenin did not record his feelings on paper. He had given up many pleasures for 'the cause': material comfort, profession, chess, classical music and cycling. He had avoided a permanent association with Inessa: the Revolution for him was always dominant. But he grieved deeply when her corpse was delivered from Nalchik.

By his side were friends and associates who thought that he was never the same again. Some said that he would have lived longer had he not lost Inessa. Shaken he certainly was; yet he had not lost the power of his will. Since 1912 he had accustomed himself to living apart from her. He could also cope with the *froideurs* of Nadya. Throughout his career he displayed an ability to be undistracted by matters of the heart. Usually it had been his physical health or his polemics that had thrown him off balance. 'Romance' did not get in his way, and Inessa's death did not destroy him. If his external reaction is any guide, he was hurt worse than by any other event since his brother's execution in 1887. But he quickly recovered. He had an enormous capacity for emotional self-suppression. He loved politics and lived for the political life. He was fixated by the importance of ideas. He was not a robot and did not deny, at least to himself, the benefits of a deep relationship; but personal love – the love of a man for a woman – was secondary to him, and, if politics so demanded, he thought he could survive without it.

Inessa's funeral was held on 12 October; her corpse was buried alongside other deceased Bolshevik heroes beneath the Kremlin Wall. A fortnight earlier Lenin had faced the Ninth Party Conference. The invasion of Poland had turned into a rout. The economy was a shambles. There were industrial strikes and peasant rebellions, and even in the armed forces there were disturbances. The Bolshevik party was restive, and its internal factions – the Democratic Centralists and the Workers' Opposition – relished the chance to attack the Politburo behind the closed doors of the Conference. Agreement about what should be party policy was absent. But there was a widespread feeling among Bolsheviks that something had gone terribly wrong in the Soviet state. It was not in Lenin's nature to walk away from a dispute: he raged to give the critics a taste of their own medicine.

Thus although he straightway confessed that a catastrophe had indeed occurred in Poland, he fudged the question of responsibility. He spoke of the approval given by the Central Committee to the invasion of 'ethnographically' Polish territory; and then he admitted that the party leadership had not taken a formal decision on the matter:[15]

When this resolution was placed before the Central Committee, there was no failure to understand the somewhat awkward character of this resolution in the sense that it appeared impossible to vote against it. How could it be possible to vote against assistance for sovietisation?

The question was rhetorical; it was meant to embarrass an audience of zealots into recognising that they, too, would have voted for the invasion of Poland. But this was a sleight of argument. Lenin had been almost alone in pressing central party colleagues into the invasion; and he now wanted to evade personal responsibility. He deliberately let his analysis wander a bit, too, when he tried to define the mistake that had been made. Was it political or strategic? He addressed the distinction, but avoided giving his conclusion. He also revealed that, on balance, the Central Committee had decided not to set up an enquiry into the military; but again he refrained from explaining why. Throughout the report he touched on sensitive points only glancingly:

> We in the Politburo during the Civil War had to decide purely strategic questions – questions that were so purely strategic that we looked at each other with smiles on our faces: how was it that we'd turned into strategists? Among us there were people who had not seen war even from a far distance.

Was this an oblique appeal for sympathy? Certainly no one in the Politburo had less experience of warfare than Lenin. Be that as it may, Lenin was claiming that he had performed pretty well – for a neophyte military planner – against Kolchak, Denikin and Yudenich. But at no point in his report – and this is the crux of the matter – did Lenin implicate himself personally in the disaster outside Warsaw. He acknowledged a mistake only on behalf of the 'Central Committee'.

Lenin said not a word against the use of 'revolutionary war'. But steadily he was coming round to the opinion that the Red Army's bayonets should remain sheathed for the foreseeable future. The logical moment had therefore arrived to reconsider policies in general. The Party Conference, however, gave no opportunity for this. The delegates had come to Moscow not to debate the whole range of options but to give the central party leaders a grilling. The conception and realisation of the Warsaw campaign was the object of harsh criticism. Here Lenin had a lucky break. The rivalry between Trotski and Stalin spilled out into vehement open dispute when Trotski denounced Stalin for misleading the Central Committee about the prospect of military victory. There had been no internal party spat of so personal a nature since the searing disagreements of 1903–4. Politburo member attacked Politburo member. Stalin, bristling at his humiliation, demanded the right of reply. Lenin decided to take sides; perhaps he genuinely agreed with Trotski, but in any case he could see that he was being offered a chance to help pick a scapegoat. The result was an unseemly row. But Lenin emerged unscathed. Indeed by the end of the Conference he was the only Politburo member not to have annoyed a large number of the angry delegates.

The other great dispute was focussed on the party itself. The Democratic Centralists and the Workers' Opposition condemned the internal practices of party life as bureaucratic and over-centralised. The Workers' Opposition added that party officialdom had opened a rift between the central leaders and the rank-and-file members and that the working class as a whole had lost faith in the party. Within the Central Committee there were figures who agreed with much of the analysis. Among them was Central Committee Secretary Yevgeni Preobrazhenski. But it was Zinoviev, despite being a very authoritarian leader in Petrograd, who spoke on the Central Committee's behalf in favour of internal party reform. His sincerity was cast in doubt before the Conference's exhausted participants agreed to give the central party leaders the benefit of the doubt. Once again Lenin, who was just as responsible as any Politburo member for the objectionable organisational phenomena, escaped without being blamed.

But the question what to do about the country's condition remained an acute one. To the outside world – and the outside world in this instance included all mortals not belonging to the central leadership of the Bolshevik party and Soviet government – it appeared that Lenin was still keen to adhere to every last detail of the policies developed in the Civil War. This is in many ways true. But the qualification must be added that he was never unidimensional in his planning. He had always wanted to sign treaties with foreign capitalist states as a means of breaking up the international phalanx ranged against Soviet Russia. Kamenev had been in London negotiating a resumption of trade at the very time when the Red Army was moving upon Warsaw. Now that he was balked in Poland, he aimed to develop commercial and diplomatic relations still further. Furthermore, Lenin in spring 1918 had declared that if Russian economic reconstruction could not be undertaken in alliance with a Soviet Germany, it should be attempted with aid from capitalist Germany. He resumed this idea in 1920 and wanted to sign concession agreements with German entrepreneurs, even to the point of granting them land in Russia where they could raise productivity by the introduction of advanced capitalist farming techniques. He also wished to tempt the Nobel oil company back to involvement in oil-extraction in Azerbaijan.

At home, too, he had some modifications he wanted to make. He recognised that violent seizure of grain from peasants by the state authorities was extremely unpopular in the countryside; and although he would not accept Trotski's proposal for a limited reversion to the legal private sale of foodstuffs by the peasantry, he wanted to coax the rural households to sow more grain. For this purpose he contemplated giving material rewards to peasants whose production could be shown to have increased.

This was not a break in the wall of the party's wartime economic policy; but many fellow Bolshevik leaders in the provinces were aghast. What, they asked, was a proposal for material reward except a backdoor method of reintroducing capitalism? And what on earth did Lenin think he was up to with his welcome for German farmers and industrialists, British timber concessionaires and – worst of all – the Nobel oil company? Had he taken leave of his senses? Could he not see that his various projects, taken together, amounted to an economic Brest-Litovsk? As the year 1920 drew to a close, there was therefore little reason for Lenin to celebrate. He had won the Russian Civil War only to lose the unnecessary Polish–Soviet War. He had become so distracted by military planning that he had ignored unrest in his party; and industrial strikes and peasant revolts were occurring with ever greater intensity across the country. His reputation for careful management of the central political machinery was going into decline. His health, never very good for decades, was decidedly shaky. He had suffered, too, the loss of the woman he had loved, Inessa Armand. And he could not even tell himself at New Year 1921 that the October Revolution had been made secure. On the contrary, honesty permitted him only to say that things were going to get worse before they could conceivably get better.

25

THE NEW ECONOMIC POLICY

January to June 1921

The winter months of 1920–21 jolted Lenin into thinking hard again about state policies. He felt no remorse about his wartime strategy. His policies had ruined the economy, induced popular revolts, isolated the country from diplomatic and financial assistance and engendered military disaster in Poland. But, while he had reluctantly acknowledged that a mistake had been made over Poland, he was singularly unrepentant about the rest. Indeed he had few regrets. But steadily he had been driven to the conclusion that mortal danger would engulf the regime without strategic change. Lenin's new idea was very simple. He proposed to replace forcible grain requisitioning with a tax-in-kind on grain. Once the peasants had delivered the fiscal contribution assigned to them, he said, they should be allowed to trade their produce in local markets. Private commerce in grain should again be allowed. Lenin successfully put this idea to the Politburo on 8 February 1921.

No great acumen was required of Lenin to invent his New Economic Policy (or NEP). In agricultural essentials it had been advocated since 1918 by the Mensheviks and Socialist-Revolutionaries and in February 1920 by Trotski, who in 1921 reminded Lenin that the change could have happened a year earlier but for his stubbornness. The NEP was the obvious way to restore the exchange of products between village and town. This was also the prerequisite for ending famine, disease, industrial ruin and popular rebellion. But, if Lenin's proposal lacked cerebral distinction, it nevertheless demanded political tenacity – and all the biographers of Lenin, despite extolling his feat in winning the Brest-Litovsk dispute in 1918, have understated the equal achievement involved in introducing the NEP.[1] The reason is probably that the dispute about the NEP was not as raucous as the controversy over Brest-Litovsk or even as the 'trade union discussion'. But this should not disguise the obstacles in Lenin's path. He had to persuade the Politburo, the Central Committee and the Party Congress, and then he had to push the legislation through the Soviet legislative agencies, and even then he had to return and defend the NEP at the Party Conference in May 1921. Without Lenin quite possibly there would have been no NEP. Without the NEP, the Soviet state would have been overwhelmed by popular rebellions.

The policy was exceptionally annoying to his party, which considered a state economic near-monopoly to be a wonderful achievement. This aspect of the party's ideology had been stiffened through the Civil War, and the Bolsheviks concurred about much more than they disagreed about. Several fundamental policies had become articles of faith. Lenin, who had been toying with ideas for reform in late 1920, was offering a programme of action that seemed to empty Bolshevism of its revolutionary content. Although he remained devoted to the one-party, one-ideology state, he appeared disgracefully keen to abandon state ownership and regulation in the economy.

At the time the party was being buffeted by its so-called 'trade union discussion'. The dispute had started with Trotski insisting that post-war economic reconstruction needed to operate on the basis of the 'militarisation of labour'. Trotski wanted to ban strikes and to reduce trade unions to the condition of state organisations. He could not care less about keeping the Bolshevik party as the main instrument of enforcement; he had ignored the party when setting up political commissariats in the Red Army in the Civil War and in 1920 had campaigned for the transference of this system to civilian needs. Trotski also demanded that transport by rail and water should be organised through just such a system.

The dispute was a nightmare for Lenin, who thought Trotski was threatening the unity that had been restored at the Ninth Party Conference. Lenin, while not intending to indulge the trade unions, saw no sense in offending them. But the dispute had got out of hand. Trotski argued that under the dictatorship of the proletariat there was no need for the workers to have a class organisation for protection against their own 'workers' state'. Lenin retorted that 'bureaucratic distortions' had taken place after the October Revolution and that trade unions still had a useful purpose. A buffer group led by Bukharin formed itself between Lenin and Trotski. The Workers' Opposition condemned Lenin, Trotski and Bukharin equally. The Democratic Centralists had no agreed position; their members sided with whichever group they fancied. Leaders of each group toured the country trying to drum up support among Bolsheviks in the provinces. Lenin was one of the few leading figures who stayed in Moscow; but even he was preoccupied by the 'trade union discussion'. As well as producing a lengthy booklet in order to win the debate, he also had to manipulate the levers of factional power to secure victory. Zinoviev travelled around the largest party organisations and Stalin kept watch over the provincial debates from the vantage point of Moscow. To Lenin's relief, the victory of his group was put beyond serious challenge by February 1921.

Much more important, he argued, was the question what to do to save the October Revolution. The 'trade union discussion' was an integral element of this question, but it was not the whole question. Lenin wanted a more direct and fundamental debate. The most effective way to start this was to tackle the policy on food supplies. Only when the party had decided what to do about the acquisition of grain could it begin to sort out its strategic orientation over the next few years.

Yet Lenin could ride two horses at once. He kept on thinking about agrarian policy even while Trotski was ripping the party apart over the trade unions. Lenin did not reveal what had caused his change of mind. But he had talked frequently to peasant representatives at the Eighth Congress of Soviets in December 1920, and he gave audiences to small delegations of peasants in subsequent weeks. He had taken little trips to Yaropolets and Modenovo in the Moscow countryside and spoken to the local villagers. He was left in no doubt that the regime's popularity stood at its lowest ebb. The evidence coming into the offices of Sovnarkom pointed in the same direction. Lenin was often compelled to absolve provinces from the need to comply with grain-delivery quotas fixed by himself and his government in Moscow. Current policy was unable to feed the country and the situation was getting worse. Soon there were Bolsheviks who were pressing the same case. One of them, V. N. Sokolov, arrived from Siberia where he had witnessed the rural disturbances. Unless the Politburo acted, he privately urged Lenin on 2 February, the problem might turn into a catastrophe.

At the Politburo on the same day a report was given by Bukharin, who had returned from Tambov province. The Politburo at last began to face the fact of 'peasant uprisings' across the Russian heartland.[2] Tambov was in the Volga region. The leadership of the revolt was a Socialist-Revolutionary, A. S. Antonov. But it was clear that the peasants, many of whom were starving because of the wartime official economic measures and a sudden drought, were infuriated with the Soviet government. Lenin had always taken a dim view of the peasantry of the Volga and in the Civil War he had practised preventive mass repression. In 1921, however, it was too late to apply prevention. The Red Army was needed to crush a rebellion that threatened to bring down the regime.

Lenin transferred Vladimir Antonov-Ovseenko as political commissar and Mikhail Tukhachevski as commander to carry out the necessary campaign. But this was not enough in itself. There had also to be some steps toward agrarian reform. The October Revolution itself was under threat.

It was the Tambov revolt that convinced Lenin that the wartime requisitioning system had to be abolished. But he did not let on to anyone as yet and went on seeing eyewitnesses of the rural scene. One such was the peasant Osip Chernov, who was surprised that the leader of world communism agreed to see him. When Lenin asked him to read out his pencil-written account of his experiences, Chernov told him some uncomfortable truths about the Siberian peasantry. In particular, he pointed out that the richer peasants in that great region had fought against Kolchak as hard as their poorer neighbours and that they were being unfairly treated as anti-Soviet. Chernov stressed that there was no kulak threat there:[3]

> When I'd finished reading, he put the question to me: 'What's your background?' I told him how I belonged to a group of exiled forced-labour prisoners, that I'd been sentenced to forced labour for having belonged to the Socialist-Revolutionary Party but that I now regarded myself as a non-party person and had my own farm in Siberia.

Chernov was precisely the kind of peasant whom the Bolsheviks were routinely designating as a 'kulak', depriving him of his entire grain stock and even killing him. Lenin needed to meet people who could talk knowledgeably and frankly. Father Gapon had opened his eyes for him in 1905, and peasants like Osip Chernov were performing the same function in early 1921.

By the time the Politburo next met, on 8 February 1921, Lenin had become a committed advocate: grain requisitioning had to be abolished. Not everyone could be present. The 'trade union discussion' was continuing and Trotski and Zinoviev were chasing each other around the Urals trying to maximise support at the forthcoming Party Congress. But four members – Lenin, Kamenev, Stalin and Krestinski – were able to attend. They regarded themselves as being quorate; and having listened to a report by Agriculture Deputy People's Commissar Nikolai Osinski, Lenin took a single sheet of paper and sketched the agreed change of policy. His 'Preliminary Rough Draft of Theses on the Peasants' was the basis for the future NEP. The die had been cast. A working party was set up under Kamenev to fill in the policy details. Not a squeak about the Politburo decision was uttered in public. But on 16

February the Politburo, with some trepidation about the party's sensitivities, sanctioned the publication of a pro-reform article in *Pravda*; the joint authors would be low-level Bolshevik activists, not Politburo members.[4] Unfortunately A. D. Tsyurupa was upsetting Lenin's progress by raising objections in the secret working party. The Politburo drew breath and handed the matter to the Central Committee. The tension was tremendous because Central Committee members were already at each other's throats over the 'trade union discussion'.

Yet Lenin need not have worried about the Central Committee's response; meeting on 24 February, its members accepted the working party's report with just a few modifications.[5] By then the depth of the political emergency in the country as a whole was evident. Strikes had broken out in Petrograd, Moscow and the other large industrial cities. There was an incipient mutiny in the Kronstadt naval garrison, and Zinoviev was unsure that he would be able to handle it from his base in nearby Petrograd. Aggravating all this were the peasant uprisings in the Volga region, in Ukraine, in southern Russia and in western Siberia. The disturbances continued even in Moscow. On 2 March, indeed, Kronstadt flared into open mutiny and the Petrograd strikes intensified. Yet still Lenin could not feel confident that his project was accepted in the party. There were plenty of Bolsheviks wishing to continue with the wartime economic programme even if it was provoking armed popular resistance. But Lenin and Trotski were together on this. The revolts were themselves the most powerful argument for reform. When the Central Committee met on 7 March, there was no serious attempt to reverse the Politburo's agrarian proposals.

The Tenth Party Congress had yet to confirm this. The proceedings started on 8 March and Lenin had prepared well by agreeing a preferred list of members of the new Central Committee at a series of meetings with Stalin and his other closest associates. While he wanted a majority for his faction, Lenin also wanted a sprinkling of Trotskyists, Democratic Centralists and Workers' Oppositionists to be included. He wanted to control but not to humiliate and exclude the critics. In his Congress opening speech, he acknowledged that a mistake had been made over Poland; he also claimed, surprisingly for a leader who was meant to be the workers' friend, that too much indulgence had been shown to the working-class consumers at the expense of disgruntled peasants. The party, Lenin said, had to accept military retrenchment, economic reform and intensified political control. He accused the Workers' Opposition, which appealed for the working class to be enabled to control the factories, of deviating from Marxism. The fact that Marx – and indeed Lenin himself in 1917 – had emphasised the need for workers to control the factories in the era of socialist Revolution was robustly ignored by Lenin. Rather than argue out the case, he announced bleakly that the regime might fall if a consensus on reform and repression did not prevail in the party. As proof he adduced the information about the mutinous talk in the Kronstadt naval garrison. The threat was greater, he declared, than when Kolchak and Denikin had been on the loose.

Towards the end of his speech of two hours he seemed to sense that the Congress, which was being told about the NEP for the first time, might think that he was going soft – or, worse, going pro-peasant and pro-capitalist. He uttered a phrase that chilled the heart:

> The peasant must do a bit of starving so as to relieve the factories and towns from complete starvation. On the level of the state in general this is an entirely understandable thing, but we're not counting on the exhausted, destitute peasant–owner understanding it. And we know you can't manage without compulsion, to which the devastated peasantry is reacting very strongly.

Plainly the NEP was not going to work by persuasion alone.

As yet there was no answer to the more fundamental question whether the Congress would sanction the NEP. The task was not easy for Lenin. The party had been torn into factions by the 'trade union discussion'. There was fury even inside Lenin's faction about the policy on foreign business concessions. There was widespread discontent about the internal organisation of the party since, while some delegates wanted looser discipline, others thought Lenin too gentle. There was confusion about the current diplomatic measures of the party leadership, and not a few delegates wondered how the victories in the October Revolution and the Civil War could be protected and enhanced. Lenin was at his wiliest in coping with the expected tumult. The fact that the Trotskyists, Workers' Oppositionists and Democratic Centralists were at each other's throats was helpful. There was no broad agreement on any policy and Lenin had the advantage of at least seeming to know where he wanted the party to go. Others such as Trotski and Shlyapnikov had their own strategy too; but they lacked Lenin's reputation in the party for getting things right. The *April Theses*, the October 1917 seizure of power and the Treaty of Brest-Litovsk had acquired canonical status inside the doctrines of Bolshevism. Lenin was regarded as having the party's wisest head. There was also an affection for him across the factions; he simply did not incur the personal rancour that was provoked by the other two most prominent Politburo members, Trotski and Zinoviev; and the entire party was aware that if it did not reseal its rifts, it would be overwhelmed by the tide of popular resentment.

Only second-rank leaders openly attacked the NEP in principle. Although it was a close-run thing at times, Lenin held out for victory, and victory was his. The NEP, foreign business concessions, Lenin's trade union policy, the condemnation of the Workers' Opposition as a deviation from Marxism: all were resoundingly sanctioned by the Congress.

His triumph would not have been achieved with such aplomb if it had not been for events outside the capital. Midway through the Congress came the news from Kronstadt. The naval garrison had risen in revolt. The mutineers demanded an end to terror, to dictatorship, to grain requisitioning and to one-party rule; they despaired of the Bolshevik party and had grown to hate it; indeed they called for 'soviets without communists'. This was the deepest internal military crisis since the July 1918 uprising of the Left Socialist-Revolutionaries. The Kronstadters, moreover, were renowned as great supporters of the Bolsheviks in 1917. It was an awful time for a mutiny to occur. The Soviet regime was threatened by peasant revolts in Russia, Ukraine, the north Caucasus and western Siberia. A terrible famine had started in the Volga and Ukraine. Industry everywhere was in ruins. Rival political parties had been suppressed, but none of them had given up hope of making a return to public life. Religious and national bodies across the former Russian Empire wanted an end to the communist regime. The great foreign powers – Britain, France, Japan and the United States – wished Soviet Russia nothing but ill. Now even Kronstadt had turned against the Bolsheviks.

In this situation it was easier than beforehand to urge the Congress that unity was the supreme requirement. Even the Workers' Oppositionists, whom Lenin was denouncing, volunteered for the military operation to cross the ice from Petrograd to Kronstadt Island. Red Army troops were camouflaged by new white uniforms and rushed north. Trotski went with them, and the fortress of Kronstadt was seized back for the Bolsheviks. Lenin stayed behind and had to wait for news. The most he could do was to produce propaganda, and his *Pravda* articles were among his most disgraceful travesties of truth. According to Lenin, the Kronstadt mutineers had been duped by the Socialist-Revolutionaries who in turn were the agents of foreign capitalist powers. Lenin, consulting with fellow Central Committee members about the punishment to be meted out to the Kronstadters, demanded ferocious reprisals. The

Kronstadt fortress fell to superior numbers. The relief of those Congress delegates remaining in Petrograd was almost palpable. The result was that Lenin's agrarian reform was not criticised as savagely as it might otherwise have been. He saw his chance and pushed through a resolution banning factional activity from the party altogether. If economic retreat was to succeed, he argued, the Bolsheviks had to strengthen their internal unity. He had won by the skin of his teeth, but he had won.

Yet he had no respite. In the last week of March 1921 the German Communist Party, egged on by the Hungarian communist leader Béla Kun on behalf of Comintern, attempted to seize power in Berlin. Almost certainly this had the support of both Grigori Zinoviev and Nikolai Bukharin, but the planning and execution of the insurrectionary measures were botched. When he heard of the 'March Action' Lenin was furious.

Even on his birthday on 23 April 1921 (according to the new calendar) he had to, or felt he had to, adhere to a punishing schedule of duties. Thus he chaired a crucial Politburo meeting, among whose items for decision were education, Siberia, Ukrainian military dispositions, the Kronstadt mutiny's aftermath and the Workers' Opposition.[6] Despite this long meeting, Lenin's day was not over. He appointed a new personal aide for himself in Sovnarkom. He wrote to the People's Commissariats for External Affairs and for Internal Affairs. He intervened in the plans drawn up for G. L. Shklovski's medical treatment; this was almost a hobby of Lenin's in relation to leading comrades: their health was regarded by him as a matter of state business. Meanwhile he followed up the previous agenda of various governmental bodies such as the Council of Labour and Defence and the Lesser Sovnarkom. In the little time he had left to himself he tried to write up some pages of his booklet on the NEP, *On the Food Tax*. It was not his busiest working day; but it was packed with duties that, he felt, could not be performed without him. He had reached the age of fifty-one and did not have a minute to himself.

Political life was the core of his existence; he was not one to feel sorry for himself when duty called. Whenever he liked, he could request Stepan Gil to drive him out to the Gorki sanatorium, but generally he just got on with politics. Nevertheless he was dreadfully weary. He had coped effectively with revolution, war and even with peace and its problems. He had survived the loss of relatives and of Inessa. But he was enormously disappointed that he had not been able to depend on his fellow party leaders. In the winter of 1920–1 they had been more interested in internal polemics than in saving the Revolution, and the polemics did not cease in spring 1921: Lenin still had a job on his hands in holding the party to the decisions taken at the Tenth Party Congress. And when the leading Bolsheviks were not fighting among themselves, they were grasping after a respite from work; the intense wartime pressures were taking their toll and each leader experienced severe problems with his health. The Politburo became inoperative as one by one the members reported sick, and Lenin, despite his own chronic ailments, had to soldier on alone. He was working at the edge of his coping capacity.

But there was nothing else for it. Trotski was in an obvious state of exhaustion and had to have a holiday. Zinoviev suffered not one but two heart attacks and Kamenev too had a cardiac problem.[7] Stalin had had to have his appendix removed. Bukharin had only recently returned from convalescence. Lenin had had lonely struggles in the past, but this one took as much mental toughness as any.

And it was in these same months that the question of the trade unions rejoined the political agenda. Alexander Shlyapnikov, the Workers' Oppositionist leader, continued to stir up trouble in defiance of the Tenth Party Congress ban on factional activity. The central party leaders – those who were not in sanatoria or under the surgeon's knife – assigned Mikhail Tomski as Chairman of the All-Russia Central Council of the Trade Unions to enforce the party's will in the Metalworkers' Union. Tomski, facing an angry audience, did his best but made several concessions to the trade union activists. Lenin plunged into a delirium at what he took to be Tomski's act of betrayal, and demanded his immediate exclusion from the Party Central Committee. In the past Lenin had often got overheated, only to calm down a day later. Nor was it unknown for him to give an exaggerated display of passion in order to secure a political result. But weeks after the Metalworkers' Union episode he was still raging to have Tomski flung out of the Central Committee and even out of the party.[8]

Lenin's nerves were in shreds; his fatigue was extreme. For Tomski was not one of his critics but quite the opposite: he had been a steadfast ally throughout the 'trade union discussion' in the previous winter. Lenin thought his luck at the recent Party Congress would hold and that leading party colleagues would recognise that the supreme priority was to realise and develop the NEP. He felt especially isolated. It was clear that the NEP, which was passed into law in April and was starting at last to be imposed across the country, was not securely accepted in the party. For many – quite possibly most – regional and central Bolshevik leaders, the reintroduction of private trade in grain was repugnant. But then Lenin and Kamenev proceeded to add various measures in order to make the reform truly workable. They went beyond the original reform project, permitting peasants to trade outside their own locality and allowing commercial middlemen to operate; they gave extensive rights to rural agricultural co-operatives; and they gave little encouragement to state collective farms. They even sanctioned the return of small-scale private manufacturers to the industrial sector. The capitalist corner of the economy was filling an ever greater space. When and where, asked the Bolsheviks, was the process going to end?

In an effort to prove his revolutionary credentials Lenin finished his booklet *On the Food Tax*. His main contention was that Sovnarkom and the Central Committee back in 1918 had recognised the need for some space to be given to capitalism in the Russian economy. Thus the NEP was not new at all, but a policy restored. The onset of Civil War had intervened and necessitated emergency measures that he now referred to as 'War Communism'. Such measures, he declared, could be suspended. Obviously there was some truth in this. But it was far from being the whole truth, and Lenin knew it, for the NEP allowed greater legal freedom for the peasantry to trade grain than had previously been available to them.

But no one was going to argue about the history of the Bolsheviks. As Lenin clearly perceived, his party was looking to him to show them why on earth they should still believe that the NEP was Marxist in orientation. *On the Food Tax* supplied arguments in abundance. He stressed above all that the NEP would not involve political concessions or ideological compromise. The supreme goal remained as previously: the consolidation of socialism and the further advance towards communism. He wanted, even under the NEP, to move towards elaborating a 'uniform economic plan for the entire state'. He retained a penchant for terror and recommended the shooting of individuals for common fraud and corruption, for bureaucratic abuses and even for commercial profiteering: '*It is impossible* to distinguish speculation from "correct" trade if speculation is to be understood in the politico-economic sense. Freedom of trade is capitalism, capitalism is speculation: it would be ridiculous to close our eyes to this.' So capitalism was not going to be done any favours. Rather it was going to be exploited by the Soviet state: capitalist tendencies in the economy would lead to the formation of larger units of production, which in turn would facilitate the incorporation of these units as state property in the near future. And capitalism would enable

Russia to rise more quickly to the technical and cultural level necessary for socialism to be attained. The NEP was consequently, in Lenin's presentation, a resumption of the road taken by the party since the October Revolution but interrupted by the Civil War, the road to socialism.

He put this case forcefully and directly at the Party Conference, held to discuss the NEP from 26 May 1921. He knew that he would have to deal with the delayed reaction of leading Bolsheviks to the NEP. As yet he could not predict the strength of feeling, but even he – the party's fiercest polemicist – was shaken by the vituperation unleashed at him. There was widespread agreement that large-scale industry was being neglected, that workers were losing out, that the central leadership had not properly explained its measures and that the kulak danger was being overlooked. Lenin's booklet did not escape criticism. It was said to be unclear and incoherent. Not a single speaker raised his voice in defence of Lenin. Not once in his long career had he been the butt of such a verbal mauling.

A furious Lenin came back next day for a debate on the recent *débâcle* in the trade union leadership. Lenin was not there at the start, but asked for the floor to express his lingering anger. After recounting the sins of Tomski, he suggested that the affair pointed to the supreme need for internal party unity. Not for the last time he argued that the basic danger to the Revolution was the clash between the respective interests of the workers and the peasants. Factions might arise in defence of one or the other social class.[9] The sole antidote was discipline. His plea was directed not only at avoiding a further trade-union *débâcle* but also at preventing a reconsideration of the NEP. Lenin's passion swayed the Conference. It had been noteworthy that, although universal objection had been voiced about aspects of the NEP and its application, not a soul had called for its replacement. Acquiescence was on the rise. Tacitly it was agreed that fundamentally there was no alternative. The Conference had things it could be enthusiastic about. In particular, it agreed that 'a merciless struggle' should be started against the Socialist-Revolutionaries. No one was happy that the party was giving up its overt military commitment to spreading socialist revolution in the West. But Lenin cheered them up: 'Of course, if a revolution occurs in Europe, we'll naturally change policy.'[10] This remark was never published. All that *Pravda* was allowed to report was Lenin's prognosis that the NEP had to be kept in place for many years.

The toughness of his Conference performance jumps off the pages of the stenographic record. It was also a bravura display. He had invited pity by reciting the list of central party leaders who had let him down or had been ill. He had challenged his critics on their own ground. Strutting up and down the platform of the Sverdlov Hall, he had shown anger and determination. He had scattered his apothegms on Marxism through his speeches. When his orthodoxy had been questioned, he had laid into his adversaries. At no point did he relax his belligerent insistence that the NEP – the expanded version of the NEP he had developed since February – was the sole means of surviving the general crisis of the regime.

The viciousness of the debates was such that Lenin decided to keep the proceedings as secret as possible. The party had confirmed the strategic options it had taken since February 1921, and he did not want others to know how tumultuous an opposition had been proffered initially. He also needed to reinforce his victory over his party with a campaign against the leftist elements in the Comintern. The fiasco of the March 1921 Action in Berlin continued to rankle. Any repetition of such 'adventurism', as Lenin described it, might jeopardise the various commercial and diplomatic agreements that Sovnarkom had authorised since the beginning of the year. To Lenin it appeared self-evident after the *débâcle* in Poland that revolutionary expansionism had to be handled with subtlety in the foreseeable future. There was too much to lose. On 16 March 1921 an Anglo-Soviet trade agreement was signed, and one of its conditions was that the Soviet authorities would desist from subversive activities in the territory of the British Empire. Two days later a peace treaty was signed with Poland in the neutral city of Riga, capital of Latvia. A diplomatic deal was done, too, with Turkey. And for Lenin it was wonderful that approaches were being made to him by business circles in the USA and especially Germany. The protection and enhancement of Soviet interests appeared to him to be on the reachable horizon.

There were phrases he occasionally used, mostly with foreigners, which gave the impression that he was satisfied with this condition. He was a good conjuror. When he said that he favoured 'peaceful coexistence', many in the West began to believe that he was some kind of pacifist. But among his fellow communists, whether Russians or foreigners, he absolutely never expressed such a non-Marxist consideration. Why should he indeed? He still believed that Soviet Russia would eventually need to be accompanied by Soviet Germany, Soviet France and Soviet Britain. But he had always prided himself on being able to make the best of a bad job. He continued to sanction the secret dispatch of money, spies and propaganda to the rest of the world, particularly to central Europe. He did what he could to divide the capitalist powers among themselves. He did not explain how the balance would be kept between a *rapprochement* with such powers and an enhancement of the interests of global socialist Revolution. He had not worked this out even for himself.

One thing was clear to him: the Comintern had to be put straight about the need to avoid any kind of insurrectionary impatience that might endanger Soviet Russia by encouraging France and the United Kingdom to organise an anti-communist crusade. His last great effort of the year after the Polish *débâcle* was devoted to binding foreign communists to this policy at the Third Comintern Congress that opened in Moscow on 23 June 1921. He kept a wary eye on influential figures in the Comintern such as Karl Radek and Béla Kun. The Communist Party of Germany objected to being criticised for the March Action; its leaders continued to feel that they had only acted as Lenin's Bolsheviks had done in 1917. Lenin quite lost his temper with them. Obviously he reckoned that they might make another ill-judged attempt to seize power. At the Congress he declared that the Bolsheviks had risen against the Provisional Government only after they had secured a 'majority of soviets of workers' and peasants' deputies' and that this was the true precedent for the German communists to follow. This was false history. It was not in fact until after the October 1917 Revolution that the Bolsheviks acquired an absolute majority even in the urban soviets. But by the end of the Civil War the myth was believed by most Bolsheviks – and perhaps Lenin himself believed it. And by the end of the Congress, on 12 July, he had got his way.

Lenin had had to be at his persuasive best. The problem was that he often lost his tactfulness. The Hungarian communists, especially Béla Kun, had taken offence at his commentary. For this, unusually, Lenin apologised; but he reasserted the correctness of his current policy and tried to suggest that he, too, had been wrong in the past:[11]

> I therefore hasten to communicate in writing: when I myself was an émigré (for more than 15 years), I several times took up 'too left-wing' a position (as I now can see). In August 1917 I too was an émigré and made too 'leftist' a proposal to the Central Committee, which fortunately was completely rejected.

This confession had been a long time in coming. Unlike his other reference to the history of 1917, moreover, it was demonstrably true. It might be added that his proposal to the Central Committee not only in

August but also in October had been disastrous. The difference was that his August 1917 proposal would have put his party's existence in jeopardy but his insistence on carrying through his October proposal doomed his country to rack and ruin.

He was never going to reconsider the whole project of the Bolshevik seizure of power. His life and career were tied inextricably to the October 1917 Revolution, and he wanted the Comintern to accept that he knew better than any living communist, Russian or foreign, how best to protect that Revolution. He had done this with ferocity at confidential meetings of the Politburo and the Central Committee. The Red Army had been dispatched to suppress the Kronstadt mutineers and to kill the leaders and transfer the rest to Ukhta forced-labour camp in the Russian far north. He had approved the transfer of political commissar Vladimir Antonov-Ovseenko and commander Mikhail Tukhachevski to Tambov with the task of rooting out the Tambov peasant rebels, if need be by use of poison gas delivered by aeroplane bombing raids. He had sanctioned violence against all those who had politically resisted the Reds as they moved into Azerbaijan, Armenia and Georgia. As in 1891–2, he had looked away when reports were made to him of the growing famine across Russia and Ukraine even though cases of cannibalism were widespread. He let the Cheka loose whenever industrial strikes took place. Not once did he give a signal that he was depressed. Not once did he say to a single associate that the October Revolution had been made in vain or that all the bloodshed was getting too much for him.

Instead he reflected on a year's satisfactory work. But for him, his party would have thrown itself off a precipice. The NEP, by combining deep military and political repression with very marginal economic reform, was the barest minimum that could save the Soviet regime. He had seen this later than he could and should have done. But no other Bolshevik could have pushed the party into it. Days before the end of the Third Comintern Congress he was exhausted, and to the disappointment of the Congress he did not appear for the closing session. But he had done what he had set out to do. He could not afford to brag about this. But the triumphs at the Party Congress, Party Conference and Comintern Congress were the products of exceptional political skill. Without Lenin, there would have been no Revolution in October 1917. Without Lenin, the Russian Communist Party would not have lasted much beyond the end of 1921.

26

A QUESTION OF SURVIVAL

July 1921 to July 1922

Most of the basic components of Lenin's New Economic Policy were in place. Peasants were allowed to sell their grain surplus to whomever they liked, and small-scale private manufacturing and commerce returned to the towns; and overt threats to subvert capitalism in Europe were put into abeyance. At the same time there was no slackening of the grip of the one-party, one-ideology state. The leading posts in public institutions were staffed by Bolsheviks, and the Cheka – redesignated as the Main Political Administration – arrested dissenters. With the exception of tsarist Poland and the Baltic states, the outlying regions of the former Russian Empire had been reconquered. Marxist tenets were given official precedence over every rival national, religious and cultural vision. The expectation in the party of Lenin was that sooner or later the world would be won for communism.

By mid-1921, however, Lenin felt inadequate to his personal responsibilities. The problem was not intellectual or political but simply physical; his health, which had never been wonderful, was in drastic decline. He could no longer put in a full day's work. The chronic headaches and insomnia had got worse, and he had suffered a series of 'small' heart attacks. Having interrogated his doctors, he saw that they were in a quandary about their diagnosis and he turned for advice instead to his brother Dmitri. This had a positive result for one of his problems. Several specialists were suggesting that Lenin was suffering from stomach illness. Dmitri Ilich thought otherwise after watching him play skittles at Gorki, and told him that he was jerking his back at the game and thereby straining the sinews of his stomach. As soon as Lenin gave up skittles, the problem with his stomach disappeared.[1] But, beyond that, Dmitri Ilich was as perplexed as everyone else and the other medical symptoms continued to give trouble. Lenin was so desperate that he stopped keeping his secret from the Politburo. He did this with reluctance since he was wary of interference by his fellow leaders. But he was caught in a trap of his own making. Having set the precedent of ordering sick colleagues to go to hospitals or sanatoria, he could not reasonably complain if the Politburo decided upon his own medical regimen.

On 4 June 1921 the Politburo instructed him to take a month's holiday,[2] and obediently Lenin moved out to Gorki. He had permission to return to Moscow only for a few sessions of the Third Comintern Congress. But the stark reality, which he withheld from all but the inner cabal of the central party leadership, was that he was seriously ill. On 8 July he himself asked for an easing of his workload over the following month.[3] The request was granted. On 9 August, his colleagues took the initiative and ordered him to extend his leave. Lenin was frank: 'I can't work.'[4] Medical examinations followed and the various specialists prescribed a lengthy abstention from work. But Lenin, who until then had been uncharacteristically docile, argued with his doctors and secured their consent to reduce but not eliminate his public activity. He interpreted this irresponsibly. He continued to chair the Politburo, Central Committee and Sovnarkom; he also appeared at the Congress of Soviets in December.

Meanwhile he moved from one former estate mansion to another in the Moscow countryside before settling at Gorki in the 'Big House', where rooms were being prepared for him. The Gorki mansion had been built in the eighteenth century at the height of the provincial gentry's passion for building splendid houses for themselves on their estates. It had been renovated in 1910 by the new owners, General and Mrs Reinbot; it therefore, unlike most such estate houses, already had central heating and electricity. A winter garden had also been added before the Great War. But the architectural beauty had been preserved. The classical façade was graced by six white columns. Inside the rooms had generous high ceilings and comfortable, well-maintained furniture. With its two storeys and spacious rooms it afforded an environment of ease. Outside there were wooded parklands where rabbits were plentiful among the birches. There was also a neat little pond where the old owners had fished. Mushrooms grew abundantly in season. Immediately to the south of the mansion there flowed the river Pakhra. The air around Gorki, which is set on high ground, was clean and tranquil. Lenin had chosen a splendid place for his convalescence.

He was joined at weekends by Nadezhda Konstantinovna and Maria Ilinichna. Determined to establish a working environment for himself, he took their Kremlin housemaid Sasha with him.[5] He gave instructions for an additional telephone line to be connected to nearby Podolsk so that he could be sure of instant communication with the Kremlin. The bookcases in the drawing room were stocked with four hundred books for his ready reference – life would not be worth living without books.[6] Then Stepan Gil brought out a Rolls-Royce saloon car and stationed it in the garage to the side of the house. This splendid vehicle, gleaming and light-grey, had been had been bought in London on Sovnarkom's behalf by Foreign Trade People's Commissar Leonid Krasin. Unfortunately the Rolls-Royce was unusable in the winter months and Lenin permitted it to be adapted for snowy conditions. This involved an act of industrial vandalism. The wheels of the vehicle were removed, and huge skis were fixed to the front of the chassis and caterpillar tracks to the back. This would enable his chauffeur to negotiate the winding path to the sanatorium without getting stuck in snowdrifts. Mr Rolls and Mr Royce would hardly have approved.

Lenin was more fastidious as a resident of the Big House itself. He stopped the servants from removing the dust covers from the furniture since he intended, at the end of his convalescence, to leave things exactly as he had found them. Such restraint was in contrast with his attempt in 1918 to light a fire in the first-floor grate as he had done in London exile in Mrs Yeo's house in Holford Square.[7] The chimneys at Gorki had not been designed for this purpose, and the result was a blaze that would have burned down the mansion if his bodyguards had not moved swiftly to put it out.

On normal days, in any case, Lenin did not like the temperature too warm. He expected his doctors too to be hardy types; the psychiatrist Professor Viktor Osipov was disconcerted to find that Lenin had ordered that the temperature should rise no higher than 15° centigrade.[8] But Osipov knew better than to complain: he had only just been released from the custody of the Cheka.[9] One day he was about to be tried, and perhaps shot, as a counter-revolutionary agent, the next he was among the chief doctors attending to the Revolution's leader. Faced with the problem of Lenin's illness, the Politburo had had to take a more pragmatic approach to suspected 'enemies of the people'. Only doctors could cure patients; and anyway the evidence against Osipov was flimsy in the extreme. People's Commissar of Health Nikolai Semashko took advice as to who were the best specialists available. Money was no obstacle to attracting foreigners to join the quest to cure the ailing Lenin. Thus it came about that a group of German professors were invited to join Osipov and other distinguished Russian doctors to diagnose what was wrong and restore him to full physical fitness.

The patient's workload since 1917 was making itself felt, and he had been foolish in not lowering it drastically in the second half of 1921. Apart from brief periods of convalescence, he had not been able to take the lengthy summer holidays he had enjoyed as an emigrant. His body and mind cried out for a rest. He was becoming frantic, and did not know whom to turn to. His experience with Russian doctors, except for his brother Dmitri, had bred mistrust, and the German doctors fetched at considerable expense by the People's Commissariat of Health had yet to agree on a diagnosis. (In fact they never did.) And all the time Lenin's condition was worsening. But one thing hurt him more than any physical pain he was suffering; this was that for the first time in his life he was losing the will to work. He got up some mornings and did not care if he looked at his papers or not.[10] This was beyond his understanding. He could scarcely believe it was happening to him. Purposefulness had been one of his cardinal characteristics since childhood. It was an unforgivable sin in the Ulyanov family to fail to get on with one's appointed tasks. To fail to want to get on with them was not just unforgivable: it was unimaginable.

Lenin's father Ilya Nikolaevich had driven himself to physical exhaustion while setting up a network of primary schools in Simbirsk province. His brother Alexander omitted to come home for the Christmas vacations from St Petersburg University so as to be able to revise for his biology exams. Nikolai Chernyshevski devoted himself to research on Russian sociology and economics while serving out years of administrative exile in Siberia. Karl Marx wrote volumes of general social theory in London. These heroes of Lenin had worked till they dropped dead. Lenin had been like them. But suddenly, in his fifty-second year, he no longer felt an automatic compulsion to go on working.

No one could explain what was going wrong. He was willing to talk about his listlessness to his doctor brother and to the specialists who tended to him. Listlessness was one of two new problems. But it was not until he had a consultation with Professor Liveri Darkevich on 4 March 1922 that he confided in him about the second. Darkevich, a gifted listener as well as a neuropathologist, elicited from him the statement that for some time he had been suffering from periodic 'obsessions'. We still do not know the exact content of the obsessions, but clearly Lenin wondered whether he was going mad. They had difficulty in discussing the symptoms in Russian, but in French they could communicate since Lenin was more accustomed to European-language medical textbooks and terminology. He was in the pit of despair. The synthesis of insomnia,

Lenin on his fiftieth birthday, 1920

Left: Lenin in 1919 recording one of his shorter speeches.

Below: Lenin addressing Red Army troops bound for the Polish front, 5 May 1920. Note the presence of Kamenev and Trotski to the right of the platform. Their images were removed from official Soviet reproductions from the late 1920s.

Right: A session of the Second Congress of Comintern. Nadezhda Konstantinovna sits to Lenin's left, Inessa to his right.

Above: Walking in Moscow: Iosif Stalin, Alexei Rykov, Lev Kamenev and Grigori Zinoviev.

Left: Nikolai Bukharin

Lenin chairing Sovnarkom in autumn 1922.

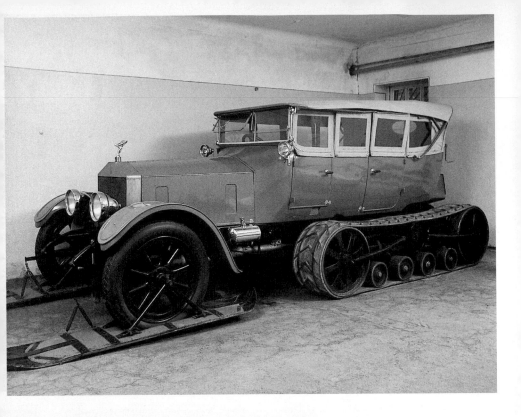

Above: The much adapted official Rolls Royce. Note the tank tracks at the back and the skis at the front.

Left: Lenin in his wheelchair in 1923, flanked by Professor Förster to the left and Dr Gete to the right.

Top right: The Big House at Gorki.

Right: Family photograph at Gorki, August 1922. From right to left: Lenin, Nadezhda Konstantinovna, the nephew Viktor (son of Dmitri Ilich), Anna Ilinichna and a girl called Vera (surname unascertained).

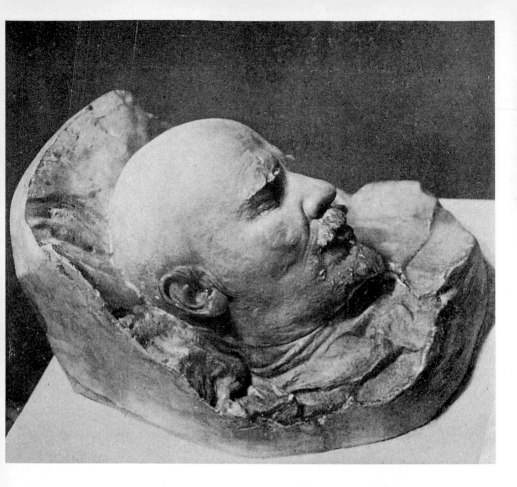

Above: Lenin's death mask, made by the sculptor Sergei Merkurov.

Left: The first mausoleum, 1924.

headache, heart seizure, listlessness, back pain and obsessiveness had produced a mood of deep pessimism. No one knew about this. He had always been secretive about his illnesses, except when he spoke to family members – and even with them he was not entirely forthcoming. But now, he recognised, something worse was happening to him than he had previously experienced. He was beginning, quietly, to panic and his thoughts turned to suicide.

He was frightened of dying the lingering death of paralysis; and for a long time he had been impressed by the similar decision in favour of self-destruction taken by Marx's son-in-law Paul Lafargue in 1911.[11] For this purpose he turned to the steeliest of his comrades: Stalin. He could not depend on relatives to put aside their emotional ties. Nor would other comrades have the necessary hardness of heart. But Lenin extracted from Stalin a promise to give him poison at whatever time he should request it. He planned to be ready when, in his judgement, the moment came.[12]

This, however, he kept secret from the medical professionals whom he consulted in these months; he feared that they would interfere with his scheme. Nevertheless he trusted them with some of his other ruminations. This is not an unusual phenomenon, especially for people who have no religious belief and therefore no priest, minister or equivalent person to whom they can unburden themselves. Lenin, once he had decided he could trust Darkevich, blurted out:[13]

> Every revolutionary, having reached the age of fifty, must be ready to leave for the side of the stage. [I] can no longer continue to work as before; it's not only hard for [me] to carry out the duties of two people but it's hard too to do just my own work; [I] don't have the strength to answer for my own affairs. It's this loss of working capacity, this fatal loss came up on me unnoticed: I've altogether stopped being a working person [*rabotnik*].

Lenin felt very depressed, saying that 'his song was sung, his role played out' and that he must hand on his post to someone else. He was also in intense pain: 'A night doomed to insomnia is a truly terrible thing when you have to be ready in the morning for work, work, work without end...'[14]

Maria Ilinichna and the Ulyanovs' family doctor Professor Gete were present and heard Lenin pour his heart out.[15] Lenin's choice of his sister rather than Nadezhda Konstantinovna to accompany him was significant; the coolness between him and his wife persisted. The consultation went on for four hours, and, when it was over, Darkevich gave his conclusions. He could find no 'organic disease of the brain' but rather a cerebral exhaustion. His proposed course of treatment was simple. Lenin needed a rest from intellectual and political work; he should take a break in the Moscow countryside and, if he liked, he could go hunting. He should give no more than one speech per month. Lenin was pleased. The shadow of an early death had passed from him. Maria Ilinichna thanked Darkevich, telling him that her brother had become 'a totally different person'.[16] In refreshed mood he kept up residence in the mansion at Gorki. Occasionally – for he would not keep strictly to Darkevich's regime – he travelled back to Moscow. His zest was too much for his chauffeur Stepan Gil. Lenin wanted the Rolls-Royce to go faster whether or not there were ruts in the road. Gil obeyed, but drew the line at endangering animal life. Lenin upbraided him for unnecessary 'reverence' for roadside chickens. This was yet another of those displays of unfeelingness than caused the official censors to withhold any reference to the conversations between Gil and Lenin for nearly seventy years.

He appeared to be following his doctors' advice. In 1921 there had been some discussion that Lenin might represent the Soviet government at the international conference planned for the following year at Genoa in northern Italy. Foreign newspapermen were already describing such a trip as an historic occasion. Outside Russia, hardly anyone knew much about Lenin. The British writers H. G. Wells and Bertrand Russell had interviewed him in 1920; their accounts left readers in no doubt that he was an extraordinary man and politician. Several very scurrilous books were also being published on contemporary Russia, and all had sections on Lenin. He was the object of the world's fascination. Excitement at the possibility of glimpsing him was mounting, and for a while the official authorities in Moscow did nothing to quieten the speculation. Even if he had been fit, however, he was unlikely to have travelled. His own People's Commissar of Foreign Trade Leonid Krasin warned him that Russian monarchists or Socialist-Revolutionaries might try to assassinate him. Lenin in response wrote from Gorki asking the Politburo to prohibit not only himself but also Trotski and Zinoviev from going. The risks were too great.[17]

It was decided at the last moment that Georgi Chicherin the Foreign Affairs People's Commissar would represent the Soviet government. Lenin suspected that the Politburo in his absence might not be aware that Chicherin needed tight control from Moscow. Essentially Lenin had already rejected the possibility of a comprehensive international settlement in Genoa. His reasons were twofold: firstly, he did not want to have his hands tied in relation to internal economic policy, and he knew that this would be the price paid for any deal with the United Kingdom and France; secondly, he had no intention of consolidating the territorial and political arrangements imposed on Europe by the Treaties of Versailles, St Germain and Trianon. To Lenin it seemed obvious that Soviet long-term interests lay in creating divisions among the various capitalist countries. He got the Politburo to order Chicherin to lend priority not to a comprehensive post-war treaty but to a separate commercial and diplomatic treaty with Germany. On 16 April the Soviet delegation under Chicherin obtained what the Politburo wanted when the negotiations with the Germans at Rapallo, nineteen miles from Genoa, yielded a separate treaty. It was a triumph for Leninist diplomatic strategy. The way was clear for trade to be boosted with the other vanquished great power on the continent without ultimately forswearing the possibility of 'European socialist Revolution'.

Chicherin had jibbed at his instructions and Lenin, with the bad temper that characterised him in these months, suggested that he had gone off his head and needed to be found a place in a lunatic asylum. This proposal was not taken seriously by the Politburo. Lenin frequently suggested that one or other of his comrades should be constrained to take a period of convalescence. To question a comrade's mental health, however, was of a different order of significance. It is hard to avoid the conclusion that, in offering a long-range diagnosis of poor Chicherin, Lenin was really expressing fears for himself. As he had said to Professor Darkevich, he felt at times that he was going mad.

The negotiations in Genoa and Rapallo were not the sole topic that undammed a torrent of rage from Lenin. He was splenetic about internal politics. Terror, he was still insisting, was integral to state policy. The Soviet regime simply could not afford to abandon it even under the New Economic Policy. Quite the opposite: Lenin asserted that the economic retreat would succeed only if the maximum of political discipline and control was maintained. Ostensibly the secret police was to be restricted in its operations, and the Extraordinary Commission was replaced by the Main Political Administration (GPU). Kamenev was pushing for justice to be meted out on a more formal, open basis. But, as soon as he heard of any potential weakening of the party's line, Lenin angrily intervened. 'Bandits' should be shot on the spot. 'The speed and *force* of the repressions' should be intensified. Any constitutional or legislative reforms should be formulated in such a fashion as to sanction the possibility of the death penalty being applied in cases involving 'all aspects of activity by Mensheviks, S[ocialist]-R[evolutionaries], etc.' He gave a warning that the regime should not be 'caught napping by a second Kronstadt'. The Civil Code, he suggested, should enshrine 'the *essence* and *justification* of terror'.

The peasant rebels of Tambov and elsewhere were still being attacked and quelled by the Red Army. In Georgia, the remnants of national resistance to the communists continued to be forcibly eliminated. Arrests of known officers of the White armies were still being carried out. Repression was conducted in abundance in the lands of 'Soviet power'. But Lenin wanted the scope widened. In the first months of 1922 he advocated the final eradication of all remaining threats, real or potential, to his state. For Socialist-Revolutionaries and Mensheviks he demanded the staging of show trials followed by exemplary severe punishment. For the Russian Orthodox Church hierarchy, or for a substantial section of it, he demanded the same. For other hostile groups he was a little less harsh. But only a little. Anti-Bolshevik figures in the intelligentsia should be exiled or deported; and if Shlyapnikov and the Workers' Opposition-ists in his own party refused to given up their collective criticism of the Politburo, they should be thrown out of the party.

His interventions were extremely ill tempered. Bukharin and Radek on a visit to Berlin saw fit to promise that if Socialist-Revolutionaries and Mensheviks were put on trial they would not be executed. Lenin castigated them in *Pravda* for having made unnecessary concessions. When he demanded repression, he meant repression. He took an interest in every possible detail. Lists of victims were scrutinised, and his judgements were crudely punitive. A book edited by the Christian socialist philosopher and former Marxist Nikolai Berdyaev was dismissed as the literary front for 'a White Guard organisation'.[18] When he turned his attention to show trials of Orthodox Church bishops and priests, he went further: 'The greater the number of the representatives of reaction-ary clergy and reactionary bourgeoisie we succeed in shooting on this premise, the better. It is precisely now that we ought to deliver a lesson to this public so that they won't dare even think about resistance for several decades.' This was Lenin writing confidentially on the strategy to be adopted in order that no Soviet citizen should be under the illusion that the communist order might be induced to moderate its ferocious ideology. Alternative ways of organising society had to be extirpated. Non-Bolshevik socialism, religion and intellectual dissent were primary potential agencies for opposition, and Lenin was determined to grind them into the dust.

He obtained at least some of what he wanted. He got a show trial of Socialist Revolutionaries, but not of Mensheviks; and the death penalty, against his wishes, was not imposed. By contrast at the trial of Orthodox Church personnel the Politburo sanctioned the executions he had demanded. Above all, the principle of using the courts and the Cheka to traumatise the opposition to the one-party, one-ideology state was enthusiastically fulfilled.

But there remained a doubt that Darkevich's reassuring diagnosis was correct across the range of symptoms. A succession of specialists came out to inspect him, including the surgeon Julius Borchardt and the physician Georg Klemperer from Germany at the daily rate of 20,000 marks apiece.[19] The entire medical file on the man came under investigation: his childhood eyesight problems, the stomach ailments of early manhood, the headaches and insomnia, the St Anthony's fire, the recent transient ischaemic attacks, the listlessness and the obsessions. The doctors were in a quandary. The only point of agreement was that rest alone would not restore him. Klemperer maintained that the bullet lodged in his neck since 1918 had to be removed if ever he was to be cured. The hypothesis was that the headaches were the result of the lead in the bullet poisoning the brain. (The fact that Lenin had suffered chronically from headaches before being shot outside the Mikhelson Factory was not taken into account.) It was noted how nervy Lenin was under medical examination, but this was thought to be a secondary problem resulting from overwork: neurasthenia. The main illness, according to Klemperer, was produced by the bullet's toxic effects. Klemperer got his way even though Professor Vladimir Rozanov, with the support of Professor Borchardt, argued against the operation. Then Borchardt, having tried in vain to hand the surgical task to Rozanov, performed the operation at the Soldatenkov Hospital on 23 April.[20]

Thus the bullet was extracted, and when Lenin awoke next morning at eight o'clock the first signs were that Klemperer's suggestion had proved successful. Lenin did not even feel pain in his neck.[21] But unfortunately this encouraging situation did not last; scarcely had a month passed after the operation when, on 25 May 1922, Lenin suffered a massive stroke out at Gorki. He was picked up and put in his bed, and the doctors waited to see whether he would survive. The whole right side of his body was rendered immobile. He had difficulty speaking. His mind was confused; he was desperate. His recovery was obviously going to be long and uncertain. Fortunately the manor house had by then been well set up for the purpose, and Nadezhda Konstantinovna and Maria Ilinichna reorganised and reduced their other duties and shared the business of looking after him.

Lenin was again seen by doctors in rapid succession, and a great concilium of them took place on 29 May. Its members included Kozhevnikov, Rossolino and Kramer as well as the Ulyanov family doctor, Fëdor Gete, and the People's Commissar of Health Nikolai Semashko. Some of them felt that Darkevich's diagnosis of over-exhaustion had been wrong. But exactly what was wrong with Lenin? The neuropathologist A. M. Kozhevnikov, who had written a study of syphilis, conducted a Wassermann test on Lenin's blood on 29 May. Next day his place was taken by the ophthalmologist Mikhail Averbakh. The official story was that these examinations conclusively rejected syphilis, especially when the Wassermann proved negative. But other symptoms left doubts. Presumably it was for this reason that Professors Kozhevnikov and Förster went on prescribing injections of arsenic-based preparations for Lenin, which was a conventional anti-syphilitic treatment at that time.[22] Unfortunately, despite the mountain of information filed on Lenin at the time, the blood analyses have gone missing.[23] These would tell present-day pathologists beyond peradventure whether he had syphilis, and their absence gives rise to the suspicion that the Soviet political leadership, wanting to preserve the image of Lenin as a morally pure individual, removed or destroyed embarrassing archives.

What can be stated with confidence is that some doctors thought that he had syphilis and others denied this. In the latter group remained Darkevich and he was joined by the neuropathologist Grigori Rossolino, a Russian of Italian descent. Rossolino bluntly told Lenin that he had been hoping that he was suffering from syphilis since it was at least curable. But, while some symptoms pointed in this direction, others surely did not. Professor Rossolino concluded that the illness was even more serious than syphilis and the general prognosis for the patient was grim.

The concilium of doctors whittled their discussions down to a small number of possibilities. One was that he had syphilis; this possibility continued to be discussed in 1923 when Professor A. Strumpel, Germany's leading specialist on neurosyphilis, concluded that Lenin was suffering from 'endarteriitis luetica'. This was the Latin term for a syphilitic inflammation of the artery linings.[24] Another possibility was that he was suffering from 'neurasthenia', or nervous exhaustion, as the result of massive overwork. Almost certainly this was what had been said to him two decades previously by a Swiss specialist; and now Förster, while identifying toxin from the lead bullet as the primary problem, affirmed that neurasthenia too was harming him.[25] The third possible diagnosis, according to some of the doctors, was that the surgical operation to remove the bullet from his neck had caused damage. Naturally Klemperer did not like this opinion since it was he who had recommended the operation. The fourth and last hypothesis was cerebral arteriosclerosis. Lenin's father had reportedly died of it in 1886 and might well have passed on the condition to his son. The subsequent medical history of the other Ulyanovs was to point in the same direction. Anna Ilinichna travelled incognito across the border to Latvia in 1922 to a sanatorium, and she died after a stroke and chronic paralysis in 1935; two years later Maria Ilinichna failed to survive a heart attack, and Dmitri Ilich died of stenocardia – the constriction of the blood vessels joined to the heart – in 1943.[26]

Nor could the doctors discount the suggestion that Lenin was suffering from a combination of the various possibilities. In truth the patient's condition baffled them and they continued to argue with each other. Only one idea united them. This was that Lenin had to cut down drastically on his political activity. A certain Professor Obukh was given the task of informing him. Failure to hearken to this advice, Lenin was told unequivocally, would result in another stroke or death. Lenin raised an objection that his daily routine was not one of great strain since he neither drank too much nor led 'a dissolute life'.[27] But Obukh would not budge. Lenin's survival depended entirely on his taking a lengthy break from his public responsibilities. While outwardly agreeing to their recommendations, in reality he was planning to trick the medical staff. His own researches in the medical textbooks convinced him that there was no hope for him. Rather than suffer paralysis, he again determined to commit suicide, and on 30 May he summoned Stalin to Gorki. They kissed in the Russian manner on greeting. Then Lenin asked his visitor to get the poison to do the job. Stalin conferred with Bukharin and Maria Ilinichna outside the bedroom. They agreed that Stalin should go back and explain to Lenin that the prognosis of the optimistic doctors should be believed. On this occasion, Lenin agreed. He would delay killing himself a little longer.[28]

But what really was wrong with him? Medical science has progressed in the ensuing decades and would be able, if Lenin were now a patient, to diagnose his illness more easily. One of the possible causes would no longer be seriously entertained: neurasthenia. Today this condition, so readily diagnosed until the middle of the twentieth century, is seldom recognised as a genuine disease. Of the three main remaining diagnoses each has something plausible about it. If it were not for the negative result of the Wasserman test, syphilis would be a credible guess. If it were not for the fact that he had had minor strokes before 1922, the surgical removal of the bullet might be credible. Yet the fact remains that some of Lenin's doctors believed he was syphilitic even though, apparently, he failed to come up positive on the Wasserman test. Nor can it be disproved that the operation on the bullet fatally worsened an existing condition. Then again perhaps Professor Osipov got it right when suggesting that Lenin was suffering from atherosclerosis or a 'hardening of the arteries'. Often it is associated with a high pressure of blood against the arterial walls. The affected arteries in Lenin's case, as was revealed after his death in 1924, were linked to the brain.

In the West this is scarcely a topic of intense interest. In Russia, however, the communist authorities propagated an image of Lenin as a morally pure individual, and the consequence is that many contemporary historians have been searching to prove that he died of a venereal disease.[29] Thus it is implied that he was sexually promiscuous. It is an understandable quest. But it is driven by motives outside the limits of medical history. And until further information comes to light, no useful conclusion may be offered.

Whatever the causes, a major stroke had occurred. The only sensible restorative measure for Lenin was his complete retirement from active politics. Even this would not bring about a cure, only the postponement of a further stroke. But, if Lenin had thought this, he would have killed himself as he had planned. Instead he was persuaded by the medical team that they would be able to restore his health and enable him to return to the Politburo and Sovnarkom. He seemed genuinely cheerful as he began little by little to recover. He read books. He wrote notes to the Politburo. He began to potter around again, and took an interest in the agricultural work at Gorki. Above all, he was kept informed about Kremlin politics since Stalin, as the party's General Secretary, travelled out to the Gorki sanatorium for face-to-face discussions. Maria Ilinichna was asked by Lenin to put out a bottle of red wine so as to make Stalin feel properly welcome. Sitting out on the sunny terrace, Lenin and Stalin could talk things over. Lenin aimed to reassure himself that all was well in the Politburo, Central Committee and Sovnarkom. For this purpose he had approved the election of Stalin as General Secretary, and the early signs were that Stalin had been a good choice.

There were abundant occasions for relaxation. A dog was obtained for him, Aida, which looked just like Zhenka, the dog he had owned in his Siberian exile.[30] Lenin was delighted. He also took gentle strolls around the woods in search of mushrooms just as he had done when first he lived with Nadezhda Konstantinovna in Shushenskoe. They paid visits, too, to the state collective farm that had been carved out of the estate at Gorki. This was not quite so happy an experience since Lenin did not think that the farm chairman was very good at his job.[31]

But Lenin did not interfere. Instead he made his own arrangements for different forms of husbandry to be introduced to the area adjacent to the sanatorium. He was keen to foster rabbit-rearing and bee-keeping. 'If I can't get involved in politics,' he said, 'then I'll have to get involved in agriculture.'[32] He had faced the choice between agriculture and politics in Alakaevka in 1889–90 when his mother wanted him as her estate manager. Agriculture had been second best in his estimation at that time, and so it remained in 1922; for he did not genuinely intend to drop politics: he was using these hobbies as a way of passing the time before he returned to his Kremlin duties. Occasionally he made this clear. When the doctors insisted that he gave up work, he replied with huge pathos: 'There's nothing else I have.'[33] Nothing, in his mind, should get in the way of his struggle to get back to normality in Moscow. He found, for example, that his nerves were set a-jangle when anyone played the piano in the house. His sensitivity to ambient sound had become more acute than ever, and Maria Ilinichna banned music from the house forthwith.[34]

His greatest pleasure came not from hobbies but from the presence of children. Dmitri Ulyanov's young son Viktor frequently came out to stay with his Uncle Volodya. So, too, did the daughter of a Moscow female worker as well as Inessa Armand's daughter Inna and son Alexander. They were by then in their twenties. It is clear that Lenin and Krupskaya would have loved to have had children of their own, and the visits of these young people brought them joy. They felt a responsibility for the Armands after Inessa's death, and Lenin gave orders for them to be well looked after.[35]

Not everyone approved of the invitation to the Armands. Maria Ilinichna, by now a crabby spinster in her mid-forties, believed that her brother needed a respite from the social round and that every such visit had an adverse effect on him.[36] It is also possible that she objected to these young people because of the relationship between Lenin and Inessa. Nadya, however, felt otherwise and a blazing row took place between the two women. Lenin, hearing Nadya's report on the incident, became so upset that he began to be afflicted by one of his severe headaches.[37] Lenin's personal bodyguard Pëtr Pakaln could see no way round the problem but to request the removal of the Armands. But this was not the end of the matter. Later in the summer Nadya wrote again to 'my sweet girl' Inna Armand – the daughter of the deceased Inessa – inviting her to stay at Gorki:[38]

> Well, why can't you stay with us? On the contrary, this year we're going to live in a more 'family-like fashion' and more 'openly' since it's impossible to occupy V.I. more than eight hours a day and anyway there's need of a break twice a week. Therefore he'll be delighted to have guests. He was very concerned when I told him you were ill and wrote a special letter to Zhidelëv about you and about [one of his secretaries] Lidia Alexandrovna [Fotieva], asking him to look after you.

It is hard to believe that Nadya was inventing Lenin's thoughts out of the air. She recognised that the visits were truly important for him, and wanted to help him.

The disagreeable atmosphere was stoked up but not created by the dispute about the children. Nadya and Maria were forever struggling with each other. Any little incident could touch off an explosion. In July 1922, the Bolshevik editor Nikolai Meshcheryakov had visited Lenin for two hours. Lenin's bodyguard Pëtr Pakaln observed the scene:[39]

> But, since comrade Meshcheryakov was not offered any tea during his visit, Nadezhda Konstantinovna complained to Ilich, who became terribly distraught and on the same day issued a rebuke to Maria and also to Sasha [the maid] for their lack of attention to visitors, and he ordered them henceforth to feed everyone coming to the house.

Maria's recollection of the events was different. Lenin's reaction had indeed been sharp: 'A comrade travelled out to a house like this and no one could even give him a bite to eat.' But Maria disclaimed responsibility, saying that she had been 'hoping' that Nadya would look after Meshcheryakov. According to Maria, Lenin's reply was: 'Well, she's too well-known a slattern [fefëla] for anyone to rely on her.'[40] While this was hardly an expression of total support for his sister, it was abusive language to use about his wife.

Nadya and Maria, his wife and his sister, were fighting for possession of Lenin. Each whispered in his ear about the shortcomings of the other. It would seem that he did not want to take sides openly and definitively. He had always used the interplay of emotions among his relatives to his advantage. The problem in mid-1922 was that he was no longer in a dominant position because of ill health. What he most needed was that Nadya and Maria calm down and find a *modus vivendi*. In subsequent months they composed themselves; but they continued to take opposite approaches to his convalescence. Maria thought it stupid of Professor Klemperer, who had not covered himself with glory by instigating surgery upon Lenin in April, to let him read newspapers and talk to visiting politicians.[41] By contrast Nadya felt that without this minimal political activity he would become demoralised, and she complied – even colluded – with his requests for information.

Nadya was bound to hold sway, if only because she was doing what her wilful husband wanted. She also had a better way of managing him. Maria taught herself how to take photographs in order to record her brother's appearance for posterity;[42] but it was Nadya who sat with him for hours and talked him round to feeling that he might recover. She helped him, too, with the manual exercises that his doctors said would be necessary. Basket weaving was among these.[43] The road to recuperation was bestrewn with obstacles. One day Lenin was progressing and seemed almost as he had been before the stroke of May 1922. The next day he could be hobbling or worse. He collapsed frequently, and had to be carried back to his bedroom. His mood, not surprisingly, was volatile. He raged to get back to the Kremlin and to resume control. He had always been reluctant to allow others to take supreme command, and the enforced convalescence made him exceedingly edgy. At the slightest resistance to his wishes, he could fly into a temper. He had had this potential even before, but in this period he was very irritable and obsessive. But, although he had admitted this to Professor Darkevich in March, he did not and probably could not restrain himself.

Thus in July he announced the need for a transformation of the entire Central Committee with its twenty-seven members elected under his aegis at the Eleventh Party Congress. He had the gall to suggest that the Central Committee should be cut down to just three members and that none of the most influential party leaders – Trotski, Stalin, Zinoviev, Kamenev, Dzierżyński and Bukharin – should belong to it. His proposed

Central Committee would consist of Central Committee Secretaries Molotov and Kuibyshev and Sovnarkom Deputy Chairman Rykov. As an additional insult, he suggested that Kamenev, Zinoviev and Lenin's least favourite colleague in the previous year, Tomski, should serve under them as candidate members. Lenin's pretext was that the Central Committee as presently constituted was too tired to discharge its functions properly. Its members, too, needed a period of convalescence.[44] The outrageous criticism of his colleagues' efficiency barely concealed an implicit claim that he alone had the talent to run the Central Committee. It was a claim to which he returned in the last weeks of 1922 when he dictated what became known as his Political Testament. His external modesty was often charming; but underneath lay the arrogance of the person who believes in his natural right to be the supreme leader.

The scheme for a three-man Central Committee was harebrained. Molotov, Kuibyshev and Rykov would have lacked the necessary authority to impose themselves on the other leaders; and, furthermore, there was nothing in the Party Rules to validate the replacement of a Central Committee in the interim between Congresses. Lenin had lost his sense of political proportion – and the Central Committee had reason on its side in refusing to dignify his scheme with a written rebuttal. The founder of the Bolshevik party and the Soviet state was best ignored until he came back to psychological normality.

27

DISPUTING TO THE LAST

September to December 1922

Despite being stuck in Gorki and feeling very poorly, Lenin still expected to dominate the making of policy. In the early months of 1922 there had been discussion on four matters of acute concern to him. On two of them he had largely obtained satisfaction before his stroke in May. The first matter had been the Genoa Conference. Without undue dissent, the Politburo accepted his guidance and gave priority to a German–Soviet agreement at the expense of pursuing a comprehensive settlement with the European powers in general. The second involved the modalities of political control in Russia. Lenin convinced his Politburo colleagues that the time was ripe to strike at the enemies of the Soviet state: the Socialist-Revolutionaries, the Mensheviks, the Russian Orthodox Church and the leading anti-Bolshevik figures in philosophy, arts and scholarship. Not every detail of policy had gone his way, but he was not balked on broad strategy. It was on the third and fourth matters that he encountered trouble in the central party leadership. One related to the limits of the state monopoly on foreign trade, the other to the inter-republican constitutional structure of the Soviet state. Neither of these matters was of fundamental significance. But the dispute over them exposed fissures in the party leadership that continued to have an impact many years later.

Stalin was among Lenin's opponents in the discussions of both foreign trade and the constitution. On the foreign-trade monopoly, Stalin simply went along with the majority in the Politburo. On the constitution, however, it was Stalin who led the opposition to Lenin. Stalin the Party General Secretary. Stalin the man whom Lenin had used as his conduit of instructions to the Politburo. Stalin who had been Lenin's ally in the internal party disputes of 1920–1. Stalin the adjutant and the loyalist. It was this same Stalin who was challenging Lenin's supremacy over policy.

Lenin was highly agitated by the proposal to repeal the state monopoly. Vladimir Milyutin and Grigori Sokolnikov, his colleagues in the Central Committee, argued that private commerce across the borders would promote internal economic regeneration. Lenin disapproved, insisting that the NEP (New Economic Policy) should be kept within the limits he had established in 1921. The Soviet state, he urged, should keep its monopoly over large-scale industry, banking and foreign trade. Previously he had been the one who had insisted that the Politburo should be pragmatic and should broaden the framework of the NEP. This is what Milyutin and Sokolnikov thought they were doing by suggesting that capitalists should be able to export and import certain goods without going through state trading institutions; and they added that the monopoly in practice induced smuggling by private traders. Among the supporters of Milyutin and Sokolnikov were some of Lenin's most prominent colleagues: Kamenev, Bukharin and Stalin. Yet Lenin persuaded himself that the debate on foreign trade involved matters of profound principle and was determined to keep the party in line with his particular version of the NEP.

The second great topic for discussion in summer 1922 was Stalin's proposal for a new constitutional structure for the Soviet state. Lenin and Stalin had already quarrelled about this in 1920.[1] Stalin believed that best plan was for the Russian Socialist Federal Soviet Republic (RSFSR) to incorporate all the other independent Soviet republics within its territory. Ukraine, Belorussia, Azerbaijan, Armenia and Georgia would become part of the RSFSR. Lenin violently disagreed, and advocated the formation of a Union of Soviet Republics of Europe and Asia. In such a Union the RSFSR would be merely one Soviet republic alongside the Soviet republics of Ukraine, Belorussia, Azerbaijan, Armenia and Georgia.

Struggle was joined over both foreign trade and the constitution. Lenin's opponents felt bewildered since none of them genuinely proposed to dismantle the entirety of the state's foreign-trade monopoly. Their objective was not total but partial repeal. Lenin not only misrepresented their purpose but also treated them as if they had offended the tenets of Marxism – and he targeted Sokolnikov with a tirade of personal abuse. Equally disconcerting was Lenin's approach to the state constitution. He did not aim to weaken Moscow's strict party and governmental control over the 'borderlands'. Lenin and Stalin were at one in their commitment to the one-party, one-ideology multinational state. Their disagreements affected secondary rather than primary aspects of policy. Yet Lenin saw fit to attack Stalin and his supporters in language of extreme bitterness, and Politburo members were at a loss to explain why.

Leading party members put this down to the effects of illness and to his distance from day-to-day political management. Even in the discussions over the Genoa Conference and over domestic political repression – discussions in which he got his way – he had been unpleasant to Georgi Chicherin, Nikolai Bukharin and Karl Radek. Thus his ill temper belonged to a pattern and his doctors were long accustomed to this. In June 1922 he had written to the Politburo demanding that he should be 'liberated' from Professor Klemperer and be 'rid of' Professor Förster, and he added: 'Russians cannot put up with German meticulousness.'[2] To his colleagues, this attitude appeared a little disingenuous since he had always been meticulous in his personal and working habits and had called upon others to be the same. If anyone – apart from Trotski – appeared to conform to the Russian popular stereotype of a German, it was Lenin. If anyone had been prominent in comparing Russians unfavourably with Germans, it had been Lenin. Unsurprisingly the Politburo ignored his request to send the German specialists back to Germany and grew accustomed to soothing him in the hope that, as he got better, he would become a more manageable colleague.

But Lenin saw things differently; he began to identify Stalin as the universal villain. In 1912 he had admired him as 'the wonderful Georgian',[3] and after the October Revolution had assigned to him tasks of state that required a ruthless, crude energy. But of Stalin's other characteristics he had a low opinion. Stalin had habits that Lenin thought vulgar and unpleasant. Once, when Stalin had been puffing on his pipe, Lenin blurted out: 'Look at the Asiatic – all he can do is go on sucking!' Stalin knocked out his pipe in deference.[4] It was unusual for Lenin to be so rude; he had been brought up to have decent social manners. Furthermore, he needed comrades to believe he thought well of them, and could see how upset people were by Trotski or Zinoviev. Within Lenin the blunt revolutionary there survived Lenin the fastidious European Russian gentleman; he was a bit of a snob in national, social and cultural terms.

It was only when his guard was down that he allowed this to show. In earlier days Lenin had acted differently, as Maria Ilinichna noted:[5]

V.I. had a lot of self-restraint. And he knew very well how to disguise and not reveal his attitude to people when he felt this to be for any reason more sensible ... All the more did he hold himself back in relation to comrades with whom his work brought him into contact. The cause for him had priority; he knew how to subordinate the personal to the cause and this personal element never obtruded or took precedence with him.

Now the angry contempt he felt for Stalin was removing such inhibitions. Maria Ilinichna was to try to warn him that his opponent was more intelligent and therefore more dangerous than he imagined. But Lenin would have none of it: 'He is absolutely not intelligent!' Thus spake the brilliant gimnazia student, the polyglot émigré and chief party ideologist. He was about to learn, in the last lesson of his political life, that intelligence was not monopolised by those who had formal cultural proficiency.

The scene was set for three political battles. Two of them intensified in the course of the summer: the struggle over the state monopoly of foreign trade and the struggle over the new constitution. In both cases Lenin identified Stalin as a standard-bearer of the campaign against the policies that had his approval. The third battle was a product of the others. And it was a struggle that Lenin had not anticipated that he would have to fight. This was the battle he eventually decided was necessary if he was to remove Iosif Stalin from the Party General Secretaryship.

These were battles that would barely have merited a footnote in the history of Soviet communism if Lenin's health had not deteriorated. The chances are that Lenin would simply have unseated 'the wonderful Georgian' from the Secretariat and replaced him with a more compliant official. Stalin would have endured a period of quiet humiliation. Even so, it is doubtful that Stalin's career would have been entirely over. For example, he would surely have retained membership of the Central Committee. Lenin had not been able to push out Tomski in 1921, even though Tomski had flouted a Central Committee policy. Stalin was guilty of no such delinquency in 1922. It was not, after all, against the rules of the party to disagree with Lenin. Nor was Stalin alone in advocating the policies that Lenin found annoying. As was usual when Lenin did not get his way, he became abusive to his rivals. The pathos of Lenin's medical condition has tended to deflect attention from the merits of the argument between the two men across that long, hot summer. We have also been affected by our retrospective knowledge of what horrors – horrors of which Lenin had no presentiment – Stalin went on to commit in the 1930s and subsequently.

Yet the discussions about the future constitution produced the first clash. Unease existed among communists in the Soviet republics about

Stalin's plan to incorporate their republics in the RSFSR. The Georgian Central Committee was outspoken. Lenin disliked Stalin's project and suspected that Stalin was bullying the Soviet republics into accepting it. Stalin wrote to Lenin in self-justification. Lenin, he felt, ought to understand that nationalism was on the rise in the borderlands and that Lenin's scheme would only encourage it and increase the complexity of administrative structures. Stalin wanted to give Soviet republics 'autonomous' status within the RSFSR and prevent them from entering a federal arrangement on equal terms with the RSFSR. A Party Orgburo commission ratified Stalin's project on 23 September 1922.

Lenin hated the idea of 'autonomisation', likening it to 'Great Russian chauvinism'. When he told Stalin of his position three days later in a conversation that lasted two hours, Stalin caved in and agreed to the abandonment of 'autonomisation' and the formation of a Union of Soviet Republics of Europe and Asia. This was the sort of project that Lenin had advocated in discussion with Stalin himself in mid-1920. Yet Stalin had not thrown in the towel. He wrote a note next day to the Politburo and proposed that the Union should not have separate organs of legislation from those of the RSFSR. He also tweaked Lenin by changing the proposed name to Union of Soviet Socialist Republics (USSR). Furthermore, he insisted that Georgia should join Armenia and Azerbaijan in a Transcaucasian Soviet Federation and that this Federation should enter the USSR on a par with the RSFSR and the Ukrainian Soviet Republic; thus he set his face against Georgia retaining a status equal to that of the RSFSR. Kamenev warned Stalin to desist from being provocative: 'Ilich has girt himself up for war in defence of [Soviet republican] independence.' Stalin was undismayed, and in the process showed himself as a leader in the making: 'What is needed, in my opinion, is that firmness is shown against Ilich.'

When Kamenev told him that he was only making things worse than they absolutely had to be, Stalin professed indifference; but, sure enough, Lenin had got his gander up: 'I declare war to the death on Great Russian chauvinism.' After a summer of convalescence, he was determined to return to the fray in Moscow. This was stupid of him because his recovery from the stroke had been interrupted by further collapses. In June he had had one after walking round the park at Gorki, and in July he had had another after doing the same thing and he lost the use of the right side of his body. In August, too, he had days of incapacity.[6] He pushed himself hard and resumed his intellectual work. Secretaries were sent scurrying to libraries for the books he wanted – in particular, he asked for Bukharin's *The ABC of Communism*.[7] He also started a contribution to Anna Ilinichna's collection of memoirs on his old Marxist friend from his Kazan days, Nikolai Fedoseev.[8] He overcame the objections of the doctors and the doubts of the Politburo, and on 2 October 1922 he left the Gorki mansion and returned by car to the Kremlin, where he resumed the occupancy of his apartment next to the Sovnarkom rooms in the old Senate Building. Next day he chaired the regular Sovnarkom meeting and on 6 October he did the same at the Party Central Committee plenum. He tried to impress everybody with his ability to take up his official duties again.

Yet Lenin was nothing like his old self and could not fool his colleagues when he had to keep up appearances at these two important meetings. His colleagues tried to avoid controversy at the Sovnarkom session. But this served only to agitate him.[9] They could do nothing right. If they disputed with Lenin, he might have another heart seizure; if they held back, the result might still be the same because he became irritated by their very politeness. The Central Committee plenum started better, but halfway through the proceedings he had a bout of toothache and had to withdraw to his apartment.[10] Although he returned for other meetings in the following days, his performance was well below normal. This in turn made him acutely nervous and he got angry at the least disturbance. His secretary Lidia Fotieva dreaded another heart attack and discreetly asked his leading colleagues not to get up from their seats or talk among themselves in meetings. Every conceivable cause of agitation had to be eliminated.[11] His mental capacity had been impaired. Sometimes he lost his place while speaking from a text and was known to repeat whole passages without knowing it.

Kamenev, Stalin and Zinoviev met to discuss his condition but came to no decision leading to action.[12] They knew that, if they ordered him back to the mansion at Gorki, he would accuse them of using his illness as a pretext for eliminating him from the discussions on foreign trade and the constitution. And so they left him alone. In fact he was already on the way to getting what he wanted on the constitution. At the Central Committee plenum on 6 October, he had had the support of Bukharin and Kamenev, and Stalin had not dared to oppose his basic demands. Only one concession had come from Lenin's side, and this was hardly a momentous one: he had accepted that the Soviet state should be designated not the Union of Soviet Republics of Europe and Asia but the Union of Soviet Socialist Republics. A party commission was established under Stalin to prepare the final text for the Congress of Soviets in December. Lenin meanwhile sent a message to Kamenev asking him to enable the Georgian communists to have access to the relevant documents in defence of their position. He wanted to clip the wings of Iosif Stalin.[13]

Lenin went on pushing himself to the limit and addressed the Fourth Comintern Congress on 13 November. The speech was incoherent in passages, but he had just enough energy and experience to get through to the end. His friends, however, were alarmed about his worsened condition. Bukharin wrote:[14]

> Our hearts were sinking when Ilich walked out on to the platform. We all saw what effort his speech cost Ilich. Then we saw him finish. I ran over to him and embraced him under my fur coat; he was completely wet from exhaustion, his shirt was drenched and there were beads of sweat on his forehead. His eyes suddenly rolled around.

The Comintern delegates applauded Lenin without suspecting that his recovery was in jeopardy. The foreign delegates in particular wanted to see and hear the man under whose leadership they expected communism to triumph around the world. But his fellow central party leaders had erred in allowing him to give a speech, and they knew it. After the Comintern Congress they increasingly tried to restrict his activities, regardless of his wishes. By then they were wondering, in their confidential discussions, whether his disease – whatever it was – was ever going to release its grip on him.

Stalin and his friends felt freer to do as they pleased. The Georgian communist leaders had annoyed Stalin beyond measure and Ordzhonikidze, close ally of Stalin, denounced them at a meeting in Tbilisi as 'chauvinistic filth'. The Georgian Central Committee protested by resigning en masse and complaining to Lenin. For a while Lenin took no notice since he too objected to the Georgian communist leadership's demand that Georgia should not be included in a Transcaucasian Federation. He also consented to Stalin's plan to send a commission of enquiry under Dzierżyński to investigate the situation in Georgia. The tension among communists in Tbilisi was enormous. In late November, Ordzhonikidze was so enraged at being accused of acting like an imperial emissary that he beat up a certain Kobachidze, who was an adherent of Mdivani. Lenin was worried about Georgia even though he had no accurate knowledge of events there, and pestered his secretaries to find out when Dzierżyński was scheduled to return. In fact Dzierżyński agreed with Stalin on the constitutional question and his report whitewashed the behaviour of Ordzhonikidze in the Transcaucasus. But, when Dzierżyński had a chat with Lenin back in Moscow on 12 December, he could not stop himself blurting out what had happened to the unfortunate Kobachidze.

For Lenin it was clear that Stalin had not surrendered on the USSR constitution and that he had to resume the battle he thought won on 6 October. There was more to this than fighting to restore an agreed official policy. Stalin's protection of Ordzhonikidze had involved him in condoning violence by one party official against another. Lenin was aghast. As long ago as 1903 he had dragged back Alexander Shotman from beating up a Menshevik on the streets of London. Now he objected to Ordzhonikidze on grounds not merely of stupidity but also of morality.

Usually Lenin had scoffed at moral codes of any kind. But at heart he was a romantic, a revolutionary believer. There were some things – just a few – that a Marxist should not do even under provocation. Marxists should be dedicated to Marxism and not take their ideas lightly. Marxists should be fighters and could assault each other verbally, but the idea that they should take to fisticuffs in order to settle a mutual grievance was anathema to him. Marxists should set an example of civil decency, and Ordzhonikidze had disgraced the party by his physical assault on Kobachidze. Already in 1920 Lenin had upbraided Ordzhonikidze for going on a drunken binge and carrying on with a group of loose women.[15] Every Politburo member knew of Ordzhonikidze's waywardness, and Lenin held it against Stalin and Dzierżyński that they had concealed the truth from him. Everything he learned about the treatment of the Georgian communist leadership pointed in the same direction: Stalin was presiding over a movement towards an authoritarian chauvinism inside the party. It did not matter that Stalin was himself a Georgian. He had acted like a Russian imperialist, and this was scandalous.

Lenin would have resumed the campaign against Stalin if he had not suffered yet another medical crisis. He underwent five collapses between 24 November and 2 December.[16] On 13 December, the day after his conversation with Dzierżyński, he suffered two severe collapses and there were fears that he would not survive the day.[17] Dr Kozhevnikov and Professor Kramer, who hurried round to attend him, told him that he would not survive unless he agreed to a regime of 'complete rest'. Their unwilling patient at last gave his consent. He called in his secretary Lidia Fotieva and made arrangements for the 'liquidation of his affairs'.[18]

He had thought often enough that his illness was fatal; but from this day, he was also improvising how to leave his impact upon his party and upon the Revolution. He refused to be taken to Gorki, where he knew it would be difficult to maintain any kind of political role. He left his medical specialists and attendants in no doubt about his intentions. He would continue to live in the Kremlin and, since he could not write legibly, he would ask his Sovnarkom secretaries to take down dictation. He understood that he might suddenly perish and that, if he wished to leave a legacy, he had to write some kind of political testament. For this purpose he had to ponder whom he should recommend as his successor – or successors. The future of the Revolution dominated his thinking. Indeed it had done so for months. In autumn 1922 his agitation made him exclaim to Maria Ilinichna: 'What scoundrel among us is going to live until the age of sixty?' Then he had explained his desire that power, when he died, should somehow be passed from his own generation to those Bolsheviks who were in their twenties.[19]

Lenin's concerns about the Revolution had burgeoned. His two remaining preoccupations with policy – on foreign trade and on the non-Soviet republics – had been joined by a political animus against Stalin. Nor was he convinced that his colleagues continued to share his priority for the maintenance of internal repression. It was beginning to seem to Lenin, in his weakened and febrile condition, that the agreed policies of the Politburo were being eroded. As he faced the probability of his imminent death, he was troubled by the general problem of ensuring that the Revolution would flourish when he was gone. Time was not on his side.

He called Fotieva to his Kremlin apartment after Kozhevnikov and Kramer had left at midday on 13 December. He was worrying less about collapsing again than about the policies of the central party leadership. One letter was about the elderly ex-Menshevik historian N. A. Rozhkov, whom Lenin had tried for months to have deported or at least exiled to Pskov (where Lenin had been confined in 1900 after his release from Siberia). Lenin treated the Politburo's postponement of this decision as a sign of a growing reluctance to sanction his strategy of appropriate repression, and he demanded that Rozhkov should finally be deported.[20] A second letter was sent to Trotski and others about the foreign-trade monopoly.[21] A third, which was about the delegation of his Sovnarkom functions, went to Kamenev, Rykov and Tsyurupa. He also talked for two hours face to face with Stalin,[22] who was left in no doubt about Lenin's obstinacy. While being reconciled to devolving his day-to-day executive responsibilities, Lenin had not abandoned hope of giving the main speech to the Congress of Soviets.[23] No deviation from his preferred policies, it was clear, was going to be tolerated. Stalin agreed to withdraw his opposition to the state foreign-trade monopoly,[24] but still Lenin did not feel confident about the policy and he waited anxiously for the Central Committee to resolve the matter in his favour.

Extreme circumstances called for desperate measures. No longer having an ally in Stalin, Lenin turned to the very person against whom he had formed the alliance with Stalin. This was Trotski. Like Lenin, Trotski supported the state foreign-trade monopoly, and Lenin asked him to speak on his behalf at the forthcoming Central Committee plenum.[25]

This was an unprecedented manoeuvre. Previously Lenin had tried to keep a wide group of allies on his side and had avoided showing a definite preference for any one of them. Even his calculated choice of Stalin as ally in April 1922 had not implied a deliberate self-distancing from Zinoviev, Kamenev and Bukharin. By achieving this *rapprochement* with Trotski, he was effectively indicating that this relationship in internal party affairs was to take precedence over all others. Such a manoeuvre was a token of Lenin's desperation. Trotski's vanity and arrogance had annoyed him before the February 1917 Revolution. The Brest-Litovsk negotiations, in Lenin's eyes, had shown Trotski as a revolutionary poseur and the 'trade union discussion' inside the party in 1920–1 had demonstrated his recklessness and impracticality. Lenin could not bring himself to like him. At times he had turned 'white as chalk' in anger at Trotski's polemical style in the central party leadership. Such arrogance seemed unnecessary to Lenin (who was incapable of recognising his own arrogance). But this had to be put to one side. *Realpolitik* demanded that Lenin should overcome his distaste and work harmoniously with Trotski.

The need became greater on 16 December, when Lenin's condition deteriorated further and for a while he completely lost mobility in his right arm and right leg.[26] Without Trotski at the Central Committee plenum on 18 December he had no guarantee that his colleagues would keep the foreign-trade monopoly. Despite his own physical pain, Lenin's mind was focussed on politics. Perhaps he already was thinking that if Trotski proved reliable at the plenum he might be able to use him in other policy discussions. Even so, he still did not completely trust him and asked another Central Committee member, Yemelyan Yaroslavski, to report to him about the proceedings.[27] In the event the Central Committee went Lenin's way with ease.[28] After the state monopoly on foreign trade was reaffirmed, Lenin wrote ecstatically to his new ally Trotski: 'It's as if we've managed to seize a position by a simple movement of manoeuvre and without having to fire a single shot.'[29] In the evening session, the broad lines of Lenin's project for a Union of Soviet Socialist Republics (USSR) were passed.[30] By then he had also had the pleasure of learning that the Politburo had agreed to his demand for Rozhkov's exile to Pskov.[31] One by one, Lenin's objectives in policy were being met.

But he still had several to achieve, and he recognised that he could not assume that he had long to live. He was right to be sceptical, especially about Stalin. On 21 December the Orgburo, of which Stalin was the leading member, ratified the Dzierżyński report on Georgia. Ordzhonikidze had escaped without censure; and, just as disturbingly, the decision was taken to withdraw Mdivani and Stalin's other opponents from their posts in Tbilisi.[32] Stalin was out for revenge and was bent upon emasculating the agreement he had made with Lenin on the formalities of the USSR Constitution. There was bound eventually to be another spat between Stalin and Lenin. The tension mounted.

In the night of 22–23 December, Lenin's health broke down again when he suffered another collapse and again lost the use of his whole right side. His relatives and doctors attended to him as best they could, but Lenin as ever was thinking about politics as soon as he regained consciousness. He had to employ low cunning since the Central Committee on 18 December had formally ordered him to withdraw from public life until he had recovered, and Stalin had been put in charge of this medical regime. Lenin, however, told his doctors that he feared he would not be able to get back to sleep unless he was allowed to dictate something to a secretary on 'a question troubling him'. The doctors relented and duty secretary Maria Volodicheva was summoned to the apartment. He was still very poorly when she arrived. But he insisted on going ahead: 'I want to dictate to you *a letter to the congress.*'[33] Although he could manage only four minutes' dictation, he had set the pattern; over the next few days, he hoped, he would put down in writing the general concerns and plans he had in mind and would make them available to the next Party Congress. Everything was to be 'absolutely secret'. The letter was typed out in five copies that were sealed in envelopes with a wax seal; Lenin stipulated that only he or, in the event of his death, Nadezhda Konstantinovna should have the right to open them.[34]

He had complete trust in his secretaries Lidia Fotieva and Maria

Volodicheva. Previously he had also been using the secretarial services of Nadezhda Allilueva, Stalin's young second wife; but, by a favourable accident, she had ceased performing such work for him since the beginning of the month. Lenin was cheered, furthermore, by the decision of Stalin, Kamenev and Bukharin on 24 December to allow him to go on dictating for five to ten minutes a day. Stalin had recognised that, if permission were to be refused, Lenin retained the capacity to do him harm by complaining that he was being unreasonably constrained.

Yet Stalin was wrong to think that he ran no serious risk by allowing the dictation. Lenin, crippled and distraught, was also angry. His bedridden existence did nothing to calm him down. He was a man in a hurry. For a couple of years he had contemplated the question of the Soviet political succession and occasionally he had given voice to this. He and Alexander Shlikhter had talked about the deaths of several of their Bolshevik acquaintances in late summer 1921. Shlikhter had said that the party need not worry about the loss of the veterans since the younger generation was ready to take over. Lenin had demurred: 'For a long, long time Lenin looked in silence without taking his eyes off me. "No, you're wrong," was his reply, "It's still too early to leave. Five more years of training are needed." '[35] These words were not casually spoken; they reflected his unease about the kind of leadership available in the party once he had left the scene. Subsequently Lenin had avoided the topic. But, fearing that he would soon die, he rushed to commit his conclusions to paper. The effort this required was enormous. He tried to prepare his argument carefully so that he would not need to redraft it. He was writing a political testament for his party and the intentions had to be expressed with clarity.

As a writer he had been used to seeing his text emerge in front of him as he wrote it out in longhand, and of course it did not help that he was so ill. Sometimes his grammar went awry and Volodicheva had to correct his drafts. She knew he found this demeaning: 'I know that I'm your necessary evil, but it's only for a short time.'[36] The problem, however, was that he had to get the contents right in his own mind and the stenographers often had to wait endlessly for his next sentence. At one point they experimented with putting the secretary in the room adjacent to Lenin's, and having him ring them up when he had composed his thoughts.[37]

One way or another he was determined to finish his testament. While Fotieva and Volodicheva supplied him with technical help, they also tried to boost his morale. Of even greater emotional importance to him were Nadezhda Konstantinovna and Maria Ilinichna. Wife and sister made sure that they were available to sit with him each day. Nadezhda Konstantinovna went further and became his unofficial political assistant. This was against the terms of the medical regime decreed by the Central Committee and overseen by General Secretary Stalin. But Nadezhda Konstantinovna enjoyed the fact that she could again fulfil the role of his political assistant, a role she had given up in April 1917. Perhaps she relished the secretiveness; it was a bit like the old days when the two of them had conspired to fool the Okhrana. Above all, Nadezhda Konstantinovna recognised that, if the Central Committee shut Lenin off from politics as the Central Committee demanded, he would not last long. He could not live without politics. She therefore went on telling him what she knew about events in the Kremlin and putting him in confidential contact with other party leaders. Steadily his feeling of well-being returned to him.

Unfortunately Stalin found out about this on 22 December. He rang up Nadezhda Konstantinovna and abused her in the language of the gutter. Nadezhda Konstantinovna, troubled by Lenin's condition, was overwhelmed by Stalin. Next day she wrote an impassioned letter to Kamenev: 'In all the past 30 years I've not heard a single obscene word from any individual comrade; the interests of the party and Ilich are no less dear to me than to Lenin.' Thus did she defend her husband's right to remain politically active and indicated that Stalin would repeat his aggression at his own peril. And Lenin, while there was breath in his body, could initiate his plan to bequeath a legacy of ideas, strategy and personnel to the Communist Party and the Soviet state.

28

DEATH IN THE BIG HOUSE

1923–1924

Lenin began dictating his political testament on 23 December 1922. He wanted to present his ideas in person to the next Party Congress, but would leave a testament in case this was impossible. His opening words ran as follows: 'I would very much advise the undertaking at this Congress of a series of changes in our political structure.' Lenin put forward two proposals. The first was that the State Planning Commission, which currently advised on economic policy, should be given a degree of legislative authority. The second was that the Party Central Committee should be increased from twenty-seven to between fifty and one hundred members.[1]

There was a political calculus behind this. The State Planning Commission's reform would strengthen the government's direction of the economy: Lenin was trying to make further use of his recent alliance with Trotski and had to pay a price. For Trotski had been demanding a reinforcement of the state's economic planning role. At the same time Lenin wanted to place a constraint on Trotski and the rest of his colleagues. To this end he urged the expansion of the Central Committee by introducing industrial workers to its membership. Lenin believed that action was needed to prevent conflicts in the central party leadership that might threaten the existence of the party and the survival of the Revolution.[2] In his next period of dictation with secretary Maria Volodicheva, he sketched the prospect of a split in the party. He had little faith in the efficacy of the Tenth Party Congress's ban on factional activity. The October Revolution, he stated, rested upon the support of two social classes, the workers and the peasants, and he insisted that the differing interests of these classes could become the basis for one section of the party leadership to engage in ruinous conflict with another.[3]

Lenin turned to the individuals who might head such sections: Trotski and Stalin. He was far from welcoming Trotski as his sole successor even though he was presently his main ally. The testament proceeded idiosyncratically. Lenin was suggesting, as no one else at the time was doing, that Stalin might be a serious contender for the succession. Trotski, Zinoviev, Kamenev and Bukharin had a sharper public profile than Stalin, who was ridiculed by the great historian of 1917, Nikolai Sukhanov, as a 'grey blur'.

Lenin was able to evaluate Stalin more accurately after recent experiences and had long ago known of the deficiencies of Trotski:[4]

> Comrade Stalin, having become General Secretary, has concentrated unlimited power in his hands, and I am not convinced that he will always manage to use this power with sufficient care. On the other hand, comrade Trotski, as is shown by his struggle against the Central Committee in connection with the question of the People's Commissariat of the Means of Communication, is characterised not only by outstanding talents. To be sure, he is personally the most capable person in the present Central Committee but he also over-brims with self-confidence and with an excessive preoccupation with the purely administrative side of things.

Continuing with these thumbnail characterisations, Lenin asserted that the behaviour of Grigori Zinoviev and Lev Kamenev before the October 1917 seizure of power had been no accident (although he added, rather paradoxically, that this should not be held against them). He castigated Nikolai Bukharin's ideas as scholastic and not entirely Marxist. He accused Georgi Pyatakov of taking too administrative an approach to politics.[5] Deftly Lenin had put his colleagues to the test and found each unsatisfactory. His implicit but unmistakable conclusion was that there was no single leader in the party worthy of succeeding him.

The hypocrisy here was stunning. Lenin too had ruled with insufficient care (Stalin), had been addicted to administrative methods (Trotski and Pyatakov), had opposed revolutionary over-optimism (Zinoviev and Kamenev) and had exhibited a dubious grasp of Marxist orthodoxy (Bukharin). Yet Lenin now contended – and obviously believed – that only his comrades were guilty of these inadequacies.

In the past he had avoided general criticism of a comrade unless a rupture of political ties was involved, and such was the affection for him among his comrades that general criticism of Lenin by one of them was almost unknown. Almost, but not quite unknown. In 1921 he had had a spat with Pyatakov about the desirability of inviting American concessionaires to take over the Donbass coalmines. Pyatakov, according to Lenin, exhibited 'a boastfulness and an adherence to the bad old Russian sect of those who seek to use swords to strike down' a dangerous and strong enemy. Back came a letter from Pyatakov, who did not mince his words:[6]

> You, Vladimir Ilich, have grown accustomed to looking at every-thing on too large a scale, deciding all the big questions of strategy at a distance of a hundred kilometres whereas our need is to resolve the little tactical questions from three kilometres away, or, ten kilometres at the very most. And this is the reason, in my opinion, why you on this question are relapsing into schematism and – if I may pay you back in kind – genuine boastfulness.

Probably this counter-accusation was at the back of Lenin's mind as he composed his testament. Pyatakov had touched a raw spot, the same raw spot probed by Nadezhda Konstantinovna when she had upbraided him for neglecting petty hooliganism among workers and over-focussing upon grand policy.

But Lenin was not engaging in self-criticism even obliquely. There is nothing in the record of his last days that indicates the slightest regret about the general course of his career. Yet, like all Bolshevik leaders, he sensed the negative propensities of Bolshevism: administrative crudity, over-optimism and boastfulness, schematism and scholasticism. The point was that each leader thought himself exempt from being influenced by such propensities. Thus Lenin simply assumed that it was only his fellow leaders who had to be warned about them.

His ideas were not much more plausible as general political theory. In 1902 he had ridiculed the notion that workers could have a positive impact on the revolutionary process merely because they were workers. Why, one may ask, did he now suppose that a change in the Central Committee's social composition by itself would save the Revolution? What had led him to believe that the next working-class generation of Bolsheviks was ready to take over from his own immediate colleagues? What induced him to think that Trotski, Stalin and the others would be unable to obviate any obstacles placed in their way by ordinary factory workers who were inexperienced in high politics? It was also surely a delusion to think that the party's power rested upon the support of the workers and the peasants. Workers had been deprived of most of their political rights; they could not even go on strike without suffering at the hands of the Cheka. Peasants across the rebellious regions were still being suppressed ferociously by the Red Army. Only about one thing was Lenin genuinely astute, and it was an important thing. He sensed that, if factional disputes were to divide the party, Trotski and Stalin would probably be the leaders of the two factions. Practically no one else would have made such a prediction about Stalin; but Lenin had observed him at close quarters and recognised the ambition he possessed.

Lenin therefore swore his secretaries to secrecy and ordered the copies to be put in a safe. This was the extent of his precautions. He went on assuming that everyone regarded him as the unchallengeable leader; he did not even bar Nadezhda Allilueva, Stalin's wife, from working as one of his secretaries. This was naive in the extreme. 'Letter to the Congress' threatened to disturb the party leadership. Maria Volodicheva was so shocked by the contents that on 23 December she asked Lidia Fotieva how to proceed. Fotieva counselled her to show it to Stalin. When Volodicheva did this the next day, Stalin grabbed the typescript and went off to discuss it with Bukharin, Ordzhonikidze and Secretariat official Amayak Nazaretyan. He returned after a few minutes and barked at her: 'Burn it!'[7] This is indeed what Volodicheva did. But then she panicked: she had directly contravened Lenin's wishes and big trouble could be round the corner. Lidia Fotieva and Maria Glyasser were equally appalled. Neither Fotieva nor Glyasser objected to the revelation of the 'Letter to the Congress' to Stalin; it was the act of destruction that gave them concern.[8] There was just one way round the problem: Volodicheva would have to re-type a fifth copy and lock it away as Lenin had told her.[9]

Stalin in fact derived little benefit from the information to which he had become privy. How he must have regretted that he had not slipped the poison to Lenin when he had begged for it. Now the situation was reversed. Stalin wanted Lenin out of the way whereas Lenin was striving to remove Stalin from office. Day after day, Lenin went on dictating notes on the institutions of the Soviet state, and with each extra section he found reason to criticise Stalin.

Yet the scope of Lenin's critique was always limited. Several influential accounts, in the West from the 1960s and in the USSR in the late 1980s, have suggested that he was advocating a massive reform of the Soviet political system.[10] They exaggerated Lenin's wish to change things. He did not challenge his own political creation: the one-party state, the one-ideology state, the terrorist state, the state that sought to dominate all social life, economy and culture. The foundations of his thought also remained in place. The October 1917 seizure of power, revolutionary amoralism, 'European socialist revolution', scientific correctness, ideological intolerance and a temperamental and political impatience: all these stayed untouched. Nothing in his testament challenged the tenet of

The State and Revolution that a classless, egalitarian, prosperous society could be established only by means of socialist dictatorship. Lenin had made many shifts in ideology, organisation and practice since 1917; he was well known for the turnabouts he had made throughout his career. But about the inevitability of the establishment of a communist society and about the general strategy for attaining this goal he had no shred of a doubt. Lenin remained a communist believer to the end; he did not feel he had lived his life in vain or on false political premises. From his sickbed he was taking a last chance to offer guidelines for the scientifically assured achievement of Marxism's global triumph.

Resuming the dictation on 26 December, he called for the Workers' and Peasants' Inspectorate to be refreshed by the recruitment of new staff from the working class. Stalin as former chairman of the Inspectorate was bound to resent Lenin's criticisms of its bureaucratic practices. Lenin added that the State Planning Commission and Sovnarkom should co-operate to increase the degree of planning and regulation in the economy. Here Lenin was hoping to appease Trotski, whom he needed as an ally in the fight against Stalin. Above all, he pondered a change of policy on the constitution. He even began to wonder whether he had been rash, in the prevailing circumstances, to approve the formation of a Union of Soviet Socialist Republics (USSR). He noted that many state officials were 'chauvinistic Great Russian rubbish', and suggested: 'There is no doubt that it would be appropriate to delay this measure until such time as we can swear by this [state] apparatus as being genuinely our own.' Yet again he singled out Stalin for his 'hastiness and administrative preoccupation'. It did not matter to Lenin that Stalin, Ordzhonikidze and Dzierżyński were not Russians. Indeed, they had become altogether too Russian, compensating for their non-Russian ethnic origins by refusing to protect the smaller nations such as the Georgians.

By then it was too late to halt the creation of the USSR, and on 30 December the Congress of Soviets in Moscow ratified the draft constitution previously approved by Lenin and the Party Central Committee. But Lenin had the bit between his teeth: on 30–31 December he dictated an article 'On the Question of the Nationalities or about "Autonomisation"':[11]

> All that's required is to call up my Volga memories about how non-Russians are treated among us, how every Pole has to be called 'a little Polak', how any Tatar is always referred to as 'Prince', any

Ukrainian as 'a Khokhol', and any Georgian or any other inhabitant of the Caucasus as 'a Capcasian person'.

Therefore internationalism on the part of the oppressing or so-called 'great' nation (albeit great only in its acts of violence, great only as a chauvinist thug can be called great) must consist not only in the observance of the formal equality of nations but also in such inequality as would compensate on the part of the oppressing nation – the big nation – for the kind of inequality that is established in real life.

This was not just a routine statement of Marxist belief. It also expressed deep feelings in Lenin that went back to his childhood. To his father's commitment to building Chuvash-language primary schools for the Chuvash children in Simbirsk province. To the condemnation of racial oppression in Harriet Beecher Stowe's *Uncle Tom's Cabin*. To the upbringing at home which taught him that the cultivated Russian should eschew narrow national pride.

In the same article Lenin made a striking apology:[12]

I am, it seems, immensely guilty before the workers of Russia for not intervening sufficiently energetically and sufficiently sharply in the notorious question of autonomisation, officially known, it seems, as the question of the union of soviet socialist republics.

Let us leave aside the fact that Lenin was saying only that it seemed he was guilty. Let us also overlook his reference to 'Russia' as if Georgia and other non-Russian countries were part of it. What is genuinely remarkable is the emotional tone. Lenin was baring his soul.

On 4 January 1923 Lidia Fotieva took down an addendum to the political testament:[13]

Stalin is too crude, and this defect which is entirely acceptable in our milieu and in relationships among us as communists, become unacceptable in the position of General Secretary. I therefore propose to comrades that they should devise a means of removing him from this job and should appoint to this job someone else who is distinguished from comrade Stalin in all other respects only by the single superior aspect that he should be more tolerant, more polite and more attentive towards comrades, less capricious, etc.

This was political war: Lenin wished to remove Stalin from the General Secretaryship. A second point deserves emphasis. This is that Lenin's addendum cut across his own earlier insistence that efforts should be directed at diminishing the rivalry between Stalin and Trotski. By himself attacking Stalin, Lenin was upsetting the balance of power among his close associates and, deliberately or not, lending weight to Trotski.

Having started with the purpose of settling party affairs after his death, he was turning his attention to present difficulties. In particular, he sought to make a last-minute modification in the agreed constitutional plan for the USSR. He urged that the sole government bodies to be unified in Moscow should be the People's Commissariats of External Affairs and of Military Affairs. All the other bodies, according to Lenin, should remain under the control of the various Soviet republics of the USSR. Rapid further centralisation of power in Moscow was to be avoided.

Lenin then reverted to general political questions. The article 'On Co-operation' took up the problem of the low cultural level of the society. Lenin wanted to reinforce the state's emphasis upon enhancing literacy, numeracy, punctuality and conscientiousness. He especially wanted peasants to join co-operatives: 'We still have to do quite a bit from the viewpoint of the "civilised" (above all, literate) European so as to make everyone, to a man and woman, participate – and participate not passively but actively in co-operative operations.'[14] At that moment, Lenin believed, the peasantry traded 'in an Asiatic fashion'.[15] He had always thought this way. But it was unusual of him to use such vocabulary openly. His words implied the notion that Asia lacked civilisation and that Russia was more Asiatic than European. Lenin had always been impatient with the primitiveness of Russian economic and social conditions. Characteristically he singled out the peasants for adverse comment. A class-based perspective remained in everything he wrote, even though most Russian workers differed little from the average Russian peasant in attitudes and technical proficiency. But of course, if he had been more realistic about Russian workers, his entire set of recommendations about the Party Central Committee and the Workers' and Peasants' Inspectorate would have been undermined.

If there was any national group in the USSR he felt positively about it was not the Russians but the Jews. According to Maria Ilinichna, he was proud of the Jewish element in his ancestry since Jews had been responsible for political, scientific and artistic achievements out of all proportion to their number. Yet he was not a Judaeophile as such. What he admired in Jews was their active and positive role in building up a Western, European, modern culture in Russia. Lenin wanted Russians – and he thought of himself as a European Russian – to do the same. Thus there remained much to do before the tasks of the October Revolution could be fully discharged.

Yet about his seizure of power in 'an inadequately cultured country' Lenin had no regrets whatever. In his review of Nikolai Sukhanov's *Notes on the Revolution*, he quoted Napoleon's dictum: 'On s'engage et puis ... on voit.' Roughly translated, this means that a commander needs to get on with the battle before being able to see what military dispositions need to be made. Lenin was urging that power had to be seized before a coherent strategy could be elaborated. He also rejected the convention of contemporary Marxism that the social and economic prerequisites for socialism – a high level of industry, technology and education – ought already to exist in a country before there should be any attempt to establish a socialist state. In fact Karl Marx had entertained the possibility that socialism could begin to be built even in a peasant society; but this was not the general understanding of Marxism held by Russian Marxists in the 1890s. Quite the opposite. Russian Marxists had traditionally insisted that an industrial economy and a literate society were prerequisites for the inception of any attempt to construct a socialist society. Historical development, they contended, proceeded in an immutable sequence of stages. Lenin stood outside the mainstream of Russian Marxism: his implicit impatience with fixed historical stages had been observable since 1905, and he had made this explicit at the Second Congress of the Comintern in 1920. As he lay dying, he wished to ensure that the party appreciated that this was no aberration. It was basic to his Marxism.

And so there was no great change of substance in the last writings of Lenin, only a change in presentation and emphasis. On 25 January 1923, *Pravda* published his article 'How We Should Reorganise Rabkrin', albeit after some tacit criticisms of Stalin had been softened. Lenin then dictated a lengthy piece, 'Better Fewer, But Better', in which he again called for more workers to be promoted to public office. At one point he touched upon the problem that workers – in his condescending jargon – were 'inadequately enlightened'; he suggested that they would have to be 'worked on for a lengthy period'. But generally he trusted in the quick results obtainable by a reliance upon class-based selection.

On foreign policy he added little to his oeuvre. He continued to believe in capitalism's inevitable collapse. While recognising the signs of economic recovery in the West, he declared yet again that the Treaty of Versailles had resulted in the enslavement of Germany and had left Europe highly unstable. Lenin, however, had been scarred by the experience of the Polish–Soviet War of 1920, and he argued that the USSR should stay clear of conflicts among the great powers in the immediate future. On an optimistic note he continued to declare that such conflicts, so long as the USSR was not drawn into them, would benefit the October Revolution by distracting foreign states from mounting an anti-communist crusade. He added that the global after-shock of the Great War had not faded. The East, he maintained, was being shaken 'out of its rut'. Colonies in Asia and Africa, even without the Communist International's intervention, would give trouble to the European imperialism. This was not an original perception: Luxemburg, Trotski, Bukharin and others had said similar things in the past. But Lenin was not claiming intellectual primacy; rather he was declaring that the ebbing of revolutionary prospects was not permanent. He added: 'These are the great tasks about which I am dreaming.'

His article 'Better Fewer, But Better' was published on 4 March 1923 and the impression was growing that Lenin's health was on the mend. This was particularly unwelcome news for Stalin. Through February, with the permission of the central party leadership, Lenin presided over the gathering of data on the Georgian affair by his assistants Nikolai Gorbunov, Lidia Fotieva and Maria Glyasser. Physically he could barely move. But intellectually he was still very sharp and his combativeness caused trepidation in the Central Committee since his *Pravda* articles had referred to tensions among the Kremlin leaders. One of the Central Committee Secretaries, Valeryan Kuibyshev, suggested that *Pravda* should give up printing Lenin's material and instead produce a dummy issue of the party newspaper containing his work, which could then be sent to Lenin alone. Thus the party could be prevented from being unsettled by his accusations against Stalin. The central party leadership rejected Kuibyshev and sent a circular letter to the party committees in the provinces bluntly asserting that unity prevailed in Moscow.

The situation was highly charged. By 3 March 1923 Lenin had received an exhaustive account of the Georgian affair from his helpers. The ammunition was in his hands and he had only to fire it at Stalin. This seemed a simple task. Around this time – we still do not know precisely when – Lenin learned from an unguarded remark by Nadezhda Konstantinovna about the verbal abuse she had suffered from Stalin. Lenin was livid. At midday on 5 March he summoned Maria Volodicheva and dictated two letters. One of these was addressed to Trotski, whom he asked to take up the Georgian Central Committee's case on his behalf. The second letter was to Stalin:[16]

You had the uncouthness to summon my wife to the telephone and swear at her. Although she has even given you her agreement to forget what was said, nevertheless this fact has become known through her to Zinoviev and Kamenev. I do not intend to forget so easily what has been done against me, and it goes without saying that I consider that something done against my wife to be something also done against me. Therefore I ask you to consider whether you agree to take back what you said and apologise or prefer to break relations between us.

The dispute with Stalin exposed aspects of Lenin that he customarily kept private. Although Lenin the revolutionary wanted men and women to be treated equally, Lenin was also a middle-class Russian husband, and such men expected their wives to be treated with gentility by other men.

There was really some excuse for Stalin's exasperation with Nadezhda Konstantinovna's pandering to Lenin's wish to stay politically active; and Stalin, too, expected other men to respect his wife. But he also expected women to know their place and had tried to get his own wife Nadezhda Allilueva to cease being a party member. Lenin himself had had to intervene to get her party card restored to her![17] Even so, Stalin had overstepped the mark in swearing at Lenin's wife. Lenin the prophet of Marxist amoralism was out to get him not only for his politics but also for his infringement of good manners.

Next day, after receiving a positive reply from Trotski about the Georgian affair, he asked Volodicheva to deliver the letter to Stalin. Then he dictated yet another letter. This one went to Mdivani and the Georgian communist group:[18]

Respected comrades,
With all my heart I am following your case. I am indignant at the uncouthness of Ordzhonikidze and the indulging of him by Stalin and Dzierżyński. I'll prepare some notes and a speech for you.
With respect,
Lenin

Little did he know that his entourage, including his wife, decided that the letter to Stalin should not be handed over to its addressee. Already on 5 March Lenin's physical condition had taken a turn for the worse, and it must be assumed that Nadezhda Konstantinovna was worried lest the dispute with Stalin should finish him off altogether. He had a bad night on 6–7 March, and again lost the use of the extremities of the right side of his body. In the morning, however, Maria Volodicheva decided that she could not disobey Lenin's wishes for ever; she took the letter across the Kremlin to Stalin. Copies were given, as Lenin had demanded, to Kamenev and Zinoviev.

Stalin was stupefied: 'This isn't Lenin speaking, it's his illness.' With some poise and much Georgian pride he wrote back: 'If my wife were to behave incorrectly and you had to punish her, I would not have considered it my right to intervene. But inasmuch as you insist, I'm willing to apologise to Nadezhda Konstantinovna.'[19] Kamenev, however, persuaded him that Lenin would be more offended by such a concession than by the original offence. Stalin rewrote his letter, but not before he had a terrible quarrel over the telephone with Maria Ilinichna. Yet he was sufficiently worried to moderate the words of his response to Lenin.

Stalin need not have bothered. By that time Lenin was in no condition to read anything. He could not even speak. Nor could he move without being carried. Nadezhda Konstantinovna and Maria Ilinichna took turns at his bedside; the doctors watched with equal anxiety. On 10 March, Lenin suffered an immense spasm. His right side was completely paralysed and he could move his left hand only with the greatest difficulty. He could not sleep, and had awful headaches. Any hope he had of recovery had virtually vanished. Nadezhda Konstantinovna and Maria Ilinichna nursed him, and Nadezhda Konstantinovna had lessons in how to teach people to talk again after a stroke. His will to survive, apart from days when he would gladly have swallowed a cyanide pill if he could, was intact. But he accepted the need to take things gently and to move to the Big House at Gorki. It took two months before the doctors thought him strong enough to be transported. But a vehicle with special springs was got ready and on 15 May 1923 it carried him, under guard, out of the Kremlin to the countryside south of Moscow.

Stalin had been let off the hook. The Twelfth Party Congress, to which Lenin had hoped to present his political testament, passed with Stalin being able to give the Central Committee report on 'the national question'. Mdivani and the Georgian communists were defeated. Lenin's remarks about Stalin in the testament were read out to the heads of delegations, but were not discussed on the floor of the Congress. Trotski failed to rise to the occasion and Kamenev and Zinoviev, worried more that Trotski might make a bid for power than that Stalin might later turn on them, supported the General Secretary. Stalin survived without irreparable damage to his authority and status. He kept the General Secretaryship. Now he had to hope that Lenin would never return to his political career. For Stalin, the signs were propitious.

Meanwhile Lenin was almost totally incapacitated; and Professor Strumpel, summoned from Germany, reasserted that he was probably suffering from an advanced form of syphilis and that the careful application of arsenic and iodine preparations should be continued.[20] Councils of doctors held in March, April and May, however, failed to produce a diagnostic consensus. No specialist could prove his point of view and several of them were in any case still baffled. The pitiful condition of the patient was obvious. British communists had bought and sent Lenin an electric wheelchair from J. A. Carter and Co. in central London. Its operational lever was positioned on the right-hand side, where Lenin had no bodily usage; in any case he refused to use the vehicle and insisted that it should be passed on to a Civil War veteran. He was dressed plainly in a khaki tunic and high-laced walking shoes. But the most he could do was sit with Nadezhda Konstantinovna and wait for her to work out what he was thinking; a few grunts and groans were all he could manage. But the usual thing was for him to say: 'Here, here, here.'[21] She was not always sure what he was trying to say; she had to make an informed guess and carry on the conversations regardless.

When it all became too much, Nadezhda Konstantinovna collapsed in tears. (Once Lenin had to give her a handkerchief.) Maria Ilinichna, a true Ulyanov, did not let her grief show. To the astonishment of Lenin's bodyguard Pëtr Pakaln, not once did she sob.[22] Yet both women experienced acute strain. After March 1923 Lenin asked first Maria and then Nadya for poison. Maria felt so coerced by him that she had to trick him by offering a phial of quinine. Nadya rejected the requests entirely, as did Lidia Fotieva.[23] None of the women could predict how the situation would develop and they had ceased bothering to ask the doctors. It was obvious to both Nadya and Maria that Lenin's condition baffled contemporary medical science. Maria felt bitter about this. If they knew so little for certain, she very reasonably concluded, they should not have experimented by allowing him back to work in October 1922.[24] Nadya, for her part, had accepted his emotional need to stay somehow involved in political activity, but she too scorned the doctors as being next to useless and wrote to friends in Moscow saying that she doubted that there was any hope left for her husband.[25]

And yet there were days when he felt a lot better. For example, he discovered that one of the comrades convalescing at Gorki, in the adjacent building, was none other than the man with whom he had debated the merits of Marxism in 1889–90, Alexander Preobrazhenski. Those days at Alakaevka in Samara seemed like a different epoch. Lenin was overjoyed to meet and embrace his old friend, who was suffering from a cardiac ailment. Indeed he refused to leave Preobrazhenski's quarters that night or the next.[26] Slumping down on the bed, he exclaimed: 'I'm done in!' A distraught Maria Ilinichna trailed after him for fear that he might collapse.[27]

This was in July 1923. Another escapade took place in October, when Lenin suddenly took it into his head to make a trip to the Kremlin. Maria Ilinichna remonstrated with him: 'Listen, Volodya, they won't let you into the Kremlin: you haven't got an entrance card.' But he only laughed and muttered incomprehensibly.[28] His chauffeur Gil brought the Rolls-Royce from the garage behind the Big House and, accompanied by Nadya and Maria, drove Lenin to the capital. As Maria had anticipated, they were not immediately granted entrance through the Kremlin gates. But again Lenin merely laughed. Back he went to his familiar rooms. To the apartment he had shared with Nadezhda Konstantinovna and Maria Ilinichna; to the Central Committee meeting room; and lastly to the Sovnarkom chamber. On the way he asked for particular books to be taken from the shelves, and checked that everything was as it should be in his absence. Just once, when he gazed around the Sovnarkom chamber with its long, green-baize table, did he become disconsolate.[29] It was there that he had directed the government through the years of the Civil War and of the early New Economic Policy. The memories unblocked his emotions; for a moment it seemed that he could not continue with the visit. But he recovered. By the time his little tour was over, it was too late to return to Gorki, and Lenin, Nadya and Maria stayed overnight in their old apartment.

This was the last such jaunt Lenin took outside the Gorki estate. Winter had set in. The countryside was covered in snow, and in the bright, low sun of the early afternoon there was no more wonderful vista in Russia. Miles and miles of leafless birch trees stretched to the horizon. The two miles of dirt road from the rail-stop at the village of Gerasimovka were cleared and relaid so that the doctors could come and go. But generally the peasants, servants, patients and their relatives were isolated from the rest of the world. They might just as well have been living at Shushenskoe in Siberian exile. No agricultural work could be done on the collective farm and no building maintenance was possible on the Big House's exterior. Time stood still.

Until mid-autumn Nadya had been able to wheel her husband around as they hunted for fungi. Lenin had loved to beat her in spotting them before her. Competitive as ever, he was pleased that he could do some things that others could not.[30] But in the last weeks of the year they went out simply to enjoy the panorama across the flat fields. Riding in a horse-drawn sleigh, they were accompanied by Pëtr Pakaln, the medical assistant Vladimir Rukavishnikov or one of the male nurses.[31] Some days Lenin was very buoyant, and Nadya wrote a postcard to the Armand children rejoicing that he could 'walk around independently (with a stick)'.[32] The doctors too were pleased with him. Indeed Pëtr Pakaln reported to the Cheka – and indirectly to Stalin in the Party Secretariat – that Lenin 'felt magnificent'.[33] As he had done in the previous winter, 'Grandad Lenin' gave orders for a fir tree to be placed in the Big House for a children's party. Anna Ilinichna's adopted son Gora Lozgachëv, now a strapping sixteen-year-old, was allowed by Maria Ilinichna to join in the fun with other invited children.[34] Lenin also welcomed visits from political associates. Among those who came out for a chat with him were party leaders Zinoviev, Kamenev, Bukharin and Yevgeni Preobrazhenski.[35]

Yet there were many counter-indications about his condition: in November and December 1923 alone he suffered seven collapses.[36] Quite what he thought about this is unknown. This was partly a technical problem of oral disability, but he had always kept his own counsel. Nadya, who had been drawn back towards him by his need for her to nurse him, resented this reticence and told Bukharin that it was as if a wall existed between them.[37] But she kept on trying to break her way through to him.

In defiance of the Politburo, she talked to him about politics; but even she dared not agitate him by telling him about a dispute that had erupted in the central party leadership. In autumn 1923 Trotski had published a series of articles, *The New Course*, in which he criticised the party's bureaucratic condition and the state's weak and inefficient control over the economy. A Left Opposition gathered around Trotski. The rest of the Politburo fought back; Stalin, Kamenev, Zinoviev and Bukharin stood shoulder to shoulder and organised their followers in Moscow and the provinces to counteract Trotski's campaign. The ascendant party leadership appealed for unity and loyalty and used every organisational trick in the book to vilify the Left Opposition. All this suited Stalin. Trotski had put himself in the role of the party splitter and could not call upon Lenin to help him out. The rest of the Politburo claimed that

Trotski lusted after personal power and wished to wreck the New Economic Policy. At the Thirteenth Party Conference, held in Moscow in January 1924, the Left Opposition went down to a crushing defeat. By then Trotski was away from the field of combat; physical exhaustion had compelled him to take a lengthy rest in Sukhumi on the Abkhazian coast of the Black Sea.

Nadya knew that this was the very schism that Lenin had predicted in his 'Letter to the Congress'. She fibbed in order to keep him calm. As she read him her selections from *Pravda*, she told him that the party had emerged united from the Thirteenth Party Conference. The deceit seemed to work. He 'felt wonderful' on 18 January 1924 and next day went out for a ride in the horse-drawn sleigh.[38] Bukharin had come out to stay at Gorki for a few days' rest and to do a bit of writing; he stayed in the building opposite the Big House. Maria Ilinichna bustled around as normal and Nadezhda Konstantinovna went on reading to Lenin. On 20 January there was reason to celebrate: it was a full month since Lenin had had a collapse.

On 21 January, too, there seemed no cause for concern. Lenin woke up at 10.30 a.m. and went to the bathroom. This was not particularly late for him during his convalescence. But then he announced that he was not feeling well and after drinking half a cup of black coffee he went back to his bed at 11.00 a.m. There he slept. At 3.00 p.m. he felt a little brighter and sipped another half-cup and a bowl of clear soup. Professor Osipov went to the bedroom to make his daily examination of the patient and found nothing especially worrisome. Lenin's pulse was a trifle fast, but his temperature was normal. His speech was no worse than for some months. But then a crisis began without warning at 5.40 p.m. Lenin, propped up in bed, felt the tremor of an incipient attack. Nausea invaded his entire body. The doctors on duty – Osipov, Förster and Yelistratov – held a hurried consultation, attended by their assistant Vladimir Rukavishnikov. Also present were Nadezhda Konstantinovna and Maria Ilinichna.[39] Lenin fell into a coma. He stayed in it much longer than in December 1923, when he had several times been unconscious for twenty minutes. His heartbeat slowed and Maria Ilinichna sent out for some camphor to restore it. This was an emergency.

Bukharin heard that something was happening and ran across to the Big House to investigate. The guards were in their customary positions around the building. But inside nothing was as normal. The lights were on upstairs and Pakaln, who usually patrolled the ground floor, was nowhere to be seen.[40] Bukharin rushed upstairs. There he discovered

Pakaln, who wanted to be with Nadezhda Konstantinovna and Maria Ilinichna as Lenin fought for his life. Lenin's temperature had risen sharply. He tossed and turned in the narrow bed and was covered in sweat. He roared in pain. Bukharin was there for the end at 6.50 p.m.:[41]

> When I ran into Ilich's room, full of doctors and stacked with medicines, Ilich let out a last sigh. His face fell back and went terribly white. He let out a wheeze, his hands dropped. Ilich, Ilich was no more.

The doctors lifted his eyelids to test whether there was still a chance. But there could be only one diagnosis. Vladimir Ilich Ulyanov-Lenin, man of struggle, had breathed his last.

A telephone call was put through immediately to the Kremlin. The Politburo had made arrangements for such an outcome and all its members except Trotski met in Zinoviev's Kremlin flat to confer. Kamenev rang Vladimir Bonch-Bruevich to instruct him to go out to Gorki to supervise the disposal of the body. On 22 January, Bonch-Bruevich went out by train to Gerasimovka with Lenin's sister Anna and brother Dmitri. Next day the coffin was carried through a line of mourning villagers down to the railway station and transported to Moscow. The corpse was laid out in the House of Trade Unions. In the biting cold, mourners moved upon Moscow from the rest of the USSR. Obituaries filled the newspapers. Everyone was gripped by uncertainty as to what would happen next. The Cheka was put on alert in case anti-Bolshevik political groups should attempt something against the regime. A solemn session of the Congress of Soviets was held on 26 January, where speeches were made in commemoration of the late leader. Central Committee leaders took turns in swearing oaths to his ideas and example. 'We swear to you, comrade Lenin,' declared Stalin, 'that we shall not spare our lives in strengthening the union of the working people of the entire world – the Communist International.'

The funeral took place on 27 January 1924, six days after Lenin's death. It was the coldest day of the year. The trumpeters had to smear vodka on their instruments to stop their breath freezing on their lips. The crowd on Red Square sang the *Internationale* as the body of Lenin was brought up from the House of Trade Unions. Zinoviev, Kamenev, Stalin, Bukharin, Molotov, Tomski, Rudzutak and Dzierżyński held the coffin; Trotski was still in Sukhumi, having been 'reassured' by Stalin that he need not return. All business was halted in Moscow. Factory whistles and hooters were sounded. The same scene was repeated elsewhere in the cities, towns and villages of the USSR. Trains were stopped in their tracks. Boats were moored. A vault had been prepared in front of the Kremlin Wall on Red Square. Lenin was lowered into the earth at four o'clock in the afternoon. It was already dark and getting darker.

LENIN: THE AFTERLIFE

The dead man did not rest in peace. On the orders of the Politburo, Lenin's corpse was kept on ice in the central Moscow morgue until scientists had completed the experiments enabling them to embalm it and put it on permanent display. Although Nadezhda Konstantinovna objected, she was getting used to her reduced authority since she knew that the Politburo decision was not subject to appeal. The decision was definitive: the body of her husband was to be housed in a Red Square mausoleum on the north-eastern side of the Kremlin. The structure would be wooden. (The present marble edifice was constructed in 1930.) The wintry conditions were so harsh that dynamite was needed to blast a hole in the frozen ground. The Bolshevik leadership announced that factory workers had written to the official authorities requesting Lenin's corporeal conservation and exhibition. This was a blatant political fabrication: the idea came not from factory workers but from the Politburo. Inside the Politburo the prime advocate was none other than Iosif Stalin, who believed that the corpse in the mausoleum would serve as an object of unifying importance for the citizens of the USSR and for the followers of communism around the world.

The Lenin Mausoleum is now such a cliché of the world's architecture that it can be hard to understand how bizarre the plan was in 1924. Although the ancient Egyptians embalmed their Pharaohs, they had then sealed them up in wooden cases and locked them in the subterranean chambers of stone pyramids outside Cairo. Lenin, dressed in a dark suit, was to be visible to visitors to Red Square. It is true that the bones of men and women designated as saints by the Russian Orthodox Church had been revered by the faithful; but no saint had been turned into a mannequin for daily public scrutiny. The perceived need for 'mausoleumisation' was a measure of the Politburo's insecurity. Lenin had been the most popular of its members; his Land Decree of 1917 and his New Economic Policy of 1921 were widely admired by fellow citizens.

Politburo members wished to deflect some of this aura of esteem towards themselves.

Simultaneously Lenin's writings acquired the status of holy writ; his collected works – whose publication had been under way since 1920 – were accorded a political and cultural significance greater than anything else in print. An Institute of the Brain was established in his honour; thirty thousand slices were collected from his cerebral tissue so that research might begin on the secrets of his great genius. A whole ideology was discovered: Marxism–Leninism. The claim was made that Lenin was no mere footsoldier in the Marxist battalion but a global thinker on a par with his heroes Marx and Engels. The October Revolution, the Bolshevik party and the USSR were his outstanding achievements. A bright new page in the story of humanity had been inscribed by Lenin. The world's governments – whether they were conservative, liberal or socialist – were trembling at the consequences of 1917; and fascism arose in several European countries in large measure in reaction to Soviet communism and its potential to be reproduced elsewhere on the continent. The twentieth century was being forged on the anvil of Lenin's seizure and consolidation of power in Petrograd. When Petrograd was renamed Leningrad in 1924, it seemed appropriate testimony to his historical significance.

Nadezhda Konstantinovna sat for a day by his coffin as it lay in state. She felt completely alone. Her parents were dead, she had no brother or sister, and she had never felt entirely comfortable with Lenin's relatives. The dearest person to her was Inessa's twenty-five-year-old daughter Inna, who was like the child she had never had. After the funeral she wrote her a letter:[1]

> My very own dearest Inochka,
>   We buried Vladimir Ilich yesterday ... Lenin's death was the best outcome. Death had already been suffered by him so many times in the previous year ... At this moment above all I want to think about Vladimir Ilich, about his work and to read him.

Nadya would not trust medical specialists again. She was certain that Lenin had suffered to the end: 'They say that he was in an unconscious condition, but now I firmly know that doctors know nothing.'[2] The Politburo annoyed her to a still greater extent. The decision to preserve the body of her husband disgusted her. Soon she was writing again to Inna:[3]

When the project arose among our people to bury V.I. in the Kremlin, I was filled with terrible indignation – what they should have done was bury him with his comrades so that they could lie beneath the Red Wall together.

The communist authorities permanently kept this file marked 'completely secret'. This is not surprising. Nadezhda Konstantinovna was not merely challenging the decision on embalming and mausoleumisation. By saying that Lenin should have had a proper burial in that precise spot, she was also recommending that his final resting-place should be near to Inna's mother Inessa Armand. Nadya had a generous spirit. Something made her want to keep the two families together even in death; she was willing for her husband to lie by his former lover Inessa in the cold Moscow ground.[4]

But this was not to be. The erection of the Lenin Mausoleum proceeded despite her anguished protests about Stalin and the Politburo. But historians have not previously been able to appreciate how much she nevertheless helped to develop the Lenin cult in other ways. Although she hated the Mausoleum, she actively propagated an image of Lenin as the perfect revolutionary, thinker and husband. Indeed she started writing a pamphlet about him immediately after the funeral.[5] This incidentally demonstrates that she lived for politics almost as much as her deceased husband had done. She mourned him, but her grief was not such as to inhibit her from writing in a fairly detached fashion about him. Furthermore, she set about this work with the full co-operation of Stalin himself. The picture we are usually given is one of permanent frostiness between Krupskaya and Stalin. The central party archives have material that tells a different story. In May 1924, once she had completed a first draft, Krupskaya took the initiative of sending Stalin a copy and asking for his opinion on it. He replied, suggesting a few factual corrections and encouraging her to go ahead with publication.[6]

This co-operation continued for years. Although Nadezhda Konstantinovna did not retire from her duties in the People's Commissariat for Enlightenment, she spent her spare time lecturing and writing about Lenin. The sanctification of his memory was her abiding preoccupation and she became virtually the high priestess of the Lenin cult. This was a personal as well as a political matter. Collecting her photographs of him, she filled an album and decorated the cover with the word Ilich, which she cut into letter-shapes from other photographs of him. She cherished, too, the leather briefcase he had given to her after he had been presented with it by a group of workers. Nadezhda Konstantinovna never got over the loss of her husband.[7]

Her rivals as high priestess of the cult were Anna Ilinichna and Maria Ilinichna. But it was a friendly rivalry. Now that the object of their affections was dead, the three women got along better. With Nadezhda, Anna and Maria as high priestesses, there was no doubt about the identity of the chief priest: Stalin himself. Meanwhile the collusion of most leading party figures in the suppression of Lenin's political testament allowed Stalin to survive as Party General Secretary, and he was quick to join in the collective effort to develop a set of doctrines explicating the core of Leninism. His series of lectures to the Sverdlov University, published as *Questions of Leninism*, were a succinct summary. Trotski, Zinoviev, Kamenev and Bukharin too made votive offerings to the memory of the party's founder and tried to expound what he had meant to world communism. Steadily his ideas were being codified. The process could not be brought to completion because Lenin had left behind – and on the public record – many contradictory ideas.

If codification was difficult, however, there was little problem about censoring what appeared about him. The need was confidentially emphasised to describe Lenin in hagiographic terms. The agencies of propaganda in party and government were deployed in the service of this objective. His works were produced in print-runs of hundreds of thousands of copies. Lenin's files were examined and Kamenev led an editorial team that published a lot of his previously unknown writings. Always the purpose was the same. Lenin was not merely to be depicted as a heroic figure in the history of Bolshevism and world revolution. He had to enjoy the mythic status of an omniscient revolutionary saint. No blemish on his record as a theorist, propagandist or party organiser was tolerable. He had to be hallowed as the sole great successor to Marx and Engels in the first quarter of the twentieth century. His foresight and determination in forming the Bolshevik party and leading it through the October Revolution and Civil War had to be laden with unconditional praise. His genius as party chief, government premier, wartime planner and global statesman had to be hailed. His humanity as a comrade, a husband and a Marxist had to be extolled.

Another criterion became more emphatic as the years rolled on. This was that anything said about Lenin had to suit the immediate interests of the communist political leadership. As the struggle for the succession was joined, the ascendant group – Kamenev, Zinoviev, Stalin and Bukharin – excised from the history books anything that even remotely reflected badly on them. Trotski suffered most in this rivalry; his opponents not only removed him and his supporters from important posts but also prevented him from publishing material demonstrating his close working relationship with Lenin. The result was the depiction of a largely imaginary Lenin, a Lenin who had had a warm association only with those who presently held power.

The main devotees of the cult – Nadezhda Konstantinovna, Maria Ilinichna and Anna Ilinichna – colluded in creating a quasi-religious myth. They understood that every publication should abide by the criteria of hagiographic and political calculation. Yet Lenin's relatives could not always predict what would fit the bill, and much of what they wrote was subsequently excised before publication. Ultimately they had to accept the judgement of Stalin. By the time others got going with their memoirs, the tacit rules of the cult had become clear and the authors knew they had to write accordingly. What is more, the Secretariat of the Central Committee under Stalin rigorously kept secret the minutes of most meetings of the supreme political leadership in the party and the government. Just a carefully vetted sprinkling of documents was allowed into the light of day. The reasons for the caution are easy to comprehend. The USSR, the October Revolution and Marxism–Leninism could have no justification unless the reverence for Lenin became a popular emotion. Thus the cult of the party's founder was not an optional matter for his successors. It was a political necessity. And so it remained until the end of the USSR.

The leading priests of the cult changed over the years. The anti-Trotski group of Kamenev, Zinoviev, Stalin and Bukharin fell apart as soon as Trotski had been defeated in 1924. Kamenev and Zinoviev opposed Stalin and Bukharin and lost. Then Bukharin opposed Stalin, and Bukharin lost. Stalin by 1928–9 was initiating his First Five-Year Plan. He herded peasants into collective farms, suppressed their resistance and arrested and imprisoned nationalists, religious leaders, critical intellectuals and internal party opponents. In 1937–8 a Great Terror raged at his instigation. Throughout this period he manufactured a 'Lenin' that fitted exactly with his current requirements. Stalin's Lenin had always been the friend of Stalin. Purportedly he had relied on Stalin for advice and had recognised Stalin as his worthiest successor. The contents of Lenin's political testament were banned from the media of public communication and opponents of the new official version of the past were executed or thrown into the Gulag system of forced-labour camps.

Stalin put it about that he was 'the Lenin of today'. His stress upon violence, hierarchy, orderliness and discipline found reflection in the historical textbooks. The complexities of Lenin's Marxism were wiped away. The Soviet mass youth organisation was named after him: the All-Union Leninist Communist Union of Youth. Further collected editions of Lenin's works were published. Pictures were painted of him to be hung in art galleries, but his image was everywhere else too: on postage stamps, on crockery, on posters draped across the thoroughfares of the great cities of the USSR. Every front page of the main central newspapers *Pravda* and *Izvestia* was adorned by his image. An Order of Lenin was founded. Excerpts from his writings were used to indoctrinate school-children so that they might grow up as committed communists, and speakers at Party Congresses quoted him in support of their proposals. If Marx, Engels and Lenin made up a secular Trinity of Marxism–Leninism, then the greatest of the three in the treatment by Soviet propagandists was not Marx or Engels but Lenin. Lenin appeared as the Godhead of Marxism–Leninism.

Increasingly it was not Marxism–Leninism but a modified ideology, Marxism–Leninism–Stalinism, that was propagated and Stalin for most purposes had himself depicted as Lenin's representative on earth. On the anniversary of the October Revolution, Stalin would stand atop the Lenin Mausoleum beneath the Kremlin Wall and look down over the parade of military personnel, youth organisations and sportsmen. He did this even in 1941 when there was danger that the Luftwaffe might bomb central Moscow. The poet Vladimir Mayakovski had once finished a piece with the words: 'Lenin lived, Lenin lives, Lenin will live!' Short of raising Lenin from death like a modern-day Lazarus, the Soviet regime did everything else to impregnate the minds of its citizens with the notion that the Leninist heritage had an inextinguishable life of its own.

So much of this 'Lenin' was an emasculated version of the historical Lenin. It was not permitted to refer to the non-Russian ingredients in his ancestry; no one except exceptionally well-informed Bolshevik veterans knew that he had grandfathers who were not Russians. Mention was never made of his noble status; even the fact that the Ulyanovs had had a comfortable existence was seldom noted. His Classical education, his agrarian-socialist terrorist sympathies and his rather privileged lifestyle even in Siberian exile were banned from public discussion. It became heretical to dwell on the fact that Lenin took ideas from other thinkers and politicians. Even the influence of Marx and Engels was played down. Accounts of tensions inside the Bolshevik party dwelt upon a struggle between Lenin, Stalin and the true Leninists on one side and a host of ne'er-do-wells – from Martov in 1903 to the rest of the Politburo in the early 1920s – on the other. The more intimate aspects of Lenin's life were not so much distorted as kept strictly hidden. His liaison with Inessa Armand was a prohibited topic. Thus his marital relationship was portrayed as a political partnership – and little more than that. The charm of Lenin for his friends and comrades was obliterated from the historical record. His astuteness as a party leader was overlooked. His alternation of bull-headed insistence with carefully calculated fudges and compromises was excised.

Outside the USSR there were attempts to describe Lenin more plausibly. Memoirs by Mensheviks who had known him were available; and after his deportation in 1928, Trotski published several pieces which challenged the crude falsehoods of the contemporary Soviet biographies. But not even Trotski had brought out all the archival information stored in Moscow, and anyway he had his own political agenda. He claimed that he, not Stalin, was the political successor preferred by Lenin. Trotski opposed 'the Stalinist school of historical falsification' with an account that was not untainted by considerations of personal interest. Obviously the Menshevik accounts, too, had their bias; no Menshevik memoirist was going to write gently about Lenin, who had locked up or deported the Menshevik leadership. Nevertheless both Trotski and the Mensheviks described and analysed Lenin in terms that reduced him from demigod to human being.

Western communists dutifully followed the lines of the picture supplied from Moscow. They took their Lenin from Stalin, and it was a shock to them after Stalin's death in 1953 that his successors announced that Lenin and Stalin had not seen eye to eye. In 1956, Nikita Khrushchëv quoted from Lenin's political testament and added that Stalin had proceeded in the 1930s to commit mass murder. Across the communist world, especially in the USSR, Khrushchëv caused a sensation. As he pulled Stalin from his pedestal, he felt obliged to elevate the status of Lenin higher than ever. A massive fifth edition of 'the complete collected works' was ordered. So, too, was a new official biography of Lenin. Khrushchëv's purpose was not to unfetter scholarship. Historians were carefully vetted before being granted access to the Central Party Archive on Pushkin Street, and were required to stick largely to the interpretation of Lenin's life that had prevailed under Stalin, except for the single major difference that they were free to expose any disagreement between Lenin and Stalin. But there were other benefits for historical plausibility. Not every instance of factional strife in the party was treated as a capitalist conspiracy, and it was also shown that Lenin was no despot over his fellow communists.

Abroad, however, further uses were made of the newer information. Some writers suggested that Lenin's last battles with Stalin demonstrated that the communism of the New Economic Policy was of a kind very different from the communism of the Civil War. Dissenting Soviet communist historians like Roy Medvedev took the same approach. Their argument was that Lenin as he lay dying envisaged a permanent communist order that involved cultural pluralism, ethnic diversity and perhaps even a mixed economy. Among the Western communist parties these ideas had a warm reception. Several so-called Eurocommunists in Italy, France and Spain proposed that, if Lenin's health had held out, then communism with a human face could have been constructed.

Other Eurocommunists, however, raised the question whether Leninism had always been flawed by its propensity for dictatorship, terror, ideological rigidity and amoralism. For anti-communists this was no great discovery: they had always believed that Lenin's impact upon his times had been malign. But what was the scope of his impact? As writers got to grips with this question in the 1970s and 1980s, they were interested mainly in his politics. Enquiries were made into the intellectual milieu of Russian revolutionaries in the late nineteenth century, into the internal divisions among Marxists of the Russian Empire, into Russian Marxism and into the limits on the power of Communist Party leaders before and after they seized power in Russia in the October Revolution. But all the time there was agreement with the conventional wisdom, Western as well as Soviet, that the course of the USSR's history was largely the product of the energies of one man: Lenin. Thus Lenin was not fundamentally redrawn as an actor on the world stage. Details were changed, but not the basic analysis. Lenin was placed alongside Hitler, Stalin, Churchill, Roosevelt, Khrushchëv, Gorbachëv and a few others as the principal actors in the history of the twentieth century.

Despite many disagreements, the opinion gained ground that Lenin was not quite the demiurge that had been claimed by both communists and their enemies since he had leaped to the world's attention in 1917. Further research on the political, social and economic environment tended to indicate that he worked to a large extent with the grain of Russian traditions. Without intending it, many writers produced an analysis that suggested that Lenin's contribution to his country's history was more as facilitator than as maker.

This was to ignore so much. There were turns in the history of Russia and the world that would not have been taken without Lenin. He decisively affected events, institutions, practices and basic attitudes. This was felt to be the case at the time, and most commentators felt the same many years later. Lenin had founded the Bolshevik faction. He had written *What Is to Be Done?*, the *April Theses* and *The State and Revolution*. He had elaborated a strategy for the seizure of power and seen to it that power was seized. Not only the October Revolution but also the Brest-Litovsk Treaty and the New Economic Policy might not have occurred without his influence – and the Soviet regime might quickly have disappeared into history's dustbin. He did not have a plan for the one-party state that was created in 1917–19, but several institutions of that state were founded by him. Among them was the Cheka, and he insisted that terror should continue to be an instrument of rule available to the communists. Above all, Lenin was the main creator of the Russian Communist Party itself, a party distinguished by commitments to centralism, hierarchy and activism. It would be odd to claim that there would have been no far-left party in Russia had Lenin not lived. But it would be equally absurd to suppose that the Soviet one-party, one-ideology state would have been born without Lenin.

Although neither Lenin nor his fellow party leaders saw in advance exactly what kind of state they would build, furthermore, there was more than random chance about their activity in the early years of the October Revolution. The Leninists carried a set of operational assumptions into power with them. Their understanding of politics gave priority to dictatorship, class struggle, leadership and revolutionary amoralism. The 'vanguard', they believed, knew what was best for the working class and should use its irrefutable knowledge of the world – past, present and future – to hasten the advent of the perfect society on earth. Lenin was not the originator of these assumptions. On the contrary, they were widespread and could be found in some form or other in Marxism, in mid-nineteenth-century Russian revolutionary terrorism and in Europe's other authoritarian revolutionary doctrines. There were traces of them in tradition of even greater longevity. Not for nothing was Leninism compared to the millenarianism of pre-Petrine Orthodox Christianity as well as to sixteenth-century Calvinism. But the point is that there was no inevitability about the recrudescence of such traditions after 1900. It took a Russian Marxist party. More particularly, it took a Lenin.

And the state created by Lenin survived intact for more than seven decades. The edifice was thrown up with extraordinary rapidity even though the architectural planning had been minimal. In 1917–19, under Lenin's guidance, the main work was already done. The foundations had been dug, the load-bearing walls erected and the roof sealed. Politics had been monopolised and centralised. The agencies of coercion were firmly under the party's control. The economy was penetrated by state ownership and state regulation. Religion was systematically persecuted. National aspirations were handled with grave suspicion. High artistic and intellectual culture was rigorously patrolled. Schooling was steadily communised. Law was introduced and suspended at the communist leadership's whim, and the legislative, executive and judicial functions of the state were deliberately commingled. The rulers treated society as a resource to be indoctrinated and mobilised. The assault was begun on all intermediate organisations that had any independence from the Kremlin.

Yet Lenin was complex as a leader and theorist. Inevitably sections of the edifice had to be added long after the building work had started; much improvisation took place and, of course, Lenin was not the sole architect: there were others in his party who had an impact on the progress of construction. The Bolshevik supreme leaders were constantly modifying their schemes. They did not drive the last surviving parties underground until 1921, and factions continued to exist in the Communist Party until Stalin's despotism after the death of Lenin. The formal panoply of censorship bodies came into existence only in mid-1922. And the policies on nationhood, which Lenin thought would allow the state eventually to fuse the various nations of the USSR into a Soviet supranational consciousness, were initially quite favourable to the national and ethnic self-expression of the non-Russians. Furthermore, the period of Civil War and the New Economic Policy was characterised by a huge amount of chaos. Communications, administration, surveillance and coercion were carried out much more haphazardly than in subsequent years. Doctrine and policy were one thing; implementation was often entirely another.

Nevertheless the basic edifice was *in situ* years before Lenin's demise. It was altered drastically by Stalin, who turned it into a personal despotism and reduced the authority of the party within the Soviet state. Stalin also practised butchery not only against the military foes and class, political and religious enemies of communism but even against the functionaries of his own government and party. Yet in truth the core of the building was left intact – and Stalin, despite being a manic rebuilder, undertook alterations that gave greater stability until his death in 1953.

But Nikita Khrushchëv altered the alterations when inaugurating de-Stalinisation and another flurry of rebuilding took place. The experimentation was gathering pace by the time of Khrushchëv's removal from office in 1964. His successor Leonid Brezhnev had a soft spot for Stalin's record, but he contented himself with undoing the more extravagant of Khrushchëv's alterations.

Yet, despite such vicissitudes, Soviet leaders were justified in claiming that they were ruling within the Leninist tradition and over a Leninist state. From 1917–19 to the late 1980s the edifice was recognisably Lenin's creation. The October Revolution, Marxism–Leninism and the USSR owed their existence to him more than to anyone else. What Lenin had built in the peculiar circumstances of wartime, revolutionary Russia was an invention that could be reproduced. Lenin wanted to export his building plans and laid down that the member parties of the Communist International should conform to principles of ideology and organisation developed in Moscow. Given the chance, he would have applied his template to revolutionary communist states. This task, however, fell to his successor Stalin. Furthermore, the Leninist template proved serviceable for Marxist revolutionaries in China, North Vietnam and Cuba. It did not much matter what kind of country was being communised. Both industrial, literate, Catholic Czechoslovakia and agrarian, illiterate, Buddhist North Vietnam succumbed. The methods of introduction varied from invasion to local communist political agitation. But the result in its essentials was the same. Lenin, by the same token, had a lot to answer for.

Already in the 1920s there was a strong reaction outside Soviet Russia against Lenin's edifice. The invention of fascism did not post-date communism; for Mussolini was already moving towards his far-right political doctrines on assuming power in Italy in 1922. But undoubtedly Hitler's Nazism fed off a visceral hostility to the Communist International, Marxism–Leninism and the USSR. To a considerable extent the history of inter-war Europe was a struggle over the consequences of 25 October 1917. The situation did not disappear after the Second World War. Rivalry between the superpowers, the USA and the USSR, was a struggle of two contrasting systems of politics, economics, ideology and military capacity – and the Soviet system was largely the one bequeathed by Lenin to Stalin and by Stalin to his successors.

It is consequently a huge paradox that the man who did most to bring the Leninist edifice tumbling down was himself a sincere follower of Lenin. Mikhail Gorbachëv came to the office of Party General

Secretary with the intention of restoring the USSR more nearly to the doctrines and practices of his idol. No less than Lenin, he improvised without reference to a detailed blueprint. He expanded his perspective on reform as he proceeded. What he and his fellow communist reformers failed to understand was that the edifice of communism was a tautly interconnected piece of architecture. Administration, politics, economics, law, ideology, welfare and even the treatment of the natural environment were heavily conditioned by the original Leninist conception. The removal of any wall, ceiling or doorway in the edifice carried with it the danger of structural collapse. Gorbachëv overlooked – indeed he was ignorant of – the risks. He abolished the Communist Party's political monopoly. He decentralised administration. He relaxed censorship and liberated religious and national self-expression. He weakened the state's mastery of the economy. He denounced the arbitrariness of Communist Party rule, and all this he did in the belief that he was restoring the spirit of Lenin to the USSR. Any single one of his reforms would have endangered the state's stability. The fact that he introduced all the reforms in a few years doomed the October Revolution, Marxism–Leninism and the USSR to extinction.

Since the end of 1991, when the Soviet Union expired its last breath and Gorbachëv resigned his presidency, there have been few attempts to show Lenin his old reverence. The communist states had already passed away in 1989, and although outward fealty to Leninism continued to be shown in the People's Republic of China, the Chinese economic reforms simultaneously reshaped the state and society in the direction of a capitalist economy. Even in Russia, where a communist party asserted itself under Gennadi Zyuganov, there was no special effort to go on defending and eulogising the historical record of Vladimir Lenin.

But is Lenin really done for? When surveys of Russian public opinion are undertaken he remains among the most popular rulers of history. His lingering popularity is such that Russia's President Boris Yeltsin in the 1990s has not dared to remove him from the Mausoleum from Red Square and bury him in conventional fashion. Respect for Lenin persists widely. While Lenin was alive, there was much admiration for him even among people who had suffered from his policies. And so peasant petitioners trusted him despite his ambition to get rid of the peasantry. After his death, he was often adduced in conversations and in folk songs as a wise tsar who would not have tolerated the abuses of power that were customary under his successors. No doubt the continuing official paeans to his greatness reinforced these popular inclinations. Nor can it be discounted that the image of Lenin will retain some considerable force in the Russian mind for many further decades. It is not even impossible that his memory might again be invoked, not necessarily by card-carrying communists, in those many parts of the world where capitalism causes grievous social distress. Lenin is not quite dead, at least not yet.

In trying to kill him off, Yeltsin the politician and indeed many anti-Leninist historians in Russia have opted for the weapons traditional among many Western writers. Nearly always this is attempted by representing him in a mono-dimensional way. Lenin the state terrorist. Lenin the ideologue. Lenin the party boss or the writer or even the lover. Not all the dimensions are given equal treatment – and this is not always the fault of the writers. Until the last few years, we could not know very much about Lenin's family and their internal tensions and mutual support. And his education and material circumstances – not to mention his physical health, his liaisons, his style of work and his day-to-day operational assumptions – were largely out of reach.

Some of these aspects were kept secret because they might reflect badly on him in terms of conventional morality. He cheated on his wife, he exploited his mother and sisters, he was maudlin about his health, he had no great opinion of Russians or even of most Bolsheviks. He relished terror and had no plausible notion about how to ensure that the Soviet Union would be able to give it up. He was still cruder in his letters and telegrams than in his books. Much of his correspondence was so cynical that Stalin prohibited its publication even in the course of the Great Terror in 1937–8. What is more, Lenin was a bit of an oddball. He was punctilious in his daily regime, being downright obsessive about silence in his office, about sharp pencils, about ridding himself of distraction to the point of denying himself chess, Beethoven and the lovely Inessa. He was an intruder on the privacy of his comrades. No other world statesman has felt as uninhibited about ordering the medical treatment of his fellow rulers. Yet Lenin kept a grip on himself less often than the rest of the world ever knew. Without his entourage of women, he would not have risen to his historical eminence. There was, right to the last, something of the spoilt child about Lenin. He was also a spoilt child who had seldom had difficulty in getting the attention he needed.

His rise to power and fame was possible because he had the luck of his family, his education, his ideology, his country's circumstances and – not the least – the personality with which he was born. But he had to make his luck work for him. He understood this; while insisting that the general political and economic circumstances had to be propitious, he never ceased to declare that revolutions did not simply happen: they had to be made. And this required leadership. Lenin might have failed, and so often – as in London in 1902 or Geneva in 1915 or even in Helsinki in 1917 – his reverses came close to being definitive. And if he had been balked over Brest-Litovsk in 1918 or the New Economic Policy in 1921, he might not be remembered now as one of the major figures of influence in the past century. And yet this short, intolerant, bookish, neat, valetudinarian, intelligent and confident politician did not stay a scribbler in the British Museum or the Geneva Public Library. His jerky gestures and lisping rhetoric did not hold him back. His lapses of prognosis did not undermine him. The brilliant student who became a gawky Marxist activist and factional leader made the most of what History pushed his way.

He led the October Revolution, founded the USSR and laid out the rudiments of Marxism–Leninism. He helped to turn a world upside down. Perhaps a few years hence he will be seen to have thrust his country and, under Stalin's leadership, a third of the world down a cul-de-sac. The future does not lie with Leninist communism. But, if the future lies elsewhere, we do not know where exactly. Lenin was unexpected. At the very least, his extraordinary life and career prove the need for everyone to be vigilant. Not many historical personages have achieved this effect. Let thanks be given.

NOTES

Introduction

1. P. N. Pospelov, *Vladimir Il'ich Lenin*; I. Deutscher, *The Prophet Armed: Trotsky, 1879–1921*.
2. N. Harding, *Lenin's Political Thought*, vols. 1–2.
3. R. H. W. Theen, *Lenin: Genesis and Development of a Revolutionary*.
4. M. Liebman, *Leninism Under Lenin*; A. Rabinowitch, *The Bolsheviks Come to Power*.
5. M. Lewin, *Lenin's Last Struggle*; S. F. Cohen, *Bukharin and the Bolshevik Revolution*.
6. E. H. Carr, *The Bolshevik Revolution*, vols. 1–3. On Lenin as a governmental co-ordinator, see also T. H. Rigby, *Lenin's Government* and M. P. Iroshnikov, *Predsedatel' Soveta Narodnykh Komissarov*.
7. A. Ulam, *Expansion and Coexistence*; O. Figes, *A People's Tragedy*.
8. R. Pipes, *Russia Under the Bolshevik Regime*; but see also his *Social-Democracy and the St Petersburg Labor Movement*, which includes an examination of the importance of ideology. My point, however, relates to Lenin's period in government.
9. A. Solzhenitsyn, *Lenin in Zurich*; D. A. Volkogonov, *Lenin: politicheskii portret*.
10. V. Soloukhin, *Pri svete dnya*.
11. R. C. Elwood, *Russian Social-Democracy in the Underground*; D. Geyer, *Lenin in der Russischen Sozialdemokratie*; L. Haimson, *The Russian Marxists and the Origins of Bolshevism*; J. H. L. Keep, *The Rise of Social Democracy in Russia*; L. Schapiro, *The Communist Party of the Soviet Union*.
12. S. Fitzpatrick, *The Russian Revlution*; R. G. Suny. *The Revenge of the Past*.
13. R. Service, *The Bolshevik Party in Revolution*; see also *Lenin: A Political Life*, vols. 1–3.
14. A. Meyer, *Leninism*; M. Malia, *The Soviet Tragedy*.

1. The Ulyanovs and the Blanks

1. A. Ivanskii (ed.), *Il'ya Nikolaevich Ul'yanov*, p. 178.
2. Zh. Trofimov, *Ul'yanovy*, p. 66.

3. D. I. Ul'yanov, 'Detskie gody Vladimira Il'icha', *VoVIL*, vol. 1, p. 121.
4. M. Shtein, *Ul'yanovy i Leniny*, pp. 13–14 and 42.
5. V. V. Tsaplin, 'O zhizni sem'i Blank v gorodakh Starokonstantinove i Zhitomire', pp. 39–44.
6. Letter from Moshko (Dmitri) Blank as quoted in M. Shtein, *Ul'yanovy i Leniny*, p. 44.
7. M. Shtein, 'Rod vozhdya. Bilet po istorii', p. 19.
8. V. Soloukhin, *Pri svete dnya*.
9. I am grateful to John Klier for his thoughts on the converted Jews of the Russian Empire in the mid-nineteenth century.
10. O. Abramova, G. Borodulina and T. Koloskova, *Mezhdu pravdoi i istinoi*, pp. 53 and 55.
11. D. I. Ul'yanov, *VoVIL*, vol. 1, pp. 322–3; M. I. Ul'yanova, *OVILiSU*, p. 230.
12. M. Shtein, *Ul'yanovy i Leniny*, pp. 110–11.
13. A. I. Ul'yanova-Yelizarova, *OVILiSU*, p. 34. I am grateful to Faith Wigzell for her thoughts on the changing significance of German culture for Russian families.
14. O. Abramova, G. Borodulina and T. Koloskova, *Mezhdu pravdoi i istinoi*, pp. 64–6.
15. ibid., p. 106.
16. M. Shtein, *Ul'yanovy i Leniny*, p. 78.
17. D. I. Ul'yanov, *VoVIL*, vol. 1, pp. 322–3; M. I. Ul'yanova, *OVILiSU*, p. 230.
18. A. I. Ul'yanova-Yelizarova, *OVILiSU*, p. 111.
19. ibid.
20. M. I. Ul'yanova, *OVILiSU*, p. 231.
21. O. Abramova, G. Borodulina and T. Koloskova, *Mezhdu pravdoi i istinoi*, p. 67
22. A. Ivanskii (ed.), *Il'ya Nikolaevich Ul'yanov*, pp. 10–12
23. M. Shtein, *Ul'yanovy i Leniny*, pp. 147–8.
24. The Russian hypothesis is examined with a degree of support in O. Abramova, G. Borodulina and T. Koloskova, *Mezhdu pravdoi i istinoi*, pp. 80–5.
25. A. Ivanskii (ed.), *Il'ya Nikolaevich Ul'yanov*, p. 8.
26. M. I. Ul'yanov, *OVILiSU*, p. 232.
27. Memoir by a teacher called Kabanova in V. Alekseev and A. Shver, *Sem'ya Ulyanovykh*, p. 16.
28. A. I. Ul'yanova-Yelizarova, *OVILiSU*, p. 130.
29. V. Alekseev and A. Shver, *Sem'ya Ulyanovykh*, p. 59.
30. ibid.
31. This was the recollection of Lyubov Veretennikova: Zh. Trofimov, *Ul'yanovy*, p. 75.
32. V. Alekseev and A. Shver, *Sem'ya Ulyanovykh*, p. 23.
33. ibid., p. 17.
34. A. I. Ul'yanova-Yelizarova, 'Vospominaniya ob Aleksandre Il'iche Ul'yanove', in *OVILiSU*, p. 29.

35. V. Alekseev and A. Shver, *Sem'ya Ulyanovykh*, p. 58.
36. A. I. Ul'yanova-Yelizarova, 'Stranichki iz zhizhni Vladimira Il'icha' [draft], RTsKhIDNI, fond 13, op. 1, d. 81, p. 20.
37. Zh. Trofimov, *Ulyanovy*, pp. 98–9.
38. See her letter of October 1901: RTsKhIDNI, fond 13, op. 1, d. 349, p. 4.
39. A. I. Ul'yanova-Yelizarova, letter to Stalin, December 1932: RTsKhIDNI, fond 13, op. 1, d. 471.
40. M. Gor'kii, 'Vladimir Lenin', *Russkii sovremennik*, no. 1, 1924, p. 241.
41. A. I. Ul'yanova-Yelizarova, 'Vospominaniya ob Aleksandre Il'iche Ul'yanove', in *OVILiSU*, p. 34.
42. Ye. K. Makarova, draft memoir, RTsKhIDNI, fond 14, op. 1, d. 350, p. 2.
43. Visit to the Gorki sanatorium, December 1998, where memorabilia of the Ulyanov family are conserved.

2. Childhood in Simbirsk

1. A. I. Ul'yanova-Yelizarova, 'Vospominaniya ob Il'iche', *VoVIL*, vol. 1, p. 19.
2. A. I. Ul'yanova-Yelizarova, 'Stranichki iz zhizni Vladimira Il'icha' [draft], RTsKhIDNI, fond 13, op. 1, d. 81, p. 21.
3. ibid.
4. ibid.
5. Draft addition to A. I. Ul'yanova-Yelizarova, 'Detskie i shkol'nye gody Vladimira Il'icha', RTsKhIDNI, fond 13, op. 1, d. 77, p. 1.
6. ibid.
7. A. I. Ul'yanova-Yelizarova, 'Stranichki iz zhizni Vladimira Il'icha' [draft], RTsKhIDNI, fond 13, op. 1, d. 81, p. 28.
8. This physical defect was a state secret in the Soviet period. I gleaned it from the consultation notes of Prof. L. I. Darkevich, who treated Lenin on 4 March 1922: RTsKhIDNI, fond 16, op. 3c, d. 6.
9. M. I. Averbakh, 'Vospominaniya o V. I. Lenine', *VoVIL*, vol. 8, p. 273.
10. A. I. Ulyanova-Yelizarova, *OVILiSU*, p. 27.
11. D. I. Ul'yanov, 'Detskie gody Vladimira Il'icha', *VoVIL*, vol. 1, p. 126.
12. A. I. Ul'yanova-Yelizarova, 'Stranichki iz zhizni Vladimira Il'icha' [draft], RTsKhIDNI, fond 13, op. 1, d. 81, p. 23.
13. ibid.
14. V. Alekseev and A. Shver, *Sem'ya Ul'yanovykh*, p. 34.
15. A. I. Ul'yanova-Yelizarova, 'Stranichki iz zhizni Vladimira Il'icha' [draft], RTsKhIDNI, fond 13, op. 1, d. 81, pp. 23 and 26.
16. V. L. Persiyaninov, Lenin's school contemporary, as recorded in V. Alekseev and A. Shver, *Sem'ya Ulyanovykh*, p. 41.
17. ibid.
18. ibid., pp. 35 and 37.
19. G. Ya. Lozgachëv-Yelizarov, *Nezabyvaemoe*, p. 132.

20. A. I. Ul'yanova-Yelizarova, 'Vospominaniya ob Aleksandre Il'iche Ul'yanove', in *OVILiSU*, p. 29.
21. V. Kalashnikov, 'Iz vospominanii domashnego uchitelya detei Il'i Nikolaev- icha Ul'yanova', in A. I. Ul'yanova (ed.), *Aleksandr Il'ich Ul'yanov i delo 1 marta 1887 g.*, p. 276.
22. A. I. Ul'yanova-Yelizarova, 'Vospominaniya ob Aleksandre Il'iche Ul'yanove', in *OVILiSU*, p. 39.
23. ibid.
24. ibid., p. 27. It ought to be added that she did once refer to her father as 'beastly Papa!'. But even then she did not think it wrong for her brother Alexander to scold her for the remark: ibid., p. 33.
25. A. I. Ul'yanova-Yelizarova, *OVILiSU*, pp. 40–1.
26. A. Ivanskii (ed.), *Molodoi Lenin*.
27. N. Hans, *History of Russian Educational Policy* p. 118.
28. A. Ivanskii (ed.), *Molodoi Lenin*, p. 196, n. 1.
29. V. Alekseev and A. Shver, *Sem'ya Ul'yanovykh*, p. 25.
30. ibid.
31. A. I. Ul'yanova-Yelizarova, *OVILiSU*, p. 117.
32. D. I. Ul'yanov, 'V gimnazii', RTsKhIDNI, fond 14, op. 1, d. 78, p. 2; A. I. Ul'yanova-Yelizarova, draft notes in RTsKhIDNI, fond 13, op. 1, d. 83, p. 6.
33. A. I. Ul'yanova-Yelizarova, *Detskie i shkol'nye gody Il'icha*, pp. 22–3.
34. A. Ivanskii (ed.), *Molodoi Lenin*, p. 33.
35. A. I. Ul'yanova-Yelizarova, draft note written later than 1922, RTsKhIDNI, fond 13, op. 1, d. 52, p. 1.
36. A. I. Ul'yanova-Yelizarova, 'Vospominaniya ob Il'iche', *VoVIL*, vol. 1, p. 22.
37. A. Ivanskii (ed.), *Molodoi Lenin*, p. 211.
38. ibid., p. 182.
39. ibid., p. 187.
40. D. I. Ul'yanov, *VoVIL*, vol. 1, p. 127.
41. D. I. Ul'yanov, *Ocherki raznykh god* (1974), pp. 153–4.
42. Anna Ilinichna's Wagner scores are kept at the Lenin Museum in Gorki.
43. A. Ivanskii (ed.), *Molodoi Lenin*, p. 136.
44. I am grateful to the Director of RTsKhIDNI, Prof. K. M. Anderson, for showing me this postcard in June 1993.
45. A. I. Ul'yanova-Yelizarova, *VoVIL*, vol. 1, p. 72.
46. V. Alekseev and A. Shver, *Sem'ya Ul'yanovykh*, p. 38.
47. N. G. Nefedev in ibid.

3. Deaths in the Family

1. A. I. Ul'yanova, letter to Shidlovskii about her father, probably written in March 1921, RTsKhIDNI, fond 13, op. 1, d. 51.
2. Zh. Trofimov, *Ulyanovy*, pp. 37, 40 and 42.

3. A. I. Ul'yanova-Yelizarova, 'Vospominaniya ob Aleksandre Il'iche Ul'yanove', in *OVILiSU*, p. 37.
4. A. Ivanskii (ed.), *Il'ya Nikolaevich Ul'yanov*, p. 246.
5. A. I. Ul'yanova-Yelizarova (ed.), *Aleksandr Il'ich Ul'yanov i delo 1 marta 1887 g.*
6. *PSU*, p. 28.
7. A. I. Ul'yanova-Yelizarova, *OVILiSU*, p. 54.
8. Although it was ice-bound, the Volga was still usable by sledges; but the journey was still a rather difficult one.
9. M. I. Ul'yanova, *Otets Vladimira Il'icha Lenina Il'ya Nikolaevich Ul'yanov*, p. 68.
10. A. I. Ul'yanova-Yelizarova, *Aleksandr Il'ich Ul'yanov*, pp. 84–5.
11. V. Alekseev and A. Shver, *Sem'ya Ul'yanovykh*, p. 24.
12. A. Ivanskii (ed.), *Molodoi Lenin*, pp. 231–3.
13. A. Il Ul'yanova-Yelizarova, *Aleksandr Il'ich Ul'yanov*, pp. 85–6.
14. D. I. Ul'yanov, *Ocherki raznykh god*, p. 54.
15. A. I. Ul'yanov-Yelizarova, *Aleksandr Il'ich Ul'yanov*, pp. 94–6.
16. ibid.
17. E. Acton, chapter 7 in R. Bartlett (ed.), *Russian Thought and Society, 1800–1917*; R. Service, *Lenin: A Political Life*, vol. 1, chapter 2.
18. R. Service, *Lenin: A Political Life*, vol. 1, pp. 40–2.
19. *PSU*, p. 36.
20. A. Ivanskii (ed.), *Molodoi Lenin*, p. 301.
21. V. Alekseev and A. Shver, *Sem'ya Ul'yanovykh*, p. 54.

4. The Ploughing of the Mind

1. V. V. Kashkadamova in *Bakinskii rabochii*, 21 January 1926.
2. *Lenin i Simbirsk. Dokumenty, materialy, vospominaniya*, pp. 65–7.
3. M. I. Ul'yanova, *OVILiSU*, p. 261.
4. A. I. Ul'yanova-Yelizarova, *OVILiSU*, p. 294.
5. A. I. Ul'yanova-Yelizarova, *VoVIL*, vol. 1, p. 69.
6. M. I. Ul'yanova, *VoVIL*, vol. 1, p. 193.
7. M. I. Ul'yanova, 'Kak? Beluyu tetradku chërnymi nitkami', *OVILiSU*, p. 46.
8. A. I. Ul'yanova-Yelizarova, *VoVIL*, vol. 1, p. 29.
9. ibid., p. 27.
10. N. K. Krupskaya, *VoVIL*, vol. 2, p. 28.
11. A. Ivanskii (ed.), *Molodoi Lenin*, p. 242.
12. A. I. Ul'yanova-Yelizarova, 'O zhizni Vladimira Il'icha Ul'yanova-Lenina v Kazani (1887–89 gg.)', *VoVIL*, vol. 1, p. 285.
13. A. I. Ul'yanova-Yelizarova, *OVILiSU*, p. 294.
14. A. I. Ul'yanova-Yelizarova, undated draft note, RTsKhIDNI, fond 13, op. 1, d. 52, p. 7.
15. D. I. Ul'yanov in *Uchitel'skaya gazeta*, 14 February 1963: see A. Ivanskii (ed.), *Molodoi Lenin*, p. 328.

16. A. Ivanskii (ed.), *Molodoi Lenin*, p. 367.
17. ibid., pp. 373–4.
18. P. D. Shestakov, 'Studencheskie volneniya v Kazani v 1887 g.', *Russkaya starina*, no. 6, 1892, p. 522.
19. A. I. Ul'yanova-Yelizarova, 'Stranichki iz zhizni Vladimira Il'icha' [draft], RTsKhIDNI, fond 13, op. 1, d. 81, p. 31.
20. A. Arosev, 'Pervyi shag', *LS*, vol. 2, pp. 439–40; A. Ivanskii (ed.), *Molodoi Lenin*, pp. 397–8.
21. Anna Ilinichna Ul'yanova to Lenin, 8 December 1922; letter: RTsKhIDNI, fond 13, op. 1, d. 43, p. 2.
22. A. I. Ul'yanova-Yelizarova, *OVILiSU*, p. 304.
23. *PSS*, vol. 1, p. 552.
24. ibid., p. 553.
25. *KA*, no. 1, 1934, p. 67.
26. *BKh*, vol. 1, p. 39.
27. *PSS*, vol. 45, p. 324.
28. N. Ye. Fedoseev, *Stat'i i pis'ma*, pp. 97–8.
29. *VoVIL*, vol. 1 (1968), pp. 106–7.
30. I. B. Sternik, *Lenin – Yurist*, p. 81.
31. I. I. Titov, *Vo glubine Rossii*, pp. 66–7.
32. RTsKhIDNI, fond 14, op. 77, d. 1, p. 46.
33. RTsKhIDNI, fond 14, op. 1, d. 74, pp. 46 and 53.
34. RTsKhIDNI, fond 14, op. 1, d. 75, p. 9.

5. Paths to Revolution

1. RTsKhIDNI, fond 14, op. 1, d. 77, p. 47.
2. N. L. Meshcheryakov (ed.), *Gleb Uspenskii v zhizni*, p. 239.
3. R. Wortman, *The Crisis of Russian Populism*, pp. 73–4.
4. A. I. Ul'yanova-Yelizarova, *OVILiSU*, pp. 294 and 304.
5. RTsKhIDNI, fond 14, op. 77, d. 1, p. 51.
6. ibid., p. 53.
7. ibid.
8. I. I. Titov, *Vo glubine Rossii*, pp. 108–9.
9. RTsKhIDNI, fond 14, op. 1, d. 77, p. 47.
10. ibid., p. 54.
11. A. I. Ul'yanova-Yelizarova, *VoVIL*, vol. 1, p. 34.
12. V. Vodovozov, 'Moë znakomstvo s Leninym', p. 175.
13. M. I. Ul'yanova, *VoVIL*, vol. 1, p. 203.
14. RTsKhIDNI, fond 14, op. 77, d. 1, p. 53.
15. ibid., p. 54.
16. ibid.
17. M. I. Semënov (M.Blan), 'Pamyati druga', p. 11.
18. ibid.

19. A. Belyakov, *Yunost' vozhdya*, pp. 31–6.
20. M. I. Semënov (M.Blan), 'Pamyati druga', p. 11.
21. M. P. Golubeva, 'Moya pervaya vstrecha s Vladimirom Il'ichem,' pp. 64–5.
22. *PSS*, vol. 55, p. 8.
23. A. I. Ul'yanova-Yelizarova, *OVILiSU*, p. 129.
24. RTsKhIDNI, fond 14, op. 1, d. 77, p. 53.
25. M. I. Semënov (M.Blan), 'Pamyati druga', p. 12.
26. D. I. Ul'yanov, 'Iz moikh vospominanii o Vladimire Il'iche Lenine', pp. 54–5.
27. ibid., p. 56.
28. *PSS*, vol. 1, p. 554.
29. ibid., p. 555.
30. *PSU*, pp. 50 and 61.
31. A. I. Ul'yanova-Yelizarova, 'Vospominaniya ob Il'iche', *VoVIL*, vol. 1, p. 36.
32. *PSU*, p. 38.
33. A. I. Ul'yanova-Yelizarova, 'Nachalo revolyutsionnoi raboty Vladimira Il'icha Lenina', RTsKhIDNI, fond 13, op. 1, d. 54, p. 24.
34. V. Arnol'd, *Sem'ya Ul'yanovykh v Samare*, pp. 29–30.
35. *PSU*, pp. 66–7.
36. A. I. Ul'yanova-Yelizarova, *OVILiSU*, p. 253.
37. M. I. Ul'yanova, 'Zhizn' nashei sem'i v Samare I Alakaevke, 1889–1893', RTsKhIDNI, fond 14, op. 1, d. 77, p. 51.
38. Photograph of diploma in I. B. Sternik, *Lenin – Yurist*, opposite p. 16.
39. *PSU*, p. 64.
40. I. B. Sternik, *Lenin – Yurist*, pp. 79–80.
41. V. Vodovozov, 'Moë znakomstvo s Leninym', p. 178.
42. M. I. Ul'yanova, *VoVIL*, vol. 1, p. 208.
43. ibid., p. 192.
44. V. V. Vodovozov, 'Moë znakomstvo s Leninym', pp. 177–8.
45. *PSS*, vol. 55, p. 2.
46. M. I. Ulyanova, *VoVIL*, vol. 1, p. 211.
47. I. B. Sternik, *Lenin – Yurist*, pp. 97–8.
48. ibid., p. 104.

6. St Petersburg

1. *PR*, no. 4, 1924, pp. 102; no. 7, 1924, p. 67; A. I. Ul'yanov-Yelizarova, 'Vospominaniya ob Il'iche', *VoVIL*, vol. 1, p. 41.
2. Letter of A. A. Sanin to A. I. Ul'yanova, 31 October 1923: RTsKhIDNI, fond 13, op. 1, d. 49.
3. S. Mitskevich, 'Stranichka vospominanii', p. 111.
4. *PSS*, vol. 55, p. 2.
5. ibid., p. 85.
6. ibid., pp. 1–2.

7. *KA*, no. 1, 1934, pp. 114–15.
8. *PSS*, vol. 55, p. 4.
9. ibid., vol. 46, pp. 1–2.
10. ibid., p. 3.
11. ibid., vol. 1, pp. 1–66.
12. V. V. [pseudonym of V. P. Vorontsov], *Nashi napravleniya*, pp. 1–215.
13. M. A. Sil'vin, *Lenin v period zarozhdeniya partii*, pp. 46–50.
14. RTsKhIDNI, fond 12, op. 2, d. 12, p. 1.
15. *KA*, no. 2, 1925, pp. 144–5.
16. D. I. Ul'yanov, *Ocherki raznykh let*, p. 71.
17. Letter of A. I. Ul'yanova to P. B. Struve, 13 July 1899, RTsKhIDNI, fond 13, op. 1, d. 45, pp. 1–2.
18. G. M. Krzhizhanovskii, *O Vladimire Il'iche*, pp. 13–14.
19. V. D. Bonch-Bruevich, *Tridtsat' dnei. 1934. Yanvar'*, p. 18.
20. RTsKhIDNI, fond 14, op. 1, d. 87, pp. 7 and 8.
21. D. I. Ul'yanov, *VoVIL*, vol. 1, p. 155.
22. O. D. Ul'yanova, 'Mariya Il'inichna Ul'yanova', in M. I. Ul'yanova, *OVILiSU*, p. 18.
23. A. I. Ul'yanova-Yelizarova, 'Vospominaniya ob Aleksandre Il'iche Ul'yanove', in *OVILiSU*, pp. 27 and 57; *PSU*, p. 94.
24. M. I. Ul'yanova, *VoVIL*, vol. 1, pp. 211–12.
25. *PSS*, vol. 1, p. 401.
26. 'Chto takoe "Druz'ya naroda" i kak oni voyuyut protiv sotsial-demokratov?', in *PSS*, vol. 1, pp. 325–31 and 460.
27. *KA*, no. 1, 1934, pp. 78 and 81.
28. ibid., p. 78.
29. *PSS*, vol. 55, p. 7.
30. ibid., p. 8.
31. M. I. Ul'yanova, *VoVIL*, vol. 1, p. 212.
32. *PSS*, vol. 55, pp. 9–12.
33. ibid., p. 13.
34. *KA*, no. 1, 1934, pp. 81 and 98.
35. A. I. Ul'yanova-Yelizarova, *Vospominaniya ob Il'iche*, pp. 47–8.
36. I. Getzler, *Martov*, pp. 21–9.
37. A. N. Potresov, *Posmertnyi sbornik proizvedenii*, p. 294.
38. *PSS*, vol. 2, pp. 70–4.

7. To Siberian Italy

1. *PSS*, vol. 55, pp. 5 and 14.
2. ibid., vol. 46, p. 443.
3. A. I. Ul'yanova-Yelizarova, *OVILiSU*, p. 148.
4. M. A. Sil'vin, letter to A. I. Ul'yanova, 18 December 1923, RTsKhIDNI, fond 13, op. 1, d. 47, p. 3.

5. *PSS*, vol. 55, p. 17.
6. ibid., p. 18.
7. A. I. Ul'yanova-Yelizarova, *OVILiSU*, p. 145.
8. D. I. Ul'yanov, *VoVIL*, vol. 1, p. 165.
9. A. I. Ul'yanova-Yelizarova, *OVILiSU*, p. 147.
10. A. I. Ul'yanova-Yelizarova, *VoVIL*, vol. 1, p. 51.
11. A. I. Ul'yanova-Yelizarova, *OVILiSU*, p. 145.
12. V. Levitskii, *Za chetvert' veka*, vol. 1, part 1, p. 51.
13. L. Martov, *Zapiski sotsial-demokrata*, p. 342.
14. R. Service, *Lenin: A Political Life*, vol. 1, pp. 62–3.
15. A. Yelizarova, 'Vladimir Il'ich v tyur'me', in N. L. Meshcheryakov (ed.), *O Lenine*, p. 71.
16. *PSS*, vol. 46, pp. 449–50.
17. A. I. Ul'yanova-Yelizarova, *OVILiSU*, p. 381; *Perepiska sem'i Ul'yanovykh*, p. 94.
18. *PSS*, vol. 55, p. 24.
19. ibid., pp. 154–5.
20. G. A. Solomon, *Lenin i ego sem'ya (Ul'yanovy)*, p. 26.
21. *KA*, no. 1, 1934, p. 122; *PR*, nos. 2–3, 1929, p. 193.
22. A. I. Ul'yanova-Yelizarova, 'Vladimir Il'ich v ssylke (ego ot'ezd i prebyvanie tam)' [draft, written in 1929], RTsKhIDNI, fond 13, op. 1, d. 69, p. 4.
23. *ZIL*, vol. 3, p. 84.
24. *PSS*, vol. 55, pp. 24–5.
25. ibid., vol. 46, p. 451.
26. RTsKhIDNI, fond 14, op. 1, d. 74, p. 36.
27. *PSS*, vol. 55, p. 30.
28. ibid., pp. 34–5.
29. *PR*, nos. 11–12, 1928, p. 242.
30. *PSS*, vol. 55, p. 32.
31. ibid., p. 54.
32. I. Getzler, *Martov*, p. 38.
33. *PSS*, vol. 46, p. 453.
34. A. I. Ul'yanova, *PR*, no. 3, 1924, pp. 109–10.
35. ibid., p. 119.
36. RTsKhIDNI, fond 13, op. 1, d. 62, p. 2: draft introduction to Lenin's letters.
37. *PSS*, vol. 55, p. 59.
38. RTsKhIDNI, fond 14, op. 1, d. 74, p. 33.
39. RTsKhIDNI, fond 12, op. 2, d. 135, p. 9.
40. S. U. Manbekova and S. A. Rubanov, *Naslednitsa*, pp. 52–4.
41. ibid., p. 62.
42. N. K. Krupskaya, *O Lenine*, p. 80.
43. *Pravda*, 18 February 1968.
44. A. I. Ul'yanova-Yelizarova, *VoVIL*, vol. 1, pp. 62–3.
45. S. L. Shatkina (ed.), *Lenin i Ul'yanovy v Podol'ske*, p. 31.

46. R. MacNeal, *Bride of the Revolution*, p. 48.
47. RTsKhIDNI, fond 12, op. 2, d. 1, p. 17: letter of 26 August 1898 to Lenin's mother.
48. D. I. Ul'yanov, *VoVIL*, vol. 1, p. 163.
49. R. McNeal, *Bride of the Revolution*, pp. 68–9.
50. N. K. Krupskaya, RTsKhIDNI, fond 12, op. 2, d. 34, p. 13: 1936 fragment.
51. *PSS*, vol. 55, p. 53.
52. D. I. Ul'yanov, *VoVIL*, vol. 1, p. 183.
53. *PSS*, vol. 55, p. 73.
54. M. I. Ul'yanova, *OVILiSU*, p. 70.
55. *PSS*, vol. 55, p. 73.
56. ibid., p. 89.
57. ibid., p. 91.
58. See the marriage certificate in S. U. Manbekova and S. A. Rubanov, *Naslednitsa*, p. 107.
59. *PSS*, vol. 45, pp. 409–10
60. ibid., vol. 55, p. 105.
61. ibid., p. 111.
62. ibid., vol. 46, p. 31: letter to Potresov.
63. ibid., pp. 25–6.
64. Letter to I. P. Tovstukha, 15 October 1923, RTsKhIDNI, fond 13, op. 1, d. 53, pp. 3–4.
65. A. I. Ul'yanova-Yelizarova, draft fragment, RTsKhIDNI, fond 13, op. 1, d. 84, p. 1.
66. *PSS*, vol. 55, p. 180.
67. *KA*, no. 1, 1934, pp. 129–30.
68. A. I. Ul'yanova-Yelizarova, draft fragment, RTsKhIDNI, fond 13, op. 1, d. 84, p. 1.

8. An Organisation of Revolutionaries

1. *KA*, no. 1, 1934, p. 134.
2. A. I. Ul'yanova, letter to Stalin, December 1932, RTsKhIDNI, fond 13, op. 1, d. 471.
3. A. I. Ul'yanova-Yelizarova, 'Tret'ii arest Il'icha' [draft], RTsKhIDNI, fond 13, op. 1, d. 67, p. 6.
4. A. I. Ul'yanova, letter to Stalin, December 1932, RTsKhIDNI, fond 13, op. 1, d. 471.
5. S. U. Manbekova and S. A. Rubanov, *Naslednitsa*, p. 129.
6. *KA*, no. 1, 1934, p. 137.
7. N. K. Krupskaya, *O Lenine*, p. 80.
8. *PSS*, vol. 4, p. 341.
9. ibid., pp. 334–52.
10. ibid., p. 342.

11. ibid., p. 343.
12. ibid., p. 345.
13. ibid., vol. 55, pp. 190 and 193.
14. ibid., p. 192.
15. ibid., p. 193.
16. ibid., p. 196.
17. See D. I. Ul'yanov, *Ocherki raznykh let*, p. 21.
18. *PSS*, vol. 55, p. 198.
19. ibid., p. 197.
20. ibid., vol. 46, p. 74.
21. N. K. Krupskaya, *VoVIL*, vol. 2, p. 199.
22. N. Valentinov, *Vstrechi s Leninym*, pp. 86 and 141.
23. N. K. Krupskaya, 'Iz otvetov na anketu Instituta mozga v 1935 godu', in N. K. Krupskaya, *O Lenine*, p. 86.
24. *PSS*, vol. 55, p. 178.
25. 'Tovarnyi fetishizm', *Nauchnoe obozrenie* (St Petersburg), no. 12, 1899, pp. 2277–95.
26. *PSS*, vol. 3, pp. 613–36.
27. ibid., vol. 6, p. 173.
28. See N. Harding, *Lenin's Political Thought*, vols 1–2.
29. N. Valentinov, *Vstrechi s Leninym*, p. 31.
30. ibid., p. 34.
31. ibid., p. 35.
32. ibid., p. 89.
33. *LS*, vol. 2, pp. 24 and 27.
34. ibid., p. 65.
35. *PSS*, vol. 6, p. 448.
36. ibid., pp. 64 and 84.
37. M. I. Ul'yanova, *OVILiSU*, p. 22.

9. 'Holy Fire'

1. *PSS*, vol. 55, p. 85.
2. N. Meshcheryakov, 'Iz vospominanii o Lenine', in N. L. Meshcheryakov (ed.), *O Lenine*, p. 45.
3. N. A. Alekseev, *Vospominaniya o Vladimire Il'iche Lenine*, vol. 2, p. 85.
4. *PSU*, p. 146.
5. N. K. Krupskaya, *VL*, pp. 56–7.
6. ibid., p. 59.
7. A. Rothstein, *Lenin in Britain*, pp. 14–15.
8. N. K. Krupskaya, *VL*, p. 59.
9. RTsKhIDNI, fond 12, op. 2, d. 14, pp. 12–13.
10. ibid., pp. 13 and 18.
11. I. Getzler, *Martov*, p. 66.

12. RTsKhIDNI, fond 12, op. 2, d. 14, p. 18.
13. N. K. Krupskaya, *VoVIL*, vol. 2, p. 57.
14. An alternative account comes from V. D. Bonch-Bruevich, who wrote a draft memoir saying that his wife diagnosed Lenin as suffering from 'sclerotic cerebral phenomena': 'Bolezn' Vladmira Ili'icha v Zheneve v 1903 g.', RTSKhIDNI, fond 4, op. 2, d. 294, pp. 2–3. Often Bonch-Bruevich exaggerated or invented things, especially when they embellished his own significance and that of his family in history. If Bonch-Bruevich's account is correct in this instance, then we must conclude that Krupskaya was lying. On balance, the latter hypothesis is less credible than the former. Just about.
15. *PSS*, vol. 46, pp. 232–4.
16. *Istoricheskii arkhiv*, no. 2, 1958, p. 10.
17. *PSS*, vol. 46, p. 190.
18. A. Rothstein, *Lenin in Britain*, p. 23.
19. *Vtoroi s"ezd RSDRP*, pp. 443–4.
20. ibid., pp. 262, 425 and 717.
21. A. V. Shotman, 'Na vtorom s"ezde partii', *PR*, nos. 77–8, 1928, pp. 62–3.
22. *Vtoroi s"ezd RSDRP*, pp. 367, 372 and 380.
23. *PSS*, vol. 8, pp. 88 and 177–8.
24. *LS*, vol. 10, p. 117.
25. RTsKhIDNI, fond 14, op. 1, d. 74, p. 45.
26. ibid.
27. 'C'est le cerveau': RTsKhIDNI, fond 14, op. 1, d. 74, p. 45.
28. N. K. Krupskaya, 'Iz otvetov na anketu Instituta Mozga v 1935 godu', in N. K. Krupskaya, *O Lenine*, p. 82.
29. N. K. Krupskaya, 'Sestra Vladimira Il'icha', *Pravda*, 13 June 1937.
30. V. D. Bonch-Bruevich, *Izbrannye Sochineniya*, vol. 2, p. 314.
31. G. M. Krzhizhanovskii, *O Vladimire Il'iche*, p. 32.
32. *LS*, vol. 10, pp. 352–3.
33. ibid., p. 117.
34. *PSS*, vol. 46, p. 355.
35. ibid., p. 378.

10. Russia from Far and Near

1. *PSS*, vol. 9, p. 35.
2. ibid., p. 246.
3. M. N. Lyadov, *O Vladimire Il'iche*.
4. *Tretii s"ezd RSDRP. Protokoly. Aprel'-mai 1905 goda*, pp. 188–9 and 193–4.
5. ibid., p. 247.
6. N. K. Krupskaya, RTsKhIDNI, fond 12, op. 2, d. 15, p. 5.
7. ibid.
8. *BKh*, vol. 2, p. 22; *PSS*, vol. 9, pp. 274–82.
9. *BKh*, vol. 2, pp. 194–5.

10. *PSS*, vol. 11, pp. 336–8.
11. ibid., p. 340.

11. The Second Emigration

1. *BKh*, vol. 2, p. 349.
2. N. K. Krupskaya, *VL*, pp. 127–8.
3. ibid., p. 128.
4. ibid., p. 129.
5. ibid.
6. *PSS*, vol. 47, pp. 119–20.
7. RTsKhIDNI, fond 12, op. 2, d. 18, p. 6.
8. M. Gor'kii, 'V. I. Lenin', in *V. I. Lenin i A. M. Gor'kii*, p. 262.
9. Ye. V. Krupskaya, letter to her nephew A. A. Krupskii, RTsKhIDNI, fond 12, op. 1, d. 1057, p. 2.
10. L. A. Fotieva, *Iz zhizni Lenina*, p. 10.
11. N. K. Krupskaya, *VoVIL*, vol. 2, p. 199.
12. G. Ya. Lozgachëv-Yelizarov, *Nezabyvaemoe*, pp. 102 and 107.
13. RTsKhIDNI, fond 12, op. 2, d. 20, pp. 9–10 and 16.
14. V. Mel'nichenko, *Fenomen i fantom Lenina*, pp. 97–8.
15. ibid., p. 109.
16. RTsKhIDNI, fond 14, op. 1, d. 74, p. 47.
17. RTsKhIDNI, fond 12, op. 2, d. 20, p. 11.
18. *PSS*, vol. 55, pp. 303 and 305.
19. ibid., p. 306.
20. *Ogonëk*, no. 10, 1989, p. 29.
21. M. Gor'kii, 'V. I. Lenin', in *V. I. Lenin i A. M. Gor'kii*, p. 253.
22. M. Gorky, *Days with Lenin*, p. 28.
23. M. Gor'kii, *Neizdannaya perepiska*, p. 48.
24. Nicolaevsky Collection, folder 1, p. 46.
25. The house which in 1908 was 21 Tavistock Place was later renumbered as 36 Tavistock Place: *Survey of London – L.C.C.*, vol. 24, *King's Cross Neighbourhood* (London 1952), p. 81.
26. *PSU*, pp. 184–5.
27. M. I. Ul'yanova, *OVILiSU*, p. 313.
28. *PSU*, p. 210.
29. N. K. Krupskaya, *VL*, p. 160.
30. M. I. Ul'yanova, *OVILiSU*, p. 121.
31. M. Gor'kii, *Neizdannaya perepiska*, p. 56.
32. Photographs of Inessa are held in RTsKhIDNI, fond 127, op. 1, d. 54.
33. RTsKhIDNI, fond 127, op. 1, d. 61.
34. ibid.
35. R. C. Elwood, *Inessa Armand*, pp. 173–89.
36. RTsKhIDNI, fond 2, op. 1, d. 24299.

37. Account of C. Rappoport's recollection in N. Valentinov, *Vstrechi s Leninym*, p. 98.
38. L. Fotieva, *Iz zhizni Lenina*, p. 10.
39. M. Body, 'Alexandra Kollontai', *Preuves*, no. 14, April 1952, p. 17.
40. Lenin's letter to Kautsky: D. Geyer (ed.), *Kautskys Russisches Dossier*, p. 344.

12. Almost Russia!

1. 'Vospominaniya', *ITsKKPSS*, no. 7, 1989, p. 171.
2. *Biblioteka V. I. Lenina v Kremle. Katalog.*
3. Nowadays it is kept at the Lenin Museum at Gorki.
4. M. S. Volin, 'Dorevolyutsionnye biograficheskie publikatsii o V. I. Lenine', *VIKPSS*, no. 7, 1970, p. 116.
5. M. S. Kedrov, *Book Publishing under Tsarism*, pp. 16–21.
6. *PSS*, vol. 55, p. 323.
7. ibid.
8. See Inessa's postcard in RTsKhIDNI, fond 127, op. 1, d. 37.
9. *VoVIL*, vol. 3, p. 319: memoir by S. Bagotski.
10. *PSS*, vol. 55, p. 328.
11. N. K. Krupskaya, *VoVIL*, vol. 2, p. 256.
12. Yu. V. Bernov and A. Ya. Manusevich, *V krakovskoi emigratsii*, p. 29.
13. M. I. Ul'yanova, *OVILiSU*, p. 296; G. Ya. Lozgachëv-Yelizarov, *Nezabyvaemoe*, p. 8.
14. M. I. Ul'yanova *OVILiSU*, p. 317.
15. *BKh*, vol. 3, pp. 52–172.
16. Stalin to Kamenev (December 1912), *Bol'shevistskoe rukovodstvo*, p. 16. See Lenin's comments on Stalin's critique in *V. I. Lenin. Neizvestnye dokumenty*, p. 109.
17. R. C. Elwood, 'Lenin and "Pravda"', *Slavic Review*, no. 2, 1972, pp. 212–14.
18. Letter of Ducos de la Haille to K. Kautsky, D. Geyer (ed.), *Kautskys Russisches Dossier*, p. 644.
19. R. C. Elwood, *Inessa Armand*, p. 96.
20. *PSS*, vol. 55, p. 339.
21. *Svobodnaya mysl'*, no. 3, 1992, p. 81.

13. Fighting for Defeat

1. RTsKhIDNI, fond 12, op. 2, d. 23, p. 5.
2. *LS*, vol. 2, pp. 173–4.
3. RTsKhIDNI, f. 12, op. 2, d. 29, p. 3.
4. ibid., pp. 3–4 and 5.
5. ibid., d. 31, pp. 7–8.
6. *PSS*, vol. 26, p. 6.

7. ibid., vol. 48, p. 155.
8. *PSU*, p. 363.
9. ibid., p. 428.
10. *PSS*, vol. 49, p. 492.
11. N. K. Krupskaya, *VoVIL*, vol. 2, p. 33.
12. *PSS*, vol. 49, p. 340.
13. *PSU*, p. 232.
14. *VoVIL*, vol. 2, p. 191.
15. *PSS*, vol. 49, p. 52.
16. ibid., p. 55.
17. ibid., p. 56.
18. F. Il'in, 'Otryvok vospominanii', *ZIL*, vol. 1, pp. 126–7.
19. *Istoricheskii arkhiv*, no. 3, 1959, pp. 38–42.
20. M. A. Moskalëv, *Byuro TsK*, p. 270.

14. Lasting Out

1. *PSS*, vol. 30, p. 328.
2. ibid., vol. 49, p. 361.
3. *PSU*, p. 419.
4. W. Gautschi, *Lenin als Emigrant in der Schweiz*, p. 178.
5. ibid., p. 328.
6. RTsKhIDNI, fond 12, op. 2, d. 55, p. 1 (Krupskaya's notes taken between 1917 and 1937).
7. N. K. Krupskaya, *VoVIL*, vol. 2, pp. 208–9.
8. *PSS*, vol. 49, p. 14.
9. ibid., vol. 27, p. 27.
10. ibid., vol. 30, p. 16.
11. ibid., vol. 29, p. 162.
12. ibid., pp. 163–4.
13. ibid., vol. 28, p. 594.
14. L. D. Trotskii, *Moya zhizn'*, vol. 1, p. 285.
15. *DZB*, vol. 1, p. 128.
16. ibid., p. 169.
17. R. Pipes (ed.), *The Unknown Lenin*, p. 31.

15. Another Country

1. N. K. Krupskaya, *VoVIL*, vol. 2, p. 220.
2. ibid., p. 221.
3. *PSS*, vol. 49, pp. 401–2.
4. F. Platten, *Lenin iz emigratsii v Rossiyu*, pp. 34–7.
5. RTsKhIDNI, fond 12, op. 1, d. 1, p. 12: E. A. Tsivilaya's account of the appeal

made by V. S. Dridzo (Krupskaya's personal assistant) and M. F. Fofanova (who hid Lenin in October 1917) to the Central Committee to secure the return of E. V. Krupskaya's ashes in compliance with Nadezhda Konstantinovna's wishes.

6. K. Radek, 'V plombirovannom vagone', *Pravda*, 20 April 1924.
7. F. Platten, *Lenin iz emigratsii v Rossiyu*, p. 57.
8. K. Radek, 'V plombirovannom vagone'.
9. ibid.
10. D. S. Suliashvili, 'Iz Shveitsarii v Petrograd vmeste s Leninym', *VoVIL*, vol. 4, p. 142.
11. K. Radek, 'V plombirovannom vagone'.
12. D. S. Suliashvili, 'Iz Shveitsarii v Petrograd vmeste s Leninym', *VoVIL*, vol. 4, p. 143.
13. G. E. Zinoviev, 'Vospominaniya: Malinovskii', *ITsKKPSS*, no. 6, 1989, p. 201.
14. V. D. Bonch-Bruevich, 'Priezd V. I. Lenina iz-za granitsy v 1917 g.' [draft], RTsKhIDNI, fond 4, op. 2, d. 3003, p. 105.
15. R. MacNeal, *Bride of the Revolution*, p. 171.
16. N. K. Krupskaya, manuscript excerpt in *VoVIL*, vol. 2, p. 229.
17. N. K. Krupskaya, 'Vospominaniya o Lenine', *VoVIL*, vol. 2, p. 229.
18. Memoir of A. A. Pushkova, RTsKhIDNI, fond 13, op. 1, d. 457, p. 1; A. I. Ul'yanova-Yelizarova, *OVILiSU*, p. 348: letter to husband, 7 June 1913.
19. G. Ya. Lozgachëv-Yelizarov [draft], RTsKhIDNI, fond 11, op. 2, d. 31, pp. 162–3.
20. G. Ya. Lozgachëv-Yelizarov, *Nezabyvaemoe*, p. 145.
21. N. A. Uglanov, 'O Vladimire Il'iche Lenine', *ITsKKPSS*, no. 4, 1989.
22. *PR*, no. 4, 1927, pp. 162–3.
23. ibid.
24. R. Service, *Lenin: A Political Life*, vol. 2, pp. 170–7.

16. The Russian Cockpit

1. *Pravda*, 14 May 1917.
2. V. P. Buldakov, 'Istoriya posnaëtsya v sravnenii', *Argumenty i fakty*, no. 45, November 1998, p. 12.
3. N. K. Krupskaya, 'Vospominaniya o Lenine', *VoVIL*, vol. 2, p. 229.
4. Extracts in I. M. Dazhina, 'Leninskie istoki zhizhni I bor'by', *VIKPSS*, no. 3, 1987, pp. 71–2.
5. A. M. Kollontai, 1950 diary entry, RTsKhIDNI, fond 134, op. 3, d. 75, pp. 19–21.
6. M. Gor'kii, 'V. I. Lenin,' in *V. I. Lenin i A. M. Gor'kii*, pp. 271–2.
7. *Pravda*, 23 April 1917.
8. N. K. Krupskaya, 'Vospominaniya o Lenine', *VoVIL*, vol. 2, p. 235.
9. ibid., p. 232.
10. *Shestoi s"ezd RSDRP(b)*, p. 41.

11. G. K. Ordzhonikidze, 'Il'ich v iyul'skie dni', *Pravda*, 28 March 1924.
12. N. I. Podvoiskii, 'V. I. Lenin v 1917 godu', *VoVIL*, vol. 4, p. 186.
13. M. S. Kedrov, 'Iz vospominanii o vserossiiskoi konferenstii voennykh organizatsii RSDRP (bol'shevikov), 16–23 iyunya 1917 goda', *VoVIL*, vol. 4, p. 223.
14. N. I. Muralov, 'I Vserossiiskii S''ezd Sovetov', *VoVIL*, vol. 4, p. 220.
15. N. K. Krupskaya, 'Vospominaniya o Lenine', *VoVIL*, vol. 2, p. 238.
16. R. Pipes, *The Russian Revolution*, pp. 419–22.
17. M. S. Kedrov, 'Iz krasnoi tetradi ob Il'iche', p. 485.
18. A. Rabinowitch, *The Bolsheviks Come to Power*, pp. 15–17.
19. M. I. Ul'yanova, 'Poiski Il'icha v pervye dni iyulya 1917 goda', *VoVIL*, p. 241.
20. G. K. Ordzhonikidze, 'Il'ich v iyul'skie dni', *Pravda*, 28 March 1924.
21. A. G. Shlyapnikov, 'Kerenshchina', *PR*, no. 7(54), 1927, p. 35.
22. M. N. Poletaev, 'V iyul'skie dni', *Petrogradskaya pravda*, 27 January 1924.
23. Fragment of memoir by A. A. Allilueva, RTsKhIDNI, fond 4, op. 2, d. 45, p. 2.

17. Power for the Taking

1. A. S. Allilueva, *Vospominaniya*, pp. 183 and 185.
2. See draft by A. S. Alliluev, RTsKhIDNI, fond 4, op. 2, d. 45, p. 6.
3. S. Ya. Alliluev, draft fragment, ibid., p. 8.
4. *PSS*, vol. 34, pp. 2–5.
5. G. Sokol'nikov, 'Kak pokhodit' k istorii Oktyabrya', in *Za leninizma*, p. 165.
6. N. A. Yemel'yanov, 'Tainstvennyi shalash', *VoVIL*, vol. 4, p. 238.
7. ibid., p. 237.
8. ibid., p. 239.
9. ibid.
10. D. I. Leshchenko, 'Kak ya snimal Lenina v podpol'e', *VoVIL*, p. 245.
11. A. V. Shotman, 'Lenin v podpol'e. (Iyul'–oktyabr' 1917 goda)', *VoVIL*, vol. 4, p. 251.
12. K. Kuusela, 'Kak artist maskiroval Lenin', in *Lenin v vospominaniyakh finnov*, pp. 79–80.
13. J. Piilonen, 'Yhteinen vihollinen yhdistää, 1908–1917', in J. Numminen (ed.), *Lenin ja Suomi*, p. 308.
14. A. V. Shotman, 'Lenin v podpol'e. (Iyul'–oktyabr' 1917 goda)', *VoVIL*, vol. 4, p. 253.
15. N. K. Krupskaya, *VoVIL*, vol. 2, pp. 244–5.
16. *PSS*, vol. 49, p. 444.
17. *Pravda*, 7 June 1917.
18. For an example see M. Liebman, *Leninism under Lenin*.
19. *PSS*, vol. 34, p. 135.
20. ibid.

21. ibid., pp. 138–9.
22. A. Rabinowitch, *The Bolsheviks Come to Power*, p. 170.
23. *PSS*, vol. 49, p. 241.
24. ibid., pp. 243–4.
25. N. I. Bukharin, 'Iz rechi tov. Bukharina na vechere vospominanii v 1921 g.', *PR*, no. 10, 1922, p. 319.
26. E. D. Stasova, 'Pis'mo Lenina v TsK partii', *VoVIL*, vol. 4, p. 288.
27. A. V. Shotman, 'Lenin nakanune Oktyabrya', *O Lenine: Sbornik vospominanii*, pp. 115–16, from *VoVIL*, vol. 4, pp. 254–5.
28. ibid., p. 255.
29. ibid., p. 256.
30. A. Kollontai, diary drafts of 1929–30, RTsKhIDNI, fond 134, op. 3, d. 48, p. 33.
31. G. Rovio, 'Kak Lenin skryvalsya u gel'singforskogo "politseimeistera"', in N. L. Meshcheryakov (ed.), *O Lenine*, p. 115.
32. Yu. Latukka, 'Lenin v podpol'e v Finlyandii', *VoVIL*, vol. 4, p. 284.
33. ibid., p. 287. The exact date is still disputed: see the editorial footnote 1, ibid., p. 187.
34. ibid., p. 287.
35. M. V. Fofanova, 'V. I. Lenin na Vyborgskoi Storone v 1917 godu', *VoVIL*, vol. 4, p. 299.
36. *PTsK*, pp. 84–5.
37. ibid., p. 85.
38. ibid.
39. L. Trotskii, *O Lenine*, p. 70.
40. *PTsK*, pp. 87–92.
41. ibid., p. 94.
42. A. A. Ioffe, 'Kanun Oktyabrya. Zasedanie v "Lesnom"', *ITsKKPSS*, no. 4, 1989, p. 203.
43. *PTsK*, p. 104.
44. M. V. Fofanova, 'V. I. Lenin na Vyborgskoi Storone v 1917 godu', *VoVIL*, vol. 4, p. 302.
45. ibid., p. 304.
46. *PSS*, vol. 34, p. 435.
47. E. A. Rakh'ya, 'Moi vospominaniya o Vladimire Il'iche', *Pravda*, 21 January 1927.
48. M. V. Fofanova, 'V. I. Lenin na Vyborgskoi Storone v 1917 godu', *VoVIL*, vol. 4, p. 304.

18. The October Revolution

1. Rakh'ya, 'Moi vospominaniya o Vladimire Il'iche', *Pravda*, 21 January 1927.
2. ibid.
3. ibid.

4. *PSS*, vol. 35, p. 2.
5. N. Sukhanov, *Zapiski o revolyutsii*, vol. 7, p. 174.
6. *PSS*, vol. 35, p. 1.
7. V. D. Bonch-Bruevich, 'Iz vospominanii o Vladimire Il'iche', *VoVIL*, vol. 4, pp. 325–6.
8. ibid., p. 329
9. ibid.
10. *PSS*, vol. 35, p. 23.
11. *PTsK*, pp. 124–5.
12. V. Mel'nichenko, *Fenomenon i fantom Lenina*, p. 67.
13. G. A. Solomon, *Lenin i ego sem'ya*, vol. 1, p. 88.

19. Dictatorship under Siege

1. N. K. Krupskaya, 'Ranenie Lenina v 1918 godu', RTsKhIDNI, fond 12, op. 2, d. 59, p. 1.
2. N. K. Krupskaya, *VoVIL*, vol. 2, p. 269.
3. ibid.
4. ibid., p. 270.
5. ibid.
6. RTsKhIDNI, fond 12, op. 2, d. 29, p. 26.
7. N. K. Krupskaya, *VoVIL*, vol. 2, p. 249.
8. The story is reprinted in Ye. Zamyatin, *Bol'shim detyam skazki*, pp. 37–8. I am grateful to Philip Cavendish for bringing this work to my attention.
9. ibid., pp. 270–1.
10. *PSS*, vol. 35, p. 57.
11. T. H. Rigby, *Lenin's Government*, p. 71.
12. ibid., pp. 179–80.
13. D. Volkogonov, *Lenin*, vol. 2, p. 200 ff.
14. *Bol'shevistskoe rukovodstvo*, p. 33.
15. *PSS*, vol. 35, p. 189.

20. Brest-Litovsk

1. *PTsK*, p. 168.
2. ibid., pp. 194–5.
3. ibid., p. 213.
4. K. Radek, *Portrety i pamflety*, p. 26.
5. *Sed'moi s"ezd RKP(b)*, p. 13.
6. Krupskaya's letter to Shirokov, 3 December 1938, RTsKhIDNI, fond 12, op. 2, d. 135, p. 30.
7. ibid.
8. ibid.

9. *PSS*, vol. 55, p. 85.
10. *BKh*, vol. 5, p. 340.
11. *PSS*, vol. 50, pp. 78–9.
12. S. Ya. Alliluev, draft fragment of memoir, RTsKhIDNI, fond 4, op. 2, d. 46, p. 1.
13. M. I. Ul'yanova, 'Otryvki', RTsKhIDNI, fond 14, op. 1, d. 87, p. 8.
14. *PSS*, vol. 35, p. 314.
15. ibid., vol. 36, p. 196.
16. ibid., p. 197.

21. At Gunpoint

1. *Sed'moi ekstrennii s"ezd RKP(b)*, p. 8.
2. *PSS*, vol. 36, p. 172.
3. (Claimed) diary entry for 18 July 1918, reprinted in *VoVIL*, vol. 6, p. 23 from *Prozhektor*, no. 4, 1924.
4. Sovnarkom, 8 and 9 May 1918: GARF, fond 130, op. 2, d. 1 (3/4).
5. *PSS*, vol. 36, p. 250.
6. N. K. Krupskaya, *VoVIL*, vol. 2, p. 312.
7. ibid.
8. ibid., pp. 312–13.
9. B. Pearce, *How Haig Saved Lenin*, p. 65; D. Volkogonov, 'Leninskaya krepost'' v moei dushe pala poslednei', *Moskovskie novosti*, no. 29, 19 July 1992, p. 20.
10. *The Last Diary of Tsaritsa Alexandra* (ed. V. A. Kozlov and V. M. Khrustalëv), p. 156.
11. N. K. Krupskaya, *VoVIL*, vol. 2, p. 309.
12. *Komsomol'skaya pravda*, 12 February 1992.
13. A. Latyshev, *Rassekrechënnyi Lenin*, p. 20.
14. N. K. Krupskaya, draft memoir on '1918': RTsKhIDNI, fond 12, op. 2, d. 30, p. 32.
15. Stenogram of M. I. Ulyanova's speech at a Lenin commemorative meeting, 16 August 1928: RTsKhIDNI, fond 14, op. 1, d. 70, p. 1; and N. K. Krupskaya, draft memoir on '1918', RTsKhIDNI, fond 12, op. 2, d. 30, p. 32.
16. *PSS*, vol. 37, p. 82.
17. Stenogram of M. I. Ulyanova's speech at a Lenin commemorative meeting, 16 August 1928, RTsKhIDNI, fond 14, op. 1, d. 70, p. 1.
18. ibid., p. 2.
19. N. K. Krupskaya, 'Ranenie Lenina v 1918 godu' [draft], RTsKhiDNI, fond 12, op. 2, d. 59, p. 6.
20. Stenogram of M. I. Ulyanova's speech at a Lenin commemorative meeting, 16 August 1928, RTsKhIDNI, fond 14, op. 1, d. 70, pp. 7–8.
21. V. N. Rozanov, 'Iz vospominaniya o Vladmire Il'iche', in N. L. Meshcheryakov (ed.), *O Lenine*, vol. 3, pp. 121–2.

22. V. N. Rozanov, *VoVIL*, vol. 5, p. 311.
23. B. S. Veisbrod, 'Bol'noi Lenin', *VoVIL*, vol. 8, p. 251.
24. Yu. M. Lopukhin, *Bolezn', smert' i bal'zamirovanie V. I. Lenina*, p. 58.
25. V. N. Rozanov, *VoVIL*, vol. 5, p. 312.
26. Previously it had belonged to Gennadi and Zinaida Reinbot and had been nationalised at Zinaida's request. Zinaida was the widow of the factory owner Savva Morozov, who had given financial help to the Russian Marxist organisations before the Great War.

22. War Leader

1. *ITsKKPSS*, 1989, no. 11, p. 168.
2. M. Gor'kii, 'V. I. Lenin', in *V. I. Lenin i A. M. Gor'kii*, p. 266.
3. A. M. Kollontai, 'Epizod vesnoi 1918 goda v Moskve' [draft], RTsKhIDNI, fond 134, op. 4, d. 18, pp. 2–3.
4. *PSS*, vol. 37, p. 243.
5. ibid., p. 245.
6. *ITsKKPSS*, no. 4, 1990. I am grateful to Arfon Rees for sharing his ideas on the influence of Machiavelli on Russian revolutionary thought.
7. *PSS*, vol. 45, p. 174.
8. Soviet political leaders, indeed, made the suggestion before historians, whether supportive or hostile, took it up.
9. RTsKhIDNI, fond 12, op. 2, d. 34, p. 49: 1936 corrections to memoirs.
10. She was, however, given a separate room of her own at Gorki: D. I. Ul'yanov, *VoVIL*, vol. 1, p. 178.
11. V. Armand, 'Zhivaya nit'', *Novyi mir*, no. 4, 1967, p. 198.
12. N. K. Krupskaya, draft memoir on '1918': RTsKhIDNI, fond 12, op. 2, d. 30, pp. 12–13.
13. 'Vospominaniya M. I. Ul'yanovoi': RTsKhIDNI, fond 16, op. 3c, d. 20, p. 1.
14. N. K. Krupskaya, draft memoir on '1918': RTsKhIDNI, fond 12, op. 2, d. 30, pp. 12–13.
15. M. I. Ul'yanova, *OVILiSU*, pp. 116–17.
16. *TP*, vol. 1, p. 228.
17. Quoted from archives by D. A. Volkogonov, *Sem' vozhdei*, vol. 1, p. 84.

23. Expanding the Revolution

1. *PSS*, vol. 50, p. 328.
2. ibid., p. 327.
3. Gorki quoted in V. Mel'nichenko, *Fenomen i fantom Lenina*, p. 70.
4. Quoted in D. A. Volkogonov, *Sem' vozhdei*, vol. 1, p. 135.
5. *PSS*, vol. 51, p. 52.
6. A. Latyshev, *Rassekrechënnyi Lenin*, pp. 44–5.

7. See M. Liebman, *Leninism under Lenin*; N. Harding, *Lenin's Political Thought*, vol. 2.
8. *Desyatyi s"ezd RKP(b)*, pp. 349–50.
9. B. M. Volin, *VoVIL*, vol. 6, p. 61.
10. N. K. Krupskaya, *VoVIL*, vol. 2, p. 284.
11. ibid., p. 270.
12. ibid., p. 301.
13. N. K. Krupskaya, RTsKhIDNI, fond 12, op. 2, d. 30, p. 15.
14. M. I. Ul'yanova, *VoVIL*, vol. 1, p. 260.
15. *PSS*, vol. 43, p. 150.
16. Kollontai's diary: RTsKhIDNI, fond 134, op. 3, d. 48, p. 33.
17. V. Mel'nichenko, *Fenomenon i fantom Lenina*, p. 53.
18. D. I. Ul'yanov, *Ocherki raznykh let*, p. 93.
19. ibid., p. 98.
20. N. Meshcheryakov, 'Iz vospominanii o Lenine', p. 45.
21. A. M. Kollontai, '1918 god' [draft memoir], RTsKhIDNI, fond 134, op. 4, d. 23, p. 2.
22. N. K. Krupskaya, *VoVIL*, vol. 2, p. 333.
23. *PSS*, vol. 55, pp. 373–4.
24. S. U. Manbekova and S. A. Rubanov, *Naslednitsa*, p. 166: telegram of V. M. Molotov to Lenin from Nizhni Novgorod.

24. Defeat in the West

1. See the Introduction.
2. A. Latyshev, *Ressekrechënnyi Lenin*, p. 40.
3. ibid.
4. Report to the Ninth Party Conference, September 1920, RTsKhIDNI, fond 44, op. 1, d. 5, pp. 11–18, 20–1, 27–8; and Lenin's memoranda, reprinted in *Izvestiya*, 27 April 1992.
5. *TP*, vol. 2, p. 278.
6. *ITsKKPSS*, no. 4, 1991, p. 171.
7. Quoted in 'Vlyublënnaya Lenina', *Literaturnaya gazeta – Dos'e*, no. 8, 1992, p. 11.
8. A. M. Kollontai, diary for 1920, RTsKhIDNI, fond 134, op. 3, d. 36, p. 12.
9. Inessa Armand's last diary, RTsKhIDNI, fond 127, op. 1, d. 61, pp. 7–8.
10. ibid., p. 8.
11. ibid., p. 14.
12. Quoted in D. A. Volkogonov, *Sem' vozhdei*, vol. 1, p. 113.
13. Ye. Drabkina, *Zimnii pereval*, p. 29.
14. A. Balabanoff, *Impressions of Lenin*, p. 14.
15. RTsKhIDNI, fond 44, op. 1, d. 5, p. 13.
16. ibid.

25. The New Economic Policy

1. See R. Service, *Lenin: A Political Life*, vol. 3, chaps 6–7.
2. RTsKhIDNI, fond 17, op. 3, d. 128, item 1a.
3. Chernov's account is given in RTsKhIDNI, fond 5, op. 1, d. 1454, p. 2; his memoir appeared in *Bednota*, no. 1729, 2 February 1924.
4. P. Sorokin and M. Rogov, 'Razvërstka ili nalog?', *Pravda*, 17 February 1921.
5. RTsKhIDNI, fond 17, op. 2, d. 58, p. 2.
6. RTsKhIDNI, fond 17, op. 3, d. 154.
7. RTsKhIDNI, fond 46, op. 1, d. 3, p. 16.
8. ibid., pp. 16 and 18.
9. ibid., p. 22.
10. ibid., p. 125.
11. *PSS*, vol. 53, p. 14.

26. A Question of Survival

1. D. I. Ul'yanov, *Ocherki raznykh let*, p. 93.
2. RTsKhIDNI, fond 17, op. 17, d. 174, p. 24
3. *PSS*, vol. 53, p. 17.
4. ibid., p. 110.
5. 'Vospominaniya M. I. Ul'yanovoi', RTsKhIDNI, fond 16, op. 3, d. 20, p. 3.
6. Rough estimate based on author's visit in June 1993.
7. N. K. Krupskaya, *VoVIL*, vol. 2, p. 317.
8. V. P. Osipov, 'Bolezn' i smert' Vladimira Il'icha Ul'yanova-Lenina', *VoVIL*, vol. 8, p. 298.
9. *Lenin iVChK*, pp. 465–6.
10. D. I. Ul'yanov, *VoVIL*, vol. 1, p. 181.
11. N. K. Krupskaya, *VoVIL*, vol. 2, p. 148.
12. 'Vospominaniya M. I. Ul'yanovoi', RTsKhIDNI, fond 16, op. 3, d. 20, pp. 11–12.
13. Darkevich's manuscript account of diagnostic examination, RTsKhIDNI, fond 16, op. 3s, d. 6, pp. 4–5.
14. ibid., p. 6.
15. ibid., p. 4.
16. RTsKhIDNI, fond 16, op. 3s, d. 6, pp. 7 and 8–9.
17. *ITsKKPSS*, no. 4, 1990, p. 189.
18. *PSS*, vol. 54, p. 198.
19. V. Klemperer, *Leben sammeln, nicht fragen wozu und warum*, vol. 1: *Tagebücher 1918–1924*, p. 577. I am grateful to Kay Schiller for alerting me to this source.
20. RTsKhIDNI, fond 4, op. 1, d. 99, pp. 1–2; V. N. Rozanov, 'Iz vospominaniya o Vladimire Il'iche', in N. L. Meshcheryakov (ed.), *O Lenine*, pp. 127–31.

21. RTsKhIDNI, fond 4, op. 1, d. 99, p. 3.
22. Yu. M. Lopukhin, *Bolezn', smert' i bal'zamirovanie V. I. Lenina*, p. 19.
23. ibid., p. 36.
24. ibid., p. 40.
25. V. Rozanov, *Krasnaya nov'*, no. 6, 1924, pp. 155–6.
26. N. Petrenko, 'Lenin v Gorkakh – bolezn' I smert'', *Minuvshee*, vol. 2, p. 195; G. Ya. Lozgachëv-Yelizarov, *Nezabyvaemoe*, p. 237.
27. 'Vospominania M. I. Ul'yanovoi', RTsKhIDNI, fond 16, op. 3, d. 20, p. 10.
28. ibid., p. 12; Kozhevnikov: fond 16, op. 2, d. 11, p. 6.
29. See V. Soloukhin, *Pro svete dnya*; D. Volkogonov, *Lenin*.
30. RTsKhIDNI, fond 5, op. 1, d. 454.
31. N. K. Krupskaya,*VoVIL*, vol. 2, pp. 334, 2.
32. 'Vospominania M. I. Ul'yanovoi', RTsKhIDNI, fond 16, op. 3, d. 20, pp. 32–3.
33. Undated speech by M. I. Ul'yanova, RTsKhIDNI, fond 14, op. 1, d. 65, p. 21.
34. M. I. Ul'yanova, *VoVIL*, vol. 1, p. 283.
35. RTsKhIDNI, fond 12, op. 2, d. 206: letter of Krupskaya to Inna Armand, 30 September 1922.
36. RTsKhIDNI, fond 16, op. 2s, d. 39, p. 17: report of P. Pakaln, 3 July 1922.
37. ibid.
38. RTsKhIDNI, fond 12, op. 2, d. 206: letter of Krupskaya to Inna Armand, 30 September 1922.
39. RTsKhIDNI, fond 16, op. 2s, d. 39, p. 17: report of P. Pakaln, 3 July 1922.
40. Memoir sketch, RTsKhIDNI, fond 14, op. 1, d. 87.
41. 'Vospominaniya M. I. Ul'yanovoi', RTsKhIDNI, fond 16, op. 3, d. 20, pp. 17–18.
42. RTsKhIDNI, fond 16, op. 3s, d. 20, p. 61: typed excerpt from M. I. Ulyanova's diary.
43. RTsKhIDNI: fond 16, op. 2s, d. 39, p. 16: report of P. Pakaln.
44. *ITsKKPSS*, no. 4, 1991, p. 188.

27. Disputing to the Last

1. See above.
2. RTsKhIDNI, fond 17, op. 2, d. 25993.
3. *PSS*, vol. 48, p. 162.
4. N. A. Uglanov, *VoVIL*, vol. 7, p. 72.
5. M. I. Ul'yanova, *ITsKKPSS*, no. 12, 1989.
6. RTsKhIDNI, fond 16, op. 2s, d. 39, pp. 7, 36, 50 and 59: reports of P. Pakaln, head of bodyguard, to the central Cheka offices in Moscow.
7. Letter of N. K. Krupskaya to L. A. Fotieva, 25 August 1922, RTsKhIDNI, fond 5, op. 1, d. 454, p. 4.
8. Letter of M. Volodicheva to A. I. Ul'yanova, 6 December 1922, RTsKhIDNI, fond 13, op. 1, d. 43, p. 1.

9. *ITsKKPSS*, no. 5, 1991, p. 189.
10. RTsKhIDNI, fond 17, op. 2, d. 84, items 1–3.
11. Her words on 25 October 1922 were '*on mozhet snova svalit'sya*'.
12. 'Dnevnik dezhurnogo vracha V. I. Lenina v 1922–1923 gg.', *VIKPSS*, no. 9, 1991, pp. 41–2.
13. Note of N. S. Allilueva to Kamenev on the basis of a message from Krupskaya on behalf of Lenin, 18 October 1922, RTsKhIDNI, fond 5, op. 1, d. 456.
14. N. I. Bukharin, 'Pamyati Lenina', *Pravda*, 21 January 1925.
15. See the text of the letter in A. Latyshev, *Rassekrechënnyi Lenin*, p. 253.
16. RTsKhIDNI, fond 16, op. 2s, d. 39, p. 92: report of P. Pakaln.
17. RTsKhIDNI, fond 16, op. 2, d. 13: A. M. Kozhevnikov's notes, as given in D. Volkogonov, *Lenin*, vol. 2, p. 333.
18. *PSS*, vol. 45, p. 471.
19. M. I. Ul'yanova diary excerpt, 2 September 1922, RTsKhIDNI, fond 16, op. 3s, d. 20, p. 65.
20. Text of letter from RTsKhIDNI, fond 2, op. 2, d. 134 given in *Rodina*, no. 3, 1992, p. 49.
21. *PSS*, vol. 54, p. 324.
22. L. A. Fotieva, 'Iz vospominanii o V. I. Lenine', *VoVIL*, vol. 8, p. 178.
23. Letter to Central Committee, 15 December 1922, *PSS*, vol. 45, p. 338.
24. L. A. Fotieva, 'Iz vospominanii o V. I. Lenine', *VoVIL*, vol. 8, p. 179.
25. *PSS*, vol. 45, p. 324.
26. RTsKhIDNI, fond 16, op. 2, d. 13: A. M. Kozhevnikov's notes, given in D. Volkogonov, *Lenin*, vol. 2, p. 333.
27. *ITsKKPSS*, no. 12, 1989, p. 189.
28. RTsKhIDNI, fond 17, op. 2, d. 86, p. 1.
29. *PSS*, vol. 54, p. 327.
30. RTsKhIDNI, fond 17, op. 2, d. 87, p. 1.
31. Politburo meeting, 14 December 1922, RTsKhIDNI, fond 17, op. 3; RTsKhIDNI, fond 5, op. 2, d. 55, pp. 202–3; L. A. Fotieva, 'Iz vospominanii o V. I. Lenine', *VoVIL*, vol. 8, p. 173.
32. *ITsKKPSS*, no. 9, 1989, p. 148.
33. L. A. Fotieva, 'Iz vospominanii o V. I. Lenine', *VoVIL*, vol. 8, p. 187.
34. ibid., pp. 189–90.
35. A. G. Shlikhter, 'Gotova li smena?', *VoVIL*, vol. 8, p. 59.
36. M. I. Ul'yanova, 'O Vladimire Il'iche', *ITsKKPSS*, no. 3, 1991, p. 194.
37. L. A. Fotieva, 'Iz vospominanii o V. I. Lenine', *VoVIL*, vol. 8, p. 189.

28. Death in the Big House

1. *PSS*, vol. 45, pp. 343–4.
2. ibid.
3. ibid., pp. 344–5.

4. ibid., p. 345.
5. ibid.
6. *Bol'shevistskoe rukovodstvo*, p. 198.
7. Quoted in G. Volkov's account of an interview with Volodicheva, 'Stenografistka Il'icha', *Sovetskaya kul'tura*, 21 January 1989.
8. A. Bek's interview with Volodovicheva and Fotieva in 1967, 'K istorii poslednikh leninskikh dokumentov', *Moskovskie novosti*, no. 17, 23 April 1989, p. 8.
9. G. Volkov's interview with Volodicheva, 'Stenografistka Il'icha'; A. Bek's interviews with Volodicheva and Fotieva in 1967, 'K istorii poslednikh leninskikh dokumentov'.
10. See M. Lewin, *Lenin's Last Struggle* and S. Cohen, *Bukharin and the Russian Revolution*.
11. *PSS*, vol. 45, p. 359.
12. ibid., p. 356.
13. ibid., p. 346.
14. ibid., p. 372.
15. ibid., p. 373.
16. ibid., vol. 54, p. 330.
17. ibid., pp. 82–3.
18. ibid., p. 330.
19. Quoted in G. Volkov's interview with Volodicheva, 'Stenografistka Il'icha'.
20. Yu. M. Lopukhin, *Bolezn', smert' i bal'zamirovanie V. I. Lenina*, p. 40.
21. V. A. Rukavishnikov's memoirs, RTsKhIDNI, fond 16, op. 2s, d. 91, p. 32; op. 3s, d. 27, p. 12.
22. ibid., p. 16.
23. Vospominaniya M. I. Ul'yanovoi', RTsKhIDNI, fond 16, op. 3s, d. 20, p. 14.
24. Diary of nurse Z. I. Zorko-Rimsha, RTsKhIDNI, fond 16, op. 2s, d. 104, p. 223.
25. Letter to A. V. Lunacharski, sometime in 1923, RTsKhIDNI, fond 12, op. 2, d. 205, p. 5.
26. V. G. Sorin, 'Bol'shoi dom', *Pravda*, 21 January 1927.
27. 'Pogib ya': 'Vospominaniya M. I. Ul'yanovoi', RTsKhIDNI, fond 16, op. 3s, d. 20, p. 14.
28. V. A. Rukavishnikov, 'Poslednaya progulka V. I. Lenina v Moskvu', RTsKhIDNI, fond 16, op. 3s, d. 27, p. 24.
29. ibid., p. 30.
30. ibid., p. 12.
31. ibid.
32. Postcard, 1 December 1923: RTsKhIDNI, fond 12 op. 2, d. 206, p. 13. The picture on the postcard is that of Bukharin in a pioneer tie. In line with Stalinist archival practice, Bukharin's face was obliterated for reasons of political orthodoxy.
33. RTsKhIDNI, fond 16, op. 2s, d. 39, pp. 93, 121 and 122.
34. G. Ya. Lozgachëv-Yelizarov, *Nezabyvaemoe*, pp. 241 and 250. For the argu-

ment against the claim that the children were mainly from the village see N. Petrenko, 'Lenin v Gorkakh', *Minuvshee*, no. 2. 1990, p. 250.

35. RTsKhIDNI, fond 16, op. 2s, d. 39, p. 92.
36. ibid., pp. 92 and 96.
37. Nurses' duty diary, note by N. S. Popov, 17 September 1923, RTsKhIDNI, fond 16, op. 2s, d. 91, p. 68.
38. RTsKhIDNI, fond 16, op. 2s, d. 39, p. 123.
39. V. A. Rukavishnikov's memoirs, RTsKhIDNI, fond 16, op. 3s, d. 27, pp. 32–3.
40. V. G. Sorin, 'Bol'shoi dom', *Pravda*, 21 January 1927.
41. N. I. Bukharin, *Pravda*, 21 January 1924.

Lenin: The Afterlife

1. RTsKhIDNI, fond 12, op. 2, d. 254, pp. 1, 5 and 6.
2. ibid., p. 1.
3. ibid., p. 7: undated letter, written before 25 March 1924.
4. This, by the way, controverts the legend originating with Yuri Karyakin at the Congress of People's Deputies to the effect that Lenin had wanted to be buried next to his mother in the Volkovoe Cemetery in Petrograd.
5. Letter to I. A. Armand, 28 January 1924, RTsKhIDNI, fond 12, op. 2, d. 254, p. 6, where she said that she had begun the pamphlet but did not give a precise date.
6. RTsKhIDNI, fond 12, op. 2, d. 41, pp. 3 (Krupskaya) and 4 (Stalin).
7. In the 1990s these articles were held at the Lenin Museum at Gorki outside Moscow.

SELECT BIBLIOGRAPHY

This Bibliography is not an exhaustive list of material on Lenin. For a fuller list of general works about his career, the reader may consult my trilogy *Lenin: A Political Life*. The following works include only those which are cited in the Notes to this book.

Abbreviations

BKh – *Vladimir Il'ich Lenin. Biograficheskaya khronika*, vols 1–12 (Moscow, 1970–82)

DZB – *Die Zimmerwalder Bewegung. Protokole und Korrespondenz*, vols 1–2 (The Hague, 1967)

GARF – Gosudarstvennyi arkhiv Rossiiskoi Federatsii

ITsKKPSS – *Izvestiya Tsentral'nogo Komiteta Kommunisticheskoi Partii Sovetskogo Soyuza* (1989–1991)

KA – *Krasnyi arkhiv* (Moscow)

LS – *Leniniskii sbornik*, vols 1–50 (Moscow, 1924–85)

OVILiSU – A. I. Yelizarova-Ul'yanova, *O V. I. Lenine i sem'e Ulyanovykh* (Moscow, 1988)

M. I. Ul'yanova, *O V. I. Lenine i sem'e Ulyanovykh* (Moscow, 1988)

PR – *Proletarskaya revolyutsiya* (Moscow, 1921–40)

PSS – *Polnoe sobranie sochinenii V. I. Lenina*, vols 1–55 (Moscow, 1958–65)

PSU – *Pis'ma sem'i Ul'yanovykh, 1883–1917* (ed. Yu. Ya. Makhina *et al.*: Moscow, 1969)

PTsK – *Protokoly Tsentral'nogo Komiteta RSDRP(b): avgust 1917 g.–fevral' 1918 g.* (Moscow, 1958)

RTsKhIDNI – Rossiiskii tsentr dlya khraneniya i issledovaniya dokumentov noveishei istorii

TP – *The Trotsky Papers, 1917–1922*, vols 1–2 (ed. J. M. Meijer: The Hague, 1964–71)

VIKPSS – *Voprosy Istorii Kommunisticheskoi Partii Sovetskogo Soyuza* (Moscow, 1962–91)

VL – N. K. Krupskaya, *Vospominaniya o Lenine* (Moscow, 1968)

VoVIL – *Vospominaniya o Vladimire Il'iche Lenine*, vols 1–8 (Moscow, 1989–91)

ZIL – *Zapiski Instituta Lenin*, vols 1–2 (Moscow, 1927)

Archives

State Archive of the Russian Federation (GARF)
  Sovnarkom, fond R-130
  People's Commissariat for Nationalities Affairs, fond 1318
  Commission on the Drafting of the Constitution (1918), fond 6890
Russian Central for the Conservation and Study of Documents of Contemporary
  History (RTsKhIDNI)
  Lenin, fond 2
  Documents on Activity of V. I. Lenin, fond 4
  Secretariat of V. I. Lenin, fond 5
  Ulyanov family, fond 11
  N. K. Krupskaya, fond 12
  A. I. Ul'yanova-Yelizarova, fond 13
  M. I. Ul'yanova, fond 14
  Lenin's Medical Archives, fond 16
  Central Committee (including Politburo and Orgburo), fond 17
  Ninth Party Conference, fond 44
  Tenth Party Conference, fond 46
  F. E. Dzerzhinskii, fond 76
  Inessa Armand, fond 127
  A. M. Kollontai, fond 134
  Stalin's Library, fond 558
  Central Control Commission, fond 613
Boris I. Nicolaevsky Collection (Hoover Institution Archives; copy held at St
  Antony's College, Oxford)
  Part 1: Towards a History of the Bolshevik Centre
  Part 2: On 'the Unity Plenum' of the Central Committee, 1909–10
  Part 3: The Struggle for the Convoking of a General Party Conference in
    1910–11
  Part 4: The Break-Up of the Bolshevik–Polish Bloc, August to November 1911
  Part 5: The Split in the General Party Centres, end of May to start of June
    1911
  Part 6: On the Prague Conference, November 1911 to January 1912

Published Documentary Collections

A. Arosev, 'Pervyi shag', *LS*, vol. 2
Biblioteka V. I. Lenina v Kremle. Katalog (Moscow, 1961)
Bol'shevistskoe rukovodstvo. Perepiska. 1912–1927 (Moscow, 1996)
V. D. Bonch-Bruevich, *Izbrannye Sochineniya*, vol 2 (Moscow, 1961)
*Chetvërtyi (Ob"edinitel'nyi) s"ezd RSDRP. Protokoly. Aprel' (aprel'–mai) 1906
  goda* (Moscow, 1959)
Desyatyi s"ezd RKP(b). Mart 1921 g. Stenograficheskii otchët (Moscow, 1963)

Devyataya konferentsiya RKP(b). Sentyabr' 1920 g. Protokoly (Moscow, 1972)
Devyatyi s"ezd RKP(b). Mart–aprel' 1920 g. Stenograficheskii otchët (Moscow, 1960)
Die Zimmerwalder Bewegung. Protokole und Korrespondenz, vols 1–2 (The Hague, 1967)
Fedoseev, Nikolai Yevgrafovich. *Sbornik vospominanii* (Moscow–Petrograd, 1923)
N. Ye. Fedoseev, *Stat'i i pis'ma* (Moscow, 1958).
D. Geyer (ed.), *Kautskys Russisches Dossier. Deutsche Sozialdemokraten als Treuhänder des Russischen Parteivermögens, 1910–1915* (Frankfurt, 1981)
M. Gor'kii, *Neizdannaya perepiska s Bogdanovym, Leninym, Stalinym, Zinov'evym, Kamenevym, Korolenko* (Moscow, 1998)
M. Gor'kii, 'V. I. Lenin', in *V. I. Lenin i A. M. Gor'kii. Pis'ma, vospominaniya, dokumenty* (2nd expanded edn: Moscow, 1961)
L. Haas, *Lenins Unbekannte, 1912–1914* (Zurich–Cologne, 1967)
W. Hahlweg (ed.), *Lenins Rückkehr nach Russland 1917*, (Leiden, 1957).
A. Ivanskii (ed.), *Il'ya Nikolaevich Ul'yanov po vospominaniyam sovremennikov i dokumentam* (Moscow, 1963)
A. Ivanskii (ed.), *Molodoi Lenin. Povest' v dokumentakh i memuarakh* (Moscow, 1964)
N. K. Krupskaya, *O Lenine. Sbornik statei i vystuplenii* (Moscow, 1983)
The Last Diary of Tsaritsa Alexandra (ed. V. A. Kozlov and V. M. Khrustalëv: New Haven, 1997)
Lenin i Simbirsk. Dokumenty, materialy, vospominaniya (Ulyanovsk, 1968)
Lenin i VChK (ed. S. K. Tsvigun: Moscow, 1975)
V. I. Lenin. Neizvestnye dokumenty. 1891–1922 (ed. Yu. N. Amiantov *et al.*: Moscow, 1999)
V. I. Lenin, *Polnoe sobranie sochineenii V. I. Lenina* vols 1 –55 (Moscow, 1958–65)
Odinnadtsatyi s"ezd RKP(b). Mart–aprel' 1922 g. Stenograficheskii otchët (Moscow, 1961)
R. Pipes (ed.), *The Unknown Lenin. From the Secret Archive* (New Haven, 1996)
Pis'ma sem'i Ul'yanovykh, 1883–1917 (ed. Yu. Ya. Makhina *et al.*: Moscow, 1969)
A. N. Potresov, *Posmertnyi sbornik proizvedenii* (ed. B. I. Nikolaevskii: Paris, 1937)
Protokoly Desyatoi Vserossiiskoi Konferentsii RKP(b). Mai 1921 god (Moscow, 1933)
Protokoly Tsentral'nogo Komiteta RSDRP(b): avgust 1917 g.–fevral' 1918 g. (Moscow, 1958)
Pyatyi (londonskii) s"ezd RSDRP. Aprel'–mai 1907 goda (Moscow, 1963)
Sed'moi ekstrennii s"ezd RKP(b). Mart 1918 g. Stenograficheskii otchët (Moscow, 1962)
Shestoi s"ezd RSDRP (bol'shevikov). Avgust 1917 goda. Protokoly (Moscow, 1958)
Tretii s"ezd RSDRP. Protokoly. Aprel'–mai 1905 goda (Moscow, 1959)
The Trotsky Papers, 1917–1922, vols 1–2 (ed. J. M. Meijer: The Hague, 1967–71)
A. I. Ul'yanova (ed.), *Aleksandr Il'ich Ul'yanov i delo 1 marta 1887 g. (Sbornik)* (Moscow–Leningrad, 1927)
Vladimir Il'ich Lenin. Biograficheskaya khronika, vols 1–12 (Moscow, 1970–82)

Vos'moi s"ezd RKP(b). Mart 1919 goda. Protokoly (Moscow, 1959)
Vospominaniya o Vladimire Il'iche Lenine, vols 1–8 (Moscow, 1989–91)
Vtoroi s"ezd RSDRP. Protokoly. Iyul'-avgust 1903 goda (Moscow, 1959)
Zapiski Instituta Lenina, vols 1–3 (Moscow, 1927)
Z. A. B. Zeman (ed.), *Germany and the Revolution in Russia, 1915–1918* (Oxford, 1953)

Memoirs and Contemporary Works

V. Alekseev and A. Shver, *Sem'ya Ulyanovykh v Simbirske (1869–1887)* (ed. with commentary by A. I. Ulyanova-Yelizarova: Moscow–Leningrad, 1925)

A. S. Allilueva, *Vospominaniya* (Moscow, 1946)

V. Armand, 'Zhivaya nit'', *Novyi mir*, no. 4, 1967

A. Arosev, 'Pervyi shag', *LS*, vol. 2

A. Balabanoff, *Impressions of Lenin* (Ann Arbor, 1964)

A. Bek's interviews with Volodicheva and Fotieva in 1967, 'K istorii poslednikh leninskikh dokumentov', *Moskovskie novosti*, no. 17, 23 April 1989

M. Body, 'Alexandra Kollontai', *Preuves*, no. 14, April 1952

V. D. Bonch-Bruevich, *Izbrannye Sochineniya*, vol. 2 (Moscow, 1961)

V. D. Bonch-Bruevich, 'Iz vospominanii o Vladimire Il'iche', *VoVIL*, vol. 4, p. 329 in *Znamya*, 1955, no. 4.

V. D. Bonch-Bruevich, *Tridtsat' dnei. 1934. Yanvar'* (Moscow, 1934)

N. I. Bukharin, 'Iz rechi tov. Bukharina na vechere vospominanii v 1921 g.', *PR*, no. 10, 1922

N. I. Bukharin, 'Pamyati Lenina', *Pravda*, 21 January 1925

O. Chernov, *Bednota*, no. 1729, 2 February 1924

Ye. Drabkina, *Zimnii pereval* (2nd expanded edn: Moscow, 1990)

M. V. Fofanova, 'V. I. Lenin na Vyborgskoi Storone v 1917 godu', *VoVIL*, vol. 4

L. Fotieva, *Iz zhizni Lenina* (London, 1967)

L. A. Fotieva, 'Iz vospominanii o V. I. Lenine. (Dekabr' 1922 g.–mart 1923 g.), *VoVIL*, vol. 8

M. P. Golubeva, 'Moya pervaya vstrecha s Vladimirom Il'ichem,' in *V. I. Lenin v Samara, 1889–1893. Sbornik vospominaniya* (Moscow, 1933)

M. Gor'kii, 'V. I. Lenin', in *V. I. Lenin i A. M. Gor'kii. Pis'ma, vospominaniya, dokumenty* (2nd expanded edn: Moscow, 1961)

M. Gor'kii, 'Vladimir Lenin', *Russkii sovremennik*, no. 1, 1924

F. Il'in, 'Otryvok vospominanii', *ZIL*, vol. 1

A. A. Ioffe, 'Kanun Oktyabrya. Zasedanie v "Lesnom"', *ITsKKPSS*, no. 4, 1989

V. V. Kashkadamova, *Bakinskii rabochii*, 21 January 1926

M. S. Kedrov, *Book Publishing under Tsarism* (London, 1932)

M. S. Kedrov, 'Iz krasnoi tetradi ob Il'iche', *Vospominaniya o Vladimire Il'iche Lenine*, vol. 1 (Moscow, 1956)

M. S. Kedrov, 'Iz vospominanii o vserossiiskoi konferenstii voennykh organizat-sii RSDRP (bol'shevikov), 16–23 iyunya 1917 goda', *VoVIL*, vol. 4

V. Klemperer, *Leben sammeln, nicht fragen wozu und warum*, vol. 1: *Tagebücher 1918–1924* (Berlin, 1996)

N. K. Krupskaya, *O Lenine. Sbornik statei i vystuplenii* (Moscow, 1983)

N. K. Krupskaya, 'Sestra Vladimira Il'icha', *Pravda*, 13 June 1937

N. K. Krupskaya, *Vospominaniya o Lenine* (London, 1968)

N. K. Krupskaya, 'Vospominaniya o Lenine', *VoVIL*, vol. 2

G. M. Krzhizhanovskii, *O Vladimire Il'iche* (Moscow, 1924)

Yu. Latukka, 'Lenin v podpol'e v Finlyandii', *VoVIL*, vol. 4

D. I. Leshchenko, 'Kak ya snimal Lenina v podpol'e', *VoVIL*, vol. 4

V. Levitskii, *Za chetvert' veka: revolyutsionnye vospominaniya, 1892–1917 gg.*, vol. 1, part 1 (Moscow–Leningrad, 1926)

G. Ya. Logachëv-Yelizarov, *Nezabyvaemoe* (Leningrad, 1971)

M. Lyadov, *Iz zhizhni partii. Nakanune i v gody pervoi revolyutsii. (Vospominaniya)* (Moscow, 1926)

L. Martov, *Zapiski sotsial-demokrata* (Berlin–Petersburg–Moscow, 1922)

N. L. Meshcheryakov (ed.), *Gleb Uspenskii v zhizni. Po vospominaniyam, perepiske i dokumentam* (Moscow, 1935)

N. L. Meshcheryakov, 'Iz vospominanii o Lenine', in N. L. Meshcheryakov (ed.), *O Lenine. Sbornik vospominanii* (Moscow, n.d.)

S. Mitskevich, 'Stranichka vospominanii', in *Fedoseev, Nikolai Yevgrafovich. (Sbornik vospominanii)* (Moscow–Petrograd, 1923)

M. Ol'minskii (ed.), *Staryi Aleksei Pavlovich Sklyrenko (1870–1916 g.g.). Sbornik statei* (Moscow, 1922)

G. K. Ordzhonikidze, 'Il'ich v iyul'skie dni', *Pravda*, 28 March 1924

V. P. Osipov, 'Bolezn' i smert' Vladimira Il'icha Ul'yanova-Lenina', *VoVIL*, vol. 8

F. Platten, *Lenin iz emigratsii v Rossiyu* (Moscow, 1925)

N. I. Podvoiskii, 'V. I. Lenin v 1917 godu', *Istoricheskii arkhiv*, no. 6, 1956

N. I. Podvoiskii, 'V. I. Lenin v 1917 godu', *VoVIL*, vol. 4

M. N. Poletaev, 'V iyul'skie dni', *Petrogradskaya pravda*, 27 January 1924

A. N. Potresov, *Posmertnyi sbornik proizvedenii* (ed. B. I. Nikolaevskii: Paris, 1937)

K. Radek, *Portrety i pamflety* (Moscow, 1927)

K. Radek, 'V plombirovannom vagone', *Pravda*, 20 April 1924

Rakh'ya [*sic*], 'Moi vospominaniya o Vladimire Il'iche', *Pravda*, 21 January 1927

G. Rovio, 'Kak Lenin skryvalsya u gel'singforskogo "politseimeistera"', in N. L. Meshcheryakov (ed.), *O Lenine. Sbornik vospominanii* (Moscow, 1924)

V. Rozanov, 'Iz vospominanii o Vladimire Il'iche', *Krasnaya nov'*, no. 6, 1924

V. N. Rozanov, 'Iz vospominaniya o Vladimire Il'iche,' in N. L. Meshcheryakov (ed.), *O Lenine. Vospominaniya* (Moscow–Leningrad, 1925), p. 127–31

M. I. Semënov (M. Blan), 'Pamyati druga,' in M. Ol'minskii (ed.), *Staryi Aleksei Pavlovich Sklyrenko (1870–1916 g.g.). Sbornik statei* (Moscow, 1922)

P. D. Shestakov, 'Studencheskie volneniya v Kazani v 1887 g.', *Russkaya starina*, no. 6, 1892

A. G. Shlikhter, 'Gotova li smena?', *VoVIL*, vol. 8

A. G. Shlyapnikov, 'Kerenshchina', *PR*, no. 7(54), 1927

A. V. Shotman, 'Lenin nakanune Oktyabrya', *O Lenine: Sbornik vospominanii* (Leningrad, 1925)

A. V. Shotman, 'Lenin v podpol'e. (Iyul'–oktyabr' 1917 goda)', *VoVIL*, vol. 4

A. V. Shotman, 'Na vtorom s"ezde partii', *PR*, nos 77–8, 1928

M. A. Sil'vin, *Lenin v period zarozhdeniya partii* (Moscow, 1958)

G. Sokol'nikov, 'Kak pokhodit' k istorii Oktyabrya', in *Za leninizm. Sbornik statei* (Moscow–Leningrad, 1925)

G. A. Solomon, *Lenin i ego sem'ya (Ul'yanovy)*, vols 1–2 (Paris, 1931)

V. G. Sorin, 'Bol'shoi dom', *Pravda*, 21 January 1927

Staryi tovarishch Aleksei Pavlovich Sklyarenko (1870–1916 gg.) (Sbornik statei) (Moscow, 1922)

E. D. Stasova, 'Pis'mo Lenina v TsK partii', *VoVIL*, vol. 4

N. Sukhanov, *Zapiski o revolyutsii*, vols 1–7 (Berlin–Petersburg–Moscow, 1922)

D. S. Suliashvili, 'Iz Shveitsarii v Petrograd vmeste s Leninym', *VoVIL*, vol. 4

'Tovarnyi fetishizm', *Nauchnoe obozrenie* (St Petersburg), no. 12 (1899)

L. Trotskii, *O Lenine. (Materialy dlya biografa)* (Moscow, 1924)

L. D. Trotskii, *Moya zhizn'. Opyt avtobiografii*, vols 1–2 (Berlin, 1930)

N. A. Uglanov, 'O Vladimire Il'iche Lenine', *ITsKKPSS*, no. 4

D. I. Ul'yanov, 'Iz moikh vospominanii o Vladimire Il'iche Lenine,' in N. L. Meshcheryakov (ed.), *O Lenine. Sbornik vospominanii* (Moscow, n.d.)

D. I. Ul'yanov, *Ocherki raznykh let. Vospominaniya, perepiska, stat'i* (Moscow, 1974)

D. I. Ul'yanov, *Ocherki raznykh let. Vospominaniya, perepiska, stat'i* (2nd edn: Moscow, 1984),

D. I. Ul'yanov, *Uchitel'skaya gazeta*, 14 February 1963

A. I. Ul'yanova, *PR*, no. 3, 1924

M. I. Ul'yanova, *O Lenine i sem'e Ul'yanovykh. Vospominaniya, ocherki, pis'ma, stat'i* (Moscow, 1988)

M. I. Ul'yanova, *Otets Vladimira Il'icha Lenina Il'ya Nikolaevich Ul'yanov (1831–1886)* (Moscow, 1931)

M. I. Ul'yanova, *O V. I. Lenin i sem'ye Ul'yanovykh: Vospominaniya, ocherki, pis'ma* (2nd expanded edn: Moscow, 1989)

M. I. Ul'yanova, 'O Vladimire Il'iche', *ITsKKPSS*, no. 3, 1991

M. I. Ul'yanova, 'Poiski Il'icha v pervye dni iyulya 1917 goda', *VoVIL*, vol. 1

A. I. Ul'yanova-Yelizarova (ed.), *Aleksandr Il'ich Ul'yanov i delo 1 marta 1887 g.* (Moscow–Leningrad, 1927)

A. I. Ul'yanova-Yelizarova, *O Lenine i sem'e Ul'yanovykh. Vospominaniya, ocherki, pis'ma, stat'i* (Moscow, 1988)

A. I. Ul'yanova-Yelizarova, *Vospominaniya ob Il'iche* (Moscow, 1934)

N. Valentinov, *Maloznakomyi Lenin* (Paris, 1972)

N. Valentinov, *Vstrechi s Leninym* (New York, 1953)

B. S. Veisbrod, 'Bol'noi Lenin', *VoVIL*, vol. 8

V. Vodovozov, 'Moë znakomstvo s Leninym', *Na chuzhoi storone*, vol. 12 (Prague, 1925)

V. V. Vodovozov, *Lenin v Samare* (Moscow, 1933)

G. Volkov's interview with M. Volodicheva: 'Stenografistka Il'icha', *Sovetskaya kul'tura*, 21 January 1989

V. V. [pseudonym of V. P. Vorontsov], *Nashi napravleniya* (St Petersburg, 1893)

N. A. Yemel'yanov, 'Tainstvennyi shalash', *VoVIL*, vol. 4

Ye. Zamyatin, *Bol'shim detyam skazki* (Berlin, 1922)

G. E. Zinoviev, 'Vospominaniya: Malinovskii', *ITsKKPSS*, 1989, no. 4

Secondary Accounts

O. Abramova, G. Borodulina and T. Koloskova, *Mezhdu pravdoi i istinoi. (Ob istorii spekulyatsii vokrug rodosloviya V. I. Lenina)* (St Petersburg, 1998)

E. Acton, chapter 7 in R. Bartlett (ed.), *Russian Thought and Society, 1800–1917* (Keele, 1984).

V. Arnol'd, *Sem'ya Ul'yanovykh v Samare. Poiski i nakhodki* (2nd expanded edn: Kuibyshev, 1983)

A. Belyakov, *Yunost' vozhdya* (Moscow, 1960)

Yu. V. Bernov and A. Ya. Manusevich, *V krakovskoi emigratsii. Zhizn' i deyatel'nost' V. I. Lenina* (Moscow, 1988)

V. P. Buldakov, 'Istoriya poznaetsya v sravnenii', *Argumenty i fakty*, no. 45, November 1998

E. H. Carr, *The Bolshevik Revolution, 1917–1923*, vols 1–3 (London, 1950–3)

S. Cohen, *Bukharin and the Russian Revolution. A Political Biography, 1888–1938* (New York, 1973)

I. N. R. Davies, *White Eagle, Red Star. The Polish–Soviet War, 1919–1920* (London, 1972)

I. M. Dazhina, 'Leninskie istoki zhizhni i bor'by', *VIKPSS*, no. 3, 1987

I. Deutscher, *The Prophet Armed: Trotsky, 1879–1921* (Oxford, 1954)

R. C. Elwood, *Inessa Armand: Revolutionary and Feminist* (Cambridge, 1992)

R. C. Elwood, 'Lenin and "Pravda"', *Slavic Review*, no. 2, 1972

O. Figes, *A People's Tragedy* (London, 1996)

L. Fischer, *The Life of Lenin* (London, 1965)

S. Fitzpatrick, *The Russian Revolution* (Oxford, 1982)

W. Gautschi, *Lenin als Emigrant in der Schweiz* (Zurich, 1973)

I. Getzler, *Martov. A Political Biography of a Russian Social Democrat* (Cambridge, 1967)

D. Geyer, *Lenin in der Russischen Sozialdemokratic* (Cologne, 1962)

L. Haimson, *The Russian Marxists and The Origins of Bolshevism* (Cambridge, Mass. 1955)

N. Harding, *Lenin's Political Thought*, vols 1–2 (London, 1977–81)

N. Hans, *History of Russian Educational Policy* (London, 1931)

B. Henderson, 'Lenin and the British Museum Library', *Solanus*, 1990, vol. 4

B. Henderson, *Lenin at the British Museum* (London, n.d.)

M. P. Iroshnikov, *Presedatel' Soveta Narodnykh Komissarov i STO, V. I. Ul'yanov-Lenin: ocherki gosudarstvennoi deyatel'nosti v 1917–1918 gg.* (Moscow, 1974)

A. Ivanskii (ed.), *Il'ya Nikolaevich Ul'yanov po vospominaniyam sovremennikov i dokumentam* (Moscow, 1963)

J. H. L. Keep, *The Rise of Social Democracy in Russia* (Oxford, 1963)

J. Klier, *Imperial Russia's Jewish Question, 1855–1881* (Cambridge, 1985)

K. Kuusela, 'Kak artist maskiroval Lenin', in *Lenin v vospominaniyakh finnov* (Moscow, 1979)

A. Latyshev, *Rassekrechënnyi Lenin* (Moscow, 1996)

M. Lewin, *Lenin's Last Struggle* (London, 1969)

M. Liebman, *Leninism under Lenin* (London, 1975)

A. S. Lindemann, *The 'Red Years'* (Berkeley, 1974)

Yu. M. Lopukhin, *Bolezn', smert' i bal'zamirovanie V. I. Lenina. Pravda i mify* (Moscow, 1997)

R. MacNeal, *Bride of the Revolution. Krupskaya and Lenin* (Ann Arbor, 1972)

M. Malia, *The Soviet Tragedy* (London, 1992)

S. U. Manbekova and S. A. Rubanov, *Naslednitsa. Stranitsy zhizni N. K. Krupskoi* (Moscow, 1990)

V. Mel'nichenko, *Fenomenon i fantom Lenina* (Moscow, 1993)

A. Meyer, *Leninism* (New York, 1957)

M. A. Moskalëv, *Byuro TsK RSDRP v Rossii: avgust 1903 g.–mart 1917 g.* (Moscow, 1964)

B. Pearce, *How Haig Saved Lenin* (London, 1987)

N. Petrenko, 'Lenin v Gorkakh – bolezn' i smert'', *Minuvshee*, vol. 2 (Moscow, 1990)

J. Piilonen, 'Yhteinen vihollinen yhdistää, 1908–1917', in J. Numminen (ed.), *Lenin ja Suomi* (Helsinki, 1987)

R. Pipes, *Russia Under the Bolshevik Regime, 1919–1924* (London, 1994)

R. Pipes, *The Formation of the Soviet Union. Communism and Nationalism, 1917–1923* (Cambridge, Mass. 1964)

R. Pipes, *Social-Democracy and the St Petersburg Labour Movement, 1885–1897* (Cambridge, Mass. 1963)

A. J. Polan, *Lenin and the End of Politics* (London, 1984)

P. N. Pospelov *et al.*, *Vladimir Il'ich Lenin* (Moscow, 1963)

A. Rabinowitch, *The Bolsheviks Come to Power* (New York, 1976)

T. H. Rigby, *Lenin's Government. Sovnarkom, 1917–1922* (Cambridge, 1979)

A. Rothstein, *Lenin in Britain* (London, 1970)

L. B. Schapiro, *The Communist Party of the Soviet Union* (2nd edn: London, 1970)

A. Senn, *The Russian Revolution in Switzerland, 1914–1917* (Madison, 1971)

R. Service, *The Bolshevik Party in Revolution. A Study in Organisational Change* (London, 1979)

R. Service, *Lenin: A Political Life*, vols 1–3 (London: 1985, 1991, 1995)

S. L. Shatkina (ed.), *Lenin i Ul'yanovy v Podol'ske* (2nd edn: Moscow, 1979)

M. Shtein, 'Rod vozhdya. Bilet po istorii', in G. Sidorovnin (ed.), *Vozhd'. Lenin kotorogo my ne znali* (Saratov, 1992)

M. Shtein, *Ul'yanovy i Leniny. Tainy rodoslovnoi i psevdonima* (St Petersburg, 1997)

D. Shub, *Lenin* (2nd edn: London, 1966)

G. Sidorovnin (ed.), *Vozhd'. Lenin kotorog my ne znali* (Saratov, 1992)

V. Soloukhin, *Pri svete dnya* (London, 1992)

A. Solzhenitsyn, *Lenin in Zurich* (London, 1975)

I. B. Sternik, *V. I. Lenin – Yurist. (Yuridicheskaya deyatel'nost' V. I. Ul'yanova) (Lenina)* (Tashkent, 1969)

R. G. Suny, *The Revenge of the Past: Nationalism, Revolution and the Collapse of the Soviet Union* (Stanford, 1993)

R. H. W. Theen, *Lenin: Genesis and Development of a Revolutionary* (London, 1974)

I. I. Titov, *Vo glubine Rossii. Ocherki istorii sela Alakaevki* (2nd, expanded edn: Kuibyshev, 1990)

Zh. Trofimov, *Ul'yanovy. Poiski, nakhodki, issledovaniya* (2nd, expanded edn: Saratov, 1988)

V. V. Tsaplin, 'O zhizni sem'i Blankov v gorodakh Starokonstantinove i Zhitomire', *Otechestvennye arkhivy*, no. 2, 1992

N. Tumarkin, *Lenin Lives! The Lenin Cult in Soviet Russia* (London, 1983)

A. Ulam, *Expansion and Coexistence. The History of the Soviet Foreign Policy, 1917–1967* (London, 1968)

Vladimir Il'ich Lenin (ed. P. N. Pospelov: Moscow, 1963)

'Vlyublënnaya Lenina', *Literaturnaya gazeta – Dos'e*, no. 8, 1992

M. S. Volin, 'Dorevolyutsionnye biograficheskie publikatsii o V. I. Lenine', *VIKPSS*, no. 7, 1970

D. Volkogonov, 'Leninskaya krepost' v moei dushe pala poslednei', *Moskovskie novosti*, no. 29, 19 July 1992

D. A. Volkogonov, *Lenin. Politicheskii portret*, vols 1–2 (Moscow, 1994)

D. A. Volkogonov, *Sem' vozhdei*, vols 1–2 (Moscow, 1995)

A. Walicki, *The Controversy over Capitalism* (Oxford, 1969)

R. Wortman, *The Crisis of Russian Populism* (Cambridge, 1967)

INDEX